WELLINGTON

By the same author

CHRISTOPHER HIBBERT

WELLINGTON

A Personal History

PERSEUS BOOKS
Reading, Massachusetts

For Pam Carpenter
With Love

Library of Congress Card Number: 99-61540

ISBN 0-7382-0148-0

Originally published in Great Britain by HarperCollins*Publishers*

Perseus Books is a member of the Perseus Books Group

Perseus Books are available at special discounts for bulk purchases in the U.S. by corporations, institutions, and other organizations. For more information, please contact the Special Markets Department at HarperCollinsPublishers, 10 East 53rd Street, New York, NY 10022, or call 1-212-207-7528.

Visit us on the World Wide Web at http://www.aw.com/gb

Cover design by Adrian Morgan/Red Letter Design
Cover photograph courtesy of Corbis-Bettmann

1 2 3 4 5 6 7 8 9—MA—01 00 99

Contents

PART II · 1815–52

ILLUSTRATIONS

Lord Castlereagh. *National Portrait Gallery, London. Photograph C. Mansell/Time, Inc.*

Harriet Arbuthnot. *Photograph Mary Evans Picture Library.*

Charles Arbuthnot. *Reproduced courtesy of the National Portrait Gallery, London.*

Frances Mary Gascoyne-Cecil, second Marchioness of Salisbury. Portrait by Sir Thomas Lawrence. *Hatfield House. Reproduced courtesy of the 35th Marquess of Salisbury and National Portrait Gallery, London. Copyright © Lord Salisbury.*

Apsley House, No. I London. *Reproduced courtesy of V&A Picture Library.*

View of the proposed Waterloo Palace. *Reproduced courtesy of His Grace the Duke of Wellington KG, Stratfield Saye House, Basingstoke, Hampshire; photograph Courtauld Institute of Art.*

Charles Greville. *Photograph Mary Evans Picture Library.*

Lady Charlotte Greville. *Copyright © British Museum.*

Oil sketch of the Duke, by Sir Thomas Lawrence. *Reproduced courtesy of His Grace the Duke of Wellington KG, Stratfield Saye House, Basingstoke, Hampshire; photograph Courtauld Institute of Art.*

"Achilles in the Sulks": caricature by Thomas Howell Jones. *Copyright © British Museum.*

Repose, a lithograph by H.B. (John Doyle). *Copyright © Museum of London.*

Punch drawing of the Duke's statue. *Pub. Vol. II, July-December 1846, p. 150. Copyright © Punch Ltd.*

Walmer Castle. *Photograph Mary Evans Picture Library.*

"The Field of Battersea": caricature by William Heath. *Reproduced courtesy of V&A Picture Library.*

Sketch by Benjamin Robert Haydon for his *Wellington Musing on the Field of Waterloo. Reproduced courtesy of His Grace the Duke of Wellington KG, Stratfield Saye House, Basingstoke, Hampshire; photograph Courtauld Institute of Art.*

Wellington Musing on the Field of Waterloo, by Haydon. *Reproduced courtesy of the Board of Trustees of the National Museums and Galleries on Merseyside (Walker Art Gallery, Liverpool).*

The First Council of Queen Victoria, by Sir David Wilkie. *The Royal Collection copyright © Her Majesty Queen Elizabeth II.*

Miniature engraving of the Duke aged seventy-five. *Reproduced courtesy of His Grace the Duke of Wellington KG, Stratfield Saye House, Basingstoke, Hampshire; photograph Courtauld Institute of Art.*

Franz Xaver Winterhalter's portrait of the Duke with Sir Robert Peel. *The Royal Collection copyright © Her Majesty Queen Elizabeth II.*

Baroness Nurdett-Coutts, by Sir William Charles Ross. *Reproduced courtesy of the National Portrait Gallery, London.*

Elizabeth Hay, later Duchess of Wellington, the first Duke's daughter-in-law. *Photograph Mary Evans Picture Library.*

Arthur Richard Wellesley, the Duke's elder son, later second Duke of Wellington. *Reproduced courtesy of His Grace the Duke of Wellington KG, Stratfield Saye House, Basingstoke, Hampshire; photograph Courtauld Institute of Art.*

Robert Thorburn's painting of the Duke with his grandchildren. *Reproduced courtesy of His Grace the Duke of Wellington KG, Stratfield Saye House, Basingstoke, Hampshire; photograph Courtauld Institute of Art.*

COLOR

Goya's portrait of Wellington painted in August 1812. *The National Portrait Gallery London; photograph Bridgeman Art Library, London.*

Wellington at Waterloo. *Copyright © British Museum.*

Equestrian portrait by Sir Thomas Lawrence. *Private Collection; photograph Bridgeman Art Library, London.*

Sir David Wilkie's *Chelsea Pensioners Reading the* Waterloo Despatch. *Reproduced courtesy of V&A Picture Library.*

Princess Lieven, by Sir Thomas Lawrence. *The Hermitage, St. Petersburg; photograph Bridgeman Art Library, London.*

The Stratfield Saye estate. *Reproduced courtesy of His Grace the Duke of Wellington KG, Stratfield Saye House, Basingstoke, Hampshire.*

The library at Stratfield Saye. *Reproduced courtesy of His Grace the Duke of Wellington KG, Stratfield Saye House, Basingstoke, Hampshire.*

The Duke's bedroom at Apsley House. *Reproduced courtesy of V&A Picture Library.*

The Duke in 1824, painted by Sir Thomas Lawrence for Sir Robert Peel. *Reproduced courtesy of Wellington College.*

Franz Xaver Winterhalter's *The First of May, 1851. The Royal Collection copyright © Her Majesty Queen Elizabeth II.*

"A Quartette in Character": caricature by William Heath. *Private Collection; photograph Bridgeman Art Library, London.*

The Duke at seventy-five: portrait by Charles Robert Leslie. *Copyright © British Museum.*

The Duke's funeral procession, after a painting by Louis Haghe. *Guildhall Library, Corporation of London; photograph Bridgeman Art Library, London.*

Author's Note and Acknowledgements

Any biographer who now attempts to write a life of the Duke of Wellington does so in the shadow, so to speak, of Elizabeth Longford whose splendid book about him was published in two volumes in 1969 and 1972. This book does not, of course, pretend to take its place; but if, as has been suggested, a person really worth writing about deserves reappraisal every twenty years, the time has certainly come for a new look at the Duke. This one skates rather quickly over his generalship and his political entanglements to concentrate more fully on those aspects of his life suggested by the book's sub-title.

The idea of my writing it came originally from the Hon. Georgina Stonor, whose knowledge of the Wellington Papers is extensive and whose library of books on the Duke and his family has been placed unreservedly at my disposal. I am extremely grateful to her for all her help, as I am to his Grace the eighth Duke of Wellington for allowing me to consult and quote from his great-great-grandfather's personal papers at Stratfield Saye and for his assistance when I was there.

I must express my thanks also to Dr C.M. Woolgar, Archivist and Head of Special Collections at the Hartley Institute, the University of Southampton, in whose care are the Duke of Wellington's official papers, and to Claire Jackson for her help when I was working at the Institute.

Southampton University and Stratfield Saye are the principal repositories of the Duke's papers; but I have also made use of letters and papers by or about him elsewhere. I have therefore to acknowledge with gratitude the gracious permission of Her Majesty the Queen to make use of material in the Royal Archives, Windsor Castle, and to express my thanks to Lord Raglan for the use of the Raglan Papers, including letters from the Duke to his brother William Wellesley-Pole, at Gwent Record Office; the Marquess of Tweeddale for use of the Yester Papers in the National Library of Scotland; the Marquess of Salisbury for use of papers at Hatfield House including the Westmeath Papers and letters from the Duke to the first wife of the second Marquess of Salisbury, her diary and the Duke's letters to the second wife of the second Marquess; Mrs M. Fry of Fulbeck Hall for a letter from the Duke to the Countess Dowager of Westmorland in the

Fane Papers: Adrian Francis for the 'Manuscript Account of the Services of John Parker, Corporal 20th Foot'; Wellington College for letters to and from the Duke and his accounts in the college's archives; and Miss S.M. Fletcher, Archivist, Hampshire Record Office for photocopies of the Duke's Lieutenancy Papers.

For helping me with these and other papers I am most grateful to Oliver Everett, Librarian, Windsor Castle; David Rimmer of the Gwent Record Office; Mr I.F. Maciver, Assistant Keeper, Manuscripts Division, the National Library of Scotland; Robin Harcourt Williams, Librarian and Archivist to the Marquess of Salisbury; and Bijan Omrani, Deputy Archivist, Wellington College.

I am also much indebted to Dr Norma Aubertin-Potter, Sub-Librarian, All Souls College, Oxford; Simon Bailey of Oxford University Archives, Bodleian Library, Oxford; Richard Olney, Assistant Keeper, the Royal Commission on Historical Manuscripts; Judith Curthoys, Assistant Archivist, Christ Church, Oxford; Dr J.N. Mills of the Historical Search Room, Scottish Record Office; Penelope Hatfield, College Archivist, Eton College Library; Dr Peter Boyden of the National Army Museum; Dr Linda Washington, Head of the Department of Printed Books, National Army Museum; and the staffs of the British Library, the London Library and the Ravenscroft Library, Henley-on-Thames.

For help in tracing the Duke's movements and activities when in the provinces I am most grateful to Elizabeth Rees, Chief Archivist, Tyne and Wear Archive Services; Rita Freeman, City Archivist, York; Jennifer Gill, County Record Office, Durham; Eileen Organ, Supervisor, Liverpool Record Office, Central Library, Liverpool; Jeremy McIlwaine, Archivist (Diocesan Records), Hertfordshire County Record Office; Richard Leonard, Research Archivist, Centre for Kentish Studies, Maidstone; Bruce Jackson, County Archivist, Lancashire Record Office; Penny Ward, Heritage Officer, Margate Library; and Janet Adamson, Heritage Officer, Folkestone Library.

For help with portraits and busts and the general inconography of the Duke I have to thank Dr Helen Smailes, National Gallery of Scotland; Dr Philip Ward-Jackson, Deputy Conway Librarian, Courtauld Institute of Art; Ian Ritchie, Archive Assistant, National Portrait Gallery; Paul Goldman, Assistant Keeper, Department of Prints and Drawings, British Museum; Liz Vance, Information Assistant, National Gallery; Fiona Pearson, Research Assistant, Scottish National Gallery of Modern Art; A.W. Potter, Information Assistant, Royal Academy of Arts; Julia Toffolo, Registrar, Government Art Collection; Helen Watson of the Scottish National Gallery; Christopher Eimer; Dr Peter Beal and Stephen Lloyd of Sotheby's; John Kenworthy-Browne; Jonathan Marsden, Deputy Surveyor of the Queen's Works of Art; Helen Valentine of the Royal Academy of Arts; Mireille

Galinou of the Museum of London; and Marjorie Trusted of the Victoria and Albert Museum.

For their help in a variety of other ways I am most grateful to the Marquess of Anglesey, Lady Marioth Hay, Lady Pamela Barbary, Major D.A.J. Williams, Regimental Secretary of the King's Royal Hussars, Captain J.G. Fergusson, Richard Way, Diana Cook, Dennis Flower, David Nugent, Peter Crane, Oliver Cooper, Margaret Lewendon, Rosemary Foster, Dr Francis Sheppard, Bruce Hunter of David Higham Associates and Richard Johnson of HarperCollins. I want also to thank Deborah Adams who edited the book; Anna Grapes who helped me choose the illustrations; Hamish Francis who read the proofs; and my wife who made the comprehensive index.

Finally I must say how grateful I am to Professor Norman Gash, biographer of Peel and author of the article on Wellington in the forthcoming *New Dictionary of National Biography*, for having read the book in typescript and given me much valuable advice for its improvement.

Christopher Hibbert

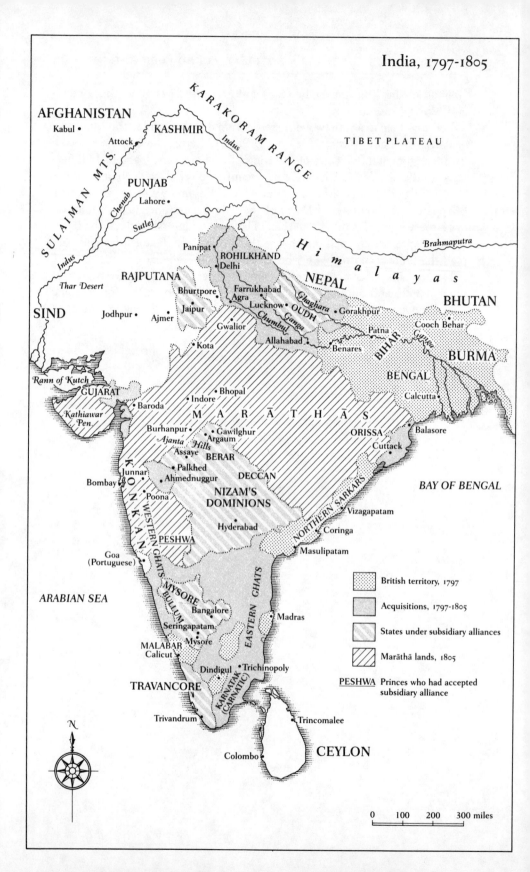

India, 1797-1805

AFGHANISTAN
Kabul •

KARAKORAM RANGE

KASHMIR
Attock •

TIBET PLATEAU

PUNJAB
Lahore •

Indus
Chenab
Sutlej

SULAIMAN MTS.

Indus

Thar Desert

SIND

RAJPUTANA

Jodhpur •

Ajmer •

Jaipur

Bhurtpore

Panipat •
ROHILKHAND
Delhi •

Farrukhabad
Agra •
Lucknow
OUDH
Chumbul
Ganga
Allahabad

Gwalior
Kota •

Himalayas

NEPAL

Ghaghara
Gorakhpur •

Brahmaputra

BHUTAN

Cooch Behar •

Benares •
Patna •
Ganga

BIHAR

BURMA

BENGAL

Calcutta •

Rann of Kutch

GUJARAT
Kathiawar Pen.
Baroda •

Indore •
Bhopal •

MARĀTHĀS

ORISSA

Balasore •

Cuttack •

Burhanpur •
Ajanta Hills
Assaye
BERAR
Palkhed •
Ahmednuggur •

Gawilghur
Argaum

DECCAN

Junnar •
Bombay

Poona •

PESHWA

Goa
(Portuguese) •

ARABIAN SEA

NIZAM'S
DOMINIONS

Hyderabad •

NORTHERN SARKARS

Vizagapatam •

Coringa •

Masulipatam •

BAY OF BENGAL

MYSORE
BULLUM
Bangalore •

Seringapatam •

MALABAR
Calicut •

Mysore •

Dindigul •

EASTERN GHATS

Madras •

Trichinopoly •

TRAVANCORE

KARNATAK
(CARNATIC)

Trivandrum •

Trincomalee •

Colombo •

CEYLON

British territory, 1797

Acquisitions, 1797-1805

States under subsidiary alliances

Marāthā lands, 1805

PESHWA Princes who had accepted
subsidiary alliance

N

0   100   200   300 miles

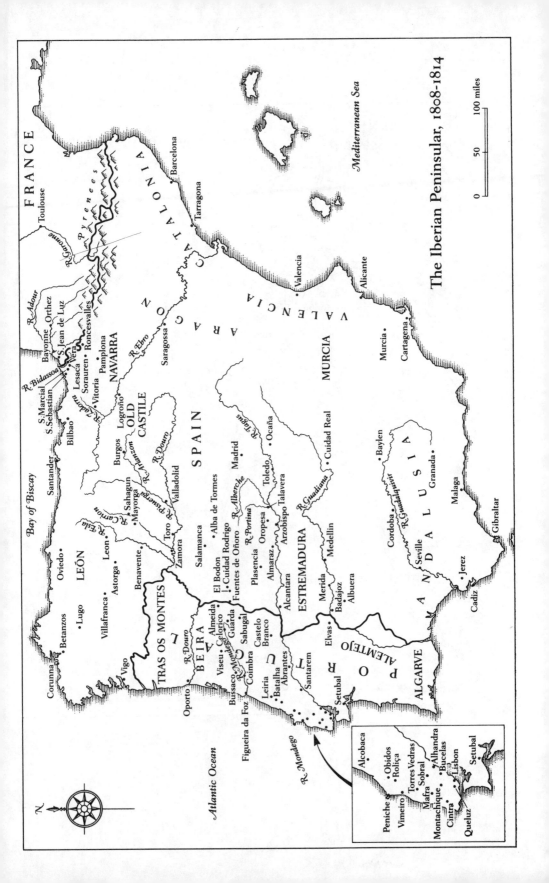

The Iberian Peninsular, 1808-1814

FRANCE

Mediterranean Sea

Bay of Biscay

Atlantic Ocean

SPAIN

PORTUGAL

CATALONIA

NAVARRA

ARAGON

OLD CASTILE

LEÓN

TRAS OS MONTES

BEIRA

ESTREMADURA

VALENCIA

MURCIA

ANDALUSIA

ALEMTEJO

ALGARVE

Toulouse • Bayonne • Orthez
R. Garonne
R. Adour
Pyrenees
S. Jean de Luz • Vera • Roncesvalles
S. Marcial • S. Sebastián • Lesaca • Sorauren • Vitoria • Pamplona
R. Bidassoa *R. Zadorra* *R. Arga*
Bilbao • Logroño
R. Ebro
Barcelona •
Tarragona •
Saragossa •
Santander •
Betanzos •
Oviedo •
Corunna •
Lugo •
Villafranca •
Vigo •
Astorga •
Leon •
Benavente •
R. Esla *R. Carrion* *R. Pisuerga*
Sahagun •
Mayorga •
Toro •
Zamora •
Burgos •
Valladolid •
R. Douro *R. Arlanzon*
Oporto •
R. Douro
Viseu • Celorico • Almeida
Mondego • Guarda
Bussaco • Sabugal
Figueira da Foz • Coimbra
Batalha • Castelo Branco
Leiria •
Abrantes •
Santarem •
Setubal •
R. Mondego
Salamanca •
Alba de Tormes •
El Bodon •
Ciudad Rodrigo •
Fuentes de Oñoro •
Plasencia •
Almaraz •
Alcantara •
Elvas •
Merida •
Badajoz •
Albuera •
Medellin •
R. Guadiana
Madrid •
R. Alberche
Toledo •
Talavera •
Arzobispo •
Oropesa •
R. Portina *R. Tagus*
Ocaña •
Cuidad Real •
R. Guadalquivir
Cordoba •
Seville •
Jerez •
Cadiz •
Baylen •
Granada •
Malaga •
Gibraltar •
Murcia •
Cartagena •
Valencia •
Alicante •

0   50   100 miles

N

Inset:
Peniche •
Vimeiro •
Mafra •
Montachique •
Cintra •
Queluz •
Alcobaca •
Obidos •
Roliça •
Torres Vedras •
Sobral •
Alhandra •
Bucelas •
Lisbon •
Setubal •

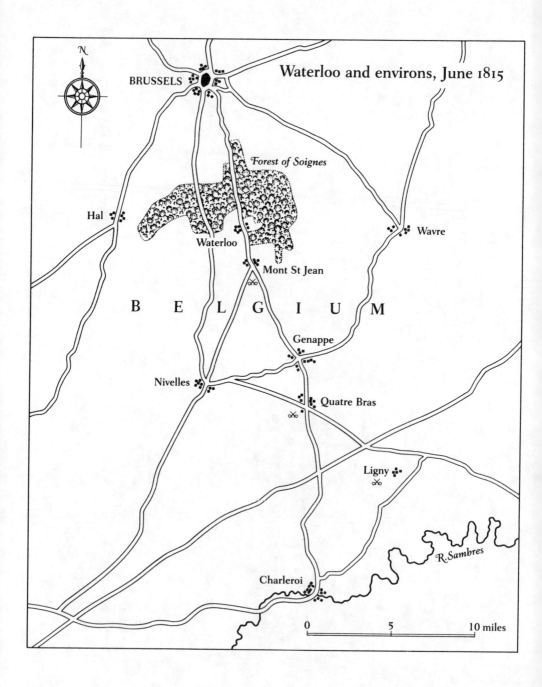

I

___

1769 — 1815

1   Eton, Dublin and Angers

1769 — 87

'My ugly boy Arthur is food for powder and
nothing more.'

AMONG THE new boys whose baggage was set down at the gates of
Eton in the autumn of 1781 were two of the five sons of the first Earl
of Mornington. The elder, the Hon. Arthur Wesley, was twelve years
old, the younger, Gerald, was nine. Neither had yet shown much
aptitude for scholarship and they were not expected to shine at Eton
in the glittering manner of their eldest brother, Richard, who had
mastered Greek and Latin with equal facility, had, afterwards at Oxford,
won the Chancellor's Prize for Latin Verse, and would, no doubt,
have taken an excellent degree had not the early death of his father
necessitated his presence at home.

His father, Garret Wesley, Lord Mornington, had not been a practical man. Descendant of an ancient English family which had been
settled in Ireland for generations, he had been a member of the Irish
House of Commons before passing to the Irish House of Lords. But
he had been more interested in music than in politics. His own father,
Richard Colley Wesley, had been a musician of sorts, playing the violin
quite well, so it was said, 'for a gentleman'.[1] There was an organ in
the hall of the Wesleys' country house, Dangan Castle, in the county
of Meath, another organ in the chapel there and a harpsichord in the
breakfast room. But Richard Colley Wesley had been essentially an
amateur, whereas his son, a composer as well as performer from his
early youth, had been able to take his place among the virtuosi of
Dublin's musical world and had been appointed Professor of Music at
Trinity College. His godmother, Mary Delany, however, while acknowledging Garret Wesley's musical talents, found him rather deficient in
'the punctilios of good breeding', and had consequently been much
gratified when he announced that he was to marry Lady Louisa Augusta
Lennox, daughter of the second Duke of Richmond. Unfortunately,

3

Lady Louisa had developed other ideas. Confessing that she had conceived 'an insurmountable dislike' for her noble suitor, she had accepted
instead the hand of a richer young man; and Lord Mornington, whose
father had died the year before, married Anne Hill, the eldest daughter
of a banker, Arthur Hill, later Hill-Trevor, the first Viscount Dungannon, a sixteen-year-old girl who, in the opinion of Mrs Delany, was
modest and good-natured but, like her husband, rather gauche in
manner,[2] and, according to Mrs Nicolson Calvert, the beautiful Irish
wife of an English Member of Parliament, a somewhat 'commonplace
character'.[3]

The young couple had appeared to suit each other well. They had
lived contentedly in the country at Dangan Castle and in Dublin in a
handsome house facing Sefton Street. Their first child, Richard, had
been born in 1760 and was styled Viscount Wellesley, that variation of
the family name, which his brothers were later to adopt, being preferred
as older and more aristocratic than Wesley with its associations of
evangelical Methodism. Other children had followed at regular inter-
vals: a second son, Arthur, who did not live long, a third son, William
in 1763, then another boy, Francis, who died in childhood, followed in
1768 by a daughter, Anne, and on 29 April the following year by a sixth
child who was named, like his little dead brother, Arthur, after his
mother's father. Arthur's younger brother, Gerald Valerian, was born
in 1770, the youngest son, Henry in 1773, and yet another child, Mary
Elizabeth, soon afterwards.

By then the family had left their house in Dublin and moved to
London where the children would grow up to speak without the Irish
accent which, it was considered, 'might be a disadvantage' to them 'in
society hereafter'.[4] They lived in rented rooms in Knightsbridge, their
father by now in debt, struggling, not very successfully, to maintain a
household befitting his rank, as well as a coach, on an income of £1,800
a year. His son, Arthur, who had been given his first lessons in a small
school in the shadow of Dangan Castle, was sent to Brown's Seminary,
later known more grandly as Oxford House Academy, in King's Road,
Chelsea. He was, by his own admission, a shy, indolent and dreamy
little boy who was often to be seen standing silently alone under a
walnut tree while the other children played their rowdy games. So he
was not sorry when, his eldest brother having mortgaged the family's
estates in Meath on their father's death, he was sent with Gerald to
Eton.[5]

*

Eton in 1781 was a school of some three hundred boys. The activities to be seen on the playing fields appeared to the uninitiated to be more like free-for-all fights than games; and so, indeed, they often were.* It was not until halfway through the next century that football rules became sufficiently standardized for public schools to play matches against each other without brawling on the pitch. An unsociable boy, quarrelsome in his reserve, Arthur Wesley seems to have enjoyed neither football nor cricket; nor is there record of his having played any of the other games with which his fellow Etonians passed the hours they spent outside the classroom, fives and hoops, hop-scotch, marbles and battledore. In later years he recalled leaping over a wide ditch in the garden of his old house, but he said he could not remember a fight he had evidently had with an older boy, Robert Percy ('Bobus') Smith, the ugly, amusing brother of Sydney Smith, the witty Canon of St Paul's, whom he had provoked by throwing a stone at him when he was bathing.[6] According to the school's historian, Arthur Wesley did 'little else', other than engage in this fight, 'to attract the attention of his schoolfellows'.[7] Certainly he did not look back upon his days at Eton with any pleasure and returned to the school but rarely.†

As for his work in class, he made very slow progress, labouring gloomily in the Fourth Form, his name appearing in the lists at number

---

* It seems improbable that Wellington ever actually observed that 'the battle of Waterloo was won on the playing fields of Eton', an aphorism regularly attributed to him in dictionaries of quotations. He had been dead for three years when Charles Montalembert, in his *De l'Avenir politique de l'Angleterre*, credited him with some such remark.

† He was to send his own two sons there, however, and after they had left, he told his niece, Lady Burghersh, that the best plan for her own two boys was to send them for 'a couple of years' to Eton, or to Harrow or Westminster, where they would mix 'with others of their own class' who would not 'flatter their Vanity . . . as all servants and their Inferiors do'. 'After that period of time' he was 'not certain that the Private Tutor is not the best system of Learning' (Wellington to Lady Burghersh, 20 Dec. 1835, Wellington College Archives). Some years before he had given different advice to his friend, Lady Shelley: 'I am astonished that you do not send your second son to the Charterhouse which I believe is the best school of them all' (*The Diary of Frances, Lady Shelley*, ii, 101).‡ Having been to see his sons on perhaps no more than two occasions, he visited Eton again in 1842 to attend the funeral of his brother, Richard, who had loved the place and had asked to be buried in the College chapel; and he was there two years later when in attendance upon King Louis Philippe, Queen Victoria and Prince Albert. 'The Duke happened to lag behind in the School Yard, and received an unexpected ovation, masters and boys alike cheering the Etonian warrior with all their might' (H.C. Maxwell Lyte, *A History of Eton College*, 448–9).

‡ Where full publication details are not given in the footnotes, these are to be found in the sources, pp. 426–38.

fifty-four out of a total of seventy-nine boys, many if not most of them younger than himself. His command of the classics, for all the hours he was required to spend poring over Ovid and Caesar, remained so highly uncertain that in later life he was to pronounce that his two standard rules for public speaking were never to take on subjects he knew nothing about and, whenever possible, to avoid quoting Latin.[8]

Early in 1784, after his younger brother, Henry, had entered the Lower Remove, it was decided that the family's finances could no longer be stretched to keep Wesley *major* at a school whose education seemed to be profiting him so little. So he left Eton and, after a short spell with a tutor, a clergyman in Brighton, he was taken by his mother to Brussels where, it was hoped, she might live more economically and he would progress in French more satisfactorily than he had done in Greek and Latin. He did learn to speak French after a fashion and with a Belgian accent; but his other studies were not pursued with noticeable vigour and he spent much of his time in the lodgings his mother had taken for them in the house of a lawyer, Louis Goubert, playing the violin with patient assiduity and some of the skill of his father: a fellow lodger in the house, the son of a Yorkshire baronet, considered that Wesley played very well, adding that it was the only species of talent that the young man appeared to possess.[9]

After a few months his mother went home, having talked to him about his future career. His eldest brother, after succeeding his father as Earl of Mornington, had made a name for himself in the Irish House of Lords and been elected to the English House of Commons as Member for Beeralston in Devonshire. His second brother, William, having served for a time in the Navy, had assumed the additional surname of Pole, on becoming heir to the estates of his cousin William Pole of Ballyfin, Queen's County, and had been elected Member for Trim in the Irish Parliament. Gerald Valerian, who had gone to Eton with Arthur, was destined for the Church and, in due course, for a prebendal stall at Durham. Henry, the youngest of the brothers, was still at Eton and had thoughts of joining the Army. Their mother, a woman now forty-two years old, rather severe in manner, ready to feel pride in her sons' achievements but incapable of demonstrating much affection for them, considered that Arthur, too, might do worse than become a soldier. Indeed, in her opinion, her 'ugly boy Arthur' was 'food for powder and nothing more'.*[10] He himself was as yet undecided about his future; but he had no objections to going to Angers in western France to enrol in the celebrated Academy there and undergo a training, as much designed for men of fashion as for future officers, which would include fencing, riding and dancing lessons as well as some instruction in French grammar, mathematics and the science of military fortifications.

It proved to be a not too demanding course. Monsieur Wesley was quite regular in his attendance at the lessons of the dancing and fencing masters and the riding instruction given by the proprietor of the Academy, M. de Pignerolle, whose great-great-grandfather had presided over it in the days of King Louis XIV. Yet the seventeen-year-old Wesley found time to take his dog, a white terrier called Vick†, for walks around the town's thirteenth-century moated castle, to play cards with M. de Pignerolle's English and Irish students, known to the French as the *groupe des lords*, to occupy idle hours by dropping coins from upstairs windows on to the heads of unwary citizens in the streets below, to sit at café tables, in the Academy's smart uniform of scarlet coat with blue facings and yellow buttons, watching the passing scene, and to accept the invitations which were readily offered to the more presentable of their number by the local *noblesse*. They were enter-

---

* The relationship between mother and son was always to remain rather strained. The Duchess of Wellington, while sitting years later for her portrait to Sir Thomas Lawrence, mentioned an incident which occurred at this time and which, she thought, had given her husband a lasting and 'painful sense of his mother's tyranny and injustice'. He and his eldest brother had gone with their mother to see some palace on the Continent. The two boys seemed to have a secret between them which may have concerned Richard's relationship with a young French woman. 'His mother got her son Arthur apart from the other and insisted on knowing this secret; the boy was firm to his promise, and said that if it had been his own secret she might have commanded it, but he had no right to betray that of his brother. Lady Mornington grew furious and declared that he should not return in her carriage. The saucy boy said, "Very well, he had no doubt he could walk", and this she actually suffered him to do.' He arrived hours later, 'whistling most unconcernedly' ('Recollections of Sir Thomas Lawrence, P.R.A. during an intimacy of nearly Thirty Years by Miss [Elizabeth] Croft', from *Sir Thomas Lawrence's Letter Bag*, 261–2).

† Although he was never a lover of animals, white terriers were a breed of which he was fond. He was to have another, named Jack, when he was in India. 'Once Jack followed Colonel Wellesley to Chitaldrug from Seringapatam, a distance of more than a hundred miles,' wrote an officer on his staff in India. 'When the Colonel arrived at the fort of Chitaldrug, they fired a salute in compliment to him. The dog was frightened and ran away, and the Colonel gave him up for lost. A few days after he received a letter from Seringapatam to say that the dog had found his way back. In India there are no beaten tracks or roads which render it the more extraordinary.' (*Memoirs of George Elers, Captain in the 12th Regiment of Foot*, 144–5.)

tained in nearby chateaux by the duc de Brissac, the duc de Praslin and the duchesse de Sabran; and Wesley afterwards related how he met not only the Abbé Siéyès, who was soon to play so prominent a part in the revolutionary deliberations of the Estates General at Versailles, but also François René Chateaubriand, who, having decided he had no vocation for the priesthood, was then a cavalry officer a few months older than himself.[11]

By the time he returned home in 1786, fluent now in French, and having impressed M. de Pignerolle as 'an Irish lad of great promise',[12] Wesley decided that he would take his mother's advice and allow his brother Richard to use his influence, as a junior member of William Pitt's administration, to obtain a commission for him in the Army.

2 An Officer in the 33rd

1787 – 93

'Those who think lightly of that lad are unwise
in their generation.'

'HE IS HERE at this moment, and perfectly idle,' Lord Mornington
wrote on his brother's behalf. It was, he added, a 'matter of indifference'
to him what commission his brother got, provided he got it soon and
it was not in the artillery which would not suit his rank or intellect.[1]
Early in March 1787, a few weeks before his eighteenth birthday, the
reply came: Arthur Wesley could be offered a commission as ensign
in the 73rd (Highland) Regiment of Foot.

His mother was delighted. She thought him much improved upon
his return from Angers, she told two friends of hers, Lady Eleanor
Butler and Miss Sarah Ponsonby, who were living together on terms
of romantic friendship, totally isolated from society in a cottage at
Llangollen in North Wales. These ladies, described by Prince Pückler-
Muskau as 'certainly the most celebrated virgins in Europe', had
already met Arthur Wesley. He had been taken to see them by his
grandmother, Lady Dungannon, who lived nearby, while still an Eton
schoolboy, and he had been awkward in their company, disturbed by
their semi-masculine attire and Lady Eleanor's top hat. But he was not
awkward now, his mother assured them. 'He really is a charming young
man,' she said. 'Never did I see such a change for the better in any
body.'[2]

She used her influence with the Marquess of Buckingham, the Duke
of Portland's successor as Lord-Lieutenant in Dublin, to have him
appointed to his lordship's staff as aide-de-camp; and she recorded
with satisfaction his promotion to Lieutenant in the 76th (Hindoostan)
Regiment of Foot, and then, since this regiment was returning to India,
his transfer to the 41st.

He called upon the 'Ladies of Llangollen' on his way to take up his
duties in Ireland; and they agreed with his mother that the eighteen-
year-old boy was now greatly improved and had much to recommend

him. He was 'a charming young man', Lady Eleanor decided, 'handsome . . . and elegant'.[3]

Not everyone in Dublin concurred with her. One young lady was thankful to be able to escape from his company; another, older woman, Lady Aldborough, having taken him to a picnic in her carriage, declined to have him with her on the return journey because 'he was so dull'; yet another refused to attend a party if that 'mischievous boy' was to be of the company: he had such an irritating habit of flicking up the lace from shirt collars. To the Napier family he gave the impression of being 'a shallow, saucy stripling'. It had to be conceded, though, that the time spent in dancing classes in Angers had not been wasted, that he rode well even if his seat was a trifle ungainly, and that, while on occasions rather stiff, his manner, when not in one of his prankish moods, was pleasant enough, his conversation interesting, though small talk was never his forte.[4]

It was quite clear that he enjoyed the company of women and, when at ease with them, was 'good humoured' in their company. He also enjoyed the excitement of gambling. Indeed, it was said of him that, like the denizens of White's club in St James's, he would bet on anything. On one occasion, for example, he won 150 guineas by getting from Cornelscourt outside Dublin to Leeson Street, a distance of six miles, in under an hour. But he lost as often as he won; and sank ever deeper into debt. He seems not to have kept a mistress as his brother, Richard, did at great expense, having chosen to live with an attractive Frenchwoman of extravagant tastes and philoprogenitive inclinations whom he later married after she had given birth to five children;[5] but Arthur does appear to have frequented a brothel, once evidently being fined for an assault upon a fellow customer of the establishment, a Frenchman whose stick he seized and beat him with.[6]

Yet Arthur Wesley had his serious and ambitious side. He took trouble to exercise his talent with the violin and to improve the quality of his playing. He read a great deal: he was once discovered studying Locke's *Essay Concerning Human Understanding*. The Hon. George Napier who had served on Sir Henry Clinton's staff in America and was then a captain in the 100th Foot, commented, 'Those who think lightly of that lad are unwise in their generation: he has in him the makings of a great general.'[7]

He was already beginning to make a name for himself, as the ambitious Richard had done so quickly. Arthur contrived to get elected at the age of nineteen to the Irish House of Commons for the family seat of Trim, formerly held by his brother William, having first become a Freemason and having publicly declared his opposition to the Corporation of Trim's decision to confer the freedom of the place upon Henry Grattan, the Irish patriot whose views on Roman Catholic emancipation were not conducive to the peace of mind of Lord Buckingham; and, although he did not speak in the House of Commons for two years, when he did so his maiden speech was quite well received. So were his subsequent interventions, even if, in the opinion of Jonah Barrington, a judge in the Irish court of admiralty, whom he met at a dinner party, he never spoke on important subjects.[8]

Lieutenant Wesley began to believe that he could become a politician if he so willed it. Yet, as revolution gained momentum in France with the storming of the Tuileries in August 1792, the September Massacres and the execution of the King, Wesley's thoughts turned again and again from politics to the Army and to service overseas. By transfers and purchase, he was advancing in his profession. From the 41st Foot he had been transferred to the 12th Light Dragoons; from the Dragoons he had returned to the infantry as a captain in the 58th Foot; from the 58th he had gone back to the cavalry as a captain in the 18th Light Dragoons; and, having appealed to his brother Richard for the money, he had bought a major's rank in the 33rd Foot.

Tired of trotting about at the Lord-Lieutenant's heels in Dublin for a paltry ten shillings a day, though this was a welcome addition to his scanty private income of £125 a year,* he was anxious to go to war. He gave up gambling; he paid off what debts he could, including one to the boot-maker with whom he lodged; he resigned his Trim seat, and gave away his violin, believing, so a friend later recorded, that playing the fiddle was 'not a soldierly accomplishment and took up too much of his time and thoughts'.[9]

He wrote to Richard to ask him to approach the authorities on his behalf and tell them that, if any part of the Army were to be sent abroad, he wanted to go with it. 'They may as well take me as anybody else.'[10]

For the moment they did not take him. He was kept in Ireland drilling the soldiers of the 33rd and supervising the logging of the regimental accounts, a responsibility he did not find as tedious as might have been expected, for he had a good head for figures, a respect for

---

* Because of the fluctuating rate of inflation and other reasons it is not really practicable to translate eighteenth-century sums into present-day equivalents. Multiplying the figures in this book by about sixty should give a very rough guide for the years before 1793. For the years of war between 1793 and 1815 the reader should multiply by about thirty, and thereafter by about forty.

detail and a pride in his talent for 'rapid and correct calculation'.[11] In the autumn of 1793 he made a brief visit to England where he witnessed his brother's signature to the deed of sale of Dangan Castle; but he was soon back in Ireland, a lieutenant-colonel by then, in command of the 33rd, frustratingly confined to regimental duties while news came from Paris of the horrors of the Terror and the blade of the guillotine rose and fell.

3 The First Campaign

1794 — 5

'I was on the Waal, I think from October to
January and during all that time I only saw once
one General from the headquarters.'

THE WAR which France had declared on Britain after the execution
of the King was not going well. The British army had been ejected
from Dunkirk and was soon to be thrown out of Flanders, through
which it was vainly hoped an attack could be made on the heart
of France; while the French, commanded by the young generals of the
Revolution, brave, impromptu and *roturier*, occupied Holland. The
British troops – led by the Duke of York who was quite at home at the
Horse Guards, the headquarters of the general staff in Whitehall, but
as inexperienced in the field as most of his regimental officers – were
ill-clothed and ill-fed, less than competently served by a Royal Waggon
Corps, whose men, raised from the rookeries of Blackfriars and Seven
Dials, were known as the Newgate Blues. For the sick and wounded, to
be carried to such military hospitals as there were was to be consigned
to a probable death. Surgeons' mates were slipshod, negligent and very
often drunk. A Dutchman counted forty-two bodies thrown overboard
from a hospital barge on which they had been left unattended on the
open deck. Officers were likely to go as hungry as their men. Colonel
Wesley was warned by an old Guards officer, 'You little know what you
are going to meet with. You will often have no dinner at all. I mean literally
no dinner, and not merely roughing it on a beefsteak or a bottle of wine.'[1]

Arthur Wesley, twenty-five years old, was at last to find this out for
himself. The orders for which he had long been waiting had come;
and in the middle of June 1794 he disembarked the 33rd Foot on the
quayside at Ostend from a ship that had brought them over from Cork.
At Ostend he was given command of two other battalions as well as
his own and handed orders to take them over post haste to Antwerp

to reinforce the Duke of York's position. But the Duke's position was not tenable for long; and, as the summer weather gave way to a cold autumn and a freezing winter, the British fell back in slow retreat. The 33rd were briefly in action in September at Boxtel where their Colonel handled them well; and later, in the depths of winter, they fought their way through another small town with bayonets fixed. Yet for most of those weeks officers and men alike struggled merely to keep warm and alive in the dreary, frozen countryside of polder and canal. 'We turn out once, sometimes twice every night,' the Colonel reported in a letter to a cousin. 'The officers and men are harassed to death ... I have not had my clothes off my back for a long time; we spend the greater part of the night upon the bank of the river [the Waal] ... Although the French annoy us much at night, they are very entertaining during the day time; they are perpetually chattering with our officers and soldiers, and dance the *carmagnole* upon the opposite bank whenever we desire them; but occasionally the spectators on our side are interrupted in the middle of the dance by a cannon ball from theirs.'[2]

Utrecht fell; French trees of liberty were set up in Amsterdam; and the ragged British army straggled back, leaving broken carts and dead animals in its wake, towards the Ems and the Weser at Bremen. Colonel Wesley did not wait to see his battalion embark. Leaving a junior officer in charge, he set sail in March for London.

His first campaign had been a most unpleasant experience; but at least, so he comforted himself, he had learned 'what one ought not to do, and that is always something'.[3] He had also learned that, while many of the British regiments were 'excellent', the generals had little idea how to manage an army. 'I was left to myself with my regiment ... thirty miles from headquarters which latter was a scene of jollifications,' he recalled, 'and I do not think that I was once visited by the Commander-in-Chief.'[4] He remembered, too, an occasion when a dispatch was brought in after dinner in the mess. 'That will keep till tomorrow,' said the senior officer complacently, returning to the port decanter.[5]

'I was on the Waal, I think from October to January,' Wesley complained, 'and during all that time I only saw once one General from the headquarters ... We had letters from England, and I declare that those letters told us more of what was passing at headquarters than we learned from the headquarters themselves ... The real reason why I succeeded in my own campaign is because I was always on the spot – I saw everything and did everything myself.'[6]

*

While his battalion went into camp in Essex, Colonel Wesley resumed without enthusiasm his duties as aide-de-camp to the Lord-Lieutenant in Dublin. Before leaving for Ostend, he had done his best to settle his debts, assigning his income to a tradesman who agreed to pay them off by instalments. But he returned to find that they had not yet all been discharged, while his lieutenant-colonel's pay and his allowances as an aide-de-camp were meagre in the extreme for a man without private fortune who wished to cut a figure in the world. His brother Richard was generous: he did not seek repayment of the sums he had advanced for the purchases in rank from captain to lieutenant-colonel; but there were limits to what he could ask of him and what Richard himself could afford. As it was, Richard was doing all he could to press his brother's claims to some office of profit under the Crown. He wrote to the Lord-Lieutenant, an appointment now held by the second Earl Camden, proposing that Arthur was ideally qualified to fill the situation of Secretary-at-War which was 'likely to be opened soon'. Colonel Wesley himself approached Camden to suggest that he might be appointed to fill vacancies on the Revenue or Treasury Boards, or, perhaps, he might be considered for the post of Surveyor-General of the Ordnance for Ireland when the present incumbent resigned. But Camden was not responsive; nor did he show due appreciation when his aide-de-camp, as Member for Trim, rose to answer Henry Grattan and defend the record of Lord Camden's predecessor as Lord-Lieutenant, the 10th Earl of Westmorland, who had been recalled in 1795 because of his firm opposition to the emancipation of the Roman Catholics.

Despairing of getting any help from Lord Camden, Colonel Wesley sought leave of absence from Dublin and returned to England to his battalion which was now stationed near Southampton under orders to sail for the West Indies. He wrote to say that he intended to set out with his men; but, if he hoped to receive some opposition to this plan, he was disappointed. Lord Camden was 'very sorry to lose him' but quite approved of his decision to go to the West Indies, being 'convinced that a profession once embraced should not be given up'. 'I shall be very glad if I can make some arrangement satisfactory to you against you come back, but if a vacancy should happen in the Revenue Board I fear the Speaker's son must have the first.'[7]

So, all hopes of employment in Ireland or England abandoned, Wesley prepared to sail. He was not feeling at all well. As a boy he had repeatedly suffered from minor illnesses, colds and low fever; and his recent campaigning on the Continent had exacerbated what his doctor called his 'aguish complaint'. He was advised to take calomel and cinnamon, opium and quassia, camphorated spirit of wine and tincture of cantharides.[8] Doubtless wary of these prescriptions, he consulted another doctor but this physician also seems to have been unable to effect a cure, while finding his patient a remarkable personality. 'I have been attending a young man whose conversation is the most extraordinary I have ever listened to,' he is said to have observed. 'If he lives he must one day be Prime Minister.'[9]

The chances that he would at least live were much improved when fortune decided that he was not, after all, to go to the West Indies, the graveyard of so many British soldiers.

Twice the ships of the convoy were swept back by winter gales, on the second occasion after tossing for seven weeks in seas so heavy that one of them was sent scudding helplessly through the Strait of Gibraltar and on to the Spanish coast, while others were scattered across the Atlantic or into the Solent.

4   A Voyage to India

1796 – 8

'In person he was about 5 feet 7 inches with a
long pale face, a remarkably large aquiline nose, a
clear blue eye and the blackest beard I ever saw.'

COLONEL WESLEY was aboard one of the ships that were blown
home. He stepped ashore in poorer health than ever in January 1796.
He went to see his doctor again when he returned to Dublin to settle
his affairs there before taking the 33rd on their next tour of duty, this
time in the East Indies rather than the West.

There was much to do before they sailed: he had to instruct his
successor in the duties of the Lieutenant-General's aide-de-camp, to
write a paper for the guidance of the man who was to take over as
Member of Parliament for Trim, to give instructions to the agent who
was managing the family's estates in Meath which had not been sold
with the castle, to make such arrangements as he could about the
liquidation of his debts, which now stood at over £1,000. He was still
busy in Dublin when the 33rd were on the point of sailing for India
by way of the Cape of Good Hope. He let them go without him. The
voyage would take several weeks and, if he sailed after them in a fast
frigate, he would be able to catch them up before they got into the
Arabian Sea.

He left Dublin for London in June and, taking rooms at 3 Savile
Row, he set out for the shops to equip himself for what might prove
to be a long absence in the East. There were clothes to buy and,
equally important, there were books. For these he went to Faulders,
the booksellers and book-binders in Bond Street, and from here and
other shops he came away with a library that could surely not have
been packed in its entirety in the trunk, complete with 'Cord Etc.',
which he bought from Mr Faulder for £1 11s 6d. There were histories
of warfare, sieges and military campaigns, an account of the topography
of the Indian sub-continent, a copy of the Bengal Army List, books
about Egypt and the East India Company, maps and German, Arabic

17

and Persian grammars and dictionaries, as well as two volumes of Richardson's Persian dictionary costing the extraordinarily large sum of twelve guineas. There were three volumes of Adam Smith's *Wealth of Nations*, four of the works of Lord Bolingbroke and of Sir William Blackstone's *Commentaries on the Laws of England*, five of the theological expositions of William Paley, six of Plutarch's lives, nine of the philosophical works of John Locke, thirteen of David Hume's *History of England*, fifteen volumes by Frederick the Great and, for lighter reading, twenty-four volumes of the works of Jonathan Swift. There were books by Voltaire, Crébillon and Rousseau, Samuel Johnson's dictionary and the memoirs of Marshal Saxe. Listed between books by Smollett and the licentious *Amours du Chevalier de Faublas* were nine volumes of *Women of Pleasure*. Between a history of France and Cambridge's *War in India* was a medical treatise on venereal disease.[1]

With these and many other books safely corded in their trunks, Wesley, by now a full colonel, sailed from Portsmouth when the wind was sufficiently fresh and rejoined the 33rd at the Cape. Here he also found two young ladies, not long out of their schoolroom, on their way to India. The elder of the two, Jemima Smith, was described by a young officer who met them at this time as 'a most incorrigible flirt, very clever, very satirical, and aiming at universal conquest. Her sister, Henrietta [aged seventeen] was more retiring, and I think more admired . . . with her pretty little figure and lovely neck [that was to say bosom] . . . She made a conquest of Colonel Arthur Wesley who had arrived at the Cape with the 33rd Regiment.'*[2]

Certainly in the company of these two girls, the Colonel, so studious in the frigate on her long passage down the west coast of Africa, became lively and entertaining, 'all life and spirits'. A captain in the 12th Regiment, Maria Edgeworth's cousin, George Elers, who had recently arrived at the Cape, provided this sketch of him:

> In person he was about 5 feet 7 inches [actually more like 5 feet 8 or 9 inches] with a long pale face, a remarkably large aquiline nose, a clear blue eye and the blackest beard I ever saw . . . I have known him shave twice in one day, which I believe was his constant practice . . . He was remarkably clean in his person . . .
>
> His features always reminded me of [the tragedian] John Philip Kemble, and, what is more remarkable I also observed the great

---

* The 33rd Foot (West Riding Regiment) was renamed the Duke of Wellington's Regiment in 1853, the year after the Duke's death. The instruction from the Adjutant-General was dated 18 June, the anniversary of the battle of Waterloo.

likeness between him and the performer, Mr Charles Young, which he told me he had often heard remarked. He spoke at this time remarkably quickly, with a very, very slight lisp. He had very narrow jaw bones, and there was a great peculiarity in his ear, which I never observed but in one other person, the late Lord Byron – the lobe of the ear uniting to the cheek. He had a particular way, when pleased, of pursing up his mouth. I have often observed it when he has been thinking abstractedly.[3]

Colonel Wesley was not detained at the Cape for long: in the middle of February 1797, at the age of twenty-seven, almost eight months after leaving England, he went ashore at Calcutta after a more than commonly tedious passage across the Indian Ocean and up the Bay of Bengal in an East Indiaman, named after Princess Charlotte, King George III's eldest daughter. As soon as he could he called upon the Governor-General, Sir John Shore, a schoolfellow of the playwright Richard Brinsley Sheridan at Harrow, who had started his career as a writer in the service of the East India Company by which his father had also been employed as a supercargo. Shore was a conscientious and hard-working though unremarkable man and 'as cold as a greyhound's nose'; but he was astute enough to recognize in Colonel Wesley a promising young man of strong common sense who might well one day be a person of distinction.[4]

The Colonel, Shore added, also had about him an air of 'boyish playfulness'; and it was this quality which struck William Hickey, the memoirist, then practising as an attorney in Calcutta and a popular and highly hospitable member of the British community there. Hickey saw him first at a St Patrick's Day dinner in Calcutta at which the Colonel had been asked to take the chair, a duty which he performed 'with peculiar credit to himself'.[5]

'On the 20th of the same month [March 1797],' Hickey continued, 'a famous character arrived in Bengal, Major-General John St Leger, who had for a long period been a bosom friend and companion of the Prince of Wales. From having lived so much with His Royal Highness, he had not only suffered in his health, but materially impaired his fortune, and was therefore happy to get out of the way of the Prince's temptations by visiting Bengal, upon which Establishment he was placed upon His Majesty's staff.'

As soon as St Leger arrived, Hickey, who had known him in England, invited him to join a party of guests he was to entertain at his house at Chinsurah. Colonel Wesley was also of the party which, Hickey congratulated himself, was a great success.

We rose early every morning making long excursions from which we returned with keen appetite for breakfast. That meal being over we adjourned to the billiard room . . . When tired of that game [we played] Trick Track [backgammon] . . . Thus the morning passed. At about half past three we retired to our respective rooms, of which I have seven for bachelors, to dress, and at four precisely sat down to dinner.[6]

Hickey gave another party at Chinsurah on the King's birthday, 4 June; and again on that occasion Colonel Wesley was one of the guests. Their host had procured a 'tolerably fat deer' and a 'very fine turtle' and engaged 'an eminent French cook from Calcutta to dress the dinner'. He had taken 'especial care to lay in a *quantum sufficit* of the best champagne that was procurable'; his 'claret, hock, and madeira', he knew, were 'not to be surpassed in Bengal'. The party accordingly went off with the 'utmost hilarity and good humour'. 'We had several choice songs . . . followed by delightful catches and glees . . . and General St Leger in the course of the evening sang "The British Grenadiers" with high spirit.' The party did not break up until between two and three o'clock in the morning; and nearly all the guests woke up with dreadful hangovers.

Freely as the claret was pushed about at Chinsurah, however, the drinking there was moderate when compared with that in the officers' mess of the 33rd Foot, over which Colonel Wesley presided, and in the house of Wesley's second-in-command, Lieutenant-Colonel John Sherbrooke, at Alypore, three miles from Calcutta. Here the drinking of the 33rd's officers was astonishing. One of the 33rd's parties, so Hickey wrote, consisted of eight as strong-headed fellows as could be found in Hindustan, including Colonel Wesley.

During dinner we drank as usual, that is, the whole company each with the other at least twice over. The cloth being removed, the first half-dozen toasts proved irresistible, and I gulped them down without hesitation. At the seventh . . . I only half filled my glass whereupon our host said, 'I should not have suspected you, Hickey, of shirking such a toast as the Navy,' and my next neighbour immediately observing, 'it must have been a mistake,' having the bottle in his hand at the time, he filled my glass up to the brim. The next round I made a similar attempt, with no better success, and then gave up the thoughts of saving myself. After drinking two-and-twenty bumpers in glasses of considerable magnitude, the [Colonel] said, everyone might then fill according to his own discretion, and so *discreet* were all of the company that we continued to follow the Colonel's example of drinking nothing short of bumpers until two o'clock in the morning, at which hour each person staggered to his carriage or his palankeen, and was conveyed to town. The next day I was incapable of leaving my bed, from an excruciating headache, which I did not get rid of for eight-and-forty hours; indeed a more severe debauch I never was engaged in in any part of the world.[7]

For Colonel Wesley these days in Calcutta were a pleasant interlude; but he had not studied McKenzie's *War in Mysore* and General Dirom's *Narrative of the Campaign in India* to sit drinking bumpers of claret at camphor-wood dinner tables under gently swishing punkahs and passing the mouthpiece of hookahs to the wives of Company officials on lamplit verandas. There was talk of an attack on the Pacific colonies of Spain which had recently come into the war on the side of France, or upon the Dutch, now also England's enemies, in Java, and Wesley hoped that if such an assault were to be mounted, he might be given a command in it, perhaps the chief command. Yet, as a recent arrival in India, he did not want to appear too importunate. So, when it was suggested he might command such an expedition, he demurred, proposing the name of another more senior officer, with the proviso that if anything should prevent that officer taking it, he would be prepared to accept the command himself, 'taking chance,' as he told his brother Richard, 'that the known pusillanimity of the Enemy' and his own exertions would 'compensate in some degree' for his lack of experience. 'I hope,' he added, not troubling to hide his low opinion of them, 'to be at least as successful as the people to whom Hobart [Lord Hobart, Governor of the Presidency of Madras] wishes to give command . . . Of course, the Chief Command of this expedition would make my fortune; going upon it at all will enable me to free myself from debt, therefore you may easily conceive that I am not very anxious for the conclusion of a peace at this moment.'[8] As though to confirm his qualifications as commander, he sent Sir John Shore a résumé of what was known of the places which were to come under attack and information he had gleaned about the harbours where the expeditionary force might be put ashore.

His hopes, however, were not to be realized; he was not given the chief command but went instead as commanding officer of the 33rd with orders to land them at Manila in the Philippines, and then launch an attack across the Sulu and Celebes Seas and through the Straits of Makassar upon the Dutch garrison in Java. But the expedition was as inconclusive as the 33rd's attempted crossing of the Atlantic in 1795.

It got off to an unfortunate start: a young clergyman, the nephew of a friend of William Hickey, appointed by Colonel Wesley at Hickey's request as chaplain of the 33rd, turned out to be 'of very eccentric and peculiarly odd manners'. A day or two out of Calcutta he got 'abominably drunk' and 'gave a public exhibition of extreme impropriety, exposing himself to both soldiers and sailors, running out of his cabin stark naked into the midst of them, talking all sorts of bawdy and ribaldry, and singing scraps of the most blackguard and indecent songs'. Overcome with remorse when sober, he took to his bunk and, though kindly assured by Colonel Wesley that his behaviour was 'not of the least consequence', that no one would think the worse of him for 'little irregularities committed in a moment of forgetfulness', 'that the most correct and cautious men were liable to be led astray by convivial society', and that 'no blame ought to attach to a cursory debauch', the poor young clergyman remained inconsolably penitent, refused to eat and 'actually fretted himself to death'.[9]

A week or so later the entire expeditionary force was recalled. There were reports of spreading unrest in British India, while Napoleon Bonaparte, appointed to the command of the French Army of Italy, was triumphantly justifying the trust the Directory in Paris had reposed in him. There had, besides, been mutinies in the British Navy at Spithead and the Nore which were so serious in the eyes of the First Lord of the Admiralty that the Channel Fleet was now 'lost to the country as much as if it was at the bottom of the sea'. It had consequently been decided in Calcutta that the British forces in the East must be concentrated, and the 33rd brought home forthwith across the Indian Ocean. So it was that before long Colonel Wesley – who had planned his regiment's part in the expedition with characteristic care and attention to detail – was once more back in India in the company of William Hickey.

But, having been denied the opportunity of distinguishing himself, he felt even less inclined to fritter his afternoons and evenings away at dinner tables or to be satisfied with the undemanding routine of regimental life. He found time to study his books on Indian affairs and even produced a long and detailed refutation of a work that had recently appeared entitled *Remarks upon the Present State of the Husbandry and Commerce of Bengal*. He also became a familiar figure in the corridors of both Fort St George, where Lord Hobart exercised his authority as Governor of the Presidency of Madras, and Fort William, the headquarters of the Governor-General of India.

5 The Tiger of Mysore

1799

'Had Colonel Wellesley been an obscure officer
of fortune he would have been brought to a
court-martial.'

SHORE'S DAYS as Governor-General were now coming to an end. As
the recently created Baron Teignmouth, he sailed home in March 1798,
leaving the Government in the hands of the Commander-in-Chief,
General Sir Alured Clarke, until his successor arrived in India.

This successor, whose ship, carrying a huge quantity of his baggage,
docked at Calcutta on 17 May 1798, was the thirty-seven-year-old
Richard Wesley, Earl of Mornington, soon to be created Marquess
Wellesley of Norragh in the peerage of Ireland. The Marquess insisted
upon that spelling of the family name which his brother Arthur now
adopted, as did Henry whom the new Governor-General had brought
out as his Private Secretary.*

The Marquess, stately and patrician, long desirous of a marquessate,
did not consider an Irish title at all adequate; nor did he hesitate to
inform Mr Pitt, the Prime Minister, of his feelings in the matter. But
he was well satisfied with his appointment which was, indeed, in his
estimation, 'the most distinguished situation in the British Empire after
that of Prime Minister of England'.[1] He was also satisfied that he had
'firmness enough to govern the British empire in India without favour
or affection to any human being either in Europe or Asia'.[2]

As though prompted by this assertion, his brother Arthur hastened
to assure him that even he would not expect to derive any more advantage from his close relationship to the Governor-General than he would
had any other person been appointed.[3] All the same, he offered his
services to Richard who, anxious though he was to avoid all imputations

---

* The name was originally spelled Wellesley. A man of that name obtained a grant of
land near Wells in Somerset from Henry I in 1104. A descendant of his was Justice
Itinerant in Ireland in 1261. The family began to spell the name Wesley in the seventeenth
century (Iris Butler, *The Eldest Brother*, 25).

of nepotism, employed him as an unofficial Military Secretary, seeking
his advice on matters that might well have been supposed the province
of the staff of the Commander-in-Chief, and receiving in return
detailed papers and memoranda on all manner of subjects of which
Colonel Wellesley had taken the trouble to inform himself, from strategic considerations to fortifications and supplies, even to such problems as the methods which should be employed in the collection of
adequate numbers of bullocks.

The Colonel's energetic activity led him to step on a number of
sensitive toes. He much offended General St Leger by opposing his
scheme for the creation of an Indian Horse Artillery, bluntly pointing
out that there were insufficient horses for such an establishment: bullocks were the answer. He was also on extremely bad terms with Lord
Hobart, Governor of the Presidency of Madras, whom he had much
annoyed by openly opposing the appointment of General John
Braithwaite to the command of the abortive expedition to Manila.
Hobart had given the command to Braithwaite on the grounds that he
was the senior officer and would be well supported by a reliable staff
and a good army. 'But he is mistaken,' Colonel Wellesley objected, 'if
he supposes that a good, high-spirited army can be kept in order by
other means than by the abilities & firmness of the Commander-in-
Chief.'[4] Colonel Wellesley's forthright criticism of the Governor's
decision had resulted in his receiving in reply such a letter as, 'between
ourselves', he indignantly told his brother Richard, 'I have been
unaccustomed to receive & will never submit to'.[5]

It was considered 'most unfortunate' that there should be quarrels
and disagreements like these in high places when affairs in India were
in such a critical state.

The area of the sub-continent administered by the British authorities
was a very small proportion of the whole. There were still enormous
princely states from Oudh in the north to Mysore and Travancore in
the south with the sprawling territories of the Marāthās and the Nizam
of Hyderabad between them. Relations between these states and the
East India Company were very uncertain, while French influence in
India was still strong. There had been persistent outbreaks of hostilities,
most recently between the British and Mysore whose Sultan, Tippu,
known as the 'Tiger of Mysore', remained an inveterate enemy of British
power.

The Governor-General proposed a pre-emptive strike against Tippu.

He had heard that the French, who had landed a large expeditionary force in Egypt, were preparing to support the Sultan in an attempt to drive the British out of India. It would surely be wise to attack Mysore before the French alliance materialized. Colonel Wellesley disagreed. He did not take the threat of immediate French intervention too seriously. There were, at present, very few French troops available; and, if more were to be sent from France, they would have difficulty in evading the attention of the British fleet. It would be far better, he argued, to leave the Sultan in no doubt as to the Governor-General's determination not to tolerate French interference in India and to give him an opportunity to deny that he wished to encourage it. 'In the meantime,' he concluded, 'we shall be prepared against all events.'

In August 1798 he sailed with the 33rd for Madras. It was a highly unpleasant voyage in which his ship sprang a leak and an impure supply of water led to an outbreak of dysentery which cost him the lives of fifteen men and days of illness himself. He had already had cause to complain of the management of the sick soldiers by ships' surgeons at sea, and had issued regimental orders for the supply of clean water, the fumigation of the lower decks, the scrubbing of hammocks, regular exercise with dumb-bells, the washing of feet and legs every morning and evening and the frequent dowsing of their naked bodies with bucketfuls of water, as well as the dilution of their allowance of spirits with three parts of water. He now castigated the commissariat for supplying his men with bad water: it was 'unpardonable' and he would be forced to make 'a public complaint' of the men responsible.[6]

In Madras Colonel Wellesley found Lord Clive installed as Governor of the Presidency in succession to Lord Hobart. Lord Clive was a very different man from his father, the great Governor of Bengal. Had he been born with a different name it is most probable that he would not have risen so high in the service of the East India Company. 'How the Devil did he get there?' asked Lord Wellesley.[7] It was a question difficult to answer; for Lord Clive was ponderous in both thought and speech, though, it had to be conceded, of a remarkable physical vigour which was to last him into old age when, in his eightieth year, by then the Earl of Powis, he could be seen digging in his garden in his shirtsleeves at six o'clock in the morning. Despite his apparently stodgy temperament, he struck Colonel Wellesley as being probably not as dull as he appeared or as people in Madras took him to be. 'Lord Clive opens his mind to me very freely upon all subjects,' Colonel Wellesley reported. 'The truth is that he does not want talents, but is very diffident of himself ... He improves daily.' So the Governor-General was persuaded to change his mind about Lord Clive. Indeed, it was not long before the Governor-General was convinced that he was 'a very sensible man'. Certainly, as Governor, Lord Clive was quite ready to cooperate fully with the military men, both in Calcutta and in his own Presidency of Madras, in whatever were considered to be the best interests of British India.[8]

For the moment, in Colonel Wellesley's sustained opinion, the best interests of British India lay in not provoking Tippu Sultan. 'Nothing,' the Colonel proposed, 'should be demanded of him [which was] not an object of immediate consequence'; and it was his advice that the demand should, for the moment, be limited to his receiving a British ambassador in his capital of Seringapatam.[9] In the meantime Colonel Wellesley continued to do his best to ensure that, were force found to be necessary, the means at the Governor-General's disposal would be adequate to the task. The work was peculiarly frustrating: there were so many officers and Company officials whose inefficiency was an almost constant exasperation. Commissaries were in general 'a parcel of blockheads'; two particular officers of the Company were worse than useless, one of them 'so stupid' that he was unfit for the simplest tasks, the other 'such a rascal' that he had to be watched all the time; neither of them understood 'one syllable of the language'.[10] The Colonel experienced as much difficulty in getting the siege-train moved nearer to the frontier between Mysore and the Madras Presidency as he did in having supplies placed in depots along the planned route of the army's proposed march.

Exasperated as he was by inefficient subordinates, the Colonel was further troubled by the scandalous quarrelling of regimental officers, one of these quarrels resulting in a duel in which Colonel Henry Harvey Aston of the 12th was mortally wounded. There had followed a court of enquiry which had occupied hour upon hour of Colonel Wellesley's time and kept him at work far into the night.[11]

The General who was to command the army which Wellesley was so conscientiously helping to prepare for action was Lieutenant-General George Harris, a parson's son who had trained as an artilleryman and had fought with distinction in the war in America where he had been wounded more than once. He was a good-natured man of no remarkable talents but deemed perfectly capable of conquering Mysore.

That Mysore must, indeed, be conquered was decided towards the end of 1798 after a lengthy, convoluted and entirely unsatisfactory correspondence between the Governor-General and the Sultan had merely widened the breach between the two men and failed to settle the question as to whether or not a representative of the King of England would be accepted in Seringapatam.

In General Harris's army of some 50,000 men Colonel Wellesley was given a large command. As well as his own 33rd he was to have six battalions of the East India Company's troops, four 'rapscallion battalions' of the army of Britain's ally, the Nizam Ali of Hyderabad, which were accompanied by no fewer than 120,000 bullocks, and 'about 10,000 (which they called 25,000) cavalry of all nations, some good and some bad, and twenty-six pieces of cannon'.[12] Wellesley was soon to decide it was, all in all, 'a strong, a healthy and a brave army with plenty of stores, guns, etc.', but he did not want the staff at Fort William in Calcutta to suppose victory was a foregone conclusion. They must be prepared for a failure; it was 'better to see and to communicate the difficulties and dangers of the enterprise, and to endeavour to overcome them, than to be blind to everything but success till the moment of difficulty comes, and then to despond'.[13]

He was somewhat despondent himself, not having felt very well of late in Madras and soon to be pulled down by another attack of dysentery. He was also rather short tempered: when his brother the Governor-General asked him whether he should join the expeditionary force himself, he responded curtly, 'All I can say upon the subject is, that if I were in General Harris's situation, and you joined the army, I should quit it.'[14]

The Colonel was still feeling unwell when, on a moonless night on the outskirts of Seringapatam, the column which he was commanding entered a dense thicket of bamboos and betel palm where they came under heavy fire in the darkness. The men fled in all directions, stumbling into irrigation ditches, shouting to each other across the thick undergrowth as rockets exploded around them and musket balls whistled through the foliage. Several of them were captured, some later killed by strangulation or by having nails driven into their skulls. The Colonel, hit on the knee by a spent musket ball, unable to see anything in the blackness of the night, and despairing of the possibility of reforming the column, limped away to report the disaster in the camp where the fires were still flickering at midnight.[15]

Some officers, disliking what they took to be Colonel Wellesley's bumptious arrogance and jealous of his close relationship with the Governor-General, were not sorry to learn of his failure. His second-in-command was one of them. Captain Elers, in a book published after he had fallen out with Wellesley, reported that, having gone to make a report to General Harris, he was turned away at the tent by a servant

who told him that 'General Sahib had gone to sleep'. 'Overcome
with despair and in a state of distraction, Colonel Wellesley threw
himself, with all his clothes on, *on the table* (at which a few hours
before he had dined), awaiting the dawn of day.'[16] In fact, so
General Harris noted in his journal, at about midnight Colonel
Wellesley came to his tent 'in a good deal of agitation to say he had
not carried the tope [thicket]. It must be particularly unpleasant to
him.'[17]

It undoubtedly was so. Ashamed of a failure that he was to remember
for the rest of his life, he bitterly blamed himself for entering
the thicket in darkness without reconnoitring it first. He told his
brother Richard that he was determined never to make such a mistake
again. 'Had Colonel Wellesley been an obscure officer of fortune,'
commented Captain Elers, 'he would have been brought to a court-
martial and perhaps received such a reprimand for bad management
as might have induced him in disgust to have resigned His Majesty's
service.'[18]

The next morning when the advance to Seringapatam was resumed
Colonel Wellesley was late in starting off because of a message which
failed to reach him. General Harris, accordingly, told another officer
to lead the attack instead. This officer was Major-General David Baird,
a tough, blunt Scotsman, twelve years Wellesley's senior. He had never
been an even-tempered man. As a young captain in the 73rd Highlanders on a previous campaign he had been wounded, taken prisoner and
held captive by Tippu Sultan for three years and eight months; and,
with the bullet still in his wound, he had been chained to a fellow
prisoner. When the news reached his mother in Scotland that her son
was treated in this way, she acknowledged the fact of his savage temper
in an observation of maternal percipience. 'God help,' she said, 'the
puir child chained to our Davie.'[19]

Age had not mellowed him. 'He is,' one of his officers declared, 'a
bloody old bad tempered Scotchman.' He had no reason to regard
Colonel Wellesley with benevolence. He considered that he should
have been offered the command of the expedition to Manila which it
had seemed likely at one time would be given to the far junior Colonel
the Hon. Arthur Wesley; he also thought that he should have been
given command of the Nizam of Hyderabad's troops which had been
assigned instead to the well-connected young Colonel and, in his disappointment, he had unwisely sent General Harris 'a strong remonstrance'. Even so, according to his biographer, he demurred when the
offer of superseding Wellesley was made to him. 'Don't you think, Sir,'

he said to Harris, 'it would be but fair to give Wellesley an opportunity of retrieving the misfortune of last night.'*[20]

So Colonel Wellesley was given his chance; and over the next few days, his knee less painful, he made amends for the débâcle of that miserable night. Having driven the Sultan's men from the wood, he successfully attacked one of Seringapatam's defensive works, as the army settled down to the formalities of a siege. He was not, however, to lead the final assault, for this duty was assigned to General Baird so that he might take revenge for the privations and ignominy of his long captivity. Waving his sword and shouting, 'Forward, my lads, my brave fellows, follow me and prove yourselves worthy of the name of British soldiers!', he led his men over the walls and into Seringapatam where Tippu Sultan – having put to death as oblations various animals, including two buffaloes, a goat, a bullock and an elephant, as well as, so it was said, various women of his court – was found dead, shot through the temple.[21]

---

* General Harris's biographer, Stephen Lushington, his son-in-law, maintained that Colonel Wellesley's reputation was saved by Harris independently changing his mind: 'On further consideration I think we must wait a little longer for Colonel Wellesley' (Stephen Lushington, A Life of Lord Harris, London, 1840, 291–8).

6   The Governor of Mysore

1799

'I must say that I was the *fit person* to be selected.'

GENERAL BAIRD expected to be placed in command of the captured city in which much treasure had to be guarded and a terrified populace reassured. But he was not considered a suitable officer for the task. 'He had no talent, no *tact*,' Colonel Wellesley said later, while acknowledging his bravery and the regard in which he was held by his men. 'He had strong prejudices against the natives, and was peculiarly disqualified from his manner, habits and temper for the management of them. Having been Tippoo's prisoner for years, he had a strong feeling of the bad usage which he had received during his captivity.' 'I must say,' Wellesley added, 'that I was the *fit person* to be selected. I had commanded the Nizam's army during the campaign, and had given universal satisfaction. I was liked by the natives.'[1] General Harris, who had not forgiven Baird for his 'strong remonstrance' over the command of the Nizam of Hyderabad's troops, accepted that this was the case.

So, while Baird and his staff were having breakfast in the Sultan's palace, news that he was not to be left in command at Seringapatam was broken to him by the Colonel himself who displayed on the occasion just that want of tact of which he accused the bluff Scotsman.

'General Baird,' he said to him, 'I am appointed to the command of Seringapatam, and here is the order of General Harris.'

'Come gentlemen,' replied Baird, rising angrily from the table and ignoring Colonel Wellesley, 'we have no longer any business here.'

'Oh, pray,' said the Colonel. 'Finish your breakfast.'[2]

Baird stormed from the palace and sat down to write a furious letter to General Harris which elicited another reprimand for once more displaying '*a total want of discretion and respect*'. Baird was told to go back to Madras. He stormed out of Seringapatam; but Colonel Wellesley had not yet seen the last of him.[3]

*

As it happened it was just as well that Wellesley not Baird was appointed to command in Seringapatam; for the situation demanded talents and insights that the brave, blunt Scotsman did not possess. At first there was much looting and frantic selling of treasures and gold bars stolen from the late Sultan's palace before order was restored by the hanging of four men and the flogging of others. Even then, the Colonel thought it would be best if most troops were withdrawn from the town since their presence, and their insatiable taste for plunder, occasioned 'great terror and confusion among the inhabitants', tending not only to obstruct the 'settlement of the country' but also to destroy the confidence which, he was pleased to say, the people reposed in him.

He had no particular affection for the Indian peoples in general. Indeed, not long after his arrival in Calcutta he had decided that the climate and the natives combined to make India a 'miserable country to live in', and he came to the conclusion that a man might well deserve some of the wealth that was brought home as a reward 'for having spent his life here'.[4] The natives were 'the most mischievous, deceitful race of people [he had] ever seen or read of'. 'I have not yet met with a Hindoo who had one good quality,' he added, 'and the Mussulmans are worse than they are. Their meekness and mildness do not exist.'[5] When he was offered two half-caste officers for the 33rd, he replied that they might well be 'as good as others', but he had been told that they were 'as black as my hat' and he declined to have them.[6] And when he heard that the Resident of Hyderabad was openly living with an Indian princess he delivered himself of the outraged opinion that it was 'a disgrace to the British name and nation'. Yet he was well aware how unwise it would be to offend against Indian customs and susceptibilities, and was determined not to tolerate in Mysore any of the 'dirty things' which he had been told, soon after his arrival in India, were 'done in some of the commands'.[7] On being informed that the Commander-in-Chief had issued an order for a search of the Sultan's zenana for hidden treasure, he strongly disapproved of it and, in carrying out his instructions, took 'every precaution to render the search as decent and as little injurious to the feelings of the ladies as possible'.* In the same way, when the Abbé Dubois, who was making a vain

---

* Among the objects discovered was a mechanical contraption representing a tiger clawing at a figure in European clothes. A pipe organ inside the metal bodies of the animal and its victim rendered the sounds of growls and screams. This gruesome toy was presented to the Court of Directors of the East India Company and is now in the Victoria and Albert Museum.

attempt to convert Hindus to Roman Catholicism under the auspices of the Missions Etrangères, asked for the return of two hundred Christian women from the zenana, the Colonel, having satisfied himself that they were not ill-treated there, refused the request on the grounds that it was 'not proper that anything should be done which can disgrace [the East India Company] in the eyes of the Indian world, or which can in the most remote degree cast a shade upon the dead, or violate the feelings of those who are alive'.[8]

Throughout his administration in Mysore he displayed this concern for Indian feelings. He asked the headquarters in Madras for a chaplain for the British garrison; but the people of Seringapatam were to be left free to practise their religion in their own way, and to be governed by their own laws in separate Muslim and Hindu courts.

While the tenor of Indian life in Seringapatam was allowed to continue undisturbed, there was much for the British Governor to do. There were the Sultan's tigers to care for; there was the reconstruction of buildings damaged during the siege and assault; there was the surrounding country to pacify; there were forts to inspect, punitive expeditions to control and punishments to ameliorate. There was advice to be given on the partition of the conquered state of Mysore and on the vexed question of the Marāthās' frontier: 'I recommend it to you not to put the Company upon the Mahratta frontier,' he wrote, showing how well he had studied his texts on Indian affairs. 'It is impossible to expect to alter the nature of the Mahrattas; they will plunder their neighbours, be they ever so powerful . . . It will be better to put one of the powers in dependence upon the Company on the frontier, who, if plundered, are accustomed to it, know how to bear it and retaliate, which we do not.'[9]

The Colonel had personal problems, too. It was an expensive business being Governor. To be sure, he had his share of prize money which amounted to £4,000, a very welcome sum if hardly to be compared with General Harris's £150,000. But his expenses were heavy, and he thought that people probably did not get quite as rich in India as was imagined in England. Indeed, he began to believe that he was ruined – certainly he was not yet able to pay off all his debts – and he enquired about the prospects of other more profitable appointments.[10] His brother, the Governor-General, offered him the opportunity of commanding an expedition against the Dutch in Java, where he would be sure to get more prize-money, if he could 'safely be spared from Mysore'. But he did not think he could be spared from Mysore. Some of his troops were in the field; and who, after all, could replace him? British generals were, for the most part as he had so often said, 'so confoundedly inefficient'. Besides, he was conscious that in Seringapatam he was rendering a 'service to the public'; and that service was not yet completed.[11]

Moreover, there was trouble to the north of Mysore where the warlord Dhoondiah Waugh, *soi-distant* 'King of the Two Worlds', was threatening the peace by assembling an army of warriors in the territory of the Marāthās. In the middle of 1800, Colonel Wellesley marched out of Seringapatam with a large force to deal with him. He proved an elusive quarry. Rivers were crossed, forts stormed, forests encountered (though not entered until reconnoitred). But nearly four months had passed before Dhoondiah Waugh was brought to bay, and forced to face his pursuers who were able at last to mount an attack in which Colonel Wellesley, for the first and last time in his life, led a cavalry charge.[12]

'We have now proved (a perfect novelty in India),' he reported with pride having sent the enemy scattering away, 'that we can hunt down the lightest footed and most rapid armies as we can destroy heavy troops and storm strong fortifications.'[13]

Soon there came an opportunity for the Colonel to demonstrate his prowess on a more prominent stage. The Governor-General, deeply concerned by the French threat, had been considering ways of dealing with it. Bonaparte, by now First Consul, had left his army in Egypt and on 14 June had overwhelmed the Austrians at Marengo. A British force was to be assembled in Ceylon with a view to an attack on the French in Egypt; and, despite 'the great trouble' that would be caused in consequence among the general officers in India, Colonel Wellesley was to lead it. 'I employ you because I rely on your good sense, discretion, activity, and spirit,' his brother told him, 'and I cannot find all those qualities united in any other officer in India.'[14] Besides, in his brother's opinion, Arthur should have been promoted long ago, and the fact that, now thirty years of age, and despite his distinguished services, he was still a colonel, reflected badly upon himself as Governor-General, just as the British Government's fobbing him off with a mere Irish marquessate had done. Colonel Wellesley's being 'not only unnoticed but his promotion protracted so studiously', the Marquess had written earlier, had led to 'every Intriguer' in India believing it 'to be delayed for the express purpose of thwarting me'.[15]

Seemingly undisturbed by the thought that older and more

experienced generals in Madras and Calcutta would not take at all kindly to his appointment, Colonel Wellesley sailed for Trincomalee in Ceylon towards the end of 1800, leaving behind in Seringapatam, for the guidance of his successor, detailed notes on all manner of subjects from the administration of Mysore to the relevant features of its topography.

By the time Colonel Wellesley landed in Trincomalee, the proposal for an assault on French troops in Egypt by way of the Red Sea had been superseded by plans for an attack upon the French island of Mauritius. But differences with the naval Commander-in-Chief in the area led to the abandonment of Mauritius as an object of attack and its replacement by Java. Plans for an attack on the Dutch were, however, also abandoned when definite orders came from England for the implementation of the original operation, a landing on the southern Egyptian coast in the region of Suez and a march from there against the French in Lower Egypt.[16]

Colonel Wellesley welcomed the opportunity to command such an expedition and was chagrined to learn that the Governor-General had been overborne by the army chiefs who had impressed upon him the impropriety of appointing – indeed the outrage to military tradition which would be occasioned by appointing – so junior an officer to the command over the heads of others so senior to him in rank and so much more seasoned by experience. The command was to be entrusted instead to General Baird.

Wellesley, who was already on his way to Egypt by way of Bombay, was furious on receipt of the new orders which placed him second-in-command and determined that, whatever orders he was subsequently to receive, he would endeavour to interpret them in such a way that they would not deny him this opportunity of advancing his career. The apologetic tone of his brother's letter breaking the news and offering him the alternative of returning to Seringapatam did nothing to mollify him.[17] He wrote to Calcutta to express his indignation, angrily and unreasonably refusing to accept his brother's reasons for what he took to be his degradation in the eyes of the world. He had not, he wrote, been informed of the possibility that he would be superseded. It was all very well for his brother to plead that he could not now employ him 'in the chief command of so large a force' which was now to proceed to Egypt 'without violating every rule of the service'. How could the Governor-General think that General Baird would ever allow him to be of the smallest service to him? He stood 'publicly convicted of incapacity' to do more than equip a force to be led by others.[18]

At first he decided he would return to Mysore rather than serve under Baird; but then he learned that Sir Ralph Abercromby had landed at Abū Qir Bay with some 15,000 men and had advanced on Alexandria. Wellesley, therefore, determined to leave Bombay immediately for the Red Sea, although General Baird had not yet arrived, since delay would entail the loss of the opportunity of cooperating with Abercromby in a pincer movement which would drive the French from Egypt. As soon as Baird appeared he would, of course, hand over the command to him, although, as he reported to the Governor-General's office, this would much annoy him as his former letters would surely have shown. However, he had 'never had much value for the public spirit of any man who does not sacrifice his private views and feelings, when it is necessary'. It was, therefore, his 'laudable and highly disagreeable intention' to obey his brother's instructions.[19]

As it happened, he was not able to obey them. He was suddenly taken ill and became feverish with a complaint known as Malabar Itch, a kind of ringworm, a 'breaking out all over [his body] of somewhat of the same kind as venereal blotches', which entailed an unpleasant treatment of nitric acid baths in Bombay.[20] When this drastic remedy, which burned the towels used to dry him, had at least partially cured him, he returned to Mysore, still deeply resentful of his brother's first giving him an independent command, then removing it from him. The angry resentment continued for months, the few letters he wrote to the Governor-General at this time being formal in the extreme, hints of intimacy being limited to his correspondence with his brother Henry, from whom he was gratified to learn that he was considered 'still top of the tree for character', and that Henry had never heard any man 'so highly spoken of, so generally looked up to'.[21] He corresponded also in a friendly manner with David Baird, with whom he had had companionable talks in Bombay before the General's departure for Egypt, finding the Scotsman more sympathetic and understanding than he had expected, and ready to listen to what the Colonel had to tell him about Egypt, the Nile and the Nubian and Libyan Deserts, being not much of a reader himself. Accordingly he learned of Baird's subsequent successes in Egypt without the rancour that continued dislike of the man might otherwise have aroused in him.

7   The Sultan's Palace

1800 – 1

'If we are taken prisoner, I shall be hanged as
brother to the Governor-General, and you will be
hanged for being found in bad company.'

RECOVERED FROM the Malabar Itch, Colonel Wellesley returned to
Seringapatam in more cheerful mood than his companions might have
expected in so disappointed a man. But he was still not very well, one
of them thought; and, although he was no more than thirty-two years
old, his closely cropped, wavy, light brown hair, parted in the middle,
was already touched with grey.[1]

> He never wore powder [one of his staff recorded], though it was at that
> time the regulation to do so. I have heard him say he was convinced the
> wearing of hair powder was very prejudicial to health as impeding the
> perspiration ... His dress at this time consisted of a *long coat*, the
> uniform of the 33rd Regiment, a *cocked hat*, white pantaloons, Hessian
> boots and spurs, and a large sabre, the handle solid silver.[2]

Having taken ship south from Bombay he rode towards Mysore
ahead of his escort, nonchalantly observing to Captain Elers who
accompanied him, 'If we are taken prisoner, I shall be hanged as brother
to the Governor-General, and you will be hanged for being found in
bad company.'[3]

One night the two men were sitting drinking wine after dinner and,
as Elers recalled, 'congratulating ourselves that we had arrived safely
... in the country of the Coorga Rajah ... when, looking through the
tent doors, we saw the forest suddenly illuminated with torches and
many men carrying all sorts of game on Bamboos', including cheetahs,
jackals, tigers, foxes, a boa constrictor sixteen feet long, eleven elephants' tails and three carp.

The next day the Rajah's green and red striped tents were pitched
nearby and from these were sent over to the British officers presents
of 'backgammon boards of the handsomest sort, inlaid with ebony and

36

ivory' and a chess board with pieces of 'the finest kind, carved in ivory'. The Rajah himself then appeared wearing Indian pantaloons but 'the rest of his dress was English including English boots'.

'In one part of the conversation,' Elers wrote, 'I admired Colonel Wellesley's quickness in detecting [the interpreter] giving an erroneous translation of a speech of his to the Rajah. The Colonel was clever in quickly acquiring languages but spoke none very correctly.'[4]

The Colonel settled down to his duties in Seringapatam if not with enthusiasm certainly with diligence, restoring order to a regiment which, while in the incapable hands of his second-in-command during his absence, had become notorious for drunkenness and quarrelling. He wrote letters and memoranda on a familiar variety of subjects, dealing with breaches of discipline and occasional criminal conduct, 'scenes of villainy which would disgrace the Newgate Calendar',[5] involving commissaries – a breed of men, so he once threatened, he would hang at the rate of one a day were he ever to be in a position to do so – and even implicating army officers, one of whom had been selling the East India Company's supplies of saltpetre, which was used in the manufacture of gunpowder, as well as copper bands stripped from the pillars of the Sultan's palace, while another had been disposing of new firearms from the weapons store and replacing them with ancient firelocks bought cheaply from native dealers. Also involved in this illicit arms dealing was an elderly lieutenant-colonel of previously good character who had been court-martialled and ruined. Taking pity on him, Colonel Wellesley, in a long and carefully worded letter, offered a plea of mitigation in view of the old man's former good conduct, asking for a small pension to enable him – once he had repaid the Company's officials the sums due to them – 'to support himself on account of his long services and his present reduced situation'.[6]

Wellesley remained equally sympathetic towards the feelings and interests of the natives, though he still did not entertain a very high opinion of their probity. He came down firmly on soldiers who mal-treated them, taking the opportunity presented by the case of an officer who had merely been reprimanded for flogging an Indian for refusing to supply him with free straw for his horse, to remind all ranks that they were 'placed in this country to protect the inhabitants, not to oppress them'. He made it clear to headquarters, too, that he strongly disapproved of such disgraceful behaviour being so lightly punished. When a lieutenant, who had forced a group of Indians to hand over money by making them stand in the sun with heavy weights on their heads, and who was believed to have flogged one of them to death, was given no more severe a punishment than a reprimand and six months' suspension of pay, he protested against such leniency, emphasizing the disgrace which would fall upon the whole army were the man not to be discharged from the service.[7]

Stern as he could be on occasions, he was a friendly and easy companion in the officers' mess in the Sultan's palace, tolerant without being over-indulgent of occasional drunkenness, believing 'a drunken quarrel is very bad, and is always to be lamented, but probably the less it is enquired into the better'.[8] He did not drink as much himself as he had done in Calcutta and as officers customarily did in India, where half a bottle of Madeira a day, with a complementary amount of beer and spirits, was considered abstemious. But he drank four or five glasses of wine with his meal and about a pint of claret afterwards. It was noticed, however, that he was quite incapable of distinguishing a fine wine from a *vin ordinaire*. Nor was he much interested in food, though he had a marked partiality for rice and for roast saddle of mutton with salad.

> He was very even in his temper [Captain Elers recalled], laughing and joking with those he liked, speaking in his quick way, and dwelling particularly upon the few (*at that time*) situations he had been placed in before the enemy, the arrangements he had made, and their fortunate results, all of which were applauded by his staff ... This generally formed the topic of conversation after dinner.[9]

The Colonel, it was also said of him, liked to be in the company of ladies whenever he could; and there was no doubt that they in turn found him attractive. He was not considered to be conventionally handsome; but he was alert and vital, attentive and eager; his body was lithe and strong, and the lingering gaze of those 'clear blue eyes' was pleasantly unsettling. He had a 'very susceptible heart', a fellow officer thought, 'particularly towards, I am sorry to say, married ladies'. There was, for example, a Mrs Stephenson, 'pretty & lively', who had special apartments assigned to her at headquarters; and Mrs Gordon and Mrs Coggan; and the wife of another officer, Captain J.W. Freese, 'his pointed attention' to whom 'gave offence to, *not her husband*, but to an aide-de-camp [Captain West] who considered it highly immoral and indecorous, and a coolness took place between him and West and they did not speak all the time I lived with the Colonel. Lady Tuite, then Mrs Goodall, interfered in the same officious way, which the

Colonel did not forget; for, in after times, upon meeting him at a large party, when she held out her hand to shake hands with him, he put both his hands behind his back and made a low bow'.* [10]

When there were no ladies to entertain at Seringapatam or to talk to with brisk intimacy, Colonel Wellesley would enjoy a game of billiards; but, having steadfastly set his mind against gambling, he still did not play cards for money, nor did he enjoy the idle chat of fellow officers, preferring to talk of the business of soldiering, his own experiences of it, and of the affairs, successes and misdemeanours of the East India Company and its officials. He could not hide his love of gossip, though; and when amused his loud whoops of laughter, 'easily excited', would reverberate around the room, 'like the whoop of a whooping-cough often repeated'†.[11] He enjoyed the mess's amateur theatricals well enough to send for the texts of plays suitable for officers and their ladies to perform.[12]

From time to time, when his duties permitted, he clambered up into a 'very handsome howdah, entirely covered with superfine scarlet cloth, hanging within two feet of the ground', and went hunting antelope with the Sultan's leopards which, together with their keepers, he maintained at his own expense, since the Government declined to pay for them.[13]

Often he would go for long, fast rides in the countryside for the peaceful administration of which he was responsible. It was essential to take exercise in India, he thought, just as it was necessary 'to keep the mind employed', to eat moderately, drink little wine, and, if possible, to keep in good company with the world. 'The last is the most difficult,' he decided, 'for there is scarcely a good-tempered man in India.'[14]

He was all the better tempered himself when news reached him that he had been promoted major-general. He had long hoped for this, once telling Captain Elers that to achieve that rank was his 'highest

---

* In July 1802 Mrs Freese gave birth to a son whom she named Arthur and to whom Colonel Wellesley was godfather. When he was four years old the boy was brought home to live with an aunt who had died by the time he arrived in England. Wellesley consequently agreed to take care of the boy who was brought up in his own family. He was sent to Charterhouse and had a successful career in India with the East India Company.

† His loud and ready laugh remained distinctive for most of the rest of his life. One day in 1817 while talking to Thomas Creevey about the Duke of Kent, fourth son of George III and father of Queen Victoria, he suddenly took hold of a button on Creevey's coat and said, 'God Damme! D'ye know what his sisters call him? By God! They call him Joseph Surface!' and 'then sent out one of his hearty laughs, that made everyone turn about to the right and left to see what was the matter' (*The Creevey Papers*, 284).

ambition',[15] and he had been much disappointed on his way back to Seringapatam from Bombay to find, on eagerly looking through the latest Army List, that his own name had not been included in a roll of colonels to be promoted. In April 1802, however, the promotion came through at last, much to the satisfaction of Marquess Wellesley, who had continued to regard his brother's earlier failure to obtain it as a slight upon his own dignity and who was to consider a decision to reduce Arthur's allowances as commander of the troops in Mysore, Malabar and Canara as another affront, a 'most direct, marked and disquieting personal indignity'.

Marquess Wellesley held his dignity in high esteem. He was conscious of having merited the gratitude of both the British government and the Court of Directors of the East India Company. He was, after all, in the process of consolidating the empire of which Lord Clive had laid the foundation; and he much resented criticisms of his autocratic manner and the exercise of his patronage. Certainly he lived in a grand style with a splendidly uniformed bodyguard which he increased from a mere fifty men in his predecessor's time to four hundred, together with a band. He occupied a magnificent house, 'the Kedleston of Bengal'; he entertained on a princely scale. But it was all for the glory of the Company and the empire in the East; and it irked him beyond measure to have to listen to guarded complaints from cheeseparing, pettifogging nonentities in the Company's offices in Leadenhall Street who had no conception of the workings of the oriental mind. He dismissed their rumblings of discontent and, so far as he could, he determined to carry on as he thought best or he would resign. His brother Arthur supported him. 'I hope you do not propose to stay in India longer than the end of this year,' he wrote when their relations had been more or less restored to their former amity. 'Such masters do not deserve your services.'[16]

8 Assaye

1802 – 5

'I never saw a man so cool and collected
as he was.'

EARLY IN 1802 the Governor-General authorized an expedition, to be led by his brother, against a troublesome rajah in Bullum, north-west of Seringapatam. The short campaign, which ended with the hanging of the rajah, gave General Wellesley further experience of forest warfare which was to stand him in good stead in the days to come. For the operations had not long been over when he was called upon to take to the field again. This time he was to operate in the territories of the Marāthās north of Mysore. Here the Peshwah, the titular chief of the Marāthā confederacy who had accepted the position of a prince under British protection, had been driven from Poona by Jaswant Rāo Holkar, an illegitimate son of Tukojī Holkar, Maharajah of Indore. General Wellesley's prescribed task was to restore the Peshwah to his throne in Poona and to defeat or scatter Holkar's army.

As the author of a recent 'Memorandum upon Operations in the Mahratta Territory' and as an officer with experience of that country in the pursuit of Dhoondiah Waugh, he felt himself as well qualified as any officer in India to do so; and he set about preparing for the campaign with his accustomed thoroughness and energy, paying particular and necessary attention to the problem of supplying an army which would be operating so far from its bases. He arranged for the acquisition of beef and sheep, rice and forage and bullocks to be stocked in depots in northern Mysore close to the Marāthā border. He dealt in detail with packing cases and containers, with kegs for salt, gunny bags for rice, with four-gallon, iron-hooped casks for arrack. Nothing was left to chance, no detail was overlooked.

His army of nine thousand men marched into Marāthā territory in March 1803; and the next month he was approaching Poona when he learned that the place was to be set on fire as soon as he drew near it. Making a forced night march of forty miles with 400 cavalry, he

41

arrived on 20 April in time to save it. The Peshwah was welcomed back there three weeks later.

The General now hoped that the other Marāthā chiefs would give no more trouble. 'I think,' he wrote, 'that, although there will be much bad temper and many threats, there will be no hostility.'[1] Nevertheless, he made plans for a further campaign if one proved to be necessary, and gave much thought to the outwitting of enemy forces by the swift crossing and re-crossing of rivers in the Marāthā territories by means of pontoons and basket-boats.

Throughout May and June an uneasy peace was maintained, but two chiefs in particular, the Bhonsle of Berar and Daulat Rāo Sindhia, Maharajah of Gwalior, whose troops were trained by French officers, gave him increasing cause for concern; and he was eventually authorized by the Governor-General to deliver an ultimatum to both of these chiefs to disband their armies. He set no time limit, wanting to leave himself free to decide when to 'strike the first blow' should he find 'hostile operations to be necessary'. Having received no undertakings by the end of July, he decided to deliver the first strike of the contest by making a sudden attack upon the hill fortress of Ahmednuggur which was stormed and quickly taken.

He did not expect to be able to follow up this success by bringing 'the enemy to an action'. But, as he said, 'we must try to keep him in movement, and tire him out.'[2] On 23 September, however, he did bring him to action; and he did so in circumstances that he would not have chosen. He came across Daulat Rāo Sindhia's forces unexpectedly at the village of Assaye. There were some 40,000 of them drawn up in a strong position in an angle formed by two rivers. His own army numbered no more than 7,000 men, many of them tired after a march of over twenty miles that morning. He had twenty-two cannon, Scindia over a hundred, while the enemy's cavalry outnumbered his own twenty to one. An engagement could not, however, well be avoided; and his quick, perceptive eye, which was one of the keys to his military prowess, detected a feature of the landscape that could be turned to his advantage. Guides assured him there were no fords across the river Kaitna beyond which the village of Assaye stood. But Wellesley, surveying the countryside through his telescope, caught sight of two villages close together on opposite banks, and concluded that they would not have been built there 'without some habitual means of communication between them'.[3] There was, indeed, a ford there and he took his army towards it under heavy fire of cannon shot which tore off his orderly's head.

The subsequent battle was ferocious, 'one of the bloodiest for the numbers' that he himself had ever seen, and 'one of the most furious battles that [had] ever been fought in this country'.[4] The General conducted it with energy, skill and much bravery. He was 'in the thick of the action the whole time', wrote Colin Campbell, a volunteer in the 78th. 'I never saw a man so cool and collected as he was . . . though I can assure you, till our troops got the order to advance the fate of the day seemed doubtful; and if the numerous cavalry of the enemy had done their duty I hardly think it possible we could have succeeded.'[5] He led infantry charges against the Marāthā guns, ninety-eight of which were captured; and, before the enemy's lines were broken, two horses had been shot under him. That night, having learned of the heavy casualties, the exhausted General was seen sitting outside his tent quite still, as though in prayer, his head between his knees.*[6]

The next morning, having given orders for bottles of his Madeira to be distributed to the wounded, he made ready to march off in pursuit; and at Argaum at the end of September he brought his quarry to battle once again. Once more he defeated them, this time with less bloodshed, congratulating himself afterwards that, if he had not been there to restore order to two battalions of Sepoys in panic-stricken flight, 'we should have lost the day'.[7] He followed up this second victory by capturing the fortress of Gawilghur which brought the campaign to an end.[8]

The Governor-General was delighted. He and his brother were now once more on the best of terms, their difficulties reconciled if not quite forgotten, Arthur's letters no longer coldly formal, Richard's full of praise: Arthur had done splendidly though no more than had been expected. Earlier his conduct in Mysore had secured his 'character and advancement' for the remainder of his life; now his endeavours had culminated in a 'brilliant point in the history of this country' and brought to a 'noble termination' his own 'military glory'.[9]

The General himself was well satisfied with what he had done, with his proven capacity to keep his army well supplied – with him always one of the most essential prerequisites of military success – and to move it with speed – which was 'everything in military operations'. On one memorable occasion he had moved five regiments sixty miles in thirty hours. Army officers and 'mercantile gentlemen' alike

---

* When asked at a dinner party over forty years later, 'Pray Duke what is the best thing you did in the fighting line?' he was 'silent for about 10 seconds & then answered, "Assaye". He did not add a word' (*The Conversations of the First Duke of Wellington with George William Chad*, 20).

congratulated him upon his achievements. Presentations were made to him, dinners given in his honour, speeches were delivered, letters of congratulation received and acknowledged. In Bombay an 'elegant transparency' of his coat of arms was displayed in the theatre.

He was not above enjoying the acclaim, referring to himself with satisfied amusement in a letter to Mrs Gordon in Bombay, as now being *'a great man'*. To this lady he issued an invitation:

> We get on well, but we want you to enliven us. Allow me to prevail upon you. If you'll come I'll go and meet you with my Servts. at the top of the Ghaut [mountain pass] so that you will only have 24 miles to travel in palanqueen.
>
> There is excellent galloping ground in the neighbourhood of the camp, & the floor of my Tent is in a fine state for dancing, & the fiddlers of the Dragoons & 78th & Bagpipes of the 74th play delightfully.[10]

He could also promise good food in his mess, although no epicure himself: accounts showed generous expenditure on York ham and Gloucester cheeses, oysters, pale ale and much Madeira as well as sword belts and saddlery. They also showed expenditure on presents for ladies, on a 'Brilliant hoop Ring and 2 pearl guards to ditto, 150 R[upee]s', and on a pearl necklace, bracelets and a silk-worked shawl.[11]

He was still buying books and several of these revealed a desire to be as well versed in European affairs as he was now in Indian, for in lists of volumes bought – among the 34 volumes of the *British Theatre*, the 19 of Bell's edition of Shakespeare and various French novels – were works such as *The State of Europe before and after the French Revolution,* and *Summary Account and Military Character of the Several European Armies that have been engaged during the late War,* a work which, incidentally, included the dispiriting observation that 'an English general, who returns from India, is like an Admiral who has been navigating the Lake of Geneva'.[12]

Such remarks made him all the more anxious to leave India as soon as he could be spared. He would not hesitate to stay, 'even for years', if British India were in danger. But it was not in danger now; and he had, after all, served in the sub-continent 'as long as any man ought who [could] serve any where else'. 'I am not very ambitious,' he wrote disingenuously, 'and I acknowledge that I have never been very sanguine in my expectation that military services in India would be considered in the scale in which are considered similar services in other parts of the world. But I might have been expected to be placed on the Staff in India.'[13]

As it was, he had no hand in the direction of such operations as were being conducted, and conducted most incompetently. Colonel William Monson was defeated by Jaswant Rāo Holkar, Maharajah of Indore, who pursued the greatly outnumbered British forces from the banks of the Chumbul to Agra which only a few hundred of them survived to reach; while Lord Lake, Sir Alured Clarke's successor as Commander-in-Chief, lost nearly 400 men killed and two thousand wounded in an unsuccessful siege of the fortress of Bhurtpore, the stronghold of an ally of Holkar, the Rajah of Bhurtpore.

General Wellesley's desire to go home was increased by failing health. He had recently undergone another bout of fever; and, having been 'much annoyed by the lumbago' in the early months of 1804, was now, at the end of the year, suffering from rheumatism.

At the beginning of 1805 he wrote to Madras to enquire about shipping. He would prefer 'the starboard side of a quiet ship', he said, but he was 'not very particular about accommodation' and did not 'care a great deal about the price' or who the captain was, so long as he could sail soon. 'I am anxious to a degree which I can't express,' he said, 'to see my friends again.'[14]

While awaiting notification of a berth, he said his goodbyes, gave portraits of himself to friends,* made arrangements for the welfare of two elephants which had been given to him by a grateful rajah, settled a sum of money on the son of Dhoondiah Waugh whom he had undertaken to look after on his father's death; and, in the shops of Madras, bought presents to take to England, including ten pairs of ladies' shoes. He also bought more books to while away the hours of the long voyage, not the instructive volumes with which he sailed out but much lighter reading: *The Letters of Madame de Pompadour*, for example, and *Beauties of the Modern Dramatists* as well as a number of novels with such titles as *Illicit Love, Lessons for Lovers, Fashionable Involvements, Filial Indiscretion or the Female Chevalier* and, in five volumes, *Love at First Sight.*[15]

He sailed in March 1805, not too sorry to see the last of India and convinced that, if he had not left when he did, he would have had a 'serious fit of illness'.[16] All the same he was grateful to have had the opportunity of displaying his talents as an officer there and, so he said

---

* Robert Home, the Scottish painter who had settled in India at Lucknow and made a fortune working for the King of Oudh, painted at least fourteen portraits of General Wellesley between 1804 and August 1806. Several of these were engraved (Mildred Archer, *India and British Portraiture 1770–1825* (London, 1979), 317; Richard Walker, *Regency Portraits*, 525).

years later, of learning 'as much of military matters' as he had 'ever done since'. Moreover, it was certainly true that his command at Seringapatam had afforded him 'opportunities for distinction, and then opened the road to fame'.[17]

Nor did he go home unrewarded. He had left England impecunious; he was returning with a fortune of between £42,000 and £43,000.[18] He was also going home as a Knight Companion of the Order of the Bath, the insignia of which his friend, Sir John Cradock, who had brought it out from England, got a servant to pin to his coat while he was asleep in bed. He was also presented with the thanks of Parliament, a sword of honour given by the people of Calcutta, a service of plate embossed with *Assaye* from the officers of his division, and an address from the 'native people of Seringapatam' who, having lived for 'five auspicious years' under his protection, trusted that the 'God of all castes and all nations' would 'deign to hear with favour' their prayers for his health, glory and happiness.[19]

9   Return to London

1805 — 6

'What, child! do you think that I have nothing
better to do than to make speeches to please
ladies?'

MAJOR-GENERAL Sir Arthur Wellesley sailed home in the *Trident*,
walking briskly about the deck in the morning, reading the novels he
had bought in Madras in the afternoon, writing papers on farming and
famines in India and on the possible uses of Indian troops in the West
Indies and of West Indian slaves in India. He went ashore at St Helena
where he was much taken with the beauty of the island, its 'delightful
climate' and much amazed by the Governor, a most eccentric gentleman 'of a description that must have been extinct for nearly two centuries'. Sir Arthur had never seen 'anything like his wig or his coat'.[1]

The *Trident* reached England in September 1805; and the General
listened eagerly to detailed accounts of what had happened in the world
in his absence. He heard and read about the Treaty of St Petersburg by
which Britain and Russia, later joined by Austria, had agreed to form
a European coalition for the liberation of the northern German states;
he learned that Napoleon, who had assumed the title of Emperor the
year before, had been crowned King of Italy in Milan Cathedral, that
the soldiers of the Grande Armée had abandoned their camps around
Boulogne and, turning their backs on the English Channel, had
marched towards the Danube, and that Lord Nelson had chased a
French fleet under Admiral Pierre de Villeneuve across the Atlantic
to the West Indies and back again, forcing Villeneuve to seek shelter
in Cadiz.

One of his obligations on landing was to settle his debts now that
he was in a position to do so, being in possession of what he called 'a
little fortune'. Already in India he had been generous in his unaccustomed wealth, lending over 9,000 rupees to the son of an old friend,
a junior employee of the East India Company, who had got himself
into trouble by extravagance in bad company. Now, so George Elers

heard, he went to thank and repay a tradesman who had lent him £300 or £400 before he had left for India. 'Can I be of any service to you?' the General asked him.

> 'Nothing for me, but I have a son.'
>
> 'Give me his name,' said Sir Arthur, 'You did me a kindness once and I do not forget it.'
>
> He got the man's son a place of £400 per annum ... Sir Arthur also sent £400 to Mrs Sturt, wife of an officer in the 80th [Major William Sturt] who had committed all sorts of follies [which included marrying this pretty woman, a former member of the establishment of the procuress, Mrs Porter, in Berkeley Street].[2]

It seems that Sir Arthur had himself been a visitor to Mrs Porter's house in Berkeley Street in the 1790s and that Mrs Sturt may well have been one of the young women then employed there. It is also most likely that he now went back to this house on his return from India and that it was by way of an introduction from Mrs Porter that he met the celebrated courtesan Harriette Wilson.[3]

He was known to be a man of strong sexual appetite, and his reputation of being 'a ladies' man' as well as a beau had returned with him from India. Indeed, he was already known to many as 'The Beau' and the nickname was commonly used for years thereafter. He was reputed to have had affairs with women, usually married women, of his own social class; but it was supposed that, by discretion as much as by taste, he was more inclined at this time to seek sexual pleasure in the arms of such professional coquettes as Harriette Wilson and the girls at Mrs Porter's.

Harriette Wilson was the daughter of a man of Swiss extraction who had a small shop in Mayfair. She spoke French as well as English, though neither very fluently; and was renowned not so much for her beauty as for her easy manners, gaiety and flighty charm. Sir Walter Scott who once met her at the house of the lively, goggle-eyed author Matthew Lewis, in Argyle Street, described her as being 'a smart, saucy girl, with good eyes and dark hair, and the manners of a wild schoolboy'.[4] Having, according to her own account, become the mistress of Lord Craven at the age of fifteen, she had numbered amongst her lovers and admirers the Marquesses of Lorne and Worcester, Lord Frederick Bentinck, Lord Ponsonby, Lord Alvanley, the Hon. Frederick Lamb, Tom Sheridan and George Brummell. In describing these men, and in relating her talks with Sir Arthur Wellesley in her memoirs, their manner of speaking, as Sir Walter Scott acknowledged, was 'exactly imitated'. Her recollections of her earliest conversations with Wellesley certainly catch his abrupt manner of talking and his inability to indulge in small talk:

> He bowed first, then said 'How do you do?' then thanked me for having given him permission to call on me; and then wanted to take hold of my hand.
>
> 'Really,' said I, withdrawing my hand, 'for such a renowned hero you have very little to say for yourself.'
>
> 'Beautiful creature! where is Lorne?'
>
> 'Good gracious,' said I, out of all patience at his stupidity – 'what come you here for?'
>
> 'Beautiful eyes, yours!'
>
> 'Aye, man! they are greater conquerors than ever [you] shall be; but, to be serious, I understood you came here to try to make yourself agreeable?'
>
> 'What, child! do you think that I have nothing better to do than to make speeches to please ladies?'
>
> '*Après avoir dépeuplé la terre, vous devez faire tout pour la repeupler,*' I replied.
>
> 'You should see me where I shine,' he observed, laughing.
>
> 'Where's that, in God's name?'
>
> 'In a field of battle,' answered the hero.
>
> '*Battez-vous, donc, et qu'un autre me fasse la cour!*' said I.[5]

Sir Arthur soon became her 'constant visitor', a 'most unentertaining one, Heaven knows!' she thought; and, 'in the evenings, when he wore his broad red ribbon [of the Order of the Bath], he looked very like a rat-catcher.'[6]

It was not long after his arrival in London that Sir Arthur encountered Lord Nelson who was on a few days' leave and had come up from Merton Place, his country house in Surrey, to see Lord Castlereagh. Wellesley also happened to have been called for interview with the Secretary for War and the Colonies on the same day, and the two men found themselves waiting together in a room in the Colonial Office in Downing Street.

Years later the General recalled this meeting with 'a gentleman, whom from his likeness to his pictures and the loss of an arm, I immediately recognized as Lord Nelson'.

He could not know who I was [Wellington told John Wilson Croker], but he entered at once into conversation with me, if I can call it conversation, for it was almost all on his side and all about himself and, in reality, a style so vain and so silly as to surprise and almost disgust me.

I suppose something that I happened to say may have made him guess that I was *somebody* and he went out of the room for a moment, I have no doubt to ask the office-keeper who I was, for when he came back he was altogether a different man, both in manner and matter.

His 'charlatan style' had quite vanished and 'he talked of the state of the country and of the aspect and probabilities of affairs on the Continent with a good sense and a knowledge of subjects both at home and abroad'.

The Secretary of State kept us long waiting [Wellington continued] and certainly for the last half or three-quarters of an hour, I don't know that I ever had a conversation that interested me more. Now, if the Secretary of State had been punctual . . . I should have had the same impression of a light and trivial character that other people have had, but luckily I saw enough to be satisfied that he was really a very superior man; but certainly a more sudden or complete metamorphosis I never saw.*[7]

Wellesley was the same age as Castlereagh; they came from similar Irish backgrounds, and had sat together in the Irish House of Commons. They had been fellow guests at Sir Jonah Barrington's dinner table in Dublin. The General felt at ease with the Minister, and spoke freely to him about Indian affairs and personalities, confiding his belief that the Government were not supporting his brother as Governor-General in the way they should. He said as much to Lord Camden, Castlereagh's predecessor as Secretary for War, and now Lord President of the Council. In fact, Lord Wellesley, severely criticized for the disasters of the recent Marāthā war, had been recalled and was on his way home; and his brother went to see his friend, the proud, touchy and extremely fat Marquess of Buckingham, the former Lord-Lieutenant of

---

* Wellington's opinion of another distinguished naval officer, Admiral Sir Sidney Smith, did not change on closer acquaintance. He remained of the view that 'of all the men whom I ever knew who have any reputation, the man who least deserves it is Sir Sidney Smith . . . At first, out of deference to his name and general reputation, I attended to him, but I soon found he was a mere vaporizer. I cannot believe that a man so silly in all other affairs can be a good naval officer' (*The Croker Papers*, i, 348).

Ireland, to seek his advice about the attitude which Richard should adopt when he arrived in England. 'Bucky' said that opposition to the Government was 'the best political game of the day'. 'He was very anxious that you should belong to the opposition,' Sir Arthur reported. 'He urged every argument to induce me to inflame your mind against Pitt, particularly that he had not given you the Garter.'[8]

But Sir Arthur did not agree with 'Bucky'; and bored beyond measure by the tedium of the two days he spent at Stowe, he told his brother that he and Lord Bathurst, a friend of Pitt and future Secretary for War, both believed that he ought to remain neutral for the moment, biding his time and observing the course of events.[9]

On leaving Stowe, and while his brother was still at sea, the General went to see Richard's children. They were all in good health, he reported to their father, the boys manly and well-behaved 'fine fellows', the girls 'very handsome and accomplished (particularly the youngest)'. This 'must surely be at least some consolation' to Richard, even though his services in India had not been treated as they deserved.[10]

The General could not give such favourable reports of the rest of their family. Their grandmother, Lady Dungannon, had long since died, having been arrested for debt, taken away to a sponging house, and from there to a French convent from which she had been brought back to England, apparently not in the least ashamed of her misdemeanours. Her widowed daughter, the General's mother, was living a completely self-absorbed life in her house off Cavendish Square, evidently quite unaffected one way or another by her son's return from India, her letters addressed to her offspring there having been so impersonal, so Henry Wellesley said, that they could have been read aloud at Charing Cross.[11]

When Sir Arthur called at the Horse Guards his reception by the Duke of York was even more off-hand than that accorded to him by his mother. He had never felt at ease with the Duke in the way that he did with Castlereagh and Camden. It rankled with him that his promotion to major-general in the East India Company's service had not immediately been confirmed in London; and he believed that the Duke had wanted General Baird to have the command at Seringapatam rather than himself. Captain Elers heard that the Duke of York made this plain enough when General Harris returned from India and attended a reception at the Horse Guards. 'Harris, who was not very quick in a difficulty, was asked suddenly by the Duke, 'Pray, General Harris what reason had you for superseding General Baird in the command at Seringapatam and giving it to a junior officer?' Poor Harris stammered and the Duke turned his back on him and began a conversation with some officers.'*¹²

General Wellesley got on much better with the Prime Minister than he did with the Commander-in-Chief and went to see Pitt more than once at his house in Putney. He also had opportunities of talking to other ministers at Camden Place, Lord Camden's house at Chislehurst in Kent. They all found the young General sensible and extremely well informed, Pitt deciding that he wisely stated every difficulty before performing any service, though none once he had undertaken it, a complimentary view Sir Arthur felt incapable of returning since the fault of the Prime Minister's character was being 'too sanguine': he conceived a project and then imagined it was done, and did not enter enough into the details.¹³

The General on the contrary was now well known for his close attention to detail; and it became recognized by the Cabinet that his clear, succinct and well-considered opinions were well worth seeking when any new stroke against the French was in contemplation. When asked, for example, what he thought of a plan, favoured by the Prime Minister, of urging the Prussians to attack the French in rear, he said on reflection that it would be at least three months before a sufficient force could be raised and equipped and be in position on the Danube.

As it happened, in the middle of October the French overwhelmed an Austrian army under Karl Mack at Ulm. But on the day after Ulm's surrender, Nelson, mortally wounded during the battle, destroyed the French and Spanish fleets at Trafalgar. The ailing Prime Minister, so cast down by news of Ulm that Lord Malmesbury believed his death to be imminent, was given fresh hope by the news of Trafalgar; and on 9 November, at the Lord Mayor's banquet at Guildhall, he was observed to be in good spirits. Sir Arthur Wellesley was among the guests who heard him respond modestly to the toast, 'The Saviour of the Nation', with the memorable words, 'Europe is not to be saved by any single man. England has saved herself by her exertions; and will, as I trust, save Europe by her example.'¹⁴

'That was all,' Sir Arthur commented admiringly. 'He was scarcely up two minutes; yet nothing could be more perfect.'¹⁵

After being so well received by members of the Government, it came as all the more of a disappointment to General Wellesley when in

---

* In a conversation with the Duke of York in 1824, the diarist Charles Greville, who had been his racing manager, was left in no doubt that the Duke much disliked General Wellesley, just as he disliked Castlereagh (*The Greville Memoirs*, i, 138–9).

December he was told what was to be his own contribution to Europe's salvation: he was to be given command of a brigade to be sent to Hanover. After three weeks in rough seas, including Christmas Day in a gale off Heligoland, his brigade was landed at Bremen where he endured a further six weeks of cold, rain and inactivity before being ordered home again.

By the time of his return, Napoleon had won his greatest victory over the combined Austrian and Russian armies at Austerlitz; and Pitt had been even more distressed by this than by Mack's defeat at Ulm. He had been brought home from Bath on 9 January 1806 to his house at Putney where, glancing at a map of Europe on the wall, he is said, perhaps apocryphally, to have given voice to the most quoted of all his utterances, 'Roll up that map. It will not be wanted these ten years.'[16] He died a fortnight later, to be succeeded as First Lord of the Treasury in the so-called 'Ministry of All the Talents', by his cousin, Lord Grenville, with Charles James Fox as Foreign Secretary, and William Windham as Lord Castlereagh's successor at the Colonial Office.

After the abortive expedition to Bremen, General Wellesley, for all the confidence that Pitt's ministers had appeared to have reposed in him, was found no employment more responsible by the new Government than the command of a brigade at Hastings. Here, conscientious as always, he studied the problems of the Rye inundations and examined the possibilities of Winchelsea Castle being strengthened as a military fortress. 'We are not actually in opposition,' he wrote to a friend in India, 'but we have no power.'[17] He did, though, now have a wife.

10 Kitty Pakenham

1790 – 1806

'She has grown ugly by Jove!'

HE HAD first set eyes on the Hon. Catherine Dorothea Sarah Pakenham, daughter of the second Baron Longford, years before in Ireland where her father, a post-captain in the Royal Navy, had, for a few months before he had come into the family title, been Member for County Longford. Arthur Wesley had often called at the Longfords' house in Rutland Square in Dublin and had made his feelings for Kitty known. She was a small, slim, vivacious and generous girl, indiscreet in her gossipy talk, much given to condemning the failings of others and to making dogmatic statements on matters which her knowledge of them did not justify. She read a great deal, sermons and books on religious matters as well as popular novels. An occasionally haughty manner concealed an inner uncertainty; but she was a well-liked young figure in Dublin society.[1]

Her parents had not at that time taken kindly to Arthur Wesley's interest in their daughter. A younger son in a large family, his prospects had not then seemed bright and his reputation, like his eldest brother's, was far from unblemished. This was the attitude also of Kitty's brother, Thomas, who became the third Baron Longford upon their father's death at the age of forty-nine in 1792.

So all thoughts of marriage had to be abandoned; but Arthur Wesley assured Kitty that, should those prospects become more certain, and her brother become more kindly disposed towards him, his own mind would 'remain the same', a promise that he afterwards felt to be binding upon an honourable man. The years passed. He seemed almost to have forgotten her; certainly he never once wrote to her from India; none of the shoes he bought were destined for her feet, nor jewels for her throat, nor shawls for her shoulders. But she evidently had been thinking of him as she later admitted one day to Queen Charlotte at court. 'I am happy to see you at my court, so bright an example of constancy,' the Queen said to her, according to Kitty's own account given to her friend, Maria Edgeworth. 'If anybody in this world deserves to be happy, you do. But did you really never write *one* letter to Sir Arthur Wellesley during his long absence?'

'No, never, madam.'

'And did you never think of him?'

'Yes, madam, very often.'[2]

Yet there had been a time, when, hearing nothing from him, so Kitty told her best friend, the Hon. Olivia Sparrow, the wife of a rich, elderly soldier, General Bernard Sparrow, she had begun to suppose 'the business over'. Another officer, Galbraith Lowry Cole, second son of the Earl of Enniskillen and three years younger than Arthur Wellesley, had fallen in love with her and had asked her to marry him. She had hesitantly accepted him. But then she was given to understand by her friend, Mrs Sparrow, who was in correspondence with him in India, that Arthur Wellesley was still attached to her. He had written to Mrs Sparrow to say that notwithstanding his good fortune and 'the perpetual activity' of his life in India the disappointment he had met with eight years before, and 'the object of it and the circumstances' were still as fresh in his mind 'as if they happened only yesterday'. 'When you see your friend,' he had added, 'do me the favour to remember me to her in the kindest manner.'[3]

When told of this letter, Kitty replied, 'Olivia, you know my heart ... and can imagine what gratitude I feel, (indeed much more than can be expressed) for his kind remembrance ... You know I can send no message; a kind word from me he might think binding to him and make him think himself obliged to renew a pursuit, which he might not then wish or my family (or at least some of them) approve ... Do you not think he seems to think the business over?'[4]

Although still unsure about Arthur Wellesley, after much worry and consideration and to the annoyance of his family, she had broken off her engagement to Lowry Cole, greatly to his sorrow. 'I had expected that before this Lowry would have married,' one of his brothers wrote to another member of their family in October 1802. 'At present I see not the smallest chance of it ... Since that love affair with Kitty Pakenham, Lowry seems like a burnt child to fear the fire and not to have any wish to hazard his happiness by paying attention to anyone else.'*[5]

The distressing contretemps had undermined Kitty's health; she had

---

* Almost thirteen years were to elapse before Lowry Cole married Lady Frances Harris, second daughter of the first Earl of Malmesbury.

grown thin and worn and had lost much of the prettiness and most of the bouncy sprightliness of her younger days. In October 1803 she had gone to Cheltenham to try to recoup her strength. Lowry Cole was there at the same time and his brother wrote, 'Kitty is in Cheltenham. I am beginning to think she wishes to bring on the subject again with Lowry, but he fights shy. She will deserve it, as she treated him cruelly.'[6]

Only too well aware that she had much changed, Kitty was extremely nervous when she heard that, in a letter to Olivia Sparrow dated August 1804, Arthur Wellesley had declared that his 'opinion and sentiments respecting the person in question' were the same as they had ever been; and she was even more apprehensive when she learned that he had arrived in London and had authorized Olivia 'to *renew the proposition* he had made some years ago'.

Kitty did not know what to say in reply. She would be 'most truly wretched', she replied to Mrs Sparrow, if she had cause to believe that Sir Arthur was repeating his offer in fulfilment of an undertaking he had made so long ago. The letter from him which she had been shown did not contain 'one word expressive of a wish that the proposition should be accepted'. There was no indication that '*Yes* would gratify or that *No* would disappoint'. Besides, she added, 'I am very much changed and you know it within these last three years, so much that I doubt whether it would now be in my power to contribute [to] the comfort or happiness of any body who has not been in the habit of loving me for years like my Brother or you or my Mother.'[7]

Someone else warned Sir Arthur that he would find Kitty Pakenham, now aged thirty-four, 'much altered'; but he maintained that 'he did not care. It was her mind he cared for', he said, 'and that would not alter'.[8] So, having obtained permission from her brother to do so, he wrote to her formally proposing marriage. She was reluctant still. She told him that she did not think it fair to engage him before he had seen her, until he was 'quite positively certain that [she was] indeed the very woman [he] would chuse for a companion a *friend* for life'. 'In so many years I may be much more changed than I am myself conscious of,' she concluded. 'If when we have met you can tell me . . . that you do not repent having written the letter I am now answering I shall be most happy.'[9]

Undeterred but quite without evident enthusiasm, Sir Arthur departed for Ireland in April 1806 at the age of thirty-seven to marry a woman with whom he was not in the least in love. He had been in no hurry to leave England where he had been busy with private as well as public affairs, paying visits to Cheltenham, where he stayed at the Plough, to Stowe to see the Marquess of Buckingham and Cirencester to call upon Lord Bathurst. Taking temporary lodgings at 18 Conduit Street, he had gone out to buy music at Robert Birchall's shop in New Bond Street—romantic songs, light operas. Mozart and Bach—and dinner and breakfast services at Flight and Barr's china shop in Coventry Street.[10]

He was described by Kitty's friend. Maria Edgeworth, who saw him now for the first time, as being 'quite bald'; but this was only because his unpowdered hair was cut so very short. Extremely plain herself, Miss Edgeworth also wrote of him as being 'handsome, very brown . . . and a hooked nose'.[11]

Sir Arthur could find nothing remotely handsome about his anxious bride who, in Miss Edgeworth's words, 'coughs sadly and looks but ill'. Mrs Calvert thought that he 'must have found her sadly altered, for she was a very pretty little girl, with a round face and fine complexion. She is now very thin and withered . . . She looks in a consumption.'[12] A few years before, the Prince of Wales, on meeting his bride for the first time, had murmured to Lord Malmesbury who had brought her over to England from Brunswick, 'Harris, pray bring me a glass of brandy', before retiring to a far corner of the room. Similarly disappointed, Sir Arthur was said to have whispered to his brother, now the husband of the eldest daughter of Earl Cadogan, the Rev. Gerald Wellesley, who was to conduct the marriage service in the drawing room of the Longfords' house in Rutland Square, 'She has grown ugly by Jove.'[13]

Having already overstayed his leave, Sir Arthur remained in Dublin for less than a week before sailing back to London after the briefest of honeymoons from which he was seen returning on the box of the carriage while his bride remained inside. She followed him to England later in the care of his brother, Gerald; and, having stayed with Mrs Sparrow for a time, while her husband still occupied his bachelor rooms, she set up house with him at 11 Harley Street, a smart residential street first rated in 1753 and not yet favoured by doctors.[14] Here she settled down uneasily to begin her married life, her husband's solicitors having drawn up a settlement by which he would contribute £20,000 and she £4,000 with a further £2,000 from her mother. Sir Arthur's hopes that she would prove as exact in money matters as he was himself were not to be realized.[15]

11   Ireland and Denmark

1806 – 7

'Show me an Irishman and I'll show you a man
whose anxious wish it is to see his country
independent of Great Britain.'

GENERAL WELLESLEY returned to his duties in Hastings, but his
eyes were now firmly set on that more imposing stage on the Continent
which Lord Longford had rather doubted he would ever ascend. His
brother, the Marquess, however, now returned from India, was in much
need of his family's support in the House of Commons where he was
under sustained attack from the Member for Newtown who was intent
upon blackening Wellesley's name and record as Governor-General in
India. This disputatious Member was James Paull, the dapper little
son of a Scottish tailor who had done very well for himself as a merchant
in India where he had fallen foul of the Governor-General. The Marquess's brother William had been Member for Queen's County since
1801; but William needed support in his defence of the reputation of
the family which, if lost, would damage the prospects of them all. So
Sir Arthur offered himself as candidate for Parliament at Rye and was
duly elected, after paying for much wine and many dinners for the
electors and their wives and families, and contributing £50 to the 'Poor
in lieu of Garlands etc., etc.'[1]

In Parliament he staunchly defended his brother against the accusations of Mr Paull, and when Paull widened his charges to include
condemnation of the behaviour in India of the 'indiscreet Knight of
the Bath', he firmly defended himself, asserting roundly that 'what he
did in India was in obedience to the orders he had received; and for
the manner of that obedience, and its immediate result, he was ready
to answer whether to the House or to any other tribunal in the realm'.[2]

Throughout the session he was regular in his attendance at the
House and could often be seen walking with brisk step across St James's
Park. He spoke upon Indian affairs when called upon to do so and
occasionally upon military matters, once warmly supporting a proposed

increase in the pay of junior officers; and, when he returned to his brigade at Hastings during the summer recess, he still concerned himself with Parliamentary business and his brother's affairs, helping to bring in two new supporters of Lord Wellesley at the St Ives election at a cost of £3,500, considerably more than he had found it necessary to lay out himself upon the electors at Rye.[3] At the same time he strongly advised his brother to seek friends among the newspaper editors, since it appeared 'that the Newspapers [had] made such good progress in guiding what was called publick opinion in this Country that no Man who [looked] to publick station [would] attain his objects, without a connection with & assistance from some of the Editors'.[*4]

His heart was not in politics, though. He was, after all, a soldier; and so long as other soldiers were gaining honours in fighting Napoleon and his allies, he could not comfortably live out his days on the south coast, however fully he contrived to occupy them.

Month by month Napoleon was extending his hold upon Europe. Joseph Bonaparte had become King of Naples in March 1806, Louis Bonaparte King of Holland in June. Their brother defeated Prussia at Jena and Saxony at Auerstädt in October and went on to occupy Berlin and Warsaw.

British victories that year were comparatively trivial. Buenos Aires surrendered to a small British force at the end of June but was retaken by the Spanish in August. In Calabria, Sir John Stuart attacked a French army at S. Pietro di Maida on 4 July and defeated it, but had no cavalry with which to follow up a victory which was celebrated beyond its deserts in London where Maida Hill and Maida Vale were named in honour of it and General Sir John Stuart, Count of Maida, received the freedom of the City.

In Hastings, General Wellesley wrote to Lord Grenville to offer his services in the hope that the Secretary for War would press his claims upon the Duke of York. He did not care in what situation he served, he wrote in another letter; he would be 'very sorry to stay at home when others went abroad' just because he could not be appointed to the chief command.[5] But no suitable command of any sort was given him. To be sure he was offered the opportunity of going to attack the

---

* Wellington generally affected to consider most journalists and nearly all newspapers as troublesome mischiefmakers and to be, as far as possible, ignored. But he later came to believe that he had 'committed a great error in not paying more attention to the Press, and in not securing a portion of it on his side and getting good writers into his employment, but he never thought it necessary to do so and was now [in 1831] convinced what a great mistake it was' (*The Greville Memoirs*, ii, 106).

Spanish in Mexico which was, according to a highly complicated plan formed by the Cabinet, to be seized by two armies falling upon it simultaneously, one from Jamaica on the coast of the Gulf of Mexico, the other – sailing by way of Singapore, the Philippines (where Manila was to be captured on the way) and Australia – on the Pacific seaboard somewhere in the region of Manzanillo.

But when he came to study this scheme, Sir Arthur was convinced of its wild impracticality as a military operation, apart from the difficulty of maintaining a government in Mexico should the operation be successful, 'particularly against the attempts which might be made upon it by the United States'.[6]

So, for the moment, politics seemed destined to claim him. The death of Charles James Fox in September had unsettled 'the Ministry of All the Talents'; and when Fox's successor as Foreign Secretary, Lord Howick, later Earl Grey, introduced the Roman Catholic Army and Navy Service Bill, which proposed opening both services to Roman Catholics and Dissenters alike, the King, convinced that to agree to such a measure would be a betrayal of his coronation oath, announced he would never consent to it and demanded an assurance that Ministers would never press upon him any concessions to Roman Catholics in the future. The Cabinet declined to give any such assurance; so in March 1807 the King summoned the Duke of Portland, old, ill and sleepy as he was, to form a new government.

The Duke appointed George Canning Foreign Secretary, Spencer Perceval as Chancellor of the Exchequer and brought back Lord Castlereagh as Secretary for War and the Colonies. Sir Arthur Wellesley was invited to accept the post of Chief Secretary for Ireland, at a salary of £6,566 a year, the Duke of Richmond being Lord-Lieutenant, two other Dukes, Rutland and Beaufort, having declined that unwelcome duty.

Sir Arthur, who had re-entered Parliament as Member for the Cornish borough of Mitchell in January, decided to accept the appointment in Dublin, provided that he might give it up should there be an opportunity of employment in the Army. The Duke of Portland agreed to this condition, and Sir Arthur took up his new post in March 1807.[7]

Sir Arthur and Lady Wellesley, with their baby son, Arthur Richard, who had been born at 11 Harley Street on 3 February, together with the child's nursemaid and their other servants, moved into the Chief Secretary's house in Phoenix Park from which the Chief Secretary rode across each morning, accompanied by the Lord-Lieutenant's daughters, to his office in the Castle. It was ten years since he had last lived in Dublin and much had changed. In 1798 a rebellion led by the Society of United Irishmen, who were dedicated to the establishment of an independent Irish republic and sought military help from France, had persuaded Pitt that union between Great Britain and Ireland was essential; and union had accordingly been authorized by legislation of the English and Irish Parliaments in August 1800.

The union, as Sir Arthur immediately recognized in Dublin, was far from universally popular. The Irish were 'disaffected to the British Government', he reported to London. They did 'not feel the benefits of their situation'. 'Show me an Irishman,' he wrote on a later occasion, 'and I'll show you a man whose anxious wish it is to see his country independent of Great Britain . . . Independence is what the Irish really aim at.' To achieve that independence from Britain they were looking eagerly for a French invasion; and in the event of such an invasion 'the operations which the British army would have to carry on would be of the nature of those in an enemy's country'. He was 'positively convinced that no political measure' that the Government could adopt would 'alter the temper of the people' of Ireland, and he was ultimately forced to the conclusion that the Irish should be 'kept down by main force', for they had too much power already and would 'only use more to obtain more and at length separation'. Now and later, as a member of the Anglo-Irish gentry, he clung steadfastly to the belief – perhaps more firmly held than any other in politics apart from his conviction that the worst evil that could befall a nation was civil strife – that the political supremacy of Great Britain over Ireland should be maintained.[8] In the meantime he settled down to his duties in the Castle with his usual conscientiousness, dealing with mounting piles of correspondence, writing memoranda for the Government on such matters as Ireland's coastal defences, granting, or more often declining, the numerous, frequently importunate requests for the Government's patronage which were made to him, regretting the fact that in Ireland 'almost every man of mark had his price', refusing permission for the Yeomanry to celebrate their part in the suppression of the 1798 rising on the grounds that it would be an unnecessary provocation to the dissidents, organizing the elections of 1807, which followed upon the dissolution of Parliament, buying some seats, exchanging favours for others, observing the drunkenness, violence and chicanery when seats were contested and a 'man who registered a vote without a cracked pate was regarded as a kind of natural phenomenon'. In Wexford, he wrote in a matter-of-fact manner in one of his dispatches to London, one candidate killed another in a duel, but as that was 'reckoned fair in Ireland, it created no sensation'.[9]

He himself was now Member for Newport in the Isle of Wight, having given up his Cornish seat; and in June he sailed for England, returning to the house in Harley Street, leaving his wife in Dublin to join him later.

The marriage was proving to be no more successful than it had seemed likely to be at the start. He spent much of his time away from home, allowing it to be supposed that he preferred to accept invitations to stay in country houses without his wife, spending as much time in the hunting field as his duties allowed, leaving her to entertain members of her family and other guests on her own. Soon after the birth of their son, Arthur, in rather uncertain health and thirty-five years old, Kitty became pregnant again and gave birth to her second son and last child on 16 January 1808. Thereafter her relationship with her husband became increasingly strained, he finding her dull and incapable, she being fond and admiring but so nervous and shy in his company that she appeared almost frightened of him and thus irritated him all the more. It was obvious to everyone who knew them that she exasperated him on occasions, particularly when she fussed about his health or tried to hide her ignorance by dogmatic assertions. When their baby, Arthur, had contracted measles at the age of five months, his mother had cause to be anxious; but the father, who had been hunting at Hatfield within three days of his birth and had told her that his return depended upon the likelihood of frost, dismissed her concern. He had 'no apprehension for the Meazles, being convinced that it is a mild disorder'. All that was needed was 'common care during the recovery'.[10]

His letters to her were addressed to 'My dearest Kitty' and customarily ended in the same affectionate way, but their contents often read as though they were addressed to a steward and a not very competent steward at that:

> I enclose a letter from a Bricklayer. I thought you had paid him. Let me know whether you have or not ... Let the Gardener [who had been dismissed] be taken back ... I am much concerned that you should have thought of concealing from me any want of money ... I don't understand how this want occurred or why it was concealed ... I acknowledge that the conclusion I draw from your conduct upon the occasion is that you must be Mad, or you must consider me to be a Brute, & most particularly fond & avaricious of money. Once for

all you require no permission to talk to me upon any subject you please; all that I request is that a [fuss] may not be made about trifles ... & that you may not go into tears because I don't think them deserving of an uncommon degree of attention ... It is to be hoped that at some time or other I shall be better understood.[11]

Fifteen years later, while walking in a garden after supper with his dear friend Harriet Arbuthnot, he confessed that he had been 'a damned fool' to have married 'such a person'.

He assured me that she did not understand him [Mrs Arbuthnot recorded in her journal], that she could not enter with him into the consideration of all the important concerns which are continually occupying his mind, and that he found he might as well talk to a child ... He told me ... that his tastes were domestic, that nothing w^d make him so happy as to have a home where he could find comfort; but that, so far from that, she made his house so dull that nobody w^d go to it ... & that it drove him to seek abroad that comfort & happiness that was denied to him at home ... At his home he had no creature to speak to, for that discussing political or important subjects with the Duchess was like talking *Hebrew* to her.[12]

Busy as he was with these political affairs which he could not discuss with his wife, Sir Arthur reminded Lord Castlereagh more than once of his determination not to give up the military profession, of his fear that were he to let an opportunity to serve slip by for the sake of clinging to 'a large civil office', he might lose 'the confidence and esteem of the officers and soldiers of the army'.[13]

His chance came towards the end of July 1807 when an expedition was being planned to force the Danes to give up possession of their fleet to the British before it was seized by the French. General Wellesley was offered the command of a division in this expedition, and eagerly accepted it. He sailed almost immediately in the fire-ship *Prometheus* for Copenhagen.

It was decided at the Horse Guards, however, that his experience of European warfare was too limited to allow his being given command of one of the leading divisions. He was to be in command of the reserve, and was, moreover, to have a more seasoned officer as second-in-command. As Wellesley knew only too well, the Horse Guards thought 'very little of any one who had served in India'. Besides, he was not only a politician but also 'a Lord's son, *"a sprig of nobility"* who came into the army more for ornament than use'. 'When the Horse Guards are obliged to employ one of those fellows like me, in whom they have no confidence,' he later told a friend, 'they give him what is called a *second-in-command* – one in whom they do have confidence – a kind of dry nurse.'[14]

Wellesley's 'dry nurse' was a Brigadier named Richard Stewart. An efficient officer and a tactful man, Stewart supervised both the embarkation of the division and its disembarkation north of Copenhagen; but he did so in such a manner as not to cause offence to his superior who 'saw no kind of objection to anything he suggested'. So 'all went *à merveille'*. But when the division had landed, the men giving 'one simultaneous and tremendous cheer', General Wellesley insisted upon leading it against the Danish force which had been sent out from Copenhagen against the invaders. 'Come, come,' he said when Stewart offered his advice as to how the advance should be conducted, "Tis my turn now.'[15]

'I immediately made my own dispositions,' he afterwards related, 'assigned Stewart the command of one of the wings, gave him his orders, attacked the enemy [at Köge on 29 August], and beat them. Stewart, like a man of sense, saw in a moment that I understood my business, and subsided with (as far as I saw) good humour into his proper place.'[16]

Copenhagen was now satisfactorily invested; and Wellesley would have liked to remain outside its walls until the place was forced to surrender. But the commander of the expedition, Lieutenant-General Lord Cathcart, the son of the ninth Lord Cathcart, a former Ambassador at St Petersburg, an officer who had been at Eton before General Wellesley was born, had no doubt that a bombardment of the city was required. Despite this, Wellesley's relations with the Danes he encountered were uniformly amicable: one of these was named Rosencrantz, and the General confessed that he had a strong temptation to ask after Guildenstern; another thanked him for ensuring the good behaviour of his troops while they lay in the neighbourhood, though he himself considered that they behaved only 'tolerably well' and were 'very unpopular in the country'. A Danish general expressed his regret that 'political views should counteract the private feelings of individuals'; while a lady, some of whose property was looted but returned to her with many apologies, made Sir Arthur a present of fruit and invited him to shoot on her land.[17]

On 6 September Copenhagen surrendered. General Cathcart was created a viscount and he and Admiral Gambier – who had been in command of naval operations and was raised to the peerage for his considerable efforts – were awarded prize money which was estimated to amount to £300,000.[18]

General Wellesley returned to his duties as Chief Secretary for Ireland, preceded by a mare which had been taken on the expedition by Major-General Thomas Grosvenor who had not known that the animal was in foal.*

* The mare was sent home by Grosvenor to Eaton Hall to the care of his cousin, Earl Grosvenor, later first Marquess of Westminster. At Eaton she foaled the chestnut colt named Copenhagen. Copenhagen came into the possession of Sir Charles Stewart, later third Marquess of Londonderry, Adjutant-General in the Peninsular War, who sold him to Wellington while they were serving together in Spain. He became Wellington's favourite charger and survived the Napoleonic Wars when many other horses died under their demanding master. Copenhagen himself died in 1836 and was buried at Stratfield Saye. In his retirement there he was often ridden by the Duke and by the Duke's grandchildren and their friends even though the horse, according to the Duke's friend Frances, Lady Shelley, was 'the most difficult to sit' of any she had ever ridden. 'If the Duke had not been there I should have been frightened,' she wrote in her diary. 'He said, "I believe you think the glory greater than the pleasure in riding him"' (The Diary of Frances, Lady Shelley, 133). The Duchess 'used regularly to feed him with bread, and this kindness had given him the habit of approaching every lady with the most confiding familiarity' (Sporting Magazine, quoted in Wellington Anecdotes, 61).

The Duke was asked by the Secretary of the United Services Museum if the horse's skeleton might be presented to the Museum as a companion exhibit to the skeleton of Napoleon's horse, Marengo. The Duke replied that he did not know for sure where Copenhagen was buried, though the funeral had, in fact, taken place with full military honours and, according to an account given by the second Duke to Sir William Fraser, the Duke had seen the horse's body just before the burial and had flown into 'a most terrible passion' when he noticed that one of the hooves had been cut off. Years later it transpired that this had been done by a servant who, thinking no one would notice, had taken the hoof as a memento (Fraser, Words on Wellington). Before his death the servant returned it to the second Duke who had it made into an inkstand. Mrs Arbuthnot and other ladies, so Lord Ellesmere said, had bracelets made of the horse's hair (Ellesmere, Personal Reminiscences of the Duke of Wellington, 89). It was the second Duke who erected the inscribed gravestone still to be seen at Stratfield Saye in the Ice-House Paddock beneath the Turkey Oak planted on the grave in 1843 by the first Duke's housekeeper, Mrs Apostles, who had entered his service twenty years before.

Copenhagen's dam, Lady Catherine, was uniquely honoured by becoming the only half-bred broodmare in the General Stud Book (Gordon Fergusson, The Green Collars, 102–4). Wellington said of Copenhagen, 'There may have been many faster horses, no doubt many handsomer, but for bottom and endurance I never saw his fellow' (John Codman Ropes, The Campaign of Waterloo, New York, 1892, 240).

12 Portugal

1808

'Sir Harry, now is your time to advance.'

'I HAVE GOT PRETTY high upon the tree since I came home,' Sir Arthur Wellesley wrote contentedly from the Lodge in Phoenix Park soon after his return to Dublin. 'I don't think it probable that I shall be called upon [to return to India] . . . Men in power in England think very little of that country, and those who do think of it feel very little inclination that I should go there . . . They think I cannot well be spared from objects nearer home.'[1]

There was, indeed, much to concern them in Europe. Following the French victories over the Prussians at Jena and Auerstädt and over the Russians at Friedland, France and Russia had become allies by agreements reached at Tilsit and had resolved to divide Europe between them, reducing Austria and Prussia to impotence. Britain thus stood alone against Napoleon. Denmark joined France in October; and Spain undertook to assist in a French attack upon Portugal which had refused to join Napoleon's Continental System, a form of economic warfare designed to ruin British trade by excluding British ships from Continental ports.

French troops invaded Portugal on 19 November under General Andoche Junot, a wealthy farmer's truculent son who had become Governor of Paris; and ten days later the Portuguese royal family fled to Brazil. While Ministers anxiously discussed the measures that might be taken to break the Continental blockade, General Wellesley took every opportunity to remind them of his presence in Dublin and to offer his services in 'any part of the world at a moment's notice'.[2]

Meanwhile he had to turn his attention to the perennial and insoluble problems of Ireland, to Irish education, to the maintenance of civil order, to the creation of a Dublin police force, to a law requiring absentee clergymen to return to their parishes, to protests against excessive rents and tithes, to the dangers of a French invasion, sometimes voicing the views of a high and impatient Tory – 'we want discipline, not learning' – at others speaking with the voice of liberal enlightenment – 'the great object of our policy in Ireland should be to endeavour to obliterate, as far as the law will allow us, the distinction between Protestants and Catholics, and that we ought to avoid anything which can induce either sect to recollect or believe that its interests are separate and distinct from those of the other.'[3]

When he left Dublin for London to attend the House of Commons he was kept equally busy, defending the reputation of the Army when it was assailed by Samuel Whitbread, an energetic member of the Whig opposition; and, as a *willing horse* upon whose back every man thinks he has a right to put the saddle', continuing to provide the Cabinet with detailed advice about their proposed military operations.[4]

He was asked to comment on an expedition to Sweden, to suggest ways in which to counter a rumoured Franco-Russian assault on India, and to confer with General Francisco de Miranda, a Venezuelan revolutionary, living in exile in London, who had recently returned to the country of his birth where he had unsuccessfully endeavoured to lead the peasants in an uprising against the Spanish authorities.

Wellesley did not take to Miranda; nor did he like the Foreign Office's idea of making another attempt to foster revolution in Venezuela. He wrote a report on its military aspects, but made it clear that he 'had always had a horror of revolutionising any country for a political object'. If they 'rose of themselves, well and good'; but it was 'a fearful responsibility' to 'stir them up'.[5]

Despite these reservations as to its wisdom, a small British force of 9,000 men was assembled at Cork for an invasion of Venezuela, and Sir Arthur, who had been promoted lieutenant-general on 25 April, was appointed to command it. He set about his plans and preparations with his familiar thoroughness, 'making out in his own handwriting lists of all the stores required, down to the very number of flints for small arms'. But then came news of a Spanish revolt. On 2 May the people of Madrid turned furiously on the French garrison and shot or stabbed every soldier they could find; and, although the revolt was soon put down by the ruthless fire of French guns, little more than a fortnight later the anger broke out again in other towns, in other provinces. Spanish officials who had collaborated with the French were dragged out into the streets and murdered; governors were lynched; committees were organized; administrative councils known as *juntas provinciales* were established; troops were enrolled; proclamations, promising support to Prince Ferdinand, heir to the deposed King and Queen of Spain, and death to the French, were read to cheering crowds.

When representatives of the Asturian *juntas* landed in England with appeals for help to a country with which Spain was still officially at war, they were greeted sympathetically; and the Foreign Secretary, George Canning, declared that 'Britain would proceed upon the principle that any nation in Europe which stirs up with a determination to oppose [France] . . . becomes immediately our ally.' The revolt spread to Portugal; and General Junot was forced to concentrate his scattered forces around Lisbon.

General Wellesley immediately recognized – and conveyed his belief to the Cabinet – that here was 'a crisis in which a great effort might be made with advantage'. It was 'certain that any measures which [could] distress the French in Spain' would oblige them to 'delay for a season' the execution of their other plans. He proposed that the force being collected at Cork for a landing in Venezuela should be diverted to the Iberian peninsula, much as this would distress General Miranda who, indeed, became so 'loud and angry' when he encountered Sir Arthur in the street that Wellesley told him that they should 'walk on a little so that we might not attract the notice of everybody passing'.[6]

In the hopes of being given orders for the Peninsula, Wellesley saw to it that instructions were sent to Cork to ensure that the troops there were properly equipped for such a campaign, with adequate transport and cooking equipment, and that, for the sake of their health, they were to be landed frequently from the crowded ships in the harbour.[7]

In daily expectation of orders to sail, Wellesley handed over the business of the Chief Secretary for Ireland's office to John Wilson Croker, a garrulous, up-and-coming lawyer and notorious gossip born and educated in Ireland and since 1806 Member of Parliament for Downpatrick.

One evening after dinner in Harley Street, when the two men were sitting over the wine and Lady Wellesley had gone upstairs to the drawing-room, Sir Arthur fell into a ruminative silence. Croker asked him what he was thinking about.

'Why, to say the truth,' he replied, 'I am thinking of the French that I am going to fight. I have not seen them since the campaign in Flanders, when they were capital soldiers, and a dozen years of victory under Bonaparte must have made them better still. They have besides, it seems, a new system of strategy which has out-manoeuvred and overwhelmed all the armies of Europe. 'Tis enough to make one thoughtful; but no matter: my die is cast, they may overwhelm me, but I don't think they will out-manoeuvre me. First, because I am not afraid of them, as everybody else seems to be; and, secondly, because, if what I hear of their system of manoeuvres is true, I think it is a false one against steady troops.'[8]

Before leaving London for Cork, he went to see various friends and relations in England. He went to dinner at Coombe Wood with Lord Hawkesbury, the Home Secretary; he called upon his sister Anne, whose first husband, a son of Lord Southampton, had died in 1794, and who was now married to Culling Charles Smith of Hampton; on his way to Holyhead he went to Llangollen to see his family's old friends in their little house there and he came away with a Church of England prayer book in Spanish which had once belonged to the Duke of Ormonde and which he was to study on the voyage out, for linguistic rather than liturgical reasons.[9]

By the time he returned to London his orders had been given him: he was to drive Junot out of Portugal. On 12 July 1808 he set sail for Corunna in the *Donegal*, soon transferring to the faster *Crocodile*, with high hopes of doing so.

Assured by the Spanish authorities in Corunna that the French grip on their country was faltering day by day, General Wellesley sailed on in the *Crocodile* around the coast of Coruña province, coming up with his transports off Cape Finisterre, then sailing down past the shores of Pontevedra to land in Portugal at Oporto by the mouth of the Douro river.[10]

The Portuguese were less sanguine than the Spaniards in Corunna; but the Bishop, who was the head of Portugal's Supreme Junta, was amenable and listened politely to the British General's request for five hundred mules for the transport of the British army when it landed sixty miles further south in Mondego Bay. The General was most insistent about these animals. Supply, he well knew, would be as vital a consideration in the wide expanses of Spain as it had been in India where, as he said, 'If I had rice and bullocks I had men, and if I had men I knew I could beat the enemy.'[11] The Bishop was clearly surprised by the request for so many animals but agreed to make arrangements to supply them. He was evidently impressed by the bearing and directness of the young General and was clearly much gratified by the proclamation he undertook to give to the Portuguese people, assuring them that their allies, the British, had come to restore their 'lawful Prince' to the throne, and guaranteeing the independence of their Kingdom and the preservation of their 'holy religion'. The General emphasized the need for respect for religious susceptibilities in Portugal in a

General Order to his men which forbade them to enter a church during the performance of divine service without permission, and which required them to take off their hats should they wish to enter a place of worship 'from motives of curiosity', when a service was not being performed. Officers must remove their hats when the Host passed them in the streets and soldiers must salute. Should the Host pass a guard-post the sentries must turn out and present arms.[12] Soldiers were allowed to attend Mass; but, in fact, as the General was to discover: 'Although we have whole regiments of Irishmen, and of course Roman Catholics, nobody goes to Mass . . . I have not seen one soldier perform any act of religious worship, excepting making the sign of the cross to induce the people of the country to give them wine.'[13]

Dismayed as the Bishop may well have been by the irreligion of his allies, he cannot have failed to be gratified by their General's order as to the respect to be shown to the 'holy religion' of his flock. Nor can he have failed to be much gratified, as the General certainly was, by news which reached them from Andalusia.

This news seemed to confirm the blithe optimism of the authorities in Corunna. For west of Córdoba the French General Pierre Antoine Dupont, recently created a count by Napoleon in recognition of his previous successes in the field, had been trapped and forced to surren-der by a Spanish force at Baylen.

In expectation of beating the French themselves, the British army, 13,000 strong, began to land on the Portuguese shore of Montego Bay a hundred miles north of Lisbon in the first week of August 1808. The soldiers, sitting four by four on the thwarts of the heavily laden boats, their packs and muskets gripped tightly between their knees, plunged violently through the Atlantic breakers towards the burning sand of the beach where sailors, the white surf frothing round their thighs, stood naked at the water's edge, watching the boats sweep forward through the spray. In the instant that the waters rushed back under the foam of a broken wave, the sailors ran out towards the boats to hurl a rope to them.

On shore piles of food and ammunition, equipment and forage lay waiting for transport to take them inland. A harassed German commis-sary, scribbling an inventory in his notebook, looked in consternation at the guns and wagons, 'the mountains of ships' biscuits, haversacks, trusses of hay, barrels of meat and rum, tents', and all the impedimenta of an invading army. Around him officers shouted orders, sergeants sweated and cursed, soldiers picked about in the wreckage of splintered boats, orderlies looked around for suitable sites for tents, aides-de-camp with nothing better to do paddled barefoot in the surf, while frightened horses, released from weeks of confinement in the dark and stuffy holds of ships, galloped wildly along the shore, snorting, panting, neighing, biting one another, and rolling over in the sand, as dragoons chased after them, bridles in hand.

Brown-skinned peasants, their long hair falling to their shoulders beneath enormous three-cornered hats, carrying goads six feet long, led the Bishop's bullock carts through the din and muddle, making a fearful screeching noise of their own, a squealing of axles so cacophonous that the German commissary thought the scratching of a knife on a pewter plate was like 'the sweet sound of a flute' beside it. Watched by scores of monks and friars carrying huge and luridly coloured umbrellas, the peasants offered pumpkins and figs, grapes and melons, wine and apples for sale to the thirsty troops.

Two days after landing Sir Arthur Wellesley was riding down the road to Leiria in what one of his aides-de-camp noticed was a disconsolate mood. He had received dispatches from London informing him that he was not to command the army after all. It transpired that Lord Castlereagh, and those other Ministers who had supported his claims, had been overborne by the Duke of York and senior officers at the Horse Guards who – with the approval of the King who 'always stood up for old Generals & disliked aspiring young ones'[14] – demanded that a more senior officer be appointed. Wellesley was, after all, they argued, a very recently promoted lieutenant-general, not yet forty, most of whose experience had been in India. There were numerous other names on the Army List more senior to his. One, indeed, was already in the Peninsula as Governor of Gibraltar. This was Sir Hew Dalrymple, fifty-seven years old, a grandson of Viscount Stair and son of a distinguished Scottish lawyer, a Guards officer who had been promoted major-general as long ago as 1794, though he had only once been on active service. Then there was another veteran Guards officer whose claims to high command could likewise not be ignored, Sir Harry Burrard, who was also in his fifties and had been a reliably Tory Member of Parliament for Lymington for several years as his uncle and grandfather had before him. The appointment of Dalrymple and Burrard to the army in Portugal was not, however, so much to prevent the young Wellesley being given the credit for winning what might prove to be an important battle, as to prevent the command passing into the hands of a man the Government had good cause both to dislike and to fear. This was Sir John Moore, a particularly handsome, upright and tactless man of Whiggish persuasions, somewhat haughty in manner and given to expressing disturbing criticisms of the Government and particularly of the Foreign Office. Moore had been sent to Sweden to help King Gustavus who was threatened not only by France but also by Denmark and Russia. He had quarrelled with the King whose sanity was questionable and had brought his army home. He was now ready to command some other enterprise. It was hoped that if he were told that his services would be welcome in Spain as a subordinate to two other officers whose names would be almost unknown to him he would feel compelled to refuse the opportunity. But this was to reckon without regard to Moore's strong sense of duty. After a frosty interview with Lord Castlereagh, he agreed to serve under the two Guards officers both of whom were, indeed, senior to him but neither of whom had even a small share of his presence or talent.

Before Moore arrived in the Peninsula, however, and before either of his two superiors reached Portugal, General Wellesley, advancing with six British and one Portuguese brigade, had come across the French near the village of Obidos, on either side of the road to Lisbon. Here his eager skirmishers charged forward with such impulsive excitement that many of them were killed before the enemy, commanded by the astute General Henri François, Comte de Delaborde, choosing not to make a stand, sensibly fell back to a stronger position at Roliça. Anxious to waste no further lives unnecessarily, Wellesley ordered a cautious flanking movement; but his centre, with the impetuosity his skirmishers had shown near Obidos, surged forward before the out-flanking manoeuvre had developed. Delaborde withdrew once more, having not only gained valuable time for Junot to concentrate and regroup his forces but also having inflicted nearly 500 casualties on the British army which outnumbered his own almost four to one.

When Wellesley reached Vimeiro, fifteen miles nearer Lisbon, he had been reinforced by about 4,000 British troops who had just landed in the sandy estuary of the river Maceira and thus commanded an army quite capable of beating the one which Junot was marching towards him. He was anxious to attack at once; and he rode down the coast to seek permission to do so from Sir Harry Burrard who had just arrived in the sloop *Brazen*. Sir Harry demurred; better to wait, he said, until Moore arrived with his 2,000 additional men. He would not himself go ashore for the moment as he had letters to write. 'I only wish Sir Harry *had* landed,' Wellesley gloomily reported to Castlereagh, 'and had seen things with his own eyes.'[15]

His gloom, however, was soon dispelled. The French moved forward that night, and the next day, 21 August, in their white summer uniforms they marched up the hill towards the British line 'with more confidence', so Wellesley recalled years later, smiling with satisfaction, 'seeming to *feel their way* less than I always found them to do *afterwards*'. 'I received them in line,' he added, 'which they were not accustomed to.'[16] And after two and a half hours' bitter fighting, the British victory was complete: the French, who had suffered nearly 2,000 casualties, were everywhere in full retreat.[17] Wellesley, whose own losses were just over 700, turned in his saddle to Sir Harry Burrard, who had come up from the *Brazen* but had not interfered with his subordinate's conduct of the battle, having been, as he generously reported to London, 'perfectly satisfied' with General Wellesley's dispositions and 'the means he proposed to repulse the enemy'.[18] 'Sir Harry,' Wellesley said in a loud voice, 'now is your time to advance. The enemy are completely beaten and we shall be in Lisbon in three days.'[19]

Once again Sir Harry demurred. Excessively wary by temperament, he had been made more cautious still by the uniformly unsuccessful expeditions in which he had previously been engaged. Believing that Junot had a stronger force in reserve than Wellesley supposed, he ordered the return of Sir Ronald Ferguson's brigade which had already been sent in pursuit. Annoyed beyond measure, Wellesley remarked to his staff as he rode away that they might just as well go off to shoot partridge. The next day 'Dowager' Dalrymple, as his subordinate was to refer to him, came from Gibraltar to approve of the action that 'Betty' Burrard had taken.[20]

Wellesley's position, as he told Lord Castlereagh, was now a 'very delicate one'. He had never met Dalrymple before and it was 'not a very easy task to advise any man on the first day one meets him'.[21] It was particularly difficult to offer an opinion to Sir Hew who showed himself not merely unwilling to listen to advice but resentful of its even being offered, especially by a young Irish general of no ingratiating manner. He certainly did not welcome Wellesley's tart comments during his negotiations with the French General François-Etienne Kellerman, the extraordinarily ugly son of Marshal Kellerman, who rode into the British lines on 22 August, escorted by two squadrons of dragoons carrying white flags, his face patched with bits of black sticking-plaster.[22]

The discussions lasted 'from about half past two till near nine at night, with the exception of a short time [they] sat at dinner'; and Wellesley, by his own account, said little. 'I beg you will not believe that I had any hand in wording [the armistice],' he told Lord Castlereagh. 'It was negotiated by the General himself in my presence and that of Sir

Harry Burrard; and after it had been drawn out by Kellerman himself, Sir Hew Dalrymple desired me to sign it.'[23]

Wellesley did sign it, commenting that it was 'an extraordinary paper', an observation which elicited a cross response from Sir Hew that there was nothing in it which had not been agreed in the negotiations. In its details it was, indeed, an extraordinary document, although Wellesley afterwards admitted that in substance it was defensible. It provided for the evacuation of the French from Portugal; but they were to be taken home in British ships with all their stores and all that they had acquired in the country which they had invaded, including, in the event, much plunder, some of it melted-down plate from Spanish churches.

Anxious to escape from Sir Hew Dalrymple's jurisdiction as soon as possible, Wellesley made it clear in letters to London that he wanted to go home without delay. He would stay if the Government wished it; but he was 'sick of all' that was going on in Portugal and heartily wished he had never left home. Were he to serve in the Peninsula with Sir John Moore, that would be a different matter altogether, even though, as he told Castlereagh, he had 'been too successful with this army ever to serve with it in a subordinate position'.[24] Moore had followed up a warm letter of congratulation to Sir Arthur on his victory at Vimeiro with an offer to 'waive all pretensions as senior' and 'take any part' that might be offered him 'for the good of the service'. Sir Arthur himself had no doubt that Moore ought to succeed Dalrymple in command and he offered to write to the Cabinet to say so. But Moore would not allow this: it smacked too much of intrigue.[25]

So Sir Arthur was more than ever determined to go home. 'It is quite impossible for me to continue any longer with this army,' he told Lord Castlereagh; 'and I wish, therefore, that you would allow me to return home and resume the duties of my office, if I should still be in office, and it is convenient for the Government that I should retain it; or if not, that I should remain upon the Staff in England; or, if that should not be practicable, that I should remain without employment.' In effect, he would do anything rather than remain in Portugal under the command of generals whom he described in a private letter as being of 'stupid incapacity'.[26]

He could certainly not look forward to a hero's welcome in England, however. His victory at Vimeiro had been heavily overcast by what was seen in England as the subsequent disgrace of the Convention of Cintra to which he had been a party.

*

'I arrived here this day, and I don't know whether I am to be hanged drawn & quartered, or roasted alive,' he wrote to his brother Richard from Harley Street on 4 October, having landed at Plymouth a few hours before. 'However I shall not allow the Mob of London to deprive me of my temper or my spirits; or of the satisfaction which I feel in the consciousness that I acted right.'[27]

It was not only the displeasure of the London mob, however, that he had cause to apprehend. The many enemies of his too successful family were making the most of their opportunity to blacken the Wellesley name. The Duke of Richmond told Sir Arthur not to bother about the 'whispers of those who dislike the name of Wellesley'; but it was difficult to ignore the barbs of such men as Samuel Whitbread, the rich brewer and Radical Member for Bedford, who rejoiced 'to see the Wellesley pride a little lowered',[28] and William Cobbett, that other leading Radical, a former sergeant-major in the Army and publisher of the influential *Weekly Political Register*, who confessed himself to be delighted to have the 'rascals on the hip'. It was evident, Cobbett wrote, that Sir Arthur Wellesley was 'the prime cause – the only cause – of all the mischief, and that from the motive of thwarting everything *after he was superseded*. Thus do we pay for the arrogance of that damned infernal family.'[29]

In the columns of his *Weekly Political Register*, Cobbett went so far as to declare that Sir Arthur Wellesley had come home 'for the purpose of avoiding another meeting' with the French.

Sir Arthur Wellesley claimed that he read the abuse of himself 'with as much indifference as [he did] that of the great General', Sir Hew Dalrymple. But his brothers did not hide their distress at the charges and insults to which the family was being subjected. William spent his time 'cursing and swearing'; Henry fell ill; Richard at first wept, then, in Arthur's words, took to whoring.* Even Arthur, indifferent to previous insults as he had contrived to appear, was stung painfully enough by Cobbett's charges of cowardice to threaten suing him for libel.[30] He also appears to have followed Richard's example and, censorious of Richard's 'whoring' as he was in his letters to William, to

---

* 'I am convinced,' Sir Arthur wrote of him to his brother William, 'that his fornication has kept him out of office. In spite of his idleness he would have been in office now if he had not taken to *Whoring*. . . I wish that he was castrated; or that he would like other people attend to his business & perform too. It is lamentable to see the Talents & character & advantages that he possesses thrown away upon Whoring' (Raglan Papers, 6 Nov. 1808, 6 April 1810).

have sought relief in his agitation in the arms of Harriette Wilson. At least Harriette Wilson maintained that this was so; and, if it was, he surely found her body more exciting than she claimed to have found his conversation:

'Do you know,' said I to him one day,' do you know the world talks about hanging you?'

'Eh?'

'They say you will be hanged in spite of all your brother Wellesley can say in your defence.'

'Ha!!' said [he] very seriously, 'What paper do you read?'

'It is the common talk of the day,' I replied . . .

He called on me the next morning before I had finished my breakfast. I tried him on every subject I could muster. On all, he was most impenetrably taciturn. At last he started an original idea of his own.

'I wonder you do not get married, Harriette!'

(By the by, ignorant people are always wondering.)

'Why so?'

He however, gives no reason for anything unconnected with fighting, at least since the convention of Cintra; and he, therefore, again became silent. Another burst of attic sentiment blazed forth.

'I was thinking of you last night, after I got into bed.'

'How very polite to [Lady Wellesley],' I observed. '*Apropos* to marriage, how do you like it?'

[Sir Arthur] who seems to make a point of never answering one, continued, 'I was thinking – I was thinking that you will get into some scrape.'

'Nothing so serious as marriage neither, I hope!'

'I must come again tomorrow, to give you a little advice.'

'Oh, let us have it all out now, and have done with it.'

'I cannot,' he said putting on his gloves and taking a hasty leave of me.

I am glad he is off, thought I, for this is indeed very uphill work. This is worse than Lord Craven.[31]

13 Board of Enquiry

1808

'This is Sir Arthur (whose valour and skill, began
so well but ended so ill).'

To ADD TO Sir Arthur's other worries, there was talk of an enquiry
into the Convention of Cintra being set up by a Board of General
Officers who were to examine General Wellesley's part in formulating
it. So long as the verdict of the Board was unknown, Lord Castlereagh
doubted the wisdom of Sir Arthur's attending the levee at St James's
Palace; and when the General asked the Secretary for War if he would
drive him there, Castlereagh 'hemmed & hawed, and said that there
was so much ill-humour in the public mind that it might produce
inconvenience, and, in short, he advised me not to go.'[1]

But Sir Arthur was determined to go. He had intended to do so as
'a matter of respect and duty to the King' and he was not the kind of
man to shrink from showing his face on account of 'ill-humour in the
public mind'. He now looked upon his attendance as a 'matter of
self-respect and duty' to his own character. 'I therefore insist on knowing whether this advice proceeds in any degree from His Majesty,' he
replied to Castlereagh's letter, 'and I wish you distinctly to understand
that I will go to the levee tomorrow, or I never will go to [another]
levee in my life.'[2]

He did go and the King was perfectly amicable. His Majesty was
not in favour of a public enquiry into the Convention of Cintra and
when such a tribunal was first suggested he rejected the proposal out
of hand. He was eventually obliged to tolerate one, however; and in
November a Board of General Officers was convened in the Great Hall
of Chelsea Hospital under the presidency of an intimate friend of the
Duke of York, the tall, austere, Scottish General Sir David Dundas,
Governor of the Hospital, who had been a captain in the Dragoons
long before Sir Arthur Wellesley was born. Sir Hew Dalrymple was
recalled from the Peninsula to answer the Board's questions; Sir Arthur
Wellesley returned from Ireland where he had briefly gone to see his

family and to consult Croker, still his deputy in the Chief Secretary's office. Sir Harry Burrard was already in England.

All three had been the subject of endless calumny, ridicule and jokes, in broadsheets, pamphlets and verse, both Byron and Wordsworth eventually adding their voices to the general condemnation.

They were shown in caricature dangling grotesquely from gallows with white feathers in their hats; they were depicted as inmates of Bedlam drinking toasts over the prostrate body of a dishonoured Britannia. James Gillray caricatured kneeling British officers kissing Junot's bottom. Charles Williams parodied 'The House that Jack Built' in seven designs, one of which was inscribed 'This is Sir Arthur (whose valour and skill, began so well but ended so ill)'.[3] In another caricature George Cruikshank showed Sir Arthur kneeling before Junot and asking him abjectly, *'May it please your Highness to accept these terms as a Convention & should any of them seem to you Ungrateful, dictate according to your Noble Will.'*[4]

Charles Williams presented Dalrymple as the butt of a fellow officer singing,

> *'T was You Sir Hew – 'T was Hew who let the French escape*
> *That makes you look so blue Sir Hew.*[5]

Newspapers took to printing comments on the Convention surrounded by thick black funereal borders. William Cobbett lambasted all responsible for agreeing to it in the pages of his *Weekly Political Register*. Indignant people told each other that Walter Scott's friend, the author George Ellis, had summed it up nicely when he said that in future he would spell 'Humiliation' with a 'Hew'.[6]

The Board examined the three Generals who were the object of all this ridicule with the most ponderous and elaborate diligence. Sir Hew Dalrymple answered questions which seemed to reflect adversely upon his good sense or honour with a touchy hauteur, occasionally revealing his animus against a junior colleague who, while a signatory to the agreement, wished to dissociate himself from it. Sir Arthur Wellesley, while taking care to exonerate Sir Harry Burrard from all blame, did not trouble to disguise his disdain for Dalrymple whom he considered wholly responsible for the pernicious document. 'I gave him my opinion when he asked for it, and when I thought it desirable to give it to him,' he deposed. 'But I was not the negotiator, and could not be, and was not so considered, the commander of the forces being present in the room, deciding upon all points . . . If the commander had given me instructions to negotiate this instrument and I had then negotiated it,

I might have been responsible for its contents ... but as it is my signature is a mere form.'[7]

Day after day the members of the Board listened to such speeches, examined witnesses, pored over bundles of papers, read transcripts, deliberated among themselves; and in December, anxious not to ruffle any feathers or hurt anyone's feelings, they issued a report which, commenting upon a number of matters other than that which they had been called upon to examine, concluded that 'no further military proceeding was necessary on the subject'.[8] When the Duke of York pointed out that their verdict scarcely answered the question which they had been asked to determine, they met again; and, after lengthy deliberation, came to the conclusion, by four votes to three, that they approved of the Convention.[9]

Wellesley was free to return to Dublin. His duties there were more irksome than ever now; and he longed to serve in the Army again. 'I shall go to England for the meeting of Parliament,' he wrote, 'and mean to join the Army as soon afterwards as I shall be allowed to go.'[10]

He was back in London by the beginning of 1809 and took up his seat in the Commons again, gratified to receive the thanks of the House for his defeat of Junot at Vimeiro; and, with an eye no doubt on his future career, he spoke in defence of the Duke of York whose witty, pretty and wildly extravagant mistress, Mrs Mary Anne Clarke, had been accepting money for recommending officers to the notice of her lover, although Wellesley expressed the view in private that the Duke had been most indiscreet and had laid himself open to the charge that he had 'manifested so much weakness and had led such a life' that there were grounds for doubting that he was a 'proper person to be trusted with the execution of the duties of a responsible office'.[11] In the event the Duke of York felt obliged to resign as Commander-in-Chief and was succeeded by the dour old General Dundas who, because of his friendship with the Duke, as well as his age, would be ready to hand the Horse Guards back to him when the scandal had subsided.

In the month of Dundas's appointment, Wellesley learned that he was to be given a new command. There had been some doubt as to whether the King would approve of so young a lieutenant-general being given such responsibility. But Castlereagh, to whom Wellesley sent long and useful memoranda on the likely future course of fighting in the Peninsula, was a strong advocate; and, as his Majesty was informed, the Cabinet 'humbly conceived' that Sir Arthur was the General most likely to succeed in the campaign that lay ahead, and therefore proposed that 'His Majesty's service (without prejudice to the claims of the distinguished officers in His Majesty's Army who are his seniors) may have the benefit of Sir Arthur Wellesley's being employed where he has had the good fortune of being successful.'[12]

There were, after all, few alternatives. Sir John Moore, who had been left in command in the Peninsula, having advanced from Lisbon towards Valladolid, had been forced to retreat to Corunna when the French advanced upon him with 70,000 men after the fall of Madrid; and at Corunna he had been mortally wounded in a battle against Marshal Soult. Moore's successor, Lieutenant-General Sir John Cradock, was believed to be insufficiently capable. Dalrymple and Burrard were not even considered. So Wellesley was appointed to the command and made his preparations for departure.

One of his last missions, so Harriette Wilson said, was to say goodbye to her.

> He called to take a hasty leave of me [she wrote], a few hours before his departure.
>
> 'I am off to Spain directly,' he said.
>
> I know not how it was but I grew melancholy. [He] had relieved me from many duns which else had given me vast uneasiness. I saw him there, perhaps for the last time in my life . . . I burst into tears . . .
>
> 'If you change your home,' [he] said kissing my cheek, 'let me find your address at Thomas's Hotel as soon as I come to England; and, if you want anything in the meantime, write to Spain; and do not cry; and take care of yourself; and do not cut me when I come back.
>
> 'Do you hear?' he said, first wiping away some of my tears with my handkerchief; and then, kissing my eyes, he said, 'God bless you!' and hurried away.[13]

It was at least true that he had given her money. When her memoirs were published in 1825 he was asked by his friend Harriet Arbuthnot if what had been written about him could possibly be accurate. He had known Harriette Wilson, he admitted, 'a great number of years ago, so long that he did not think he should remember her again, that he had never seen her since he married tho' he had frequently given her money when she wrote to beg for it'.[14]

*

In April 1809, having waited for a wind, Sir Arthur Wellesley set sail for the Peninsula once more in the *Surveillante* in heavy seas that by nightfall had been lashed into fury by a gale. Heedless of the captain's fear that he would have to run the ship ashore on the Isle of Wight, he was undressing when Colin Campbell, his aide-de-camp, whom he had first seen, as a volunteer in the 78th, clambering to the top of a scaling ladder at Ahmednuggur, dashed into his cabin to say that all was over with them.

'In that case,' said the General, 'I shall not take off my boots.'*[15]

* A different version of this story was related by John Cam Hobhouse. In his account the aide-de-camp rushed into the cabin when the General had already removed his boots and advised him to put them on again as the captain thought he should come on deck since the ship was in danger of sinking. Wellington replied that, in that case, he would leave his boots where they were: he could swim much better without them (Lord Broughton, *Recollections of a Long Life*, iii, 254).

14   Across the Douro

1809

'*Ma foi! La discipline anglaise est bien sévère.*'

As SOON AS he landed at Lisbon, 'the most Horrible Place that ever was seen',[1] Wellesley threw himself into work on those administrative details which he always regarded as essential to the proper conduct of a military campaign. He turned his attention to bullock carts and food supplies, to horse transport and forage, to blankets and kettles. He commandeered all the boats he could lay his hands on so that Marshal Soult, whose army was quartered in and around Oporto, some two hundred miles to the north, could not attack him across the Tagus; and he arranged for all his brigades to have a company of riflemen attached to them.

He had studied the way in which France's Revolutionary armies had swept across the plains of Central Europe in dense columns behind a screen of *voltigeurs* and *tirailleurs*, both protective and destructive. Their new formations had proved highly effective against the ranks of infantry that opposed them. Wellesley had also studied the tactics employed in the forests of America by Colonel Bouquet, the brilliant Swiss officer who commanded the 60th (Royal American) Regiment, later the King's Royal Rifle Corps, and who had taught his men to fight the French as the American Rangers had done, not as unthinking parts of a clumsy whole but as intelligent men with individual duties to perform in a scheme of warfare that had no rigid rules.[2]

The Duke of York, always ready to listen to new ideas as a reforming Commander-in-Chief, had instructed various regiments to send officers and men for a course of instruction in light infantry tactics at the newly created camp of the Experimental Rifle Corps at Horsham. Two years later, in 1801, the 95th Regiment (later the Rifle Brigade) was formed and the green jackets which the men wore so proudly gave a name to their own and other regiments which were to become among the finest in the Army.

Wellesley had cause to regret that so many of the soldiers in his regiments of the line were far from being as good soldiers as his companies of riflemen. Several of the best battalions in the Army had been held in England for a proposed – and, as it was to prove that summer, disastrous – attempt to send troops up the Scheldt to seize Antwerp from the French; and in the British army in Portugal there were many soldiers, a large proportion of them Irish, whom Wellesley considered, as he was to say of those of a later army, 'the scum of the earth'. 'We are not naturally a military people,' he wrote; 'the whole business of the army upon service is foreign to our habits . . . particularly in a poor country like this.'[3] Yet he saw in that poverty an advantage since the French armies would find it difficult to raise supplies in enemy territory, as was their usual method, while the British could be supplied by sea and the navigable rivers of Portugal.[4]

So Wellesley marched north with confidence against Marshal Soult who he knew had lost the trust of many of his officers and was in a bitter dispute with his fellow Marshal, the brilliant, courageous and temperamental Michel Ney. Wellesley had learned about this dispute from a traitorous French officer, Captain d'Argenton, who crept into the British lines to inform the General that Soult – who had already been created duc de Dalmatie and now had ambitions to declare himself King of Northern Lusitania – was to be deprived of his command in a mutiny. Wellesley, sceptical but curious, listened to d'Argenton in the flickering light of a camp fire; he provided him with papers to assist him in his conspiracy, but assured Castlereagh, who had advised him to treat d'Argenton cautiously, that he 'would not wait for revolt'. Instead he would try his 'own means of subduing Soult'.[5]

On the road north the British army and its Portuguese allies were greeted enthusiastically by the people of the towns and villages through which they passed. Flowers were thrown upon them from windows and cups of wine pressed into their eager hands. They reached the Douro beneath the cliffs of Oporto in the second week of May. It was a broad river here; but Soult had not ensured – as Wellesley had by the Tagus – that no boats could be found by the enemy. The British troops were ferried across in daylight, thirty at a time, in wine-barges which had been discovered concealed from view beneath overhanging cliffs by a Portuguese barber; and Soult, who had no idea that the British were so close, was sent flying out of the town in the pouring rain, abandoning guns and stores, as well as chests of bullion, sick soldiers in the town's hospitals and an excellent meal which General Wellesley and his staff ate instead.

The French army, in a retreat almost as arduous as Sir John Moore's to Corunna, struggled through the harsh landscape of Tras os Montes into Spain, stragglers from their columns being attacked by Portuguese peasants who, in retaliation for the cruelties inflicted upon their people in the villages through which the French passed, burned wounded men alive, pushing them into piles of burning straw with pitchforks.

'The ball is now at my foot,' Wellesley wrote contentedly having cleared the French out of Portugal, inflicting upon them losses of over 4,000 men, 'and I hope I shall have strength enough to give it a good kick.'[6] He could not speak highly of his allies. He believed that, had the Portuguese been 'worth their salt', the French might well not have escaped from Oporto.[7] His Spanish allies seemed to promise no better, when, because of an officer's oversight and a misleading map, the British General arrived late for a review and had to inspect them by the light of flaring torches. When it came to fighting, he afterwards decided, they were no better than they looked. 'They would fire a volley while the enemy was out of reach, and then all run away.' 'They were, no doubt, individually as brave as other men,' he conceded. 'I am sure they were vain enough of their bravery, but I never could get them to stand their ground.'[8] It was largely the fault of their officers, he decided on another occasion. 'This would ruin any soldiers – and how should the Spaniards have confidence in officers such as theirs?'*[9]

As for the guerrillas, they looked formidable enough with their fierce moustaches, their heavy belts and bands of ammunition strung round their waists and across their shoulders beneath heavy cloaks; but, while he did not doubt their bravery, he could not but wonder how reliable they might prove to be.†

---

* Evidently the Spanish soldiers would obey Wellington more readily than their own officers: 'At this moment [the British General] appeared, when the Spaniards, scarcely kept steady by their own officers, now shouting forth a cheer of recognition rushed forward to the charge with such impetuosity that their opponents were swept down the hill as if by a torrent' (A Boy in the Peninsular War: The Services, Adventures and Experiences of Robert Blakeney, Subaltern in the 28th Regiment, 306).

† They were to prove themselves as ruthless as they were brave. Wellington told Harriet Arbuthnot that they believed the French to be devils as well as Jews: 'Once he had a Guerilla come to him, who told him he had had to guard three French officers from one post to another & that, in crossing a bridge, he thought the best thing to do was to upset them into the river. This he did, carriage & all, "& do you know," he said, "they were all Jews for, as they were drowning, I saw their tails"!!' (The Journal of Mrs Arbuthnot, i, 214).

The Spanish regular troops were equally ruthless when Frenchmen came into their hands. Ensign John Mills of the Coldstream Guards argued with a Spanish soldier who 'murdered sixteen large carts full of wounded after the Battle of Fuentes. Instead of being ashamed of it, he considered it as a great feat . . . He said that the wounded were Frenchmen, and that he was justified in killing them wherever he could find them' (For King and Country: The Letters and Diaries of John Mills, Coldstream Guards, 1811–1814, 61).

The Spanish generals, too, their medals clanking on their exotic uniforms, were an unknown quantity, although it was at least certain that the one with whom Sir Arthur had so far had the closest contact – the aged, frail and very vain Don Gregorio Garcia de la Cuesta, Captain-General of Estremadura, 'as obstinate as a gentleman at the head of an army needs to be' – had led his troops far less often to victory than to defeat.[10]

Wellesley was asked for his opinion of another Spanish General, Francisco de Castaños, who had brought about the surrender of Dupont's troops at Bailén. Surely he was an able man?

'Oh, no, no!' he said, 'lowering his voice and gently shaking his head as he usually did whenever giving an opinion unfavourable to any one.'[11]

If Don Gregorio and Francisco de Castaños and their troops did not impress him, Sir Arthur was still little more content with his own men, despite their success at Oporto. On the march towards Spain they behaved abominably. 'They have plundered the country most terribly,' he had to report. 'I have long been of the opinion that a British army could bear neither success nor failure, and I have had manifest truth of this opinion in the recent conduct of the soldiers of this army . . . They are a rabble.'*[12]

He endeavoured to bring discipline into the ranks by the most severe punishments, issuing and repeating orders that the first man caught in the act of plundering should be hanged on the spot.[13] But, as he related years later, he was 'famously taken in on one occasion':

> One day just as we were sitting down to dinner three men were brought to the door of the tent by the prévôt. The case against them was clear, and I had nothing for it but to desire that they should be led away, and hanged in some place where they might be seen by the whole column in its march next day. I had a good many guests with me on that occasion, and among the rest, I think, Lord Nugent. They seemed dreadfully shocked, and could not eat their dinner. I didn't like it much myself, but, as I told them, I had no time to indulge my feelings, I must do my duty. Well, the dinner went off rather gravely, and next morning, sure enough, three men in uniform were seen hanging from the branches of a tree close to the high road. It was a terrible example,

---

* Now and later Wellington excepted the army's sergeants from this general condemnation. 'I have served with all nations,' he was to say when his fighting days were over, 'and I am convinced that there is nothing so intelligent, so valuable as that rank of man in the English service.' He felt constrained to add, however, 'if you could get them sober, which is impossible' (Hatfield House Papers, 9 July 1837).

and produced the desired effect ... But you may guess my astonishment, when some months afterwards I learned that one of my staff
took counsel with Dr Hume, and as three men had just died in hospital,
they hung them up, and let the three culprits return to their
regiments.[14]

'Weren't you very angry?' someone asked him. 'Well, I suppose I was
at first,' he replied. 'But as I had no wish to take the poor fellows' lives,
and only wanted the example, and as the example had the desired
effect, my anger soon died out, and I confess to you that I am very
glad now that the three lives were spared.'[15]

On occasions, however, he made sure that plunderers' lives were
not spared. One of his aides-de-camp recorded an instance of this
when two soldiers were found looting a shop and assaulting a woman
who was attempting to protect her property. 'Having satisfied himself
as to the guilt of the soldiers, Wellington turned round to the Provost-
Marshal, and in that brief expression which ever characterized him,
said, "In ten minutes report to me that these two men have been
executed".' When the French under Junot entered the town, the two
bodies were still hanging there. An English surgeon, who had remained
behind under a flag of truce to attend to the wounded, was questioned
as to the offence for which the soldiers had suffered. '"Plundering
and violence towards an inhabitant," responded the surgeon. "*Ma foi!*"
exclaimed Junot, shrugging his shoulders, "*la discipline anglaise est bien
sévère.*"'[16]

It did not altogether surprise Sir Arthur that the soldiers were inveterate plunderers since the army's commissaries were 'incompetent to
a man'; and to add to his difficulties the Treasury were being more
than commonly dilatory in sending him the currency he so urgently
needed. He would advance into Spain immediately, he wrote, but he
could not 'venture to stir without money'.[17]

'We are terribly distressed for money,' he wrote on another occasion,
voicing a complaint he was often to make in the future. There were
other grumbles, too; and he expressed and continued to express them
with petulant irritability, complaining that the Cabinet did not 'repose
confidence' in him, and that he was unable to obtain any 'specific
instructions from the Minister of War',[18] whereas he had earlier
expressed satisfaction in being given a free rein, a 'general object' which
allowed him to consider himself 'authorized to pursue any other object
... likely to conduce to the benefit of the Spanish and Portuguese
nations'.[19]

The Government were, in fact, giving him their full support: George Canning, the Foreign Minister, wrote of Wellesley's 'frankness – honesty – quickness – and military Ability' being 'not only beyond those of any other military Commander that could be chosen but perhaps possessed by him alone, of all our Commanders, in a degree that qualifies him for great undertakings'.[20] Yet Sir Arthur professed unreasonably to 'suspect that the Ministers in England [were] very indifferent to our operations in this country'. He wrote to complain of their supposed attitude in an angry letter to his brother William who replied, 'I am perfectly satisfied that you are mistaken in supposing that you do not possess the confidence of ministers. If there is anything like truth in man, there never was more implicit confidence felt in any General officer than is felt by [the First Lord of the Treasury and the Secretary for War] and I firmly believe by all the other members of the Cabinet in you.'[21]

Sir Arthur was not to be mollified. He continued to suspect strongly that some members at least of the Cabinet were blaming him for allowing Soult to escape into Spain. It was most unreasonable that they should do so, he thought: 'From the force I had & the force opposed to me what right had they to expect that I should do so much?' he asked William. After all, he never asked the Government for more than he thought they could reasonably allow him, on one characteristic occasion concluding a request for craft for river crossings with the assurance that he would expect them only if they were not needed elsewhere. Surely he had a right to be rewarded for such moderation.[22]

He could derive some comfort at least from the unhappy state of the French marshals and generals who were constantly at loggerheads, each going his own way, despite the occasional efforts of King Joseph to impose some common plan and the directives that successively arrived from Napoleon's camps in Central Europe and from Vienna's Schönbrunn where the Emperor had installed himself, having entered the city on 12 May after driving the Austrians out of Ratisbon.

Faced by a choice of operations against these French generals, Wellesley decided to move against Marshal Victor, who had given a drubbing to Cuesta's army at Medellin on the south bank of the Guadiana at the end of March. Indeed, Sir Arthur had already told Castlereagh, 'I should prefer an attack on Victor, in concert with Cuesta, if Soult were not in possession of a fertile province of this

Kingdom, and the favourite town of Oporto.' Now that Soult had been deprived of Oporto, the attack on Victor in New Castile could begin.

So, on 27 June 1809, Wellesley left Abrantes on the Tagus north-east of Lisbon with some 20,000 men, and having crossed the Spanish frontier on 4 July, he was riding a fortnight later into Oropesa where he joined forces with Cuesta's army of more than 30,000 men. The old hidalgo, who had broken several bones when his retreating cavalry had ridden over him in one of his various defeats, was lifted from his mule-drawn coach and placed upon a pile of cushions from which he conversed with the British General by means of an English-speaking officer on his staff named O'Donoju.

Sir Arthur proposed that they jointly attack the French the next morning. Marshal Victor had already withdrawn his troops some miles towards Madrid; and it was essential that an attack be launched before they combined forces with King Joseph's army in and around the capital. Cuesta could not be persuaded to agree. Day by day, he was 'more and more impracticable', Wellesley said; it was 'impossible to do business with him, and very uncertain that any operation' would succeed in which he had 'any concern'.[23]

Eventually, however, he was persuaded to advance; but by then Victor had made a further retreat, and the opportunity to attack him before he joined forces with the King was lost. So Wellesley declined to go with Cuesta. He was bound 'to get in a scrape', Wellesley said; any movement by the British army to assist him was 'quite out of the question'. In any case he had heard that Cuesta's officers were 'all dissatisfied with him' and that there was a movement afoot to have him dismissed from the command.[24]

Denied the help of his allies the headstrong, gallant and obtuse old man took his men unsupported against the French until, near Toledo, they came upon almost the entire French army in New Castile; and, startled by this unfortunate and unexpected encounter, he brought them scurrying back again towards the Alberche river, furiously pursued by Imperial cavalry.

Deeply concerned as to what might happen to the Spaniards should they be brought to battle with their backs to the Alberche, Wellesley went in search of their commander to ask him to move further back to a stronger position at Talavera. He found him in the middle of the afternoon fast asleep. Stubborn as ever, he declined to retreat any further; Wellesley begged him to do so; he remained adamant. Wellesley, so Cuesta said, went so far as to kneel down in supplication before him; and at last he gave way.[25]

It was not before time. French skirmishers were already approaching his own lines. They came upon the men of a British brigade as fast asleep in the hot July sun as Cuesta had been and killed many of them before they were fully awake. Many more were killed before they could be rallied; in all Wellesley lost over 400 men before the battle proper began.

He was almost killed himself. He had climbed to the top of a tall building to survey the surrounding countryside beyond the cork and olive groves when, at the very foot of the tower on which he and his staff were standing, French troops suddenly appeared at the base of the wall. Dashing down the steps, they rushed across the courtyard to their horses and galloped away, as the French fired at their backs.

The battle fought at Talavera on 27 and 28 July 1809 was the 'hardest fighting' Sir Arthur Wellesley had 'ever been a party to'.[26] Indeed, he declared with unaccustomed hyperbole, 'it was the hardest fought battle of modern times . . . Never was there such a Murderous Battle!!'[27] He had lost over 5,000 men, inflicting more than 7,000 casualties on the enemy.[28] General Sir Alexander Mackenzie, one of the most reliable of his field commanders, whom he had known since his days at the Academy at Angers, had been killed; he himself had been hit in the chest by a spent bullet. During a brief truce in the fierce battle, his soldiers, overcome by heat and thirst, had been driven to run down to drink the brackish water of the stream between the opposing lines before carrying away for burial the bodies of the dead and dying. The day before, Cuesta's Spanish troops, whose officers seemed to be endlessly smoking cigarettes, suddenly unleashed a terrific volley of musketry fire at some distant French dragoons who were taking occasional shots at their pickets. 'If they will but fire as well tomorrow,' Wellesley said to a member of his staff, 'the day is our own; but as there seems nobody to fire at just now, I wish you would stop it.'[29]

The officer galloped away to carry out the General's order; but, before he reached the inexperienced Spanish levies, they had taken sudden fright and had run off in panic to the rear, plundering some British baggage-wagons on their way. General Cuesta, infuriated by the shameful behaviour of his men, gave orders that two hundred of them should be shot after the battle. General Wellesley put in a word for them; but Cuesta insisted that at least forty of them must suffer, and on the morning of the 29th they did.

Throughout the battle General Wellesley had insisted upon carrying out himself most of the duties usually assigned to staff officers as well as being his own intelligence officer; and he had consequently been obliged to ride about from one vantage point to another. Some of his officers questioned the wisdom of this, yet none denied that he had won an undoubted victory – though there were those who considered it a Pyrrhic one – a French army, almost twice as large as his own, had been forced into retreat; and, reinforced by Robert Craufurd's Light Brigade, which had marched and run over sixty miles in less than twenty-six hours, he was justified in hoping now to move towards Madrid.

Yet this hope was not to be realized: Sir Arthur was informed that another French army was fast approaching and would soon be across his lines of communication with Portugal. His men were disastrously short of supplies as it was; and for this he angrily blamed his selfish and incompetent allies who 'allowed a brave army, that was rendering gratuitous services to Spain, that was able and willing to pay for everything it received, to starve in the centre of their country . . . and who refused or omitted to find carriages to remove the officers and soldiers who had been wounded in their service, and obliged me to give up the equipment of the army for the performance of the necessary duties of humanity'.[30]

'We are starving and are ill-treated by the Spaniards in every way', he added, making no allowances for the difficulties of gleaning provisions in a poor countryside already plundered by the French; 'and a starving army is actually worse than none. The soldiers lose their discipline and their spirit. They plunder even in the presence of their officers.'[31] His complaints were echoed by his brother Richard, who had been sent to Spain to represent the British Government in a more authoritative manner than had so far been displayed by John Hookham Frere, the British Minister at Seville. Although Sir Arthur did not think his brother would 'be able to do any good', the Marquess was certainly a match in haughtiness for the proudest of hidalgos and did not hesitate to protest that he would 'not trust the protection of a favourite dog to the whole Spanish army'. And so long as his brother Arthur had cause to complain that his army wanted everything and could get nothing, that the Spanish treated their allies without respect, he 'might almost say not even as friends', he agreed that there was no alternative but to retreat towards Portugal.[32]

Complaining that he had 'fished in many troubled waters, but Spanish troubled waters [he would] never fish in again',[33] Sir Arthur withdrew through Estremadura towards the Guadiana river and the Portuguese frontier near Badajoz, more annoyed than ever with the Spanish when it transpired that General Cuesta, who had undertaken to look after the 1,500 British wounded left behind in Talavera, had been obliged to abandon them there and march towards him at the approach of the French.

The Spanish authorities, as though wishing to make amends for Cuesta's having enabled the enemy to take so many prisoners, tendered the British General tokens of their gratitude and regard: they presented him with six Andalusian horses and offered him the rank of Captain-General in their Army, an honour he accepted while declining to accept a Captain-General's pay. The British Government rewarded him also: he was granted an income of £2,000 for three years, and, with the King's approval, was created Baron Douro of Wellesley and Viscount Wellington of Talavera.* Lord Wellington had now to justify the honours bestowed upon him.

* Since there was no time to ask Sir Arthur himself about a suitable name for his title, the College of Heralds consulted his brother William, who, 'after ransacking the Peerage and examining the map', chose Wellington. It was, William told his brother, a town 'in Somerset not far from Welleslie'. 'I trust,' he added, 'you will not think there is anything unpleasant or trifling in the name of Wellington . . . I long much to hear that I ought not to be hanged for my arrangement. God bless you' (*Wellington Dispatches*, viii, 148). Although Lady Wellesley, who had not been approached, did not much like the name, 'for,' she said, 'it recalls nothing', Sir Arthur himself thought it 'exactly right'. 'I think,' he told William, 'you have chosen most fortunately' (Raglan Papers, 13 September, 1809). Lady Wellesley came to approve the Douro part of the title; and when her husband was raised a step in the peerage and the title became their elder son's, she wrote to Lady Hood, 'My little boy's title is Baron Douro. They wanted to change his title and raise his rank, but I roared and screamed. The passage of the Douro, the most brilliant and least bloody of all his father's achievements, shall not be forgotten, and he shall keep the name' (Wellington Papers, Stratfield Saye; Joan Wilson, *A Soldier's Wife: Wellington's Marriage*, 124).

15 'A Whole Host of Marshals'

1809 — 10

'They really forget everything when plunder or
wine is within their reach.'

ALMOST a hundred thousand men of the Imperial army were marching
through France for the Pyrenees. There were rumours that the Emperor
himself, having finally overwhelmed the Austrians at Wagram at the
beginning of July 1809, would come with them to direct personally
the expulsion of his tiresomely persistent enemy from the western
peninsula of the Continent which he had otherwise almost made his
own.

Wellington was at least spared the personal attention of Napoleon.
But there was still 'a whole host of Marshals' in Spain, among them
Edouard Mortier and Michel Ney as well as Soult, Victor and
Kellerman.[1]

Threatened as he was by the immense power of France, Wellington
felt his position also endangered by the reconstruction of the ministry
in London and the departure from office of his friend Lord Castlereagh
on whose support he had always been able to rely. The new Prime
Minister was to be Spencer Perceval, a man of whom little was generally
known and scarcely anything known at Wellington's headquarters in
the Peninsula. Nor did Wellington know very much about the new
Foreign Secretary, Lord Bathurst, nor the Secretary of War, the Earl
of Liverpool. It was not long, however, before it was decided to recall
Marquess Wellesley home from Seville to replace Lord Bathurst as
Foreign Secretary and to send out his brother Henry as British Minister
in Lisbon. So Wellington was able to comfort himself with the thought
that by these changes he had at least two friends at court.[2]

He would need all the support he could contrive to obtain in the
months ahead, for his position in the Peninsula, as he well recognized,
was an ever more precarious one, while praise in England for his victory
at Talavera was being overcast by grumbles that it had merely been
the prelude to a defeat. The utter failure of the attempt to seize Antwerp

from the French, the withdrawal of most of the troops from Belgium, and the death from malaria of so many more who had been left behind as a garrison, were humiliating enough; but now there was retreat in Spain to contemplate as well. *The Times* was far from being alone in questioning Lord Wellington's fitness for command. The extreme *Independent Whig*, a Sunday newspaper, described the Peninsular War as 'the frantic and visionary pursuit of treachery and folly. Every success which may accompany the valour of our armies we can consider as HUMAN BUTCHERY, perpetrated for the PERSONAL SPLEEN AND VINDICTIVE RAPACITY of the British Ministry.'[3] As at the time of the enquiry into the Convention of Cintra, pamphleteers, satirists and caricaturists were let loose upon Wellington's reputation. Cobbett became more vehement than ever, ridiculing Wellington's dispatches and choosing instead to propagate the version of events printed in the French paper, *Le Moniteur universel*, while, in a characteristic satirical print attributed to Thomas Rowlandson, which pilloried him for his conduct of the war in the Peninsula, the General was portrayed outside a fairground booth advertising plays by Beaumont and Fletcher and August von Kotzebue, *The Wild Goose Chase* and *The Wanderer*.[4] In the army, too, there was much discontent and, among both officers and men, there was widespread feeling that the Commander was not as able as had earlier been supposed.[5]

Wellington assured Lord Liverpool that he cared not a straw for vilification, but he was anxious that the Prime Minister should be in no doubt as to the difficulties of his position and the disadvantages under which he laboured. 'If I succeed in executing the arduous task which has devolved upon me,' he wrote to him, 'I may fairly say that I had not the best instruments, in either officers or men, which the service could have afforded.'[6]

He had by then decided that he could not defend the long Portuguese frontier, but must stand closer to the sea; and, with this in mind, he and his Chief Engineer had closely inspected the high ground north of Lisbon on either side of Torres Vedras between the river Tagus and the Atlantic Ocean. Here he could make a stand; and here he set his Engineers to work in constructing, with the help of several thousand Portuguese labourers, the extensive fortifications of gun emplacements, earthworks, palisades, fascine-lined trenches, gabions and ravelins which were outlined in memoranda of careful exactitude.[7]

The French marched on, brushing aside resistance at Tamamès and Ocaña, the incompetently led Spanish forces, in Wellington's contemptuous words, 'doing Bonaparte's business for him as fast as possible'.[8] At least the Portuguese promised to be better soldiers. Submitting themselves to British discipline under the command of a British officer, William Carr Beresford, a natural son of the Marquess of Waterford, who had learned to speak Portuguese while Governor of Madeira, they underwent training in British drill and British tactics.* Wellington hoped they might even prove a match for the French who would find the going more and more difficult and hunger harder to bear as they marched through the wide plains and black mountains of central Spain towards the Portuguese frontier.

Occupied and anxious as he was, Wellington found time to spare from his maps and reports and inventories, his letters and reconnaissances. He sought permission to shoot royal coverts beside the Caya; he went hunting red deer around Elvas; he read books about Portugal and warfare in Portugal; he wrote to his mother and sent her a shawl which, 'bad as it is', he commented dismissively, 'is the only manufacture of Spain I have seen'.[9] He also found time to talk informally to those members of his staff, his 'family', with whom he was on intimate terms; and even to perform some of their duties for them.

One day one of his staff officers returned from an unprofitable visit to the estate of a noble Spaniard to whom he had been sent to procure forage. The General asked him why he had been unable to get any. 'I was told I would have to bow to the noble owner,' the officer said, 'and of course I couldn't do that.'

'Well I suppose I must get some myself,' Wellington said.

Soon carts full of forage were being carried into camp. Wellington was asked how he had managed it.

'Oh,' he said easily, 'I just bobbed down.'[10]

Since the departure of his senior aide-de-camp, Major Colin Campbell, to become Assistant Adjutant-General of a division,† most of the officers chosen for staff appointments were of aristocratic birth and

---

* Wellington expressed the opinion more than once that Beresford was 'the best officer we have for the command of an army' (*The Croker Papers*, i, 337). He was 'far superior to all in talents' (*The Journal of Mrs Arbuthnot*, i, 13). Mrs Arbuthnot agreed that he was 'clever & agreeable, but vulgar & *dirty*. He boasted to me one evg that he never was 5 *minutes* dressing. I do not envy Mad^me Lemos . . . the Portugueze woman to whom he has been attached for many years' (*The Journal of Mrs Arbuthnot*, ii, 51).

† The absurdly mispronounced and incompetent French of this Scottish officer – of whom Wellington once remarked that he spoke no language except his own, and that not very correctly – was a source of constant amusement to other members of the staff. Later, in France, when the Mayor of St Jean de Luz inadvertently picked up Campbell's umbrella after a dinner party, 'Colin seized the other end of it', Wellington was fond of relating, 'took it away, and said with a low bow, "C'est moine"' (G.R. Gleig, *Reminiscences*, 430).

three were related to him by marriage. One of these was his wife's brother, the Hon. Edward Pakenham, who had been a lieutenant in the 92nd Foot at the age of sixteen, had commanded a battalion of the 7th Royal Fusiliers in Denmark when he was nineteen, and, before being given command of the 3rd Division, had served on the staff as Deputy Adjutant-General. Another was the Marquess of Worcester, later seventh Duke of Beaufort, a dashing young man whom Harriette Wilson had hoped to marry and who made a more suitable marriage with one of Wellington's nieces, Georgiana Frederica Fitzroy, and after her death, with another of his nieces, Emily Frances Smith. The third was Lord Fitzroy Somerset, the fifth Duke of Beaufort's youngest son, the future first Lord Raglan, who was to marry Lord Wellington's niece, Emily Harriet, second daughter of the third Earl of Mornington.

Lord Fitzroy bore so marked a resemblance to his wife's uncle that, when they had sailed out to Corunna together in the *Donegal* in July 1808, men had taken them for father and son. Their friendship, formed then, was never to be broken. The General was once asked why he reposed such confidence in Lord Fitzroy whom he appointed his Military Secretary at the age of twenty-two in succession to Colonel James Bathurst whose responsibilities had driven him to a nervous breakdown. Wellington replied that, while Fitzroy Somerset, whom he always addressed as Lord Fitzroy, though he had known him since childhood, certainly had no very exceptional talents, he could always rely upon him to tell the exact truth and to carry out his orders with precision and promptitude.[11]

Other favoured members of his staff were Captain the Hon. Alexander Gordon, brother of the fourth Earl of Aberdeen; Lord Burghersh, only son of the tenth Earl of Westmorland, who was one day to be Resident Minister in Berlin; Captain Ulysses Burgh, later second Baron Downes; and Charles, Lord March, son of Wellington's friend, the fourth Duke of Richmond, whom the General, though painfully bruised in the thigh, was to ride several miles to see when he heard that the young man had been severely wounded. He hobbled out of the patient's room, supporting himself on two sticks, with 'tears trickling down his cheeks'.[12]

Yet while Wellington, 'in looking for able young men for his personal staff, preferred ability with a title to ability without'[13] – and, indeed, was 'all for having gentlemen for officers'[14] since the British Army was what it was 'because it [was] officered by gentlemen'[15] – he would not tolerate inefficiency in any member of his staff however nobly born and whether related to him or not. His brother William's only son, also

William, an extravagant and dissipated young man, was dismissed and sent home shortly after his appointment to his uncle's staff, for being 'lamentably ignorant and idle' and for 'doing things he has no right to do'.[16]

Apart from the disreputable and incompetent William Wellesley-Pole and a few other dissidents, Wellington's young staff officers greatly respected him. So did most of his brigade and divisional commanders, if few could bring themselves to feel that affection for him which he inspired in the inner circle of his 'family' and in one or two more senior officers who knew him well such as Galbraith Lowry Cole, Lady Wellington's former suitor, now in command of the 4th Division, who thought that he had never served any chief he liked so much, apart from Sir John Moore. 'He has treated me with much more confidence than I had a right or could be expected from anyone,' Cole went on. 'Few, I believe, possess a firmer mind or have, as far as I have heard, more the confidence of the Army.'[17]

It could not be said, however, that the army inspired much confidence in Wellington. He was 'apprehensive of the consequences of trying them in any nice operation before the enemy, for they really forget everything when plunder or wine is within their reach'.[18] The general officers were 'very bad'; indeed, some of them were 'a disgrace to the service'. The man who had been sent out as his second-in-command was 'very unfit for his situation'. All in all, he told his brother William in confidence, 'I sincerely believe that in every respect, with the exception of the Guards and one or two other Corps, this is the Worst British Army that was ever in the field.'[19]

The most severe punishments could not stop the men plundering, an activity which many of them seemed to consider part of the natural process of soldiering. Throughout the war in the Peninsula numerous general orders were issued on the lines of the following:

> The Commander of the Forces requests the General officers commanding divisions will take measures to prevent the shameful and unmilitary practice of soldiers shooting pigs in the woods, so close to the camp and to the columns of march as that two dragoons were shot last night . . . The number of soldiers straggling from their regiments for no reason excepting to plunder, is a disgrace to the army, and affords a strong proof of the degree to which the discipline of the regiments is relaxed, and of the inattention of the commanding and other officers of regiments to their duty, and to the repeated orders of the army . . .
> The Commander of the Forces desires that notice may be given to

the soldiers that he has this day ordered two men to be hanged who were caught in the fact of shooting pigs.[20]

'On the other hand', so the commissary August Schaumann said, 'Lord Wellington frequently showed himself merciful towards regiments of which he was fond. On one occasion, for instance, he came upon the 1st German Hussars ... one of whose men came riding up with a bleating sheep. The moment Lord Wellington saw the man, however, he only smiled, and turning his back on him, pretended not to have noticed anything, although the officers at his side were shuddering with fear.'[21]

Similarly, it gave Wellington wry pleasure to recount the story of a man he himself caught with a stolen beehive, a popular species of loot.[22] Where did he get it? he asked. Oh, the man said blithely, just over the hill; but it would be as well to get over there quickly: they were nearly all gone.[23]

The women were quite as bad as the men, if not worse. General Orders had frequently to be issued in an effort to stop them misappropriating army as well as Spanish or Portuguese property and making the life of the commissaries more difficult than it was already. Female camp followers were occasionally beaten on their bare bottoms; but they continued looting just the same. Nor were most officers above looting themselves. A soldier in the 71st recorded the looting of a mill by his regiment whose colonel forced the men out, 'throwing a handful of flour on each man as he passed out of the mill. When we were drawn up he rode along the column looking for the millers, as we called them. At this moment a hen put her head out of his coat-pocket, and looked first to one side, then to another. We began to laugh; we could not restrain ourselves. He looked amazed and furious ... Then the colonel in his turn laughed ... and the millers were no more looked after.'[24]

As for the general officers, when Wellington reflected that 'these were the persons on whom [he was] to rely to lead columns against the French Generals, and who [were] to carry [his] instructions into execution', he confessed that he trembled. 'And, as Lord Chesterfield said of the Generals of his day,' he added, '"I only hope that when the enemy reads the list of their names he trembles as I do."*[25] Sir William

---

* A similar remark has been attributed to King George III; and when General Wolfe was appointed to the command in Canada and someone protested that the man was mad, King George II is said to have observed, 'Oh, he is mad, is he? Then I hope he will bite some others of my Generals' (Francis Thackeray, *History of William Pitt*, London, 1827, 1, ch. 15).

Erskine and General [William] Lumley will be a very nice addition to this List.'[26] So would General Lightburne and Colonel Sanders, from whom he prayed to God and the Horse Guards to deliver him. Erskine, in fact, was 'generally understood to be a madman', and committed suicide in 1813 by throwing himself out of a window in Lisbon.

Particularly tiresome for Wellington were those senior officers who came out to join the army with recommendations from the Prince of Wales or cronies at the Horse Guards. One of the most exasperating of these was a reckless and troublesome Hussar officer at one time Groom of the Bedchamber to the Duke of Cumberland, Sir Colquhoun Grant, whom Wellington would have liked to send home but who was instead promoted by the Horse Guards.

The commissary August Schaumann found the arrogant Grant intolerable in his impossible demands and in his haughty astonishment that these demands should be questioned. 'Was he not six feet high, and had he not a huge black moustache and black whiskers? . . . His whole manner bore the stamp of unbounded pride and the crassest ignorance, and he tried to conceal the latter beneath positive assertions which he did not suffer to be contradicted.' Schaumann was delighted one day when the great man was treated cavalierly by Wellington who galloped past him shouting out an invitation to dinner which he did not wait to be acknowledged and which left 'the black giant' looking 'crestfallen' and . . . 'silently shaking his head' before riding off 'gesticulating violently'.[27]

Quite as bad as the madmen and incompetents, in Wellington's opinion, were what he called the croakers, officers who muttered criticisms of his strategy, spreading doubt and resentment in the army and conveying gloom in letters home. Among these was his so-called second-in-command, the Irish General Sir Brent Spencer, a great favourite of King George III but, in Wellington's opinion, an 'exceedingly puzzle-headed man' who, in Portugal, had constantly referred to the Tagus as the Thames, and had once told an aide-de-camp to trot down to the Thames to see what was going on there. The aide had answered that he wished with all his heart that he could.[28]

'As soon as an accident happens,' Wellington complained, 'every man who can write, and has a friend who can read, sits down to write his account of what he does not know.' And, what was worse, newspapers in England got hold of these letters which could not but spread disquiet at home.[29]

One of the most *intrigant* of Wellington's senior officers was the Adjutant-General, Charles Stewart, the handsome son of the Marquess of Londonderry by his second wife, and half-brother of Lord Castle-reagh. He had accepted the staff appointment with reluctance and was repeatedly asking for a cavalry command which Wellington declined to give him on account of his defective sight and hearing.[30] Stewart insisted that the cavalry was not well handled and insinuated that the army was not being well managed either. Eventually, after Stewart had insisted that as Adjutant-General 'the examination of prisoners belonged exclusively to him', Wellington had summoned him to an interview and told him that if his orders were not obeyed he 'would dismiss him instanter and send him to England in arrest'. 'After a great deal of persuasion', Wellington said, 'Stewart burst out crying and begged my pardon, and hoped I would excuse his intemperance.'[31]

Despite his differences with some of his senior officers and his low opinion of his soldiers, Wellington maintained that he was 'prepared for all events'; and, if he were in a scrape, he was determined to give the impression that he was confident he could get out of it. 'I am in no scrape,' he wrote to his brother William, 'and if Mr Pitt were alive, or if there were anything like a Government in England, or any publick Sentiment remaining there, Buonaparte would yet repent his invasion of Spain.'[32]

It was widely held in England, though, that he was, indeed, in a scrape. The Earl of Liverpool, Secretary for War, told Wellington that 'a very considerable degree of alarm existed respecting the safety of the British army in Portugal'; and went on to say that he 'would rather be excused for bringing away the army a little too soon than, by remaining in Portugal a little too long, exposing it to those risks from which no military operations can be wholly exempt'.[33] In subsequent letters Liverpool wrote of the probability of the enemy's being soon enabled to employ such overwhelming force that evacuation would be inevitable; and he also told Wellington that officers who had returned from the Peninsula 'entertained and avowed the most desponding views as to the result of the war'.[34]

Yet Wellington felt that if he were, in fact, in a scrape, the French might soon be in one too. He doubted that they 'could bring a large force to bear upon Portugal without abandoning other objects, and, exposing their whole fabric in Spain to great risks'. If they invaded Portugal, and did not succeed in obliging the British army to evacuate the country, they would be 'in a very dangerous situation'. The longer he could oppose them and 'delay their success', the more likely they would be 'to suffer materially in Spain'.[35]

He did not underestimate his opponent. Marshal Andrea Massena, duc de Rivoli and prince d'Essling, born in Nice, the son of a wine merchant in a poor way of business, had enlisted in the Royal Italian Regiment at the age of seventeen, after serving as a cabin boy. At the outbreak of the French Revolution he had been a sergeant at Antibes. Scarcely more than three years later he was a general. He had greatly distinguished himself in Italy, in Switzerland and in Austria, had helped Napoleon to win the battle of Marengo and had paid a crucial part in the battle of Wagram. He was one of the Emperor's most successful marshals. Indeed, Wellington considered him the 'ablest after Napoleon'.*[36] He was not as alert as once he had been, however, and was said not only to be in poor health but also distracted from his duties by his demanding mistress whom, to the annoyance of his generals, he had brought to the Peninsula with him, dressed in the uniform of an aide-de-camp.[37] Wellington believed he could out-manoeuvre him.

* He said so more than once. But he also said, 'Clauzel is the best general, perhaps, that the French have. I never, during the period he commanded the French army, caught him napping' (*The Reminiscences and Recollections of Captain Gronow*, ii, 189).

16   From Bussaco to El Bodon

1810 — 11

'The whole ground was still covered with the wrecks of an army.'

MASSENA CAME on steadily with some 70,000 men; and Wellington, sorely outnumbered, withdrew beyond the Coa towards the valley of the Mondego, Robert Craufurd, commanding the rearguard and leading it in an unnecessarily aggressive way, repeatedly attacking the leading French columns and losing men to little purpose. After the loss of the fortress of Ciudad Rodrigo to Massena's dashing second-in-command, Marshal Ney, Wellington hoped to make a stand at Almeida – a fortress twenty-five miles west of Ciudad Rodrigo on the other side of the Spanish frontier – which Massena began to bombard on 26 August 1810. But an enemy shell ignited a trail of gunpowder which had been left by a leaking barrel between the cannon on the walls and the powder magazine in Almeida Cathedral. Masonry and shattered casks were sent flying high into the sky in a thunderous explosion which killed or wounded hundreds of the men of the garrison; and Wellington was obliged to withdraw fifty miles further down the Mondego to Bussaco.

His army took up position on the ridge at Bussaco on 27 September and at dawn that day he made his rounds, removing from his command the colonel of a regiment who had drunk too much brandy in an attempt to steady his nerves. He was anxious enough himself: he remained outwardly calm as always; but it was noticed that he kept gathering up blades of grass and chewing them.

At about six o'clock the French launched their first attack on the centre of the long British line.

Facing Massena's 65,000 men were about 25,000 British and the same number of Portuguese. Both stood their ground well, the Portuguese, in Wellington's words, 'worthy of contending in the same ranks as British troops'. Massena, despite his greater numbers, could not dislodge them, hard and persistently as his commanders led their men against the allies on the ridge, losing some 4,500 men in the process.[1]

The day after the battle, with a loss calculated at precisely 1,252 men, divided equally between British and Portuguese, Wellington withdrew towards his lines at Torres Vedras with Massena at his heels, both armies looting where they could, one British soldier struggling to carry out of Coimbra an immense looking-glass which was strung up beside him when he was hanged by order of the Provost Marshal.

On 14 October, Massena came to a halt beneath Wellington's defensive lines in surprise and anger. Why had no one told him of this defensive system, blocking the way to Lisbon? he asked. One of his staff officers, by way of apprehensive explanation, told him that Lord Wellington had made them, as though this were an excuse for their existence. The devil he did, the Marshal angrily retorted; and did he make the mountains, too?[2]

The lines were far from being a single row of gun emplacements, bastions and entrenchments. Behind the first line of earthworks another stretched across the mountains; and beyond this was yet another. The French army ground to a halt. The days of October passed slowly in intermittent rain; the French, waiting for the enemy to attack them, could get their hands on little food in the inhospitable Estremaduran countryside, though more than Wellington had hoped the Portuguese would allow them to discover. 'All is abandoned,' Massena wrote. 'Our soldiers find potatoes and only live to fight the enemy.'[3]

From time to time Wellington was tempted to attack him, feeling fairly confident that he 'could lick those fellows any day'.[4] But then he reflected it would cost him 10,000 men and, since he had been entrusted with the last army England had, he must take care of it. 'They won't draw me from my cautious system,' he told a friend in England. 'I'll fight them only when I am pretty sure of success.'[5]

In England, while Lord Liverpool assured Wellington that the Government were still 'most fully and completely satisfied with all that you have done and all that you are doing',[6] there were rumbles of discontent as there had been when the battle of Talavera had been followed by retreat. 'The croakers about useless battles will attack me again about that of Bussaco,' he had written to his brother William at the beginning of October; and so, indeed, they did. Lord Auckland maintained that Massena had 'out-generalled us and turned our position' and expressed doubts as to Wellington's 'truth as a writer of despatches'.[7] Lord Grey thought that, as at Talavera, mistakes at Bussaco had forced the 'necessity of an immediate retreat'.[8] Lord Carlisle told Countess Spencer, 'Ld. W. was no general at all, and fell from one blunder to another, and the most we had to hope was his being able to embark quietly and bring his troops back to England which he thought very doubtful.'[9]

Wellington heard that the Prince of Wales, under the influence of his Whig friends, was now amongst his critics. 'I condole with you heartily, my dear Lord, upon poor Arthur's retreat,' the Prince said to Marquess Wellesley one day at Windsor. 'Massena has quite outgeneralled him.'[10] It often seemed to Wellington that, as well as the King's eldest son, the King's Government had lost whatever confidence in him they had formerly expressed: ministers declined to reinforce him, he complained, although there were, in fact, no reinforcements available except a corps in Ireland which Lord Liverpool promised to send out as soon as it could be relieved.

Despite all criticism of his conduct, Wellington remained determined not to fight until he was fairly certain of winning; and he was still not sufficiently sure when, at the beginning of March 1811, Massena, his army reduced to about 46,000 men, withdrew towards Santarem. He crept after them, 'determined to persevere in [his] cautious system'.[11]

His aim, he said, was 'to operate upon the flanks and rear of the enemy with my small and light detachments, and thus force them out of Portugal by the distresses they will suffer, and do them all the mischief I can upon this retreat. Massena is an old fox, and is as cautious as I am; he risks nothing.'[12]

The more prudent and sensible of Wellington's officers admired his control. 'His ability is universally acknowledged,' said Lowry Cole, 'and I hope the good folks in England will do him equal justice.'[13]

At Santarem, Marshal Massena held his ground, to Wellington's astonished admiration. It was, he thought, 'an extraordinary instance of what a French army can do. It is positively a fact that they brought no provisions with them, and they have not even received a letter since they entered Portugal . . . I assure you that I could not maintain one division in the district in which they have maintained not less than 60,000 men and 20,000 animals for more than two months.'[14] A further two months passed and Massena still stubbornly stood his ground, though the uniforms of his men were ragged now, their shoes worn out, their rations reduced to the meagre supplies that reached them by way of the long routes that stretched east for mile upon mile across the mountains or from what foraging parties could bring in from broken farms and deserted villages. Junot was badly wounded; Ney quarrelled bitterly with Massena who soon dismissed him from his command; and the French at last turned their backs on Lisbon.[15]

Wellington followed them cautiously. His duty was clear: he would not risk the army entrusted to his care by unnecessary fighting; he must get it across the road which led out of Spain towards the French frontier at Bayonne. Once he had cut across that road, north of Madrid at Burgos, not only Massena's army but all the French troops in Spain would have to fall back towards the narrow gap that separated the foothills of the Pyrenees from the waters of the Bay of Biscay. Yet there must be no sudden dash towards León and old Castile. Portugal must be safe behind him; he had to retake Almeida in the north and Badajoz in the south, and, in the meantime, keep his 'own army entire', for if he weakened it by a rash advance he might find himself 'so crippled as not to have the ascendant over the French troops on the frontiers'.[16]

The French, fighting actions when they had to, marched slowly and painfully towards the Portuguese frontier in the gently falling rain, losing hundreds of men on the way, hungry soldiers torturing peasants, women and children as well as men, to discover hidden stores of food and wine. Exhausted stragglers fell with a kind of relief as prisoners into the hands of their wily pursuers.

On 10 April 1811 Wellington felt able to issue a proclamation declaring that the 'cruel enemy' after suffering 'great losses' [of 25,000 men] had retired across the Agueda into Spain. The inhabitants of Portugal were 'therefore at liberty to return to their homes'.

Having supervised the close investment of the French garrison in Almeida, Wellington, anxious as always to see things for himself, galloped south to reconnoitre Badajoz, killing two horses on the way, exhausting the soldiers of his escort, two of whom were swept away and drowned in a torrent, pausing to write letters and orders before leaping once more into the saddle. Leaving Beresford to besiege Badajoz, he rode back again as fast as he could towards Almeida – which Massena had determined not to lose without a fight – his arrival welcomed with relief by both officers and men who had been uneasy to be commanded in his absence by Sir Brent Spencer, as always perfectly agreeable, but less noted than ever for 'military quickness' and certainly not considered to be a match for 'that old fox', Marshal Massena.

South of the town, the two armies met at Fuentes de Oñoro on 3 May 1811. It was a hard and savage battle, in which Craufurd's Light Division performed brilliantly executed service in rescuing the shattered battalions of the 7th Division from what seemed for a time almost certain defeat. The British infantry, drawn up in squares, held firm against the charges of the French cavalry; but the outnumbered British cavalry were no match for Massena's lancers and hussars.[17] The British line did not break, however, and Almeida fell, though its garrison was allowed to escape through the incompetence of several officers, among them the brave, unbalanced Sir William Erskine and the commanding officer of the 4th Foot, Colonel Bevan, who, late in obeying orders then losing his way, was selected as a scapegoat by Erskine, and, rather than face a court-martial, blew his brains out.[18] Another officer behaved so recklessly that Wellington decided that 'there was nothing on earth so stupid as a gallant officer'.[19] It was all very well 'to want to be forward in engaging the enemy'; what was wanted was 'cool, discriminating judgement in action'.*[20]

The whole operation outside Almeida had left Wellington furiously angry and bitterly dissatisfied. It was 'the most disgraceful military event that has yet occurred'.[21] He was driven to conclude that the Prime Minister was 'quite right not to move thanks for the battle at Fuentes'.[22] 'It was the most difficult one I was ever concerned in,' he told his brother William.[23] 'We had very nearly three to one against us engaged; above four to one in cavalry; and moreover our cavalry had not a gallop in them; while some of that of the enemy were fresh and in excellent order. If Boney had been there, we should have been beaten.'†[24]

Wellington was just as displeased when he learned how Beresford had fared south of Badajoz at Albuera. There had been a fierce fight here, too. Beresford's men had held their ground under heavy bombardment from Soult's artillery, and had withstood the attacks which his infantry and cavalry had launched against them. But so many men had been killed or wounded – 4,000 out of 10,000 engaged – that Wellington felt obliged to complain that another such battle would ruin his army.[25]

---

* His cavalry, Wellington considered, were particularly lacking in this quality; and it was with this in mind that he maintained in later years – much to the annoyance of King George IV – that the French cavalry were the 'best in Europe' (*Reminiscences and Recollections of Captain Gronow*, ii, 4).

† In 1824, while staying with Charles and Harriet Arbuthnot at their house in Northamptonshire, the Duke expressed the opinion, while talking of some of his engagements, that 'the battle of Fuentes d'Honoro was the most glorious he ever fought', an observation at odds both with his comments at the time and with his remark about Assaye to George Chad (*The Journal of Mrs Arbuthnot*, i, 281). Ten years later he told J.W. Croker, 'I look upon Salamanca, Vittoria and Waterloo as my three best battles; those which had great and permanent consequences' (*The Croker Papers*, ii, 235).

As for this one, he refused to allow the 'croakers' in England to make capital out of it. When Beresford's gloomy dispatch arrived at headquarters he declined to send it on. 'This won't do,' he said to the staff officer who brought it to him. 'Write me down a victory.' 'The dispatch was altered accordingly.'[26] 'If it had not been for me,' he explained, 'they would have written a whining report upon it, which would have driven the people in England mad. However, I prevented that.'[27]

At the same time, to comfort and reassure Beresford, he wrote him a kind letter: 'You could not be successful in such an action without a large loss, and we must make up our minds to affairs of this kind sometimes, or give up the game.'[28]

Just how terrible the slaughter at Albuera had been was brought home vividly to Wellington when he went there himself to supervise another siege of Badajoz. The men of one regiment were 'literally lying dead in their ranks as they stood', a phenomenon he had never encountered elsewhere.[29] A French officer had already seen the blood-stained bodies of hundreds of his countrymen, 'all of them naked, the peasants having stripped them in the night'. An English officer who visited the ground a year later found it was still covered with white bones. A soldier recalled that the 'whole ground was still covered with the wrecks of an army, bonnets, cartridge boxes, pieces of belts, old clothes and shoes; the ground in numerous ridges, under which lay many a heap of mouldering bones. It was a melancholy sight; it made us all very dull for a short time.'[30]

With another large French army not far away, Wellington did not have long to conduct his operations against Badajoz; and he felt compelled to order an assault upon its walls before his guns, antiquated brass cannon removed from the obsolete fortifications of Elvas, had made adequate breaches. Mistakes were made similar to those which had enraged Wellington outside Almeida: officers again lost their way, and, when the breaches were at last reached, the scaling ladders proved too short.

The attack failed and, learning that the French were now within a day or two's march of him, Wellington felt obliged to withdraw across the Portuguese frontier into the Alentejo. He now turned his attention once more to the north and to the town just beyond Fuentes de Oñoro, Ciudad Rodrigo. He surrounded the garrison there in August, hoping it would soon be forced to surrender. But the French appeared in strength to drive the British off. They were commanded now by Massena's successor, Marshal Marmont, the thirty-seven-year-old duc de

Raguse. There was a short engagement at El Bodon on 25 September after which Wellington was forced to withdraw, finding himself in a predicament from which General Craufurd made no noticeable effort to extricate him.

'I am glad to see you safe, General Craufurd,' he said to him coldly the next morning.

'I was never in danger.'

'Oh! I was.'

As they parted after this brief exchange, Craufurd was heard to mutter, 'He's damned crusty this morning.'[31] Wellington took no notice. 'He knew Craufurd's merits and trusted him', though the Advocate-General thought it was 'surprising what he bore from him at times'.[32]

Despite his irritability after the setback at El Bodon and his disappointment after Fuentes de Oñoro, Wellington felt justified in congratulating himself when he withdrew to the Coa in Beira: the French were no longer in Portugal.

'We have certainly altered the nature of the war in Spain,' he reported to the Cabinet. 'It has become, to a certain degree, offensive on our part. The enemy are obliged to concentrate large corps to defend their own acquisitions; they are obliged to collect magazines to support their armies ... and I think it probable, from all that I hear, that they are either already reduced, or they must soon come, to the resources of France for the payment of those expenses which must be defrayed in money. As soon as this shall be the case ... you may be certain that Bonaparte will be disposed to put an end to it ... I think it is not unlikely that peace is speculated upon in France.'[33]

Wellington's feelings towards the Government had changed of late. He was still short of money but satisfactory numbers of reinforcements were being sent out to him – against the advice of the Duke of York who feared that England was being left undefended – and he looked with confidence to the future.

17   Life at Headquarters

1810 — 12

'He was in the best of spirits, genial and *sans
cérémonie*; in fact, just like a genuine country
squire.'

IN THOSE WINTER months of 1811 when the fighting died away and
the guns were silent, Wellington remained with his army in Portugal.
He showed no inclination to go home as so many of his senior officers
had done from time to time: he had, after all, no pressing reason to
return, no one whom he could not wait patiently to see again, no
brother or sister whom he sorely missed, nor wife whom he longed to
hold in his arms.

To those who did want to go home, he listened without much sympathy, whether it was business that called them, or family ties or illness.
One morning when James McGrigor was with him and he was in a particularly bad humour after listening to various gloomy reports from the
heads of other departments, two officers came in to request leave to go
to England. 'One of them, an officer in the Engineers, first made his
request; he had received letters informing him that his wife was dangerously ill, and that the whole of his family were sick. His Lordship quickly
replied, "No, no, Sir! I cannot at all spare you at this moment." The captain, with a mournful face and submissive bow retired. A general officer
of a noble family next advanced, saying, "My Lord, I have of late been
suffering much from rheumatism –" Without allowing him time to proceed further, Wellington rapidly said, "And you must go to England to
get cured of it. By all means. Go there immediately." The general, surprised at his Lordship's tone and manner, looked abashed, while he made
a profound bow; but to prevent his saying anything in explanation, his
Lordship immediately addressed me.'[1]

Wellington had no objection to officers going off to Lisbon for a day
or two; once cheerfully giving leave to an officer to do so for forty-eight
hours 'which is as long as any reasonable man can wish to stay in bed
with the same woman'.[2] But when he received a letter from England

on behalf of a young lady who was said to be pining away for love of an absent major, he replied sardonically that, while there were believed to be 'desperate cases of this description', he himself could not say that he had 'ever yet known of a young lady dying of love'. 'They contrive, in some manner to live, and look tolerably well, notwithstanding their despair; and some even have been known to recover so far as to be inclined to take another lover, if the absence of the first has lasted too long.' He did not suppose that this particular lady could ever recover so far, but he hoped that she would 'survive the continued necessary absence of the Major, and enjoy with him hereafter many happy days'.[3]

As for the demands of family business and private concerns, his own opinion was that there were no such that could not 'be settled by instruction and power of attorney'. Indeed, he eventually prevailed upon the Horse Guards to send him no general officers who were not prepared to undertake that they would not ask for leave to attend to private business at home during their term of absence. He might occasionally feel obliged to grant leave of absence to an officer, but he could never approve of it. Why, were he to grant all requests for leave that were made to him, 'between those absent on account of wounds and sickness, and those absent on account of business or pleasure', he would have no officers left. A characteristic rebuff was delivered to Lieutenant Gurwood of the 52nd Regiment:

> The Commander of the Forces cannot grant leave of absence to any officer in the army, except for recovery of health or for the arrangement of business which cannot be settled without his presence, and the settlement of which is paramount to every other consideration in life. As Lieutenant Gurwood's application solely implies private affairs as the plea, without stating their nature, it is not in his Excellency's power to comply with his request.[4]

There were those who condemned him for being hard and unfeeling. Certainly he always endeavoured to keep his emotions firmly under control and was ill at ease in the company of those who could not. Stories about his restraint were constantly repeated in the army: once, early one morning when excitedly informed that the enemy were withdrawing after he had waited long for them to do so, he paused for a moment, his razor motionless against his chin, murmured, 'Ay, I thought they meant to be off; very well,' and continued unhurriedly with his shaving.[5] When told with equal excitement that his advance-guard had suddenly come upon the entire French army, he observed conversationally, 'Oh, they are all there, are they? Well, we must mind a little what we are about.'[6] Distressing news was greeted with the same imperturbable self-control as the most joyous intelligence, although those who knew him best were well aware when his innermost feelings were aroused. The death, for instance, of a brave and talented young Intelligence Officer, Major Edward Somers-Cocks, son of Earl Somers, affected him deeply. Colonel Frederic Ponsonby, commanding officer of the 12th Light Dragoons, recorded how Wellington had suddenly entered Ponsonby's room to break the news, how he had paced up and down in silence, opened the door again, and left, announcing abruptly, 'Poor old Cocks was killed last night.' His look of despair at the funeral was such that no one liked to talk to him.[7]

On less emotional occasions, men were often wary of approaching him, for fear lest they were met with one of those rebuffs which the General would deliver, apparently unconscious of how wounding they could be. The Judge-Advocate General, Francis Seymour Larpent, observed that some officers were 'much afraid of him'. Larpent himself when going up to him with his papers for instructions – which would always be given in a 'civil and decisive' way – felt 'something like a boy going to school'.[8] Yet there were times enough in the headquarters mess, as there had been in the mess of the 33rd in India, when the General seemed quite prepared to tolerate a jovial informality, when his highly distinctive laugh could be heard, 'very loud and long'. He also tolerated much informality in dress. He himself was usually clothed in a well-cut grey frock-coat, rather shorter, like his boots, than was the normal fashion and slightly tighter so that, now he was in his early forties, he could be seen to be as lithe and trim as he had been as a subaltern. 'He is well made and knows it,' Larpent wrote home to his step-mother, attributing entirely to vanity what was also dictated by practical requirements, 'and is willing to set off to the best what nature has bestowed. In short, like every great man present or past, almost without exception, he is vain . . . He is remarkably neat and most particular in his dress . . . He cuts the skirts of his coat shorter to make them look smarter: and only a short time since, on going to him on business, I found him discussing the cut of his half-boots and suggesting alterations to his servant.' In wet weather his cocked hat was carefully encased in an oilskin cover.[9]

His officers were permitted the same kind of latitude as he allowed himself in matters of dress. 'Scarcely any two officers were dressed alike,' one of them said. 'Some wore grey braided coats, others brown: some again blue; many (from choice, or perhaps necessity) stuck to the old "red rag".'[10] Nor was much attention paid by the General to the uniform of the soldiers. 'Provided we brought our men into the field well appointed with their sixty rounds of ammunition each,' this same officer recorded, 'he never looked to see whether trousers were black, blue or grey.' 'I think it indifferent how a soldier is clothed,' Wellington wrote himself in a letter to the Horse Guards, 'provided it is in a uniform manner, and that he is forced to keep himself clean and smart, as a soldier ought to be.'[11]

Visitors to headquarters were sometimes astonished by the amateurish, almost disorderly look of the place. Not only did officers walk about in a variety of clothes, some smart in their regimental uniform, others dressed in an individual manner which would have horrified their King had he seen them at a levee. The whole atmosphere, so a German commissary recalled, was 'strikingly' informal. 'Had it not been known for a fact, no one would have suspected that [General Wellington] was quartered in the town. There was no throng of scented staff officers with plumed hats, orders and stars, no main guard, no crowd of contractors, actors, valets, cooks, mistresses, equipages, horses, forage and baggage waggons, as there is at a French or Russian headquarters. Just a few aides-de-camp, who went about the streets alone and in their overcoats, a few guides, and a small staff guard; that was all. About a dozen bullock-carts were to be seen in the large square of Fuente Guinaldo, which was used for bringing up straw to Headquarters; but apart from these no equipages or baggage trains were visible.'[12] What was not to be missed, however, was the Commander-in-Chief's marquee which enclosed the tent in which he slept. This 'large Marquee' also served as 'a sitting and dining room', wrote his cook, James Thornton. 'The gentlemen of the staff had a tent each . . . I had a round tent to sleep in, the Butler one also, my two Assistants had one between them, the Duke's footmen and all the staff servants had one tent for two servants, all the servants' tents were round ones, the gentlemen's small Marquees.'[13] The cooking was done 'in a Room made with poles and a Tarpolain . . . There was a mound of earth thrown up, and niches cut round this in which we made fires and boiled the saucepans. We had a larger niche cut out for roasting. We stuck a pole in that and dangled the meat. When it rained hard, they had nothing but cold meat and bread.'[14]

Thornton's cooking, the General had to concede, was not very good: 'Cole gives the best dinners in the army; Hill the next best; mine are no great things.'[15] However, the wine at Wellington's headquarters was better than that at any other; much of it, including champagne, being sent out from England.

Sometimes the General was seen walking up and down in the company of one or other of the staff or with another General or perhaps a civilian visitor; and the conversation would range over all manner of topics, not all of them military, politics perhaps, or that night's theatricals, or the prospects for next day's hunting, for he still allowed himself his hunting days and kept a pack of hounds, known as 'The Peers' ', which had been brought out for him by two aides-de-camp, Lord Tweeddale and Lord Worcester. Indeed, as often as he could he went hunting in the uniform of the Hatfield Hunt, a black cape and sky-blue coat, which Lady Salisbury had given him, chasing after the quarry – which once turned out to be a load of salt fish – not much caring what the hounds ran so long as he could 'enjoy a good gallop', tumbling off often enough to give a Guards officer grounds for commenting, 'He will certainly break his neck someday.'[16]

August Schaumann remarked how different he appeared on one of his hunting days when compared with his demeanour in times of stress in battle when, although always in control of his emotions, he 'seemed like an angry God under whose threatening glance every one trembled'. By contrast, on his hunting days, when Schaumann 'often used to meet him with his entourage and a magnificent pack of English hounds', he was 'in the best of spirits, genial and *sans cérémonie*; in fact, just like a genuine country squire. No one would have suspected at such moments that he was the Field-Marshal of three nations.'[17]

He was liable at such times to dash off at any moment, even in the middle of a conversation. The Spanish General Castaños was once much surprised to have an 'earnest conversation' with him interrupted in this way when a 'brace of greyhounds in pursuit of a hare' passed close to them as they rode along together 'under a fire of artillery and accompanied by a numerous staff'. The instant Wellington observed the hare and greyhounds, he 'gave the view hallo and went after them at full speed, to the utter astonishment of his foreign accompaniments. Nor did he stop until he saw the hare killed; when he returned and resumed the commander-in-chief as if nothing had happened.'[18]

The air of informality which pervaded headquarters was deceptive. The General worked hard, unwilling to leave much to his second-in-command – an appointment he chose not to recognize – though more willing to do so when Sir Brent Spencer went home and was succeeded by the more trustworthy Sir Thomas Graham, the future Lord Lynedoch. He kept himself fit and expected his hardworking staff to keep fit too. He needed little sleep and grew impatient with those who pleaded the necessity of more. He was up at six o'clock, having been

Lieutenant-Colonel the Hon. Arthur Wellesley, 33rd Foot. A portrait by John Hoppner painted in 1796 when Wellesley (then Wesley) was twenty-seven.

Anne, Countess of Mornington, the Duke of Wellington's mother.
A portrait attributed to François Théodore Rochard.

The Hon. William Wellesley-Pole, later third Earl of Mornington, Wellington's elder brother. A portrait by John Hoppner.

The Rev. the Hon. Gerald Valerian Wellesley, Wellington's younger brother, Prebendary of Durham.

Richard Colley, Marquess Wellesley, Wellington's eldest brother.

The Hon. Henry Wellesley, later first Baron Cowley, Wellington's youngest brother. A portrait by John Hoppner.

A caricature of soldiers on the march by Thomas Rowlandson. A limited number of women were permitted to accompany a regiment on active service, usually six per company, but most units accumulated more common-law wives and camp-followers who were, it was said, 'averse to all military discipline'.

'Blücher the Brave extracting the Groan of Abdication from the Corsican Bloodhound.'
A caricature by Rowlandson published in April 1814. The news that Napoleon had agreed to abdicate and to retire to Elba, after Blücher's victorious entry into Paris, had reached London that month.

The Duke of Wellington and Marshal Blücher greet each other on the late evening of 18 June 1815 on the Brussels road between Rossomme and the inn of *La Belle-Alliance*. *'Mein lieber Kamerad,'* Blücher said, leaning forward in his saddle to kiss Wellington on the cheek, *'Quelle affaire!'*

'The Master of the Ordnance Exercising his Hobby!' A caricature by Isaac Cruikshank published in April 1819. Wellington, then Master General of the Ordnance, bestrides a phallic cannon in St James's Park with Buckingham House in the background. He playfully threatens three ladies, one of whom cries out in affected alarm, 'Bless us! What a spanker! – I hope he won't fire it at me – I could never support such a thing!'

Robert Stewart, Lord Castlereagh.
A portrait of the Foreign Secretary by
Sir Thomas Lawrence.

Right: Frances Mary Gascoyne-Cecil,
second Marchioness of Salisbury, aged
twenty-seven. A portrait by Sir Thomas
Lawrence painted in 1829 and exhibited
at the Royal Academy that year.

Catherine (Kitty), the short-sighted Duchess of
Wellington sketching in her room. A drawing by
John Hayter.

Harriet Arbuthnot, the Duke's intimate
friend and confidante, after a portrait by
Sir Thomas Lawrence.

A portrait by Spiridore Gambardella of
Charles Arbuthnot, Wellington's close
friend, 'Gosh', who was cared for by the
Duke after Harriet Arbuthnot's death.

Apsley House, No. 1 London, the Duke's house at Hyde Park Corner, now the Wellington Museum.

Benjamin Dean Wyatt's perspective view of a proposed palace, Waterloo Palace, at Stratfield Saye, which was designed for the Duke when it was intended that the existing house should be demolished.

Left: Charles Greville, the diarist, was the brother of Algernon Greville, the Duke's secretary, and the son of Lady Charlotte Greville. Known as 'Punch' and 'the Gruncher', he was exceptionally well informed about the politics and fashionable society of his day.

Right Lady Charlotte Greville, an 'excellent woman' in Lord Minto's opinion, was the eldest daughter of the third Duke of Portland who was twice Prime Minister.

in bed for no more than six hours, sometimes for only three. He was at his desk writing until nine o'clock when he had breakfast, a spare, plain meal as all his meals usually were since he had such scant interest in food and was little concerned if he passed twenty-four hours without eating anything at all other than the crust and boiled egg he sometimes stuffed in his pocket when riding out of a morning.*[19]

The Duke's abstinence often upset the Spanish aide-de-camp at his headquarters, Miguel Ricardo de Alava y Esquivel, later Spanish Ambassador in London, who, as he confessed, grew to dread those days when the General was asked what time the staff were to set off in the morning and what they were to have for dinner, since Alava knew that 'the Peer' would reply, as he never failed to do, 'At daylight. Cold meat.' The Spaniard held those four words *'en horreur'*.[20]

After breakfast the General received in turn the heads of the various departments of the army, making it clear that he preferred them to speak without recourse to notes, since hesitation while they were look-ing at them clearly annoyed him and made him 'fidgetty'.[21] He then mounted one of his horses, upon which he expended large sums of money, and rode off to inspect an outpost or to see a divisional com-mander. At six he dined, 'never alone, nor with members of his personal staff exclusively about him', wrote the Rev. G.R. Gleig, son of the Bishop of Brechin, at that time an officer in the 85th. 'Everybody recommended to his notice [who happened to be passing through] was sure to receive an invitation . . . The conversation was most interesting and lively. The Duke himself spoke out upon all subjects with an absence of reserve which sometimes surprised his guests . . . He was rich in anecdote, most of them taking a ludicrous turn, and without any apparent effort put the company very much at their ease.'[22]

About nine o'clock he would order coffee which was accepted as a signal for breaking up; and he then returned to his writing table where he studied papers and resumed his correspondence, remaining at work far into the night.

Occasionally there were performances in a makeshift theatre and evenings of great jollity.[23] On one memorable occasion, during a lull in fighting, a grand party was given to celebrate Lowry Cole's investiture

---

* Wellington once greatly shocked the duc de Cambacérès, one of the most celebrated gourmets of the day, with whom he dined in Paris, by replying to an enquiry as to how he had enjoyed some exceptionally delicious dish, 'It was excellent; but to tell you the truth, I don't care much what I eat.' 'Good heavens!' exclaimed Cambacérès, 'Don't care what you eat! Why then did you come here?' (A.H. Brialmont, *Histoire du duc de Wellington*, i, 327).

with the Order of the Bath. Wellington lent his plate for the dinner which was followed by a dance attended by forty ladies and 200 officers and other gentlemen guests. The band of the 52nd played tirelessly. The wine 'both at dinner and supper having circulated freely', at about two o'clock in the morning 'a number of Spanish officers insisted upon carrying Lord Wellington round the room in a chair. He suggested that they should begin with the person of highest rank present, and named the Prince of Orange [one of his aides-de-camp]. The Prince was immediately seized, and General [Sir John Ormsby] Vandeleur, coming up to remonstrate, was seized in like manner. Each was placed in an arm-chair, and hoisted on the shoulders of four bearers. The inevitable consequence soon followed. The bearers had not taken many steps before they with their burdens came down.'[24]

The Advocate-General thought that there were rather too many of these parties. 'Great dinners' were held on the anniversaries of victories and on the birthdays of members of the Royal Family, indeed on any occasion considered worthy of celebration. 'The Commander-in-Chief's victories and successes will soon ruin him in wine and eating,' Larpent thought, 'and if he goes on as he has, he had better keep open house at once every day, and his calendar of feasts will be as full as the Romish one with red letter days.'[25]

Many of the papers which Wellington studied in those early morning hours in his room or tent at headquarters were orders written by Napoleon to his marshals in Spain and sent on to the *Inglese* by the guerrillas who kept careful watch upon the roads that led to France, pouncing down by night on horsemen and convoys with sharp knives in strong brown hands. Their contribution to the Spanish cause Wellington valued more highly than that of the Spanish levies.[26] He listened with admiration, if sometimes with a frisson of horror, to stories of their exploits, of the achievements of such guerrilla leaders as one known as Moreno who was said to have once killed seven French soldiers with a single shot from his huge blunderbuss, the recoil of which dislocated his shoulder, and who, in presenting some captured silver to the town of his birth, arranged upon one of the pieces a selection of French ears. 'It is probable,' Wellington had written to Spencer Perceval at the beginning of 1810, 'that, although the [Spanish] armies may be lost and the principal Juntas and authorities of the provinces may be dispersed, the war of partizans may continue.'[27]

It had continued. So had the dangerous work and intelligence activities of Wellington's scouts and spies who cooperated with the guerrillas, of men like Sir John Waters, who could 'assume the character of Spaniards of every degree and station', and Patrick Curtis, Rector of the Irish College at Salamanca, Professor of Astronomy there and future Archbishop of Armagh, who was arrested by the French in 1811, and John Grant, known as a 'master of disguise', and his namesake, Colquhoun Grant, a brilliant linguist (unlike his other namesake, the arrogant Hussar), one of those 'exploring officers' of whom Wellington said 'no army in the world ever produced the like', adding, 'Grant was worth a brigade to me.'[28]

The Imperial commands which, intercepted by guerrillas, were handed to these 'exploring officers', were almost invariably impracticable and sometimes absurd, based upon faulty intelligence and misconceptions as to the nature of the Spanish terrain. They ignored the fact that the British now held the initiative in the Peninsula, and that the French, with limited supplies and transport in the bleak terrain of western Spain, could not possibly seize Lisbon, as Napoleon so insistently demanded.

Wellington, however, was free to move against the French; and in January 1812 he did so, marching towards Ciudad Rodrigo, digging trenches in front of it and, on the 19th of the month, after a most hastily conducted siege, storming it.[29]. The assaulting troops charged into what one of them called 'an inferno of fire'. The Connaught Rangers were sent forward by the gruff Welsh commander of the 3rd Division, Thomas Picton, with the order, 'It is not my intention to spend any powder this evening. We'll do this with the cold iron.'[30]

Their Colonel, Henry Mackinnon, was blown up and killed by a mine. Other officers fell around him: the fiery-tempered General Craufurd of the Light Division was wounded in the back; Colonel John Colborne of the 52nd, tall and patrician with a nose like Wellington's, was shot through the shoulder; Lieutenant John Gurwood, one day to be Wellington's private secretary, was severely wounded in the skull; Major George Napier, who had volunteered to command the storming party, lost his right arm which had already been broken by a shell fragment three days before.

The heavy casualties were not in vain. The operation was completely successful and – as Wellington, in a dispatch of unusual though well-justified self-congratulation, reported to the Cabinet – was performed 'in half the time' he had told them it would take, and 'in less than half that which the French spent in taking the same place from the Spaniards'.[31] He did not, however, mention the scenes which had marred the success once the British soldiers entered the town. Many were soon incapably drunk and, firing at doors and windows in the square beneath the twelfth-century cathedral, they killed and wounded some of their comrades. Neither the oaths of Picton, in Wellington's opinion 'the most foul-mouthed fellow that ever lived', nor the calls of trumpets nor yet the efforts of officers who hit the men over the head with the butt ends of broken muskets could restore order or prevent the pillaging of the joints of meat, loaves of bread, clothes and shoes which the men, marching out of the town the next morning, hung round their necks or carried on the points of their bayonets. Passing Picton they demanded a cheer. 'Here then, you drunken set of brave rascals,' he replied indulgently. 'Hurrah! We'll soon be at Badajoz!'[32]

There were many who were never to get to Badajoz. Over a thousand men had been killed or wounded; an uncertain number of deserters found hiding in the town were shot as they knelt beside their shared grave; General Craufurd, his spine shattered, anxious in his last moments to be reconciled to Wellington with whom he had had his differences, begged forgiveness for having sometimes been a croaker in the past, talking, so Wellington said, in puzzled sorrow, 'as they do in a novel', before dying after five days' agony and being buried in the breaches through which his men had stormed.[33]

18 Badajoz, Salamanca and Madrid

1812

'I assure you I actually could not help crying.'

IN ENGLAND, Craufurd was mourned as a national hero. His brave death was recognized by votes of both Houses of Parliament; and monuments were erected to him and to Colonel Mackinnon in St Paul's Cathedral.

Wellington was highly honoured also. Over the past few months he and his army had been severely criticized. General Sir Banastre Tarleton, who had achieved fame as a ruthless cavalry commander in the American War, had been tireless in his sniping; the Whigs had been eager to seize upon any setback; Henry Brougham had been unable to hide his pleasure upon learning of the failure of the assault on Badajoz; Creevey had reported that Lord Wellington and the campaign in Portugal were now 'out of fashion' at court; and the Prince of Wales, who had become Prince Regent now that his father was considered incurably insane, had declined to discuss the matter. When someone had spoken of Wellington's campaigns in the north of the Peninsula, the Regent, his mind preoccupied with the behaviour of his detested wife, had exclaimed, 'Damn the north! and damn the south! and damn Wellington! The question is, how am I to be rid of this damned Princess of Wales?'[1]

Now all past failures and disappointments were forgiven and forgotten. The British Government, the Prince Regent and the Spanish Cortes all agreed that the capture of Ciudad Rodrigo was an achievement in which Wellington could justifiably take pride. The Cortes created him Duque de Ciudad Rodrigo; the Government asked a willing Parliament to grant him another annuity of £2,000. Even General Tarleton joined in the universal praise; only the radical Sir Francis Burdett voiced doubts as to the hero's ability;[2] and on 28 February 1812 the Prince Regent created him Earl of Wellington.

Yet there were further setbacks and sorrows soon to be borne. With Ciudad Rodrigo now safely in his possession, Wellington turned south for Badajoz. Anxious to take the place before Soult or Marmont reached

it, he hurried forward the necessary preparations for siege warfare –
the digging of trenches and parallels, saps and mines, the building of
batteries and bulwarks.

The assault was launched on the dark night of 6 April and, as some
had thought at Ciudad Rodrigo, Wellington launched it too soon.[3] The
first storming column struggled to clamber up the slopes and across
the imperfect breaches, treading on to the sharp spikes of caltrops and
planks studded with the points of nails, being blown apart by mines,
mutilated by shells and grenades, burned by fire-balls and knocked
over by powder barrels, coming up against chevaux-de-frise made from
Spanish sword blades, carrying scaling ladders, many of which proved
too short, taunted by the shouts of the French troops on the walls and
with the piercing sound of their own bugles ringing in their ears.

They were driven back with appalling losses. The second storming
column suffered the same fate. When Wellington was given reports of
these failures and the dreadful carnage that accompanied them, he
remained outwardly calm; but those close to him saw the colour drain
from his face. The surgeon James McGrigor, standing nearby, thought
that he would never forget the 'countenance of Lord Wellington at
that moment lit up by the glare of the torch held by Lord March':

> The jaw had fallen, and the face was of unusual length while the
> torchlight gave his countenance a lurid aspect . . . Suddenly turning
> to me and putting his hand on my arm, he said, 'Go over immediately
> to Picton, and tell him he must try if he cannot succeed on the castle.'
> I replied, 'My Lord, I have not my horse with me, but I will walk as
> fast as I can, and I think I can find the way; I know part of the road
> is swampy.' 'No, no,' he replied, 'I beg your pardon, I thought it was
> De Lancey' [an aide-de-camp]. I repeated my offer, saying I was sure
> I could find the way, but he said, 'No.'[4]

Later he was seen to be in tears when he saw the heaps of dead
lying piled upon the broken walls; and the next day, when handed the
casualty returns, he read them with tears pouring down his cheeks.
He admitted as much when his life as a fighting soldier was over:

> He told us that the day after the storm of Badajoz, which had been
> most bloody, Sir Thos. Picton, who, he said, was as hard as iron, came
> to congratulate him, & [Wellington told Mrs Arbuthnot] I assure you
> I actually c^d not help crying. I bit my lips, did everything I c^d to stop
> myself for I was ashamed he sh^d see it, but I could not; & he so little
> entered into my feelings that he said, 'Good God, what is the matter?'!

& I was obliged to begin swearing & cursing the Government for giving me no sappers & miners as an excuse for my agitation.[5]

Wellington's confusion and emotional breakdown soon turned to anger when, after men of the 3rd and 5th Divisions had clambered up scaling ladders and into the Castle, the town became a scene of appalling riot, as soldiers broke into houses, dragged cases of wine into the streets, raped women, robbed and murdered men, bayoneted children, and abandoned themselves to a frenzy of looting which such moderate General Orders as that issued from headquarters on 7 April – 'It is full time that the plunder of Badajoz should cease' – were not likely to quell.[6]

A young officer in the 28th wrote of

the shrill shrieking of affrighted children, the piercing shrieks of frantic women, the groans of the wounded, the savage and discordant yells of drunkards firing at everything and in all directions, and the continued roll of musketry kept up in error on the shattered gateway . . .

Every house presented a scene of plunder, debauchery and bloodshed, committed with wanton cruelty on the persons of the defenceless inhabitants by our soldiery; and in many instances I beheld the savages tear the rings from the ears of beautiful women who were their victims, and when the rings could not be immediately removed from their fingers with the hand, they tore them off with their teeth . . .

Men, women and children were shot in the streets for no other apparent reason than pastime; every species of outrage was publicly committed in the houses, churches and streets, and in a manner so brutal that a faithful recital would be too indecent and too shocking to humanity. Not the slightest shadow of order or discipline was maintained; the officers durst not interfere . . . A sergeant struck me with his pike for refusing to join in plundering a family; I certainly snapped my pistol in his face, but fortunately it missed fire or he would have been killed.[7]

For three days and nights the riot continued, the men, some accompanied by their women, so drunk as to behave as though insane: a nun was dragged into the street by two men, one of whom was disposed to spare her; so the other man shot him dead.*

---

* Another of the soldiers' victims was more fortunate. The fourteen-year-old Juana Maria de los Dolores de León was seized with her elder sister, a Spanish officer's wife, and their earrings were torn from their ears. They managed to escape to the British camp outside Badajoz where they claimed the protection of two officers, one of whom was Harry Smith, a captain in the 95th. Both men wished to marry the younger sister who

Wellington himself was almost shot by a soldier firing distractedly into the air as his comrades called out to the General, 'Old boy! Will you drink? The town's our own. Hurrah!' 'I remember entering a cellar,' Wellington recalled in later years, 'and seeing some soldiers lying on the floor so dead drunk that the wine was actually flowing from their mouths.'[8]

It was not until after a gallows had been erected in the Plaza that sufficient order was restored for the army to march off once more against the enemy. The objective now was Salamanca in León on the right bank of the River Tormes. Wellington explained his reasons for having chosen to make this move against Marmont, instead of sweeping to the south against Soult in Andalusia: 'The harvest in all countries north of the Tagus . . . is much later than it is to the southward. We shall obtain our advantages for a longer period of time in these countries than we should to the southward' where Soult would be able to feed his men sooner than Marmont in León.[9]

So in June 1812 the British army marched for Salamanca from which the French withdrew, leaving strong garrisons in the town's forts. Ordering detachments to besiege these forts, Wellington moved on to occupy the ground to the north of Salamanca on the ridge of San Cristobal. Here, in this strong position, he hoped that Marmont would attack him; but Marmont, aware of the dangers, declined to oblige him. Once the French columns came close and Wellington thought for a moment of attacking them himself. 'Damned tempting', he said to an aide-de-camp. 'I've a great mind to attack 'em.'[10] But the idea was soon dismissed. He had already made up his mind not to engage the enemy 'unless under very advantageous circumstances'; and these had not yet occurred. So it seemed that, since neither side was prepared to provoke it, there would be no battle outside Salamanca after all. The headquarters staff felt sure of this when one of them courageously approached the General with a request for leave and, to everyone's astonishment, was granted it. 'You have seen the end of it,' he was told. 'I shan't fight him without an advantage, nor he me, I believe.'[11]

Even so the staff were not quite sure what Wellington intended to

chose Smith. She accompanied him for the rest of the campaign. Wellington was much taken with her and called her 'Juanita'. In 1847 Smith, by then created a baronet after distinguished service in India, was appointed Governor of Cape Colony. His wife went out with him to South Africa where Ladysmith in Natal was named after her (*The Autobiography of Sir Harry Smith*).

do next. 'We hear little or nothing of Ld. Wellington, who keeps not only the Portuguese but the Officers of his Staff in the dark with regard to his Intentions,' Lieutenant William Bragge of the 3rd Dragoon Guards had written home not long before; 'and I understand at his own Table he rattles away to the General Officers etc, and fills them full of Humbug Accounts which they have scarce time to repeat to their confidential Friends before an order arrives for the Brigades to march without Delay at least 20 Points of the Compass from the one expected.'*12

Anxious as always to ensure that no idle talk or information in indiscreet letters should reach the enemy, Wellington paid no regard to insinuations of secretiveness, just as, in his anxiety not to give the political opposition at home any ammunition which would help them unsettle a Government by no means secure, he resisted all temptation to take risks which might end in political as well as military ruin. In the meantime he liked to keep his own counsel. Years before in India he had once declared, 'I like to walk alone.'13 He had not changed.

On 17 June 1812, the French in the forts of Salamanca having surrendered, Lord Wellington rode across the Roman bridge that spanned the Tormes into the ancient university town. He was greeted with rapture. Beneath the brown walls of the splendid Plaza Mayor, built at the beginning of the century and large enough to hold 20,000 spectators of a bull-fight, the cheering crowds thronged the pavement and surged around the ninety arches of Andres Garcia de Quiñones's arcade. The General was besieged by women crying with joy, endeavouring to kiss him, tugging at him so that he was almost toppled from his saddle as, unresponsive to their excitement, he contrived to write

* This secretiveness was a trait which remained an essential part of his make-up for the rest of his life. As Charles Greville said, 'One of his peculiarities was never to tell anybody where he was going; and when my brother [Algernon Greville, Wellington's Private Secretary] or his own Sons wished to be acquainted with his intentions or his whereabouts, they were obliged to apply to the Housekeeper, to whom he was in the habit of making them known, and nobody ever dared to ask him any questions on the subject' (The Greville Memoirs, vi, 364).

Like Greville and others, his friend Mrs Arbuthnot, to whom he entrusted many secrets, complained that she often did not know what he intended to do or why he intended to do it. The servants at Apsley House 'never would say where the Duke was to be found'. He explained rather lamely that he 'did not desire his servants to conceal where he was, but he had no doubt they did it to keep his name out of the newspapers, for that reporters had often come to his house to know where he was, pretending to be Gov^t messengers' (The Journal of Mrs Arbuthnot, ii, 53).

orders on his sabretache. 'It is almost impossible to describe the enthusiasm of our reception,' wrote Captain George Bowles the next day. 'Lord Wellington was in great danger of being smothered by the crowds of women who aspired to the honour of not only seeing him but, I believe, kissing his Excellency. The nunneries were all thrown open and the repeated shouts of "*Viva los Ingleses*" have almost made my head ache.'[14]

Outside the town the manoeuvring continued in the hot summer days, the British soldiers weary and grumbling, eating raw onions for breakfast, filtering brackish water from the streams through their teeth, shivering in the bitterly cold nights when, failing to find firewood in a landscape almost bereft of trees, they went digging in graveyards and, tipping out their contents, burned coffins. Their Commander, 'Atty' and 'Nosey' as they alternately called him, was as cold as any of them. He had never been so cold, he said, and never so tired.[15] Insisting upon seeing everything for himself and personally superintending all the work of headquarters, he was always up now at four o'clock in the morning, however few hours he had slept. Fortunately he had the ability to go to sleep for an hour or so during the day, even when the enemy army was on the move. 'Luckily,' he said, 'I have the power, very generally, of going to sleep when I choose.'[16] He had managed to get to sleep for a few hours on the ground in the night before the fierce fighting at Talavera; and now one day as he watched the French manoeuvring through his glass, he suddenly lay down, wrapped himself up in his cloak, placed a newspaper over his face and told Lord Fitzroy Somerset to wake him up when they reached 'that copse'.[17]

'Fagged' as he complained of being, he remained fully alert. He also contrived to appear perfectly composed. Once, while he was observing the French manoeuvres, a French gun sent several volleys of shot hurtling through the air to the ground where Wellington sat in his saddle, glass and map in hand. He 'moved a few paces, and continued his directions'.[18]

The enemy manoeuvring continued, 'nobody knew with what object,' until it appeared that Marmont was endeavouring to get across the road to Portugal and force Wellington to withdraw to protect it. The leading French troops advanced at a smart pace; those behind marched less quickly after them; the line became extended as it moved across the front of Wellington's army, three of whose divisions were concealed from the enemy's view. Wellington watched them closely through his glass as he munched on a leg of chicken in a farmyard in the little village of Los Arapiles, his back to the broken, undulating ground that stretched away six miles north to Salamanca. 'By God!' he broke out suddenly, throwing the remains of the chicken leg over his shoulder, 'That will do.'[19]

He galloped away to get a better view, then turned to his Spanish aide-de-camp and exclaimed triumphantly, '*Mon cher Alava, Marmont est perdu.*'* He rode off to Edward Pakenham, who had taken over command of the 3rd Division since Picton had been wounded at Badajoz. 'Ned,' he said to him, 'do you see those fellows on the hill? Throw your division into column and have at them. Drive everything before you.'

'I will, my Lord, if you will give me your hand.'[20]

In offering his hand to his brother-in-law, it was noticed that Wellington, as though rather embarrassed by his display of emotion, did not relax his 'usual rigidity'. But as Pakenham immediately galloped off to begin his attack on the unsuspecting French, Wellington observed to his staff almost affectionately, 'Did you ever see a man who understood so clearly what he had to do?' He then galloped away himself to give orders personally to the other divisional commanders.[21]

It was a fierce engagement; but Wellington seemed never to be in doubt of the result. He was seen all over the field that day, a surprisingly cool day for July in León, galloping about from one scene of action to another, apparently oblivious of the enemy's fire, anxious to give orders personally, now with the infantry, now with the cavalry. 'By God, Cotton,' he called out with unusual excitement to the commander of the cavalry, Sir Stapleton Cotton, as Major-General Le Marchant, commander of one of Cotton's brigades, led a charge in which he was to be mortally wounded by a musket ball in the groin. 'By God, Cotton! I never saw anything so beautiful in my life. The day is *yours*.'[22]

It was undoubtedly a triumph for Wellington and would have been a greater one still, had not the Spanish garrison evacuated the castle and abandoned the ford at Alba de Tormes, allowing the defeated enemy to escape to the east. The French lost over 13,000 men, twelve guns, two eagles and several standards.[23] He had 'never seen an army take such a beating'.[24] Marmont was badly wounded, his second-in-command, Bertrand Clauzel, who took over from him, less severely so. Although 'everywhere' in the battle and having 'Sadly Exposed himself', 'the Peer' had escaped serious injury, being slightly hurt by a spent bullet that hit his thigh.[25]

---

* When the war was over, Alava gave an amusing description of the events of this day in Wellington's presence, 'the Duke sat by with his head inclined, quite silent, but with a quiet smile which seemed to say that the narration was a good deal pleasanter than the reality had been' (*The Croker Papers*, 120).

I saw him late in the evening of that great day [wrote William Napier, at that time commanding officer of the 43rd], when the advancing flashes of cannon and musketry stretching as far as the eye could command showed in the darkness how well the field was won; he was alone, the flush of victory was on his brow and his eyes were eager and watchful, but his voice was calm and even gentle.[26]

To Francisco de Goya y Lucientes, the Spanish painter who was at Alba de Tormes, so he claimed, when Wellington rode into the place that night, he looked as though he might well have been badly wounded; and the drawing he made of him at that time shows him gaunt, exhausted, the beard unshaven on his cheeks, his hair plastered to his forehead, like a man suddenly wakened from a terrifying nightmare.*

The following morning Wellington contemplated his next move: he could make north for Burgos, or he could turn south for Madrid. He chose Madrid, well aware that his army needed rest and food, and believing that the capture of King Joseph's capital would not only be a coup of great political importance, but also that the threat to Madrid would draw Soult out of Andalusia.

At his approach King Joseph rattled away in his carriage for the Mediterranean coast at Valencia, preceded by an escort and followed by two thousand carts and carriages; and on 12 August British soldiers marched into the city to a welcome even more uproarious than that which had greeted them at Salamanca. They were besieged by what a private soldier described as 'deffening shouts of "Vivi les Angoles, Vivi les Ilandos"',[27] by the inhabitants offering them wine and sweetmeats, waving scarves, palm branches and olive leaves, as the bells of the city clanged overhead, scarcely heard in the din of human voices. 'The inhabitants testified their Joy by hanging all their Curtains, Tapestry etc out of the windows,' wrote Captain Bragge. 'This had a very pretty effect and was greatly increased by a splendid Illumination with Immense Wax Candles.'[28]

'But amidst all this pleasure and happiness,' complained Private William Wheeler of the 51st, 'we were obliged to submit to a custom so unenglish that I cannot but feel disgust now I am writing. It was to be kissed by the men. What made it still worse, their breath was so highly seasoned with garlick, then their huge mustaches well stiffened with sweat, dust and snuff, it was like having a hair broom

---

* This drawing in red chalk over pencil, which was done within days, if not on the eve, of Wellington's victory at Salamanca, was used as a basis for the portraits at Apsley House and in the National Gallery. It is now in the British Museum.

pushed into ones face that had been daubed in a dirty gutter.'[29]

Wellington himself was surrounded by girls, eager to touch him, to kiss him, and even, so Lowry Cole said, to cut pieces off the skirt of his coat to keep as relics;[30] while those unable to reach the silent, unsmiling figure in the saddle, kissed the horse instead. Thereafter he was to be seen riding about the streets of Madrid in a coach drawn by six mules, followed by 'an immense crowd eager to get a glimpse of him' and accompanied, so an ensign in the Coldstream Guards observed, by 'two or three of the prettiest girls'. 'Lady Wellington would be jealous,' this officer added, 'if she were to hear of his proceedings. I never saw him in his carriage without two or three ladies.'[31]

The Spanish bestowed further honours upon him by admitting him to the Order of the Golden Fleece, one of the greatest and most ancient knightly orders in Europe, by presenting him with an extensive estate near Granada and by appointing him Generalissimo of their forces. There was talk in England of promoting him field marshal; but this was opposed by the Duke of York who countered that it would provoke much jealousy among senior officers.[32] The Prince Regent did, however, see fit to raise him a step higher in the Peerage. Wellington did not value this greatly. 'What the devil is the use of making me a Marquess?' he wanted to know.[33] But he did take kindly to a grant of £100,000 towards the cost of a country estate in England and to the Prime Minister's intention of buying for him the Manor of Wellington.* He also took sufficient interest in his coat of arms to protest when his brother, Marquess Wellesley, proposed that he augment it with a French eagle. This, he thought, would be ostentatious, a fault of which he hoped he was not guilty. He agreed with those who suggested that the Union Jack would be more appropriate.[34]

---

* 'I should be glad to know your sentiments as to the description of estate you would wish us to purchase,' Lord Liverpool wrote in his letter confirming the grant, 'whether you would look to any particular county or counties . . . If a well-conditioned property could be found in the neighbourhood of Wellington, you would perhaps prefer it to any other situation. But I believe land in general sells higher in Somersetshire than in many other parts of England' (Wellington Supplementary Dispatches, vii, 505).

19　Retreat to Portugal

1812

'Oh, by God, it was too serious to say anything.'

THERE WAS NO TIME for Lord Wellington to rest on his laurels, though. The French were still in Spain and the key town of Burgos was still in their hands. He set out for Burgos in September; and, at the sight of its strong fortifications, the confidence he had felt in Madrid deserted him. 'Matters go on well,' he had written while there, 'and I hope before Christmas, if they turn out as they ought, and Boney [who had invaded Russia in June 1812] requires all the reinforcements in the North, to have all the gentlemen safe on the other side of the Ebro.'[1] But how, he began to wonder. He doubted that he had the means to take the castle at Burgos which was 'very strong'.[2]

Moreover the French governor of Burgos was considered to be 'a very clever fellow' who knew his business only too well; and, to add to Wellington's concern, a strong enemy force was reported to be marching fast towards him. He realized that he would soon have to 'discontinue this operation in order to collect the army'.[3]

Before doing so, however, he mounted an attack upon a hornwork which, after the loss of over 300 casualties, fell into his hands. Encouraged by this expensive success, he decided to attack the fortress itself, even though it had not yet been bombarded and only eight heavy guns had so far been brought up for this purpose. Predictably, the attack on the fortress failed; and almost 200 more casualties were incurred.

It was now clear that if Burgos were to be taken, an orthodox siege would be required. But as trenches were dug and mines ineffectively exploded, the autumn rains poured down, flooding the siege works. Transport, unusually under his command, was inadequate; so was the army's siege equipment; and, worst of all, ammunition was running short.

After a more satisfactorily placed mine blew a wide breach in the wall, storming parties were sent forward again; and, after further loss of life, they gained a foothold in the outer defences of the fortress.

From these, however, they were soon thrown back by French troops who, before retiring to the safety of their main defences, did much damage to the besiegers' excavations. Despite this depressing evidence of the strength of the fortress and the determination and spirit of its defenders, Wellington decided upon yet another assault. This too failed, the storming parties being repelled with further heavy casualties.

There was no doubt now that the British army would have to be withdrawn, and withdrawn it was in such a hurry that several of its heavy guns had to be abandoned; while the engineers, in their haste to demolish the captured hornwork, laid mines which failed to explode.

Wellington, conscious of having suffered a serious and costly defeat, was thankful to see the last of 'the damned place'. His losses in dead and wounded were over seven times as high as those of the enemy. 'The whole operation had been a tragic farce and had served no useful purpose,' Dr David Gates, the most recent historian of the Peninsular War, has commented severely. 'Wellington's complacency and ineptitude [had] cost his troops dear . . . Now, as an immense Imperial army advanced to regain Madrid, the scattered Allied forces were pressed into headlong retreat.'[4]

They marched back to the Douro at Valladolid, through the wine country renowned for its Cigales and Ribera del Duero. It was late autumn now and the huge tanks and vats were full of newly fermented wine. Wellington often said that his soldiers enlisted only for drink; and certainly now they displayed a wholesale propensity to drunkenness. Over a thousand of them got so helplessly inebriated at Torquemada that they collapsed as though dead by the roadside.

> The conduct of some men would have disgraced savages [wrote Private William Wheeler of the 51st]. Drunkenness prevaled to such a frightful extent that I have often wondered how it was that a great part of our army were not cut off. It was no unfrequent thing to see a long string of mules carrying drunken soldiers to prevent them falling into the hands of the enemy . . . From Burgos to Salamanca is chiefly a wine country and as there had been a good harvest, and the new wine was in tanks particularly about Validolid the soldiers ran mad. I remember a soldier fully accoutred with his knapsack on in a large tank, he had either fell in or had been pushed in by his comrades, there he lay dead. I saw a Dragoon fire his pistol into a large vat containing several thousands of gallons, in a few minutes we were up to our knees in wine fighting like tigers for it.[5]

When his men at last reached San Cristobal, where he had vainly hoped that Marmont would attack him in the summer, the Commander-in-Chief, who had been increasingly ill-tempered of late, was relieved beyond measure that he had got clear of the enemy. It had been 'the worst scrape that he ever was in'.[6]

He held his ground for a week at San Cristobal, hoping for a French attack even though his army, while strengthened by that of Sir Rowland Hill who had now joined him after operating in the south, was still greatly outnumbered by the French. But their commanders would not oblige him; and, when his lines of communication with Portugal were once again threatened, he decided he must fall back still further towards Ciudad Rodrigo and the frontier.

Day after day the rain poured down; and, largely through the incompetence of a socially well-connected, recently appointed and soon to be dismissed Quartermaster-General, supplies ran so short that men were driven to chewing acorns until they came across an immense number of black pigs which they attacked so recklessly that many of them were taken prisoner as they chased after them, firing wildly at their hindquarters. Yet hard as they found food to come by, the men seemed always able to get their hands on wine and were often as drunk as they had been during the withdrawal to San Cristobal. The officers, so the Commander-in-Chief considered, were quite as reprehensible as the men; and on one occasion three major-generals, William Stewart, the Earl of Dalhousie and John Oswald, all decided to disobey the Commander-in-Chief's orders.

Almost nothing could have been calculated to annoy Wellington more, since his determination to keep all matters under his own control made obedience to his orders essential. The chief of the army medical staff, James McGrigor, remembered only too clearly the rebuke he had himself received when he had redirected a party of wounded and medical supplies away from the route the Commander-in-Chief had laid down for them. On hearing what McGrigor had done, Wellington exploded in fury. 'I shall be glad to know who is to command the army, I or you?' he demanded 'in a passion'. 'I establish one route . . . you establish another . . . As long as you live, Sir, never do so again; never do anything without my orders.'

'But my Lord, the case was urgent: there was no time to get your orders.'

'That don't signify. Never act again without orders, be the consequences what they may.'

Even when Dr McGrigor's decision proved to be the right one,

Wellington was not prepared to overlook the disobedience. 'It is all right, as it turned out,' he conceded reluctantly. 'But I recommend you still to have my orders for what you do.'*[7]

So it was with the disobedient major-generals. When he discovered that, ignoring his orders, they had taken the infantry on a different road from the one prescribed, thus endangering the whole army, he was speechless with anger when he came upon them. What had he eventually said to them, Lord Fitzroy Somerset was asked. 'Oh, by God,' Somerset replied, 'it was too serious to say anything.' Yet the incident was forgotten before long; the Commander-in-Chief remained on perfectly amicable terms with the three men, all of whom served with him until the end of the war in the Peninsula; and 'no further allusion was made to what had occurred'.[8]

Upon the army's arrival in Ciudad Rodrigo, however, the Commander-in-Chief was not prepared to allow the general disobedience of officers to go unnoticed. They were reminded of the necessity of paying 'minute and constant attention' to the orders they received. They were reminded of much else besides in a circular addressed to commanding officers which was much resented when its contents became more widely known and were actually printed in the 'rascally London newspapers'. It was written, so Dr McGrigor said, just before its ill-humoured author had read an issue of Cobbett's *Weekly Political Register* which his wife might well have omitted from the packets she sent him. Although he knew only too well what to expect from Cobbett's pen, he read the paper before throwing it into the fire. He then read out to the doctor what he had written in his circular.

He reprimanded officers for losing 'all control over their men', for their 'habitual inattention to their duty'. He declared that the army had suffered no privations which 'trifling attention on the part of the officers could not have prevented'. Then, having offended the officers, he annoyed the men by complaining of their disgraceful behaviour during the withdrawal and of their slowness in cooking when compared with that of French soldiers – a complaint that seemed to them particularly unjust having regard to the efficiency of the equipment that the French

---

* It should be added that Wellington was as ready to forgive a good man as to upbraid him, provided that he did not actually have to apologize to him. After this altercation with Dr McGrigor he asked him to dinner and had him sit next to him, showing him 'unusual civility and marked attention' (*The Autobiography and Services of Sir James McGrigor*, 302). At the end of the war he gave full credit to the doctor as 'one of the most industrious, able, and successful public servants' he had 'ever met with' (Gurwood, *Dispatches*, vii, 643).

carried about with them compared with the clumsy iron kettles with which the British army was inadequately supplied, let alone the fact that on the withdrawal to Ciudad Rodrigo there had been precious little to cook anyway.[9]

It was a sad end to an otherwise successful campaign. It was better not to think of the disastrous failure at Burgos and the subsequent retreat. Yet even the withdrawal was a creditable achievement: Wellington had brought back his army with Soult's men, almost twice as numerous, close upon its heels; and had sent home almost 20,000 French prisoners. Since he had set out from Portugal after Massena in April the year before, he had won notable victories over the French and inflicted many casualties. Soult had been drawn out of Andalusia, southern Spain was free and guerrilla bands were active wherever the French were encamped. Above all, while the Grande Armée had perished in the Russian snow, his own army was still in existence. It would soon be ready for the long march to the Pyrenees.

The men, well fed again and able to buy cheap wine and tobacco, forgot their recent grumbles and almost forgave old 'Nosey' for his strictures upon their conduct. He was, perhaps, they were prepared in their more contented moments to concede, not such a bad fellow really. They heard how, after the assault on Ciudad Rodrigo, he had ridden thirty miles to see some wounded men who, so he had been told, were lying in roughly constructed and bitterly cold bivouacs. He had given orders for them to be carried inside the officers' quarters and had gone back the next night to ensure that his orders had been carried out. They had not been: he had seen to it himself that they were and had the officers responsible brought to a court-martial. Since then bivouacs had not been seen. They had been replaced by tents which were carried by mules; and officers who had been using these animals to carry their personal baggage had to find other means of transport.

> The army have Lord Wellington to thank principally for this [the Advocate-General commented]. Last year the mules per company allowed by Government were employed in carrying the heavy iron camp-kettles, and our men had no tents; though they were allowed them, they could not be carried. This year Lord Wellington had light tin kettles made, one for every six men, for the mess, to be carried by one of the men, each having a small cooking machine of tin besides.

This plan sets the mules free and disposable, and thus three tents have been carried for every company, and allowing for absentees, guards, officers' servants, sentries, &c.; this now nearly houses or covers all our men, and contributes much to the health of the army. It was entirely an arrangement of his own.[10]

'We were not pleased with Lord Wellington at the beginning of the Winter,' Captain Bragge commented. 'He has now given the Infantry Tents . . . Therefore he is again a fine Fellow.'[11]

Soon after being appointed Generalissimo of the Spanish forces and created Duque da Victoria by the Portuguese, Wellington learned that the Prince Regent had added to his English honours by conferring upon him the Order of the Garter, whose blue ribbon he was not sure should be worn over the right shoulder or the left. But no honour appeared to please him more than his appointment as Colonel of the Royal Regiment of Horse Guards, an appointment which elicited from him the grateful comment that there 'was never so fortunate or so favoured a man'.[12]

He was certainly an active one. His command of the Spanish forces took him to Cadiz where he was greeted rapturously by the inhabitants and presented with trappings for his horse, richly embroidered by the ladies of the town. He conferred with the Spanish Regency, delivered a speech to the Cortes in their own language, which he spoke forcefully with a strong accent; he gave orders to Spanish generals; and he came away with a profound distaste for the murky waters of Spanish politics and an undiminished distrust of the efficiency of Spanish army officers. However, he would, of course 'fight for Spain as long as she [was] the enemy of France, whatever might be her system of government'.[13]

He then rode back to Lisbon for further conferences, more negotiations, prolonged discussions. His time was not given over entirely to business, though. On the anniversary of the capture of Ciudad Rodrigo he presided over a grand banquet; also there were performances at the opera to attend; there were theatricals performed by the Light Division at Gallegos; there was a ball at Rodrigo, attended by two hundred guests, from which the Commander-in-Chief rode the seventeen miles back to headquarters by moonlight.

At headquarters he gave due thought to the coming spring's campaign which would, he hoped, rid all Spain of French troops. Many had already been withdrawn in obedience to the Emperor's calls for drafts to reinforce his armies beyond the Pyrenees; but there were a good 20,000 still left in the Peninsula. There was a strong rearguard in Madrid; there were known to be several brigades around King Joseph's headquarters at Valladolid. Marshal Clauzel was still in Spain; so was General Gazan; so was Comte d'Erlon who had distinguished himself at Jena and Friedland; and so was King Joseph's military adviser, Marshal Jourdan.

To force the French back across the Pyrenees would need great skill; and there were few, very few generals upon whom Wellington could rely to help him in his task. Certainly there were only three or four at present in the Peninsula whom he could trust to carry out his orders as unquestioningly as Pakenham did. He contrived to get some of the worst sent home without too much damage to their self-esteem and made it clear that he needed no replacements to serve in the forthcoming campaign.[14] 'Really,' he said, 'they do but little good.' As for seconds-in-command, he still 'would not admit their existence'.[15]

What form the new campaign was to take no one knew, for the Commander-in-Chief was as unwilling as ever to allow his staff to know what he had in mind.

He had, in fact, decided to make the attempt to 'hustle the French out of Spain' by sweeping northwards and, by repeated threats to their lines of communication, to push them back beyond the Ebro. He would avoid all frontal attacks on strong positions where the enemy might invite him to battle, but he would oblige them to withdraw by feeling his way around them until he could bring them to fight on his own terms with their backs to the mountains.

20 From Vitoria to the Frontier

1812 – 13

'No officer dared to interfere.'

WELLINGTON left for the Spanish frontier in May 1813, turning in his saddle as he rode across it and waving his hat – in one of those theatrical gestures to which he was occasionally and unexpectedly prone – as he called out, 'Farewell, Portugal I shall never see you again.'[1]

As the French withdrew across the Douro, his men marched into Spain, greeted excitedly in village after village where church bells pealed, flowers were scattered on the soldiers' heads from windows and balconies, girls beat tambourines, young men stamped their heels as they kept pace with the soldiers down the streets, performing fandangos and boleros as accompaniments to the rhythmical tramp of the marching feet.

The tiring march went on through Zamora and Léon towards the fast-flowing river Esla, a tributary of the Douro. This was a formidable obstacle, and several men were swept away in the torrent as they tried to cross the ford of Almendra before a pontoon bridge was erected for the rest of the British force. But soon after the last man was across the entire British army – which Wellington had divided so that the French might be left in doubt as to which of the two columns was the main thrust – was reunited near Tordesillas and ready to march together for Burgos, supplied now through the port of Santander on Spain's northern coast.

The enemy, having evacuated Valladolid and Palencia, were prepared to make a stand here; but Wellington saved himself a siege by manoeuvring them out of the town and obliging them to blow up the castle which was destroyed in a thunderous explosion that blew out the windows of the white Gothic Cathedral, founded in the thirteenth century by Ferdinand III of Castile.

Over the Ebro the British troops tramped and into the small Basque province of Alava, through fertile valleys, beneath mountains clothed in oak and chestnut trees until, at last, having marched 400 miles in forty days, they came to face the French at Alava's capital, Vitoria.

King Joseph's army, 60,000 strong, stood here, with 150 guns, in extended lines almost twelve miles long south of the river Zadorra over which none of the bridges had been mined. Wellington brought against them some 80,000 men with 70 guns and he unleashed them against the enemy in four immense columns.[2] The battle was fiercely fought from ten o'clock in the morning of 21 June 1813 till past six in the evening, the Commander-in-Chief exhibiting throughout what one of his officers called 'the sangfroid of an indifferent spectator'.[3] At one point in the battle, so Captain Kincaid of the 95th recorded:

> One of their shells burst immediately under my nose, part of it struck my boot and stirrup-iron, and the rest of it kicked up such a dust about me that my charger refused to obey orders; and while I was spurring and he capering, I heard a voice behind me, which I knew to be Lord Wellington's, calling out, in a tone of reproof, 'Look to keeping your men together, sir!' and though, God knows, I had not the remotest idea that he was within a mile of me at the time, yet so sensible was I that circumstances warranted his supposing that I was a young officer, cutting a caper, by way of bravado, before him, that worlds would not have tempted me to look round at that moment.[4]

The French, compelled at last to give way, retreated towards Pamplona to scurry over the Pyrenean passes, abandoning all but seven of their guns and an immense amount of ammunition and stores as well as baggage, wagons, three thousand carriages, chests full of money, eagles, standards, horses, mules, pet monkeys and parrots.[5] King Joseph's coach, from which its occupants had fled when fired upon, was captured by Captain Henry Wyndham of the 14th Light Dragoons and Wellington's aide-de-camp, the Marquess of Worcester. Inside were discovered a number of rolled-up canvases looted from the palace of the Spanish King, as well as a large number of state papers, several love-letters written to King Joseph by his mistresses, a quantity of other letters addressed to him by his wife and three daughters, and his silver chamber pot.*

* The chamber pot is still in the possession of Captain Wyndham's regiment which is now, by amalgamation with other regiments, known as the King's Royal Hussars. Called 'the Emperor' it is sent for by the commanding officer of the Regiment just before the end of a guest night. He drinks a toast to 'the Emperor' from the pot which contains champagne. The pot is then taken by the Mess Sergeant Major to other members and guests who repeat the toast. The commanding officer then selects an officer to finish the champagne in the pot. If he cannot do so he is expected to tip what is left over his head.

Also abandoned were several of the numerous women who had been following the army and King Joseph's court and had led to the whole host being described by one of their number as '*un bordel ambulant*'.[6] 'Most of these ladies,' August Schaumann reported, 'were young and good-looking Spanish women, dressed in fancy hussar uniforms and mounted on pretty ponies . . . All they wanted was protection and a new lover, both of which they soon obtained, and they were to be had for the asking.'[7]

One of those left behind was Mme Gazan, General Count Gazan's wife, whom Wellington later invited to dinner. She was asked if another well-dressed lady was also a General's wife and perhaps should be invited too. '*Ah, pour cela*,' Madame Gazan replied, '*non. Elle est seulement sa femme de campagne*.'[8]

As well as these women and most of their treasure, the French had lost some 5,000 killed and wounded and 3,000 prisoners, the casualties of the allies being also about 5,000, of whom 1,600 were Spanish and Portuguese.[9]

Hundreds of the survivors of the battle poured into Vitoria to plunder the treasure and paraphernalia that the French had left behind. They ransacked cases of Spanish dollars and tried on French generals' uniforms and ladies' dresses 'richly embroidered in gold and silver'.[10] In the Campillo they held an auction to dispose of pictures, books, tapestries, church plate, watches, jewels, silver brandy cups, medals and all the trinkets and bric-à-brac that had fallen into the allies' hands.

> The ground all round the town was littered with broken wagons of all kinds [August Schaumann wrote], boxes, cases, trunks and baggage, while masses of papers, maps, account books, and letters lay about as thick as snow . . . I saw huge and beautifully kept ledgers belonging to the Royal Treasury, wonderful maps and expensively bound books trodden under foot and sodden with the rain . . . [Over this loot] men fought to the death. In short, more thorough and more scandalous plundering has never been known, and I heard later that Lord Wellington was most indignant and angry about it.[11]

King Joseph's letters from his wife and daughters, having been handed over to the Commander-in-Chief, were subsequently sent back to France by the seventh Duke of Wellington (*Archives de Joseph Bonaparte, roi de Naples, puis d'Espagne*, Inventaire par Chantal de Tourtier-Bonazzi, Paris, 1982).

'In the midst of all this hurly burly, frolic and fun, the belley was not forgotten,' wrote Private Wheeler. 'An hundred fires were occupied in preparing food . . . One of our men walked into camp having a large table cloth tied by the four corners, it contained dishes, tureens, plates, knives and silver forks. He had found it ready laid.'[12]

Marshal Jourdan's marshal's baton was packed up and, together with King Joseph's sword, despatched in the Commander-in-Chief's name to the Prince Regent who replied with extravagant grace, 'You have sent me, among the trophies of your unrivalled fame, the staff of a French Marshal, and I send you in return that of England.'[13] The rank was welcome enough, but its symbol had to wait, since, as the Regent's brother, the Duke of York, could have told him, there was no such thing as a British field marshal's baton, a desideratum which the Regent said he would satisfy by designing one himself.*

While his soldiers were filling their pockets and knapsacks with what they could conveniently carry and pushing what they could not take with them onto wagons, the pursuit of the French was being very inefficiently conducted. The Commander-in-Chief, who had, as usual, been galloping about the battlefield, supervising attacks, delivering orders personally, rushing from one vantage point to another to get a better view of the developing movements of his troops, now endeavoured to direct the pursuit in the same way.

As always, one officer grumbled, voicing a common enough complaint, he was reluctant to trust officers to act on their own initiative, 'according to circumstances'. 'I am not quite clear if he approves of much success, excepting under his own immediate eye.'[14]

The sometimes unfortunate consequences of his determination to keep operations under his own control, and his insistence upon having his orders implicitly obeyed, were demonstrated after the battle by his dealings with an artillery officer, Captain William Norman Ramsay, who, through some misdirection of orders, was marching up the wrong road. Wellington personally ordered him to stop and to remain where he was until the Field Marshal himself came back with further instructions. After Wellington had galloped off, Ramsay received further orders which he wrongly presumed had come from the Commander-in-Chief.

---

* 'It does not appear that there ever has been an English baton,' Colonel Henry Torrens, Military Secretary at the Horse Guards, explained; 'and no better occasion can ever occur of establishing one than the present. I am therefore getting one prepared to present to each of our Marshals; and if I am not interfered with from *the fountain of taste*, I trust it will be found an appropriate badge of command' (Wellington Supplementary Dispatches, viii, 95).

He moved off in obedience to them, and was consequently put under arrest by Wellington, since he had 'disobeyed a positive order' given to him by the Commander-in-Chief. After both Colonel Frederic Ponsonby, commanding officer of the 12th Light Dragoons, and Sir Thomas Graham had interceded with Wellington on Ramsay's behalf, he was released from arrest, though not before the Commander-in-Chief had explained that there had been so much disobedience by officers of late that he 'had determined to make an example of Captn. Ramsay'. Ramsay's promotion, soon afterwards requested by the Horse Guards, was blocked and, despite his distinguished services, he had risen no higher than the rank of major two years later at Waterloo where Wellington 'spoke kindly to him as he rode down the line'. 'Ramsay did not answer, merely bowed his head gravely' and at four o'clock was killed by a bullet which, passing through his snuff box, entered his heart.[15]

To organize a proper pursuit after the allied victory at Vitoria proved quite impossible. Surrounded by such tempting plunder, so many thousands of dollars spilling from boxes, such enticing treasures and such a profusion of delicacies intended for French officers' mess tables, the men were uncontrollable. 'No officer dared to interfere,' said one observer of the scene who might have added that several officers were too busy helping themselves to think of interfering, and that others had got so drunk the night before on the fine French wines discovered in a hotel that their fearful hangovers virtually incapacitated them.[16] Only a few men from two of the nine cavalry brigades took any part in what should have been a close pursuit of the retreating enemy.

We started with the Army in the highest order, & up to the day of the Battle nothing could get on better [Wellington reported to the Secretary for War]. But that event has as usual totally annihilated all order and discipline. The soldiers of the Army have got among them about a million sterling in money, with the exception of about 100,000 dollars which were got for the military chest. The night of the Battle, instead of being passed in getting rest and food, to prepare them for pursuit the following day, was spent by the soldiers in looking for plunder. The consequence was that they were incapable of marching in pursuit of the Enemy, & were totally knocked up . . .

This is the consequence of the state of discipline of the British Army. We may gain the greatest Victories; but we shall do no good until we shall so far alter our system as to force the officers of the junior ranks to perform their duty, & shall have some mode of punishing them for Neglect.[17]

A month after the battle of Vitoria, Wellington was standing in the churchyard at Lesaca a few miles from the French frontier waiting for news from San Sebastian which Sir Thomas Graham's parties had assaulted at dawn. At eleven he was told that the attack had failed with heavy losses; and later that day he learned that the centre and right of his own line were under heavy attack.

Marshal Soult – whom Napoleon had sent to Bayonne after the disaster at Vitoria with orders to 're-establish the Imperial business in Spain' – having pulled the French army together with remarkable speed and efficiency, had resolved on an ambitious plan. Instead of going to the relief of San Sebastian, as Wellington had expected he would, he had decided to launch an attack on the allied centre and right, to advance to the relief of Pamplona and then sweep round behind Wellington's rear towards the coast.

By 28 July he had almost succeeded. Wellington's subordinates, spread out on so long a front and lost without the guidance of their leader, had felt obliged to fall back almost as far as Pamplona. Lowry Cole, after two sleepless nights, was out of his depth in command of the 4th Division. General Picton of the 3rd was far from confident when unable to rely upon Wellington's decisive hand. Sir William Stewart of the 2nd was also in his mind when Wellington complained, 'They are really heroes when I am on the spot to direct them, but when I am obliged to quit them they are children.'[18] He had to confess, though, that he should never have attempted to take San Sebastian and Pamplona at the same time. It was, he thought, 'one of the greatest faults he had ever committed in war'.[19] He hated these 'extended operations which he could not direct himself'.[20]

He soon made amends, however. Galloping across to Sorauren, six miles from Pamplona, to reach his right wing before Soult attacked it, he arrived just in time. Fierce battles were fought here on 28 and 30 July and the British troops, so their Commander said, had never behaved so well. The Spanish, too, fought bravely, while the Portuguese were 'the fighting cocks of the army'.[21] For a time it had been 'rather alarming', so Wellington admitted when recalling this 'close run thing',[22] but the enemy was repulsed at Sorauren; and, although the pursuit was again bungled – provoking Wellington to observe that if he had 'any others but Gallant Officers to deal with' he could have taken the whole French army[23] – Soult failed in his attempt to march across the British flank to the relief of San Sebastian, was mauled again and had no alternative but to retreat beyond the Spanish frontier into France.[24]

Wellington was ready to go after him, though he hesitated for the time being to do so, much concerned that the 40,000 unpaid and ill-fed Spanish troops under his command 'must plunder and set the whole country against us', and that an invasion of their homeland might arouse a fierce patriotism among the French people.[25] He was not much less worried about the British soldiers' likely plundering; and, in the mood of despondency that occasionally overcame him that summer, he would rail at the behaviour and character of his men. They were 'the scum of the earth as common soldiers', he was later to maintain, since 'none but the worst description of men enter the regular service ... The English soldiers are fellows who have all enlisted for drink ... People talk of their enlisting from their fine military feeling – all stuff – no such thing. Some of our men enlist from having got bastard children – some for minor offences – many more for drink. But you can hardly conceive such a set brought together.' And the non-commissioned officers were quite 'as bad as the men'. There was 'no crime recorded in the Newgate Calendar' that was not committed by these soldiers 'who were constantly quitting their ranks in search of plunder'.[26]

They had done so after the storming of San Sebastian which had been taken on 31 August 1813 with the loss of some 3,500 allied soldiers after a heroic resistance by the French under General Louis Emanuel Rey, Wellington having sent men clambering over the breaches of the walls as though they were, in the words of Field Marshal Sir William Gomm, then a lieutenant-colonel in the 9th Foot, 'no more than mice in an air pump'.[27] The capture of the town, due more to good fortune than tactical skill, was followed by a three-day orgy of looting and atrocities quite as horrifying as those witnessed at Badajoz in 1811 and characterized by what Sir William Napier described as 'the most revolting cruelty' by the drunken, uncontrollable British troops.[28] 'One atrocity of which a girl of seventeen was the victim, staggers the mind by its enormous, incredible, indescribable barbarity.'[29]

August Schaumann later visited San Sebastian and found the 'traces of the siege visible everywhere'.

All the roofs were off the buildings. The doors, windows, staircases and floors of the houses had been used as fuel, the walls were perforated by the cannon-balls from the castle, the gardens were devastated, and the whole place was deserted. A stillness as of death reigned everywhere.

The roads were blocked by *débris*, broken furniture, heaps of rags, crushed shakos, bandoleers, cartridge boxes, broken weapons, shells, fragments of bombs, and corpses already in an advanced state of decomposition; and a pestilential stench hung about the ruins. Apart from a few survivors among the inhabitants who, with faces grown wild and haggard from hunger, anxiety and sorrow, were groping about among the ruins of their former homes, there was nobody to be seen.[*30]

In his less censorious moods, Wellington felt constrained to admit that, for all their passion for drink and plunder, provided they could 'only be kept in their ranks during battle', British soldiers constituted 'an unrivalled army for fighting'. His was, in fact, he eventually decided, an army which was 'probably the most complete machine for its numbers now existing in Europe'. He would 'venture to say, there never was an army in the world in better spirits, better order or better discipline'; he could have 'done *anything*' with it, it was 'in such splendid order'.[31] It was 'really wonderful', considering the raw material upon which their officers had to work, that they were turned into the 'fine fellows' they were. Even the officers were now as likely to be praised as castigated. There appeared to be 'a new spirit among the officers' who were now much more capable of keeping the troops in order. As for the general officers, they found the Commander-in-Chief far more willing than in the past to let them have a certain independence of command. On the last day of the fierce fighting on the Nive, Sir Rowland Hill, in command of the right of the army, defeated the French

---

* 'Virtually all of the great port was destroyed,' Dr Gates comments, 'deliberately, many Spanish believed, for it had always been a rival to Britain's own commercial centres. The issue soured Anglo-Spanish relations for months to come' (David Gates, *The Spanish Ulcer: A History of the Peninsular War*, 426). When it was suggested in a Cadiz newspaper that St Sebastian 'had been ill-treated because its former trade had been exclusively with the French nation to the disadvantage of Great Britain', Wellington angrily denied the charge. The soldiers could not be expected to know anything about the trade of St Sebastian, while 'so far from the principal officers having harboured so infamous a wish as to destroy the town from motives of commercial revenge, they had done all in their power to prevent it'. He told his brother Henry he was 'never so much disgusted with anything as with this libel' ([Lord William Lennox], *Three Years with the Duke . . . by an Ex-Aide-de-Camp*, 178–9).

at St Pierre unaided and was warmly congratulated by Wellington for having done so: 'My dear Hill, the day's your own.'[32] He had always liked and approved of Hill, who was, in fact, an officer of no very exceptional skill but who had one great merit in Wellington's eyes: 'Hill always does what he is told.'[33]

While readier than he had been in the past to give due credit to his officers, Wellington never relaxed in his efforts to take due care of their men. He saw to it that, so far as it was possible, they were decently clothed, well supplied and well fed; and he took great pride in the belief that they had never been reduced to eating horseflesh, as the French had been. He had himself seen French soldiers at the battle of Fuentes de Oñoro driving off dead horses in bullock-carts 'to be cooked and eaten in another part of the field'.[34] But then the French would eat anything, even rats and – so a Portuguese assured him – cats.[35]

It was 'very necessary to attend to all this detail of proper food supply', he said, and 'to trace a biscuit from its being landed at a Peninsular port into the man's mouth, and to provide for its removal from place to place, by land or by water'.*[36] It was also necessary, he insisted, that the Government should pay allowances to soldiers' families to encourage more decent men to enlist, to get into the Army the kind of men that the French got into theirs by conscription, a method of enlistment which called out 'a share of every class'. As it was, the families of British soldiers were as often as not left to the mercy of the parish or, in the case of Irish soldiers, 'on a dunghill to starve'.

Knowing that he looked after their interests in this way, his men

---

* Despite his efforts to keep the army well supplied, his soldiers were frequently hungry; and their accounts of their experiences in the Peninsula make reference to this. The anonymous author of the *Journal of a Soldier of the 71st*, for example, writes much of his hunger during the campaign and describes how thankful he was to be able to steal a bit of beef from a comrade's haversack, how another soldier in his regiment was caught chewing a piece of meat which was seen to be the forearm of a man discovered outside a hospital – 'the man threw it away but never looked squeamish; he said it was very sweet' – and how, when sent on fatigue to 'break biscuit and make a mess for Lord Wellington's hounds', he eagerly took the opportunity to assuage his own hunger (Hibbert, *A Soldier of the 71st*, 74, 76). It was generally recognized, however, that Wellington did all he could to ensure that his men were as well fed as possible. 'It is true that we were sometimes badly off for biscuit,' Private Wheeler wrote. 'But taking everything into consideration no army could be fed better. Indeed it is a mystery to thousands how we were supplied so regular as we were ... If England should require the service of her army again, let me have "Old Nosey" to command. Our interests would be sure to be looked into ... and we should always be as well supplied with rations as the nature of the service would admit' (*The Letters of Private Wheeler*, 196).

were prepared not only to obey the orders that came down to them from him, but on occasions to demonstrate their regard. They might refer to 'Atty' slightingly, insultingly on occasions, or, as one of them did in the presence of a shocked staff officer, as 'that long-nosed bugger that whops the French'.[37] They might, when painfully wounded, even curse him to his face as did an Irish soldier who had had both of his legs shot off at Burgos and who called out to him, 'Arrah, may be yer satisfied now, you hooky-nosed vagabond!'[38] But when they saw the easily recognized, frock-coated figure sitting straight-backed upon his horse before a battle they were comforted by the sight of him and on occasions ready to cheer him. 'Where's ar Arthur?' a fusilier had asked of another at Albuera. 'I don't know. I don't see him.' 'Aw wish he wore here.'[39] Their officers felt the same. When he had come back from his visit to Beresford in the south in May 1811, just in time to take over from Sir Brent Spencer in command of the army at Fuentes de Oñoro, Captain Kincaid of the 95th had voiced the general relief at his return. 'I'll venture to say,' he wrote, 'that there was not a heart in that army that did not beat more lightly when we heard the joyful news of his arrival.' From the moment he joined the army Kincaid had harboured 'an intense desire' to get a look at his 'illustrious chief'. 'My curiosity did not remain long ungratified; for as our post was next the enemy, I found, when anything was to be done, that it was his also. He was just such a man as I had figured in my mind's eye; and I thought that the stranger would betray a grievous want of penetration who could not select Wellington from amid five hundred in the same uniform.' 'We would,' Kincaid added, 'rather see his long nose in the fight than a reinforcement of ten thousand men any day.'[40]

It could not be said, though, that Wellington was regarded with much affection by most regimental officers and their men; but they respected him and, in their way, they were proud of him. They would do for him, Wellington once said with satisfaction, 'what perhaps no one else can make them do'.[41] Years later he was asked how he could account for having so consistently beaten the French marshals. 'Well, the fact is,' he replied, 'their soldiers get them into scrapes, mine always got me out.'[42]

Under his leadership the army crossed the Bidassoa and the Nivelle and before the end of 1813 drove the French beyond the Nive. An ensign in the First Foot Guards who saw him for the first time as he crossed the frontier into France described him as looking 'very stern and grave; he was in deep meditation so long as I kept him in view and spoke to no one ... He rode a knowing-looking, thoroughbred horse, and wore a grey overcoat, Hessian boots, and a large cocked hat.'[43]

21   St Jean de Luz

1813

'I began to believe that the finger of God is
upon me.'

HEADQUARTERS were established at St Jean de Luz. It was for a
time almost as though the war were already over. Officers strolled along
by the Biscayan shore; church parades were held on the beach, dances
at the Mairie. If campaigning in an enemy country was like this, one
English officer observed, he never wanted to campaign in a friendly
one again. St Jean de Luz was such a pleasant contrast to Lesaca, the
town he had just left on the other side of the frontier. There the place
had been full of 'wounded and prisoners and mules and muleteers
innumerable, besides all the country people' who came 'to turn all they
had got into money':

> Noises of all sorts; *aguardente* being cried about; lemonade (that is
> dirty water and dark-brown sugar); here a large pig being killed in the
> street; another near it with a straw fire singeing it, and then a number
> of women cutting up and selling pieces of other pigs killed a few
> hours before. Suttlers and natives with their Don Quixote pigskins,
> all pouring wine to our half-boozy, weary soldiers . . . bad apples and
> pears, sour plums all offered for sale at the same moment.
>
> Perpetual quarrels take place about payment for these things
> between the soldiers of the three allied nations and the avaricious and
> unreasonable civilian natives; mostly however between Spaniards and
> Spaniards.[1]

In St Jean de Luz, on the other hand, there were 'as few quarrels as
there might have been in a garrison town at home'.[2] The Commander-
in-Chief could occasionally be seen riding about in the little town,
sometimes in a top hat rather than the cocked hat which usually
distinguished him, once or twice in the sky-blue coat of the Hatfield
Hunt which Lady Salisbury had given him. Occasionally he was to be
found playing whist, though not for high stakes.

He was anxious to ensure that the friendly relations between the French civilians and the invading allies were maintained.[3] The depredations of the troops after crossing the frontier had at first been appalling. One private, tried and hanged for rape, endeavoured to excuse himself with the plea that 'as he was now in France, he had thought it must be in order'.

Drunkenness was quite as prevalent in France as it had been in Spain, if not more so. 'Our Brigade is fortunately not Quartered in the Town,' wrote an officer in the 3rd Dragoons, 'or we should have lost half of the Men from Intoxication as the Vessels wrecked were full of Brandy, Rum and Beer. Two of our Men *are dead* and many more Dead drunk. I believe amongst Soldiers and Sailors 15 lost their lives from Drinking last Night.'[4] The Spanish troops had behaved with exceptional bravery at San Marcial above San Sebastian where, commanded by General Manoel Freire, they had defeated Soult's men without help from the British, Wellington having declined Freire's request for reinforcements with the words, 'Look, if I send you the English troops you ask for, they will win the battle; but as the French are already in retreat you may as well win it for yourselves.'[5]

But subsequently, the Spanish behaved quite as badly as Wellington had feared they might; and most of them had to be sent back across the border.

They seem verily to have pledged themselves to wreak vengeance on France, and to repay her for all she had done to them [wrote August Schaumann]. Their eyes were aflame. Every Frenchman who fell into their hands was ill-treated or secretly murdered. Before leaving a village they always plundered it and set it on fire ... But Lord Wellington, who was clever enough to see where such behaviour would lead [and could not spare troops to fight French partisans or to guard his supplies and lines of communication] issued one or two furious general orders, and, constituting his brother-in-law, General Pakenham, head of the military police, gave him the most stringent and solemn instructions to hang without trial or mercy any who were caught red-handed in *actu flagrante*. Pakenham, supported by a powerful guard and the provost-marshal, then began to ride up and down our columns like a raving lion seeking whom he might devour. His command, 'Let that scoundrel be hanged instantly!' was executed in a twinkling ... I saw the body of a Spanish muleteer, who had entered a house to steal apples, hanging from the window of that house as a warning to all marauders. In his mouth, which had fallen open in the process of strangulation, they had stuck an apple to show what he had coveted![6]

Within a short time such punishments had helped to restore order and 'the whole neighbourhood could not cease from singing the praises of our army, and its good behaviour and discipline'.

There were lapses, of course. After the crossing of the Nivelle, the men of the 52nd relieved a farmer of his pigs and poultry.

'Although the Brigade have even more than usually distinguished themselves, we must respect the property of the country,' Wellington told the 52nd's Commanding Officer, Colonel Colborne.

'I am fully aware of it, my Lord . . . In the very heat of action a little irregularity will occur.'

'Ah, ah! Stop it in future, Colborne.'[7]

The shopkeepers of St Jean de Luz – who were happy to exchange goods for sugar, of which the blockade had deprived them for several years – and the Gascon girls – who came down into the town from the surrounding farms wearing wooden clogs and red checked handker- chiefs on their heads, to sell butter and milk, eggs and chickens – looked upon the English soldiers, who were required to pay a fair price for their produce, almost as liberators. Certainly the soldiers now treated them far more considerately than the soldiers of the French army had done, and bought their produce with proper money rather than with the flattened regimental buttons which they had endeavoured and often contrived to pass off on to unsuspecting Spaniards.

> The French lasses are up with the sun [wrote a young officer in the King's German Legion], and ten or twelve of them are seen skipping along the road, with milk and butter, singing and laughing as uncon- cernedly as if all was peace and tranquillity; and when receiving their scanty demand for their articles of commerce they smile upon the hand which probably has curtailed some beloved relative's existence . . . The French Emperor has seized all capable of carrying arms and none but females and aged men are to be met with here.[8]

Unfortunately, it was quite impossible to talk to them since their language was 'utterly incomprehensible', being said to be 'the language spoken by Tubal, Noah's nephew', who came to these parts '143 years after the flood'.[9] Besides, the girls, though they would 'sing and dance and play the tambourine', were 'very shy of Englishmen'. The commis- sary Augustus Schaumann said that in Navarre he had to make do with the beauties among the soldiers' wives. He had, like others, been far luckier in Spain where, making a claim which was far from exceptional, he had 'plenty of love affairs'. In one town alone, so he said, he had had affairs with five different women at once. Two of these women were the daughters of a wealthy landowner and had proved 'very responsive', one was the wife of a Spanish colonel, the fourth a pretty girl who paid him 'many visits', and the fifth 'the legitimate spouse of an organist', who always availed herself of her husband's duties in the church in order to come to him.[10]

Amicable as relations were between the civilians and the soldiers in St Jean de Luz, so were they at the front where officers and men alike were anxious to avoid 'unnecessary waste of life in petty outpost bickering'. Not only was there very little interference with sentries once the two lines of pickets had been laid out, there was a great deal of fraternization. Indeed, there had also been in Spain where French and British soldiers had been seen laughing and joking together as they dug up potatoes with their bayonets between the opposing lines, and where, at Fuentes de Oñoro during a truce agreed for carrying off the wounded and burying the dead, men shook hands with their opponents and, having run back to their own lines, took off their caps and cheered each other.

Time and again French outposts would give British pickets notice of an imminent attack by shouting across the lines, 'Courez vite, courez vite. On va vous attaquer.' Wellington encouraged his own men to do the same. 'The killing of a poor fellow of a vedette or carrying off a post could not influence the battle,' he told J.W. Croker, 'and I always when I was going to attack sent to tell them to get out of the way.'[11]

To shoot an exposed sentry was unthinkable, and if a French or British officer thought an enemy outpost was too far forward he would send a message through the hedge or across the stream that divided the two armies with a request that the outpost be moved farther back. Often cheerful conversations were carried on in pidgin Spanish and the bartering of food and liquor was common. Once a bullock, issued as rations to a French regiment, escaped from the butcher and charged into the British lines. A French delegation came over and begged to have it back, as they had been without meat for a week; so the English sent half of it back with a bucket of loaves as compensation for the rest and with the apology that they had felt obliged to cut the animal in half as beef was 'not too common' in their quarters either. On another occasion a company of riflemen 'clubbed half a dollar' each to send a man across to the French to buy brandy. The representative unfortunately sampled so much of his large purchase that he was incapable of carrying the remainder back, and the French had to shout for the other members of the syndicate to come and get him. It was not impossible to find a sentry with French and English muskets slung over his shoulder guarding a bridge on behalf of both armies.[12]

'The most unbounded confidence existed between us,' wrote William Surtees, a quartermaster in the 95th Rifles. The French 'used to get us such things as we wanted from Bayonne, particularly brandy . . . and we in turn gave them a little tea of which some of them had learnt to be fond. Some of them also who had been prisoners of war in England sent letters through our army-post to their sweethearts in England.'

Concerned that the enemy might learn more than he wished them to know by means of this fraternization, Wellington ultimately issued an order putting an end to the friendly conversations between the two sides, Surtees recorded, 'for, as all these conversations were necessarily conducted in French, (very few indeed of their officers being able to speak English), he was apprehensive they might gain such information from our people, from their imperfect knowledge of the French language, as might materially injure our future proceedings.'[13]

The carefree attitude of units in the allied army is illustrated in an entry in the diary of Edmund Wheatley, a subaltern in a line battalion of the King's German Legion.

> About one o'clock in the morning I was reading in my tent when who should come in but Llewellyn [a fellow officer]. Surprised at this early visit and more so when he enquired where the Sentry was and said that no body was round the fire, out I sallied with a candle and found the Sentry dead drunk and Corporal Einer insensible by the fire with one man, and the other man missing. All the kicking possible could not revive them and I was obliged to stand Sentry myself till day break, Llewellyn cooking the coffee.
>
> On arousing Corporal Einer, I discovered a couple of muleteers had been treating them with aqua dentae, a bottle of which I discovered under some furze . . . And after a fatiguing search, I found [the missing man] in a bush stripped naked and frozen to death.
>
> Not knowing how to conceal this unpleasant business from the Colonel I determined to screen the poor fellows. So digging a deep hole we buried the man and I reported him as having deserted to the enemy. The other three would go to the Devil for me now. But should it be discovered I shall go to Him myself I fear.[14]

*

Towards the end of February the lull in the fighting came to an end. The allied army crossed the Adour and encircled Bayonne, where the garrison was left to be blockaded by Sir John Hope of whose attainments Wellington 'had long entertained the highest opinion'. In the final sortie of the French garrison, Hope was wounded and, for a short time, held prisoner.

Not long before, Wellington had almost been captured himself while undertaking a personal reconnaissance on the banks of the Adour. It was not the first time that this had happened of late. At Sorauen he and Lord Fitzroy Somerset had galloped ahead of the rest of the staff towards the bridge over the Lanz and, leaning over the parapet, Wellington had scribbled orders for the 6th Division on a sheet of paper with which Lord Fitzroy dashed off. Wellington also galloped away a minute or two before the French light cavalry entered the village.[15] 'I escaped as usual unhurt,' he reported to his brother William. 'I began to believe,' he added, using a phrase which he was often to repeat in the future, 'that the finger of God is upon me.'[16]

He was not so lucky in France. He was riding along one day with Alava when the Spaniard cried out that he had been struck in the bottom. Amused by the poor man's predicament, Wellington burst out laughing – or, so another version of the story went, both men were laughing at a Portuguese soldier who said he had been '*offendido*' by a French shot – when Wellington himself was hit by a spent bullet which knocked the hilt of his sword into his thigh, causing a most painful injury. He was advised not to ride until it was better; but he was soon in the saddle again making for the Garonne.[17]

The war was almost over now. By the Treaty of Chaumont signed at the beginning of March, Austria, Russia, Prussia and Britain had undertaken not to negotiate a separate peace but to continue the struggle against Napoleon until he was overthrown. At the end of that month strong forces of the allies arrived on the outskirts of Paris; and, when Napoleon moved out to attack their rearguard, the Parisian authorities entered into negotiations with them. Prince Talleyrand, as president of a provisional government, declared the Emperor had been deposed and invited King Louis XVIII to ascend the throne which his executed brother had occupied before the Revolution.

Rumours of all this reached the British headquarters in Gascony and on 10 April there came unconfirmed reports that the Prussian Commander-in-Chief had actually entered Paris. It was 'earnestly hoped' at the Horse Guards in London that there would be no further action by the British army in France. But Wellington, who had told an officer not to believe anything he might hear in France, had already issued orders for an attack upon Toulouse.

He had some 49,000 men under command with over fifty guns. They faced 42,000 French troops. The assault began in the early hours of the morning of 10 April, Easter Sunday. It was to be one of the fiercest battles of the whole war, a 'very severe affair', as Wellington himself termed it.[18] The allies lost 4,600 men, the French 3,200. When Soult quietly withdrew to Carcassonne during the night of 11 April, Napoleon had already abdicated.[19]

The news was brought to Wellington by Colonel Frederic Ponsonby soon after the Commander-in-Chief had ridden into Toulouse. Ponsonby found him in his shirt sleeves, dressing for dinner.

'I have extraordinary news for you.'

'Ay, I thought so. I knew we should have peace. I've long expected it.'

'No. Napoleon has abdicated.'

'How abdicated! Ay, 'tis time indeed,' Wellington declared. 'You don't say so, upon my honour! Hoorah!'

Then, giving way to that exuberance which had prompted him to wave his hat in the air on coming into Spain from Portugal the year before, he spun round snapping his fingers in a lively parody of a Spanish dance.[20]

It was a time for celebration. There was a dinner at the Préfecture that night, followed by a ball. Wellington proposed a toast to King Louis XVIII of France; Alava responded with one to 'El Liberador de España'. Others stood up to toast the Liberator in their own languages. The uproar lasted for ten minutes at the end of which Wellington stood up, 'bowed, confused, and immediately called for coffee'.[21]

There were more loud cheers and shouting at the theatre where, during a performance of Grétry's *Richard Coeur de Lion*, Wellington displayed his hat on the front of the box to show that he had placed in it a cockade in the royal colours of France.

22 In London Again

1814

'It's a fine thing to be a great man, is it not?'

'I BELIEVE I forgot to tell you,' Wellington ended a letter to his brother Henry, 'I was made a Duke.'[1]

He was also appointed Ambassador in Paris, a post which Henry thought he would find 'very pretty amusement'. Wellington considered it a situation for which he would 'never have thought [himself] qualified'; but he knew that he 'must serve the public in some manner or other', and he had, after all, by now a good deal of experience of diplomacy in dealing with the allies in the war. Nor did he particularly want to go home: although he had 'been so long from England', he felt 'no objection to another absence in the public service'.[2]

He arrived in Paris at the beginning of May, entering the city, in strong contrast to the many other generals there, in civilian clothes of a blue frock-coat, white neck-cloth and top hat. It seemed to be a city en fête rather than the capital of a defeated country. There were military parades, balls, receptions, picnics, parties. English officers prided themselves on 'imitating the Duke of Wellington in nonchalance and coolness of manner', observed Sir Walter Scott whose admiration of the Duke was unbounded.

> So they wander about everywhere with their hands in the pockets of their long waistcoats or cantering upon cossack ponies staring, whistling and strolling to and fro as if all Paris was theirs. The French hate them sufficiently for the hauteur of their manner and pretensions but these grounds of dislike against us are drowned in the detestation afforded by the other powers.[3]

King Louis XVIII, complacently accepting the throne which had been restored to his family, was host to three other European sovereigns, the King of Prussia, the Emperor of Austria and the Czar of All the Russias. Numerous statesmen were gathered there, too, as well as generals. Lord and Lady Castlereagh had come over from England. With them was Castlereagh's half-brother, Major-General Sir Charles Stewart, soon to be appointed British Ambassador in Vienna. Also in Paris were Klemens, Fürst von Metternich, the Austrian Foreign Minister, the French cavalry general, Marshal Ney, in Napoleon's words 'the bravest of the brave', who had thrown in his lot with Louis XVIII, as well as the Russian Cossack leader, Count Platov, and the elaborately moustached Prussian Field Marshal Gebhard Leberecht, Fürst Blücher von Wahlstatt. Wellington encountered all of them. He praised Platov's horsemen as they marched past: 'Well, to be sure, we can't turn out anything like this'; and he tried to pay a compliment to Blücher but, though an interpreter offered his services, conversation was difficult and the old Field Marshal looked as though he could not understand a word that was said. So the two men contented themselves with holding each other's hands and with 'a great deal of hearty smiling'.[4]

Before the end of May, the Duke, as men were learning to call him rather than 'the Peer' or 'the Beau', left Paris for Madrid to see King Ferdinand VII, that impulsive, sly and erratic monarch, recently released from Napoleon's imprisonment, whose bulbous nose and mock-pugnacious chin have been preserved for posterity in the portraits of Francisco de Goya. The Duke thought him 'by no means the idiot he is represented'; but he found his reactionary ministers exasperating and the formalities of the court irritating to a degree. The palace guards stamped their feet in saluting him. 'That is only done for a Grandee of the first order,' the King told him, as though this were the greatest of honours the world could bestow. 'You must, indeed, be a happy man.'[5]

He was glad to get away to the north again, across the Pyrenees and back through Gascony to Bordeaux where he wrote a last Order to the army which was now to be dispersed, the Spanish and Portuguese women who had followed it being left behind to make their own way home 'with much weeping and wailing on the part of the signoras'.[6]

He congratulated the men upon the 'recent events which have restored peace to their country and to the world'. 'He assures them,' he added with a rashness he was later to regret, 'that he shall never cease to feel the warmest interest in their welfare and honor; and that he will at all times be happy to be of any service to those to whose conduct, discipline, and gallantry their country is so much indebted.'[7]

It was a rare compliment. Time and again complaints had been made about the Commander-in-Chief's reluctance to recognize the distinguished services of individual officers and regiments. 'I don't like Lord Wellington's despatch,' runs one characteristic objection. 'I don't want to brag, but the best thing done . . . was the attack of the 43rd and he has not done the honour to mention our names.'[8] The Duke 'had great success', wrote another officer, Charles Napier, who had served in the Peninsula as aide-de-camp to General Craufurd and on Wellington's staff, 'but he repulsed the soldiers, and there are few of those who served under him who loved him as much as I do. He feels that he owes all to his own abilities, and he feels that justly; – but he should not show it, for his soldiers stood by him manfully.'[9]

Very rarely he was prevailed upon to add a word or two of praise to his dispatches. 'Is it usual?' he once abruptly asked Dr McGrigor, who had suggested that the untiring labours of the medical department might be given some sort of recognition.

It was certainly not usual; but McGrigor suggested it could do nothing but good. So, although he had finished his dispatch, Wellington agreed to 'add something about the doctors'.[10]

The Duke was as reluctant to praise individual officers in ordinary conversation as he was in his dispatches, 'though free enough in discussing the merits of those to whom he had been opposed'. 'Being pressed on one occasion to say which among them all he considered to be his most promising pupil,' George Gleig said, 'he replied, "That is not a fair question. It is not for me to answer it" . . . "But was not Moore a first rate officer?" "Moore was no pupil of mine. He was as brave as his own sword; but he did not know what men could do or could not do." "And Hope?" "He was but a short time with me, but I found him to be very intelligent." "And Hardinge?" "Well, Hardinge is a very clever fellow." Beyond this the Duke could never be prevailed upon to go.'[11] On another occasion when asked by George William Chad about the Prince of Orange he said, 'The Prince is a brave young man but that's all.'[12]

Having bidden his troops farewell at Bordeaux, Wellington went back to Paris where, on the night of his arrival, he attended a party at Clichy given by the brilliant woman of letters Mme de Staël, who, upon the restoration of the monarchy, had returned to the city of her birth from which she had been forced to flee when persecuted by Napoleon's police. The Duke, in an unaccustomed gesture of obeisance, knelt before her on one knee.

Five days later he stepped ashore in England for the first time in over five years. News of his coming had preceded him: there were crowds to greet him in the port at Dover and all along the route his carriage took through Kent and Surrey to London. People peered in at the windows as the coach rattled by, cheering and waving, holding children up to catch a sight of the silhouette of the long curved nose and prominent chin of the forty-five-year-old hero whose expression clearly evinced his strong distaste for such demonstrations. At Westminster Bridge an attempt was made to take out the horses and have the carriage pulled by men to his house just off Piccadilly, Number 4 Hamilton Place, where his wife and two sons were awaiting him. He could not bear to be dragged along the streets in this way. So, mounting a horse, he trotted off at a brisk pace towards St James's Park.

Neither husband nor wife was looking forward to the meeting. Before he had left for the Peninsula, Kitty had begun complaining to her relations about the coldness of his manner towards her, the severity of his demands. Since then, during his absence, there had been little in the way of personal correspondence between them. Very occasionally, he had family news to impart: for example, Kitty's brother Hercules, who had been wounded as an officer in the 95th at Obidos, had been wounded again at Badajoz. But her husband's infrequent letters were less likely to contain news of her relations than criticisms of her inefficiency as a housekeeper and business-woman or anger at the indulgence of her thoughtless largesse to members of her family and others in need. In September 1810, for example, she had received a letter which most deeply wounded her. 'I was originally to blame,' she wrote in her diary, 'but I think I could have felt more forgiveness, more indulgence.' In March the next year she had received a letter which made it clear that she had not done all that was expected of her. 'Must try,' she had recorded, 'to make up my mind to repeated disappointments.' One day Lady Liverpool had brought her a shawl which, she was told, had arrived as a present for her from her husband; but she had felt constrained to wonder 'if it really was from him'.[13]

He remained her 'dearest Arthur'; she read of his achievements with pride. 'They are mine!' she cried when shown the French eagles captured at Salamanca, kissed them, then fainted.[14]

'She appeared to have suffered a great deal from the uncertainty which everybody had been in for more than a fortnight,' wrote Mary Berry, the diarist, who called upon her not long before her husband's return from France, 'and she spoke with an enthusiasm and a worship of her hero which was truly edifying.'[15]

Yet she could not face being fêted as the hero's wife, being held up 'en spectacle' and obliged to make it plain that she knew no more of her husband's activities than anyone else. Unable to bear the thought of attending the ceremony at which the French eagles were handed over, she left town for Sevenoaks and from there sent her apologies to Lady Liverpool. Nor could she bring herself to face going to a ball given in honour of 'Lord Wellington's victory and taking possession of Madrid'. Her brother-in-law William was 'very angry' with her for not going but she really 'could not go'. She could not go to Lady Olivia Sparrow's ball either. 'I cannot bear,' she wrote, 'the questions and observations, to which I am subjected.'[16]

She was only too conscious of her weakness. Her diary's pathetic entries reveal how unhappy her inadequacies made her feel, how she longed for that affection which her husband could not find it in his heart to give her. She occupied her time with giving lessons to her children, making them shoes, playing the harp, going to the theatre, to the library and to church, taking the boys to the seaside at Ramsgate and Broadstairs, going to Tunbridge Wells, paying evening calls – 'Dined alone. Went to Lady Harington in the evening . . . very dull' – writing to her husband, sending him newspapers, treasuring the brief letters she had from him.[17]

'I am fatigued by a regular course of insignificant occupations & dissatisfied with myself when idle,' she recorded in her diary. 'Much as yesterday, languid and dawdling . . . Too late for Church . . . very shamefully late . . . Still too late . . . I am tired . . . I can hardly account for the languor, the depression that preys upon me . . . It has pleased God to deny me one blessing: on that one I had fixed all my hopes of happiness . . . Perhaps in time God will pity the agony I suffer . . . Oh Merciful Father, forgive and pity a very weak and suffering Being . . . My fault is great, but my punishment is most severe . . . From the time the Children go to bed, I find my mind torn with the most painful recollections.'[18]

As well as her own boys and Arthur Freese, her husband's godson, these children included Gerald Valerian Wellesley, the son of her brother-in-law Henry's wife, Lady Charlotte Wellesley, who had eloped with General Lord Paget soon after the child's birth. Henry declined to acknowledge the child as his own; and so Kitty, with her husband's agreement, and conscious of the 'dreadful evil which the loss of a Mother inflicts upon Children', had taken him into her home, since no one else would agree to look after the 'miserable little Being'. 'My darling Children,' she wrote in her diary, 'may no degree of suffering tempt me to forget my duty to you. I little imagined the extent of my crimes when I so earnestly wished to die.'[19]

For his own part, Wellington was astonished that Lady Charlotte's brother, Colonel Henry Cadogan, allowed his sister to return to Henry, to live 'and perform' with him, after she had gone off with Paget and Henry had divorced her.*

Nor could Wellington understand how his eldest brother, Richard – having married his Frenchwoman and subsequently paid a large sum of money to get her out of his house – could afterwards openly live with another woman whom he took with him to Spain when appointed British Minister there.

As for Wellington himself, no one who knew him well could suppose that, having regard to his temperament, he had remained celibate during his five years in Spain and Portugal. There had been talk of a Spanish Duchess in Madrid, of a French lady, the wife of the owner of the house where he stayed in Toulouse, and, earlier, of an English lady at his headquarters. But he was the very model of discretion; and, while vague rumours of his infidelities reached England, they could never be corroborated by those who would dearly have liked to be able to do so.

At 4 Hamilton Place he greeted the two sons he had not seen for so long, Arthur, now Marquess Douro, aged seven, and Charles who was six. He could, of course, scarcely recognize them. Their mother was, unfortunately, much the same as he remembered her, though she had become rather dumpy and her hair was going grey. At once retiring and fussy, her clothes, too young for her age – she was well over forty now – were as unsuitable as ever; she still wore no make-up; she had become extremely short-sighted.

Her husband did not stay with her long. He escaped as soon as he could for his mother's house in Upper Brook Street, leaving by a back door into Hyde Park to avoid the attentions of the crowd outside the front of the house in Hamilton Place.

*

* In fact, Colonel Cadogan had done all he could to save his sister from Lord Paget. He offered to sell his commission and leave the Army so that he could protect her. She refused to give Paget up, so Cadogan challenged him to a duel. This took place on Wimbledon Common. Paget declined to return Cadogan's shot (Marquess of Anglesey, One-Leg, 100–4).

He was to remain for only five weeks in England; and he was determined to make the most of them. One day he was seen in Portsmouth, the next back in London. He took his seat in the House of Lords; he made a speech to the House of Commons whose Members stood up at his entrance. With similar respect the crowds stood back for him at the Opera where he was overheard to remark cheerfully to the pretty woman on his arm, the wife of the much older Sir John Shelley, 'It's a fine thing to be a great man, is it not?'[20] He was to be seen 'in great good humour' at a masquerade held in his honour at Burlington House where amongst two thousand guests, Byron appeared as a monk and Lady Caroline Lamb flitted about in green pantaloons and masked 'but always trying to indicate who she was to everybody', while playing the 'most extraordinary tricks'.[21]

The Duke was seen also at Almack's Assembly Rooms in King Street, St James's from which he was at his first appearance turned away because he was wearing trousers instead of the knee breeches and white cravats required by the seven ladies of high rank who ruled the establishment with draconian authority.*[22]

He went to the Guildhall where the Common Council of London presented him with a sword. He went to St Paul's Cathedral in the Prince Regent's carriage, bearing the Sword of State, to attend a thanksgiving service; he went to Oxford to receive the honorary degree of Doctor of Laws, and to Hertfordshire to receive the freedom of the county town and, while staying nearby with the Salisburys at Hatfield, he marched across the park to the railings to shake hands with the

---

* 'The Duke, who had a great respect for orders and regulations, quietly walked away' (*Reminiscences and Recollections of Captain Gronow*, i, 32). He always prided himself, as Mme de Lieven said, 'on knowing how to obey as well as to command' (*The Unpublished Diary of Princess Lieven*, ed. Harold Temperley, 111). As an example of this it was related that, while riding at Stratfield Saye, his path had been blocked by a yokel standing beside a shut gate. On being asked to open the gate the man replied that he had been told to keep it shut by the farmer who employed him. 'Quite right,' said the Duke, obediently turning his horse's head, 'always obey orders.' His own respect for orders seems on occasions to have been carried to extremes. The son of one of his gamekeepers recorded such an occasion:

> One day Jonathan, our headkeeper, who had to tell everyone which way he was to walk and where to stand when we were pheasant shooting – he orders the Duke which way he was to go. And his Grace never said a word, but away he goes, just as if he was a private soldier and keeper was Commander-in-Chief; and the Duke went straight on right through the wood, and when he came out on the other side, you never saw such a sight in your life as the Duke's nose, it was that full of thorns. Father had quite a job getting them out. And keeper said, 'Why, Your Grace, I can't think how you came to walk through all those bushes.' And the Duke said, 'You ordered me to go that way, so go I did' (J.G. Witt, *Three Villages*, 95–6).

cheering crowd, impressing one spectator, a friend of Kitty, with his 'modesty and unaffected simplicity of manner'.[23] Kitty herself was rarely to be seen.

The Duke returned to London where he was clearly in happy mood at Carlton House. Observing some of his young officers and aides-de-camp on the dance floor, he remarked with complacent contentment to Lady Shelley, 'How would society get on without all my boys?'[24]

The Prince Regent, his host at Carlton House, was a guest at Wanstead in Essex where Wellington's nephew, his brother William's son, gave a grand party in honour of his uncle. This young nephew, briefly Wellington's incompetent aide-de-camp, had recently married an heiress, Catherine Tylney-Long, whose surname he hyphenated to his own and whose immense income allowed full rein to his extravagance. Among his guests, apart from the Prince Regent and the Duke, were Blücher and Platov, three of the royal dukes, and several members of William Pole-Tylney-Long-Wellesley's family. Lady Shelley was there, too, and she recorded how the Duke rose after the Prince Regent had proposed his health and how he had hesitatingly begun, 'I want words to express . . .' The Regent had interrupted him with easy affability, 'My dear fellow, we know your actions, and we will excuse you your *words*, so sit down'; and how the Duke had complied with this royal command 'with all the delight of a schoolboy who has been given an unexpected holiday'.[25]

The five weeks were not altogether a holiday for him. Parliament had voted £400,000 for him to purchase an estate, £300,000 more than the sum granted to him for this purpose after the battle of Salamanca in 1812, and over four times as large as the amount granted to Lord Nelson's brother after the Admiral's death at Trafalgar. It represented a figure which would be worth about £15,000,000 today. So a property of great distinction could be bought; and the Duke sought the advice of Benjamin Dean Wyatt, the eldest son of the architect, James Wyatt. This young man had been trained in his father's office after having worked in Calcutta in the office of the Governor-General, Lord Wellesley, and in Dublin as private secretary to Wellington. He had set up his own practice in 1809 and had recently been in charge of the rebuilding of Drury Lane Theatre after its destruction by fire.[26]

He left London on the Duke's behalf in search of what his client described as 'a very fair house' which he would be able to make 'as magnificent as it ought to be'. He went to Buckinghamshire but decided that there was nothing there which would not be overshadowed by the Duke of Buckingham's place at Stowe; the same applied to the neighbouring county of Oxfordshire where Vanbrugh's and Hawksmoor's Blenheim Palace could brook no opposition, certainly not from Great Tew. Longford Castle in Wiltshire, which had been altered and enlarged a few years before for the Earl of Radnor, was considered but eventually rejected. So was Standlynch Park in the same county which was bought instead by Earl Nelson and renamed Trafalgar House. So, now and later, were Somerhill near Tonbridge, Kent, Houghton Hall in Norfolk, the Marquess of Bute's estate at Luton, Radley Hall near Abingdon, Fonthill in Wiltshire, Exton in Rutland, the Duke of Queensberry's estate in Wiltshire, Lord Stourton's in Yorkshire and Lord Sage's in Gloucestershire. Lord Fitzwilliam's Harrowden was no good for hunting; Lord Egremont's Busbridge was too small.[27]

While Wyatt continued his house hunting, the Duke had much other business to attend to, since his advice was constantly sought about military matters, in particular about the unreasonable war with the United States which had broken out in 1812 and was not going well. It was proposed to employ the British forces in America in an attack upon New Orleans, a venture which Wellington roundly condemned as ill-advised and impracticable. His advice was ignored and the results were as he had feared they might be: the Americans, commanded by one of their best generals, Andrew Jackson, drove the British back, inflicting upon them over three thousand casualties, among them Wellington's brother-in-law Edward Pakenham, who was killed, shot through the spine, in the unsuccessful attack.

The Duke mourned the loss of a man who had greatly admired him and of whom he had grown fond;[28] but there was much else to occupy his mind. He had returned to Paris where he had arranged for the purchase of the Hôtel de Charost in rue du Faubourg St Honoré, a delightful house, also known as the Hôtel Borghese which had belonged to Napoleon's sister Pauline, the wife of Prince Camillo Borghese, a ravishing and eccentric woman who sold it, together with its contents, for 861,500 francs, over twice what she had paid for it.[29]

23 Paris and Vienna

1814 — 15

'There is nobody but myself in whom either
yourselves, or the country, or your Allies would
feel any confidence.'

IN PARIS THE DUKE found himself as much in demand as ever: he
had a finger, as he put it himself, in every pie. He was asked about
French attitudes to the war in America, about the policies to be pursued
by the British representatives at the Congress in Vienna, about the
Princess of Wales whose extremely dubious behaviour on the Continent
was being investigated by her husband's agents. It was 'worth considering', was the Duke's worldly advice, 'whether it [was] not desirable that
every facility should be given to the Princess of Wales to enjoy herself'
so that she would not be tempted to return to England.[1]

The Duke was also much concerned with the French slave trade
against which public opinion in England, where the trade had been
abolished in 1807, was running strong, and which he had been
instructed to persuade the French government to abolish.[2] He studied
all the books he could find upon the subject including the *History of
the Abolition of the African Slave Trade by the British Parliament* by
the anti-slavery agitator Thomas Clarkson; and, a more pleasurable
task, he discussed the problem with the knowledgeable Mme de Staël
who translated for him English anti-slave trade pamphlets into French.
He came to the conclusion that, of course, the slave trade was wrong;
but he sympathized with the French who could not understand why
the English were making such a fuss and strongly suspected that they
were motivated less by humanitarian reasons than by jealousy of French
commerce. Wellington sensibly proposed that French public opinion
should be moulded by the same kind of anti-slavery propaganda that
had been so effective in England and, in the meantime, he succeeded
in persuading King Louis XVIII to press for the abolition of the slave
trade within five years.

His relations with the gouty King were friendly enough even though he described him as 'a perfect walking sore', 'selfish and false in the highest degree'.[3] 'He was a man of education and information', said the Duke, who admired his scrupulous punctuality, the manner in which, when he was wheeled into dinner, the doors were thrown open, and his chair was seen to enter 'while the clock was actually striking six'.[4] His behaviour at table, however, was not so praiseworthy. He was very greedy. Once when the Duke was dining with him en famille 'there was a dish of very early strawberries, which the King very deliberately turned into his own plate, even to the last spoonful, without offering any to the ladies'.*[5]

The Duke also got on perfectly well with the King's nephew, the duc d'Angoulême, though he was alarmed by his behaviour when they were out together on a deer hunt, for his aim was most erratic, so much so, indeed, that the gamekeeper would take aim at the quarry at the same time as Angoulême and call out, *'Monsieur tire à merveille,'* when his shot brought the animal down.[6]

It was the attractive duchesse d'Angoulême, whose parties he attended at the Pavillon de Flore, whom the Duke found the most pleasing of the members of the Royal Family. Indeed, in these months in Paris, his delight in the company of attractive, lively, intelligent women, who found him attractive and lively in return, had never been more apparent. He prided himself upon his intimacy with Mme de Staël whom he considered far less tiresome than did Byron who never went near her if he could help it. 'Her books are very delightful,' Byron wrote, 'but in society I see nothing but a plain woman forcing one to listen, and look at her, with her pen behind her ear and her mouth full of ink.'[7] 'She was a most agreeable woman,' Wellington said of her, 'if only you *kept her light*, and away from politics. But that was not easy. She was always trying to come to matters of State. I have said to her more than once: *"Je déteste parler politique"*; and she answered, *"Parler politique pour moi c'est vivre"*. She and I were great friends.'[8]

The Duke was also on easy terms with the charming and witty Mme Récamier, daughter and wife of rich bankers, who, exiled from Paris by Napoleon, had gone to stay with her friend, Mme de Staël, in Geneva and had now returned to preside once again over the Parisian salon whose conversation she so skilfully directed from the daybed named in her honour.

---

* When told by Lord Mahon that this was 'exactly what Queen Anne relates William the Third to have done with a dish of early green peas, she being then Princess and at table with her sister Queen Mary, the Duke laughed. "Aye – I hope it is not a Royal custom"' (Stanhope, *Notes of Conversations with the Duke of Wellington*, 126).

The Duke saw a good deal, too, of Talleyrand's niece by marriage, Dorothea, Countess of Périgord, later Duchess of Dino, also of Marshal Ney's pretty wife, Aglaé Ney, the daughter of a chambermaid, and, on far more occasions than with either of these, of Giuseppina Grassini, the opera singer from La Scala who had followed Napoleon's soldiers out of Italy and, as '*La Chanteuse de l'Empereur*', had become one of the Emperor's mistresses. It was widely supposed in Paris that she became Wellington's mistress, too. Certainly he kept a portrait of her in his room; but then he kept pictures of Pauline Borghese and Pope Pius VII there as well. He was so often to be seen in Giuseppina Grassini's company that Lady Bessborough, who was staying in Paris that autumn, complained not so much of the immorality of the liaison as of the 'want of procédé and the publicity of his attentions'.[9]

He also saw much of another of Napoleon's former mistresses, the *tragédienne* Joséphine Weimer, a big, buxom, sensuous woman whom the Emperor had considered the best actress in Paris where she performed under the name Mademoiselle Georges. He had invited her to come to St Cloud after seeing her give a splendid performance as Clytemnestra. She had obeyed the summons, had stayed the night and had later received a present of 40,000 francs which Napoleon had stuffed between her breasts. He presented her with a special kind of garter made of elastic which he found easier to undo than the usual kind of garter with a buckle. She made no secret of her affair with Napoleon, and liked it to be known that she had afterwards been the mistress of Wellington who, she declared, was '*de beaucoup le plus fort*'.[10]

According to Harriette Wilson, the Duke also saw her at this time as she was 'taking a solitary drive one day up the Champs Elysées on [her] road to the Bois de Boulogne'.

'I thought it was you,' said Wellington, 'and I am glad to see you are looking so beautiful. I'll come and see you. How long have you been in Paris? When may I come? Where do you live? How far are you going?'

> 'Which of these questions do you desire to have answered first, Wellington?' I enquired.
> 'I want to know where you live?'
> 'At thirty-five Rue de la Paix.'
> 'And may I pay you a visit?'
> 'When you like.'
> 'I'll come tonight at eight o'clock. Will that suit you?' I assented, and shook hands with him. His Lordship was punctual . . .

'The ladies here tell me you make a bad hand at Ambassadorship,' said I to him.

'How so?'

'Why, the other day you wrote to ask a lady of rank if you might visit her, *à cheval*? What does that mean pray?'

'In boots, you foolish creature! What else could it mean?'

'Why the lady thought it just possible that the great Villainton, being an extraordinary man, might propose entering her drawing-room on the outside of his charger, as being the most warrior-like mode of attacking her heart.'

'You are a little fool,' said Wellington, kissing me by main force. Wellington was no inducement for me to prolong my stay in Paris.[11]

As well as old and new-found friends, Paris was full of the Duke's former enemies, among them Marshal Ney whose wife often came home at night in tears because of the snubs she received from the returned émigrés at court.[12] Massena was here, too; and one evening, after looking in Wellington's direction uncertainly for some time, the old, one-eyed Marshal came up to his former adversary and declared in French, 'My Lord, you owe me a dinner – for you made me starve *furieusement*.'[13]

'You should give it to me, Marshal,' the Duke laughed as he replied in the same vein, 'for you prevented me from sleeping.'

There was no possibility of the Duke and Marshal Soult, now the Minister of War, not recognizing each other; for the Duke had watched the Marshal closely through his telescope as he sat in his saddle on the ridge at Sorauren, and Soult had peered through the Duke's carriage window as their horses were being changed at an inn near Toulouse when they were both on their way home.

It was not expected that the Duchess of Wellington would choose to appear at these parties in Paris where her husband hobnobbed with Marshals and took actresses in to dinner. He had asked her if she would like to come; and she had been so gratified by the invitation that she had replied enthusiastically: 'To an Ambassador's wife there are no difficulties which I do not feel myself equal to overcome, no duties which I am not willing to perform, and I may venture to add that you shall never have reason to regret having allowed me, on this subject, to decide for myself.'[14] When the time for departure came she was, as might have been expected, reluctant to go and became distressed at the thought of leaving her children behind until they could come out to the Embassy for the Christmas holidays. Nor, when she did arrive, did her husband take the kind of notice of her that would have enabled her to feel at home. 'I am afraid he is behaving very ill to that poor little woman,' Lady Bessborough wrote: 'and he is found great fault with for it' because of his attentions to Giuseppina Grassini.[15]

The apparent gaiety of Parisian life concealed much foreboding. Royalists were becoming increasingly disillusioned with the incompetence of Louis XVIII's government, comprising, as the Duke of Wellington put it, 'Ministers but no Ministry'; while Bonapartists were becoming ever more clamorous in their opposition to a regime which they condemned as being propped up by a foreign, indeed an enemy power. The French army would almost universally have endorsed the lament of General Maximilien Foy, the son of a Picardy post-master, who had risen through the ranks to become one of the Emperor's most distinguished generals and was now a leading spokesman of the liberal opposition: 'O Napoléon où est tu?'[16]

Although he liked Wellington personally and enjoyed talking to him about military affairs, Foy could not but consider him an interloper, the commander of an occupying army, the unwelcome symbol of a nation's disgrace. These views were widely shared: one day a shot was fired at the Duke during a review on the Champs de Mars.

As reports of an imminent insurrection in France reached London, Lord Liverpool's Government became concerned for the Duke's safety. His life was too valuable to risk; but for the moment there seemed no other place to send him. It was suggested that he might be given supreme command in America. The Regent was in favour of this plan, since 'his name alone [would] reconcile the whole view & opinion of the Country';[17] and the Duke himself was not altogether averse to the idea, provided he were given authority to carry out negotiations when appropriate and bring the war to an end.[18] It was high time this was done: the burning of several of Washington's buildings after the defeat of an American force at Bladensburg in August 1814 had caused deep revulsion in France – though when Mme de Staël expressed this revulsion at a gathering in the Duke's presence he 'silenced her'.[19]

But Wellington was too conscious of his own worth to believe he could be spared from Europe at such a time. 'In case of the occurrence of anything in Europe,' he told the Government in London, confident of his own indispensability, 'there is nobody but myself in whom either yourselves, or the country, or your Allies would feel any confidence.'[20] In any case he did not want it to appear that he was being 'frightened away'.[21] So it was decided that Lord Castlereagh should be brought home to resume his seat in the Cabinet and that the Duke should replace him as Britain's chief diplomatist in Vienna where the Congress convened to redraw the map of Europe after Napoleon's downfall and exile to Elba had so far achieved little of importance. Lord Fitzroy Somerset and his wife were to occupy the Embassy in Paris until the Duke's return. The Duchess of Wellington was to remain in Paris with them.

The two aides who accompanied the Duke from Paris to Vienna found the journey an arduous one. One of them, Lord William Pitt Lennox, wrote:

> The Duke travelled in an English carriage, with his valet, Tesson, on a seat on the roof, and a courier in advance. Anxious to lose no time on the road, we breakfasted and dined in the carriage.
>
> With the exception of four hours during the night, we never stopped upon the road between Paris and Vienna, and here the Duke's powers of falling at once to sleep came into effect; for no sooner had we reached the inn, than, the courier having made preparations, his Grace went immediately to bed, and at the hour named for starting, he appeared perfectly refreshed, having slept, dressed, and breakfasted during that brief period; while we, the two *attachés*, looked what is called, with more truth than elegance, 'extremely seedy,' having passed our time in eating supper, and then lying down in our clothes before the hot German stove.[22]

They arrived in Vienna on 3 February 1815 and without delay went to Prince Metternich, the Austrian Emperor's Minister of Foreign Affairs. 'What have you done?' Wellington asked. 'Nothing,' Metternich replied, 'absolutely nothing.'[23] Both he and Metternich were agreed as to what should be done: legitimate monarchs must be restored to their thrones, a balance of power maintained, and popular movements discouraged everywhere. They differed however in their diplomatic approach to these ends. Wellington believed in going 'straight forward without stratagems or subterfuges', allowing no more than an occasional affectation of lofty unconcern to disguise his diligent watchfulness. Metternich – like the French Foreign Minister, Talleyrand-Périgord, the former Bishop of Autun, now Prince of Benevento, a crafty, ill-favoured, born trimmer and survivor – was more devious.

Wellington and Talleyrand were both careful to ensure that the Congress, as well as being a diplomatic conference, was a social event. Parties, dinners and balls, theatre performances, drives to the Prater and Augarten and promenades on the ramparts kept amused those who might otherwise have disrupted the work in hand. To Wellington, it seemed, there were quite enough mischief-makers, meddlers and profligates in the city as it was. The Regent's unpleasant brother, the trouble-making Duke of Cumberland, was here. So was Wellington's philandering and disreputable nephew William Pole-Tylney-Long-Wellesley. To make matters worse, that old intriguer from the Peninsula, Lord Castlereagh's half-brother Sir Charles Stewart, who had been raised to the peerage as Lord Stewart the year before, had taken up his appointment as British Ambassador in Vienna and was indiscreet enough to have become the lover of Wilhelmine, daughter of the Duke of Courland, who had once been one of Metternich's many mistresses. Her sister, Dorothea, Countess of Périgord, publicly announced her devotion to the Duke; while two of Wilhelmine's other sisters, Pauline and Jeanne, were known to be having affairs with Congress officials, one of them its Secretary-General. Although well aware of the dangers of such liaisons, the Duke was not a man to find the concupiscent atmosphere in Vienna uncongenial.

Soon, however, the kissing had suddenly to stop.

24 Brussels

1815

'Duchess, you may give your ball with the greatest
safety without fear of interruption.'

ON THE EVENING of Monday 6 March 1815 Prince Metternich
received various representatives of other Continental powers at his
official residence. Among them was the Duke of Wellington. There
were many important matters to discuss, and the meeting did not break
up until three o'clock on the Tuesday morning. Metternich then went
to bed, giving orders that he was not to be disturbed. At six, however,
he was woken by a servant who handed him a dispatch marked *urgent*.
He left it unopened on his bedside table and tried to go to sleep again;
but, restless now, he could not do so. He opened the dispatch and
read its contents: Napoleon had disappeared from the island of Elba.[1]
   The Duke's days as a diplomat were for the moment over. He was
to be a soldier again. By the beginning of April he was in Brussels
preparing for war, while careful to give the impression that he thought
war might be averted. There were numerous foreign visitors in Brussels,
enjoying a continental holiday in what was then considered 'one of the
most brilliant cities in Europe'. Wellington's mother was there until
her son advised her to leave for Antwerp. So, to the Duke's great
pleasure, was Lady Frances Wedderburn-Webster, the alluring, emotional daughter of the Earl of Mountnorris. She was married to a rather
stupid officer of Hussars who once told his friend Lord Byron that he
thought 'any woman fair game', that 'every woman was his lawful prize'.
He could '*depend* upon' his wife's principles, he said. She was 'all moral
. . . very like Christ!!!' *She* couldn't go wrong, therefore *he* could. Byron,
however, knew her better. Admittedly she said 'prayers, morning and
evening, besides being measured for a new Bible once a quarter'. But
she was far from being as virtuous as she seemed; and at two o'clock
one morning at Newstead Abbey she told Byron she was entirely at
his mercy. 'I own it,' she said. 'I give myself up to you. I am not cold
whatever I seem to others . . . Now act as you will.' Byron confessed

that she was his 'present idol', that he was for the moment 'totally absorbed in this passion'. Yet in the end he 'spared her'.[2]

This was in October 1813. Now, in Brussels, the Duke of Wellington seemed almost as much taken with Lady Frances as Lord Byron had been then. Once a young officer saw them meeting in the Park, having descended from separate carriages, then going down together into a hollow in the ground where the trees hid them from view.[3]

Also in Brussels at this time was the Whig politician Thomas Creevey, who, deeply in debt, was living there with his wife and two stepdaughters on an annuity paid by his friend Samuel Whitbread.

The Duke met them at a ball given by Lady Charlotte Greville; and Creevey was both surprised and relieved when – as though Creevey's organization of a petition against Wellington's being granted a pension after Talavera had been forgotten – the Duke approached him with his hand outstretched.

Creevey thought that, while the Duke gave 'no indication of superior talents', he was 'very natural and good-humoured', his behaviour characterized by 'the most marked civility and cordiality'. He appeared to 'be confident that it would never come to blows' with Napoleon.

'We had much conversation about Buonaparte,' Creevey recorded, 'and the Duke would have it that a Republick was the thing which he was sure was to be got up at Paris – *that it would never come to fighting with the Allies.*'[4] This, though, was mere talk for Whig consumption; and the Duke expressed quite different opinions to the diplomat Sir Charles Stuart, Minister at the Hague and soon to be Ambassador in Paris. All the same, he maintained an attitude in public of cheerful unconcern.

> The Duke during this period was for ever giving balls [Creevey recalled]; and very agreeable they were. On one occasion, there having been a ball in his house on a Saturday night, old Blücher and his staff came over to the town on the next day – Sunday – and the Duke sent out instantly to all who had been there on the preceding evening to come again that night to meet Blücher, and he kept making everybody dance to the last.[5]

He had disconcerting worries, though. His army numbered twice as many foreign troops as British; and he did not think highly of either the Dutch or the Belgians as soldiers. Besides, the British were as inexperienced as the foreigners: only six out of twenty-five British battalions had served in the Peninsula, and these were not what 'they ought to be to enable us to maintain our military character'.[6] Sir Henry

Torrens agreed with him. 'I wish to God,' he wrote, 'You had a better army.'[7]

The cavalry were adequate, although he would have preferred as their commander Sir Stapleton Cotton, now Lord Combermere, with whom he had served in the Peninsula and who offered his services,* rather than Henry Paget, since his father's death the Earl of Uxbridge, who had been foisted upon him by the Prince Regent and the Duke of York.[8] He had no objection to Uxbridge on moral grounds. When it was suggested to him that he 'might have forgotten' Paget's elopement with the Duke's sister-in-law, Lady Charlotte Wellesley, he replied, 'Oh no! I had not forgotten that.'

'That is not the only case, I am afraid. At any rate Lord Uxbridge has the reputation of running away with everybody he can.'

'I'll take good care he don't run away with me: I don't care about anybody else.'†[9]

---

* His good opinion of Lord Combermere was evidently not maintained. When, years later, the Government was contemplating the dispatch of an expedition to Burma with a view to taking Rangoon, the Cabinet, it is said, asked for Wellington's advice as to a suitable commander. He instantly replied, 'Send Lord Combermere.'

'But,' it was objected, 'we have always understood that your Grace thought Lord Combermere a fool.'

'So he is a fool, and a damned fool; but he can take Rangoon' (G.W.E. Russell, *Collections and Recollections*, 42).

† This is characteristic of the Duke's attitude to sexual impropriety. He was warned in Brussels that Lady John Campbell had a very poor reputation in this regard. 'The Duke of W—— has not improved the *Morality* of our society,' Lady Caroline Capel, Lord Uxbridge's sister, told her mother. 'He makes a point of asking all the Ladies of Loose Character [to his parties] – Everyone was surprised at seeing Lady John Campbell at his House, and one of his Staff told me that it had been represented to him her not being received for that her Character was more than Suspicious. "Is it, by God," said he, "then I will go ask her Myself." On which he immediately took his Hat and went out for the purpose' (Anglesey, *The Capel Letters*, 102).

When Lord Melbourne was charged with having seduced the Hon. Mrs George Norton in 1836, Charles Greville asked the Duke whether or not he thought Melbourne would resign. 'O Lord no! Resign? Not a bit of it. I tell you all these things are a nine days' wonder . . . It don't signify a straw' (*The Greville Memoirs*, iii, 290). The Duke was not usually so tolerant, however, when his own family were involved. He much disapproved, for example, of Lord Worcester who, before his marriage to his niece Emily, had been married to her half-sister. There had been fallings out in the family as a consequence. Worcester, the Duke had told Harriet Arbuthnot, was 'the most extraordinary person about women he ever knew'. He had been 'much disgusted by his gross want of feeling and common decency' in becoming engaged to Lady Jane Paget the day after Lady Worcester's funeral. In Paris he wrote every day to Lady Jane while 'flirting violently' with Lady Mildmay, 'making love to a French girl who lived with her, & had besides affairs going on with two or three girls at the Opera' (*The Journal of Mrs Arbuthnot*, 4 November 1821).

The Duke could comfort himself with the thought that, although he had no personal knowledge of Uxbridge as a cavalry commander and although he distrusted his dashing hussar qualities, the man had fought with distinction in the retreat to Corunna under Sir John Moore who had written in warm commendation of the cavalry's services, in whose praise it was 'impossible to say too much'.

Yet if the cavalry seemed to be adequate, the artillery was well under strength, and try as he would he could not persuade the Horse Guards to send him the twelve-pounders by which he set such store. Nor was the Duke much comforted by some of the names of the generals which were proposed to him. One of these, the well-intentioned son of an army surgeon, Sir Hudson Lowe, he had already decided was a 'damned old fool'.[10] Another, Sir Thomas Picton, brave if impulsive in the past – 'as rough, foul mouthed a devil as ever existed'[11] – who was bitterly disappointed not to have been granted a peerage as other Peninsular generals had been, was said to have lost his nerve and, having a strong presentiment of death, had recently jumped into a grave with the words, 'Why, I think this would do for me.'[12]

As for the general staff, it was 'very inexperienced' and 'overloaded with people' he had never seen before. He crossly complained that it appeared to be 'purposely intended to keep those out of [his] way whom [he wished] to have'.[13]

All in all it was 'an infamous army, very weak and ill equipped'. In his opinion they were 'doing nothing in England'; they had 'not raised a man' nor called out the militia. 'To tell you the truth,' he told the authorities in London, 'I am not very well pleased . . . with the manner in which the Horse Guards have conducted themselves towards me. It will be admitted that the army is not a very good one.' However, he would do the best he could with 'the instruments' which had been sent to 'assist' him.[14]

As it happened, these 'instruments' were not so ineffective as he feared they might prove. Several highly competent senior officers joined him, including Sir Rowland Hill, Sir James Kempt, Sir Frederic Ponsonby and Lord Edward Somerset. And, by dint of much badgering and exhortation, he did get more British troops than the numbers at first offered him, as well as a satisfactory staff on which there were only two officers who had not served him well on the Peninsula.

So Wellington's apprehension was gradually replaced by a guarded optimism. He still felt the want of more British troops; but, as he said, 'I can now put 70,000 men into the field, and Blücher 80,000; so that I hope we should give a good account even of Buonaparte.'[15] He well knew how vital Napoleon's presence would prove to be. He was, he considered, 'unquestionably the greatest military genius that ever existed':[16] his presence on a battlefield was the equivalent of 40,000 men.[17]

'Will you let me ask you, Duke, what you think you will make of it,' Thomas Creevey asked him when they met one day while walking in the Park.

He stopt, and said in the most natural manner: – 'By God I think Blücher and myself can do the thing.' – 'Do you calculate,' I asked, 'upon any desertion in Buonaparte's army?' 'Not upon a man,' he said, 'from the colonel to the private in a regiment – both inclusive. We may pick up a marshal or two, perhaps; but not worth a damn.' – 'Do you reckon,' I asked, 'upon any support from the French King's troops at Alost?' – 'Oh!' said he, 'don't mention such fellows! No: I think Blücher and I can do the business.' – Then, seeing a private soldier of one of our infantry regiments enter the park, gaping about at the statues and images: – 'There,' he said, pointing at the soldier, 'it all depends upon that article whether we do the business or not. Give me enough of it, and I am sure.'[18]

As the pleasant summer days passed by in Brussels, conflicting reports came into the city about Napoleon's movements and intentions. He was even said to be in Cherbourg waiting for a ship in which to sail to the United States. Wellington himself did not think that Napoleon who, without a shot being fired against him, had entered Paris on 20 March, would for the moment leave the city from which King Louis XVIII had fled to Ghent. But in case Napoleon did march north against the Allies in Belgium, the Duke did his best to ensure that he would be ready for him. Frequently he rode out with an orderly to reconnoitre the ground south of Brussels where the conflict, if it were to come, would be likely to take place.

In the meantime he was careful to maintain an appearance of confidence and calm in a city full of spies. 'We are getting on pretty well here,' he claimed on 6 June. Even when it was known for certain that Napoleon was, indeed, on the march, he did not hesitate to agree that the Duchess of Richmond should go ahead with a ball she was planning to give for the cosmopolitan society still in Brussels at the house she was renting in the rue de la Blanchisserie.

'Duke,' the Duchess had said to him, 'I do not wish to pry into your secrets ... I wish to give a ball, and all I ask is, may I give my ball? If you say, "Duchess, don't give your ball", it is quite sufficient, I ask you no reason.'

The Duke, who had himself intended to give one of his own balls on 21 June, the second anniversary of the battle of Vitoria, replied, 'Duchess, you may give your ball with the greatest safety without fear of interruption.' Indeed, he undertook to attend the ball himself.[19]

> Although the Duke affected great gaiety and cheerfulness [wrote one of the other guests at this ball], it struck me that I had never seen him have such an expression of care and anxiety on his countenance. I sat next to him on a sopha for a long time, but his mind seemed quite preoccupied; and although he spoke to me in the kindest manner possible, yet frequently in the middle of a sentence he stopped abruptly and called to some officer, giving him directions ... Despatches were constantly coming in to the Duke.[20]

Another guest at the ball, Captain William Verner of the 7th Hussars, who arrived rather late, was accosted on entering the ballroom by a fellow officer who said to him urgently, 'Verner, the Prussians have been attacked and defeated, and I am going to order the Duke's horses.' Verner found the ballroom in the 'greatest confusion'. 'Officers were hurrying away as fast as possible, in order that nothing might prevent their joining their regiments. At this moment Lord Uxbridge came to the door and said, "You gentlemen who have engaged partners had better finish your dance, and get to your quarters as soon as you can." '[21]

The Duke still appeared perfectly composed, far too composed, in fact, for the Belgian Marquise d'Assche who sat opposite him at the supper table. 'I would,' she wrote, 'willingly have throttled him from the impatience which his unconcern caused me,' as he sat talking easily to his neighbours, Lady Frances Wedderburn-Webster, 'to whom he paid ardent court', and the Duchess of Richmond's daughter, Lady Georgiana Lennox.[22]

Even when he was interrupted by the agitated Prince of Orange, the young commander of the Dutch troops, the Duke maintained his appearance of sangfroid. The Prince 'whispered some minutes to his Grace, who only said he had no fresh orders to give, and recommended the Prince to go back to his quarters and go to bed'.[23]

> The Duke of Wellington remained nearly twenty minutes after this, and then said to the Duke of Richmond, I think it is time for me to go to bed likewise; and then, whilst wishing him good night, whispered

to ask him if he had a good map in his house. The Duke of Richmond said he had, and took him into his dressing-room. The Duke shut the door and said, Napoleon has *humbugged* me, by Gad! He has gained twenty-four hours' march on me. The Duke of Richmond said, What do you intend doing? The Duke of Wellington replied, I have ordered the army to concentrate at Quatre-Bras; but we shall not stop him there, and if so, I must fight him *here* (at the same time passing his thumb-nail over the position of Waterloo). He then said adieu, and left the house by another way out.[24]

25 Waterloo

1815

'It is a bad thing to be always fighting.'

IT WAS NOW past two o'clock in the morning; but it was not long after dawn that an English lady's maid caught a glimpse of the Duke – who had managed to get two hours' sleep in his hotel in the rue Montagne du Parc – trotting down the street beneath a bedroom window as she was opening the shutters. 'O, my lady, get up quick. There he goes, God bless him, and he will not come back till he is King of France!'[1]

At about ten o'clock the Duke reached Quatre Bras and three hours later he joined Field Marshal Blücher's staff on the heights of Brie above the village of Ligny.

He did not much like what he saw: the Prussians, 84,000 strong facing 80,500 French, were drawn up on an exposed slope and, if attacked there, so he said to Sir Henry Hardinge, the British military commissioner at Blücher's headquarters, they would be 'damnably mauled'. 'I told them so myself,' the Duke later informed Lord Mahon, 'but of course in different terms. I said to them, everybody knows their own army best; but if I were to fight with mine here, I should expect to be beat.'[2]

Irritated by this observation, General Count von Gneisenau, Blücher's Chief of Staff, testily replied that his men liked to be able to see the enemy.[3]

Wellington's discussions with the Prussian staff lasted rather more than an hour; and, before returning to his own army, he promised Gneisenau that he would come to his assistance if he were not to be attacked himself at Quatre Bras. But when he returned to Quatre Bras, he found his troops in a dangerous position. They had come up to the front in the most appalling confusion: some had received orders; others had not. Many officers had not even had time to change out of the uniforms they had been wearing at the Duchess of Richmond's ball which some had left in their dancing pumps.

Marshal Ney, however, was slow to take advantage of his opponent's

disorganization and missed his opportunity of overwhelming Wellington's far smaller force. It was not until a quarter to twelve that he
acted in obedience to the dispatch he had received from the Emperor
three-quarters of an hour before; and, by the time the two armies were
actively engaged, Wellington's reinforcements had come up to prevent
Ney from breaking through the allied front.

As he had been in the fighting in Spain, so now at Quatre Bras,
Wellington was seen galloping about the field from one battalion to
the next, giving orders as though he were a regimental officer – '92nd,
don't fire till I tell you' – once finding himself – when well in advance
of his own front line – threatened by a troop of French cavalry and
obliged to shout to the Highlanders lining a ditch behind him to lie
down while he came galloping back to leap over their heads.

His troops, once steadied, held their ground; but by nightfall he had
lost 4,800 of them, rather more than the French. He rode back to the
Roi d'Espagne at Genappe to have a meal, hoping that that 'damned
fine old fellow' Blücher had succeeded in halting the French advance
at Ligny.

Blücher, however, was not at Ligny. He was lying in a farmhouse
five miles to the north at Mellery; his horse had been killed under
him; he had been trampled underfoot; and he would have been taken
prisoner had not an aide-de-camp saved him from being recognized by
throwing a cloak over him to hide his medals. He had lost 16,000 men
and half that number were still in retreat.

Before going to bed at midnight in the Roi d'Espagne, Wellington
had been given some intimation of this disaster by a Prussian officer
sent to him by Gneisenau. He had listened to his reports, as shot flew
around them, with a sangfroid which the Prussian found remarkable;
but he allowed himself less than three hours in bed before riding hard
back to Quatre Bras and sending his aide-de-camp, Alexander Gordon,
to Ligny to find out exactly what had happened there.

When Gordon returned at about half past seven on the morning of
17 June, he gave his dismaying report to the Commander-in-Chief in
a low voice little above a whisper. When he had finished, the Duke
said, 'Old Blücher has had a damned good hiding, and has gone back
to Wavre, eighteen miles to the rear. We must do the same. I suppose
they'll say in England that we have been licked; well, I can't help
that.'[4]

So the Allied troops withdrew towards Brussels, marching discon-
solately in the now heavy rain, to occupy the ridge in front of Waterloo.

Away we went, helter-skelter [wrote an officer of the rearguard] –
guns, gun-detachments and hussars, all mixed *pêle-mêle*, going like
mad, and covering each other with mud, to be washed off by the rain
which . . . came down in splashes rather than drops, soaking us to the
skin . . . The obscurity caused by the splashing of the rain was such
that . . . I could not distinguish objects more than a few yards distant.
Of course, we lost sight of our pursuers altogether, and the shouts
and halloos, and even laughter, they had at first sent forth were either
silenced or drowned in the uproar of the elements and the noise of
our too rapid retreat; for in addition to everything else, the crashing
and rattling of the thunder were almost awful and the glare of the
lightning blinding.[5]

Dawn on Sunday 18 June 1815 found both armies in a pitiable state.
The torrential rain was succeeded by a drizzling shower which ceased
as the morning advanced. Both officers and men in their wet, dirty
uniforms 'looked blue with the cold'.[6] Only a few regiments in the
British lines had an adequate breakfast. Most men had nothing but
biscuits, a little rum stirred up in oatmeal, or perhaps a little soup.
The Duke rode past them in his low cocked hat with its black cockade,
a cloak thrown over his blue frock-coat, since he had always made it
a rule never to get wet if he could help it.[7] Ensign Gronow, of the
First Foot Guards, a dressy man himself, noticed also his white cravat,
leather pantaloons and Hessian boots.[8]

Having gone to bed not long before midnight, he was up again at
three o'clock, writing letters by candlelight, an occupation upon which
he was still engaged six hours later. He warned the royal family that
they might have to move from Ghent; he advised Lady Frances
Wedderburn-Webster to leave for Antwerp, and suggested to the British
Ambassador that all the British in Brussels ought to be ready to leave
at a moment's notice while keeping calm, 'neither in a hurry or a fright'.
His own calm was still unruffled, the only sign of apprehension being
the occasional bite he gave to the riding whip which he carried in his
right hand and from time to time brought to his mouth. The day before
he had been sitting on the ground after a reconnaissance actually
laughing at some item of idle gossip he had read in a page of the *Sun*,
a newspaper devoted to such chit-chat, and had even contrived to go
to sleep for a while with the newspaper over his face.

He had momentarily revealed his anxiety by suddenly losing his
temper when an artillery battery rashly replied to shots from a French
battery, giving away the position of the British guns; and he had shown

another flash of irritation when, having refused permission for the major in charge of the army's rockets to bring the unreliable weapons into action, a senior officer interceded on the major's behalf saying that it would break his heart 'to lose his rockets'.

'Damn his heart, Sir,' Wellington exploded in fury. 'Let my order be obeyed.'[9]

He had, however, immediately calmed down, and given permission for the rockets to be brought into action. In the same way, he had recovered himself almost immediately when he flared up at Lord Uxbridge who – mindful of the fact that if 'any accident' happened to the Duke he would suddenly find himself Commander-in-Chief – asked him what he proposed to do on the morrow.

'Buonaparte has not given me any idea of his projects,' Wellington replied tartly; 'and as my plans will depend upon his, how can you expect me to tell you what mine are?' Then, relenting, he stood up, laid his hand on Uxbridge's shoulder and said with a kind of apology, 'There is one thing certain, Uxbridge, that is, whatever happens, you and I will do our duty.'[10]

At least he had been able to get his army into the sort of position he liked, on a ridge with a gentle slope running down towards the enemy and with shelter and concealment for the troops behind the crest. 'Now,' he said to Baron von Müffling, the Prussian liaison officer at his headquarters, 'Now, Bonaparte will see how a general of sepoys can defend a position.'[11] He had between 67,000 and 68,000 men in that position with 156 guns. Napoleon had almost a hundred more guns and at least 4,000 more men. But Blücher's troops were on the march towards them, their seventy-four-year-old commander, his bruised body having been bathed in brandy, riding beside them, insisting that he would rather be tied to his horse than miss the battle, exchanging jokes and banter with the men, sustained by large doses of garlic-flavoured rhubarb washed down by schnapps.[12]

After earlier lethargy, Napoleon was now in confident mood. He seemed satisfied, Blücher having been so badly mauled at Ligny, that there was no need to pursue his defeated troops with vigour. When Soult advised him to summon reinforcements, he dismissed the suggestion out of hand. 'Just because you have been beaten by Wellington you regard him as a great general,' he said. 'I tell you that Wellington is a bad general, that the English are bad troops and that this battle will be a picnic.' 'We have ninety chances in our favour and not ten against.' The Prussians and English could not possibly join forces for at least two days. When one of his generals made some remark about the tenacity and steady aim of English infantry when well posted by Wellington, Napoleon turned away from him and marched off. There would be no need for complex manoeuvring with this sepoy general; a frontal assault would settle the issue. It would all be over before nightfall. 'Nous coucherons ce soir à Bruxelles.'[13]

So the Emperor 'did not manoeuvre at all', as Wellington said himself. 'He just moved forward in the old style.'[14] It was not as simple as that, though. There were times that day – as the cannon thundered in the thick smoke and soldiers, their faces blackened by powder, were mown down in their hundreds – when defeat seemed as likely as victory. During the battle the squares in which the infantry were drawn up to resist the charges of the French cavalry presented 'a shocking Sight', in the words of an ensign in the 1st Foot Guards.

> Inside we were nearly suffocated by the smoke and smell from burnt cartridges. It was impossible to move a yard without treading upon a wounded comrade, or upon the bodies of the dead; and the loud groans of the wounded and dying was most appalling.
>
> At four o'clock our square was a perfect hospital, being full of dead, dying, and mutilated soldiers. The charges of cavalry were in appearance very formidable, but in reality a great relief, as the artillery could no longer fire on us; the very earth shook under the enormous mass of men and horses. I shall never forget the strange noise our bullets made against the breastplates of the cuirassiers, six or seven thousand in number, who attacked us with great fury . . .
>
> One might suppose that nothing could have resisted the shock of this terrible moving mass . . . In an almost incredibly short period they were within twenty yards of us shouting 'Vive l'Empereur!' The words of command, 'Prepare to receive cavalry', had been given. Every man in front ranks knelt, and a wall bristling with steel presented itself to [the enemy] . . .
>
> I should observe that just before the charge the Duke entered by one of the angles of the square, accompanied by one aide-de-camp; all the rest of the staff being either killed or wounded. Our Commander-in-Chief, as far as I could judge, appeared perfectly composed, but looked very thoughtful and pale.[15]

Another officer, a lieutenant in the 30th Foot, confirmed that the Duke was 'coolness personified'. 'As he crossed the rear face of our square,' this officer remembered, 'a shell fell amongst our grenadiers, and he checked his horse to see its effect. Some men were blown to bits by the explosion, and he merely stirred the reins of his charger, apparently as little concerned at their fate as at his own danger. No leader ever possessed so fully the confidence of his soldiers, "but none did love him". Whenever he appeared, a murmur of "Silence – stand to your front – here's the Duke!" was heard through the columns, and then all was steady as on a parade.'[16]

As at Quatre Bras, Wellington rode about the field on Copenhagen, apparently ignoring danger, scribbling messages, temporarily taking the command from colonels, even from majors, bestowing terse compliments, giving brief orders: 'Drive those fellows away . . . There, my lads, in with you – let me see no more of you . . . Ah! That's the way I like to see horse-artillery move . . . They must hold their ground to the last man . . . Stand fast . . . Stand to the last man, my lads. We must not be beat. What will they say in England . . . Hard pounding this, gentlemen; try who can pound the longest . . . Life Guards, I thank you . . . Now, gentlemen, for the honour of the Household troops! . . . Adam, you must dislodge those fellows . . . Go on, Colbourne. They won't stand . . . Now, Maitland, now's your time . . . Stand up Guards!'

Despite his calm, Wellington recognized that he came close to defeat that day; and it was not until late in the afternoon that he was heard to say ruminatively, 'I believe we shall beat them after all.' Even the bravest and strongest of his soldiers had by then reached the limits of their endurance. He contrived to look unconcerned, continuously appearing wherever the fire was hottest, an immediately recognizable and reassuring figure as he loomed out of the dense smoke in his civilian clothes and cocked hat. Once, when attempting to rally some Dutch troops who had lost their nerve and were beginning to run away, a few of them opened fire on him. He ignored the shots, and continued to go about his business as though 'riding for pleasure'. His staff also seemed to be 'as gay and unconcerned as if they were riding to meet the hounds in some quiet English county'.[17] Talking unconcernedly to the commanding officers of an infantry square, the Duke remarked, 'Oh, it will be all right. If the Prussians come up in time, we shall have a long peace.' It was noticed, though, that for all his apparent unconcern and unaccustomed geniality, he kept glancing at his watch, and, later, that he repeatedly tapped his telescope in and out of its case.

But Napoleon was anxious, too. One of Soult's staff officers thought how sadly changed he was from the dynamic figure whom he had so deeply admired at Austerlitz.

> During his stay on Elba, Napoleon's stoutness had increased rapidly. His head had become enlarged and more deeply set between his shoulders. His pot-belly was unusually pronounced for a man of forty-five. Furthermore, it was noticeable during this campaign that he remained on horseback much less than in the past. When he dismounted, either to study maps or else to send messages and receive reports, members of his staff would set before him a small deal table and a rough chair made of the same wood, and on this he would remain seated for long periods at a time . . .
>
> His stoutness, his dull white complexion, his heavy walk made him appear very different from the General Bonaparte I had seen at the start of my career during the campaign of 1800 in Italy, when he was so alarmingly thin that no soldier in his army could understand how, with so frail a body and looking as ill as he did, he could stand such fatigue.[18]

Despite his age, Blücher seemed far from tired. Urging his hungry men on through the rain-soaked countryside, as their guns sank axle-deep in the mud, he said repeatedly, 'I have promised Wellington. You would not have me break my word.'

He did not break his word; and that night, after Wellington had watched a last desperate charge of the Imperial Guard falter and fail, Blücher was able to write to his wife:

> In conjunction with my friend, Wellington, I put an end to Napoleon's dancing. His army is completely routed, and the whole of his artillery, baggage, caissons, and equipages are in my hands. The insignia of all the different orders he had won have just been brought to me, having been found in his carriage in a casket.[19]

He and Wellington had met earlier that night on the Brussels road between the appropriately named Belle-Alliance and Rossomme. 'We were both on horseback,' Wellington recalled; 'but he embraced and kissed me, exclaiming, *Mein lieber Kamerad* and then *quelle affaire!* which was pretty much all he knew of French.'*[20]

---

* Blücher, in fact, spoke French rather better than Wellington then knew. A year or so later the Prince of Wahlstatt, as Blücher had by then become, called upon the Duke in Paris. '*Je sens un éléphant là,*' he told his former comrade-in-arms, tapping his stomach. He had, he added, been made thus inconveniently pregnant by a French soldier (Stanhope, *Conversations with the Duke of Wellington*, 119–20).

Wellington rode slowly back to the inn where he was staying, passing in the moonlight the corpses of the dead and the bodies of those still struggling to breathe in the sickly sweet air of the battlefield, the detritus of twisted swords and scattered uniforms, saddles and harness, mutilated horses, smashed guns and broken carts beneath the shattered trees, and looters creeping from body to body, feeling for valuables and money, watches and lockets, tearing off epaulettes and gold braid, cutting out teeth to sell to dentists and makers of dentures. At the inn door the Duke gave Copenhagen a pat on his hindquarters as if to offer thanks for a hard day's work. The horse responded with one of those savage kicks of which soldiers in the Peninsula had learned to be wary.[21]

Inside the inn, the aide-de-camp whom he liked so much, Sir Alexander Gordon, his leg amputated, lay dying. 'Thank God you are safe,' the young man said. The Duke told him something of the victory, then left him with the gruffly spoken words, 'I have no doubt, Gordon, you will do well.' There were a few other officers in the entrance passage and the Duke said to them, 'How are you?'; then, catching sight of his cook, James Thornton, he called to him, 'Is that you? Get dinner.'[22]

The dinner table was laid in the Duke's bedroom upstairs. Various members of the staff who had not been wounded were there; so were Alava and Müffling; and so were Lord Apsley and Sir Sidney Smith who, now retired from the Navy, had happened to be in Brussels that June and was thenceforward given to boasting that he had been 'the first Englishman that was not in the battle' who shook hands with the Duke after his victory.[23]

It was noticed that the Duke looked up quickly every time the door opened, hoping to see a familiar face; but no other officer appeared. Towards the end of the meal he raised both his hands in one of those theatrical gestures to which he was occasionally given, and said, 'The hand of Almighty God has been upon me this day.' Then, after giving a single toast – 'To the memory of the Peninsular War' – he stood up, left the room, lay down unwashed on a mattress and was soon asleep, his face begrimed with the dust and powder of the battle.

He was woken by the surgeon, John Hume, who brought with him a long list of casualties. The Duke stretched out his hand as though in need of comfort. Hume took it and held it in his own as he read the names on the list. The surgeon soon became aware of tears dropping on their clasped fingers. He looked down to see them coursing down the Duke's still dirty face, and paused in his reading. 'Go on, go on, for God's sake go on,' the Duke said. 'Let me hear it all. This is terrible.'

'Well, thank God,' Wellington added, when Hume had finished, brushing the tears with his hand, 'I don't know what it is to lose a battle; but, certainly nothing can be more painful than to gain one with the loss of so many of one's friends.'[24] Sir Thomas Picton, commander of the 5th Division, was dead, shot through the top hat which he invariably wore in action to protect his eyes, as he galloped at the head of one of his brigades, two of his ribs already broken, shouting encouragement. The American-born Deputy Quartermaster-General, Sir William De Lancey, whom Wellington had known since they were boys together, was also dead, knocked from his horse by a cannon ball as he was talking to the Duke. Sir William Ponsonby, Commander of the Union Brigade of heavy cavalry, and his brigade major were both cut down by French lancers, Ponsonby hacked from his horse to the ground where he lay with a miniature of his wife in a locket revealed by his slashed coat. Sir James Kempt, who succeeded Picton in command of the 5th Division, was severely wounded; so were Denis Pack, commander of a brigade in that Division, and General Halkett, shot through the mouth. The names of Generals Edward Barnes, Frederick Adam, George Cooke, Charles von Alten, Duplat and Grant were also on the casualty lists. So were those of Colonel John Elley, who was said to have killed more than one cuirassier in single combat, and Colonel Sir Frederic Ponsonby who, suffering from seven wounds, was robbed, ridden over by Prussian troops, used as musket rest by one French soldier then as a pillow by another who was dying, and Edward Whinyates, commander of the rocket troop whose efficacy the Duke had so strongly doubted. It seemed astonishing that the Duke himself had remained unhurt. 'The finger of Providence,' so he told Lady Frances Wedderburn-Webster, using a favourite expression, was upon him.[25]

Officers, maimed for life, bore their suffering without complaint. Lord Fitzroy Somerset, wounded by a musket ball which smashed his right elbow as he rode along next to his chief, walked back to a cottage used as a field hospital to have his arm cut off between the shoulder and the elbow. He did not even murmur. The Prince of Orange, lying wounded in the same small room, was unaware that an operation had been performed until the arm was tossed away by the surgeon and Lord Fitzroy called out, 'Hey, bring my arm back. There's a ring my wife gave me on the finger.'*[26]

---

* The Duke temporarily replaced Somerset with another one-armed officer as an assurance to him that his disability would not prevent his returning as principal aide-de-camp when he was recovered.

Lord Uxbridge behaved with comparable aplomb when one of the last cannon balls to be sent flying from the French guns hurtled into his right knee. Uxbridge, according to a well-aired account, looked down and said to Wellington who was sitting in his saddle beside him, 'By God, sir, I've lost my leg!' Wellington, lowering his telescope for a moment to inspect the wound, retorted, 'By God, sir, so you have!' Then, having resumed his survey of the field, he helped Uxbridge to remain in his saddle before men came to bear him away; and immediately galloped off himself.[27]

Uxbridge bore the amputation as quietly as Lord Fitzroy Somerset had undergone his, never moving or complaining except to observe that the surgeon's knife was not very sharp and, after the operation was over, asking someone to look at the mangled leg to reassure him that it could not have been saved.[28]

The next morning Uxbridge was carried on a stretcher into the house of the Marquise d'Assche. 'Well, Marquise,' he remarked to her conversationally. 'You see I shan't be able to dance with you any more except with a wooden leg.'[29]

The Duke's acknowledgement of Uxbridge's services in the dispatch he addressed to Earl Bathurst, the Secretary for War, the day after the battle was perfunctory to say the least, so perfunctory, in fact, that Uxbridge's sister, Lady Caroline Capel, described the dispatch as an 'odious' report in which 'no one is done justice to'.[30] She was far from being its only critic, since Wellington, to whom hyperbole was abhorrent and high praise not easy to bestow, could not bring himself to write in terms other than those which came naturally to him. Having read the dispatch, the American Minister in London suggested that it might as well have served as the report of a defeat. To be sure, Sir Thomas Picton was described as having fallen 'gloriously leading his division in a charge with bayonets, by which one of the most serious attacks made by the enemy on our position was repulsed'. Other Generals, including Kempt and Pack, Alten, Halkett and Cooke, Maitland and Byng had 'highly distinguished themselves'. He had 'every reason to be satisfied' with the conduct of the Adjutant-General and the Quartermaster-General, while the artillery and engineer departments had been conducted much to his satisfaction. Sir John Byng's brigade of Guards had behaved with 'the utmost gallantry'. Lord Edward Somerset's brigade of the Life Guards, the Royal Horse Guards and 1st Dragoon Guards had 'highly distinguished themselves'; as had Sir

William Ponsonby's Union Brigade. Also the dispatch gave due credit to the 'cordial and timely assistance' given by the Prussian army to which the successful result of the arduous day could be attributed. But of the British Horse Artillery there was no mention; nor was there mention of the regiment of Hussars, not even of Sir Hussey Vivian's Hussars whose services were particularly meritorious. The regiments of Foot received scant attention, while John Colborne's 52nd whose charge and routing of the Old Guard was held by some – and most insistently by the Regiment's historian, William Leeke[31] – to have been the decisive action of the battle, was not mentioned at all.

These omissions caused widespread and lasting resentment; and it seems that, towards the end of his life, the Duke admitted that he should have given more praise. But it was an admission that he had not made earlier. When asked by John Gurwood, an officer severely wounded in the battle, about the services of the various regiments engaged at Waterloo, he replied curtly that he knew nothing about them: 'there was glory enough for all.'[32] He stood by his original assertion that there was 'no officer nor description of troops that did not behave well'.[33]

He had never seen 'such a pounding match', and the numbers of dead grieved him sorely. His army had suffered casualties of almost 15,000; some battalions, such as those of the 27th and the 73rd, had been almost wiped out. In addition the Prussians had lost 7,000 men killed and wounded, the French 25,000. The sight and thought of the dead overshadowed his pride and gratitude in victory. Years later when a woman of his acquaintance commented, 'What a glorious thing must be a victory, sir,' he was said to have replied in his abrupt way, 'The greatest tragedy in the world, Madam, except a defeat.'[34]

He said much the same thing at the time to Lady Shelley. During the battle as in all his battles, he had far too much to think about to 'feel anything'. 'But it is wretched just after. It is impossible to think of glory. Both mind and feelings are exhausted.'[35]

Much as he enjoyed talking about and being questioned about his military campaigns, he did not like to discuss his emotions, his reactions. Another of his lady friends, Lady Salisbury, pressed him to tell her what he was thinking about after the battle when he rode back very early on the Monday morning from Waterloo to Brussels, having had a cup of tea and some toast and left poor Alexander Gordon dead in his bed at the inn. He was not communicative. 'But now! While you were riding there!' Lady Salisbury pressed him. 'Did it never occur to you that you had placed yourself on such a pinnacle of glory?'

'No,' he said, 'I was entirely occupied with what was necessary to be done. I have no recollection of any sensation of delight.'[36]

He was rather more communicative with Thomas Creevey who, on hearing that the Duke had returned to Brussels, hurried round to see him at his hotel. But then Creevey was anxious to know what had happened at Waterloo, not what the Duke thought about it.

> I saw the Duke upstairs at his window [Creevey recollected]. Upon his recognising me, he immediately beckoned to me with his finger to come up ... The first thing I did, of course, was to put out my hand and congratulate him upon his victory. He made a variety of observations in his short, natural, blunt way, but with the greatest gravity all the time, and without the least approach to anything like triumph or joy.
>
> 'It has been a damned serious business,' he said. 'Blücher and I have lost 30,000 men. It has been a damned nice thing – the nearest run thing you ever saw in your life' ... As he walked about he praised greatly those Guards who [stood firm] against the repeated attacks of the French; and then he praised all our troops, uttering repeated expressions of astonishment at our men's courage. He repeated so often its being *so nice a thing – so nearly run a thing*, that I asked if the French had fought better than he had ever seen them do before – 'No,' he said, 'they have always fought the same since I first saw them at Vimeiro.' Then he said: – 'By God I don't think it would have been done if I had not been there.'[37]

'It was the most desperate business I ever was in,' he wrote in the same vein to his brother William, reporting upon his 'Desperate Battle and Victory over Boney!!' 'I never took so much trouble about any Battle; & never was so near being beat. Our loss is immense particularly in that best of all Instruments, British Infantry. I never saw the Infantry behave so well.'[38]

He trusted that he would never have to see such slaughter again. 'Nothing except a battle lost can be half so melancholy as a battle won.' 'I hope to God that I have fought my last battle,' he said to Lady Shelley. 'It is a bad thing to be always fighting.'[39]

II

1815 — 52

26 The Ambassador

1815

'The Duke's conduct to the Parisians was kind
and considerate.'

THERE WAS, as Wellington hoped, to be no more fighting for him.
For the moment he was to be a diplomat in Paris where Baron von
Müffling had been installed as Military Governor.

Both the Prussians and the British troops had a mind to take advantage of their victory. So, indeed, had the British Government, which,
like the army, were somewhat impatient of what they considered to
be the Duke's leniency towards their former enemies. 'It is quite right
to prevent plunder of every description,' wrote Lord Liverpool, 'but
France must bear a part of the expenses of war . . . We do not exactly
know what course in this respect the Duke of Wellington has been
following . . . I trust however that [he can be persuaded] that the
French nation ought to bear a part of the expense.'[1] The French, in
fact, were being asked to pay a fine of 100 million francs; and, as for
the Duke of Wellington, it was quite clear that he strongly disapproved
of any excessively harsh penalties which would antagonize the French
people. He recognized that the Bourbons were far from universally
popular in France; yet he insisted that 'the establishment of any other
government than the King's in France [would] inevitably lead to new
and endless wars'.[2] He also insisted that if King Louis XVIII were to
be returned to his throne with the help of the nations who had so
recently fought against his people, the Allies must do nothing to offend
those people: the humiliation of France, or its dismemberment as some
recommended, might lead eventually to another war and, as the Duke
had once said, 'Take my word for it, if you had seen but one day of
war, you would pray to Almighty God that you might never see such
a thing again.' When it was proposed to demolish one of Paris's bridges,
the Pont d'Iéna, named after Napoleon's great victory on the Saale, a
request to spare it was made to Blücher on behalf of the French Foreign
Minister. 'I have resolved upon blowing up the bridge,' Blücher replied

in his own handwriting. 'And I cannot conceal from you how much pleasure it would afford me if M. Talleyrand would previously station himself upon it; and I beg you will make my wish known to him.'

In the hope of saving the bridge, Wellington placed a British sentry on it, trusting that the Prussians would not blow up an Allied soldier. The bridge, subsequently renamed the Pont des Invalides, was saved, however, not by such hoped-for squeamishness but by the incompetence of the Prussian engineers who – having failed to persuade the imperturbable British sentry to get off the bridge until relieved by his corporal – succeeded only in damaging an arch and toppling one of their own sentries into the river.*[3]

The Duke also intervened in a less contentious matter when he heard that the Duke of Queensberry's friend, Colonel John Woodford, was taking advantage of his appointment to the army of occupation by digging up the field of Agincourt to uncover the armour of French knights killed by British archers in 1415. Wellington sent him 'a strong hint' to abandon his provocative excavations.[4]

'The Duke of Wellington's conduct to the Parisians was kind and considerate,' wrote Rees Howell Gronow, who entered the city with a battalion of the 1st Foot Guards on 25 June. 'But Blücher was not so moderate.'

> His troops were billeted in every house [Gronow continued]; he obliged the inhabitants to feed and clothe them; and issued an order (which I well recollect seeing) commanding the authorities to supply each soldier with a bedstead containing a bolster, a woollen mattress, two new blankets and a pair of linen sheets. The rations per day, for each man, were two pounds of bread of good quality, one pound of butcher's meat, a bottle of wine, a quarter of a pound of butter, ditto rice, a glass of brandy and some tobacco . . . Blücher's generals occupied all the best hotels in the Faubourg St Germain . . .
>
> The Russian and Austrian armies, with the two Emperors, [the Tsar Alexander I and Francis I, Emperor of Austria] entered Paris soon after our arrival. The Emperors imitated Blücher in some respects; they refused to quarter their soldiers in the large and wholesome barracks which were in readiness to receive them: no; they preferred billeting them with peaceable merchants and tradespeople, whom they

---

* The Pont d'Austerlitz was also threatened with destruction and also saved, unlike Napoleon's statue on its pillar in the Place Vendôme. This, however, was not smashed by the Prussians but by a group of rabid Royalists.

plundered and bullied in the most outrageous manner. Wellington, all this while, showed great moderation; and his army paid for everything they required. Blücher, on the other hand, threatened to take possession of the Bank of France and the Government offices: which threat was not carried into execution, owing to the wise and timely interposition of the Duke.[5]

Gronow was not surprised to find the inhabitants of occupied Paris 'sulky and stupified' at first; but after a time they were friendly enough towards the British, though the Parisian women disapproved of the Scottish regiments – which were bivouacked in the muddy Champs Elysées – declaring that their 'want of *culottes* was most indecent'.[6]

Gronow himself enjoyed his time in Paris immensely. He dined at the Café Anglais on the Boulevard des Italiens and beneath the gilt-framed looking-glasses of Beauvillier's restaurant in the rue de Richelieu; he went to receptions at the British Embassy; he frequented the Café Foy in the Palais Royal; he saw François-Joseph Talma, the most famous tragedian of his day, on the stage of the Comédie Française; he paraded about in the corridors, gardens and saloons of the Palais Royal amidst the 'countless foreigners from all parts of the world', the *filles de joie* who strolled up and down, 'ornamented with mock diamonds and pearls, casting their eyes significantly on every side', and the Allied officers in their garish uniforms.

'Prussian and Russian officers were in blue or green uniforms', an English officer wrote, 'waists drawn in like a wasp's, breasts sticking out like a pigeon's, long sashes, with huge tassels of gold or silver, hanging halfway down their legs . . . lancers in square topped caps and waving plumes; hussars in various rich uniforms . . . Austrian officers in plain white uniforms, turned up with red'.[7]

Many of these uniforms were displayed to good effect in July when a grand review was held on the plains of St Denis. As bands played and 'a mass of men, numbering not less than two hundred thousand' were drawn up around the field, the Duke arrived 'mounted on a favourite charger; and, strange as it may appear, on his right was observed a lady in a plain riding-habit, who was no other than Lady Shelley. Immediately behind the Duke followed the Emperors of Austria and Russia; the Kings of Prussia, Holland, Bavaria, and Württemberg, and several German princes and general officers – the whole forming one of the most illustrious and numerous staffs ever brought together. The Duke of Wellington, thus accompanied,

took up his position, and began manoeuvring, with a facility and confidence which elicited the admiration of all the experienced soldiers
around him.'[8]

Ensign Gronow, being on duty near the Duke, overheard the Austrian
Field Marshal Fürst zu Schwarzenberg say to him, 'You are the only
man who can so well play at this game.'[9]

On 8 July King Louis XVIII arrived in Paris, and Wellington was
once again in the limelight, playing a principal part in the reception of this fat and gouty monarch of fifty-nine whose greediness in
eating oysters prompted the French to render XVIII as 'Dix-Huîtres'.
As the Duke had hoped, the King – although entering the capital 'in the baggage train of the allied armies', as his enemies put it –
was received with great enthusiasm. 'The people in the streets
and at windows displayed the wildest joy,' one spectator observed,
'shouting "Vive le Roi" amidst the waving of hats and handkerchiefs,
while white sheets or white rags were made to do the duty of a
Bourbon banner.' 'The King's portly and good-natured appearance,'
this witness commented, 'seemed to be appreciated by the crowd.'
There were, however, others, among them the novelist Fanny Burney,
now married to an officer in the corps de garde, General D'Arblay,
who thought there were more sullen than cheerful faces in the
streets.[10]

The next day Wellington, accompanied by the Foreign Secretary,
Lord Castlereagh, paid the King his personal respects. Captain Gronow,
on duty in the Salle des Maréchaux when they passed through on their
way to the reception room where the King was waiting to receive them,
was much impressed by the respect paid to the Duke by 'a number of
ladies of the highest rank' who 'formed an avenue, through which the
hero of Waterloo passed'. The position of the Duke was a difficult one,
Gronow added. He not only had to 'curb the vindictive vandalism of
Blücher and his army', but 'at the same time a spirit of vindictiveness
pervaded the restored Court against Napoleon and his adherents, which
the Duke constantly endeavoured to modify'.[11]

If the sovereigns wished to put Napoleon to death, Wellington said,
'they should appoint an executioner which should not be me'.[12] And
he was much relieved when demands that the former Emperor should
be executed were eventually refused, as was Napoleon's own request
that he should be allowed to live in England, where, as Lord Liverpool
said, declining the petition, he would become 'an object of curiosity
immediately, and possibly of compassion in the course of a few months'.
The Prince Regent approved of the Cabinet's decision, though – noting

that Napoleon had referred to him in his request as 'the most powerful, the most constant and the most generous' of his enemies – he declared approvingly, 'Upon my word, a very proper letter: much more so, I must say, than any I ever received from Louis XVIII.'[13] So Napoleon was dispatched to exile on the island of St Helena; and Wellington was never to meet his great contemporary – three and a half months younger than himself – as he had wanted to do.

This was a disappointment to him but a disappointment far outweighed by his satisfaction in having played so large and successful a part in placing Louis XVIII on the throne which Napoleon had been obliged to vacate. The King – for whom the Duke now 'cherished a strange personal affection'[14] – rewarded him lavishly: he was admitted to the ancient Order of the Holy Ghost founded in 1578, his Majesty removing the wide, sky blue ribbon of the Order from his own well-filled coat to present it to him. He also offered him a country estate; but this the Duke thought it as well to refuse, particularly as the British Government, having no honours to bestow that he did not already possess, had increased the grant already made to him for an estate in England. Other foreign monarchs were as generous as the French: from Prussia came the Order of the Black Eagle founded by the Elector of Brandenburg, Frederick I; from Denmark, the Order of the Elephant, established in 1462 and limited to thirty knights; from Russia the Order of St Andrew, founded by Peter the Great. The Netherlands created him Prince of Waterloo. The Prince Regent rewarded him with the Royal Hanoverian Guelphic Order.*

He affected to take such honours lightly; but he was very fond of dressing up. When he discarded the familiar blue frock-coat for his field marshal's uniform, the red cloth looked particularly well, adorned with the white and gold Maltese cross of the Order of St Esprit and the orange ribbon of the Order of the Black Eagle. He was proud of the figure he cut; he did not mind being known as 'the Beau' and spent a large amount on his clothes: an annual bill presented by William

---

* The Duke eventually accumulated so many Orders that he could not remember what they all were. On one occasion, according to Sir William Fraser, having been invited to Windsor Castle to meet a foreign royal visitor, he asked his servant to take the box in which he kept his Orders to the foreign prince's valet and to ask which was the one presented to him by the Prince's country. 'Either by the maladroitness of the Duke's servant, or more probably of the servant of the foreign Prince, the Duke's drawer of Orders was carried up to the latter, no doubt to his disgust' (Sir William Fraser, *Words on Wellington*, 26).

Moore of Old Bond Street, 'Town Manufacturers of Hats, Hosiery and Gloves', lists sixteen pairs of kid gloves as well as many other items, including flannel gloves.[15]

Occupied though he was with his work in the daytime, he found time for occasional alfresco luncheons and horse races on the plains of Neuilly where Blücher was once thrown to the ground while galloping headlong over the course; and in the evenings there were fancy dress balls and, since the Duke, in the words of one of his aides-de-camp, was 'devoted to music' there were numerous occasions upon which he 'got together the best private and professional talent that could be found in Paris'.[16] At formal receptions he talked easily with diplomats and field marshals, kings and the ministers of kings, with the allied generals for whom he gave 'a great dinner in a low room at Verrey's, the most celebrated Restaurateur', and with the French Foreign Minister, Prince de Talleyrand, and with Joseph Fouché, duc d'Otrante, the great survivor, formerly Napoleon's Minister of Police, now President of the provisional government. At one of these receptions, given in the Duke's house, the Hôtel de la Reynière, which had once belonged to Marshal Junot, the Order of the Bath was bestowed upon Marshal Blücher. The novelist Sir Walter Scott was there and the Duke sent for him to sit down by him. Scott asked him if he had ever actually seen Napoleon. 'No,' the Duke replied; but he had been near enough to him to hear repeated shouts of 'Vive l'Empéreur!' Scott asked him other questions to which he got 'very direct replies'. 'He is,' reported Scott to his daughter, 'the most downright person you ever knew.' He was also, thought Scott, rather formidable. Indeed, the novelist told Lady Shelley that Wellington was the only person he had ever encountered who made him feel shy.[17]

The Duke enjoyed these receptions well enough, just as he enjoyed the parties at the British Embassy and at Lord Castlereagh's where Lady Castlereagh, no longer beautiful but as much given to laughter as ever, wore the star of her husband's Garter in her hair. But the Duke preferred less formal affairs, particularly those he gave at the Hôtel de la Reynière. 'I must always have my house full,' he said. 'For sixteen years I have always been at the head of our army, and I must have these gay fellows around me.'[18]

Despite these sixteen years, he was still only forty-six, lithe, eager, alert and personable, though his carefully shaven cheeks were sunken now from his having lost his back teeth. For all his abrupt manner, women found his company enchanting, none more so than Lady Shelley who so obviously worshipped him, who had almost fainted on first encountering him.* He liked to go riding with her – 'stick close to me', she was once delighted to hear him say – and on more than one occasion he let her ride Copenhagen. He liked to tell her about his campaigns, to explain to her how the infantry squares were formed at Waterloo, to show her his possessions, the Orders and the gold boxes which had portraits of European sovereigns on the lids. He let her watch him working at his desk; and she wrote down everything of interest he said to her and everything she saw him do, how he had told her that the finger of God had been upon him at Waterloo, that he hated soldiers to cheer him: 'I hate that cheering. If once you allow soldiers to express an opinion, they may on some other occasion hiss instead of cheer.'[19] She described how they had dinner at Malmaison, and had afterwards walked together in the garden and looked into the Empress Josephine's conservatory; how she had once watched him playing with a dirty little child, taking a bite of the infant's apple and sitting her upon his knee; how they had gone to a fair and ridden on a merry-go-round, the ladies on swans, the Duke on a horse; how she had been allowed, with her husband looking on, to cut off a lock of his hair.[20]

The complaisant acquiescence and frequent presence of her husband saved her from scandal, Lady Granville thought. The two of them 'ran after the great Duke in a very disgusting way', she told one of her correspondents, 'but as they were together, "sans peur et sans re-proche"'.[21] The husband was not always there, though: the Duke had once taken the wife in his arms and danced a polonaise with her all round the house, downstairs and upstairs.

Yet no one supposed the Duchess of Wellington, left behind in London, had any real cause to be jealous of the simple, pretty little blonde Lady Shelley. The same could not be said, however, of the Duke's relationship with Lady Frances Wedderburn-Webster. Lady

---

* Many others worshipped him from afar, as Charlotte Brontë had done since she was a child, naming a toy soldier after him, introducing him into the stories she wrote for the little magazine her brother produced at Haworth, collecting pictures of him, reading all she could find about him in newspapers and periodicals and concluding in an essay that his character equalled in grandeur and surpassed in truth 'that of all other heroes, ancient and modern'.

The character of Robert Gérard Moore in her novel Shirley is loosely based on him; and the compelling, masterful, sardonic Edward Fairfax Rochester in Jane Eyre was a man who clearly emerged from her fascinated regard for him. There are echoes of the Duke's character, too, in Heathcliff, the central figure in Wuthering Heights by Charlotte's sister Emily (Rebecca Fraser, The Brontës: Charlotte Brontë and Her Family, London, 1988, 33–66; Juliet Barker, The Brontës, London, 1994, 154–5, 159–60).

Shelley was convinced they were not and never had been lovers; but others, including the Duchess of Wellington's friend Maria Edgeworth, who hoped that the glory of Kitty's husband would not 'be tarnished like Nelson's glory', were not so sure.[22] One of these was Mme de Lieven who reported to Metternich, 'Lady Frances [is] married to a jealous husband who has reason to be jealous. She is a young and rather pretty woman, although a little too washed out for my taste. But my taste has nothing to do with it, and other people admire her; for instance the Duke of Wellington, who had certain passages with her at Brussels five or six years ago, and nearly forgot in her company that he had the battle of Waterloo to win. There was talk of a lawsuit but he avoided the scandal by paying some thousands of guineas.'[23] Soon the alleged continuing affair between the Duke and Lady Frances was being hinted at in English as well as Continental newspapers. The *St James's Chronicle*, a London evening Opposition paper founded in the 1760s, informed its readers that the 'cessation of warfare [had] enabled scandal to resume her usual influence on the public mind' in Paris where a report was 'very prevalent that a distinguished commander' had 'surrendered himself captive to the beautiful wife of a military officer of high rank, in a manner to make a very serious investigation of his offence indispensable'.[24] Another newspaper repeated the story that 'after the battle of Waterloo (which, *en passant* ought to be called the battle of Mont St Jean) the Duke went to visit the wounded – perhaps the wounded heart was meant. A word to the wise.' Elsewhere a 'Fashionable Alliteration' was reported as being current at Brussels:

> *In the letter W there's a charm full divine,*
> *Wars, Wellington, Wedderburn-Webster, and Wine.*

The *St James's Chronicle* suggested that the injured husband was instituting proceedings for divorce and seeking damages in the sum of £50,000 and that the 'unfortunate lover' had offered to pay this amount.

His aide-de-camp, Lord William Pitt Lennox, was with the Duke when a newspaper carrying a similar report of the alleged affair was brought to his notice by Alava. While Alava was turning over the pages looking for the report the Duke stood 'playing with his watch-chain which he often did when absorbed in thought'. Then, having read the article himself, he declared furiously, 'That's too bad! The writer's a walking lie. Never saw her alone in my life. This must be checked.'[25]

Eventually it *was* checked. It seems that for a time Wedderburn-Webster, still notorious as a womanizer himself, considered divorcing

Lady Frances; but instead he joined with her in bringing an action for damages against the proprietor of the *St James's Chronicle*, Charles Baldwin, a printer said to be worth £100,000.[26] The Wedderburn-Websters' counsel was William Draper Best, Sergeant-at-Law and Member of Parliament for Bridport, whose style of speaking was said to be 'forcible and pointed' and his arguments 'remarkable for their clearness'. He called upon the Duke's friend, the Duke of Richmond, to testify to Lady Frances's good character, her 'singularly amiable and decorous manners' and referred to the Duke of Wellington himself as the 'saviour of Europe', the 'greatest commander of any age and country', one who should be revered 'by Christendom as the tutelar saint of the World'. As though stunned by these encomia, Baldwin's counsel, John Lens, who had been a close friend of Charles James Fox, produced no credible defence.

Sir Vicary Gibbs, the small, thin Chief Justice of the Common Pleas, a man entirely devoid of humour, was clearly in favour of substantial damages when he summed up for the jury. The Wedderburn-Websters were awarded £2,000; and two years later Lady Frances became intimate with Byron's friend, the dandiacal philanderer Scrope Davies, who decamped to the Continent in 1820 leaving twenty-one of her melodramatic letters to him in a brass-studded leather trunk.[27]

While people were still whispering about the relationship between the Duke and Lady Frances, there were rumours too that he was still casting a far from platonic eye on Lady Caroline Lamb who had burst upon the Parisian scene 'tormenting everybody', laughing, occasionally screaming, galloping about in the Bois in a violently purple riding habit, setting her cap at him.

'I am convinced she is ready primed for an attack upon the Duke of Wellington,' Lady Granville told her sister, 'and I have no doubt but that she will to a certain extent succeed, as no dose of flattery is too strong for him to swallow or her to administer. Poor William [Lady Caroline's husband] hides in a small room while she assembles lovers and tradespeople in another ... [Later, she could be heard giving occasional] screams of delight as she dined alone with the Duke and Sir Walter Scott.'

'She arrived dying by her own account, having had French apothecaries at most of the towns through which she passed. She sent her maid immediately for a doctor, but by mistake they went for the Duke of Wellington.'[28]

There was also talk that the Duke was interested in the Countess of Westmeath, daughter of the Marquess of Salisbury, who was then in Paris with her husband. Her husband's mother, by then divorced and remarried as the Hon. Mrs Augustus Bradshaw, was anxious to promote the interest the Duke showed in her daughter-in-law whom he had known since her childhood. 'Now, my dear soul,' she said to her, according to Lady Westmeath's account. 'You are very silly; there is but one step from friendship to love with a man for a pretty woman, and if you would make use of your prettyness as other women do, you might put [your husband] at the top of the tree.'[29]

'I am willing to consider this by way of a joke,' Lady Westmeath replied, 'but it is a very bad one, and I must request you never to mention such a subject to me again.'

She told her husband what his mother had proposed. He had a mistress himself and was 'not unwilling' that his wife should become the Duke's; but he knew that she was far too much of a prude. 'Oh, my poor dear mother,' he commented. 'She did not know what an old square-toes she was speaking to when she said that to you.'[30]

Much as the Duke enjoyed whiling away the hours in the company of attractive young ladies, he never neglected either his duties or his private study, having made it a rule, so he said, 'to study by himself for some hours every day'. He was kept busy with both military and diplomatic affairs. He constantly concerned himself with the state of the army which, with the exception of the infantry that had fought in Spain, so he told Lord Bathurst, was now worse equipped, composed of the worst troops and 'with the worst Staff that was ever brought together'. He personally attended to the General Orders which dealt in detail with such matters as the necessity for officers to appear properly attired in their regimental dress when walking about in Paris, their obedient submission to the search made at the barriers for contraband articles carried by their postilions, and the circumstances in which commanding officers of regiments might allow soldiers to help farmers with the harvest and to accept payment for this assistance. He concerned himself with the award to officers of the various classes of the Order of the Bath and with the foreign decorations which he was asked to distribute. He conscientiously dealt with the problem of prisoners of war, and wrote letters to the families of wounded officers still in hospital. He submitted his advice upon the concessions and reparations to be extracted from the French and upon the securities to be demanded for the performance of the treaty of peace. He was required to reject as tactfully as possible the Tsar's eccentric proposal for a Holy Alliance inspired by that 'old fanatic' Baroness von Krüdener, a mystic visionary, even more crack-brained, in the Duke's opinion, than her imperial convert whom she reduced to tears in her Bible classes. The Duke found it difficult to listen with 'becoming gravity' to the Tsar's plans for his Holy Alliance which Castlereagh described as 'a piece of sublime mysticism and nonsense'.[31]

Finding it as tiresome as any of his other duties, Wellington had also to deal with the question of the works of art looted by the French during their continental campaigns. From Italy alone, among other treasures removed to Paris, had come the ancient Roman horses taken from the Basilica di San Marco in Venice in 1797 and placed over the Triumphal Arch of the Carrousel, the Laocoön, the Belvedere Apollo and countless other masterpieces brought from Rome, including works by Raphael, Caravaggio and Bernini, as well as the Medici Venus sent to the Louvre from Florence.

It was the British Government's opinion that they should either be restored to the countries from which they had been taken or divided amongst the Allies, the Allied armies, so Lord Liverpool said, having 'the same title to them by conquest as that by which the French authorities acquired them. In any case,' Liverpool added, 'it is most desirable, in point of policy, to remove them if possible from France, as whilst in that country they must necessarily have the effect of keeping up the remembrance of their former conquests, and of cherishing the military spirit and vanity of the nation.'[32]

It was Wellington's opinion that 'the Allies could not do otherwise than restore them to the countries from which, contrary to the practice of civilised warfare, they had been torn during the disastrous period of the French Revolution and the tyranny of Buonaparte.' The French did not agree: Paris was 'the fittest depository' for these works of art. King Louis declared that they would not be handed over; if the Allies insisted on removing them from Paris they would have to seize them by force. Wellington, at first conciliatory, speaking of a gradual restoration, soon lost patience with French intransigence. The King and his people must be taught 'a great Moral Lesson'.[33]

So British soldiers were sent to the Louvre as a guard for the men instructed to bring the treasure out. William Grattan of the Connaught Rangers described how angry and distressed the Parisians were to see the parade of pictures and statues emerging into the Jardin des Tuileries. Was it not unworthy of the English General, one citizen asked, to sanction the removal of these exquisite works 'collected by the Emperor with paternal care from every country in Europe' and now 'so well calculated to be seen by all those nations, and free of expense, too?' Another onlooker protested that the operation might at least have been conducted at night to spare the citizens the horror of seeing the Louvre's collections being torn apart like this.[34]

Wellington decided that to avoid any further trouble the Venetian horses of St Mark's would be removed at night and he sent a party of men under a British officer to carry out the operation as quietly as they could under the cover of darkness. They had no sooner set to work, however, than a crowd of Parisians, led by troops of the National Guard, burst into the Place du Carrousel, bringing the hammering to a sudden end. The next day the angry Duke ordered several hundred Austrian and Hungarian troops into the Place and, while these troops cheered and Parisians shouted and hooted in protest, the hammering and chiselling was resumed until all four horses had been brought to the ground.

Austrian troops were again called upon by Wellington to act as custodians in the Louvre in case any unauthorized attempts were made to remove works either by the French or by representatives of the Allies laying dubious claims to them. A party of Sardinians did make such an attempt one day when the Austrians were off duty; but they were sent packing by cleaners brandishing brooms.

> For the last two days I have been at The Louvre, fearing that the pictures might be gone before I could see them [Lowry Cole's wife, Lady Frances, wrote home]. For the Bavarians, Prussians and Spaniards are taking away what was stolen from them and have already got about a hundred. I think this mortification of their vanity chafes the French more than anything, particularly when inflicted by the Germans whom they detest . . . Their vanity is wounded in the most susceptible spot.[35]

A fortnight before Lady Frances had been driven to watch a review in the Duke's carriage which was 'much stared at' as it passed along. 'There is no doubt,' she had thought then, that the Duke was 'by far the most popular of the commanders'. He was far from being so now: 'The Duke's wonted popularity is quite at an end and they abuse him as much as they worshipped him before. And all this because as commander-in-chief he sent some English soldiers to protect the workmen in the Louvre.'[36]

One of the Duke's most unpleasant dilemmas was whether or not to interfere in the punishments decreed by the new regime for those whom they deemed 'traitors'. He had a constitutional dislike of interference, largely for fear of being rebuffed when he did intervene. In obedience to the wishes of the Cabinet he declined to interfere to save the life of Napoleon's former aide-de-camp, Charles de la Bedoyère, who had been arrested when he slipped into Paris to say goodbye to his wife and little son before attempting to escape abroad. Even when the pretty Georgine de la Bedoyère pleaded with the Duke to save her husband's life, he insisted that he could not help her.

He was equally unwilling to become involved when Marshal Ney's wife, Aglaé, begged him to use his influence to have her husband spared. He was unable to help her, he said; he was the servant of his Majesty's Government and the representative of the Allies. Besides, so he told not her but Lord Alvanley long after Ney's execution, he had been snubbed at the Tuileries before the Marshal's arrest by the King who had twice turned his back upon him at his approach. 'I immediately left the Palace,' the Duke said, 'feeling very angry and saying to myself, "I'll be hanged if I come here again to be insulted by the King or anyone else": for there were others . . . who were immediately cold and distant to me that evening . . . My belief is that they had offended me on purpose to drive me away, that I might not interfere to prevent Ney's death.'*[37]

When the uncompromisingly outspoken and tactless Major-General Sir Robert Wilson and two companions, Robert Bruce, later Lady Hester Stanhope's lover, and Captain John Hely-Hutchinson of the 1st Foot Guards, afterwards third Earl of Donoughmore, helped another Frenchman, Napoleon's former Director of Posts, Count de Lavalette, to escape the guillotine by hiding him away after he had walked out of prison in his wife's clothes, the Duke did intervene, however, and by his intervention helped to ensure that the three men received only three months' imprisonment each instead of the far heavier punishment the prosecution had demanded.

---

* The second Duke of Wellington told Sir William Fraser that when Napoleon III attempted to introduce Ney's son to the Duke after a dinner at Windsor Castle where the Emperor was a guest of Queen Victoria, 'Marshal Ney's son clearly indicated that he did not wish to make the Duke's acquaintance' (Sir William Fraser, *Words on Wellington*, 116).

27 Cambrai and Vitry

1815 — 18

'The Shelley is arrived in great beauty!'

BY THE END of October 1815 the Duke's orders and dispatches were being dated regularly from Cambrai; for he had been appointed Commander-in-Chief of the Army of Occupation with over 150,000 men, Russians, Austrians and Germans as well as British, under his command. The diarist Mary Berry met him at this time and, while impressed by the 'simplicity and frankness of his manners', she noticed how easily he spoke of himself as a man on a par with the sovereigns of the soldiers he commanded. 'Talking of the allied sovereigns,' she observed, 'he says *we* found so-and-so – *we* intend such-and-such a thing – quite treating *de Couronne à Couronne*.'[1] Fully and naturally conscious of his importance as he was, however, he did not consider himself indispensable; and, when he returned to Paris for a wedding in the French royal family, he spoke of going back to England to take a course of the waters at Cheltenham.

While waiting to leave, he did not let his rheumatism interfere with his pleasures. He went riding with Lady Shelley and took her out to tea. He attended the garrison races. Private theatricals were performed 'under the immediate patronage of Wellington' whose 'shouts of laughter' rang round the temporary theatre.[2] He gave a dinner for the Spaniards and put on his splendid Spanish uniform; and when Lady Shelley took leave of him to go on from his house to a late reception at the duchesse de Berry's, he urged her to stay: his own entertainment was far from over yet. She needed little pressing. Besides, the Duchess's party was sure to be 'monstrous dull'.

He asked her to a ball he was giving at the Hôtel de la Reynière; and, when she arrived, as instructed, earlier than the other guests, she found him busily rearranging all the chairs. Going in to supper he gave his arm to the wife of Marshal Marmont whose husband had been rewarded for deserting Napoleon by being created a peer of France; but after the meal he once more gave his attention to Lady Shelley with whom he sat until four o'clock in the morning, telling her before he went to bed that she must have dinner with him every day until he went home to England.[3]

In England the Duke's social round continued apace. He had dinner with the Prince Regent who put his arm round him affectionately and called him Arthur. He received invitations from the Arbuthnots, from the Salisburys and from the Earl and Countess of Westmorland. He went to Almack's; and, always ready, as Charles Greville said, to get involved in other people's affairs, particularly those of attractive young women, he took the side of various ladies on the committee of that establishment against the haughty bossiness of the Regent's former mistress, Lady Jersey, who stubbornly refused to accede to the Duke's request that Lady Caroline Lamb should be admitted to it.

Much concerned with the tangled affairs of the wildly excitable Lady Caroline, who had not recovered from her passionate attachment to Lord Byron, the Duke endeavoured to persuade her to be reconciled with her husband, William Lamb, who was worth 'half a score' of poets such as Byron. 'There never existed a more worthless set than Byron and his friends.' He hated the 'whole race of poets', he declared on another occasion. 'There is no believing a word they say . . . I have the worst opinion of them.'[4]

The Duke also involved himself in the matrimonial affairs not only of his niece Anne, his brother Richard's daughter – who had left her husband, eloped with Lord William Charles Augustus Bentinck, son of the Duke of Portland, and having returned home, eloped with him again – but also with those of his brother, the Rev. Gerald Wellesley, whose wife, Emily, the daughter of the first Earl Cadogan, had deserted him, as her sister, Charlotte, had deserted Henry Wellesley.

Much as he disliked making such applications on behalf of his relatives, the Duke approached the Prime Minister with a suggestion that Gerald might be considered for a bishopric. Liverpool was not responsive; and, as when the Duke was rebuffed by King Louis XVIII before Marshal Ney's execution, he became extremely angry, refusing to intercede on behalf of two of his other brothers, William and Henry, when the one wanted help in obtaining the Presidency of the Board of Control and the other had an opportunity of becoming British Ambassador in Paris. Declining to make any overtures in either case, he said he had been 'unworthily treated' by Lord Liverpool once; and he was certainly not going to expose himself to such treatment again.

In July 1816 the Duke left London for Cheltenham; and here, although he was greeted with the by now familiar cheers, triumphal

arches and illuminations, he led a far quieter life than he had done in
London, sipping the unpleasant sulphated waters from the Montpellier
spring in the hope that these might cure the lumbago which had been
intermittently troubling him since the closing stages of the Peninsular
War, talking to fellow officers and their ladies on the benches of
Well Walk and in the pump rooms, and pleasing his wife, who had
accompanied him to the spa, by showing little of that irritation which
her fussy, diffident manner so often aroused in him and by behaving
easily and affectionately with the boys, Arthur, now aged nine, and
Charles, eight.

> He for whom all the world is so justly anxious is considerably better
> both in looks & spirits since his arrival in England [the Duchess wrote
> to her friends at Llangollen].
> I think I perceive an amendment every day. This happens to be the
> time of the holidays of our Boys [it was July 1816], and I say with
> delight they are as fond of and as familiar with their noble & beloved
> Father as if they had never been separated from him. They accompany
> him in his walks, *chat* with him. In short they are the chosen com-
> panions of each other.[5]

But soon he was back in London where he went to see David Wilkie
at his studio in Lower Phillimore Place about the purchase of a painting.
Wilkie, 'a raw, tall, pale, queer Scotsman', had come down from his
native country some ten years before and had soon established himself as a highly successful painter of such anecdotal pictures as
The Alehouse Door and *Distraining for Rent* which had led to, his
election as a Royal Academician. It was just such a painting, with a
military flavour, that the Duke was after. Accompanied by Lady Argyll,
Lord Lynedoch and the Duke and Duchess of Bedford, so Wilkie told
his friend Benjamin Robert Haydon, he walked about the painter's
studio, looking at the canvases, delivering himself of an occasional
comment, 'very good – capital', but without 'entering into conversation
further than by expressing a general approbation'. Eventually he proposed a painting of 'a parcel of old soldiers' drinking and chewing
tobacco and reminiscing outside an inn, perhaps an inn in the King's
Road, Chelsea. David Wilkie said that he liked this idea, but he would
just have to think of 'some story to connect the figures together'. The
Duke suggested they might be playing skittles. Wilkie countered with
the proposal that one might be reading a newspaper to the others. He
eventually decided upon the subject of the painting now at Apsley

House entitled 'Chelsea Pensioners Reading the Gazette of the Battle of Waterloo'.*

Before they went downstairs, the Duke asked Wilkie, 'Well, when shall I hear from you?' Wilkie said that, in view of his other commitments, he would not be able to get it done for two years.

'Very well,' said the Duke with characteristic decisiveness. 'That will be soon enough for me.' He went downstairs to the front door, bowed to the artist, noticed Mrs Wilkie, the artist's mother, at the parlour window, bowed to her, too, mounted his horse and rode back through Kensington to London. The Wilkie family tied ribbons to the chair in which the great man had sat and contemplated having an inscription placed upon it, 'descriptive of the honour it has received'.[6]

The Duke paid £1,260 for Wilkie's picture when it was finished in 1822. A most generous patron, he was to pay a similarly large sum to the Scottish historical painter Sir William Allan for his painting *The Battle of Waterloo from the English side* which was completed in 1843. When Allan went to collect his fee, he was surprised to find the Duke laboriously counting out banknotes.

'Your Grace might prefer to draw a cheque on your bank to save time and trouble,' Allan said.

'Do you suppose,' the Duke replied, continuing to count the notes, 'I am going to let Coutts's people know what a damned fool I've been.'[7]

Edwin Landseer and Sir Thomas Lawrence were also beneficiaries of Wellington's generosity. Asked to pay 600 guineas for Landseer's painting of the lion-tamer Van Amburgh, the Duke, so Landseer told William Frith, gave the artist twice that amount;[8] and after Lawrence's death, Mrs Arbuthnot accompanied the Duke to the painter's studio where they saw two or three hundred pictures, some, so she thought, twenty years old, still unfinished. 'The Duke wanted to find some belonging to him. He has paid Sir Thos 1500 £ for pictures & has got

* The painting, which is in the Piccadilly Gallery at Apsley House, created such a stir when it was first exhibited at the Royal Academy in 1822 that barriers had to be erected around it to protect it from the thousands of people who flocked to see it. A marvellously spirited and crowded picture, it celebrates in its details British military triumphs other than Waterloo as well as the various peoples who helped to achieve them.

Among the English men and women here depicted are Irishmen and Scotsmen; a man from a Welsh regiment rides in with news of the victory; a black military bandsman leans forward to read the gazette.

Wilkie, 'a Scotsman, painted a London street scene in celebration of a victory won by an Anglo-Irishman'. 'War, this picture contends, has been the making of Great Britain' (Linda Colley, *Britons: The Forging of the Nation*, 365–7).

none.'[9] Landseer told a dinner party that he could 'relate many more instances of the Duke's liberality'.*[10]

After his visit to Wilkie, the Duke was soon in France again, issuing orders from Cambrai, setting out the regulations to be observed 'for the review of infantry in column', reminding staff officers and aides-de-camp about the rules concerning dress, forbidding chaplains 'to marry anyone without permission, in writing, of the Field Marshal', repeating orders that officers should not ride over cultivated ground when hunting, since the country was 'becoming so exasperated on the subject' that he would be 'obliged to forbid in General Orders hunting and coursing altogether, excepting in the woods and forests', expressing his astonishment and concern that 'in so many recent instances of robbery and disorder, the non-commissioned officers themselves have either been accomplices in the offences committed or privy thereto' and reprimanding officers who were the object of frequent complaints because of their habit of 'striking individuals with their fists' which was 'quite inconsistent with their duty, and with their character as British officers'. 'The Field Marshal,' these officers were told in a general order, 'has repeatedly given orders that the officers of the army may not quit their quarters without their side arms, an obedience which would certainly preclude the supposed provocation for making use of fists, if anything can be a provocation for a British officer so far to forget himself.'[11]

At the same time the Field Marshal told Sir Henry Torrens at the Horse Guards that he believed 'nothing could be more desirable than to teach officers the use of the sword' which was 'essentially necessary to every officer who is to wear one', and he sought and obtained permission for a fencing master to be employed to give instruction to those officers in need of it.[12]

---

* As with artists so with others, the Duke was on occasions almost eccentrically generous in his determination not to take the opportunity of striking an advantageous bargain. The well-informed merchant Thomas Raikes, who spent most of his time with his fellow dandies in the clubs of the West End, recorded in his diary:

> Some years ago it was proposed to [the Duke] to purchase a farm in the neighbourhood of Strathfieldsaye, which lay contiguous to his estate, and was therefore a valuable acquisition, to which he assented. When the purchase was completed, his steward congratulated him upon having had such a bargain, as the seller was in difficulties, and forced to part with it. 'What do you mean by a bargain?' said the Duke; the other replied, 'It was valued at 1100£., and we have got it for 800£.' 'In that case,' said the Duke, 'you will please to carry the extra 300£. to the late owner, and never talk to me of cheap land again' (A Portion of the Journal Kept by Thomas Raikes, iv, 343).

There were many other matters, other than the discipline of the army of occupation, that required Wellington's attention. He was bothered with questions about the bad behaviour of the Bonapartist exiles in Brussels, about the maintenance of the fortresses on the Brussels frontier, about the concerns of government ministers and officials, of diplomats and army officers who, passing through Cambrai, sought his opinion or advice, as, for instance, did George Canning, at that time Ambassador in Lisbon. Canning suggested that British help for Portugal, which had been devastated in the recent war with France, should depend upon what support that country gave to the abolition of slavery. This, in the Duke's succinct opinion, was nothing but 'nonsense and folly'.

Yet he always found time for amusement in the evenings. Lady Shelley was not available, having gone on to Vienna, and he wrote to tell her how much he missed his 'absent A.D.C.', but there were other young ladies to entertain him. The Duchess of Richmond came out with a selection of her fourteen children to stay at his house at Cambrai. Among these children was her third daughter, the pretty, lively Georgiana who was to marry the twenty-third Baron de Ros. With her and her mother and sisters, the Duke rode and danced the mazurka and supervised amateur theatricals and played a rowdy game called 'riding in the coach' in which the young ladies sat on carpets to be dragged about the corridors by the officers of the headquarters staff.

The house is as full as it can hold [he wrote one day]. Yesterday . . . I understand they hunted Lord C—— through all the corridors, even that in the roof. At night we had an improvement on ['riding in the coach']. Two goats were brought in and harnessed, but instead of being horses and assisting to draw, they chose to lie down and be drawn. The night before, the ladies drew me the *petty* tour, and afterwards Lord Hill, the *grand* tour, but the 'fat, fair and forty' and M—— were so knocked up that some of us were obliged to go into the harness, although we had run many stages.[13]

'It is quite impossible to imagine any school boy in higher spirits or up to any sort of fun than the Duke of Wellington,' reported Captain George Bowles. 'He has just taken a large chateau about twelve miles from hence [Cambrai] . . . His plans [for it] are quite *en prince*. He has sent for a pack of hounds.'[14]

He hunted as often as he could until he thought it as well to call a halt to this favourite activity so as to remain on 'tolerable terms' with the local inhabitants. He sent to England for stags and hinds as well as hounds and a spaniel; and once he speared a huge boar, a feat, so he told a friend, of which he was more proud than he was of the Battle of Waterloo. It was 'a feat of Horsemanship as well as management of the spear.'[15]

He took obvious pleasure in the company of three attractive American girls of Irish descent, Louisa (later Duchess of Leeds), Elizabeth (later Lady Stafford) and Marianne, great-granddaughters of Charles Carroll, a rich lawyer from Maryland, the only Roman Catholic to sign the Declaration of Independence. He took all three of these sprightly young women on an expedition to explore the field of Waterloo, an excursion which he evidently little enjoyed, since it aroused so many painful memories: the battlefield resembled a fair with tourists wandering about, searching like beachcombers for bullets and buttons, buying boots and badges and bits of uniform from the stall-holders at Hougoumont and La Belle Alliance.[16] On his return, so Marianne noticed, the Duke was unusually silent at dinner.

It was clear that of the three sisters, it was Marianne, the wife of an American merchant, Robert Patterson, who was the Duke's favourite. Indeed, according to both the Duchess's friend, the Hon. Mrs Nicolson Calvert, and the Duke's friend, Mrs Arbuthnot, he was much in love with her and was widely supposed to be her lover.*[17] Certainly he paid

---

* When the by then widowed Mrs Patterson, having returned from America, announced that she was going to Ireland to marry the Lord-Lieutenant, the Marquess Wellesley, whose French wife had died in 1816, the Duke was furious. Indeed, Mrs Arbuthnot had 'never seen him more annoyed'. She herself considered that Mrs Patterson, who 'had come to this country on a matrimonial speculation', had done pretty well for 'the widow of an American shopkeeper to think of marrying a Marquis and a Knight of the Garter'. But the Duke maintained that the match was 'preposterous'. His brother had no money, no house to take her to outside Ireland, and 'moreover, was of a most jealous disposition, a violent temper & had entirely worn out his constitution by the profligate habits of his life'. The Duke was sure that, after the marriage, his brother would never allow him to associate with Marianne 'for reasons of Jealousy' and that 'all intercourse with her' was consequently 'entirely at an end'. He wrote to her in what Mrs Arbuthnot supposed was an attempt to persuade her to change her mind (The Journal of Mrs Arbuthnot, i, 421). When the Duke had calmed down he brought himself to send his brother his good wishes, telling him that 'in disposition temper sense acquirements and manners' Marianne was the 'equal if not the superior to any Woman of any Country with whom [he] had ever been in Society' (Wellington to Wellesley, 13 October 1825, Add. MSS 37415, Wellesley Papers, quoted in Thompson, Wellington after Waterloo, 51). But he refused to attend the wedding, this 'very strange and awkward event', as Liverpool described it (Aspinall, George IV Letters, iii, 126). It was not, at first, a successful marriage, largely because of the interference of one of the Marquess's illegitimate sons, Edward Johnston, who lived at Vice-Regal Lodge and for long could not be persuaded to leave it. The Duke wisely persuaded the Marchioness not to insist on the dismissal of Johnston, his younger brother and their friends, 'the Parasites' as he called them. The Marquess eventually quarrelled with Johnston who was shaken off; and the Wellesleys settled down together in harmony.

particular attention to her; and, according to Lady William Russell, he was much distressed when she returned to America. 'The Duke of Wellington looks horribly ill,' Lady William told Mary Berry. '*Si dice* that it is . . . love. He declares he never knew the meaning of the word until he saw Mrs Patterson, and her departure for America *déchire son tendre coeur* in a terrible manner. He really looks mighty sick.'[18]

There were, however, several other lady friends to console him, among them, now and later, Lady Granville, daughter of the Duke of Devonshire, who flattered herself that, upon one occasion at least, he behaved to her as devotedly as he did to Mrs Patterson, even though she treated him, as she put it, '*des haut de ma grandeur*'. 'He called me to sit by him,' she told her sister, 'and was quite *à mes pieds*. . . The fact is that I really believe the Duke finds so few women that do not kneel to him that he must feel a sort of respect for any who do not make up to him. Granville, who has rather suffered at seeing us sit through two dinners *dos-à-dos*, will be rather pleased to hear of my successes, obtained *d'après ma façon*, for an ugly good sort of woman to be attended to by a man into whose good graces beauties force themselves by dint of *bassesse*.'[19]

The Duke was clearly also attracted to the haughty Lady Jersey as well as to Harriet Arbuthnot and Olivia Kinnaird – wife of the eighth Baron Kinnaird and youngest daughter of the second Duke of Leinster – and Lady Georgiana Fane – Mrs Arbuthnot's cousin and Lady Jersey's half-sister – and Lady Caroline Lamb, whom he called 'Calatha' after the heroine of *Glenarvon*, her first and most rhapsodical novel which contains a caricature portrait of her erstwhile lover Lord Byron – and Lady Frances Cole and Lady Charlotte Greville, both frequent visitors at a house the Duke rented at Mont-Saint-Martin.

He was particularly attracted to Lady Charlotte Greville, the Duke of Portland's daughter and the diarist's mother, who came to stay on her own, leaving her husband and children behind in Brussels, and who was soon known to be having a passionate affair with him. This affair came to an end when Lady Charlotte's husband heard of it and protested strongly. Seeking revenge on his mother's behalf, Charles Greville wrote an anonymous letter to Mrs Arbuthnot, accusing her also of being the Duke's mistress. Mrs Arbuthnot showed the letter both to her husband and to the Duke, who recognized Charles Greville's handwriting: and it was decided that the two friends, innocent though their relationship was, must be more discreet in future. 'In public,' Mrs Arbuthnot wrote, 'we will not talk much together, but go on just the same in private. The anonymous writer wd. be surprised if he knew how amicably we three had discussed his amiable letter.'[20]

The Duke also saw much once more of Lady Shelley who had now returned from Vienna. 'The Shelley is arrived in great beauty!' he told Mrs Arbuthnot. 'I have a capital story of her which I must tell you when we meet. I dare not write it.' Evidently Lady Shelley had rejected the advances of a fat Austrian nobleman, expostulating with 'pride & Indignation', 'Know, Sir, that I have resisted the Duke of Wellington and do not imagine, etc. etc. etc.!!!' 'In my own justification,' Wellington commented when relating this story to Lady Burghersh, 'I must say that I was never aware of this resistance!!'[21]

For these and other ladies and 'assorted gentlemen' he gave large parties at Mont-Saint-Martin; while at an inn at Vitry he gave less formal parties in far more simple surroundings. At one of these Thomas Creevey was once a guest:

> We got to Vitry about ten. The Duke had driven much faster than us, so as to have time to answer his letters, and to have the return dispatches ready . . . The inn we found him in was the most miserable concern I have ever beheld – so small and so wretched that after we had entered the gate I could not believe that we were right till the Duke, who had heard the carriage enter, came out of a little wretched parlour in the gateway, without his hat, and on seeing me said: – 'Come in here, Creevey: dinner is quite ready.' Dinner accordingly was brought in by a couple of dirty maids; and it consisted of four dishes – 2 partridges at the top, a fowl at the bottom, fricassee of chicken on one side and something equally substantial on the other . . .
>
> The Duke had left Paris at 5 in the morning, and had come 130 miles, and a cold fowl was all that had been eaten by his party in the coach during the day. Altho' the fare was so scanty, the champagne the commonest of stuff, and the house so bad, it seemed to make no impression on the Duke. He seemed quite as pleased and as well satisfied as if he had been in a palace . . .
>
> In the morning we all breakfasted together at five o'clock punctually. Our fare was tea in a great coffee-pot about two feet high. We had cups to drink out of, it is true; but no saucers. The Duke, however, seemed quite as satisfied with everything as the night before; and when I observed, by way of a joke, that I thought the tea not so very bad, considering it was made, I supposed, at Vitry: – 'No,' said he, with that curious simplicity of his, 'it is not: I brought it with me from Paris.'[22]

The Duke's outings were never made at the expense of work. There were regular inspections to be made, reviews to be held, matters concerning French reparations to be discussed with the bankers Alexander Baring and Nathan Rothschild, meetings to attend with allied leaders whose claims for heavy war damages were more rigorously pressed than Wellington in his sensible moderation thought advisable. There were also constant differences to resolve between British officers and French and Belgian property owners in dispute over claims for damages. On occasions the Duke would lose his temper with what he considered to be an unreasonable claim, once turning in fury upon an importunate landlord who followed him up his headquarters' steps with a bill in his hand. 'What the devil do you want, sir,' he shouted at him; and when the bill was pressed into his hand told his aide-de-camp to 'kick the rascal downstairs'.

Normally, however, he treated the foreigners' claims sympathetically, ensuring that fair reparation was made for damage caused by soldiers. He also saw to it that the French and Belgians had no cause to complain that he had a less than even hand when he was called upon to settle disputes: when, for instance, there was an affray on the stage of a theatre in Boulogne in which a British officer was knocked down by a French actor, the Commander-in-Chief ensured that the officer took the blame for the uproar since his insults had provoked it.[23]

Yet, although the Duke advocated moderation, imposed a discipline upon British troops that was not so strictly enforced upon the soldiers of his allies, endeavoured to keep the cost of the occupying army as low as possible, and – strongly encouraged to do so by his dying friend, Mme de Staël – recommended a reduction in its strength by 30,000 men, it was he who, as Commander-in-Chief of that army, deeply resented by Bonapartists and ultra Royalists alike, was seen as being largely responsible for France's ignominy. He was condemned as 'le tyran de Cambrai', and was threatened with death at the hands of an outraged people. Wellington, as he confessed, thought it unwise to 'go into any blackguard mob or place in which a fellow might insult' him with impunity. 'But in other respects,' he said, 'I ride and walk alone.' His life was consequently held to be in constant danger; and more than once in fact it was. In Brussels two French journalists hid themselves in the park one night intending to shoot him as he walked home from dinner and would no doubt have done so, had he not taken a route different from the one he usually followed. Some time later in Paris, as he was being driven home from a party, he was fired at as his carriage was turning into his *porte cochère* by 'a well-dressed person who ran away and immediately made his escape'.[24]

A Bonapartist named Cantillon was later arrested and, having been acquitted by a French jury since there were no witnesses to his crime, lived to be left 10,000 francs in Napoleon's will.*[25] But, while the intended victim made light of the matter, as he had always made light of 'everything of this kind', in the words of his Chief of Staff, great concern for his safety was expressed by others. His wife wrote of her profound relief at his narrow escape and asked why a footman had not seized the varlet since it appeared 'that he stood near the sentry box and must have seen him'. But, she added, the Duke had 'none but French footmen'; and that was, no doubt, the reason.[26]

The King of France congratulated him warmly upon his escape and sent him a present of Sèvres china as a token of his continuing regard. The Prince Regent wrote of his shock at hearing that his 'dear friend' Arthur had been so exposed to danger and was gratified to be informed in a most courtly reply that if anything could reconcile the Duke to such attempts upon his life, it was the concern expressed by one to whom he owed all his success.

The Duke was urged to leave Paris permanently for Cambrai;[27] but he declined to move, refusing to comply with a specific order from the Prince Regent requiring him to do so.[28] He would become 'the ridicule of the World' by appearing to run away, he said, and his flight would 'give the most fatal shake to everything that is going forward'. He had 'no hesitation in stating' that 'after assassination, the greatest public & private calamity which could happen would be for me to obey the order of the Prince Regent'. He wished the Cabinet would 'lay aside the notion that [he was] anxious to be assassinated by a French mob'.[29]

So he remained in Paris and altered the conduct of his life not at all.[30]

---

* Lord Mahon once told Wellington that he thought the 'greatest blot' on Napoleon's character was this 'shocking bequest in his will'. The Duke agreed, 'shaking his head with a sad and very serious expression' (Stanhope, *Notes on Conversations with the Duke of Wellington*, 5 November 1831). According to William Siborne, the historian of the Waterloo campaign, who was then serving in the army of occupation as a lieutenant in the 9th Foot, Wellington himself had had an opportunity of ordering Napoleon's death: 'An officer of the artillery came up to the Duke, and stated that he had a distinct view of Napoleon ... that he had the guns of his battery well pointed in that direction, and was prepared to fire. His Grace instantly and emphatically exclaimed, "No! No! I'll not allow it. It is not the business of commanders to be firing upon each other"' (William Siborne, *History of the War in France and Belgium in 1815*).

28 Stratfield Saye

1818 – 20

'A miserable imitation of a French château.'

FROM PARIS the Duke paid visits to London. On one of these, on the second anniversary of the battle of Waterloo, he was present at the opening by the Prince Regent of John Rennie's Waterloo Bridge, originally known as Strand Bridge, which, almost six years in the building, was described by Canova as 'the noblest bridge in the world, worth a visit from the remotest corner of the earth'.[1] On this occasion it was draped in the flags of the allied nations; and, as the sun shone down in a cloudless sky, there was a salute of 202 guns, the number of French cannon captured in the battle.

As a further celebration of his victory at Waterloo, the Duke was asked to sit for a portrait by James Ward who, although far better known as a painter of animals than of historical scenes, had been awarded a prize by the British Institution for a sketch of an *Allegory of Waterloo* and had been commissioned to paint a picture from it four times the size of the sketch. Wellington – evidently wary of being portrayed by a man whose *Alderney Bull and Cow* was considered the best of the four hundred works he exhibited at the Royal Academy, and many of whose later commissions came from the Royal Agricultural Society – made the excuse that he was on the point of returning to France. Ward said he would follow him there; but the Duke was adamant: he had so many troops under his command that he did not know where he would be 'one day after another'. He would, however, sit for Mr Ward on his return, as he had already sat for Hoppner, Beechey and Sir Thomas Lawrence.*

Despite all his other commitments, the Duke found time to study Benjamin Dean Wyatt's proposals in their continuing search for a country estate; and, having considered the Jacobean Bramshill House near Hartley Wintney and Misserden Park in Gloucestershire as well

---

* The Duke did eventually sit for James Ward whose portrait, painted in 1829, is now at 10 Downing Street (Richard Walker, *Regency Portraits*, i, 537).

as Uppark near Petersfield, where the young Emma Hamilton was said to have danced naked on Sir Harry Featherstonaugh's dining-room table, his eye eventually lighted upon Stratfield Saye in Hampshire, an estate of some five thousand acres between Basingstoke and Reading, which was offered to him by George Pitt, the second Lord Rivers, from whom it was bought for £263,000, less than half the amount of £600,000 which had eventually been voted for the purpose by Parliament.

The house had been built about 1630, on the site of an earlier one, by Lord Rivers's great-great-grandfather, Sir William Pitt, Comptroller of the Household to King James I. The red brick exterior had been stuccoed and painted white, while the interior had been remodelled in the late eighteenth century by the first Lord Rivers who had served briefly as British Ambassador in Madrid and had been one of King George III's Lords of the Bedchamber.

It was a pleasant enough property, though few people shared the Duke's own enthusiasm. Lord Francis Leveson-Gower described the house as a 'miserable imitation of a French château'; a later visitor thought it 'a wretched' house, 'wretchedly furnished', though admittedly 'warm and not uncomfortable'. Another guest considered it an 'indifferent' house for him, 'not a nice place', its site 'damp & low'. Lady Wharncliffe, whose husband was a grandson of the Earl of Bute, agreed that it was damp and low, not at all pretty and stood 'in the worst place possible for the view'.[2]

At this time, however, the Duke intended to demolish the house and erect on higher ground in the north-east corner of the park a splendid building to be called Waterloo Palace – an idea never realized. Benjamin Dean Wyatt, Charles Heathcote Tatham, who designed Cowdray Park in Sussex and the sculpture gallery at Castle Howard, and C.R. Cockerell, Samuel Pepys Cockerell's son, who was to be responsible for the Ashmolean Museum, Oxford, all drew up plans for a house on a most lavish scale. Wyatt's estimate, most precisely calculated, came to £216,850 15s 3d.[3]

The Duke also bought a house in London, Apsley House, a handsome property at Hyde Park Corner known as No. 1 London since it was the first house to be encountered after passing the gates and toll-houses at the top of the road from Knightsbridge. It was the property of his brother Richard who was given £42,000 for it, a sum which Richard found extremely useful in his financial difficulties and which – generally considered a good deal more than the house was worth – was certainly £26,000 more than had been paid for it in 1807.[4]

It had been built between 1771 and 1778 by Robert Adam for Henry Bathurst, second Earl Bathurst and first Baron Apsley, the Lord Chancellor universally recognized as the most inefficient holder of that office in the eighteenth century, whose commissioning of Adam as architect was described by Lord Campbell as 'perhaps the most memorable' act in an otherwise undistinguished life.[5] The house – which had already been altered for Lord Wellesley by James Wyatt and Thomas Cundy, and was to be greatly enlarged and lavishly improved to the design of Benjamin Dean Wyatt and his brother, Philip, faced with Bath stone and provided with a huge Corinthian portico – was to be the Duke's London home for the rest of his life. Here from 1830 in the Waterloo Gallery – a room ninety feet long on the walls of which hung well over a hundred paintings* – were to be held those grand banquets on the anniversary of his great victory, banquets attended by up to eighty-five guests, most of them officers who had served under him that day. At one end of the long table – on which stood the magnificent silver and silver-gilt centrepiece presented to the Duke by the Portuguese Council of Regency – was displayed the Waterloo Shield designed by Thomas Stothard, who also designed the silver-gilt Waterloo Vase which stood on the sideboard at the opposite end.†[6]

The Duke had little time to enjoy Apsley House yet. Back in France, he was soon busy with arrangements for a congress at Aix-la-Chapelle which was to open in September 1818 and which, it was hoped, would result in the signing of a declaration by France and the Allies which would settle all their differences. The Duke and Lord Castlereagh, still Foreign Secretary in Lord Liverpool's administration, were the principal British delegates; and the dandyish Lord Palmerston, who was at the

---

* According to the painter William Frith, it was 'a small weakness' of the Duke to demonstrate his ability to name all these pictures without reference to the catalogue. 'So long as the pictures followed in regular sequence, and were named one after the other in order, the effort of memory was successful'; but if for any reason the sequence was interrupted 'he was at fault'. Landseer once asked him who was represented in the portrait of a 'sour-looking woman in the costume of the time of Elizabeth'. The Duke muttered something and left Landseer's side. He was gone for a few minutes and when he returned Landseer was studying another picture. A voice close to his ear announced, 'Bloody Mary!'

Frith added that it was the Duke's habit to examine every picture in the exhibitions at the Royal Academy with equal attention and 'show the same interest – and no more – over pictures in which he figured gloriously, as he did in all others. If a friend were with him, he would make a remark, as I heard him on [Sir William] Allan's picture of the "Waterloo Fight." "Too much smoke!" said the Duke' (W.P. Frith, R.A., *My Autobiography and Reminiscences*, i, 324–5).

† All these objects are still on display at Apsley House.

congress in his capacity as Secretary at War, was much impressed by the manner in which the Duke conducted himself, quite without pretension but perfectly at ease with kings and emperors. Palmerston noted the 'extreme respect and deference paid by all to the Duke' as well as the 'manly but respectful manner with which the Duke treated the sovereigns'. He was also pleased to recall how well the Duke behaved towards him, talking to him about military tactics and telling him more than once just how effective was the firepower of steady British infantry.[7]

As a mark of their respect the sovereigns granted the Duke yet another honour to add to all those he had already received from them. He was made a Marshal in the armies of both Emperors as well as in that of King Frederick William III of Prussia. There were now few further honours left in Europe to bestow on its greatest and most celebrated soldier.

With his days as a fighting man behind him Wellington now turned his mind to a new career in politics. There was no doubt that Lord Liverpool would welcome the support of a man of international reputation whose victories had helped in the past to keep his Government in office and whose final triumph at Waterloo had ended the Chancellor of the Exchequer's fears that the country might not be able to pay the bill for another year of war.[8]

In December 1818, the offer came: would the Duke accept the post of Master-General of the Ordnance with a seat in the Cabinet?

He was certainly prepared to agree to the appointment, but it would have to be on his own terms. It must be understood that he was not a party man. He was 'sincerely attached' to the present Tory Government and their interests, but if they were to be removed from power he hoped ministers would allow him to consider himself 'at liberty to take any line' he might think proper.

> The experience I have acquired during my long service abroad has convinced me that a factious opposition to the government is highly injurious to the interests of the country [he explained]; & thinking, as I do now, I could not become a party to such an opposition . . . I wish this may be clearly understood by those persons with whom I am now about to engage as a colleague in government.[9]

Ministers were prepared to accept these conditions, since they strongly believed that they had need of the Duke's reputation and authority, of his 'great name in council'. His talents, 'as they were then understood, were not exactly of the kind most required by the Cabinet,' Benjamin Disraeli was to write; 'and his colleagues were careful that he should not occupy too prominent a post; but still it was an impressive acquisition, and imparted to the Ministry a semblance of renown.'

As it was the Ministry had no such reputation at that time and there were those who doubted that the Duke's renown, splendid as it was upon the European stage, was such as would help the Tory Government to gain sympathy and respect in the England of 1819.

The country at large was increasingly dissatisfied and turbulent. In London multitudes of people in the elaborate fashions of the last months of the Regency still flocked to Vauxhall Gardens and to fêtes in the royal parks. Vast fortunes were still won and lost around the tables at White's and Boodle's. But England was changing fast. In the country men and women were leaving the hand-looms in their cottages to sit at machines in workshops; towns were growing fast – Birmingham's population had risen from about 12,000 at the beginning of the eighteenth century to 45,000 in 1800. Windmills and watermills were fast disappearing and the tall chimneys of William Blake's 'dark satanic mills' were pouring forth a thick black smoke over the surrounding fields. In many of these factories, in mines and sweat-shops, conditions were appalling: children were employed as well as men and women and were pushed into tubs of cold water to keep them awake during their interminable hours of labour.

There were increasing protests and uprisings against these conditions, riots against the Corn Laws – which had been passed in 1815 to protect British agriculture by forbidding the entry of foreign wheat until the domestic price had risen to 80 shillings a quarter – and demonstrations against the savage punishments imposed upon machine-breakers whose activities, it was feared for a time, might provoke national revolution.

Wellington was not unsympathetic to the plight of the poor, and believed that the upper classes and the gentry were just as much to blame as the lower orders for the country's distress; but he had a profound distaste for demagogues and agitators. His entire experience as a soldier and a diplomat had made him wary of democrats and contemptuous of the mob. Nor did he trouble to hide his contempt; and amongst the common people there arose the feeling that the great Duke of Wellington was no longer to be revered as the hero of Waterloo but to be reviled as the enemy of democratic aspirations. In Piccadilly gentlemen might deferentially raise their hats to him as the supreme general who had saved them from the tyranny of Bonaparte, but in many of the homes of the working people he was seen in a quite different light and the mobs that hooted him for having put his signature to the Convention of Cintra were now ready to hoot again.

On 16 August 1819, not long after the Duke's return to England, a large crowd of people in St Peter's Field, Manchester, many of them hand-loom weavers attending a rally in support of parliamentary reform, were charged by mounted troops. Eleven people were killed and hundreds more wounded in what became known as the 'Peterloo Massacre' in ironic allusion to the battle of Waterloo.

The Prince Regent congratulated the Manchester magistrates on their action in ordering the arrest of the radical orator Henry Hunt, who had agreed to address the rally in St Peter's Field; while the Government, deciding that it had been an illegal assembly – and with Wellington's firm support – brought in six Bills designed to suppress radicalism and prevent revolutionary outbreaks in the future. The Duke was convinced that a stern hand was necessary if a revolution such as that which had torn France apart was to be prevented. It was 'very clear' to him that agitators like Hunt would 'not be quiet till a large number of them "bite the dust", as the French say, or till some of their leaders are hanged, which would be the most fortunate result'.[10]

The year after the Peterloo Massacre a group of radicals, meeting in a stable loft in Cato Street near Old Marylebone Road, conspired to murder the Duke and all his colleagues in the Cabinet while they were having dinner at Lord Harrowby's house in Grosvenor Square and to carry off the heads of the Home and Foreign Secretaries in bags. When the luridly murderous conspiracy became known to the authorities the Duke proposed that the Cabinet should arm themselves with pistols, lock themselves in Harrowby's house together with soldiers dressed as servants, and resist the would-be assassins until troops arrived to catch them red-handed.[11] But this was not a plan that recommended itself to his less adventurous colleagues. The dinner was held elsewhere. The conspirators were arrested and five of the ringleaders were hanged, two of them, a bankrupt butcher and Arthur Thistlewood, a former estate agent, expressing particular hatred for 'that damned villain, Wellington' whom Thistlewood would rather have killed, so he said, 'than any of them'.[12] Another of the conspirators, a former trooper in the Household Cavalry, had been prepared to 'swear after the massacre that the Duke of Wellington turned out to be the biggest coward in the room, and begged for mercy on his knees'. This would, he thought, have been 'very degrading' for the Duke's relatives.[13]

The would-be assassins were spared being drawn and quartered because of public sympathy; but even so the hangman was attacked in the street and almost castrated.*

Wellington's life was again threatened when he was going home one night from the Ordnance Office. An assassin planned to stab him to death while he was walking across the Park; but the Duke happened to encounter Lord Fitzroy Somerset, and the sight of two men passing by arm in arm was too much for the nerves of the intending murderer who abandoned his scheme and made off.[14]

The unpopularity of the Government and, with it, that of the Duke was much increased when on 29 January 1820 the poor old white-bearded King, after years of pottering about his rooms at Windsor, 'greatly emaciated', though still finding 'amusement in the inexhaustible resources of his distempered imagination', died at last and the Prince Regent became King George IV.

---

* Voicing a sentiment common amongst the upper ranks of society, the Duke's friend Mrs Arbuthnot thought that 'one really ought to thank God that the world is rid of such monsters'. Her brother, Cecil Fane, a Commissioner of the Court of Bankruptcy, who had never seen an execution, had 'a great curiosity' to see this one. But when the time came he could not bear to watch it, retiring into a corner of the room, 'which excited much contempt in the people who were in the room with him; amongst whom was one woman, young & pretty & very decent looking who kept her eyes fixed on it all the time & when they had hung a few seconds exclaimed, "There's two on them not dead yet"!!' (*The Journal of Mrs Arbuthnot*, i, 15–16).

29 King George IV and Queen Caroline

1820 – 1

'God save the Queen – and may all your wives be like her.'

THE DUKE SAW little to admire in the new King. Indeed, he had not long expostulated to Creevey, 'By God! You never saw such a figure in your life as he is! Then he speaks and swears so like old Falstaff, that damn me if I am not ashamed to walk into a room with him.'[1] As for his brothers, the royal dukes, they were, 'My God! the damnedest millstones about the necks of any government that can be imagined. They have insulted – *personally* insulted – two thirds of the gentlemen of England.'[2] Yet the Duke, as an inveterate enemy of republicanism, as a member of the King's Cabinet and a loyal servant of the Crown, felt himself in duty bound to support his Majesty in any way his conscience would allow. So that when the King made it known that he wanted to divorce his detested wife, who returned to England on 5 June 1820, he gave the most careful consideration to the problems which the King's decision raised.

The Cabinet had already made it known that they were against a divorce since this was possible only by Act of Parliament or by a trial for treason on grounds of the Queen's adultery with her Italian majordomo, Bartolommeo Bergami – or, as he preferred to spell his name, Pergami. The ecclesiastical courts could only grant a separation and, in any case, an action there would entail recriminatory evidence being given against the King. The Cabinet had accordingly endeavoured to persuade his Majesty to agree to a settlement which would not only keep his wife abroad but would also contain a formal enactment depriving her of her powers and privileges as queen consort.[3] On behalf of the King, Wellington and Castlereagh had met the Queen's representatives to discuss the possibility of the Queen accepting an income of £10,000 a year and agreeing to undertake to remain abroad and not insist that her name should be included in the Liturgy. But from the outset their talks had been unpromising, the Queen – in Wellington's opinion 'the most impudent devil that ever existed'[4] – had been insistent that her name should be kept in the Liturgy, and, on this point, as Castlereagh remarked, the King was as 'immovable as Carlton House itself'.[5] So the Queen's lawyers had been warned that, if she returned to England, proceedings would be started against her. When she did return and further negotiations failed, the Cabinet decided that they must carry out their threat.

A Bill of Pains and Penalties, a Parliamentary method of punishing a person without recourse to a court of law, was chosen as the best method of proceeding against the Queen, since it put the emphasis on depriving her of her powers and privileges, leaving the matter of divorce as a second-ary and, indeed, dispensable issue. The Bill was introduced first in the House of Lords because the forms of the Lords allowed the use of pro-fessional counsel to argue the case pro and con before the bar of the House and to introduce witnesses.[6] This, it was hoped, would effectually prove the adultery of the Queen of whose outrageous behaviour in Italy the British public was still largely unaware.

As they waited for the proceedings to begin, people throughout the country lost no opportunity of displaying where their sympathies lay, toasting the Queen in taverns and ale-houses and so alarming the King with shouts of 'Nero!' beneath the windows of Carlton House that he retired to the Royal Lodge in Windsor Park, a move which heightened the feeling against him for, as Lord Liverpool said, he was condemned as 'a coward for not showing himself'.[7]

Those who had known the Queen personally in the past had little doubt that she was as guilty as Wellington felt convinced she was. But as William Cobbett put it, so unpopular was the King, 'the people, as far as relates to the question of guilt or innocence, did not care a straw'.[8]

'The common people, and I fear the soldiers, are all in her favour and I believe the latter more than is owned,' Emily Cowper told her brother. 'As for her virtue, I don't think they care much about it.'[9] The 'military in London', Charles Greville confirmed, were showing more and more 'alarming symptoms of dissatisfaction', so much so that it was doubtful how far even the Guards could be trusted. A battalion of the 3rd Guards had been heard shouting, 'God save the Queen!' If they survived these dreadful times, Lord Grey told Lord Holland, they would see 'a Jacobin revolution more bloody than that of France'.[10]

When the public enquiry began on 17 August, the excitement grew more intense than ever; and the crowds that gathered outside the house where the Queen was staying in St James's Square were uproarious and immense. So were they in the streets around the House of Lords where they greeted Ministers with cat-calls and abuse. Wellington, the windows of whose carriage had already been smashed by demonstrators, was hissed and booed with exceptional violence as he rode his horse through a gap in the fence that had been erected around the approaches to the House. Later a mob tried to pull him off his horse;[11] and outside the House they shouted, 'No hero! We want no hero', which seemed to amuse him very much.[12] 'They look upon him particularly as the Queen's enemy,' Emily Cowper observed, 'I suppose they think he is against everybody's wife as well as his own.'[13] Mme de Lieven reported to Metternich, 'Your friend Wellington did something in very bad taste. He was the only person who kept his hat on, during the whole of the first hearing, in the Queen's presence.'[14]

One day upon his return to Apsley House a gang of roadmenders was said to have stopped his horse in Grosvenor Place and demanded that he repeat, 'God save the Queen!' 'Well, gentlemen,' he – or, so some reports say, the almost equally abused Lord Anglesey, or Lord Londonderry or Theodore Hook – replied with characteristic aplomb, 'Since you will have it so, God save the Queen – and may all your wives be like her.'*[15]

He was growing accustomed to the abuse of the populace; but he affected to think nothing of it. Certainly his contempt for the mob was much deepened. 'The mob are too contemptible to be thought about for a moment,' he told Lady Shelley. 'About thirty of them ran away from me in the Park this morning, because I pulled up my horse when they were hooting! They thought I was going to fall upon them and give them what they deserved!' At the same time he comforted himself and his friends with assurances that he was still esteemed outside London. At Dover he was received with 'great Respect by everybody'; he did not meet a 'respectable Man who did not pull off His Hat'. Riding home from Hatfield 'all along the Road the people turned out to see [him] pass, and were better than enthusiastick and noisy. They were very respectful.' Even at Hounslow 'there was not a Man in the Street who did not pull off his Hat' to him.[16]

Despite the rude treatment of him by the Queen's champions in

---

* She was, of course, irresistible as a butt for such jokes. Lord Norbury, when asked how she had enjoyed herself in Algiers, replied, 'She was as happy as the Dey was long.' When someone wondered what newspaper she read, Norbury suggested that she took in the Courier (The Greville Memoirs, i, 115).

London, the Duke remained on perfectly amicable terms with her Whig supporters. One night he came across Thomas Creevey and spoke to him with 'his usual frankness'. They talked about 'the trial' with 'the most perfect freedom' and when Creevey observed that the foreign witnesses whom the King's party were going to produce 'would find very few believers in this country, the Duke said: – "Ho! But we have a great many English witnesses – officers"'; and this, Creevey confessed, 'was the thing that almost frightened [the Queen's supporters] the most'. Some weeks later, when the proceedings were nearly over, Creevey heard the people in the Park booing the Duke again. Creevey received 'a very good-humoured nod' from him.[17]

Good-humoured or not, the Duke was far from pleased with the progress of the proceedings in the House of Lords. Sensible men could not but conclude that the Queen had been guilty of gross impropriety; but several of the witnesses called against her were most unsatisfactory and the Government was gradually forced to the conclusion that, even if the Bill passed in the Lords, it would never do so in the Commons. Besides, Brougham had got hold of the copy of a will which the King had made and in which he had referred to Mrs Fitzherbert as his 'dear wife'. Brougham was threatening to produce this will as an argument that the King had forfeited his legal right to the throne. The Government also knew that Brougham, who had found numerous witnesses to swear to the King's own sexual escapades, intended to bring direct recrimination against him.

Wellington expressed himself as being quite unimpressed by this recriminatory evidence; he told the Duke of Portland that 'the King was degraded as low as he could be already'.[18] But Ministers, for the most part, feared the dangers of further opprobrium and, after it had passed its third reading in the Lords, the Bill was withdrawn because the narrowness of the winning margin indicated that it would almost certainly be defeated in the Commons where the Government had much less control.

The King was furious. For weeks he had been venting his ill-humour in abuse of his Ministers, his 'language and manner', according to Charles Arbuthnot, being 'those of a Bedlamite'.[19] Yet rage against them though he did, the King, so Wellington believed, never really intended to replace his Ministers. The Duke's sister-in-law, Mrs William Wellesley-Pole, one of his Majesty's guests at Brighton, reported that the King's language was 'beyond anything indiscreet and improper, that the language there now [was] not whether the Ministers would be changed but only as to the time'.[20] Wellington was not persuaded by such reports.

He considered the King's tirades 'just talk': his Majesty liked people to suppose that his Prime Minister was a kind of maître d'hôtel whom he might dismiss at any moment it happened to suit him.[21]

Wellington was right: the Government survived the abandonment of the proceedings and was still in office when on 19 July 1821 the King was crowned in Westminster Abbey, the doors of which were shut against the Queen. The ceremony, for which Parliament had voted the astonishing sum of £243,000, lasted for almost five hours; and the King, very pale, seemed at any moment likely to collapse, weighed down as he was by his heavy, cumbrous robes. But, revived by sal volatile, he behaved on occasions in the most improper fashion, according to Wellington, 'even in the most important and solemn' parts of the ceremony – 'soft eyes, kisses given on rings! . . . God alone knows what . . . which everyone observed'.[22] These 'follies' and *oeillades* were noticed also by Lady Cowper, who being 'in the line of fire had a full view',[23] and by the Duke's friend Harriet Arbuthnot, who accused the King of kissing a diamond brooch to an admirer in the Abbey and then 'continually nodding and winking' to this same lady, his kindly, amply proportioned, intimate friend Lady Conyngham.[24]

Yet when the crowning ceremony was over the congregation in the Abbey showed their enthusiasm by waving their caps and coronets, their purses and handkerchiefs and by shouting at the tops of their voices, 'God bless the King!' His Majesty was clearly 'much gratified', and, some thought, astonished by the vociferousness and evident sincerity of their acclamations. The people in the streets outside were prepared to join in the general enthusiasm. They 'were all in good humour', Lord Denbigh told his mother. 'The King was *excitedly* and most enthusiastically cheered, and seemed in the highest spirits' in Westminster Hall where the coronation banquet was held and the Duke of Wellington played his part as Lord High Constable, riding a horse which had been trained at Astley's Circus to walk backwards from the King's presence to the great doors of the Hall, undisturbed by cheering and the waving of hats. But the horse unfortunately, upon entering the Hall, took the roar of welcome to be the signal to turn round and would have approached his Majesty back to front had not – so the Page to the Lord High Steward recorded – 'some of those in attendance with great difficulty succeeded in "slewing" the animal round and enabled the great Duke to approach George the Magnificent in a decorous and orderly manner'.[25]

*

The Queen was almost forgotten and, ill and vexed, her spirit broken, she was dead within the year. Her husband – who, when Napoleon had died on St Helena three months before, on 5 May 1821, was said to have responded to the intelligence that his 'greatest enemy' was dead with the words 'Is she, by God!'[26] – was not expected to display much grief at his bereavement. Nor did he. Four days after her death he set sail for a visit to Ireland, leaving a country which, if not entirely tranquil, was at least less turbulent than it had been for many months.

30   Husband and Wife

1821

'She made his house so dull that nobody w^d go
to it.'

THE DUKE, who had been busy formulating plans for a police force
when the Guards had seemed on the verge of mutiny the year before,
could now devote more of his time to the decorations and furnishings
of Apsley House and Stratfield Saye. He had brought furniture with
him from Paris, pictures from Spain, *objets d'art* from Belgium. At
picture galleries and auction rooms he had purchased several paintings
of the Dutch school and other Old Masters. In the hall at Apsley
House stood Canova's huge nude statue of Napoleon, which, rejected
by Napoleon, had been stored in the Louvre until bought by the British
Government for 66,000 francs and presented to the Duke by the Prince
Regent. In the rooms above were numerous works of art given to the
Duke as well as those bought by him and the treasures found in
Joseph Bonaparte's carriage after the battle of Vitoria,* paintings, busts,
trophies, decorations, plate and porcelain, snuff boxes and field marshal's batons from every major army in Europe. There were two
diamond-mounted swords, one of them a present from the Tsar, the
other from the inhabitants of Bengal after the battle of Assaye.† There
were dessert services given by the Emperor of Austria and the Kings
of France, Prussia and Saxony, as well as the Portuguese service of
silver parcel-gilt in the Waterloo Gallery. In display cases on the ground
floor were silver-gilt table ornaments given by the City of London, by
the British army in India and by officers who had fought with the Duke
at Waterloo.[1]

These splendid possessions so prominently displayed heightened his

* The Duke offered to return these treasures from the royal Spanish collection, which
included four paintings by Velasquez and a particularly fine Correggio, to the King of
Spain who, 'touched by the Duke's delicacy, begged him to keep property which had
come into his hands in a manner as just as it was honourable' (Gerald 7th Duke of
Wellington, *Collected Works*, 96–7).
† This was stolen in 1948 while on display in the Victoria and Albert Museum.

guests' feelings that Apsley House was more of a museum than a home. It was also sadly evident that the Duke and Duchess were more peculiarly ill-matched than ever, that he found her shyness, her short-sightedness, her fussy concern for his welfare, her tearful, timid jealousies, her gaucheries and incompetent management of the household, all profoundly irritating. So also did he find her occasional, unexpected, petulant outbursts against certain of his friends and members of his family, that 'insufferable puppy', William Long-Wellesley, for example, and the 'insignificant, chattering blockhead', Lord Burghersh.[2]

One visitor to Stratfield Saye found the house 'not very comfortable, the park ugly, the living mediocre, the whole indeed indicating the lack of sympathy existing between the Duke and Duchess'. He occupied rooms in the south-west corner of the ground floor; her bedroom was on an upper floor, about as far removed from her husband's as it well could be; and here, unable to win the affection of the husband she so much admired and of whom she stood so much in awe, she grieved alone, her unhappiness exacerbated rather than alleviated by the sympathy of well-meaning friends.

While walking with one of his own intimate women friends, Harriet Arbuthnot, one evening after supper in the summer of 1822, the Duke complained bitterly of the distress it was to him 'to be united to a person with whom he could not possibly live on any terms of confidential intercourse'.

He assured me [Mrs Arbuthnot wrote in her diary] that he had repeatedly tried to live in a friendly manner with her . . . but it was impossible . . . She did not understand him, that she could not enter with him into the consideration of all the important concerns which are continually occupying his mind, and that he found he might as well talk to a child. He added too, that she had so high an opinion of herself and thinks herself so excessively clever that she never stirs even to accommodate herself to him, & never for an instant supposes that, when their opinions differ, she may be the one in the wrong. He said her mind was trivial and contracted . . . He told me . . . that his tastes were domestic, that nothing w^d make him so happy as to have a home where he could find comfort; but that, so far from that, she made his house so dull that nobody w^d go to it . . . & that it drove him to seek abroad that comfort & happiness that was denied to him at home. [He added that] I must have seen how much he preferred to any other the quiet visits that he paid to us at Woodford, how eagerly he always accepted our invitations, because he felt that he could do as he liked, that he could ride & walk with us & discuss with us any subject that occupied him; but that, at his home, he had no creature to speak to, for that discussing political or important subjects with the Duchess was like talking *Hebrew* to her.[3]

Mrs Arbuthnot 'could not at last help' expressing her astonishment at his ever having 'married such a person'. Nor could she help laughing at his answer: 'Is it not the most extraordinary thing you ever heard of! Would you have believed that anybody could have been such a *damned fool?* I was not in the least in love with her. I married her because they asked me to do it & I did not know myself.' Mrs Arbuthnot then said she had never heard of anybody doing so absurd a thing. He 'agreed cordially' and assured her that she could not think him a greater fool than he did himself.[4]

She herself later came to the conclusion that the Duchess was 'the silliest woman' she had ever met. 'She does not comply with any of his fancies in the arrangement of his house,' she wrote in her journal in October 1825, '& in truth it is so bad a ménage it is quite disagreeable to be in the house . . . She is totally unfit for her situation. She is like the housekeeper & dresses herself exactly like a shepherdess, with an old hat made by herself stuck at the back of her head, and a dirty basket under her arm. The Duke says he is sure she is mad.'[5]

There were persistent differences between them, not infrequently about money and the Duchess's erratic methods of accounting. He went through her accounts, frequently finding discrepancies and making sardonic remarks or placing exasperated exclamation marks in the margins.[6]

There were numerous poor people, mostly former servants, to whom she gave occasional presents or paid regular pensions; and she was constantly overspending her allowance. She admitted to her husband that she did so 'very injudiciously'; but she was not, in fact, an extravagant woman: she spent hardly anything on clothes or on her appearance or on jewellery. At the Coronation she had chosen to wear cornelians instead of the diamonds or more precious stones with which the other ladies were bedecked. Yet she was constantly in a muddle about money. She wondered whether he might increase her allowance from £500 a year to £670 to set her straight. No, he would not: £500 was a perfectly proper sum for a lady in her position.[7] She turned to others for help, borrowing £4,000, for example, from the Russian-born merchant and philanthropist John Julius Angerstein.[8]

The Duchess tried to find out to whom her husband had himself made charitable gifts and donations, so that those whom she wished to help did not appear on her lists as well as his. But she was too nervous of him to ask him directly about the objects of his charity; and when she approached others for the information he wrote to her furiously, protesting that she was questioning his undoubted generosity, accusing her of prying into all his personal affairs with which she had no business to interfere, of adopting 'a dirty way of trying to find out something' which, if it were to be found out, might cause her 'the greatest uneasiness'. Every day's experience convinced him that she did 'more foolish things' – which, upon reflection, she 'surely must regret' – 'than any woman in the world'. Her modes of enquiry into his transactions really made his life 'a Burthen' to him. If it went on he 'must live somewhere else'. It was 'the meanest dirtiest trick' of which anyone could be guilty.[9]

She replied with that occasional flash of spirit and acerbity with which she, as a high Tory, responded to what she took to be the impertinence of Whigs. She told her husband that she hoped she would not again be subjected to offensive accusations for which there was 'positively no grounds whatever'. In returning two of his letters to him, she wrote, 'I am sure I could have made you happy had you suffered me to try, but thrust from you I was not allowed . . . For Christ sake do not use another woman as you have treated me. [Never] write to a human being such letters as those from you which I now enclose. [They] have destroyed me.'

It was true that she did try hard to please him. One day she encountered him unexpectedly upon her return, windswept after a boating trip on the Thames with her sons. He ran his fingers through her tangled grey hair. Could she not do something about the greyness? he asked her. But she thought he had always 'hated everything approaching a wig'. 'Oh, no,' he replied, 'I am sure you would look better.' So she hurried off to a hairdresser and returned not only with a wig but also with rouge on her pale cheeks. She intended to appear like this at Devonshire House that night. She hoped he would notice that she had lost no time in complying with his wishes; and 'O', she thought, 'if only she had done so about rouge 16 years ago'.[10]

It was really too late now. Mrs Arbuthnot astutely put her finger on the problem when – having advised him to be more civil to his wife and received the tart response that he was 'always very civil to her and never said a harsh word to her in his life' – she said that he did not realize just how uncivil to her he was. He was abrupt with everyone but exceptionally so with her. 'She is frightened to death at him (a thing he detests) she always seems *consterné* when he comes near her . . . Poor woman I am sorry for her . . . I am sorry for him too; it drives him from his home.'[11]

Five years after the Duchess's death, the Duke confided in his friend Lady Salisbury how tiresome he had found her, a subject he had never broached with her before.

> He said she was one of the most foolish women that ever existed . . .
>
> She was very vain. She thought herself the *prettiest* woman in the world (she had been pretty in her youth), and the cleverest. She used to buy a great many books, and write her name in the title page, but never read them. She always professed a wish to do everything to please me, but if I desired anything might be done, the wish was complied with at the moment and then it was always neglected afterwards.
>
> In her observations upon other women (and she was very censorious), there never was anything that showed observation or discrimination of character. The remarks she made upon *one* would have done equally for half a dozen others. She spoilt my sons by making everything give way to them, and teaching them to have too high ideas of their own consequence.[12]

Unhappy as she was in her marriage, the Duchess had her comforts, though. She loved her sons and loved her adopted children not much less, and they in turn loved her. There were four of these adopted children: Arthur Freese, son of the pretty army wife whom the Duke had known so well in India; Gerald Valerian Wellesley, the Duke's nephew; the Duchess's niece, Kate Hamilton; and Lord Arthur Lennox, son of the Duke of Richmond who, appointed Governor-General of British North America, had died the following year of hydrophobia after being bitten by a fox. Two other children were later to be taken into the Wellingtons' care, the Duke's great-nephews, William and James Long-Wellesley, Wards in Chancery.

They had a pleasant life at Stratfield Saye, although as a parent, godparent and guardian the Duke was, of course, strict and demanding, concerned to ensure, so he told Mrs Arbuthnot, that his sons at least did not take after their mother. Certainly the Duke – worried that his elder son, Marquess Douro, was falling into bad company at Eton, and that the younger, Lord Charles, was incorrigibly idle – was far readier to find fault with them than to praise them. When they wrote to him from Eton they were likely to have their letters returned to them with mistakes in spelling and punctuation corrected without further comment.[13]

After their father's death, Douro was asked by the Duchess of Cleveland if his father had been an affectionate parent. 'No,' Douro replied, according to the Duchess, 'he never even patted me on the shoulder when I was a boy, but it was because he hated my mother.'[14] Douro came in time to revere his father, 'treasuring up every reminiscence of him, and considering every memorial as sacred';[15] but the relationship between them was never easy and, as a young boy, so he confided in his mother, he thought his father the 'most severe disciplinarian that ever lived and consequently avoided and feared him accordingly'. This fear he never fully outgrew.[16] Nor could he overcome the feelings of inadequacy which his father's great name and reputation aroused in him. 'Think,' he once said sadly, considering the prospect of his own situation after his father's death. 'Think what it will be like when the Duke of Wellington is announced and only I come in.'[17]

Unwilling or unable to show much affection for his sons, the Duke was undoubtedly fond of other people's young children; and, in their houses, he was often to be found playing with them. He spent as much time in these houses as he could, going to stay as an ever-welcome guest with the Arbuthnots at their unpretentious farmhouse, Woodford Lodge near Thrapston in Northamptonshire, or with the Bedfords in the comparative splendour of Woburn Abbey, or with the Granvilles at Wherstead in Suffolk where he enjoyed games of piquet with Dorothea Lieven. 'He knows as little about [piquet] as I do,' Mme de Lieven wrote; 'and the only difference between us is that I play badly and know it, and he plays badly and thinks he plays well. It is incredible how his pride has a share in everything that he does. It plunges him into despair not to be able to do something, or to do it badly. It is a strange vanity. Men have a great deal of it, a hundred times more than we have.'[18]

He never lost his pleasure in the company of young women, not only better looking but also far more intelligent than his wife, young women to whom he could talk about war or politics or to whom he could even read aloud papers and pamphlets he had written about political and military matters, presuming that he would be understood and found interesting.

He needed little encouragement to talk about his campaigns, an activity he clearly relished. 'His countenance lights up,' a fellow guest once said of him, 'his eyes flash fire & his whole appearance is as if he was inspired.'[19] Not all his listeners found his accounts so enthralling, however, particularly those who had heard them before. 'Since dinner,' Robert Peel once wrote to his wife from Sudbourne, Lord Hertford's house in Suffolk, 'the Duke of Wellington has been giving a long account of all that happened at Waterloo and afterwards.'[20]

When, 'in order to kill time', a guest in his own house in 1821, Mme de Lieven, asked him to tell her something of his military career, he related it in detail from his days in India to Waterloo, 'the most difficult battle he ever fought'.[21] 'He had never been wounded,' wrote Mme de Lieven when describing the Duke's monologue to Prince Metternich.

> He has never lost a battle ... His first feat of arms was as follows. He was sent out on an expedition near Calcutta. He mistook the direction, and let a fortress be captured which he ought to have defended. He shut himself up in despair, and what do you think he did? He fell asleep. I suppose that it was in his sleep that he made up his mind to be a great man. He said to your ambassador, who declared that all would end well in the neapolitan campaign: 'But, my dear Prince, I have always noticed that, in order to end, you have to begin.' We all laughed.[22]

He would scribble plans of besieged cities or battle formations on bits of paper, even on the knee of his breeches, and explain how the French had been beaten, gradually enlarging their numbers, so it was noticed, in relation to his own and firmly contradicting stories such as that he was surprised at Waterloo. 'Surprised!' he once expostulated to someone bold enough to put forward the proposition, perhaps to Mrs Arbuthnot, or as Lord Wilton suggested, to the portrait painter H.W. Pickersgill, who asked the provocative question so as to bring animation to his sitter's expression. 'Surprised! Not half so surprised as I am now.'[23] 'Supposing I *was* surprised,' he protested on another occasion, 'I won the battle; and what could you have had more even if I had been surprised?'* He was always inclined to be acerbic when

---

* The Duke of York insisted that Wellington had, indeed, been surprised at Waterloo. Charles Greville, who knew the Duke of York well, having managed his racing establishment, said that his prejudice against Wellington was excessively strong. 'He does not deny his military talents, but he thinks that he is false and ungrateful, that he never gave sufficient credit to his officers, and that he was unwilling to put forward men of talent who might be in a situation to claim some share of credit, the whole of which he was desirous of engrossing himself. He says that at Waterloo he got into a scrape and allowed himself to be surprised, and he attributes in great measure the success of that day to Lord Anglesea, who, he says, was hardly mentioned, and that in the coldest terms; in the Duke's dispatch' (*The Greville Memoirs*, i, 120).

his military acumen was even hesitantly questioned or some naive remark hinted that he had had a less than complete grasp of the operations in which he had been engaged. When Sir Watkyns William Wynn asked him if he had a good view of the battle of Waterloo, he replied dismissively, 'I generally like to see what I am about.'[24]

He was a most welcome guest though. He was very rarely moody, the 'most unpretentious, perfectly natural and amiable person' one of his hostesses, Lady Granville, had ever met with; and in Mrs Arbuthnot's eyes, 'the pleasantest person possible in a house, so simple & so easily amused and pleased'.[25] Lady Salisbury agreed with them: the Duke was 'never bored for an instant, always gay, always cheerful, entering with interest into everything that passes, even the most absolute trifles, and extracting amusement from them'.[26]

Encountering him at a party, Mrs Calvert found him just the same good-humoured, unaffected creature he ever was.[27] Lady Granville described how he enjoyed playing charades at Wherstead, 'happier than when he won his battles', as he carried his niece, Lady Worcester, in his arms across a river represented by a row of cushions.[28]

At the dinner table he ate his food without apparent interest but was pleasant and attentive to the ladies who sat on either side of him; and he could always be relied upon to talk to them afterwards in the drawing-room.* 'There is no subject you can mention,' observed the rich dandy and diarist Thomas Raikes, 'on which the Duke is not always prepared to relate some curious anecdote which shows his extraordinary memory.'[29]

He played with the children of the house with whom he never made the mistake of condescending. At Lady Shelley's as at Wherstead he cheerfully joined in the charades and when she played waltzes at the piano he accompanied her on the triangle. He enjoyed dancing and

---

* He often, indeed, evinced a strong preference for the company of women rather than that of men. He saw enough of men in the course of his work. He was a member of several gentlemen's clubs in London; but he was rarely seen in them, even in his favourite, the United Service Club, although the horse blocks in Waterloo Place were specially erected there for him. He sometimes went to Crockford's but did not gamble there; and he took a lively interest in the formation of the Carlton Club, which was founded as a meeting-place for Tories in 1832 as a consequence of the general election of 1831 which had given a massive majority to the Whig ministry to enable them to pass a reform bill. But the Duke did not go to the Carlton very often either. Nor was he often to be seen in either the Athenaeum or the Oriental Club of both of which he was a founder member in 1824. He was also a member of the Kildare Club in Dublin where he was supposed to have said, 'very well, think what you are about. But if you let in the bishops, mind your umbrellas' (Elizabeth Longford, *Wellington: Pillar of State*, 150).

once at Belvoir Castle Lady Wharncliffe – who could not tell how odd it seemed 'to be in a Country House with the Duke of Wellington like *any other visitor*' – saw him 'with perfect good humour, dancing down two *immensely* long country dances'.[30] At Lord Bridgewater's and elsewhere he settled down happily to whist, his luck at cards, a fellow guest thought, 'quite extraordinary'; it seemed 'as if his good genius accompanied him in every, the most trivial concerns of life'.[31] He liked to be shown pictures and objects of art and made acute remarks about them, if not always flattering to their owners at least sensible and to the point. He took pleasure in walking and riding. He liked shooting, and was credited with killing eighty head one day at Ashridge Park.[32] 'I have been shooting pretty well lately,' he told Lady Shelley in 1820. 'I killed twenty-seven head at Woburn; and the Duke of York, with his five guns, only killed thirty-five.'[33] Earlier while shooting with Louis XVIII and the Dauphin, so he told J.W. Croker, he 'killed 280 pieces to his own share': he could not say 'to his own gun, for he had ten guns and ten Swiss soldiers to load them. His shoulder was all contused, and his hands and fingers cut, and he says the force of practice was so great that latterly he *could not* miss a shot.'[34]

These triumphs were most exceptional, though: generally he was considered a most indifferent shot, once frightening Lady Shelley's little daughter by blasting away in all directions.

'What's this Fanny,' her mother chided her. 'Fear in the presence of the Lord of Waterloo! . . . Stand close behind the Duke of Wellington,' the mother wisely added. 'He will protect you.' When he managed to bag a pheasant, this was considered so memorable an event that the bird was stuffed and placed in Lady Shelley's dressing-room which was already well supplied with ducal memorabilia.[35]

If pheasants were generally safe within range of the Duke's gun, human beings were not always so. Having peppered a gamekeeper, he once 'had the misfortune' of putting several shots into the face of Lord Granville, an accident about which Lady Granville was 'very good humoured'.[36] On another unfortunate occasion, having already wounded a dog and struck a gamekeeper's gaiters, he shot an old woman doing her washing by an open window.

'I'm wounded, Milady,' the woman shrieked to her landlord's wife.

'My good woman,' Lady Shelley replied, 'this ought to be the proudest moment of your life. You have had the distinction of being shot by the great Duke of Wellington!' The woman was no doubt more gratified by the guinea which the great Duke apologetically pressed upon her.[37]

Lady Shelley's undisguised, almost reverential admiration of the

Duke never seemed to pall upon him, nor, for a time, did the company of another attractive young woman, Maria Tollemache, daughter of the Hon. Charles Tollemache, who claimed that she had declined to marry him and who subsequently refused to invite him to her wedding when, in 1833, she married a widower, the elderly first Marquess of Ailesbury. But it was observed that the Duke far preferred talking to Harriet Arbuthnot, the good-looking, agreeable if rather strait-laced woman whom everybody supposed – almost certainly incorrectly – to be his mistress or, at least, to have been so in the early days of their friendship. Charles Greville referred to her as such, as though it were an incontrovertible fact; Thomas Creevey called her 'the Beau's flirt', though Lady Shelley considered her 'devoid of womanly passions'.[38] She was the second wife of Charles Arbuthnot, a well-liked, discreet and sensible Secretary of the Treasury, known universally as 'Gosh', twenty-six years older than his wife to whom he was as devoted as she was to him. She had 'a clear, good head', Lady Wharncliffe said, 'and was well-informed on many subjects', particularly on political subjects on which, indeed, she could be rather a bore. Prince Pückler-Muskau, for one, found her 'very clever' when he sat next to her at a dinner party at the Rothschilds', but she was 'an *enragée* politician . . . I hate politics at dinner.'[39] The Whig Lady Cowper thought her an 'odious little woman';[40] but she nevertheless invited her to parties at Panshanger to please the Duke since, as she said, 'There is nothing I would not do to please him, he is such a love.'[41]

Although highly intelligent Mrs Arbuthnot was a rather unimaginative young woman, undeviatingly Tory in her opinions and with a strict regard for the proprieties of social conduct and the importance of rank. George Canning's 'want of principle' was to be attributed to the inferior stock from which he sprang;[42] while Robert Peel's inability to control the disorderly young men in the House of Commons was the consequence of his 'low birth and vulgar manners'.[43] There was also in Mrs Arbuthnot's character a certain coldness of feeling, as she readily admitted herself: 'I sometimes think it is most unfortunate but it is quite true that, excepting my husband & his children, I have no feeling of warm interest for any human being but the Duke. There is something about him that fascinates me to a degree that is silly, but which I cannot resist. He is so amiable, so kind hearted with a degree of roughness, & so frank that I always feel I w^d die for him.'[44]

Fond of her as he was, the Duke, like Prince Pückler-Muskau, occasionally found Mrs Arbuthnot's passion for politics rather overwhelming, and her manners sometimes a little bossy. He and Lady

Shelley enjoyed pretending that 'La Tyranna' ruled him with an iron rod and that he was frightened to death of her. 'I have taken advantage of a favourable moment and have obtained *permission*,' he once wrote to Lady Shelley. '*When the cat's away the mice go and play*, and as she is at her brother's in Lincolnshire . . . I have taken leave to ask you to Stratfield Saye.'[45]

Dorothea de Lieven was also well informed as well as attractive and 'a very clever woman of intrigue', in Nathan Meyer Rothschild's opinion, amusing, quick-witted and fascinated by politics on which the King would talk to her at exhausting length during her frequent visits to his Majesty's Marine Pavilion at Brighton. One day there Mme de Lieven found him 'in a more talkative mood than ever . . . on the subject of high politics'. She wished that she could remember 'his ideas and the order in which he gave them'. 'I know that three times I bit my lip so as not to laugh,' she told Metternich. 'And that I ended up by eating all the orange-peel I could find, so as to give my mouth something to do to hide its twitching if the danger grew too great . . . Everything was plunged in such confusion . . . The whole speech was addressed to me; but in a tone of voice which obliged everyone else to listen in silence. We should be there still if Admiral Nagle ['a bold, weather-beaten tar' who was Groom of the Bedchamber] had not begun to snore so loudly that the King lost patience and broke up the meeting.'[46]

Wellington was quite as bored as Admiral Nagle during these dinner parties at Brighton where the loquacious King talked away inconsequentially, stopping occasionally to take pinches of snuff placed for the purpose upon Lady Conyngham's dimpled shoulder.

The Duke was there in January 1822 when the King, suffering from a severe attack of gout and most cantankerous, could scarcely hobble to the dining-room table where he ate very little, and could eat nothing at all without imbibing cherry brandy in quantities 'not to be believed'.[47]

The rooms were infernally hot; the air reeked of scent; the lights were dazzling; the guests spent their evenings half-lying on cushions playing patience, sipping liqueurs, listening to music or to the King singing, which he did, it had to be admitted, tolerably well but with only a shadow of his former verve and force.

'Devil take me,' Wellington exclaimed to Mme de Lieven, 'I think I must have got into bad company.' He behaved, she thought, 'in a lordly way with his master' who nevertheless pressed him to stay when he wanted to leave. Wellington made the excuse that he had to go back for a meeting of the Privy Council. '*Damn the Council*,' was all the King said. The Duke grumbled to Mme de Lieven that he would now have to write a long letter of excuse to his colleagues; so she undertook to do this for him and wrote, '*By his Majesty's command, Damn the Council.*' He signed the note and sent it off.[48]

There was no escaping the King, though, and when his Majesty left on a visit to Hanover, the Duke was required to go with him as far as Brussels so that he could be conducted over the battlefield of Waterloo. For Wellington the tour was not a success. Lady Shelley would have been a delightful audience, but the King showed scant interest as he was taken from one vantage point to the next in the pouring rain. He 'took it all very coolly', the Duke reported disapprovingly; 'indeed never asked a single question, nor said one word, till I showed him where Lord Anglesey's leg was buried, and then he burst into tears.' Recovering himself, he pottered about for some time, poking at the ground with his stick, hoping to find the bones. Failing to do so he gave orders that a tree whose branches had been shattered by gunfire should be cut down, made into a chair for Carlton House and inscribed with the glorious legend: GEORGIO AUGUSTO EUROPAE LIBERATORI.[49]

The King returned from Hanover well satisfied with his reception there; and in contented mood he turned his mind to the possibility of getting rid of his irritable and incompatible Prime Minister, Lord Liverpool, and replacing him with Lord Sidmouth, Wellington or Castlereagh. He favoured Castlereagh with whom he had got on well during his trip to Hanover; but was reluctantly forced to conclude that Liverpool, with a wider measure of support than any other member of the Cabinet could command, was indispensable. His indispensability made him all the more objectionable to the King who was constantly finding fault with him.* But after some satisfactory rearrangements in appointments in the Royal Household had been made with the Government's help, there had been a rapprochement with Liverpool who was received at Brighton '*with cordiality*'. 'Such a changed man as the King you never saw,' Castlereagh reported. 'He is in the highest spirits and says Liverpool is again! entitled to all his confidence.'[50]

But Castlereagh was not well. He had begun to display inordinate

---

* 'Depend upon it if he lives till Doomsday,' runs a characteristic letter of complaint from the King to Wellington, 'Lord Liverpool will never be corrected or made fit for the high office to which I raised him, and I should consider it a mercy to be spared the irritations to which he continually subjects me' (Wellington Papers, Hartley Institute, WPI/766/14, 17 July 1823).

suspicion of his colleagues, particularly of Wellington. He also began to talk wildly. In conversation with the King he had gripped his arm and kissed his hands, accused himself of all sorts of crimes, wept, declared that he was being accused of homosexual practices, that he was going to fly away to Portsmouth 'and from there to the ends of the earth'.[51]

He displayed similar symptoms of derangement and persecution mania to Wellington, referring to the case of Percy Jocelyn, a son of the Earl of Roden, who had been deposed as Bishop of Clogher after having been found in flagrante delicto with a soldier in an inn in Westminster. Castlereagh accused himself of a similar offence, although in reality he was being persecuted by blackmailers who had burst in upon him in a brothel into which he had been enticed by a male prostitute dressed as a woman.[52] After listening to Castlereagh's distressed ramblings for some time, Wellington said bluntly, 'I am bound to warn you that you cannot be in your right mind.'

Castlereagh covered his face with his hands and began to cry. 'Since *you* say so,' he sobbed, 'I fear it must be so.'[53]

Wellington offered to stay with him; but Castlereagh refused the offer: no one must suspect what was happening. So the Duke went to see Castlereagh's doctor to tell him that his patient was 'very unwell'. Afterwards he wrote to the Arbuthnots, asking them to go to see Castlereagh as soon as they could. In the meantime all razors and pistols were removed from the poor man's dressing-room, but, having attacked his wife whom he accused of being involved with Wellington in the conspiracy against him, he summoned his doctor, then, making use of 'a little nail knife which he carried in his pocket-book', cut his carotid artery with 'anatomical accuracy'. The doctor, so he told Wellington, found his patient standing in his dressing-room with his back to him, his head raised to the ceiling, the knife in his hand. 'Let me fall upon your arm,' he said, ''Tis all over.'[54]

Castlereagh's suicide forced upon the King the unwelcome business of approving a new Foreign Secretary. Wellington would have been the King's choice; but, as the Duke told Mme de Lieven, he did not want the post: he would be compelled to adopt the opinions of a party. Besides, he had been 'out of England too long not to have lost the habit of speaking in the House'. In any case, Lord Liverpool was convinced that George Canning would have to be given the appointment if his Government were to survive. He would, indeed, have brought Canning in long ago had not grief at Lady Liverpool's death made him feel incapable of coping with the King's violent objection to a man who, his Majesty believed, had been one of Queen Caroline's lovers and who had certainly gone abroad before her trial, resigning as President of the Board of Control. The King had hoped to get rid of Canning for good and had warmly welcomed his appointment as Governor-General of India.

Unfortunately the man had not yet sailed to take up his appointment; and the King insisted that his departure should not be delayed. 'The immediate object of my writing to You is that You will not interrupt & *on no account impede*, the Arrangements which are already settled *respecting India*,' the King told Liverpool in a letter which arrived on the day of Castlereagh's funeral. 'It is *my Decision* that they should remain *final* & *conclusive*'.[55]

Emphatic as this letter was, having listened to the Prime Minister's arguments in favour of Canning, the King felt obliged to consult other members of the Cabinet to ask them if they shared Liverpool's views. He remained sulky, reluctant and unconvinced, complaining of the difficulty in being reconciled to a man whom he said he 'never wanted to see again'. Wellington urged the King to give way. He would have to forgive Canning and agree to his appointment. The King protested that his 'honour as a gentleman' prevented him from doing any such thing. Wellington at that time disliked the clever, self-confident, sarcastic upstart Canning almost as much as the King did and at various times accused him of being 'one of the idlest of men',[56] 'the slowest & worst man of business he ever knew'.[57] Even so, the Duke replied, the King's duty as a monarch made it essential for him to take the man whom those in high office considered most suitable, astutely reminding him of the fundamental difference between his situation and that of a private individual. Subjects of his Majesty might call other men to account when their honour was impugned, a sovereign could only demean himself by demanding explanations. 'The honour of your Majesty,' the Duke said, 'consists in acts of mercy and grace, and I am convinced that your Majesty's honour is most safe in extending your grace and favour to Mr Canning upon this occasion if the arrangement in contemplation is beneficial to your Majesty's service.'[58] At length the King gave way. 'Very well,' he said, 'since you are determined to have him, take him in God's name, but remember I tell you he will throw you all overboard.'[59]

So Canning was informed by the King that 'the brightest ornament' of his Majesty's crown was 'the power of extending grace and favour to a subject who may have incurred his displeasure'.[60] This manner of appointing him deeply offended Canning who said at first that in the circumstances he would refuse to accept office: it was as though he had been given a ticket to Almack's and found written on the back, '*Admit the rogue*.'[61] Wellington, however, advised him to disregard the rebuke. So Canning swallowed his pride, agreed to rejoin the Cabinet and took up his duties as Foreign Secretary, while Lord Liverpool wrote to the Duke to thank him for all that he had done. 'It might never have been brought to such a result' without his assistance.[62]

Having helped to smooth down ruffled feathers in London, the Duke now prepared to leave England to practise his diplomacy on a foreign stage.

Francisco Goya's portrait of Wellington painted in August 1812 soon after the British army entered Madrid after the battle of Salamanca. The Order of the Golden Fleece and the Peninsular Gold Cross were added later. The Duke is also wearing the pink sash and star of the Order of the Bath.

Ten minutes after the retreat of the Garde
Impérial at Waterloo, Wellington snapped his
telescope shut, took off his hat and waved it
as a signal for the advance to victory.

Right: An equestrian portrait by Sir Thomas
Lawrence of the Duke in 1816 when he was
Commander-in-Chief of the Army of
Occupation on the Continent.

HANC
ARTHURI DUCIS DE WELLINGTON
IMAGINEM
QUALEM ESSE HABUIT PROELIO 1815
APUD WATERLOO
QUOAD VESTITUM, ARMA, EQUUM, HABITUM,

Above: Sir David Wilkie's *Chelsea Pensioners Reading the Waterloo Despatch* was commissioned by the Duke who paid the artist £1,260 for it. It still hangs at Apsley House.

Left: Dorothea Benckendorff, Princess Lieven, painted in the early 1820s by Sir Thomas Lawrence.

Top right: The library at Stratfield Saye has changed little since the Duke's time. The design and decoration of the room, attributed to William Kent, date from about 1740. Many of the books are from Napoleon's library. The picture over the fireplace is Tintoretto's *Ascension*.

Middle right: The Duke's bedroom at Apsley House from an illustration by Thomas Shotter Boys in Richard Ford's *Apsley House and Walmer Castle* (1853). In reply to a comment about the narrowness of his bed at Walmer Castle, the Duke famously replied, 'When it's time to turn over it's time to turn out.'

Right: The Stratfield Saye estate in Hampshire was bought by the nation in 1817 for £263,000 and presented to the Duke, who added the conservatory on the left in 1838 and the two outer wings in 1846. His great-great-grandson, the eighth Duke, who lives here, has opened the house to the public.

Jarvey Jarvey — Here I am your Honor — Rum tum tiddi idde — High gee wo —

A QUARTETTE in Character — Pub May 1829 by Tho Maclean 26 Haymarket Sole Publisher of H Heaths Original Caricatures

'A Quartette in Character.' A caricature by William Heath published in May 1829 depicting King George IV, the Duke as a coachman, the King's fat friend, Lady Conyngham, blowing a horn and Sir Robert Peel. The print is one of a number issued at the time of the debate on Roman Catholic emancipation portraying the Duke as the driver of the sovereign. It was published shortly after the King had given way to Wellington's pressure.

The Duke at seventy-five when he was bent with arthritis. A pencil and watercolour portrait by the anecdotal painter, Charles Robert Leslie.

The Duke's funeral procession passing Hyde Park Corner on 18 November 1852, after a painting by Louis Haghe. On the left is the portico of Apsley House, on the right Decimus Burton's Triumphal Arch, which was moved to the top of Constitution Hill in 1882. Matthew Cotes Wyatt's huge forty-ton statue of Wellington on his horse Copenhagen was moved to Aldershot three years later.

31   Vienna and Verona

1822 — 4

'There is nothing so improper as for one
government to interfere in the internal affairs
of another.'

BEFORE HE LEFT for the Continent the Duke had a duty to perform
as Master-General of the Ordnance, an office which required him to
supervise the Army's equipment, armaments, fortifications and barracks. Various howitzers were to be tested at the beginning of August
and his presence was required by the Artillery. There had been a
deafening explosion dangerously close to where the Duke was standing
and a month later he was still suffering from earache and a ringing,
such as that caused by tinnitus, in his left ear. Wellington's physician
was Dr J.R. Hume, the uncomfortably hearty Scotsman now living in
Curzon Street who had served with distinction in the Peninsular War
and at Waterloo. Hume, unable to cure the complaint himself, called
in Dr John Stevenson, a well-known aurist who had been apprenticed to
his father, a surgeon, at the age of sixteen and had attended both Queen
Caroline and the Duke of Saxe-Coburg. Stevenson treated the Duke's
ear with so strong a caustic solution that the patient suffered such distress
from inflammation for forty-eight hours that he could neither sleep nor
eat. 'I don't think I ever suffered so much in my life,' he said. 'It was not
pain: it was something far worse. The sense of hearing became so acute
that I wished myself stone deaf. The noise of a carriage passing along the
street was like the loudest thunder, and everybody that spoke seemed to
be shrieking at the very top of his voice.'[1]

Dr Hume called the next morning and was shown into the Duke's
room where he found his patient sitting at his table, 'unshaved and
unwashed with blood-shot eyes and a flushed cheek and he observed
that when he rose he staggered like a drunken man. His whole appearance, indeed, to use Dr Hume's expression, "was that of one who had
recovered from a terrible debauch".'[2]

'Indeed, I never was so unwell,' he wrote to Mrs Arbuthnot when
he was slightly better. 'I do not remember before in my life having

passed a day in bed . . . Strange to say I was near fainting in the effort to dress myself, & was obliged to give it up.'[3]

'I doubt my ear ever recovering the consequences of the accident,' he told his brother Richard. 'At present I don't think I hear at all with my left ear, though I do with my right. But the loss of the sense of one ear has deranged my power of hearing very much indeed; and I cannot tell from where a sound comes.'[4]

For days after the accident he looked worn out. During his military service he had lost all his back teeth and this had already altered the shape of his mouth, giving it a sunken look not apparent in his portraits, a look which the painter, Benjamin Robert Haydon, described as being like that of 'a helpless infant learning to whistle'.[5]   Also, the damage to his ear affected his sense of balance; and he was often thereafter seen to stumble, as he did one day in the street when he was knocked down by a gig and was lucky to escape with his life.[6]   Some time later he 'had a most terrible fall' upon getting out of his cabriolet at the Opera and was 'most frightfully cut and swelled about the nose and face'.[7]   And in 1836 he was to hurt his knee badly when he fell off his horse after running into a water-cart.[8]

He was still unwell when he set out for the Continent on 17 September 1822 at the age of fifty-three. He was appointed Britain's representative at a new international congress to be held in Vienna before being transferred to Verona. He felt as though he were drunk, he said, and could not walk properly. 'I am very tired of being sick,' he complained, 'never having been so before.'[9]   It was reported that 'persons who had not seen the Duke of Wellington for some years, have perceived a great alteration in his features and a great change in his person'.[10] Thomas Creevey described him as appearing like 'a perfect shadow, and as old looking as the ark'.[11]

Yet he was determined not to let his poor health interfere with his efforts to obtain 'a satisfactory result' and 'preserve the Peace of the World'. Metternich had hoped that Castlereagh would attend the conference as an influential member of Liverpool's administration with a strong sense of Continental unity, as the 'only person in his country with experience in foreign affairs', and as a man with sound views on the maintenance of a conservative monarchical Europe. But Wellington was a perfectly acceptable substitute – a distinguished man with a European reputation,* the only member of the English Cabinet

---

* Not long before, in Italy, the Countess of Blessington had been delighted to observe that mass-produced busts of Wellington were on sale in Carrara. 'Long, long may England preserve the original,' she wrote in her diary, 'and glory in his achievements' (Michael Sadleir, *Blessington-D'Orsay*, 88).

considered to be able to hold his own with the Tsar and the Emperor of Austria, as well as the King of Prussia, all of whom were to be present at Verona in person. Also to be there were all the rulers of Italy (apart from the Pope), twenty ambassadors, fifteen ministers, two Barons von Rothschild, one cardinal and, from France, the Vicomte de Montmorency, the Foreign Minister, and the Vicomte de Chateaubriand, the recently appointed French Ambassador in London.

Chateaubriand's friend, Madame Récamier, Metternich's mistress, Mme de Lieven, and Napoleon's widow, Marie Louise, who had been granted in perpetuity the Duchy of Parma, were among the many ladies also assembled in Verona. They were to be seen in the audience listening to Angelica Catalini sing in Rossini's operas, conducted by the composer himself, and at the card tables in Mme de Lieven's salon. The Duke sat down with them to play écarté; the Duchess of Parma won, and he paid his debt to her in napoléons. He went to dine with her and she apologized for not serving mutton which she knew was with him a favourite dish. He responded by inviting her to be guest of honour at a musical evening to be given by himself with his niece, Lady Burghersh, as hostess.

Wellington was more than a diplomatic host and card player in Verona. The King of Spain had asked for armed help against the liberals in his country. The Russians were eager to intervene. But the Austrians had no wish to see the Tsar's army marching across Europe to the Pyrenees. Nor had the French, though they were quite prepared to intervene themselves and the following year did, in fact, do so, restoring King Ferdinand VII to absolute power. For his part, and for the moment, Canning told the Duke 'frankly and peremptorily to declare that to any such interference, come what may, His Majesty will not be a party'. Wellington was quite sure that the King should not be a party. He made it clear that the British Government had 'insuperable objections to interfering in the internal concerns of any country', and would not give any 'moral support' whatsoever to any other power prepared to intervene. These were his own views: 'There is nothing,' he said, 'so improper as for one government to interfere in the internal affairs of another.' A civil war in Spain was to be avoided at all costs. 'He would,' he once declared, 'lay down his life rather than endure a single month of civil war.' The other diplomats in Verona were clearly impressed by the Duke's patent sincerity, his common sense and outspokenness, his direct honesty and what Thomas Creevey called his 'comical simplicity' in a devious world.[12] He left Verona on the day before the Congress ended and by Christmas he was back in London, congratulated by *The Times* for his part in arranging the suspension of hostilities for the time being and carrying a blouse he had bought in Paris as a present for Lady Shelley.[13]

On his return to London he suffered a relapse in his health which had been somewhat improved in Verona. He confessed to Mrs Arbuthnot that he did not feel very secure in his 'Balance'; and one day he was knocked down when crossing the street and almost killed for the second time within a few months. Lord Liverpool told Arbuthnot that he had had 'a strong warning' and really ought to alter his mode of life. It was 'most unlucky' that he could not find in 'domestick comforts a proportion at least of that repose' of which he was so much in need.[14] As it was he was an extremely difficult patient, refusing to cut down on his dining out, declining to be bled when Dr Hume recommended such treatment and denouncing all doctors as charlatans. 'I know what is good for me as well [as] Dr Hume or any Doctor of the Profession,' he told Mrs Arbuthnot. 'I am never unwell but at night; and I get well from the moment I rise in the morning, & am better till I go to bed again. The whole Medical profession cannot tell the reason any more than they can tell . . . whether I shall ever hear again.'[15]

In defiance of Dr Hume his round of house-parties was resumed. Usually taking his camp-bed with him, he went to Hatfield to stay with the Salisburys, to the Westmorlands at Apethorpe, the Beauforts at Badminton, to Ashridge Park in Hertfordshire, to Combermere Abbey in Cheshire, to Gunton Park in Norfolk, Beaudesert in Staffordshire, Maresfield in Sussex and, more often than he cared to do, to the Pavilion at Brighton and the Royal Lodge, the large Gothic *cottage orné* which John Nash had created for the King in Windsor Great Park. At Windsor the party would be driven down to Virginia Water in the afternoon to one or other of the Moorish and Chinese pavilions which his Majesty had had built by the shores of the lake.

> They meet at three o'clock [Lady Shelley recorded] at which hour five or six phaetons come to the door, each to receive a lady and gentleman who drive about the country until five. At that hour the whole party dine [then] sit at table until between nine and ten o'clock, then they return to the Cottage [Royal Lodge] dress *presto*, and go into the saloon where they play at écarté and other games until midnight. It is every day the same: Oh! monotony![16]

Wellington was desperately bored by these parties, this perpetual *'junke thing'* which lasted 'from morning till night'. 'We embarked yesterday at three, and were upon the lake of Como, either in the boat or dining, till nine,' he complained one summer day to Mrs Arbuthnot. 'We then returned, dressed as quickly as possible and passed the night at Ecarte and supper from which we broke up about one, thus passing ten hours in company! In my life I never heard so much nonsense and folly or so many lies in the same space of time . . . One is obliged to listen to [them] with a certain degree of complacency if one does not intend to offend . . . We are to have a repetition of the same today, as I see that unfortunately it is a fine day . . . I am not astonished that Lady C[onyngham] is tired out of her life.'[17]

Wellington continued to be a regular visitor at Windsor, however, 'as he prided himself upon being able to settle differences as well as any man and loved being consulted', so Charles Greville said, and 'mixed up in messes'. He was particularly needed this summer because Lady Conyngham's eldest son, Mount Charles, was dying on the Continent; she wanted to go out to see him, and the King insisted on accompanying her. If he followed her, Wellington protested, the public would have the impression that 'it was neither more nor less than abdication of his high duties'. But the King remained adamant: if she went, he would go too. It appeared to Wellington that he was more in love with her than ever, a state of mind that the Duke found incomprehensible, for he had never seen so vulgar a woman as Lady Conyngham, though he recognized her shrewdness, and the advisability of consulting her before approaching the King on matters of importance. She gave him the feeling that he thought he would have if he were ever 'to experience a revulsion of blood'; 'every time she spoke [he] trembled lest [he] should hear some fresh vulgarity'.[18] He could not conceive why the King wanted to go abroad with her. By the beginning of September the crisis was over; Lady Conyngham had agreed to remain in England, and a member of the King's household had left for France to take Lord Mount Charles to Italy.[19]

Wellington endeavoured to ensure that house-parties at Stratfield Saye were more enjoyable than those held at the Royal Lodge; and Lady Wharncliffe testified to his success. The 'simple & cordial civility of his manner' as a host she thought was 'charming'.[20] He had the Shelleys there and Mme de Lieven and the Arbuthnots and Prince Esterhazy, the Austrian Ambassador, though occasionally he felt constrained to ask less entertaining company, Lord Liverpool, for example, a man of 'disagreeable, cold manner', in Mrs Arbuthnot's opinion, 'and a most querulous temper', and Liverpool's second wife, and Prince Leopold, son of the Duke of Saxe-Coburg-Saalfeld, a handsome and 'most honourable young man', charming in a solemn kind of way but bland, rather unctuous and shifty.

When such men as Prince Leopold were of the party, it was as well to have sparkling young ladies to cheer the company up. It was not always possible for the Duke to do so. 'We are here with a crowd of bores,' Mme de Lieven reported to Metternich in January 1821, 'the Castlereaghs, the Esterhazys, the Arbuthnots, some princes I do not know and bad weather into the bargain ... It is absolutely essential on a country visit to like the people with whom you are going to spend three times twenty-four hours; for short of an affair, which nobody here would risk, you are certain to be bored. However, I do all I can to look as if I were enjoying myself, for I should hate the Duke of Wellington to think I were not; he goes at it wholeheartedly himself.'[21] 'You have no idea how much [staying here] bores me and puts me out,' she wrote in another letter. 'The Duke has unfortunately taken it into his head that his house is the most comfortable in the world. Well, there are two very definite drawbacks to that comfort. It is always cold, and his wife is stupid. What's to be done?' 'The house is ugly,' she continued, 'and the park rather barren ... The Duke took me into his study; there are two portraits there, one of Lady Charlotte Greville and one of Mrs Patterson, the American [who married Lord Wellesley]. How can one have two passions at the same time, and how cán one bear to parade them before the world at large?'[22]

Sir Robert Peel agreed with her about the house: it was 'a wretched' place, he thought, 'wretchedly furnished'. The drawing room, in particular, was very small and very low. He had to admit, though, that the library, separated only by columns from the billiard room, was 'handsome'.[23]

The Duke himself had to confess that he was often 'bored to death' by these house parties at Stratfield Saye. 'During these visitations (for I must call them such) I am literally a *Slave*,' he complained to Mrs Arbuthnot, 'and all the objects of my Life are necessarily lost sight of ... I declare to you that I am worn out by it ... You'll say, how do other Men do? I answer, other Men have a Wife or a Son, with whose attentions the World are satisfied. They are not required always to be *en Presence*... I cannot even take up a Newspaper. If I do everybody is bored.'[24] 'And,' as he added to Priscilla Burghersh, 'I can bear anything but to bore people.'[25]

'My Company are still here,' he told Mrs Arbuthnot on another occasion. 'It is however very difficult to amuse them, and I am sometimes quite at a loss.' One night Mme de Lieven sat down at the harpsichord, and he felt obliged to 'fulfil the ignoble office' of turning over the leaves for her. 'But after she had played for some little time, others began to talk, & she got up immediately saying that she played very seldom, but that if she was not attended to she would not play at all. As the Duchess does not like cards on a Sunday, I was then obliged to amuse them as I could until they went to bed.'[26]

The days were as bad as the evenings: 'I like to go hunting, but I cannot go. If I do, nobody will go shooting. Then the sport is bad; everybody is dissatisfied and out of Temper.'[27]

It was generally conceded that, while country house parties at Stratfield Saye were not always of the most enjoyable, the Duke's conversation could be enthralling, particularly when talking about interesting men and women he had known and great events in which he had participated. Charles Greville for one remembered fascinating talk about subjects ranging from Louis XVIII's astonishing memory to George IV's equally astonishing extravagance. 'Met the Duke at dinner yesterday,' Greville recorded in his journal, 'and afterwards had a long talk with him, not on politics. I never see and converse with him without reproaching myself for the sort of hostility I feel and express towards his political conduct, for there are a simplicity, a gaiety, and natural urbanity and good-humour in him which are marvellously captivating in so great a man.'[28]

Hard as he worked to keep his guests amused, the Duke could never forget that he was a man in busy public life. He once told Lady Shelley that there was 'nothing like never having an idle moment'; and if he were not reading or playing cards, or if he were not out riding or shooting, he could usually be found amidst the clutter of papers in his room, dealing with the often tedious work of the Ordance Office or the problems faced by the Cabinet or in private study. He was consulted constantly on foreign affairs, on Ireland, on the oppressions of the Turks and the disturbing expansion of Russian influence, on Spain and South America.

He was worried by Canning who was so eager to lend Britain's support to South American revolutionaries. 'Considering what is passing in Ireland,' he wrote, 'and what all expect will occur in that country before long . . . we must take care not to give additional examples in these times of the encouragement of insurrection . . . If you hold that the people of Colombia have been guilty of no crime, and that Bolivar is a hero and no rebel, then you ought not to prosecute O'Connell.'[29]

When Canning decided that the time had come for the formal recognition of the South American republics, Wellington argued strongly against it; and, when the rest of the Cabinet had given way to the Foreign Secretary's arguments, he continued to protest against them. In the end, however, he had to give way. 'The fight has been hard, but it is won,' Canning reported in triumph to the immensely rich liberal Lord Granville. 'The deed is done. The nail is driven. Spanish America is free; and if we do not mismanage our affairs she is English.'[30]

The Duke was also concerned by Canning's policies in Europe, his strong reluctance to allow Britain to become too deeply involved in Continental politics and, condemning the Continental sovereigns for their attempts to suppress liberal movements, he advocated an independent Britain outside the so-called Holy Alliance. 'Every nation for itself,' Canning declared, 'and God for us all.'[31]

'Mr Canning poses as a Radical to please the populace,' Mme de Lieven observed. 'The other Ministers smile approvingly to keep their places. The Duke of Wellington alone is prepared to break a lance for the good cause.'[32]

Certainly the Duke, a supporter of close ties with the continent of Europe, had no patience with Canning's insular and isolationist policies; nor did he care for the demagogic and theatrical manner in which he presented them, a manner one might indeed expect, the Duke thought, from a man, admittedly an Old Etonian, whose widowed mother had gone on the stage, had married an actor and, after his death, had become the wife of a linen-draper. Wellington much regretted having encouraged the King to consent to Canning's appointment. The man 'knew no more of foreign politics than a child'.*[33]

'We are radically defective in our diplomatic headquarters here,' Wellington complained to his brother Henry in 1824. Robert Peel, the Home Secretary, agreed with him. So did the King. 'I do not like Canning any better than I did,' his Majesty told Mme de Lieven. 'I recognise his talent, and I believe we need him in the Commons; but

---

* Canning was, however, ready to listen to the Duke's views on such matters. 'I hope you will never stand on such ceremony again,' Canning wrote to him after learning that Wellington had refrained from offering advice because he had not been invited to do so 'Pray believe in the sincerity of this assurance once for all' (Wellington Papers, Hartley Institute, WP1/756/10, 11 Feb. 1823).

he is no more capable of conducting foreign affairs than your baby. He doesn't know the first thing about his job: no tact, no judgement, no idea of decorum. But what is to be done? Can I change my Minister! No, for I should only get someone worse. That is the fix I am in. The best is bad; but the worst would be hateful, and there is nothing in between.'[34] He was still talking of Canning in similar terms to Wellington in May 1824, saying that he was 'the damnedest fellow in the world and that he could not bear him', while admitting that it 'would not do to turn him out'.[35] 'Think of that damned fellow wanting me to have the King and Queen of the Sandwich Islands to dinner,' he expostulated the next month, 'as if I would sit at table with such a pair of damned cannibals.'[36]

At the end of the previous month the man had behaved abominably in the King's eyes by attending a dinner given by supporters of the late Queen. He had drafted a letter of protest so heated in its intemperance that Canning would have had no alternative but to resign on receiving it. When Wellington went to Windsor to advise the King not to send the letter, he was immediately greeted with the words, 'Ah, I know what you have come to say. You think that, if I want to get rid of Mr Canning, this is not a proper opportunity, that at all events I ought not to write such a letter as will force him to resign.' The Duke told Mrs Arbuthnot that the King was so pleased by this display of his prescience that he 'had less difficulty with him than he had expected' and a far milder letter was dispatched.[37]

His disagreements with the Foreign Secretary were made all the worse, so the King complained to Wellington, by the 'absurd, weak and disgusting conduct' of the Prime Minister to whom he had 'always had an aversion' and whom, if Wellington had been willing to succeed him, he would have endeavoured to replace.[38] The man was quite as bad as Canning in his way. Indeed, there was not a single minister, apart from the Duke, with whom the King felt satisfied. 'You are my friend,' he wrote to him in July 1824,' and the only person I completely rely upon in the Cabinet . . . You [act] in everything perfect.'[39]

The differences between the King and Canning were strongly emphasized in 1824 when the Cabinet proposed negotiating a commercial treaty with Buenos Aires which had ceased to acknowledge the sovereignty of the King of Spain. Encouraged by Wellington, the King informed the Cabinet that he very much regretted this move which would 'carry with it the appearance and promise of an early recognition of the different insurrectionary States of South America'. In a long letter to Lord Liverpool the King roundly condemned the 'new political liberalism' which – since he firmly believed that the monarchs of Europe shared a common interest and ought to support each other in their struggle against revolutionary movements – he considered so dangerous a policy that for a time he refused to talk about it personally to Canning who was required to communicate with him in writing. When, at the end of the year, Buenos Aires, Mexico and Colombia – and shortly afterwards Brazil – were all recognized as independent countries, the King was so annoyed by the Government's action that he resolutely refused to read the speech announcing it at the opening of Parliament. He let it be known that his gout was so bad that he could not walk. He could not speak either, so he said, because he had lost his false teeth.[40]

There were also private worries for Wellington to contend with. His family were still feeling aggrieved that Gerald was denied the bishopric which they considered his worth merited; and the Duke, persuaded to overcome his reluctance to approach Lord Liverpool with such a request, made another plea on his brother's behalf. The Prime Minister curtly replied that no clergyman separated from his wife ought to be raised to the Bench. He told Arbuthnot that he had already done more for Wellington's family than he had done for his own in the way of pensions for his mother and sister, a good office for his brother-in-law and a Cabinet appointment for his brother, Wellesley-Pole. Liverpool could not in all conscience find a bishopric for Gerald; but he did eventually provide him with a prebendal stall at Durham.[*41]

* When the Duke later successfully solicited a peerage for his brother Henry, Ambassador in Vienna, Gerald was the only one of his brothers without a seat in the House of Lords.

32 St Petersburg and the Northern Counties

1825 — 7

'We have some great diplomatic characters here, but I believe they are all as much in the dark as I am.'

HAD HE BEEN in better health, the Duke might well have been thankful to be able to escape from England for a time when he was asked in 1825 to undertake a diplomatic mission to Russia where the Tsar Alexander had died and been succeeded by Nicholas I. But, as it was, he had not yet fully recovered from the incompetent ministrations of Dr Stevenson. He had almost collapsed from dizziness while shooting one day, and, most unusually for him, he had been suffering from sleeplessness, which another course of the Cheltenham waters had failed to alleviate. He had also had a bout of cholera. Not long before Mrs Arbuthnot had recorded in her journal, 'He is so terribly thin & gets so little sleep I cannot but feel very anxious & uneasy about him.'[1]

With his health so poor he dreaded the prospect of a winter's journey to St Petersburg. He almost doubted that he would survive it. But he could not see how he, who had 'always been preaching the doctrine of going wherever' a man in public life 'was desired to go', 'could decline to accept the offer of this mission'. So he did accept it, going so far as to assure Canning that he had never felt better in his life and was ready to leave at a moment's notice.[2] He said goodbye to his family and friends with such unaccustomed emotion that General Alava, exiled now in England, had never seen him so moved; nor had Lady Burghersh from whom he parted in tears. Charles Greville was surprised to hear that he was also 'deeply affected when he parted from his Mother'.[3]

Everybody was sorry to see him go, he told Mrs Arbuthnot, who was herself 'so unhappy at parting from him'. Even Mme de Lieven 'had cried & kissed him & told him that there was nobody in the world she loved so much as him'. 'It is impossible to know him well without loving him,' Mrs Arbuthnot commented. 'He is so kind to everybody, so affectionate & so good-natured, & I must say I never did know any man so universally beloved.'[4]

'His friends did all they could to keep him [in England],' she wrote in her journal, 'and realising that this was impossible, resigned themselves to the grief of never seeing him again. It seemed to them that this rough journey undertaken in a very weak state of health would be fatal to him. The enemies of Canning said that he wanted to kill the Duke.'[5]

As it happened the discomforts of the journey were not so arduous as Wellington had feared; but he was not buoyed up by any hopes of success in his mission. His orders were to dissuade the Russians from going to war with Turkey over the attempts of the Greeks to gain their independence from the Turkish Empire. This was the cause embraced by Lord Byron who had died of a fever, aggravated by his doctor's insistence on bleeding, at Missolonghi in April the year before. It was a popular cause in England as well as in Holy Russia; and Wellington had no sustained hope of being able to persuade the Tsar not to go to war in defence of it; but at least he might, so it was hoped in London, come to some arrangement in St Petersburg whereby a war involving the whole of Europe might be avoided.

He arrived in St Petersburg, 'the most beautiful town in the World',[6] at the beginning of March 1826, after three weeks on the road, having taken with him his own bed with 'a mattress made of silk in order to prevent vermin penetrating into it and of a light colour that they might be seen upon it'.[7]

He was greeted amicably by the Tsar, entered into friendly discussions with the Tsar's Foreign Minister, Vasilievich Nesselrode, the son of a German count who had served as Russia's Ambassador in Portugal, was entertained at dinners, obediently responded to toasts, accepted the colonelcy of a regiment of infantry and presents of furs and malachite, much admired 'the double windows which kept the rooms warm and might with advantage be copied at home', and inspected a girls' seminary where the young ladies curtseyed politely and twenty-five of them played pianos in unison.[8]

It was rather tedious and rather tiring; and on occasions the Duke became confused by the labyrinthine processes of Slavic diplomacy. 'It is difficult to judge of matters here,' he wrote to his brother, 'and who is the adviser. We have some great diplomatic characters here, but I believe they are all as much in the dark as I am.'[9] 'Except by way of conciliation,' he added in a letter to Lord Bathurst, 'I don't expect to do much good in my mission.'[10]

However, he managed to quash all suggestions of the kind of Continental congress which Canning so much disliked; and helped to bring about an agreement by which Greece was guaranteed a very modified form of independence under the joint auspices of Russia and Britain. But, although the agreement had been accepted by the Russians without compromising the Duke's own belief that the Turkish Empire should be preserved intact for the sake of European stability, and although another European war had at least been averted, no one was really satisfied: Canning, 'as anti-Turk as it is possible to be', let it be known that he thought Wellington had been outwitted by wily Russian diplomacy, while Mme de Lieven, whose husband had been summoned to St Petersburg from the Russian Embassy in London, considered that the Duke had failed lamentably to ensure that the kind of 'hierarchical discipline' which she herself advocated had not been imposed upon the troubled region.

In the past she had told her brother how 'charming, agreeable and accommodating' the Duke was. He was 'the finest and noblest character of the day', 'proud, simple and great'. England could not send to Russia 'an Ambassador more worthy of the great occasion'.[11] But now, all had changed: he was 'obstinate as a mule', 'Turkish from head to foot', 'thoroughly mediocre, though not without guile';[12] while the Duke for his part considered Mme de Lieven a mischievous intriguer who would 'betray everybody in turn if it should suit her purpose'. Ever since his embassy to Russia she and her husband had 'taken pains to represent [his] conduct in the most unfavourable light in St Petersburg'. They 'wrote all the evil that they thought and much more than they knew'.[13]

'The Duke has had violent quarrels with the Lievens,' Lord Palmerston told his brother, the Hon. William Temple, who was chargé d'affaires at St Petersburg. 'A great many things have contributed to set him against [them] . . . He has a strong personal dislike to Russia . . . and thought himself not civilly used at St Petersburg . . . Mrs Arbuthnot and Lady Jersey, who both have influence over him, both hate Mme de Lieven.'[14]

As the months passed, however, the Duke once more won over Mme de Lieven by his charm and attentions to her. They 'talked on every subject except Turkey'. She found in him 'a remarkable change –

much gentleness, and great friendliness'. She was again on 'the best of terms with him and in full enjoyment of his confidence and friendship'.*[15]

Thankful to be leaving Russia, the Duke travelled home in contented mood, carrying in his baggage various presents for his lady friends, including a handsome and heavy porphyry vase for Harriet Arbuthnot. He looked much improved in health, 'quite fat and fresh', and in 'amazing health and spirits'.[16] But the England he found on his return in the spring of 1826 was far from as content as he was. Canning was being as difficult as ever; businesses in the City were facing heavy losses; there was agitation about the proposed relief to be afforded to Roman Catholics and the repeal of the Corn Laws; machine-breakers had again been active in the North and Midlands. In the Russia he had left behind the workers were kept in dreary vassalage, yet they seemed to be happier than British workers 'with their comparatively refined, but discontented ill-informed minds'.

The Duke also learned that there was uproar in Portugal where, against his advice, Liverpool and Canning had decided to intervene and dispatched a brigade to the Tagus.

Then there was the behaviour of the Duke's sons who had gone up to Christ Church, Oxford when Douro was seventeen and Lord Charles sixteen. At the beginning of their first term in October 1824 the Duke had written from Hatfield to their private tutor, the Rev. H.M. Wagner, a clergyman of Swiss descent, severe manner and conscientious disposition who had accompanied the boys to Eton.

> After all the enquiries which I have made, I believe that the allowance which they ought to have and which would go nearest to provide for the expenses of their Education at Oxford ... would be for Douro, who will be entered a Nobleman, £800 per annum and for Charles, who will be entered a Gentleman Commoner, £500 per annum ...
> I intend that these Allowances should cover all their [expenses] of

---

* After her affair with Metternich was over, Mme de Lieven asked the Duke to help her get back the letters she had written to him. Metternich agreed, provided she returned his letters to her. Mme de Lieven's letters arrived in a 'great box' at Apsley House where she 'inspected them very carefully and carried them off'. Lady Salisbury asked the Duke how she had come to apply to him for such a service in view of their past disagreements. 'Because,' Wellington replied with grand complacency, 'I am the Duke of Wellington and because they knew I was an honest man' (Hatfield House Papers, Lady Salisbury's journal).

every description, and I have reason to believe them to be so ample that I expect they will not run into debt, particularly as I begin by paying them in advance.[17]

Mr Wagner agreed that they were ample, and gave credit to the Duke not only for the trouble he had taken to establish the fact but also for the attention he paid to his charges' upbringing, never failing to answer by the very first post any enquiry or letter connected with their well-being.[18] The Duke was therefore all the more distressed to hear that Charles had been in trouble with the Dean of the College, Dr John Bull, for helping to paint the dons' doors red, then for breaking open the College gates 'in the dead of the night with great and premeditated violence'.[19] He had been rusticated for a year, a punishment which his father, in an angry letter to the Dean, deemed excessive, particularly so as he was led to suppose that the ill discipline at Christ Church arose from the incompetence of the governing authorities who allowed their charges to 'have suppers in their Chambers every night, at which large quantities of Wine are drunk and at which other irregularities are committed [including gambling]'. It seemed to the Duke 'astonishing that irregularities are not more frequently committed in the College' than they already were.[20] Charles was removed from Christ Church and, having failed to find a place at New College, Magdalen or Oriel, was sent with his brother to Trinity College, Cambridge, after a period of instruction with Mr Wagner at Brighton.

Charles's childish pranks did not, however, worry his father nearly so much as what he took to be his elder son's laziness, his haphazard womanizing and his avoidance of him during the university vacations. Charles, in fact, according to Mrs Arbuthnot was 'very well with his father' and not the least afraid of him. Certainly he was a 'wild, rattling, high spirited boy, full of tricks'; but the Duke, she thought, was 'amused' rather than annoyed by his 'nonsense'.[21]

'Charles is a good Humoured, well meaning fellow,' the Duke wrote himself. 'But his whole Mind and time are employed running after Ponies and Puppy Dogs and Mrs Browne [wife of Captain Browne who rented a small house on the Stratfield Saye estate]. What I cannot bear is [his and his brother's] grovelling partiality to low Company.'

I wanted Charles to go to Oatlands [at that time the country house of Lord Francis Leveson-Gower] with me if I had gone. No! he would not. But he will go into any Cottage in the County in which Candles are lighted. It quite breaks one's Heart. Yet they have had every advantage of Education, position, fortune &c. Douro has 2,500£ a year, and no House to keep anywhere. Charles has not less than 700£ a Year; lodged, lighted, and fed if he pleases, and His Horses kept for him in the Country. Yet they go about like two Scamps, and in their appearance are scarcely clean; and one cannot get them to take their place among the Young Men of their own Rank and Position in Life.[22]

Douro's behaviour in his father's eyes was particularly reprehensible. He was 'very much disappointed' in him.

Ld. Douro went abroad with him this year [Mrs Arbuthnot recorded] & he thinks that he shewed no curiosity or eagerness about any thing. During the whole month they were absent he did nothing and slept almost the whole way in the carriage . . . The Duke says he is listless & indifferent & does nothing but 'loll on a sofa and chatter'. I think the Duke judges him too severely. He is but 18, just let loose from school, falling in love with every woman he gets near . . . No longer *forced* to study, he is not yet man enough to do it of his own accord. But he is remarkably gentlemanlike & pleasing, very sensible in his conversation, and I believe I am prejudiced in his favour because he is so wonderfully like the Duke not only in face, but in every action . . . I have understood the Duke himself was not a clever boy and, besides that, he must not expect that a young man born in the highest rank & heir to a princely fortune will exert himself & turn all his talents to account in the same way that he, a younger brother without fortune, did.[23]

'I think,' Mrs Arbuthnot added, 'the Duke's unfortunate marriage has pursued him even in his relations with his children.' Certainly the Duke imagined that Douro had been set against him by his mother. This, Mrs Arbuthnot commented, only made him the more irritated with his wife. 'It mortifies him to the greatest degree,' she thought. 'He is unjust, for the Dss. would do anything she possibly c^d to put him & his children well together if she knew how, but she is such a fool she does not.'[24]

While he expressed the opinion that it was impossible that his sons 'could do that of which they [were] guilty without being excited to it by their Mother', since he himself had 'spoken to them so often', the Duke felt quite confident that he could be accused of no fault as a father 'excepting excess of Indulgence'.[25] He had been determined never to quarrel with either of them; and the result was that, were he ever to be employed again in command of an army, he would be 'under the necessity of disgracing them both', since they were 'so inefficient and useless' he could employ neither.[26]

The Duke endeavoured to improve his sons' minds by a long letter of stern parental admonition containing advice on how to conduct their lives and improve their minds and providing them with a formidable reading list of books, in French as well as in English, on ancient and modern history, geography, law, political economy, the art of warfare, biographies of great men from Marlborough and Washington, to Henry VIII and Sir Robert Walpole, politics, British possessions, foreign countries and 'all Burke's Works on the French Revolution and the questions of that day'. In all there were nearly a hundred works on the list; but the Duke had in time sadly to conclude that they had not done the boys much good, if, indeed, they had even glanced at them.[27]

At Windsor the King was not feeling well, spending much of the day in bed, an indulgence which, according to Mme de Lieven, he liked 'better than anything'; and at the beginning of 1827 he was much cast down by the death of his brother, the Duke of York, whose funeral sent many others to bed, some never to leave it. It was a bitterly cold day and the congregation, which included most members of the Cabinet and many of the Royal Family, stood shivering in the gloom. There was no matting or carpeting on the floor, and Canning presumed that whoever had filched it had had bets on the duration of the mourners' own lives. Lord Eldon sensibly followed Canning's advice and stood on his cocked hat and then 'in a niche of carved work where he was able to stand on wood'. The Duke of Sussex caught a severe cold; so did the Lord Chamberlain of the Household and William Huskisson, President of the Board of Trade. Canning contracted rheumatic fever; the Bishop of Lincoln subsequently died; and it was alleged that the soldiers who had made up the guard of honour expired at the rate of half a dozen a day.[28]

Wellington became so seriously ill that when Sir Robert Peel, who was staying at Stratfield Saye at the time, tried to comfort the Duchess by telling her that he was sure to get better soon as he had been looking so well of late, she burst into tears. 'I am so short-sighted, I cannot remark his features,' she said. 'I can only judge by the colour, and when I look at *that precious face*, it seems to be very pale.'[29]

This pathetic statement and the tears that accompanied it much upset Peel. He was himself devoted to his wife, a general's daughter, and strongly disapproved of Wellington's relationship with women other than the Duchess. 'What wickedness,' he exclaimed to Lady Peel, 'and what folly to under-value and to be insensible to the affection of a wife!'[30] Such things make me still more hate the sight of those who can find it in their hearts, even if they have no sense of virtue, to usurp her place.' He was thinking of Mrs Arbuthnot in particular. 'I see no signs of the influences of Mrs A. having abated,' he told his wife on a later occasion. 'She takes her place next to him at dinner as if it were a matter of course . . . But let us leave these odious things.'[31]

Lord Liverpool, at the age of fifty-seven, was already chronically ill at the time of the Duke of York's funeral. On the morning of 17 February he had a stroke, and, though he did not die until the end of the following year, he was thereafter totally incapable of continuing in office.

'What the devil is it to come to?' asked Thomas Creevey in exasperation on hearing that the King – agitated beyond measure at the news of Liverpool's stroke and the tiresome business of having to replace him – had retreated to Brighton where for over a fortnight he had not left his dressing-room and was refusing to see anyone, 'servants, tailors and doctors excepted'.[32] Wellington had already heard that the doctors disagreed about the use of laudanum by the King, some arguing that the huge doses he took would drive him mad, others contending that spirits would drive him mad if laudanum were not given and that, in any case, he would insist on taking the drug in even larger quantities if it were not prescribed in the usual amounts. 'He drinks spirits morning noon and night,' Wellington told Mrs Arbuthnot, 'and he is obliged to take laudanum to calm the irritation which the use of spirits occasions.'[33] After an immense dose of spirits one day the King exasperated the Duke by being 'very drunk, very blackguard, very much out of temper at times, and a very great bore'.[34]

'Was there ever such a child or Bedlamite?' Creevey wondered, not for the first time, 'or were there ever such a set of lickspittles as his Ministers to endure such conduct?'[35] The ministers were, in fact, in total disarray. There seemed no possible candidate for the office of Prime Minister who could hold the two wings of the Tory party together as Liverpool had succeeded in doing. Although he had been Home Secretary for five years, Peel was considered too inexperienced, and was also thought to be too advanced in his views except on the Roman Catholic question. Wellington, who had succeeded the Duke of York as Commander-in-Chief while retaining, at the King's request, the

Master-Generalship of the Ordnance, was not at first supposed to be in the running from which, in any case, he was believed to have disqualified himself by accepting command of the Army.[36] He himself dismissed the idea of becoming Prime Minister, although he confided that 'circumstances might be conceived under which it would be his duty to accept the situation if he was called upon by the King to do so'. In public, however, he made himself quite clear on the point. As he was to express it in the House of Lords, he was 'unaccustomed' to such political duties; he was 'not qualified'; he would be 'worse than mad if [he] thought of such a thing'.[37] He knew his limitations as an orator – Thomas Carlyle said he was the 'worst speaker' he had ever heard – and, while he was on occasions capable of making highly effective speeches – 'gruff', 'husky', 'quaint', 'unusual' and 'telling' are some of the adjectives Disraeli used to describe them – they were certainly often as ill delivered as they were confused in construction.

So that left Canning who was certainly on far better terms with the King than he had been in the past, having appointed Lady Conyngham's brother to an Under-Secretaryship of State and having offered an agreeable diplomatic post far away in South America to Lord Ponsonby with whom Lady Conyngham had once been in love and of whom she still seemed disturbingly fond. Besides, much as he had disapproved of Canning's foreign policy in the early stages of its development, the King had come to recognize that it had raised the standing of Britain in Europe and that his own reputation had been enhanced in consequence.

On 28 March the King invited Canning to come to stay at the Royal Lodge at the same time as Wellington. First he interviewed the Duke; and as the morning wore on and his rival did not reappear, Canning grew more and more gloomy. When the Duke did reappear, Princess Lieven approached him and later recorded this conversation in her journal:

'Ah, well, M. le Duc, you have talked for two hours with your master. What news?'
   'Devil take me if I know.'
   'Has he named you First Minister?'
   'Listen, Madame Princess, let us be frank. You know the difficulties well. I will be wholly frank. The difficulty lies with one man.'
   'Canning. Are you resigned to having him as head?'
   'Never.'

'Then it is really very difficult for he wants to be it.'

'My word, we shall see.'[38]

At luncheon the King continued to show particular attention to Wellington; and after luncheon Canning feared that his hopes were to be disappointed when arrangements were made for the guests to drive out in the Park in the little two-seater pony carriages which were brought up from the stables. All the seats were allocated to the satisfaction of the King who, ignoring Canning's presence, said to Princess Lieven, 'I am sure you and the Duke would like to go out together.' Just as everyone was ready to drive off, and the King was expected as usual to seat himself beside Lady Conyngham, he went up to Canning, took him by the arm, and said, 'I want to talk with you. I shan't go out.'[39]

There was a difficulty in appointing Canning, though: it was doubtful that any of the right-wing Tories would agree to serve under him. Certainly Wellington would not; nor would Peel, and the King, thoroughly annoyed with both of them, told Canning with a kind of desperation to 'prepare with as little delay as possible a plan for the reconstruction of the Administration'.

Canning again approached Wellington, telling him that the Duke's continuance in office was essential to the stability of the new Government. The Duke asked who was to be Prime Minister in that Government. With the approval of the King, Canning sent an extremely caustic reply:

My dear Duke of Wellington,

I believe it to be so generally understood that the King usually entrusts the formation of an Administration to the individual whom it is His Majesty's gracious intention to place at the head of it, that it did not occur to me . . . to add that, in the present instance His Majesty does not intend to depart from the usual course of proceeding on such occasions.

Ever my dear Duke of Wellington,

Your Grace's sincere and faithful servant,

George Canning.[40]

Stung by Canning's sardonic tone, Wellington responded by resigning not only as Master-General of the Ordnance but also as Commander-in-Chief, an appointment which the King himself undertook to fill until, as he said, Arthur recovered his temper.[41]

Unable to form an exclusively Tory government – since so many of the Duke's former colleagues, wary of Canning's soundness on the matter of Roman Catholic relief, were unwilling to serve under him – the new Prime Minister had to turn to the Whigs for support, much to the annoyance of the King who, holding Wellington to a large extent responsible, was for weeks in no mood to forgive him. The Duke, for his part, was 'convinced that no man ever had such a hold upon the King' as that 'charlatan' Canning whom he now disliked more than ever and whom he constantly denigrated, becoming so heated in his denunciation of him during a conversation with Creevey that he nearly pulled a button off Creevey's coat in his animation.[42] The man was not only idle, his rages when he could not get his own way were deplorable; the Duke feared that the burdens and worry of office might unhinge his mind as they had that of poor Castlereagh.[43]

There would surely not be long to wait before Canning's administration collapsed. It was known as 'the ministry of the warming pans';[44] the Morning Chronicle suggested it was 'like people going to keep places for the first act of a play'.[45] While the country waited for the end of the play 'one heard nothing at table, at the opera, even at the ball', so Prince Pückler-Muskau reported, 'but Canning and Wellington from every lovely mouth; indeed Lord Ellenborough complained that his wife plagued him with politics even at night. She had terrified him by crying out suddenly, in her sleep, "will the Prime Minister stand or fall?"'[46]

Canning's health was not strong enough to allow him the energy to keep his Cabinet together. He had never properly recovered from the rheumatic fever that had assailed him after that bitterly cold day of the Duke of York's funeral in St George's Chapel. In July the Duke of Devonshire asked him to Chiswick for a change of air. But he felt no better there; he told the King that he did not know what was the matter with him: he felt 'ill all over'. He died the following week in the house in which Charles James Fox had died twenty-one years before. His administration had lasted a bare three months.[47]

There was talk that the King would now be obliged to send for Wellington; and the Duke himself half expected the summons, thinking it best not to leave home to stay with the Arbuthnots in case he was called to Windsor. His Majesty, however, had other ideas, and decided that it would be better for his own peace of mind if Canning's Government were to remain in office with a reshuffled Cabinet under the leadership of Lord Goderich, an attractive, good-natured, easy-going man who had been Canning's Secretary for War and the Colonies. It was an ill-advised decision: Goderich was, indeed, a most pleasant man; but he was also hesitant and indecisive, quite incapable of control-ling the disparate forces in his Cabinet and so little recovered from the recent death of a beloved daughter that his problems often reduced him to tears. In Princess Lieven's opinion he was 'as cowardly as the most timid woman'.[48]

Convinced that he could not remain in office for long, the high Tories proposed that the Duke should strengthen his claim to succeed him by going to stay at a few grand houses in the north and by appearing before assembled crowds in the nearby industrial and market towns. He agreed to go and sought an invitation from the Marquess and Marchioness of Londonderry at Wynyard Park, County Durham. His tour, which began at Stockton on 24 September 1827, was considered a great success. In all the towns through which he passed the horses were removed from his carriage and he was pulled through the streets by men wearing blue ribbons inscribed 'Wellington for Ever' to the cheers of admiring crowds. Triumphal arches of laurel covered with flowers and flags had been erected and from their summit girls dressed in white dropped roses on the hero's head. Splendid dinners were given in Guildhalls and Exchanges emblazoned with banners bearing the names of the great Duke's victories and with brightly flickering gas lamps. Balls were held in Assembly Rooms; speeches were made and toasts were drunk; his Grace was assured that 'no event in the district in the memory of man had created so much ardent excitement and enthusiastic feeling in every mind as that which had sprung from his expected coming'.

Guards of honour were inspected; cannon thundered, bands played and church bells pealed. Ships in the rivers had 'all their decorations floating in the air'; while 'the windows of every house were filled with well-dressed females, and the very roofs of the houses were covered with spectators'. At Stockton, Newcastle, Durham and Sunderland he was welcomed and bidden farewell 'to the most deafening cheers'.[49] At York the Duke himself said that he had had to undergo a 'very heavy fire'; Lord Grey wrote of 'one continued scene of rejoicing'.[50]

There were those, however, who doubted that the tour had been well advised. Some suggested that the people had flocked to see the Duke more out of curiosity than in support of a future Prime Minister, others that they cheered the great soldier not the statesman. Sir Walter Scott thought that this kind of electioneering was beneath the Duke's dignity. The *Manchester Guardian* spoke for many in the north when it declared that the Duke of Wellington combined 'inveterate preju-dices, very mediocre abilities, and an unteachable disposition'.[51]

Soon after the Duke's return, Lord Goderich, that 'blubbering fool' as the King called him, made one of his periodical visits to Windsor. 'Quite unnerved and in a most pitiful state', he 'ran true to form' by breaking down and weeping as he endeavoured to explain to the King that he felt incapable of carrying on. The King handed him his pocket handkerchief and sent for the Duke of Wellington.[52]

33 The Prime Minister

1828 — 9

'He will do everything himself. He wishes to be
the universal man.'

WELLINGTON found the King in bed wearing a dirty silk jacket and
an even scruffier turban night cap.[1] He had been ill for some time,
suffering from gout and rheumatism; and was deeply concerned by the
resurgence of Harriette Wilson, now living in Belgium as Mme Rochfort, who was threatening to publish further stories about his murky
past. He cheered up at the sight of the Duke, however, called
out, 'Arthur, the Cabinet is defunct', and proceeded to entertain
him with imitations of its members so skilfully executed that he contrived not merely to sound like them but actually to look like them too.
The Duke had 'never seen anything like it'. It was all 'so lively, so
exact and so amusing'. 'It was quite impossible to restrain from fits
of laughter.'[2]

But the King's cheerful mood did not last long. He listened to the
Duke's proposed candidates for office with increasing gloom, objecting
particularly to Peel, whom he had never liked, and positively refusing
to consider Lord Grey. It was not long before Wellington, having
got his own way about Peel, who became Home Secretary, wished
that he had never undertaken the task with which the King, more
peevish and fretful day by day, had entrusted him: he might have
avoided 'loads of misery'. He was particularly upset that he had been
unwillingly induced to relinquish his resumed appointment as
Commander-in-Chief, it being considered incompatible with that of
Prime Minister.

At the first meeting of his Cabinet, one of his Ministers thought
that they all displayed to each other 'the courtesy of men who had just
fought a duel'.[3] Most of them were at least in agreement that the Prime
Minister himself was 'domineering', a verdict with which the King at
that time concurred. Already of the opinion that Wellington was
'incapable of flexibility', that he set about a question 'like a battery of

cannon', he now declared that either 'King Arthur must go to the Devil or King George to Hanover'.[4]

Wellington and Peel had agreed that they could not fight a party and a half with half a party, so they had decided upon including in the Cabinet four leading Canningites, Huskisson as Secretary for War and the Colonies, Palmerston as Secretary at War, Charles Grant as President of the Board of Trade and, although he was extremely eccentric and shortly to be declared insane, the Earl of Dudley as Foreign Secretary.

In choosing men to form his Government, Wellington had had to disappoint several who had felt that they could rely upon him for satisfactory appointments, including a much disgruntled Lord Eldon, and the Duke's brothers, Richard and William, both of whom had hoped to be given offices, as well as Charles Arbuthnot who had expected his long and faithful friendship with the Duke to be rewarded with something better than the renewal of his appointment as First Commissioner of Woods and Forests. When Arbuthnot did not trouble to hide his disappointment, the Duke became 'dreadfully annoyed'; while Mrs Arbuthnot also expressed her annoyance that her husband had been denied a seat in a Cabinet which included such 'rif raf' as the Duke had appointed to it.[5]

'God knows,' the Duke commented, 'that I have disgust enough in all these affairs to avoid the augmentation of that which must be the consequence of the break up of the only private & confidential Relation I have in Life.'[6]

He had long been well known for the curt dismissal of appeals made upon him by men who laid claim to favours for past services real or imagined or who were considered unworthy of his regard.

He was once approached in Staffordshire by a man whose face was unfamiliar to him. 'Ah, your Grace,' this man said. 'I have served with you.'

'Where?'
    'Why, in Spain.'
    'What regiment were you in?'
    'In the Regiment of Artillery.'
    'Well and when did you go to Spain?'
    'In 1801.'
    'Oh,' said the Duke before striding off, 'that will never do.'

Those he did know were as likely to be rebuffed as those he did not. Captain George Elers, who had been with him at Seringapatam, wrote to the Duke at this time soliciting employment of any kind and enclosed a letter which his Grace had written to him and which he had 'constantly preserved' for twenty-six years. He received this reply:

The Duke of Wellington presents his Compliments to Mr Elers and begs leave to acknowledge the Receipt of his letter of this day [28 February 1828].

The Duke returns the inclosure, and regrets very much that he has it not in his power to be of any service to him.[7]

A later letter from Captain Elers offering the Duke a dog which had come into his possession as residuary legatee of a relative, a parson in Northamptonshire, received an even shorter reply: 'The Duke has no occasion for a Newfoundland Dog, and will not deprive Mr Elers of him.'[8] A letter from a clergyman who complained of the 'disrespect' in an earlier brief and dismissive note from the Duke, received the reply: 'I know nothing of you nor ever heard your name. Therefore I could feel no disrespect towards you.'

In writing to those Tories whom he felt obliged to disappoint upon becoming Prime Minister, the Duke was rather more tactful, assuring them of the pain he felt at having nothing to offer them, though complaining exasperatedly to Croker that he had no time left to attend to the affairs of the country since all his time was 'employed in assuaging what gentlemen call their *feelings*. In short, the folly and unreasonableness of people are inconceivable.'[9]

The mixture of political views in Wellington's Cabinet neither promised harmony nor achieved it; there were constant differences and arguments both about foreign and domestic policies. The Cabinet was described as 'meeting to debate and dispute and separating without deciding'.[10]

The Prime Minister confessed that he was 'very unhappy and uncomfortable', although Lord Lyndhurst, the Lord Chancellor, said he was 'a good man to do business with, quick and intelligent';[11] and, unlike Peel, who would 'take up his newspaper and sulk' if his opinion were not adopted, the Duke 'was always candid, reasonable and ready to discuss fairly every subject'.[12] Peel himself described him as being 'most reasonable and friendly and satisfactory in every way'.[13] Acknowledged to be exceptionally well informed about foreign affairs, if not about public opinion in his own country, he soon familiarized himself with the business of the Government's other departments and was recognized as a leader of quick perception, orderly habits of mind and remarkable industry. Thomas Creevey told his niece, 'The Beau is rising most rapidly in the market as a practical man of business. All the deputations come away charmed with him. But woe to them that are too late! He is punctual to the second himself, and waits for no man.'*[14] 'I trust in God we shall never lose the Duke,' Lord Ellenborough, Lord Privy Seal, commented. *'If he should fall, all falls.'*[15]

The Duke himself told Mrs Arbuthnot that he hoped eventually to establish a strong Government in the country and he could then 'retire with Honour'. For the time being, so he claimed, he usually got his own way in Cabinet. Charles Greville described him in August as being 'all powerful'.[16] He recorded with self-satisfaction after one prolonged argument with his colleagues that he had 'everything [his] own way as usual after a *seance* of 3½ hours'.[17] When his decisions were questioned he 'looked staggered', wrote one of these junior colleagues, '& with that air, which he always has, of a man very little accustomed to be differed from or contradicted'.[18]

Always self-reliant and undismayed by difficulties, he was certainly not frightened by responsibility. 'The people of England,' he said, 'must be governed by persons who are not afraid.' Nor was he in the least in awe of experienced and well entrenched civil servants, treating them as though they were recalcitrant staff officers. An official at the Treasury was said to have informed the Duke that a certain change in the department's methods of accounting was impossible to achieve. 'Never mind,' the Duke replied. 'If *you* cannot accomplish it, I will send you half a dozen pay-sergeants who will.'[19]

Yet despite Charles Greville's contrary opinion and his own self-confident assertions, the Duke did not always have his way in Cabinet whose members, so Mme de Lieven heard, blackguarded 'one another

---

* Nor did he make allowances in this regard for members of the Royal Family. Lord Ellesmere gave an example of this:

> He was a great admirer of Mrs Butler (Fanny Kemble), and constantly took a stall when she acted. When she acted in *The Hunchback*, in Belgrave Square, he told us he was engaged to the Beauforts to meet the Duke and Duchess of Cambridge, and that he would keep that engagement, provided they kept theirs, and that there were signs of dinner at the time specified in the invitation. He went, but finding no sign of dinner at a quarter to eight, very deliberately drove off to us, leaving them in the lurch, Royalties and all (Ellesmere, *Personal Recollections of the Duke of Wellington*, 79).

like draymen'. The Prime Minister was on friendly terms with few of its members. He certainly did not get on very well with Peel whom, so he confided in Mrs Arbuthnot, he did not find it at all easy to deal with although outwardly their relationship at this time seemed quite amiable. The two men were, after all, temperamentally ill suited to each other: the one was gregarious and unhappily married, the other uxorious and, as he admitted to his wife, 'really quite uneasy in society'.[20] Nor did the Duke get on well with Palmerston who opposed him more strongly than any of the other Canningites and who answered a question as to why he and his fellow Canningites had joined Wellington's Government with the comment that he had not done so: 'they came and joined ours'. Nor yet did he work harmoniously with Charles Grant who resigned as President of the Board of Trade and was persuaded to withdraw his resignation with difficulty. Huskisson also resigned and was not asked to reconsider his decision as he had expected to be. His resignation was followed by that of all the other Canningites, so Wellington's Government, *nolens, volens*, became exclusively Tory.

A particularly intractable bone of contention was Roman Catholic emancipation. The King, insisting that his Coronation Oath bound him to entertain the same opinions on this matter as his 'revered and excellent father', had informed Goderich that his conscience must 'not be disturbed upon that painful question'.[21] He had trusted that the Duke would agree to let the matter rest for the time being. But Wellington had come to the view that the problem of the Roman Catholics, whose claims he had long known would one day have to be satisfied, was becoming a question which would have to be faced. In May 1828 the House of Commons had carried, by a majority of six, Sir Francis Burdett's resolution affirming the expediency of considering the laws affecting Catholics. The next month the Irish political leader Daniel O'Connell offered himself as a candidate at a by-election in County Clare where the Protestant candidate was Vesey Fitzgerald, the Duke of Wellington's choice as successor to Charles Grant as President of the Board of Trade. A Catholic could not, as the law then stood, take up his seat in the House of Commons; but there was nothing to prevent him being elected to it, which, indeed, O'Connell was by a large majority. It was a result welcomed by the Lord-Lieutenant, Lord Anglesey, who had earlier suggested that the provocative 1825 Act against the Catholic Association, which O'Connell had founded to work for Catholic emancipation, should not be renewed. Anglesey now suggested that if O'Connell could force himself upon the House of Commons it would be 'a most fortunate event'.[22]

Wellington certainly had not thought so. When Sir Francis Burdett's resolution had come up to the Lords from the Commons, he had declared, 'There is no person in this House whose feelings are more decided than mine are with regard to the subject of the Roman Catholic claims; and until I see a great change in that quarter, I shall certainly oppose it.'[23] He later gave it as his opinion that Lord Anglesey must have been bitten by a lunatic Papist, for he had certainly gone mad.[24] Peel, hovering on the brink of resignation, was just as much a worry to the Duke. So was the King.

Throughout the late summer and autumn of 1828, Wellington, who had gradually come round to the belief that, with civil war threatening in Ireland, something must be done for the Catholics, persisted in his efforts to bring the King round to less intransigent views about them. The King avoided him as often as he could, pleading illness; and when the Duke did manage to see him he talked with exhausting garrulity on any matter other than the one upon which his Prime Minister wished to consult him.

The Duke felt quite exhausted by it all. Life was becoming a burden to him, he complained to Mrs Arbuthnot who agreed with Princess Lieven that he wore himself out by insisting on doing so much work that might have been left to subordinates. 'He will do everything himself,' Princess Lieven said. 'He is in everything . . . In a word he wishes to be the universal man.'[25] Guests at Stratfield Saye – even Mrs Arbuthnot who spent two weeks there – saw little of him except at dinner after which he would immediately return to his writing-table where he would remain until midnight.[26]

Towards the end of August Princess de Lieven heard that he had gone to Cheltenham to 'recoup'. 'He is looking very ill,' she reported gloomily. 'Prime Ministers don't live very long.'[27]

At Cheltenham, however, he could not bring himself to rest, insisting upon still dealing personally with his correspondence, giving advice upon foreign as well as domestic issues. He protested that he felt much better, though 'not very firm' upon his legs. But when he returned to London he seemed as much agitated as ever; and one day, while walking down the Mall with Harriet Arbuthnot, he became so heated over a critical letter from the Duke of Richmond which she had shown him that she thought the people they encountered would think he had gone mad. Not long after his return Lord Farnborough, a former Postmaster-

General, expressed the opinion that the Duke was 'in a very disturbed state of mind'.[28]

At Windsor, however, his patience with the King was remarkable. By making it 'a rule never to interrupt him', by allowing him 'to talk himself out',[29] Wellington had, by the beginning of 1829, persuaded his Majesty to agree that the Cabinet should at least discuss the Roman Catholic question; and on 21 January, Charles Greville reported the Duke as being 'in very good spirits' at dinner, 'and agreeable as he always is'.[30]

But then the King's brother, the Duke of Cumberland, 'the most mischievous fellow' that Wellington had ever known, announced his intention of coming home from Germany where he was then living. The man had already done harm enough by his letters, reinforcing his brother's prejudices, helping to turn him into 'the most Protestant man in his dominions'.[31] Wellington did all he could to stop Cumberland coming home from Berlin and succeeded in persuading the King to write to his brother to put him off. Wellington also wrote to Cumberland himself; but the exciting prospect of stirring up trouble was too much for the tiresome man to resist. The Duke of Cumberland arrived to the welcome of crowds of cheering Protestants on 14 January and was soon skilfully working on the King's emotions and provoking him to make a stand against his better judgement. Wellington well understood how Cumberland did so: the King was afraid of nothing that was 'hazardous, perilous or uncertain'; but he dreaded ridicule, and the Duke of Cumberland's powers of ridicule were unrivalled.[32]

As the weeks passed at Windsor, the King, who had been relentlessly pressing for the recall of Lord Anglesey from Ireland, became more and more unreasonable upon the subject of Roman Catholic relief, working himself up into a fury whenever the subject was mentioned. Indeed, he became so hysterical on occasions that Lady Conyngham's son, Lord Mount Charles, 'verily believed he would go mad'.[33]

At the end of February Wellington went down to Windsor with a letter to be handed to the King as soon as he was awake. When shown into his presence, Wellington bluntly informed the King that if the Duke of Cumberland were to remain in the country, his Majesty would do well to recommend an immediate change of government. The Prime Minister had heard a rumour that Cumberland was planning to assemble a large mob of Protestants to march on Windsor and frighten the King into refusing any measures of Roman Catholic relief. If these rumours proved to be well founded, Wellington would have Cumberland sent to the Tower 'as soon as look at him'.[34]

The next day Wellington went down again to Windsor where he found the King was in 'a very agitated state'. He remained with him for five hours, at the end of which, having listened to threats of abdication and watched tears slip down the royal cheeks, Wellington felt he had made some progress. But the Duke of Cumberland was still at Windsor, constantly appearing in his brother's room and insistently pressing his views upon the King who was all the more encouraged to listen to them when Robert Peel, formerly an opponent of emancipation, changed his mind after weeks of uncertainty, consequently offered himself for re-election as Member for Oxford University and was defeated by a rampantly Protestant concourse of Masters of Arts.

Wellington drove down to Windsor yet again on 2 March. His Majesty seemed quite distracted by worry, not only about the Roman Catholic Relief Bill but also about Harriette Wilson and by reports that a Captain Thomas Garth – rumoured to be an illegitimate child of his Majesty's sister, Princess Sophia, either by an elderly general or even by the Duke of Cumberland – was threatening to make scandalous disclosures. Wellington felt quite sorry to see 'the poor old man's distress and agitation', and wondered, not for the first time, if perhaps he was losing his mind or was, indeed, insane already.[35] Certainly he astounded his Ministers by declaring that he had fought at Waterloo and had helped to win the Battle of Salamanca, 'when things were looking very black indeed', by leading a magnificent charge of dragoons disguised as General Bock. He had also, so he claimed, ridden Fleur-de-Lis for the Goodwood Cup.[36] When recalling these stirring events the tears would often start to his eyes, and no one was quite sure whether or not he was making some elaborate joke. Sometimes it seemed that he had succeeded in persuading himself that he had actually participated in the sagas he so vividly described. The Duke usually listened to such tales in silence, though once after hearing an account of how the King had made a body of troops charge down a particularly sharp declivity, he was heard to observe, 'Very steep, Sir.'[37] Throughout the interview on 2 March, which lasted for three hours, the King was in one of these strange moods which left Wellington feeling quite exhausted.

After his next interview with the King, which took place two days later, Wellington was even more exhausted and more than ever convinced that the King was insane. He talked almost continuously hour after hour, constantly sipping brandy and water, occasionally breaking down in tears, rambling on about the Coronation Oath and threatening to abdicate. After five and a half hours of this he asked for the

Government's resignation. It was granted immediately. After Wellington had gone, however, the King had to face the fact that the Tory
opponents of the dreaded Bill were not strong enough to form an
alternative government and, urged to do so by both Sir William Knighton, his Majesty's influential Keeper of the Privy Purse, and Lady
Conyngham, he wrote Wellington a letter before going to bed:

> My dear Friend, As I find the country would be left without an Admin-
> istration, I have decided to yield my opinion to that which is considered
> by the Cabinet to be for the immediate interests of the country. Under
> these circumstances you have my consent to proceed as you propose
> with the measure. God knows what pain it causes me to write these
> words. G.R.[38]

Fearing that the King might change his mind the next day, or at
least call for the Government's resignation as soon as the Bill was
passed, Wellington felt anger rather than relief. He 'abused the King
most furiously', castigating him as 'the worst man he ever fell in with
in his whole life, the most selfish, the most false, the most ill-natured,
the most entirely without one redeeming quality'. He would be *'damned'*
if he would stay in office.[39]

Yet few doubted that he would remain as Prime Minister so long as
his sense of duty required it, so long as it remained true that 'nobody
could manage the King' other than himself;[40] and when, in calmer
mood, having made an exceptionally persuasive speech in the Lords –
standing with arms folded and speaking 'slowly but without hesitation
or embarrassment of any kind . . . for an hour and a quarter'[41] – he
returned to Windsor in the second week of April, he was able to
persuade the King to give his consent to the Roman Catholic Relief
Act. It was generally conceded that, as his former staff officer, now
Major-General Sir Colin Campbell, put it in a letter to the Duchess,
the Duke had achieved a triumph and that he was 'the only Man living
who could have carried the measure'.[42] Charles Greville concurred that
he had managed the business with 'firmness, prudence and dexterity.
There was hardly any other feeling than that of satisfaction, except on
the part of the ultra-Tories . . .'[43] The Irish and the Catholics were duly
grateful: when a Wellington Testimonial Committee was established
in Dublin for the purpose of adding bas-reliefs to the Wellington obelisk
in Phoenix Park, the name of Daniel O'Connell appeared in the list
of subscribers.

34   Battersea Fields and Scotland Yard

1829

'Last week the Mob were roaming, hooting,
abusing your father, now they are cheering him
again.'

THE DUKE'S VICTORY had not been achieved without casualties. He
had had to dismiss the furiously Protestant, ultra Tory Attorney-
General, Sir Charles Wetherell; he had been harangued in speeches
in the Lords, in letters and in newspaper articles by Thomas Burgess,
the zealous old Bishop of Salisbury;[1] he had made an inveterate enemy
of the Duke of Cumberland who, the following year, made plain his
dislike of Wellington at a dinner in Windsor Castle by ostentatiously
turning his glass upside down when his health was proposed;[2] and he
had had to contend with Lord Eldon, the reactionary Lord Chancellor
who had declared that the moment a Roman Catholic sat in Parliament,
'the sun of Great Britain would be set' and who presented himself at
Windsor Castle with armfuls of petitions from people of the same
opinion.[3] The Duke had also had sharp differences of opinion with
Lord Anglesey who, as Lord-Lieutenant in Ireland, had had cause to
complain of the Duke's reluctance to keep him informed of his changing attitude towards Roman Catholic relief. Lord Anglesey had, so the
Duke believed, been on terms of too familiar intimacy with members
of the Irish Catholic Association. Having allowed a letter from Phoenix
Park to the Archbishop of Armagh, in which he admitted to differences
with the Duke, to appear in the press, Anglesey had been summarily
recalled from Dublin.[4]

In addition the Duke had had to deal with two other vehemently
Protestant peers, the ninth Earl of Winchilsea and the fourth, ultra
Tory Duke of Newcastle, who proposed leading the members of the
London and Westminster Protestant Society in a march upon Windsor
Castle in the manner of Lord George Gordon, the procession of whose
Protestant Association had precipitated the fearful Gordon Riots in
London in 1780.

Lord Winchilsea, who always ranted in the House of Lords as though he were 'shouting to a mob on a windy day upon Pennenden Heath', had been particularly offensive to the Duke in letters to the editor of the *Standard* and the Secretary of King's College, London. This college had been founded the year before, as a rival to University College, the godless institution in Gower Street, by the Duke of Wellington, the Archbishops and thirty Bishops of the Church of England. In announcing the withdrawal of his subscription to the college fund, Winchilsea alleged that Wellington's motives in helping to establish the institution were highly suspect, that 'under the cloak of some coloured show of zeal for the Protestant religion', he was carrying on 'an insidious design for the infringement of our liberties and the introduction of Popery into every department of the State'.[5]

After the exchange of angry letters, Winchilsea refused to apologize for his words and Wellington accordingly called upon him to give him 'that satisfaction for [his] conduct which a gentleman has a right to require, and which a gentleman never refuses to give'. Lord Falmouth, a diehard Tory, agreed to act as Winchilsea's second; the Duke's was Sir Henry Hardinge, now Secretary at War, who asked Wellington's doctor, John Hume, to bring a case of pistols to Sir Henry's house at precisely a quarter to eight on the morning of Saturday, 21 March 1829. Hume obeyed the summons, not knowing who the 'persons of rank and consequence' referred to in Hardinge's instructions were; and having been driven away in a carriage towards Battersea Fields, he was surprised to see riding towards him the Duke of Wellington who said to him conversationally, 'Well, I daresay you little expected it was I who wanted you to be here.'

'Indeed, my Lord,' replied Hume. 'You certainly are the last person I should have expected here.'

The Duke seemed perfectly calm as they waited for Winchilsea and Falmouth to appear; and, after jumping over a ditch to escape the notice of some labourers at work in the Fields, he said with his usual briskness, 'Now then, Hardinge, look sharp and step out the ground . . . I have no time to waste.'

Hardinge strode out the customary twelve paces, and indicated where Winchilsea was to stand.

'Damn it!' Wellington called out. 'Don't stick him up so near the ditch. If I hit him he will tumble in.'

He intended aiming at the man's legs, and, being a notoriously bad shot with a pistol, he was not likely to hit him; but it was as well to be on the safe side.

Hume retrieved the pistols from under the hedge where he had concealed them; and, since Hardinge had lost his left hand at Waterloo, he loaded them for him. He also loaded Winchilsea's because Falmouth was shivering so badly with cold and nerves he could not perform the task himself.

Hardinge gave the order to fire. Wellington noticed that Winchilsea's arm remained straight at his side. So, instead of taking aim at his legs, he shot well to the side. Winchilsea raised his arm above his head and shot into the air. A suitable apology was then accepted by the Duke who bowed in turn to his opponent and his opponent's second, touched his hat, said, 'Good morning, my Lords' and rode away to make his report to Mrs Arbuthnot.[6]

Anxious as the participants had been not to be discovered, the news of the duel was soon all over London. There were reports of it in newspapers and, in the windows of the print-sellers, caricatures appeared depicting the Duke variously in civilian clothes firing straight at Winchilsea with grim determination and, with a lobster's claw for a head, wearing a monk's habit with a rosary hanging from the girdle.[*7] Leading opponents of Roman Catholic emancipation expressed their disappointment at the outcome of the duel. 'One is almost tempted,' said the Duke of Newcastle, 'to wish that a life so dangerous had been taken away, but one must not indulge in such unChristian feelings . . . The Duke of Wellington's time may not yet be come, but it may, and that shortly, for assuredly he is a villain.'[8]

The Duke himself was afraid that 'many good men' were shocked by the duel. But the King was not among them: he would, he said, have fought a duel himself under such circumstances.[9] For her part, Mrs Arbuthnot thought the Duke had been 'quite right': 'it was a gross and unprovoked insult and, if he had passed it over, it w^d have been repeated again and again';[10] while the Duchess, distraught as she appeared when told what had happened, was thankful at least to note in a letter to her son Charles that 'last week the Mob were roaming, hooting, abusing your father, now they are cheering him again.'[11]

* Several of the Duke's friends testified to the amusement he derived from caricatures of himself. Mrs Arbuthnot once described him as roaring with laughter at one. He was, however, very loath to be discovered in a ludicrous situation which might be lampooned. Once, having found himself locked in a lavatory, rather than 'reveal his predicament to all and sundry' by shouting for help, he kept his eyes on a starling's nest in the ivy outside the window and when the birds flew out disturbed by someone walking below, he called for assistance just loudly enough to be heard.

Nothing could equal the astonishment caused by this event [Charles Greville recorded] ... The women, particularly of course L. Jersey, have been very ridiculous, affecting nervousness and fine feelings, although they never heard of the business till some hours after it was over ... Everybody of course sees the matter in a different light; all blame Ld. Winchilsea, but they are divided as to whether the Duke ought to have fought or not ... Lord W. is such a maniac ... that everybody imagined the Duke would treat what he said with silent contempt ... I think the Duke ought not to have challenged him; it was very juvenile ... beneath his dignity ... more or less ridiculous ... and a great error in judgement. [Still] it is impossible not to admire the high spirit which disdained to shelter behind the immunities of his great character and station.[12]

Having made his report to Mrs Arbuthnot, the Duke returned to his desk to consider the Metropolitan Police Bill which Peel was to introduce in the Commons in a month's time and which he was to introduce in the Lords in June. Wellington had long believed the establishment of a police force in London to be essential. At the time of the disturbances during the proceedings against Queen Caroline, he had told Lord Liverpool, 'In my opinion, the Government ought, without the loss of a moment's time, to adopt measures to form either a police in London or military corps, which would be of a different description from the regular military force, or both.'[13]

The warning had not been lost upon Liverpool who, when Lord Sidmouth had been persuaded to retire as Home Secretary, had appointed in his place Robert Peel whose views on the need for a centrally controlled police force were well known. Two months after his appointment, Peel had called for a committee to report on the police of the metropolis. This committee had concluded, repeating a traditional formula, that it was difficult to 'reconcile an effective system of police with that perfect freedom of action and exemption from interference which are the great privileges and blessings of society in this country'. The committee had, therefore, decided that 'the forfeiture or curtailment of such advantages would be too great a sacrifice for improvements in police'.[14]

Undeterred, Peel persisted; and in 1828 with the encouragement of Wellington, he had moved for another committee. This time Peel obtained the report he wanted; and the following year he was able to introduce his Bill for Improving the Police in and near the Metropolis. In his speech he reminded an attentive House that, while the population had increased by fifteen and a half per cent between 1821 and 1828, crime had increased by over forty per cent. Something must clearly be done 'but he did not intend to proceed at first on too extensive a scale. Rather he would endeavour in this, as on other occasions, to effect a gradual reformation.'[15]

This promise of caution and restraint, emphasized in the Lords by Wellington, set many uncertain minds at rest. The Bill passed both Houses without serious opposition; and within a matter of weeks the first two Commissioners of Police were established in an office at 4 Whitehall Place, the back of which opened on to a courtyard known as Scotland Yard. In less than three months Wellington was able to write to Peel to congratulate him upon 'the entire success of the Police in London'. It was 'impossible to see anything more respectable'.[16]

Satisfied as he was with the speed and efficiency with which the new police force had been established, the Duke was beset by other concerns. Since the departure of both the Canningites and the ultra Tories, his Government had never been strong; and, as Wellington's inveterate enemy, the Duke of Cumberland, declined to leave Windsor for Germany, the Duke's visits to the Castle were never pleasant interludes in his busy days which almost invariably found him at his desk by six o'clock in the morning. Nor was he in the best of health: the long debates on the Roman Catholic question had taken their toll, and for several days in March he had been obliged by a fearful cold to take an unwonted and unwanted rest while Dr Hume bled him. Peel noticed that thereafter he seemed rather feeble and dragged one leg after the other. Others observed 'a movement of his lips as if he were chewing' which arose from his artificial teeth not fitting him properly.[17] One day he fell from his horse in Bruton Street and was nearly killed by a carriage which almost ran over his head.[18] At a military review in May 1829, wearing the tall and top-heavy cap of the Grenadiers which the King had introduced, he fell off his horse at the feet of the Duke of Cumberland, much to the amusement of the ultra Tories.[19]

35 The Death of the King

1829 – 30

'I believe there never was a man suffered so much
and for so little purpose.'

STRATFIELD SAYE provided little comfort. Endeavouring to please
him, his wife invited guests to stay when he himself was coming; but
they were rarely people he wanted to see, and sometimes he did not
even remember their names. 'The Duchess,' he told Harriet Arbuthnot,
'has certainly the most extraordinary fancy in the selection of her
acquaintances.' And worse than this, it was he who was expected to
entertain them, while his wife sat at the other end of the table, dressed,
'even in winter', so Lady Shelley recorded, 'in white muslin, without
any ornaments, when everyone else was in full dress . . . She seldom
spoke, but looked through her eyeglass lovingly upon the Duke . . .
When the ladies went into the drawing-room she retired into her own
room.'[1] She could see little without the aid of her ill-fitting spectacles
or the lorgnette which she used with nervous fidgetiness. Her clothes
annoyed her husband, too. He liked women to be smartly, fashionably
dressed; but Kitty never troubled to be so. Her head-dresses were
particularly unappealing. A complaint about a head-dress was passed
on to her by her elder son who told her that his father was 'extremely
hurt' at its 'being inconsistent with and beneath the station' which she
held in the world. There seems, however, to have been no noticeable
improvement in the Duchess's style of dressing thereafter, or in the
relationship between husband and wife. While out walking one day at
Stratfield Saye with Mrs Arbuthnot, the Duke complained 'heavily'
of his continuing domestic annoyances. 'The parties at his house
are certainly spoilt by the Duchess,' Mrs Arbuthnot said, 'for she
is the most abominably silly, stupid woman that ever was born; but
I told the Duke [not for the first time] I thought he was to blame,
too, for that all w^d go on much better if he would be *civil* to her
but he is not. He never speaks to her & carefully avoids ever going
near her.'[2]

It was often a profound relief to the Duke to escape from the irritations of Stratfield Saye to the restful atmosphere of Walmer Castle on the coast of Kent.

Upon the death of Lord Liverpool, the previous holder of the office of Lord Warden of the Cinque Ports, the Duke had asked the King if he might be appointed Liverpool's successor and consequently allowed the use of Walmer Castle.

The office was an ancient one and, when established in the eleventh century, was also a highly important one, the Lord Warden being responsible for providing the nucleus of the King's fleet and overseeing the five English Channel ports of Hastings, New Romney, Hythe, Dover and Sandwich, to which Winchelsea and Rye were later added. But over the years the office had become a virtual sinecure with largely ceremonial duties, although, in applying for it, the Duke told the King that it was still of 'great influence and power though without any salary'.[3] Its chief attraction for him, however, was the right to occupy Walmer Castle as his official residence.

Rebuilt in the reign of Henry VIII, and converted for the use of the then Lord Warden in the 1730s, the Castle was, the Duke thought, 'delightful; very well furnished; and in a tolerable state of repair'. He felt much more at home here than he did at Stratfield Saye; and rarely came to stay without having invited a number of congenial guests, the Arbuthnots paying an annual visit, on the first occasion returning from Margate to London by steam boat on which they were 'all dreadfully sick.'[4]

Visitors were sometimes taken by their host to watch the drill and manoeuvres of the soldiers at Canterbury and Dover; and occasionally the Duke, in his Lord Warden's uniform, would take over the parade and demonstrate that he had lost none of his skill in marching men about, wheeling them and bringing them into line as to the manner born.

Delighted as he was with Walmer Castle, it was all the more irksome for the Duke to be called away from its pleasures and comforts to attend upon the King.

Despite his continued mutterings and grumblings about it, his Majesty, so Lady Conyngham told Wellington, was 'more easy since he had given his consent to the Roman Catholic Act'. The King's doctor, Sir Henry Halford, gave the Duke a similar report: 'his Majesty was more composed and in pretty good spirits'. When next he went to Windsor, the Duke himself found the King far less emotional and irrational. He was having his picture painted '*in a Highland dress*' and kept his Prime Minister waiting for twenty minutes. He was rather stiff in manner but 'not in bad humour'.[5]

He was, however, still capable of annoying Wellington intensely when he chose to do so; and then the exasperated Duke would complain that he was the 'greatest *vagabond* that ever existed', that he was 'always acting a part to himself'. On these occasions Wellington felt like giving him up 'as a bad job'.[6] So did other members of his Cabinet. They would go to Windsor to find the King incapacitated by cherry brandy or laudanum and unable to talk to them sensibly or even see them at all; and yet when Wellington himself did see him and found him sober, reasonable and prepared to forget their past differences, the Duke could not but respond to his insinuating charm. It had to be admitted that he was, after all, a man of very varied gifts with 'a wonderful knowledge of character' and of an essentially kind disposition. The Duke would be 'very sorry to hurt him'; he could not 'bear to see the King in distress'.[7]

But then there would arise some new difference between them; and Wellington would find the King as unreasonable as his Majesty protested that he found his Prime Minister. There was, for example, the matter of a baronetcy for the King's favourite architect, John Nash, which Wellington opposed on the grounds that it would be 'attended with the greatest inconvenience' in view of numerous other pressing applications for honours, not to mention the public's attitude towards the enormous expenses incurred by Nash's construction of Buckingham Palace.[8] Then there was the matter of the offer of the Greek throne to the King's bête noire, Prince Leopold of Saxe-Coburg, whom his daughter Princess Charlotte had married in 1816. How could the Government be 'such fools as to think [Prince Leopold] could be of any use'? The King could not but '*deeply regret* the selection': the Prince was '*not qualified* for this peculiar station'.[9]

The King was urged by the Duke of Cumberland to stand his ground on the issue. He must not give way to the 'over-bearing and dictatorial spirit of the Duke of Wellington'. To do so would be 'signing and sealing [him] not only as your Minister for the rest of your reign, but as Dictator in the country'. It was quite clear, Cumberland insisted, that Wellington was determined to show that he did not 'care a farthing for the King or any of his commands'. In the 'greatest possible rage',

Cumberland accused his brother of 'suffering himself to be turned round the Duke of Wellington's little finger'.*[10]

Once more the King was driven to 'a state of agitation beyond description'; and once more there was talk of the Government's being dismissed. But when he saw that further resistance was useless he gave way to Prince Leopold's nomination. He did so, however, very 'grumpily';[11] and afterwards, as he had done when the stern Wellington would not let him have his way over Nash's baronetcy and as on so many other occasions in the past, he took to his bed.

Arthur was King of England now, the King observed gloomily once again; and Wellington seemed content enough to be considered so. After the satisfactorily engineered recall of Lord Anglesey from his post as Lord-Lieutenant of Ireland, he seemed particularly cheerful. He was a man of good luck, he told Croker complacently. He pointed to the little red Cossack cap he wore in cold weather; that, he said, was his 'Fortunatus's Cap'.[12]

He had never trusted the plaudits of the crowd; but it was not long since that he had behaved for once out of character by saying to Princess de Lieven, 'I am the most popular Minister that England has ever seen. Take my word for it, I am very strong.'[13] He was led to believe that this was still true when he was thrown from his horse during the military review in the Park. As he stood up and remounted there were loud and prolonged cheers; and people crowded round him to shake his hand.†[14]

In these moods of complacency, he was inclined to underestimate the real distress in England, both in the industrial towns and in rural areas, even though, as a landowner himself – and one, incidentally, who refused to enclose common land and was acknowledged to be a considerate landlord even by William Cobbett – the Duke knew that his own tenants were in real need of the reductions in their rents

* The Duke of Cumberland's assertions that Wellington was endeavouring to assume dictatorial powers were reflected in numerous contemporary caricatures. A typical one by Heath portrayed Wellington trying on the royal crown in front of a looking-glass while the King, sucking his thumb, in a cradle, is rocked to sleep by Lady Conyngham, believed to be one of the Prime Minister's closest allies (*British Museum Catalogue of Political and Personal Satires*, xi, 15521).

† He was in the habit of demonstrating his indifference to such public acclamation. Princess Lieven told Metternich about his being 'cheered to the echo' upon his appearance at the theatre in Drury Lane. 'At first he did not want to take any notice; when he was compelled to go forward to satisfy the audience, he gave two little nods, as if to say, "How do you do," and then left them to clap their hands sore without giving them another look' (*Private Letters of Princess Lieven*, ed. Peter Quennell, 171).

which he accorded them. He recognized also that conditions in the north for the poor were, indeed, pitiable; and he condemned the great landowners there for refusing to deny themselves 'any gratification or luxury' while complaining of the poor state of agriculture generally and that on their own estates particularly. Yet he liked to suppose that the country was 'improving slowly'. Certainly he himself saw no need for radical reform, or for much reform at all: when it was proposed that a relief bill for Jews should follow the Roman Catholic Relief Act, he agreed with the bishops that it should not; nor did he have any confidence 'in any of these schemes to civilize Negroes'; and when Sir Henry Hardinge suggested that flogging should no longer be resorted to as a punishment in the Army, he argued strongly against a proposal which would deprive officers of the only means of instilling discipline into such men as the service, in default of conscription, had to rely on. As for Parliamentary Reform, proposed by Lord Grey, Lord John Russell and other Whigs, as well as radicals, this would do far more harm than good. The people of the country wished to go on quietly; they were tired of what he called 'novelties in Trade, Agriculture, foreign and domestic policy'; they would support any Government that would protect them from such newfangled ideas.[15]

He could not, however, disguise from himself the fact that his own Government was now far from secure: the ultra Tories, still deeply offended by what they considered his apostasy over Roman Catholicism, were now almost as strongly opposed to him as were the Whigs. Some thought he should strengthen his position by making overtures to the Canningites or even to Lord Grey, whom the King never forgave for his support of Queen Caroline.

> It really does appear [Charles Greville recorded at this time] that a notion prevails of the D. of Wellington's indifference to the state of the country, and of his disposition to treat the remonstrances and petitions of the people with contempt, which I believe to be most false and unjust. He has an overweening opinion of his own all-sufficiency, and that is his besetting sin, and the one which, if anything does, will overturn his Government; for if he would be less dictatorial and opinionated, and would call to his assistance such talents and information as the crisis demands, he would be universally voted the best man alive to be at the head of the Government. But he has such a set of men under him.[16]

Yet to recall the Canningites would entail having Huskisson as a colleague; and he had no more stomach for dealing with Huskisson than he had for cooperating with Lord Grey. If only, he thought, all his colleagues were as efficient and amenable as he now found Peel to be. He would even, he said, be prepared to serve in a Government under Peel's leadership.[17]

As it was, he carried on as Prime Minister, working harder than ever, spending long hours in the Treasury before walking over to the House of Lords, then reading and writing papers until after midnight, rushing about the country, from one house party to the next. Mrs Arbuthnot, complaining that she scarcely ever saw him nowadays, told him that if he went on like this 'he would soon have no eyes left'. When Charles Greville called at Apsley House one day, another caller sent in a card while he was there. Greville asked the Duke whose card it was. 'Oh, a man who wants to see me about a canal,' he replied. 'I can't see him. Everybody will see me, and how the Devil they think I am to see everybody, to be the whole morning with the King, and to do the whole business of the country, I don't know. I am quite worn out with it.'[18]

Even when he took a short break at Cheltenham to drink the waters, he took newspapers with him into the bathroom, folding them across a frame erected for the purpose. Nothing appeared too trivial for his consideration, be it details of foreign policy or the problem of London traffic.

Overworked as he was, he had to concede that there were advantages in holding high office which he would be loath to forgo. He enjoyed, for instance, being able to do favours for his friends or even strangers when he felt they deserved a helping hand, which, it had still to be admitted, they very often, in his opinion, did not. He arranged a pension from the Civil List to be paid to the old surviving lady of Llangollen, Miss Ponsonby;[19] to oblige the Countess of Blessington, he obtained a brigade-majorship for the son of a friend of hers;[20] and, in the face of opposition from the Foreign Office and to please Lord Alvanley and Lord Worcester, he obtained a consulship for the King's erstwhile friend George Brummell whom, it seems, the Duke had never met.[21] There were occasions, rare occasions, when he overstepped the bounds of propriety in order to oblige a friend. When Lady Salisbury's daughter, the Countess of Westmeath, was involved in proceedings against her husband, whom she accused of all manner of sexual misdemeanours, the Duke found means of rewarding three extremely dubious men who had helped her in her attempt to prove her husband's adultery. One was appointed a government solicitor; the other two were found places in the Ordnance Office. Informed of this, presumably by Lord

Westmeath, a newspaper observed, 'We may remind our readers that Lady Westmeath's sister is married to the Duke of Wellington's brother [Henry]. The Duke is Master General [of the Ordnance]. Truly it may be remarked that there are "wheels within wheels." '[22]

Later the Duke prevailed upon the King to agree to the Countess's being granted a pension of £385 on the Irish establishment. This also caused much adverse comment. The Marquess of Anglesey, still at that time Lord-Lieutenant of Ireland, had strongly objected to the pension being granted and refused to authorize it unless expressly told to do so by the King himself. It was 'an instance of political corruption at Ireland's expense which had long been a grievance'. He could not, he said, 'bear that it should stand as an act of mine'. So when the fuss had died down, the Duke secretly 'pushed the matter through by a warrant under the royal sign manual'.[23]

Despite these opportunities to help his friends, there were times when the Duke doubted that it was worth while carrying on. 'I certainly admit that I am anxious to quit office,' he confided in Charles Arbuthnot. 'Till I became First Lord of the Treasury I never had a dispute or a difference with anybody,' he continued disingenuously; 'excepting the Scum of the Earth, who defrauded the Publick or who would not do their Duty. In my office I am necessarily put in Collision with every body. Then I am obliged to keep everything and every body in order and in His Place. I have a quarrel open with Mr Huskisson and Lord Anglesey; and another ready for Lord Combermere [whose appointment as a Privy Councillor the Duke opposed]; and all for what?'[24]

He also quarrelled with Sir Herbert Taylor, Adjutant General and later the King's Private Secretary, who complained of his 'rudeness in matters of business', and with Sir Henry Hardinge, Secretary at War, who said that he was 'sometimes so harsh & so offensive' it was all he could do to bear it, notwithstanding the warm affection he entertained for him.[25]

All public affairs made him miserable, the Duke told Mrs Arbuthnot who had never known him more irritable. 'The truth is,' she wrote, 'he is worried by everybody; he is tormented by people asking for places which he has not got to give, and by complaints of the weakness of his Gov^t and the bad management of Mr Peel.'[26] She talked to him about his 'being cross with his colleagues': it was 'a thousand pities' that he should be so, because no one could be more 'amiable and attractive than the Duke when he chose to be so'. But he 'stoutly denied' that he was 'harsh and ill-tempered' with official people. 'I knew he w^d,' she commented, 'for he always denies any charge of that sort, but it is a good thing to tell him these kind of reports of him for it puts him on his guard.'[27]

'If I had known in January 1828 one tithe of what I do now, and of what I discovered in one month after I was in office,' he declared, 'I should never have been the King's minister . . . However, I trust that God Almighty will soon determine that I have been sufficiently punished for my sins, and will relieve me from the unhappy lot which has befallen me . . . I believe there never was a man suffered so much and for so little purpose.'[28]

He was not feeling at all well, he confided in Mrs Arbuthnot. One day he fell asleep in his carriage, 'always a sign of being unwell'. He was also often extremely crotchety. On 22 January 1830 Charles Greville recorded in his diary:

> The Duke has lately given audience to the West Indians [merchants] who came to complain of their sufferings and taxation and to implore relief. Murray [Secretary for War and the Colonies] and Goulburn [Chancellor of the Exchequer] were present, neither of whom (it is said) spoke a word. The Duke cut them very short, and told them that they were not distressed at all, and that nothing could be done for them.[29]

The offended merchants said that they would never go near Wellington again; and George Hibbert, their Chairman, a generous patron of arts and Member of Parliament, said that he had attended deputations to every Prime Minister since Pitt and 'never saw one so ill received before'.[30]

Exasperated as he so often was, the Duke kept reminding himself that it was something, after all, to be the King of England's first Minister, even in the service of such a King. He went over to Windsor frequently, usually finding his Majesty as heavily dosed as ever with laudanum or cherry brandy but not often completely incapable of conducting a rational conversation. The Duke was astonished by the man's resilience. He was obviously ill, suffering from what was diagnosed as 'gout, principally confined to the neck of the bladder and all along the course of the urethra'; but he stubbornly refused to adopt a way of life which might alleviate his condition. 'One night,' the Duke reported, 'he drank two glasses of hot ale and toast, three glasses of claret, some strawberries!! and a glass of brandy. Last night they gave him some physic and, after it, he drank three glasses of port wine and a glass of brandy. No wonder he is likely to die.'[31] For breakfast on 9 April 1830, Wellington said he had 'a pidgeon and beef steak pie of which he ate two pidgeons and three beef-steaks, three parts of a bottle of Mozelle, a glass of champagne, two glasses of port and a glass of brandy! He had taken laudanum the night before, again before his breakfast, again last night and again this morning.' Yet he was 'easily satisfied that he would get the better of his illness'; and, on the day that he saw Wellington for the last time, 'he said that he was getting quite well and should be able to move soon.'[32] The Duke, however, reported him as being in a 'very precarious state'.[33] Not long afterwards it was announced, 'The King expired exactly as the clock struck the quarter after three, June 26 1830.'[*34]

* Some little time before his death, the King had earnestly asked Wellington, whom he had appointed one of his executors, to ensure that he was buried in his night clothes and 'with whatever ornaments might be upon his person at the time of his death'. Wellington had assured him that this would be done. Afterwards he realized what lay behind the King's request, for noticing a black ribbon around the neck in the open coffin, he was driven by curiosity to see what was suspended from it. He drew aside the collar of the nightshirt and blushed deeply as, with some hesitation, he told Mrs Dawson-Damer what his inquisitiveness had led him to discover: it was a diamond locket containing a portrait of Mrs Fitzherbert.

As one of the King's executors the Duke was concerned to ensure that there was nothing in his papers, nor in Mrs Fitzherbert's, that might come to light and prove the fact of their marriage. The bulk of this correspondence, including letters 'expressive of ardent attachment', were burned by Wellington and Sir William Knighton, the King's other executor. But Mrs Fitzherbert, who greatly disliked and much distrusted Knighton, declined at first to hand over the King's letters in her possession; and it was not until August 1833 that she gave formal consent to their destruction (Wellington Papers, Stratfield Saye, Misc. 31, 24 Aug. 1833). Soon afterwards nearly all of these letters were burned by Wellington in the drawing-room of her house in Tilney Street off Park Lane in the presence of her friend Lord Albemarle. There were so many of them that after several hours' work, Wellington said to Albemarle, 'I think, my Lord, we had better hold our hand for a while, or we shall set the old woman's chimney on fire' (George Thomas, Earl of Albemarle, *Fifty Years of my Life*, London, ii, 71). Mrs Fitzherbert insisted on keeping some papers, including those which established her marriage to the King, and these were preserved in Messrs Coutts's vaults until 1905 when they passed into the Royal Archives. Wellington was always determined that they should never be opened, and threatened to move for an injunction from Chancery if any attempt were made to publish them. He told John Gurwood, his private secretary, that 'the publication would be mischievous, as the Prince by marrying a Catholic had by law forfeited the crown' (Sir George Seymour's annotations to Langdale's *Memoirs of Mrs Fitzherbert*, Seymour of Ragley MSS, Warwickshire County Record Office, CR 114/A/536/7). The King's marriage to Mrs Fitzherbert was not made public until after Wellington's death.

36 Riots and Repression

1830 – 2

'Beginning Reform is beginning Revolution.'

'LOOK AT THAT IDIOT!' the late King had once whispered in Mme de Lieven's ear at the dinner table, indicating his brother, the Duke of Clarence, whose red-thatched face – 'like a frog carved on a coconut' – could be seen at the other end of the table. 'They will remember me, if he is ever in my place.'[1]

Now that King William IV was in his brother's place, Wellington endeavoured to establish as reasonably satisfactory relations as he had done with George IV. There were some doubts that he would be able to do so as Wellington had already felt in duty bound to check the eccentric behaviour of King William as Lord High Admiral and had accepted his resignation in August 1828. But, as it happened, the Duke got on perfectly well with the new King whom he found, while eccentric, unpredictable and naive, quite reasonable and manageable. In fact, so Wellington told Charles Greville, he could do more business with him in ten minutes than he could in ten days with King George IV who had constantly wandered off into digressions on every kind of subject except that which was meant to be under discussion. 'If I had been able to deal with my late master as I do with my present,' the Duke said, 'I should have got on much better.'[2]

King William seemed to share the Duke's political views, and showed no eagerness to press for the admission of Lord Grey into the Government as Wellington feared he would do.

At a dinner party at Apsley House, to which his Majesty had invited himself together with the King and Queen of Württemberg, he delivered himself of one of those inordinately long and inconsequential speeches to which he was addicted, elaborating upon the virtues of the married state which, intended to please the German guests, was naturally not so welcome to their host, and, having asked the band to play *See the Conquering Hero Comes* and made allusion to the Duke's conquest of the French, had to modify his words on recollecting that the French Ambassador was in the room. He explained that the victory he referred to had been won over a republican force and not over the army of his friend, the French King. And so the speech went rambling on, in part incomprehensibly, ending at last with an assurance that the present Government would retain his confidence as long as he was King.*³

The question was, though, could the present Government survive, its supporters being so weak in Parliament? It was decided that in an attempt to strengthen it an approach must be made to the Canningites. So, although Peel thought him 'too discreditable and unsafe', Palmerston was sounded out. So was Lord Melbourne who said that he could not accept office unless Huskisson did so, too.

The Duke was reluctantly considering the problem when he left for Manchester to join Huskisson, Member of Parliament for Liverpool, to attend the opening of the Liverpool to Manchester railway. The two men were talking together, Wellington in a carriage with Mrs Arbuthnot, Huskisson standing on the line – which the 'directors had particularly requested that nobody would' – when Robert Stephenson's *Rocket* and other engines came puffing down the track. Shouts of warning rang out. Spectators jumped clear; but Huskisson, a far from nimble man who was prone to accidents and had three times broken his arm, hesitated, turning this way, then that and eventually falling back upon the rails in front of the *Dart* which ran over him, crushing his thigh. 'It's all over with me,' he cried. 'Bring me my wife and let me die.'⁴

With Huskisson dead, it was more difficult than ever for Wellington to make a deal with the Canningite party which, seriously weakened, was drawing closer to the Whigs who had made significant gains in the elections following the late King's death. The Duke, reluctant to consider a coalition, had 'got into a great rage' when Mrs Arbuthnot had urged upon him the need for allies and she had felt obliged to abandon her argument. But he was now being forced to conclude that a more formal approach must be made to Palmerston, even though that might mean asking an old friend, Sir George Murray, to stand down as Secretary for War. Palmerston was approached; he seemed willing to join the Cabinet, provided two of his Canningite colleagues were brought in with him. The thought of this deeply distressed the Duke. 'I cannot change Ministers more frequently than the coats on

* The Duke told Princess Lieven that he had had to warn the King against making such speeches and 'that when at table my master wishes to make a speech I always turn to him my deaf ear so as not to be tempted to get up and contradict him' (*Letters of Dorothea, Princess Lieven*, ed. Lionel G. Robinson, 236).

my back,' he protested to Mrs Arbuthnot, dreading the thought of dismissing faithful colleagues to make way for new men.[5] Even so, he offered Palmerston the three places he had requested. Palmerston then asked for more. The Duke thankfully used this as a reason for bringing the discussions to an end. Peel agreed that the Cabinet, weak as it was, must struggle on as best it could.[6]

The elections had shown how the mood of the English people was changing, how fast demands for reform were growing. The Duke was still generally respected: he had been greeted by cheering crowds in Lancashire. But the mood of the country was for Parliamentary Reform and the Duke was not.

To many the Duke's stand was scarcely comprehensible. Only about one man in every hundred then had a vote; and, while several large towns, such as Manchester, had no representative in Parliament at all, there were several places far smaller which had two. There were also various so-called rotten or pocket boroughs, like Salton which was no more than a park and Dunwich which had for centuries been submerged beneath the North Sea. These were mostly in the hands of landowners who nominated Members as they chose.

Wellington's distaste for Reform had been exacerbated by revolution in France from which King Charles X had been forced to withdraw to England. 'Beginning Reform,' the Duke told Mrs Arbuthnot, 'is beginning Revolution.'[7] And, on a later occasion, he declared in the House of Lords that 'from the period of the adoption of that measure [Parliamentary Reform and its attendant interference with property rights] will date the downfall of the Constitution.'[8]

He was by then inextricably associated in the public mind with the old order, with Metternich and those who had redrawn the map of Europe in its former image after the fall of Napoleon; and he was suspected of favouring the Bourbons who had been deposed in France. Certainly he did not mean to trim his sails to meet the challenge presented by the Whigs and Radicals. 'I have not leisure to discuss Parliamentary Reform either in writing or in conversation,' he stated firmly. 'If it should be carried it must occasion a total change in the whole system of that society called the British Empire, and I don't see how I could be a party to such changes, entertaining the opinions that I do . . . I am fully convinced that the country possesses at the present moment a Legislature which answers all the good purposes of legislation, and this to a greater degree than any Legislature ever has answered in any country whatever . . . I am not only not prepared to bring forward any measure of this nature, but I will at once declare that, as far as I am concerned, as long as I hold any station in the government of the country, I shall always feel it my duty to resist such measures when proposed by others.'[9]

He said as much and more in a speech in the House of Lords which, delivered in an autocratic and defiant manner, dismayed his supporters as much as it provoked his opponents. It was 'violent and uncalled for', Charles Greville commented. 'Never was there an act of more egregious folly, or one so universally condemned by friends and foes.'[10]

When the Duke sat down to a profound silence followed by a rumble of astonished discontent, he said to the grave and cautious Earl of Aberdeen, who had succeeded Lord Dudley as Foreign Secretary, 'I have not said too much, have I?' Aberdeen replied with gloomy foreboding, 'You'll hear of it.'[11]

He had not consulted Aberdeen, or, indeed, any of his colleagues before making his speech. He did not even consult Peel who was provoked into observing that the Duke was never influenced by men, though he was by women and by the silliest women at that.[12]

While Greville thought that the Duke's speech had 'without doubt sealed his fate', Wellington himself believed that his fall was most improbable and that, if he were to be forced to resign, the unrest caused by the Paris uprising in July, aided by the plots of the devious Duke of Cumberland, would be largely to blame.

He could not deny, though, that he was personally under serious threat. The country was in uproar; and his own life was in danger. He was hissed and hooted in the streets, threatened with assassination, sent numerous alarming letters, some signed, others anonymous, several from 'Captain Swing' whose name was so often invoked all over the country in protestations against enclosures, low wages, the employment of 'strangers' and of farm machines which were held to be keeping men out of work. From Wiltshire to Sussex and as far north as Carlisle, gangs of men, sometimes with blackened faces and reported to be in women's clothes, often carrying flags and blowing horns, cut down fences, destroyed machinery, burnt down ricks and barns, and demanded action and reform from the Government in London.

In London, so it was rumoured, the Lord Mayor's Day, 9 November 1830, was to be the occasion of a massive demonstration. Some said the City was to be burned down, factories blown up, gas pipes cut and, as at the time of the Cato Street Conspiracy in 1820, members of the Cabinet were to be murdered. Hundreds of workers were expected to march down from the north; Londoners were to arm themselves with staves to attack the new Police; the Guards would mutiny. On the arrival of the King at Guildhall to have dinner with the Lord Mayor elect his Majesty was to be taken prisoner and held until the Government were dismissed from office, or, failing that, the traces of the King's carriage were to be cut at the foot of Ludgate Hill and he was to be held hostage until the Reform Act was carried.

Two days before this uprising was due to take place, the King asked the Cabinet if they thought his visit to the City should be postponed. The Prime Minister and his Cabinet did think so. But the postponement of the Lord Mayor's dinner did not end the unrest. Fearing attacks upon their premises, shopkeepers locked their doors and shuttered their windows; counting-houses in the City were deserted; householders kept their servants indoors.

While the Duke's enemies made the most of his postponement of the dinner – which was described by his brother Richard as the 'boldest act of cowardice he had ever heard of '*[13] – the Duke himself made light of his own danger. It was not easy to kill a man, he said; and his life, after all, had so often been in greater jeopardy than it was now. He went personally to the Rotunda at Blackfriars to see what arrangements were being made to control the huge crowds that assembled there of an evening to listen to radical orators; and he made provision for more secure precautions for the future.

He also took precautions himself: he carried pistols with him in his carriage and had bolts fitted to the inside of the doors. At Apsley House, gates were locked; shutters were closed on ground-floor windows; armed men were stationed at the windows above and at other places set out in a detailed memorandum entitled 'Precautions to be taken to Defend Apsley House in case of Attack'. These men were ordered not to fire unless the mob broke into the garden over the rails or by pulling down the rails, then 'every effort must be made to prevent the approach to or entry of the house'.[14]

Lord Mayor's Day and the following night passed off with only minor disturbances; and the next day the Duke was assuring his friends that all would be well with his Government. Numerous as they were, the Whigs and Radicals, the Canningites, and his opponents in his own

* Lord Ellesmere was told that at a dinner party years later the Duke asked a number of young officers what crisis in his career they supposed had caused him 'the most anxious consideration'. Various suggestions were made from Assaye to Salamanca and Waterloo. 'No, gentlemen,' he said. 'It was when at a Cabinet Council I had to consider the safety of the King [William IV] in going to the dinner in the City, and I felt compelled to say No' (Lord Ellesmere, *Personal Reminiscences*, 64).

party were too divided amongst themselves to combine effectively against him. 'Lord, I shall not go out,' he said cheerfully to Lady Jersey. 'You will see, we shall do very well.' Another friend was assured, 'You may rely upon it that I shall not alter my course.' 'Everybody says we are to go out, and I don't believe a word of it. They will be beat on the question of Reform; people will return to the Government and we shall go on very well.' In giving similar assurances to Mrs Arbuthnot he went so far as to say, 'I dare say that I shall be again the most popular Man in the Country.'[15]

Mrs Arbuthnot was far too astute not to realize, however, that unless the Duke's Government were to be reinforced and Peel given more support in the Commons, her friend could not long survive in office. Yet, following the Duke's example, she assured Charles Greville, whom she encountered one day on her walk to Downing Street, that she was not in the least alarmed: 'Everybody says we are to go out and I don't believe a word of it.' Greville did believe it, though. 'The Duke talks with confidence,' he wrote, 'but he does not inspire his friends.' He had 'amazing confidence in himself' which was 'fostered by the deference of those around him and the long experience of his military successes'. He was also 'exceedingly quick of apprehension', though admittedly 'deceived by his own quickness' into thinking he knew more than he did, his 'habits of mind' not being those of 'patient investigation'. But 'one of his greatest misfortunes was his having no wise head to consult with in all emergencies'; and 'chusing with a very slender stock of knowledge to take upon himself the sole direction of every department, he completely sinks under the burden'.[16]

On 15 November – the day before there was to be a debate on a new Reform Bill – a Tory malcontent seconded a motion in the House of Commons proposing that a committee be appointed to examine the Civil List accounts, an unprecedented procedure. The Chancellor of the Exchequer opposed the appointment of such a committee. A vote was taken. The Ministers were defeated, and not only snubbed but given clear notice that they had lost control of the House. Charles Arbuthnot, accompanied by the Chancellor and by Peel – much relieved that his tribulations were over – immediately went to Apsley House where the Duke was giving a dinner party for the Prince of Orange in the Waterloo Gallery. Pressed by Peel to do so, they all agreed that the Government must resign.

The King received them 'with the greatest kindness', Greville was informed, 'shed tears, but accepted their resignation without remonstrance.'[17]

Greville later met Wellington 'coming out of his room, but did not like to speak to him; the Duke got into his cabriolet, and nodded as he passed, but he looked very grave'.[18]

'Bad business, devilish bad business,' Princess Lieven had heard the Duke remark in Peel's drawing-room;[19] and Samuel Rogers reported his words spoken by the fire at Mrs Arbuthnot's: 'They want me to place myself at the head of a faction; but I say to them, I have now served my country for forty years – for twenty I have commanded her armies, and for ten I have sat in the Cabinet – and I will not now place myself at the head of a faction.'[20]

As he had told Lord Liverpool when first accepting a place in the Cabinet, he could never see himself in factious opposition to his Majesty's Ministers; he certainly could not see himself leading such an opposition now. In Parliament, he said, he would voice his dissent when he could not approve of a measure, but he would give his approval to measures when he thought it right to do so.

His attitude naturally did not commend itself to enthusiastic Tories;* and he was consequently all the more pleased when his refusal to pay heed to party considerations in matters of national honour and interest was accorded praise, as it was at a Waterloo dinner by his erstwhile critic Lord Anglesey, who declared that it was 'superfluous to talk of his military achievements but that he must express his admiration of his conduct in civil matters'. When Anglesey sat down the Duke 'squeezed his hand hard and long, and said to him, "I cannot tell you what pleasure you have given me."'[21]

For the moment the Duke felt there was no occasion to support or censure the Government, and seemed perfectly content that this was so. Mrs Arbuthnot thought that he was much happier out of office. 'If I thought only of his own comfort and my own pleasure,' she wrote, 'I never w^d desire to see him again at the head of affairs. I have not for years enjoyed so much of his society, & seen him in so much repose . . . He has come some times & sat two hours at a time in my armchair, enjoying his idleness & the power of sitting in the *dolce far niente*; and he will never be bored, for he reads a great deal, is never tired of it,

---

* Now and later they were much annoyed by this refusal of his to toe the party line. Disraeli gave his sister an example of this when he condemned the Duke's 'damned generosity' in announcing his support of the Whigs' Canada policy: 'Great disgust in Tory ranks, even among the highest; Duke supposed to be passeé [sic] and to like being buttered with Whig laudation' (Jane Ridley, *The Young Disraeli*, 210).

has bought hunters ... & Time does not hang the least upon his hands.'[22]

Towards the end of November he decided to leave London politics behind him and go down into his county of Hampshire, of which he was Lord-Lieutenant, and do what he could to 'restore order and peace' there. For days he had been receiving reports from worried landowners and magistrates about riots and acts of arson. The Portals of Laverstoke Park wrote to him to say that their neighbourhood was 'very disturbed'; they needed 'more magistrates and military assistance'. Sir William Heathcote also complained of disturbances in his area and a lack of troops. Lord Chandos reported that 'things at Avington [were] bad' and that his troop of Yeomanry were ready to march if required. Sir Claudius Stephen Hunter gave accounts of disturbances at Brimpton, Baughurst, Sherborne and Dewhurst and suggested that 'more magistrates were needed in the area'. The Duke of Buckingham reiterated his son's fear that Avington would be attacked and that there was 'little prospect of military help'. He asked that his letter should be sent on to Lord Melbourne, the Home Secretary. Sir William Heathcote of Hursley Park reported on two consecutive days riots in his district and asked for more troops to be sent to Winchester where the militia's arms were 'at present only locked in an insecure store at the Gaol'. John Fleming of Stoneham Park proposed that the Duke stayed with him after the magistrates' meeting in Winchester to avoid returning home in the dark. Sloane Stanley of Paultons considered it 'unwise, owing to recent violent outrages', for the Duke to attend the meeting at all. The Duke replied that he would 'certainly be at Winchester' for the meeting.[23]

He acted promptly and decisively on the reports and requests made to him, arranging for reinforcements of troops for Winchester and Andover, ordering the locks of muskets and bayonets to be removed from militia depots, requesting detachments of the Buckinghamshire Yeomanry to be sent to Hampshire.

When he arrived in Hampshire the Duke was given details of the rioting and outrages that had occurred there: an iron foundry making agricultural machinery had been ransacked; much damage had been done at various country houses including Stratton Park and Grange Park, where William Bingham Baring, of the banking family, Member of Parliament for Callington, in attempting to remonstrate with a hostile crowd had been knocked to the ground and almost killed by a man wielding an iron bar; a fire had been lit beneath the Duke's pew in Stratfield Saye church; a mob had attacked the village of Itchen and been dispersed by the Duke of Buckingham's tenants headed by the village parson who had taken fifty prisoners; between three and four hundred people had marched on the Vyne near Sherborne St John, had been surrounded by troops near Baughurst and seventy-one ring-leaders had been detained and taken to Basingstoke.[24]

The Duke had no hesitation in taking strong action against the perpetrators of 'these outrages'. Urged by Lord Melbourne to 'take all measures to repress violence and outrage and to attend in person those parts of Hampshire where they are prevalent', he persuaded the magistrates 'to put themselves on horseback, each at the head of his own servants and retainers, grooms, huntsmen, game-keepers armed with horse-whips, pistols, fowling pieces and what they could get, and to attack . . . these mobs, disperse them, destroy them, and take and put into confinement those who could not escape'.[25]

Nearly seventy men who were arrested were eventually sentenced to transportation by a Special Commission sitting at Winchester; six were condemned to death and two of these were hanged. Reporting on the Commission to the King's Private Secretary, Sir Herbert Taylor, the Duke was to say that it 'had been successful . . . Few of the people convicted were agricultural labourers.'[26] He took pride in having quelled the disturbances in scarcely more than a fortnight.

On his return Wellington gave a large dinner at Apsley House for some fifty Tories, the 'most magnificent banquet' Croker had ever attended; and when the Duke of Gordon rose to propose his health – and expressed the hope that he would soon give them the word of command, 'As you were!' – he replied, 'No, not as you were, but *much better*.'[27] They must bide their time, however: the country was in a very dangerous state; he believed there existed 'a formidable conspiracy', the 'original focus' of which was at Paris. They must 'remain quiet' until they saw 'real cause to take an active part'. In the meantime it was quite clear that he still 'could not bear the idea of being in oppo-sition'. He admitted that he 'had supported the Government for nearly forty years and he did not know how to set about opposition'.[28] When he was pressed to be more active in opposing the new Government's policies, he flew off the handle. 'You draw false conclusions,' he snapped at Mrs Arbuthnot, 'either because I do not express myself clearly or because you do not read with attention what I write, or because you don't like what I write.'[29]

37 A Bogy to the Mob

1832

'I told you years ago that the people are rotten to
the Core.'

EARL GREY, an aristocrat as he described himself 'both by position
and by nature',[1] had no difficulty in forming a Government of many
political shades, with Lord Melbourne, whose views were unpredictable
but whom everyone liked, as Home Secretary, Lord Palmerston as
Foreign Secretary, Lord Brougham as Lord Chancellor, Lord Althorp
as Chancellor of the Exchequer, Lord Goderich as Secretary of War,
Lord Lansdowne as Lord President of the Council, and with seven
other peers filling all but two of the remaining places.

In the composition of his ministry, so Grey told Princess Lieven, he
was anxious to show 'that in these times of democracy and Jacobinism
it is possible to find real capacity in the high aristocracy – not that
I wish to exclude merit if I should meet with it in the commonalty;
but, given an equal merit, I admit that I should select the aristocrat, for that class is a guarantee for the security of the state and
throne'.[2]

Wellington found it far from easy to form an effective opposition to
this Cabinet which was bent on Parliamentary Reform. 'We are all
commanders,' he complained, 'and there are no troops. Nobody obeys
or ever listens to advice but myself. Then I am abused because things
do not go right.'[3] Peel was now of little help. 'One can't go on without
him,' he later told Lady Salisbury, 'but he is so vacillating and crochety
that there's no getting on with him. I did pretty well with him when
we were in office, but I can't manage him at all now. He is a wonderful
fellow – has a most correct judgement – talents almost equal to those
of Pitt, but he spoils all by timidity and indecision.'[4]

The Duke was still on occasions more than a little crochety himself.
The more inevitable Reform began to look, the more harm he saw in
it: it would 'destroy the country';[5] it spelt the 'downfall of the constitution' which had, after all, worked perfectly well, rotten boroughs

included, for centuries.[6] 'I am one of those,' he told Lord Mansfield, 'who think it very desirable to have no reform.'[7]

Nor was Reform his only worry. There were many other threats to his peace of mind: not least there was his wife. She was now seriously, he thought fatally, ill; and he felt constrained to spend much time by her bedside.

A family scandal had of late brought them closer together than they had ever been since their marriage. The son of the Duke's brother William, William Pole-Long-Wellesley, the young man who had been sent home from the Peninsula as a hopelessly inefficient aide-de-camp, had fled abroad with his wife to escape his creditors. In Italy, having spent all their available money, he seduced an English Guards officer's wife on the slopes of Vesuvius and, abandoning his own wife, had eloped with her. She had subsequently given birth to his child, while Mrs Long-Wellesley returned to England, sought the protection of two unmarried sisters, and, while endeavouring to get her own three young children, two boys and a girl, declared Wards in Chancery, had died soon after receiving an abusive letter from her husband who, hoping to get his hands on his eldest child's money, had demanded custody of them all.

When the Duke intervened in an effort to prevent his dreadful nephew obtaining custody of the children, William threatened to murder him, then issued a pamphlet and other publications accusing Wellington, and various other members of his own and his wife's family, of all manner of offences from incest to blasphemy. The children's unmarried aunts, he alleged, were lesbians; the governess employed by them for their niece was a prostitute; so was her sister. As for Wellington himself he was a notorious adulterer, having had affairs not only with Lady Charlotte Greville, Mrs Arbuthnot, and the mother of his godson, Arthur Freese, but also with the two American women, the former Marianne Patterson, now his sister-in-law, Marchioness Wellesley, and Marianne's sister, Louisa, who had married the Duke's former aide-de-camp, Colonel Felton Hervey.[8]

By the time these accusations appeared in a sensational publication, *The Rambler's Magazine or Frolicsome Companion*, the Duke had been appointed guardian of his nephew's three children; and William Pole-Long-Wellesley's appeal to have that appointment set aside was dismissed. The Duke had then asked his wife if she would look after the children; she had agreed 'with the greatest pleasure'; and had fulfilled her duties to the Duke's entire satisfaction. His gratitude and regard for the attentive care with which she studied the children's interests had evidently aroused late flickers of respect, even of affection.

Now that she was dying, her old friend Maria Edgeworth came to visit her in the ground-floor room where she lay on a sofa-bed surrounded by her husband's trophies.

> Always little and delicate-looking, she now looked like a miniature figure of herself in waxwork [Miss Edgeworth wrote]. And a little delicate death-like white hand stretched itself out to me before I could reach the couch, and when I got there I could not speak . . . But she raised herself and [noticing that her friend was looking at the gold shield, the Dresden services and other presentations made to the Duke which filled the room] exclaimed with weak-voiced enthusiasm, 'All tributes to merit! There's the value; all pure, no corruption ever suspected even. Even of the Duke of Marlborough that could not be said so truly.'
>
> The enthusiasm she feels for his character, for her own still youthful imagination of her hero, after all she has gone through is most touching.[9]

Miss Edgeworth trusted that she would not outlive the pleasure she felt at 'the Duke's returning to kindness'. 'I hope,' she said, 'she will not last too long and tire out that easily tired pity of his.'

She did not do so; and he sat beside her with unaccustomed patience. It was as though he were trying to make amends for the irritation he had in the past so often displayed in her presence, for the impression he had given to the world – as Greville said in the single reference he made to her in his voluminous memoirs – that he found her 'intolerable'.[10]

He knew she had always loved him with a kind of fearful awe; and his conscience was struck by her dreadful pallor now, the pathetic thinness of her hands as she stretched out towards his sleeve. Once she tentatively felt inside his sleeve to discover whether or not he was wearing an armlet she had given him in the early years of their marriage. 'She found it, as she would have found it any time these twenty years, had she cared to look for it,' the Duke said later. It was strange, he thought, that two people could live together for so long and 'only understand one another at the end'.[11] She died on 24 April 1831.

Unaware of her death, Maria Edgeworth returned to Apsley House six days later and was admitted by the porter at the gate into the 'great, silent hall' where the Duchess's maid, dressed in black, told her, 'Her Grace died on Saturday.'

'Was the Duke in town?'

'Yes, Ma'am, beside her.'

Not a word more, but I was glad to have that certain. Lord Charles had arrived in time; not Lord Douro . . . The poor maid could hardly speak. She went in and brought me a lock of her mistress's hair, silver gray, all but a few light brown that just recalled the beautiful Kitty Pakenham.[12]

By the time of the Duchess's death Grey's Government had introduced into the House of Commons another Reform Bill which – proposing to disenfranchise some sixty boroughs and provide seats in Parliament for over forty towns – had been passed on its second reading at three o'clock in the morning by a majority of one. The King had subsequently been persuaded to dissolve Parliament as a prelude to a General Election by which, it was hoped, the reformers would be provided with an unquestionable majority.

The dissolution and imminence of a General Election had provoked fresh riots in London. A mob, surging down Piccadilly, demanded that the windows of houses along their route should be illuminated. Those at Apsley House remained in darkness. Stones were hurled at the plate-glass panes and men set about tearing up the railings until dispersed down Park Lane by a servant firing a blunderbuss over their heads from the roof. 'They certainly intended to destroy the House,' Wellington told Mrs Arbuthnot, 'and did not care one Pin for the Poor Duchess being dead in the house.' He intended to seek damages from the parish, since no measures had been taken to prevent the outrage.[13]

'My opinion,' the Duke continued not long after this attack on his house, 'is that we are on the Eve of a great Change . . . Matters appear to be going on as badly as possible. It may be relied upon that we shall have a Revolution. I have never doubted the Inclination and disposition of the Lower Orders of the People. I told you years ago that the people are rotten to the Core. You will find that is true . . . They are not bloodthirsty, but they are desirous of plunder . . . I told you likewise that the Upper Orders and the Gentry were not prepared or in a State to resist the attack upon Property which would be made.'[14] 'It had been a dangerous experiment to educate the Lower Orders,' he told Charles Arbuthnot. 'They now say why should they not associate with us.' 'They want to resort to our private houses, our entertainments; have the run of our kitchens and dance with our wives and daughters . . . They would shortly afterwards discover that they are better qualified to be

Legislators Ministers Generals Holders of Large Properties than we are.'[15]

'Affairs are in a terrible state,' he wrote in a letter to Lord Lauderdale. 'I confess that I consider the revolution is attained.'[16] To Peel he wrote in similar gloomy terms: 'Publick affairs are now in a sad state and I don't see how the country can escape the ruin threatened by the monstrous combination of the King, the Whigs, the radicals, the dissenters and the mob against the bulk of the property, the Church and all the great establishments and institutions.'[17]

In September 1831, after a session lasting three months, the House of Commons passed the Bill; and as the Lords prepared to reject it, London was plagued by an outbreak of cholera which was to take 4,000 lives and cause the Duke further unease. 'If three or four *Notables* were to leave London for fear of it,' he said, 'they would be followed by three or four thousand, and then this country would be plunged into greater confusion than had been known for hundreds of years.'[18] As it was, when the Lords threw out the Bill after five days of debate, angry meetings were held all over the country and riots broke out in several towns, most violently in Nottingham, Derby, Birmingham, Exeter and Bristol. In London, an effigy of the Duke was burned at Tyburn and Apsley House was again attacked, this time in daylight, by a mob which, for almost an hour, hurled stones and rubbish through the windows, almost hitting the Duke as he wrote with provocative unconcern at his table, and tearing a strip out of a picture hanging on the wall behind him, a portrait by Sir David Wilkie of Lady Lyndhurst, the wife of the man who had been Lord Chancellor in his Cabinet, a beautiful woman whom the Duke of Cumberland had attempted to rape.[19] When the police at last arrived at Apsley House, the mob ran off into the Park to do what damage they could to Richard Westmacott's bronze twenty-foot-high statue of Achilles which, cast from captured French guns, had been erected by 'the women of England to Arthur Duke of Wellington and his brave companions in arms'.*[20]

---

* This statue, the first nude statue to be erected in a public place in England, provoked much ribald comment. It was derived from one of the statues then known as the horse-tamers on the Monte Cavallo in Rome and, with the addition of shield and dagger, transformed into a muscularly heroic figure of Achilles. On 8 August 1822, soon after its erection, a print by George Cruikshank entitled *Making Decent!!* was published depicting the comparatively puny figure of William Wilberforce, the philanthropist, reaching up between Achilles's legs to hold his top hat over the statue's fig leaf (British Museum *Catalogue of Political and Personal Satires*, x, 14383).

Whether or not to provide the statue with a fig leaf had been the subject of debate. Lady Holland pretended to believe that the question had been put to the female subscribers who voted by a majority in favour of it. 'The names of the *minority*,' she said,

As he had done during earlier disturbances, the Duke contrived to appear indifferent to his unpopularity and danger. 'I was hooted as usual on my way to the House,' he told Mrs Arbuthnot. 'But that is nothing more than what is conformable to the usual course.'[21] As also before, however, he had loaded pistols on the seat beside him in his carriage and there was an armed servant on the box next to Turnham, his fat coachman, whose 'pride of place and contempt for the rabble was sublime'.[22] He also carried with him an umbrella with a sharp steel spike. He received a letter from a man who threatened to shoot him the next time he appeared in Palace Yard.[23] On going down into Kent where, so he was warned, a mob intended to waylay his carriage on a lonely part of the road between Sandwich and the Deal turnpike, he was escorted by a guard armed with pistols and hunting whips.[24] 'I expect,' he said complacently, 'that those who will attack me on the road will come rather the worse out of the contest should there be one.'[25]

Until order was restored, there could be no question of a compromise over Reform. But he had once answered the question what was the best test of a great general by answering, 'To know when to retreat and to dare to do it.' And he recognized that once the country was quiet again, the time would have come to make a political retreat. After all, the King had now 'pronounced himself for Reform, and it would not be easy to govern in his name without Reform', though the Duke added the expected proviso, 'the more gentle and more gradual the reform, the better'.[26]

This proviso was to guide him in the coming months. When pressed to do so, he declined to urge the King to refuse to create sufficient peers to ensure the passage of the Reform Bill through the House of Lords. Nor would he consider a proposition that he should advise the King to form a Tory Government uncompromisingly opposed to the Bill, although he did allow him to know that if his Majesty wanted to escape from his subservience to the Whigs he would help him to do so; and he went so far as to declare, 'I am perfectly ready to do whatever his Majesty may command me.'[27]

When he spoke against the Bill in the House of Lords, his words were 'fair and gentlemanlike'. His considered opinion was that some degree of Reform was now inevitable and that 'the efforts of all ought

---

'have not transpired' (Marie F. Busco, 'The "Achilles" in Hyde Park', *Burlington Magazine*, 130, 1988, 922). It seems, in fact, that it was the men on the statue committee who had decided to advise Westmacott not to feel bound by the example of his Roman inspiration (Linda Colley, *Britons: Forging the Nation*, 258).

to be directed to render that Bill as little noxious as possible'.[28]

In the event the King refused Grey's request for the creation of new peers. The Prime Minister resigned; the King sent for Lord Lyndhurst; and Lyndhurst sought advice from Wellington and Peel.

These three men met at Apsley House to discuss the crisis. Also there was John Wilson Croker, the influential Tory recently retired from the lucrative appointment of Secretary of the Admiralty, whom Lyndhurst insisted must come into the Cabinet. Croker asked who was to be Prime Minister. Lyndhurst indicated Peel; but Peel, having changed his mind over Roman Catholic relief, felt that he could not make a similar volte-face over Reform, however moderate a Tory Reform Bill might be. Croker also declined to join a Government committed to a measure which he could not in his conscience approve and suggested the Earl of Harrowby, Canning's Lord President of the Council, for the office of Prime Minister. But Wellington did not think Harrowby could command sufficient support; and, in any event, he declined the offer when it was made to him. So did the Speaker. 'Well,' said Wellington, 'we are in a fine scrape, and I really do not see how we are to get out of it.'[29] Indeed, the only solution he could propose was that he should become Prime Minister himself and take on the responsibility of extricating the King 'from the difficulty in which he was placed'.[30]

Yet Wellington, in interview after interview, failed to find Tories willing to serve under him in a Government committed to the measures he proposed. He had a possible Chancellor of the Exchequer in the financier Alexander Baring, and two other potential ministers among his old army friends, Sir George Murray, who had succeeded Huskisson as Secretary of State for War in 1828, and Sir Henry Hardinge. But other suitable colleagues proved impossible to find, while some of those whom he approached proved almost as exhausting as the Speaker who had spent three hours in explaining why he could not make an immediate decision, leaving Lord Lyndhurst to express the succinct opinion upon his departure that he was 'a damned tiresome old bitch'.[31]

After almost a week of such tedious conversations, the Duke was forced to conclude that his efforts to help the King were all in vain: he could not persuade sufficient Tories to agree that a moderate measure of Reform was necessary to the preservation of public order. In any case he was more at ease in command than in efforts at persuasion, and confessed that he wished he had never undertaken so thankless and so impossible a task; all he had contrived to do was to make himself as unpopular as he had ever been. The only service he could now perform for the King was to persuade his colleagues to refrain from further opposition to the Reform Bill which, Grey having returned to office, became law on 7 June 1832.

The Duke remained a bogy to the mob. Wherever he went in London he was as likely to be hooted as cheered, and even attacked. Hearing rumours that he was in danger of assassination, his niece, Priscilla Burghersh, suggested that he should go to Parliament in her inconspicuous carriage. He brushed the proposal aside. 'I could no more go to the House of Lords in your Carriage after such Reports than I could crawl [there on] all fours.'[32]

'We are governed by the mob and its organ – a licentious press,' he observed, a press typified by the outpourings of the radical breeches-maker Francis Place, who, while organizing agitations that threatened civil war, had drawn up a placard with the words, 'Go for Gold and stop the Duke', which had encouraged a partial run on the Bank of England.* 'Things will be worse,' the Duke said, 'before they get better.'[33]

On 18 June, Waterloo Day, the Duke was threatened by a large mob as he rode back with his groom to Piccadilly from the City, where he had been sitting to the medallist Benedetto Pistrucci at his studio in the Mint. A magistrate offered him protection but the Duke replied, 'You can do nothing. The only thing you can help me in is to tell me exactly the road I am to take to get to Lincoln's Inn; for the greater danger would be in my missing my way and having to turn back on the mob.'

He was also offered help by two Chelsea pensioners whom he asked to march along beside his horse and face away from him whenever he was halted by the press of people. In addition two policemen came up

* The Duke had always underrated the power of the press which he held in the utmost contempt, as he did public opinion. 'The Duke has nothing to say to the newspapers,' he wrote in 1833 to a journalist who had offered to write in support of the Tories, 'and he is desirous of avoiding to have any communication of any description with them' (*Wellington, Political Correspondence*, i, *1833 – November 1834*, ed. John Brooke and Julia Gandy, 6).

'I have been abused, vilified, slandered since I was a boy,' he told Croker in 1838, 'and I don't believe that there is a living creature who thinks the worse of me for all the horrible crimes of which I have been accused, and which to this moment remain unanswered. I would much prefer to get rid of the rheumatism in my shoulder and neck than I would of all the libels of all the Jacobins, Republicans, Bonapartists, Radicals, Reformers and Whigs in all her Majesty's dominions, including her ancient Kingdom of France and her colonies in N. America' (*The Croker Papers*, ii, 330).

to protect him and were placed at his horse's head, while the driver of a tilbury brought up the rear of the beleaguered procession and much pleased the Duke by never afterwards looking to him for any favours.

Having survived an attempt to drag him from his horse in Fenchurch Street, a hail of stones in Holborn, and the appearance of a cart piled high with sacks of coal – which drew from him the wry observation, 'Hillo! Here's the Artillery coming up; we must look out'[34] – the Duke arrived at the gate of Lincoln's Inn still followed by a large and threatening crowd. He asked if there were any way out of the Inn at the other end. Told there was, he said, 'Then be so good as to shut *this* gate.' But he was separated from his pursuers for a short time only. When he emerged into Lincoln's Inn Fields, he was pursued by the mob again. A man on the steps of No. 41 shouted out, 'Waterloo! Waterloo!', a cry which seems to have imposed a brief pause for thought upon the crowd.

Lord St Leonards, the future Lord Chancellor, who had been in his chambers in Lincoln's Inn that day and joined those helping to guard the Duke, described him as being 'pale, with a severe countenance, and immovable on his saddle, looking straight before him. A butcher was bawling lustily against the Duke, when a young gentleman, a solicitor, seized him by the collar with one hand and knocked him down with the other; and the mob seemed rather amused by it.'

As we proceeded [St Leonards' account continued] the noise of the mob attracted the workmen in the shops and manufactories, particularly in Long Acre, where the upper windows were quickly opened by workmen who, with their paper caps, rushed to join the people; but nowhere was any personal violence offered to the Duke, and the respectable portions of the crowd would promptly have crushed any attempt at violence.

As their quarry, having passed along the Strand and the Mall, trotted up Constitution Hill, the mob rushed across the Park to confront him and hoot at him as he entered the gateway of Apsley House but no one ventured to attack him. He turned in his saddle by the entrance to the house and, recalling where he had been and what he had done on that day seventeen years before, he observed in his abrupt way, 'An odd day to choose. Good morning.'[35]

*

'I think I have got the better of the mobs in London by walking about the town very quietly, notwithstanding their insults and outrages,' the Duke endeavoured to persuade himself. 'It is certain that the better class are ashamed of them, and take pains upon all occasions to testify every mark of respect for me.'[36] Yet he could not but feel concerned that, as he had said more than once, the country was on the verge of eruption into another civil war. England, so he was to tell Lady Salisbury, was 'doomed to revolution'.[37] The times were 'much more similar to those of Charles I' than people supposed. 'God knows,' he said, 'what will happen to the world.'[38] He could not suppose its salvation lay with Parliament: the Lords were almost an irrelevance now and he did not trouble to attend with any regularity. As for the Commons, he decided after looking into the Chamber one day that he had never seen 'so many shocking bad hats' in his life.*[39]

---

* He had expressed a different opinion about the Lower House in conversation with Thomas Creevey in 1818: 'Nobody cares a damn for the House of Lords; the House of Commons is everything in England' (*The Creevey Papers*, 287).

38   Oxford University and Apsley House

1832 – 4

'If I could be spoilt by this sort of thing, they
would spoil me here.'

THE DUKE sometimes thought, now that he was in his mid-sixties, that he would like to live as a private country gentleman, reading, entertaining and being entertained, talking to pretty women about his campaigns in the past, undertaking further improvements at Stratfield Saye where central heating was installed under his watchful eye, riding to hounds without discontented villagers gazing upon him sullenly and, as they sometimes did, raising their voices against him. He even thought how pleasant it would be to quit altogether this 'unfortunate and unhappy country', as he advised Harriet Arbuthnot to do.[1] But then he was, after all, a public figure with public duties to perform and public responsibilities to fulfil. In the early days of his opposition to the Reform Bill he had declared that he would never again enter the House of Lords should it become law. But his sense of duty was too strong for that declaration to be taken seriously; and when, after the Bill had become law, Croker wrote to tell him that he himself would not stand for Parliament again, the Duke replied, 'I am very sorry that you do not intend again to serve in Parlt. I cannot conceive for what reason.'[2]

As for himself, he considered that the Duke of Wellington – referring to himself in the third person as though he saw the great statesman and soldier as a man apart – could not abandon the role for which he had been cast. So long as he was needed he must serve his King and country as only he could. 'I am the Duke of Wellington,' he told Croker, '*and, bon gré, mal gré*, must do as the Duke of Wellington doth.'[3]

And, after all, there were still many compensations in being the Duke of Wellington, and many agreeable functions for him to perform as a public figure. His duties as Lord Warden of the Cinque Ports were not unduly time-consuming, or unpleasant, while his visits to Walmer Castle were always welcome. He found perfectly congenial his responsibilities as a Governor of Charterhouse which he continued to believe was 'the best school of them all', as he had emphatically assured Lady Shelley.[4] He was pleased to be Master of the Elder Brethren of Trinity House, the lighthouse authority for the coasts of England and Wales; and he was even more pleased when, after the death of Lord Grenville in 1834, he was invited to succeed him as Chancellor of the University of Oxford, an honour he at first felt inclined to refuse since, as he confessed, he had 'not received a university education . . . and knew no more of Latin and Greek than an Eton boy in the Remove'.[5]

Although the Dean and canons of Christ Church decided 'to take no part as a Body in the Election' of a man who had removed both his sons from their care, the Duke was warmly welcomed by the Fellows of the other colleges at Oxford and by the undergraduates, about a hundred of whom rode out to escort his britska into the town. 'I could not make the Duke take off his hat to anyone,' wrote Croker who was in the carriage with him, 'not even the ladies; he kept saluting like a soldier. I, however, made him show himself occasionally and take notice here and there; but he is a sad hand at popularity hunting.'[6]

He appeared equally unmoved by the acclamation that greeted him in the Sheldonian Theatre where the Tory scholars were only too ready to overlook the inadequacies of his pronunciation of Latin in their pleasure at seeing him arrayed in the long, trailing robe of his office, its heavy brocade silk trimmed with gold lace.* Stumbling over some Latin words, he turned for help to the Vice-Chancellor, then, armed with his advice, he 'went at it with a plunge', in the words of Francis Buckland, the naturalist and son of a Canon of Christ Church. 'The shouts of the undergrads were never louder or more merry.'[7]

The Duke's 'false quantities were treated very indulgently', a Doctor of Divinity confirmed:

---

* This robe, made for him by William Moore of Old Bond Street, cost £157 10s. On the back of the bill for it the Duke wrote, 'Tell Mr Moore that if he charges me such a price for a Chancellor's Robe he shall be paid. But he and I part from this time forward. The price is more than double nay nearly three times what it ought to be' (Wellington College Archives).

The Duke's face had certainly a much kinder expression about it than I had expected to see. I should say that . . . he was the most respectable looking old gentleman I ever saw – not to mention any loftier qualities. He has a face that would suit any situation and character. In lawn sleeves, I have no doubt, he would look the most episcopal person on the Bench.

He was evidently sometimes much affected by the enthusiastic cheering he met with, if one can gather anything by a certain tremulous motion in the mouth.[8]

His speech is believed to have been written for him by Philip Bliss, the Registrar, and edited by his physician who, he supposed, was 'most likely, from his prescriptions, to know Latin'. It 'answered very well', he thought. 'I believe it was a very good speech.' But he had, as he confessed, little idea what it was all about.[9]

He did, however, well understand the verses which won the Newdigate Prize and, declaimed by the winner, Joseph Arnould of Wadham, contained the lines

> And the stern soul the world could scarce subdue
> Bowed to thy Genius, Chief of Waterloo

At these words the Fellows and their guests rose from the crowded benches to cheer their heroic Chancellor, stamping their feet, waving handkerchiefs and their black caps, while he 'as usual seemed quite unconcerned at the applause'.[10]

The enthusiasm was such that Croker, so he reported to his wife, had never witnessed the like:

Some people appeared to me to go out of their senses – literally to go mad. The whole assembly started up, and the ladies and the grave semicircle of doctors became as much excited as the boys in the gallery and the men in the pit. Such peals of shouts I never heard; such waving of hats, handkerchiefs, and caps, I never saw; such extravagant clapping and stamping, so that at last the air became clouded with dust. During all this the Duke sat like a statue.[11]

After sitting for a time quite impassively, he raised his own black velvet cap with its gold tassel in acknowledgement of the acclamation, and indicated to the poet that he should proceed with his reading, which he attempted to do as the cheering broke out once more.

Lady Salisbury said that she had never heard such cheering as there was that day in Oxford:

The noise was positively outstanding and continued fully quarter of an hour. As to the under-graduates and the occupants of the arena, they scarcely knew how to give vent to their feelings; they roared, they screamed, they waved hats and handkerchiefs, they actually jumped and danced with delight. It was quite overcoming.[12]

The Duke himself told Lady Salisbury afterwards that 'he had never seen anything like it'; and he said to her, 'If I could be spoilt by this sort of thing, they would spoil me here.' 'I think,' she commented, 'he feels it deeply.'[13]

His ceremonial duties as Chancellor suited the Duke well; but the responsibilities of another of his ancient offices, that of Constable of the Tower, caused him much concern: the Yeoman Warders were corrupt; the elderly medical officer declined to attend to his patients or even to live on the premises; the moat was used as a rubbish pit and sewer and when the Duke ordered it to be cleared and cleaned the attendant stench was so poisonous that people living nearby contended that the work was responsible for another outbreak of cholera.[14]

He had other worries too: it transpired that his wife had died in debt to the tune of no less than £10,000. He had no idea where the money had gone, but presumed much of it must have been given to her sister, Elizabeth Stewart, whose husband's family bank in Dublin had collapsed. In her lifetime he had questioned his wife closely about the money that seemed to slip through her hands so easily. She had denied that she had given large sums away to her family; but now he was not so sure that she had been telling him the truth. The doubt in his mind fretted him. He took the trouble to go through her accounts again and on discovering that she had been generous to his family as well as her own, he composed a memorandum, in fairness to her memory, setting out the facts as he had discovered them to be.[15]

He was a rich man and could afford to be generous.* When the prize money was distributed after Waterloo – and privates were given £2 10s each, sergeants £9, subalterns £33 and Generals £1,250 – he felt able to return £40,000 of his own £60,000 share to the Treasury. When General Alava was exiled from Spain, the Duke not only provided him with a house on the Stratfield Saye estate, but took him to Messrs Coutts and Company in the Strand and introduced him to one of the

---

* As Prime Minister the Duke had drawn a salary of £4,022 and an annual 'pension' of £13,168. This is the equivalent of about £700,000 today, a remuneration almost ten times as much as that of the present Prime Minister.

partners with the words, 'This is my friend; and as long as I have any money at your house, let him have it to any amount that he thinks proper to draw for.'[16] Since then he had lent money to his sister Anne's husband, Culling Charles Smith, who had been released from the debt when it transpired that he was threatened with bankruptcy. He had also lent to the Rev, Samuel Briscall, the curate at Stratfield Saye, who had died before repaying him.[17]

Rich as the Duke was, his enormous outgoings were a worry to him. At Stratfield Saye – where he had stopped preserving game after one of his gamekeepers had been shot and killed by a poacher – he had spent tens of thousands of pounds upon improvements, devoting all the rents from the farms on the estate to this purpose, and he laid out immense sums upon entertaining guests as well as upon maintaining the household. Every day in the 1820s over forty servants, including fourteen stable men and grooms and nine maidservants, sat down to dinner in the Stewards' Room or the Servants' Hall.[18] His steward in Hampshire was unreliable; and his estates in Spain were ill run and far less profitable than they had once been: his income from them, once reckoned to be worth £8,000, was now reduced to £800. At Apsley House his bills were quite as formidable as they were at Stratfield Saye. The cooks' expenses alone were the equivalent in today's money of about £6,000 a week; while enormous sums had been and were still being laid out on repairs and alterations to the structure. 'The Duke's house will be magnificent,' Mrs Arbuthnot had recorded in her journal after a visit to it in November 1828. 'He has quarrelled with the architect, Mr Wyatt, & begs I will manage it all with him. The truth is he is too busy to pay proper attention to such a work.'

Fifteen months later she thought the house improved beyond measure – having herself 'made the drawings for the doors and windows which Mr Wyatt had proposed in a shape & design that was frightful' – even though the yellow damask which the Duke insisted upon for the gallery was 'just the very worst colour he can have for pictures & will kill the effect of the gilding'.

When the Duke received the bill, he was appalled. It was three times over the estimate. He 'abused Wyatt furiously', so he told Mrs Arbuthnot, '& told him it sh^d be the last conversation he w^d ever have with him'.*[19] By 1831 the Duke had spent about £64,000 on improvements to the house.[20]

---

* Four years later, however, Wyatt felt able to write to the Duke asking him to re-commend his name as one of the architects to be employed upon the reconstruction of the Houses of Parliament after the disastrous fire of October 1834 (*Wellington: Political Correspondence, i, 1833 – November 1834*, ed. John Brooke and Julia Gandy, 707).

There was another terrible quarrel between the Duke and Wyatt towards the end of 1840 when the Duke accused Wyatt's clerk of the works of breaking open a box belonging to a groom and stealing the man's clothes. The Duke threatened to stop all work at Apsley House until he could be certain that 'Honest Men, and not a gang of thieves would be introduced into his house'. He would have to employ 'another Artist' in the business. 'I beg you therefore to send me in the bills for the works lately done,' a letter dated 'Decr 12 at night 1840' ended. 'They shall be liquidated forthwith, & I wish you a good morning. Yr. most obedt. Servt. Wellington.'[21]

Wyatt was not finally dismissed, however, until 1842; and, even then, there was not a final rift between the two men: in 1844 Wyatt wrote to thank the Duke for having nominated him to carry out an addition to the Duke of York's Column.[22]

As well as constantly finding fault with Wyatt, the Duke was annoyed that his son Douro, to whom he made a handsome allowance, should make himself so thoughtlessly at home at Apsley House and Stratfield Saye, sending his horses to the stables and having rooms made ready for him, without bothering to pay his respects to his father. The young man, twenty-five in 1832, was as much a source of anxiety to his father as he had ever been. Having fallen in love with Dr Hume's daughter, Elizabeth, at the age of fourteen, he now declared he wanted to marry her. The Duke granted that she was a pleasant, pretty girl; but he felt bound to warn his son that it was not a suitable match, sensibly not forbidding it but suggesting that he waited a bit. Thomas Creevey told Elizabeth Ord what he heard about this:

> I never saw Lord Douro before . . . Altogether he is very homely in his air. Do you know he is engaged to be married to a daughter of Hume, the Duke's doctor? It seems she had stayed a good deal with the Duchess which has led to the youth proposing to her. When it was told to the Duke, all he said was – 'Ah! rather young, Douro, are you not – to be married? Suppose you stay till the year is out, and then, if it's all in the same mind, it's all very well.'[23]

'The truth is that he is incorrigible,' the Duke complained to Mrs Arbuthnot, a few months later. 'His manner when I spoke to him and his shuffling excuses provoked me, because it put me in Mind of his Mother when she was in a difficulty . . . First he is afraid of me and dislikes to be in the House with me. Secondly he inherits His Mother's lightness of character.'[24]

Thomas Raikes gave an example of the kind of altercation that disrupted the relationship between the two men after Douro had come down from Oxford and joined the Army. Douro's regiment, the 60th Rifles, was stationed at Dover and the officers rode over to Walmer to pay their respects to the Duke. Supposing that, as the Duke's son, such a courtesy would not be expected of him, Douro did not accompany them. 'Shortly after came an invitation from his Grace to dinner, including all the officers, excepting *Lord Douro*. The major who received the note knew not how to act, and showed it to Lord Douro' who, thinking there must have been some mistake, then went to see his father. 'I make no distinctions in the service,' the Duke said to him. 'Those gentlemen who paid me the compliment of a visit I invited to dinner. You were not of their number, and so I omitted you from the invitation.'[25]

Lord Charles was treated more indulgently. He, too, joined the Army and, while serving abroad, was sent home with important dispatches. He arrived a fortnight later than expected. His father, presuming he had 'loitered amid the amusements of Paris, reprimanded him and for some days would not speak to him' until he heard that Charles had been delayed at Marseilles by quarantine. It was never the Duke's practice to apologize; but the next time he saw his son he said to him, in Sir William Fraser's account, 'Charles, You would like to hunt this winter would you not?'

'I have no horses, Sir.'

'I have sent £1,000 to your bankers. You can buy some.'[26]*

---

* Lord Charles became a major-general, his brother, Lord Douro, the second Duke, a lieutenant-general. All the Dukes of Wellington since have served in the Army, the third, fourth and fifth Dukes in the Grenadier Guards, the sixth Duke, who was killed at the age of twenty-one at Salerno in 1943, in the Duke of Wellington's Regiment and the Commandos. This Duke's uncle, writer, editor and practising architect, who inherited the title on his nephew's death and was for several years Surveyor of the King's Works of Art, gave Apsley House and most of its contents to the nation in 1947. Apsley House is now administered by the Victoria and Albert Museum as the Wellington Museum. The present Duke, the seventh Duke's son, formerly Lieutenant-Colonel commanding the Royal Horse Guards and subsequently commander of the RAC 1st (Br.) Corps, has opened Stratfield Saye to the public together with that part of the estate known as Wellington Country Park.

39 Lady Friends

1834

'Oh, *how* I *love* you! *How* I *love* you!'

SOON AFTER the 'gratifying day' of his installation as Chancellor at Oxford, the Duke was staying at Hatfield House when, on 2 August 1834, he received a letter which so distressed him that he crumpled it up and dropped it on the floor, then threw himself down 'in the greatest agitation' upon a sofa from which he rose to pace about the room 'almost sobbing'.[1] Harriet Arbuthnot had died of cholera. He had lost not only a woman of whom he was deeply fond but a home where he felt more completely at ease than he did in any other.

'It is a dreadful loss to him,' Lady Salisbury commented; 'for whether there is any foundation or not in the stories usually believed about the early part of their liaison she was certainly now become to him no more than a tried and valued friend to whom he was sincerely attached. Her house was his home; and with all his glory and greatness, he *never had a home*! His nature is domestic and as he advances in years some female society and some fireside to which he can always resort become necessary to him.[2]

At Woodford Lodge in Northamptonshire and at the Arbuthnots' London house in Carlton Gardens he had always been, and known himself to be, a welcome guest. He could talk freely there to a responsive and understanding listener and draw comfort in the affection of a woman of the kind of managing temperament he liked, his 'Tyranna' to whom it pleased them both to imagine he was in thrall.

As soon as he had recovered his composure he went to see the desolate widower to share his grief with him and to do what he could to comfort him. The next day Arbuthnot wrote to thank him for coming: 'I am very glad you came to me instead of writing to propose it; for had you, I must have said no. There was no one I so much dreaded seeing for the first time – She had no friend to whom she was so much attached as She was to you . . . I believe I may say that you never had such a friend before & you will never have such a one again. As for myself I . . . feel the conviction that life to me is from this day a blank.'[3]

The Duke suggested that they now share a house together. The offer was accepted; and Charles Arbuthnot lived at Apsley House for the rest of his life.*

There was never to be another confidante with whom the Duke was to feel so completely at ease as he had done with Harriet Arbuthnot, although some time after her death he asked Lady Wilton, daughter of the twelfth Earl of Derby, and wife of the second Earl of Wilton, to consider herself as his 'best friend'.[4] There were women enough who would have liked to become a new 'Tyranna' or the second Duchess of Wellington. One of the most persistent of these was the Hon. Mary Anne Jervis, daughter of the second Viscount St Vincent, a fey, flirtatious girl over forty years younger than himself, with a fine singing voice, known as 'The Syren'. But the woman who came closest to replacing Mrs Arbuthnot as a confidante was the Countess of Salisbury, only child and heiress of the rich Bamber Gascoyne, Member of Parliament for Liverpool, and wife of the second Marquess of Salisbury. A pleasant, intelligent, good-natured woman, who was to give birth uncomplainingly to eleven children before dying at the age of thirty-seven, Lady Salisbury was far from beautiful. While staying at Hatfield, Princess Lieven drew a characteristically tart portrait of her:

> We are a large party – there are diplomats, Ministers, pretty women, jealous husbands, perfumed dandies, long dark corridors, chapels, towers, bats in the bed curtains – everything you need for a romance, or, at any rate, for an affair. The owner of the place has the largest house, the largest chin, and the smallest stature you could possibly imagine. His wife has plenty of money, big languishing eyes, and big teeth. She is lucky enough to fancy she is beautiful, and unlucky enough not to be. She is not without intelligence, but entirely without charm.[5]

The Duke, however, did find her charming. She recorded with pride in her journal how he had called her his friend, 'twice over with

---

* While he was still living at Woodford the Duke visited him there as often as he could. 'Nothing can exceed his good nature and kindness in going to Woodford when every moment is precious to him,' Lady Salisbury commented. 'Besides nothing can be more irksome to a man of his active mind than a visit to the solitary, broken-hearted Mr Arbuthnot who has lost all energy and interest in everything' (Hatfield House Papers, Lady Salisbury's diary).

emphasis' and used other 'kind expressions which would never be erased from [her] remembrance'. 'He expressed a confidence in me which I feel with a gratitude and pleasure I cannot express. "With you," he said, "I think aloud."'[6] He relished his frequent visits to Hatfield, asking only that the boring Duke of Gloucester and the disreputable Duke of Cumberland should not also be of the party. He raised no objection, however, when the Duchess of Gloucester was a guest in the house for the christening of Lady Salisbury's third son, Robert, the future Prime Minister, for whom he and she were both godparents.

A few months before Harriet Arbuthnot's death, the Duke had received a letter from one Anna Maria Jenkins. It was an exhortatory missive concerning the welfare of his soul. Although he might well have made an exception in this case, the Duke had followed his usual practice and acknowledged the letter. He had done so in a hurry, miswriting a word, dropping two blots of ink on the paper, and dating it 1833 instead of 1834, an understandable mistake since it was January. But Miss Jenkins had taken the error and the blots as indications of agitation if not spiritual turmoil; and, in pursuit of the Duke's soul, she had called at Apsley House carrying a Bible which she had left for his guidance with several passages marked in pencil, including: 'Verily, verily, I say unto thee. Except a man be born again, he cannot see the Kingdom of God.'

The Duke had declined to acknowledge the gift; but shortly after Mrs Arbuthnot's death, he wrote to thank the donor for it, addressing her as Mrs Jenkins. She replied immediately to say that she was not married and, having discussed the matter with a friend, 'a perfect woman of the world', she had decided it would be in order to invite the Duke to call upon her at her lodgings in Charlotte Street. Several weeks passed. It seemed that the Duke would venture no further into this ambiguous relationship; but in the middle of November he wrote to Miss Jenkins again to say that he would, indeed, call upon her, making it clear, however, that he was not in the habit of visiting young ladies with whom he was not acquainted.

On presenting himself at Charlotte Street, the Duke was pleasantly surprised to find that Miss Jenkins had not at all the appearance of the pious spinster her correspondence might well have led him to expect. She was, in fact, an extremely attractive young woman.

It transpired that she was only twenty years old, the orphaned daughter of parents who had left her but moderately provided for. She lived at Charlotte Street with a companion, a Mrs Lachlan; she played the harp; she had been granted a glimpse of her mission in life when, the year before, she had visited a murderer in prison and had persuaded him to repent of his sins before he was taken to the gallows. She had prayed to God to give her some sign of the next mission He intended for her. 'Greater things than these,' she had been told. So she had written to the Duke, and now he had appeared before her, with his 'beautiful silver head', such a head as she had always admired from her childhood. She trusted that the Lord would, as Mrs Lachlan hoped He would, 'send His arrow into the Duke's soul'. She had prayed that He would guide her 'every moment of the time' she was with the Duke, 'directing even my dress': the divine choice had evidently fallen upon an old dark green merino gown.

'This,' she said as she came down the stairs, 'is very kind of your Grace.' He offered her his hand without replying; she indicated two chairs on either side of the fireplace; then, no sooner had she sat down, than she jumped to her feet, exclaiming, 'I'll show you my *Treasure*.' This turned out to be a large Bible which she placed on the table between them and from which, as she raised a hand in a gesture requiring silence and attention, she read verses from the Gospel according to St John, enjoining him to submit to being born again, to undergo 'a birth into righteousness'.

According to her own account, written down in detail in her journal, the Duke now took her hand again in his and, with the greatest fervency, repeated the words, 'Oh, *how* I *love* you! *How* I *love* you!' What drove him to this declaration, she asked him; and he replied with an admission well calculated to please her, 'God Almighty.'

When he left her, he promised to call again and asked her to write to him in the meantime. She said that she would do so, but, after making several attempts at the composition of a suitable letter, she decided that the correspondence was 'not the will of God'; and the Duke, by then deeply preoccupied with political affairs, did not go to see her again just yet. When he found time to do so, however, he seemed to be as strongly drawn to her as ever. He told her that he was on his way to the King, to which intelligence she replied that she wished it had been to the King of Kings. Evidently not deterred by this deflating observation, the Duke repeated protestations of his regard for her. 'This must be for life,' he said more than once. 'Do you feel sufficiently for me to be with me a whole life?' Taking this to be a proposal of marriage, Miss Jenkins replied, 'If it be the will of God.'

The Duke then left her and when he returned he was irritated to find that she had locked the door against him. She explained that she had wanted to pray without interruption. But why had she not written to him? She had been guided by God not to do so.

It appears that the Duke was growing rather tired of such protestations; and when she wrote to him to say that it would be better if he did not call again, that, for religious reasons, their friendship should remain purely spiritual, he replied – as usual by return – to say that, since she could not agree to his proposal, it would, indeed, be better for them to part.

This brought forth a cascade of indignation: how could he treat her like this? How could he so degrade himself and her? If a prince should ask for her hand she would bestow upon him as much honour by accepting him as he would in proposing to her. The Duke replied soothingly, apologetically: there was nobody more strongly impressed than he was with 'veneration for [her] Virtues, attainments, and Sentiments'. But nothing more was said about marriage or about any other relationship at which the Duke had so equivocally hinted.

Yet Miss Jenkins professed that she had no doubt that the Duke loved her 'above every other lady upon earth from the first moment' he had beheld her and that she might, despite the great disparity in their ages, one day become his Duchess.

He himself soon abandoned all attempts of making her either his wife or his mistress; but, on and off for fifteen years, he wrote her letters – 390 of them in all – and she sent him long missives in return, one of them covering 'nineteen sides of paper'.* There were tracts and sacred texts, hymns in manuscript and pious exhortations, complaints of her ailments and insufficiency of her income, accounts of her elevating conversations with clergymen and preachers, and of her attempts to convert heathen travellers in stagecoaches. She also sent him presents of pen wipers and bits of material for cleaning his spectacles, and offered to send him a Bible in large print.

In his replies he was frequently irritable: the Bible he already had served him perfectly well. When he asked for the return of his letters and she – having consulted the Lord – declined to return them, he informed her that it was 'a matter of Indifference whether Miss Jenkins has burnt the letters; or kept them; or sent them back'. When she asked him to return one of her own letters, he told her coldly that,

---

* When this correspondence was published in America in 1889 its authenticity was questioned; but Sir Herbert Maxwell, whose biography of Wellington was published in two volumes in 1899, saw the original manuscripts and declared that there was 'not a shadow of doubt that they are genuine'.

since they were 'in general long' and succeeded others so rapidly, it was his practice to destroy them; and, on being sent letters to be forwarded to Sir Robert Peel or Miss Burdett-Coutts, he returned them to her with a reprimand, reminding her that he was 'not the Post Man! nor the Secretary of Sir Robert Peel nor your Secretary!' She in turn upbraided him for sealing his letters with an ordinary seal instead of a ducal coronet and with a bare signature. He told her that he had 'always understood that the important parts of a letter were its Contents'; he 'never much considered the Signature'. However, he relented and promised her that in future his letters would be 'properly signed and sealed' to her satisfaction.

He had, after all, never objected to being bossed by a pretty young woman. Besides he was a lonely man and he was growing old; he was inclined to believe that she was more interested in him than in his dukedom; and, after all, despite her tiresome verbosity, piety and touchiness, Miss Jenkins was still extremely attractive and he was, as he once put it himself, 'but a man'. So one day he called upon her again. He had been having trouble with his knee; she asked him about it sympathetically; he drew his chair a little closer to hers; this approach was met, so Miss Jenkins said, 'with a withdrawal on [her] part due to Christianity'.

After this his replies to her letters became increasingly impatient. 'You write at great length,' he complained tartly on one occasion. On another, in 1847, he wrote, 'Field Marshal the Duke of Wellington presents his Compliments . . . He declines to [address] anything further to Miss Jenkins, being convinced that as usual any correspondence will end in his giving her Offence, however much he may desire and endeavour to please her.' At length, after a number of long letters had arrived, he was driven to tell her that 'to read one letter from you is as much as I can do'.

Yet he could not bring himself to dismiss her altogether until, after receiving a letter condemning him for giving too much of his attention to earthly ceremonies, he replied that he considered it his 'Duty to serve the Public to the best of his Ability' and begged her to write to him no more. She paid no attention to his request: a letter from her to the Duke was waiting to be posted on the day he died.[7]

40 The Foreign Secretary

1834 – 6

'His Highness the Dictator is concentrating in himself all the power of the State.'

IN THE YEAR of Harriet Arbuthnot's death, the Duke had celebrated his sixty-fifth birthday. His hair was quite white now, his face lined, his body thin; but his eyes had lost little of their bright sparkle. He kept himself as busy as ever with his public duties, attending the House of Lords within three days of Mrs Arbuthnot's death, having what Charles Greville called 'the good taste and sense' to appear there with a 'chearful aspect', though he was looking 'very ill'. He also kept himself as busy as ever with his interminable correspondence which was more voluminous than ever now since his increasing deafness was making human intercourse a strain. Often he heard little of what was said to him in crowded rooms and replied to what he did hear in an alarmingly loud voice. He heard scarcely a word of sermons in church, so, although he had always thought it a gentleman's duty to go to church and was a regular subscriber to the Society for the Promotion of Christian Knowledge, he gave up attending services in London – apart from occasional visits to the Chapel Royal, St James's – advancing as an additional excuse the coldness of London churches where he was obliged to remove his hat, particularly the chilliness of St James's, Piccadilly, the Wren church where he had once attended early service regularly. He did, however, always occupy his pew on Sundays when he was staying at Stratfield Saye or Walmer Castle, since he felt the sight of his presence there would 'operate as an example'.* He also

---

* According to Captain Gronow he also, on at least one occasion, walked from Walmer to the parish church at Deal where he 'ensconced himself in a roomy-looking pew in front of the pulpit. After a short time a lady of portly and pompous appearance, the owner of the pew, entered.' She cast a scowl at the intruder whom she did not recognize, then, since this did not have the desired effect, she told him 'bluntly that she must request he immediately leave her pew'. He obediently did so; but unused to not being recognized, and evidently disliking the experience, he said to the sexton upon leaving the church, 'Tell that lady she has turned the Duke of Wellington out of her pew' (*The Reminiscences and Recollections of Captain Gronow*, i, 266).

received the sacraments regularly, kneeling with 'unaffected devotion before the altar rails, as Samuel Rogers observed.[1] But 'he was not always attentive during the sermon. Indeed, unless the preacher were eloquent, or the subject out of the common, he used generally to gather himself up into the corner of the pew and go to sleep; when he sometimes snored audibly.'[2]

He liked to claim that he was not a person 'without any sense of religion'. This would have been unpardonable, he thought, since he had had opportunities to acquire and *had* 'acquired a good deal of knowledge upon the subject', and believed that the essence of all religion was to do no harm to one's neighbours. 'That is the wonderful part of Christianity,' he said. 'It imposes no privations, it only requires you to live without doing harm to others.'[3] He was certainly not 'a "Bible Society Man"', though, and made 'no ostentatious display either of charity or of other Christian virtues'.[4] He was to shock Queen Victoria and Prince Albert by declaring that he attended services at the Chapel Royal only out of a sense of duty and that the sooner they were over the better.[5] It was 'a duty which ought to be done' to go to church regularly when one could; and it was advisable to get the duty discharged as early in the day as possible.[6]

The Duke was at Stratfield Saye when at six o'clock on a November morning in 1834, as he was just about to go hunting, he received a letter from the King. The disintegrating Whig administration of Grey's successor, Lord Melbourne, had been dismissed and the Duke of Wellington's services were once more required. By eight o'clock the Duke was on his way to Brighton where the King asked him to form a new administration. Wellington demurred: the state of the Commons required that the Prime Minister should be a Member of that House. He 'earnestly recommended to his Majesty' that Sir Robert Peel should be appointed.[7] Peel, however, was on holiday in Italy with his wife and eldest daughter; and it would be some time before he could be summoned home. In the meantime, the King said, the Duke must hold the reins of office.

Wellington was perfectly willing to obey this command; so, 'after much fumbling for his spectacles', he was sworn in as Secretary of State. He was clearly much gratified to be 'in harness again' as he put it, and he moved about Whitehall from one government office to the next with 'unperturbable self-confidence', giving orders and making decisions in what Disraeli described as his familiar 'curt, husky manner',*[8] deeply impressing a Foreign Office official, Charles Scott, son of Sir Walter Scott, with his ability to come straight to the point, to do business promptly and to write 'short, full and *clear*' directions.[9] He had lost none of his decisiveness. His sons' tutor, the Rev, Henry Wagner, described how he had gone to see the Duke about renting a house for his sons. The following exchange ensued:

> 'The rent of the house is so much.'
> 'Take it.'
> 'The taxes are so much.'
> 'Pay them.'
> 'The furniture is so much.'
> 'Buy it. Have you anything more to say?'
> 'No, Sir.'
> 'Then good morning.'[10]

> If I have anything to communicate to his Grace [recorded the French Ambassador, Count Sebastiani] I write to ask at what hour he will receive me. The hour is instantly appointed; I find him punctual as the clock, and in half an hour he has heard my report . . . and gives me an answer without any ambiguity. Thirty minutes with him suffice to transact what can never be accomplished in as many hours with our wavering ministers of France.[11]

'It was really a moment worth living for,' wrote Lady Salisbury, 'to see that great man once more where he ought to be, appreciated as he deserved by his King, and at the head of this great country – if it does but last.'[12] This was not an opinion universally shared. 'His Highness the Dictator,' Lord Grey observed, 'is concentrating in himself all the power of the State, in a manner neither constitutional nor legal.'†[13] 'Nor was his manner of doing so too tactful. Indeed, one commentator complained of the 'unceremonious and somewhat uncourteous mode in which without previous notice he entered into the vacant offices, taking actual possession without any of the usual preliminary civilities to the old occupants'.[14] Another critic of his abrupt not to say didactic manner said that as he 'knew so much, he thought he knew everything';[15] while

---

* The description comes from Disraeli's novel *Coningsby* (1844) in which the Duke appears, as does, in the unpleasant character of Rigby, J.W. Croker, whom Macaulay detested 'more than cold boiled veal'.

† 'If there were a revolution in this country it must end by a military dictator,' Wellington told Lady Salisbury in September 1834: 'revolutions always have: that dictator would not be me – I am too old – but there would be one' (Hatfield House Papers, Lady, Salisbury's journal).

Princess Lieven considered that he had the vanity of believing 'he knew how to do everything and to do it better than anyone else'.[16] At least, so yet another commentator observed, 'we have a *United* Government'.[17]

Wellington's dictatorship, as it amused him to refer to it himself, was short-lived. On 9 December Peel, having stopped for only four nights on the road to Calais from the Hotel de l'Europe in Rome, was back in London at his desk in Whitehall Gardens, and, after a conversation with the King in which he was at his most awkward, he was soon in discussion with his colleagues about the formation of a credible Government. This was far from an easy task. He would have liked to enlist the services of Lord Stanley and Sir James Graham but both declined his offers, Stanley explaining that Wellington's having briefly been Prime Minister while Peel was on the Continent rendered it impossible for him to take up a Cabinet appointment. 'This circumstance alone,' he said, 'must stamp on the administration about to be formed the impress of [the Duke's] name and principles.' The Duke of Buckingham and his son, Lord Chandos, also declined to serve except on terms that could not be accepted; so Peel had to rely on younger men, including Sidney Herbert and W.E. Gladstone.

Wellington returned to the Foreign Office; but his short tenure was not a happy one. He disapproved of most of the policies of his predecessor, Lord Palmerston, yet was unable to reverse them or disentangle the alliances which Palmerston had engineered; and when he nominated Lord Castlereagh's half-brother, the third Marquess of Londonderry, as Ambassador at St Petersburg, he caused such an uproar in the Commons that afterwards men saw in that nomination the first of the blunders which were to bring about the collapse of Peel's first Administration. It was all very well for the Duke to protest, as he did to Charles Greville, that while he was 'not particularly partial to the man, nor ever had been', Londonderry was 'very fit' for the post, had proved himself an excellent Ambassador in Vienna and 'procured more information and obtained more insight into the affairs of a foreign court than anybody'.[18] The inescapable problem was that Londonderry, a lordly not to say arrogant High Tory, and an uncompromising and outspoken opponent of Reform, was a widely disliked figure, so unpopular, indeed, that he had been mobbed in the streets and dragged off his horse. The proposed appointment of him to represent his country in Russia was, Greville thought, the same 'old story of ignorance and disregard of public opinion'.[19] Londonderry felt obliged to withdraw his acceptance of the offer.

Before other mistakes were made, Peel was strongly urged to set out his proposed reformist policies in what John Walter, proprietor of *The Times*, called 'some popular declaration'. Well aware himself of the need of such a declaration, Peel issued it in the form of a manifesto to the constituents of Tamworth where he was offering himself for re-election in the forthcoming General Election.

In this election, which began in January 1835, the Conservatives did rather better than had been expected; but, when they took their seats in the Commons, they could never be sure of a majority, and Peel decided he must resign as soon as a suitable opportunity presented itself.

When such an opportunity seemed likely to occur, the Duke strongly urged Peel not to resign. There was a 'dreadful scene', he said: Peel was 'in a dreadful state of agitation, his countenance and all his features working and twitching in a thousand ways'. But the Prime Minister remained adamant: he was determined to go as soon as he could.[20]

When a crucial vote was about to be taken on the night of 2 April, the Duke was asked if he would like news of the result sent to him at Apsley House; but he declined the offer: he would 'just as soon wait', being quite satisfied to learn about it when the newspapers came next morning. Would not the Duke be anxious, unable to sleep perhaps? No he would not; he did not like lying awake; it did no good to lie awake; he 'made a point never to lie awake'.[21]

Defeated again in that first week of April, Peel resigned on the 8th and Lord Melbourne became Prime Minister once more.

The Duke had enjoyed his brief spell as Foreign Secretary, dispatching business with the same brisk authority as he had displayed at his military headquarters years before; but he seemed equally content when the Tories were removed to the Opposition benches again. He was looking forward to 'a quiet life', he told Lord Lyndhurst; and when he met Lady Salisbury in the Park one Monday morning in May he was 'in great spirits'. He was the 'idlest man in town', he claimed most improbably, 'nothing to do. I must say it is far the pleasantest to belong to a party in opposition – no cares or anxieties, everybody at leisure and everybody good humoured.'[22] He made up his mind not to concern himself unduly with the prejudices of High Tory peers. He could think of better things to do than attend a proposed series of dinners for disgruntled Members of the House of Lords.[23]

He could not escape involvement, however, when the Whigs introduced their Municipal Corporations Reform Bill; and, although it was agreed that this should not be a party measure, the Duke's wild objection to it as a means of creating 'a little Republic in every town' and as 'formidable instruments in case of anything like a civil war' – as well as his loss of control of the ultra Tories – so exasperated Peel that he abruptly left London for his house, Drayton Manor in Staffordshire. For months the two men did not talk to each other. Then, in January 1836, Peel was persuaded by Arbuthnot and Hardinge to ask the Duke to join a house party at Drayton. The two men greeted each other without rancour, the Duke, so he complacently told Lady Salisbury,' displaying his usual 'unaffected good temper and cordiality'.[24]

William Ewart Gladstone was also of the party and said that it was

pleasing to see the deference with which [the Duke] was received as he entered the library; at the sound of his name everybody rose; he is addressed by all with a respectful manner. He met Peel most cordially, and seized both Lady Peel's hands. I now recollect that it was with *glee* Sir Robert Peel said to me on Monday, 'I am glad to say you will meet the Duke here.' . . .

Of the two days which he spent here he hunted on Thursday, shot on Friday, and to-day travelled to Stratfieldsay, more, I believe, than 100 miles, to entertain a party of friends to dinner. With this bodily exertion he mixes at 66 or 67 a constant attention to business.[25]

The Duke remained, he was proud to think, a man of great consequence; and, although as he had to confess, he did not hear 'half that passes', he remained a highly respected figure in the House of Lords. His speeches were still rarely well delivered and sometimes difficult to follow. After listening to one which was exceptionally ill spoken, Lord Mahon recorded in his diary:

The Duke's speech is accurately given in to-day's papers, and reads extremely well. But it was distressing to hear, from the delivery. His words came out very slowly, and as it were drop by drop, and he seemed to have lost the modulation of his voice, which sometimes rose almost to a scream – sometimes sank almost to a whisper, and this without reference to the greater or lesser energy of the sentiments he was expressing.[26]

Yet despite this often poor delivery, Members listened in awe to his gruff and husky, authoritative interjections as when, for instance, he raised a bony finger as a sign of warning to Lord Brougham, the former Lord Chancellor and now an independent supporter of the Government, whom he startled with the words, 'Now take care what you say next.' 'As if panic-struck, Brougham broke off, and ran upon some other tack.'[27]

In the Commons, too, the Duke was much revered by younger men, though most were intimidated by him. Indeed, Alava said at this time that 'everybody was afraid of him, even his nearest relations'.[28] Disraeli, having received £500 from the Tory managers towards his election expenses, had been disappointed not to be elected a Member for Wycombe where he had declared himself a follower of the Duke of Wellington whom he assured with characteristic flattery that he sought 'no greater satisfaction than that of serving a really great man'.[29] Gladstone, who had been one of Peel's Junior Lords of the Treasury, noted with approval that the Duke 'received remarks made to him very frequently with no more than "Ha!" a convenient suspensive expression, which acknowledges the arrival of the observation and no more'.[30]

41   Portraits and Painters

1830 — 50

'I lament the fate of having passed my Manhood
acquiring celebrity; and of having to pass my old
Age in sitting for Busts and Artists.'

IN THE COUNTRY as a whole Wellington's former unpopularity now
appeared to have been largely forgotten. He was loudly cheered at
Vauxhall; he was joyously acclaimed by the crowds at a review in Hyde
Park; on a visit to Cambridge he was as enthusiastically welcomed by
the town as he was by the University. When he appeared at a choral
concert in London, 'the singing stopped, the whole audience rose, and
a burst of acclamation and waving of handkerchiefs saluted the great
old man. Everyone was moved except the Duke himself.' 'The feeling
of the people for him seems to be the liveliest of all popular sentiments,'
Charles Greville commented. 'Yet he does nothing to excite it, and
hardly appears to notice it.'[1]

In the streets of London gentlemen raised their hats to him; doctors
stood on the steps of St George's Hospital opposite Apsley House to
watch him pass by;[2] 'even the butcher's boy pulled up his cart as he
stopped at the gate';[3] and once a cheering crowd followed him up
Constitution Hill to Apsley House where he paused to indicate with
an ironic gesture the iron shutters on the windows which had been
smashed not so long before.* He gave a bow, touched the brim of his

---

* The Duke left the smashed windows at Apsley House unmended for a long time. He
had them reglazed in June 1833 for the annual Waterloo dinner. Some said that he did
so because the King was coming as the principal guest, others that he was provoked by
a caricature by John Doyle published on 10 June. This, entitled 'Taking an airing in
Hyde Park: Framed but not *yet Glazed*', depicted him staring defiantly through a shattered
frame. The iron shutters may have originally given rise to the soubriquet 'the Iron Duke'.
In an apparent allusion to these shutters, *Punch* referred to the 'Wrought-iron Duke' in
1842. The 'Iron Duke', *tout court*, seems first to have appeared in print in the *Mechanics'
Magazine* in 1845. Sir Herbert Maxwell (*The Life of Wellington*, i, 304) suggested that
the soubriquet originated, not so much in the Duke's iron will and often unbending
opposition to hidebound Tories, as well as to radicals, as in an iron steamship launched
on the Mersey and named *The Duke of Wellington*. This ship became known as the

hat with two fingers in a characteristic salute, and rode his horse through the gate. One day in the summer of 1835 near Apsley House Lady Wharncliffe had the pleasure of hearing him 'cheer'd as warmly & generally as in the days of his greatest favor. It was quite a triumph to his own gates, & he was obliged continually to touch his cap in acknowledgement. It was truly delightful to hear and see.'[4]

'He was such a familiar sight to Londoners,' Lord Redesdale recalled:

> To the last a spare lithe figure, smart as a young boy, dressed with scrupulous neatness, and even a tinge of dandyism, in a tight-fitting, single breasted blue frock coat, with spotless white trousers. When he passed all men doffed their hats to him as if he had been a king, and the answering salute of the forefinger raised to the brim of his hat, never omitted, never varying, became almost historic . . . London loved him.[5]

In the countryside and in provincial towns crowds gathered to cheer him, as they had done when, on one of his regular visits to the Arbuth-nots in Northamptonshire, they assembled to see him go into church '& rang the bells in token of their joy'. It was the same in every county he visited: in Bedford 'a great crowd collected round the inn and loudly cheered the Duke'; in Norwich, as soon as it was known that he was there, the 'cathedral filled to such an overflow, it was with the utmost difficulty the corporation' could get him out 'and they were obliged to stop in one of the Canons' houses and send for a carriage to get back to the inn'; in Durham and Newcastle 'the people [seemed] hardly able to pay him honours enough'.[6]

In London he was as busy as he liked to be while protesting that he was never left in peace, holding meetings and giving dinners at Apsley House; offering advice; endlessly writing letters, as many as fifty in a single day; speaking on all manner of subjects in the House of Lords, turning up papers for Colonel John Gurwood, who had served with him in the Peninsula and at Waterloo and who was occupied upon an edition of his general orders and selections from his dispatches. The Duke took the greatest interest in this work and was unaffectedly delighted to be reminded how well written the dispatches were. When told that Brougham – who had recently said of Wellington that 'that

---

Iron Duke and thence, by natural transition, the name was applied to the Duke of Wellington.

man's first object is to serve his country, with his sword if necessary, or with a pick-axe' – had added that the dispatches would be remembered when Brougham himself and other eminent men of the day had been forgotten, he commented 'with the greatest simplicity', 'It is very true: when I read them I was myself astonished, and I can't think how the devil I could have written them.'[7]

'Upon my word,' he said to Lady Salisbury, 'I was quite surprised on looking over them to see how well they were written. Tho' I was very young then I could not write them better now. I see that I had at that time all the care and foresight and attention to every detail that could forward the business which I had in charge.'[8]

As well as helping Gurwood with his edition of his dispatches, the Duke was also required to spend long hours sitting to portrait painters and sculptors, an obligation about which he constantly complained.

> Mr [John] Lilley has been here since last Monday [runs one characteristic protest to Lady Burghersh from Stratfield Saye] and has had nine sittings; eighteen at Walmer make twenty-seven. This really is too much.
>
> After painting the head at Walmer, he was to come here to sketch in the figure, the cloak, &c. He has in fact commenced a new picture altogether ... I can positively sit no longer. I do think that having to pass every leisure hour that one has by daylight in sitting for one's picture is too bad. No man ever submitted to such a bore: and I positively will not sit any longer.[9]

'I have not promised to sit for less than a score of portraits,' he wrote on another occasion in 1834. 'No portrait painter will copy the picture of another nor paint an original under fifteen to twenty sittings, and thus I am expected to give not less than four hundred sittings to a portrait painter, in addition to all the other matters I must attend to.'[10] 'I am convinced that there is no Man existing or that ever lived in this Country who has sacrificed his time, his leisure, his amusements, the best hours of his days, to the Artists to the same degree that I have,' he wrote five years later to Lord Sandys, a patron of William Salter who spent six years working on his celebrated *Waterloo Banquet at Apsley House*. 'I have sat for no less than six Pictures since the Prorogation of Parl! My House at W.C. [Walmer Castle] was full of Artists. I have had three there at a time, each taking up one, two, three hours of the best of the day & I am now called upon to receive another here in the Winter, and to devote to him possibly the only Hour of Daylight that there may be in the 24 hours. Is this fair? . . . I cannot do what is required of me.'*[11]

Yet protest as he would about the waste of his time, he undertook the obligation of sitting not altogether unwillingly, being gratified to see pictures of himself in public galleries and the houses of his friends and concerned to ensure that posterity would have no doubts as to what the Duke of Wellington looked like, although, since his distinctive features appeared in innumerable caricatures and on all manner of objects – snuff boxes, fans, bell-pulls, door-stops, clocks, knife-handles, tea services, medals, Staffordshire portrait figures, brooches, watches, barometers, even razors and chamber pots – it was highly improbable that they would not have been identified immediately.

'He would be mortified if he were not asked to sit,' Sir David Wilkie assured Benjamin Robert Haydon. 'He also complains of dining out so much and making speeches; but he would be mortified if he was not asked, and if he did not make speeches.'†[12]

He was portrayed several times by Sir Thomas Lawrence, notably in the fine portrait of c. 1815 now at Apsley House and once, also in uniform and with St Paul's Cathedral in the background, holding the Sword of State in his right hand. 'The one thing my father was vain of,' his elder son commented, 'was that he was the only man to whom the Sword of State had been given who was able to carry it upright. Everyone else, the sword and scabbard being very heavy, sloped it on the right shoulder; my father carried it upright, and he insisted upon Sir Thomas Lawrence painting him doing this', persistently as Sir Thomas urged him not to do so because of the awkwardness of the pose. In the finished portrait it does, indeed, appear that the Duke is grasping a bell-pull rather than holding a sword. When the Duke of Beaufort was asked which he thought was the best portrait of the Duke of Wellington, he replied, 'The one ringing the bell.'[13]

Lawrence also painted the Duke for Mrs Arbuthnot, who considered

---

* In 1840, however, when Lord Anglesey asked 'a great favour' – 'a full length portrait', preferably by Lawrence, for his house, Beaudesert Hall in Staffordshire – the Duke responded most agreeably and at considerable length: he was 'much flattered' to be asked; he did not know of any portraits by Lawrence, who had died ten years before, which were 'now to be sold'; but John Lucas had painted the best portraits of him since Lawrence's death. A few days later the Duke wrote to Lucas offering to give 'any sittings that may be necessary' (Plas Newydd Papers, 8 Dec. 1840, quoted in Anglesey, One-Leg, 300).

† 'I am invited to every dinner that is given,' he once complained to Lady Salisbury, having forgotten to attend one at Lady Verulam's. 'I was invited to no less than four yesterday' (Hatfield House Papers, 27 May 1836). He did not like it, though, when he was not asked.

the finished work more like him than any other portrait of him she ever saw. 'I have got the Duke's picture back,' she wrote in her journal in September 1826. 'It is hung up in the drawing-room here [Woodford Lodge] &, please God, shall never move again. It has been for two years in London with the engraver and a man I allowed to copy it in miniature for Lady Burghersh. Before it was put up I made the Duke write his name & the date of its being finished (13 Dec' 1821) on a piece of paper which we stuck on the back . . . Mr A. also wrote that it was an admirable likeness.'[14] The Duke himself described it as being as 'good a picture as any Lawrence ever painted'.[15] Lawrence also painted the Duke in 1824 for Peel who had a good collection of the artist's works. In Peel's portrait, which Mrs Arbuthnot justifiably did not like, and which is now at Wellington College, Lawrence painted the Duke holding a watch in his hand as though he were anxiously awaiting the arrival of Blücher's army at Waterloo. 'That will never do,' the Duke protested. 'I was *not* waiting for the Prussians at Waterloo. Put a telescope in my hand, if you please.' Lawrence obliged him.*

Lawrence was equally obliging when the Duke protested that the sword the artist had painted in another portrait was very ill done.

> Wellington stood for L[awrence] for three hours. After he had done he stepped down and said, 'Pshaw! That is not like my sword.'
> 'Please, your Grace, I'll do it next time.'
> 'Do it now.'
> 'I must go to the Princess Augusta's.'
> 'Oh, no. You must put my sword right. It is really bad.'
> This was done.†[16]

---

* The cloak which the Duke is wearing in this portrait is the one he wore at Waterloo. He gave it to J.W. Croker who lent it to Lawrence who, in turn, when the picture was finished 'delivered it to a lady who said she had the Duke's authority for it'. Croker complained to the Duke who 'seemed a good deal vexed but . . . with a strange misunderstanding of the real value of the cloak he had another – a perfect facsimile – made, which he gave me . . . You may be sure I was by no means satisfied with this substitution. But . . . the Duke said, "One cloak is as good as another" (*The Croker Papers*, iii, 281).
† It was, no doubt, not done quickly. Lawrence, as well as being overworked, was notoriously reluctant to put the finishing touches to a picture. In October 1822 the Duchess had begged him to let her have her husband's portrait for the library at Stratfield Saye which was 'now complete':

> The room is a handsome one . . . his favourite room . . . The Duke has done everything to [it] he could do to make it beautiful and comfortable, and my own ardent, earnest wish is to place in that room the Portrait of the Duke which yet remains unfinished, but which if you are so kind as really to undertake it, would in a very short time be completed . . . Will you do this? Pray, pray do not refuse me!!! I think I have evinced much patience . . . Pray, pray oblige me! . . . I am most anxious for an answer (*Sir Thomas Lawrence's Letter-Bag*, 172).

The Duke was also painted by Sir Edwin Landseer, John Doyle, Thomas Heaphy, John Singleton Copley, Richard Cosway, Andrew Morton, Peter Eduard Ströhling, Sir David Wilkie, who, in Lord Aberdeen's opinion, gave him the appearance of a 'Spanish beggarman',[17] and by Sir George Hayter whose *Duke of Wellington standing by his horse, Copenhagen* was shown at the Royal Academy in 1821 and whose earlier portrait of the Duke was commissioned as a present for one of his many godsons, Lord Arthur Russell. Although this picture gives his features a rather calculating expression, the sitter was sufficiently pleased with it to have a number of engravings made to give to people who asked him for a likeness.

Other artists employed to paint portraits or make busts or statues of the Duke were Salter and Turnerelli, Thomas Milnes and E.H. Baily, Thomas Campbell who made a monumental marble statue of him for Dalkeith Palace, the seat of the Duke of Buccleuch near Edinburgh;* Campbell's assistant, James Hall; John Lucas, who painted him eight times, for the Oxford and Cambridge Club among other patrons as well as for Lord Anglesey; Baron Marochetti who made studies for the statues erected in Glasgow and Leeds and at Stratfield Saye; Antoine Maurin to whom he was 'obliged to find time to sit even at Hatfield';[18] H.W. Pickersgill who produced a full-length portrait for Lord Hill and who, according to Lady Salisbury, made him look like 'a drunken undertaker';[19] and Franz Winterhalter who painted him at Windsor Castle with Peel and at Buckingham Palace with Queen Victoria and Prince Arthur. In their *Iconography of the Duke of Wellington* Lord Gerald Wellesley and John Steegmann listed no fewer than seventy-nine portraitists known to have painted or sculpted the Duke, French, Italian, American and Spanish artists as well as British. Nor does the *Iconography* list all the known likenesses of the Duke. A more recent survey enumerates over two hundred made between 1795 and 1852.[20] 'Of all the Britons who have ever lived [the Duke] has been the most portrayed.'[21]

---

* Before being commissioned to make this statue in 1828, Campbell had executed a bust of the Duke in 1827. This classicizing bust is now at Stratfield Saye. A replica in marble was purchased for the Hopetoun collection in 1833; another copy, which bears a head of Medusa on the breastplate, is at Thirlestane, East Lothian. The design of the 7ft 2ins statue which followed the bust was clearly inspired by Donatello's St George, at that time in a niche on the façade of Orsanmichele in Florence and now in the Bargello (Helen Smailes, 'Thomas Campbell and the "camera lucida": the Buccleuch statue of the 1st Duke of Wellington', *Burlington Magazine*, vol. cxxix, no. 1016, Nov. 1987, 709–14).

He did not talk much when sitting; but, on going to the St John's Wood studio of the genial, American-born C.R. Leslie for a painting commissioned for Windsor Castle he did give a firm warning: 'Now, mind the shape of my head. It's a square head. I know it, for Chantrey told me so.'*[22]

The Duke's opinion of his portrait by Leslie is not recorded; but evidently he did think highly of the statuette of him made by the gifted dandy Count Alfred D'Orsay, to whose studio at Gore House the Duke made regular visits, being much entertained by a talking crow belonging to D'Orsay's mistress, Lady Blessington, a bird which 'lived in the house and shrieked, "Up boys and at 'em," with his head on one side, to the great delight of the Duke of Wellington, who would roar with laughter at the bird's absurd gravity'.[23]

'I have just made a statuette of the Duke of Wellington on horseback which is almost causing a revolution here,' Count D'Orsay told Lord Lytton. 'The Duke declares it is the finest thing he has ever seen and the only portrait by which he would wish to be known to posterity. He comes here continually to admire himself.'†[24]

* The Duke had been asked to sit for Sir Francis Chantrey in 1833 by the Rev. John Keble, at that time Professor of Poetry at Oxford, writing on behalf of various university colleagues (W.R. Ward, *Victorian Oxford*, 85). Chantrey had already done a bust of the Duke for Lord Liverpool in 1820–3. The Duke ordered a replica of this marble bust which cost 150 guineas, the same price as the original. He did not settle the bill for twenty years, two months after the sculptor's death (Celina Fox, ed. *London: World City, 1800–1840*, Yale University Press, 1992, 245). Other replicas were ordered for Windsor Castle and Petworth House. The replica ordered by the Duke is now at Apsley House. A cast of it was given to Mrs Arbuthnot who thought it 'excessively like', but not so well done as a bust by Joseph Nollekens which, although executed before the Duke first went to the Peninsula, was still considered a most striking likeness (*The Journal of Mrs Arbuthnot*, i, 156). The Duchess of Wellington also admired Nollekens's bust above all other likenesses. 'It is, indeed,' she said, 'as like as possible' (Joan Wilson, *A Soldier's Wife: Wellington's Marriage*, 118). Her son Lord Douro, however, thought that the later bust by George Gammon Adams was the finest and he assured the artist that he, and the Duke's friends and servants, all agreed that it was the 'best likeness by far' (Lord Gerald Wellesley and John Steegmann, *The Iconography of the Duke of Wellington*, 1). Busts of the Duke by Benedetto Pistrucci and Sir John Steell can be seen at Apsley House. The bronze equestrian statue opposite Apsley House is by Sir Joseph Boehm (see note on p. 377).

† In his memoirs, the publisher and engraver Henry Vizetelly maintained that T.H. Nicholson, an artist who worked for the *Illustrated Times*, had more of a hand in D'Orsay's work than D'Orsay cared to admit. 'Nicholson modelled well in plaster, and no secret was made of Count d'Orsay's obligations to him in regard to his famous equestrian statuettes and miniature busts, the faces of which were modelled by [William Behnes] before he became celebrated as a sculptor. The statuette of the Duke of Wellington on horseback was undoubtedly Nicholson's, and the famous bust of the Iron Duke which was to make the fortune of the lucky manufacturer who reproduced it in porcelain is said to have been his and Behnes's joint work' (Henry Vizetelly, *Glances Back through Seventy Years*, London, 1893, ii, 39).

He had given several sittings to D'Orsay, which 'he had refused to that fellow Landseer ... He marched up to the bust, paused and shouted, "By God, D'Orsay, you have done what those damned busters never could do."'[25] He liked D'Orsay's work, he said, because 'he always made him look like a gentleman'.[26]

The Duke also much admired a bust – 'the best bust done of me' in his own opinion – by 'a man named Burges who is employed on the Edinburgh Statue'; and he ordered copies of this for both Eton College and Oxford University.*[27] These were rare presentations; but engravings were commonly sent by the Duke to those who asked for one or were considered worthy of having one. Not only did he have a stock of J.H. Robinson's engravings of Hayter's portrait for this purpose, but he also arranged for the Prince of Prussia to have an engraving of Hoppner's portrait framed in one of the maple frames he kept for such presentations.[28]

Long as he spent sitting for various artists – who had portrayed him, he said, in every posture except standing on his head[29] – the Duke had also to spend time writing letters refusing requests from painters and sculptors of whom he had never heard or whose work he did not admire. Those artists whom he disappointed he found as tiresomely importunate as people in the public eye now find paparazzi. At Walmer he 'could not move along the passage, or on the staircase, or the ramparts, without meeting them'. There 'was not a moment of the day or night' that he could call his own. 'I have here two Artists who occupy all my time by Day Light,' he complained to Lady Wilton in May 1841. 'I shall have a third with Brushes tomorrow; and possibly a fourth. I lament the fate of having passed my Manhood acquiring celebrity; and of having to pass my old Age in sitting for Busts and Artists, that they may profit by it.'[30]

One of his most persistent supplicants was Benjamin Robert Haydon, the eccentric historical painter, who badgered him without success for a companion piece to his portrait of Napoleon on St Helena which

---

* Burges is a mystery. The equestrian statue which stands in Princes Street Gardens, Edinburgh is by Sir John Steell who went to Walmer Castle to model a bust. 'Mr Steell,' so the *Edinburgh Evening Post* reported on 12 June 1852, 'found that the kindness and courtesy of his noble host was surprising. He would come in and give a sitting once or frequently twice a day as the modelling progressed ... The Duke highly appreciated the merits of Mr Steell's bust' (National Library of Scotland, F B. m 55). At Eton it is supposed that the bust of the Duke in the College's possession is by Steell. Oxford University has no record of being presented with a bust of Wellington by either Steell or Burges, though it still possesses the Chantrey bust. Burges is unknown as a sculptor. Perhaps he worked as a craftsman in Steell's foundry in Edinburgh.

was bought by Sir Robert Peel. Wellington refused Haydon's overtures: he really had 'no leisure to sit at present'. Besides, 'to paint the Emperor Napoleon on the rock of St Helena is quite a different thing from painting me on the field of the Battle of Waterloo', the Duke told him. 'The Emperor Napoleon did not consent to be painted. But I am to be supposed to consent; and, moreover, I on the field of the Battle of Waterloo am not exactly in the situation in which Napoleon stood on the rock of St Helena.'

Despite this rebuff, Haydon persisted with his painting and in order to borrow the Duke's clothes he called at Apsley House where he was shown into a 'waiting parlour full of pistols and muskets'. The contrast of the house with Lord Grey's was 'extraordinary. All about Lord Grey was anti-military, while everything seems to be martial about the Duke.'

When he heard that Haydon had called and that Mugford, the steward, had undertaken to send him the clothes, the Duke wrote again to protest.

Haydon was undeterred. Two thirds of the purchase money had already been paid, he told the Duke. He would have to go on with the picture. He was 'totally without other employment'. He had six children, one a midshipman, another a scholar at Wadham College, Oxford, four at home.

'I cannot be a party to or an encourager of the picture which you are painting of me,' the Duke explained with unaccustomed patience. 'Do as you please with it. But I have nothing to say to it. There can be no doubt that your communication with my servants, without my previous permission, was not regular. I cannot say otherwise.'

Four years later, however, when a new approach was made by Haydon who had been commissioned to paint another portrait of the Duke, he agreed to sit for the artist on learning that the commission came from 'a committee of gentlemen from Liverpool'. His consent was given, through rather grumpily, it always being his way, as the seventh Duke of Wellington observed, 'to do kind actions in an ungracious manner'.[31] He did, however, invite Haydon to come to stay at Walmer for the sittings, a privilege which had not been bestowed earlier on Sir George Hayter who had been advised to come down to Stratfield Saye 'by the railway and put up at the Wellington Arms'.[32]

Haydon accepted the invitation instantly and set down in his journal all the details of his visit, from his arrival by steamer at Ramsgate on Friday evening to his departure the following Tuesday morning at six o'clock, having heard the Duke go up to his room the previous night, roaring out 'Good night!' to Arbuthnot and slamming the door.

On his arrival after dinner on the Friday Haydon found the Duke in the drawing-room in conversation with Charles Arbuthnot, Sir Astley Cooper, the surgeon, and William Booth, who, having served efficiently as the Duke's deputy commissary general, had been employed to look after Wellington's estates in the Netherlands and was the proud owner of a gold pocket-watch by Bréguet which the Duke had bought in Paris after Waterloo for 1,800 francs and had presented to him in gratitude for his services.*

In what Haydon had previously described as 'his loud, distinct and military voice', the Duke spoke of Napoleon and Mme de Staël, of the encroachments of the sea at Dover, of the plundering propensities of British soldiers and their pulling down of whole houses in Spain to serve as fuel. 'The French always did so, but there was this difference; we had the houses regularly valued and paid for; the French gave nothing, and often tore off doors and windows from the whole village.'[33]

Arbuthnot began to doze; the Duke 'gave a tremendous yawn', said, 'It's time to go to bed', rang for candles and led the way upstairs, pausing in the hall by an old print of Dover to explain to Haydon the encroachments of the sea.

In his bedroom Haydon could not sleep, so excited was he to think that here he was 'tête-à-tête' with the greatest man on earth and the noblest' whose conversation had been so natural yet so enlightening. If only, Haydon thought, the Duke's public speeches were as fresh.

At breakfast the next morning the Duke kept a chair for Haydon on his right. 'Which will ye have,' he asked, 'black tea or green?' When Haydon stated his preference, the Duke gave the order, 'Bring black'; and when the tea arrived Haydon ate what he described as a 'hearty breakfast' in the middle of which six noisy children appeared at the windows. Let into the room on the Duke's instructions, they clambered all over him, crying, 'How d'ye do, Duke? How d'ye do?' One of them shouted, 'I want some tea, Duke.'

---

* Another gold watch by Bréguet was presented by Wellington to the Hon. Henry Percy of the 14th Light Dragoons, grandson of the Duke of Northumberland – the only one of the Commander-in-Chief's aides-de-camp to have escaped unscathed at Waterloo – who brought Wellington's dispatch from the battlefield to London, travelling night and day to do so. This watch is now preserved at Levens Hall, Westmorland, Colonel Percy having left it to his sister, forebear of the present owners. Also at Levens Hall is a coffee service brought back from the Continent by Wellington who gave it to his niece, Lady Mary Bagot, daughter of his brother William, Earl of Mornington. This service was ready packed in the factory at Sèvres awaiting dispatch to Napoleon's mother (Reginald Colby, *The Waterloo Despatch*, 39; Annette Bagot, *Levens Hall: Home of Robin Bagot*, Norwich, 1968, 6).

'You shall have it, if you promise not to slop it over me as you did yesterday.'

So tea was brought for them and so was toast; and three of the children gathered on one side of him and three on the other. He hugged them all; and, after they had all left the room to play outside, he threatened to run after them and catch them. So they all ran away in pretended horror.

The Duke went hunting that morning, but sat for an hour and a half for Haydon in the afternoon. 'I hit his grand, upright, manly expression,' Haydon wrote proudly. 'He looked like an eagle of the gods who had put on human shape, and had got silvery with age and service.'

That evening they dined at seven, the Duke limiting himself to half a glass of sherry in water; and after dinner he put a candle on either side of him to read the *Standard*, which he did with the deepest interest. The next day was Sunday, so they all went to church, the Duke entering his large pew near the pulpit after matins had begun and, taking up his prayer book, following the service attentively. 'At the epistle he stood upright, like a soldier, and when the blessing was pronounced he buried his head in one hand and uttered his prayer as if it came from his heart in humbleness.' Haydon noticed also how dirty the green footstools were.

After dinner that night the Duke read the *Spectator*, giving it as close attention as he had given to the *Standard* the night before. 'He then yawned, as he always did before retiring, and said, "I'll give you an early sitting tomorrow, at nine."'

Promptly at nine he appeared, looking tired and worn, much older than he had done on Saturday. 'His skin was drawn tight over his face; his eye was watery and aged; his head nodded a little.' Haydon put a chair for him. He said, 'I'd as soon stand'; but he soon sat all the same, taking his watch out of his pocket from time to time, 'and at ten up he got, and said, "It's ten".' Haydon 'opened the door for him and he went out. He had been impatient all the time.'

At breakfast he brightened at the sight of the children who were once more given tea and toast; and he agreed to give Haydon another sitting on his return from hunting. Haydon was pleased with his sketch; but, since the Duke had said that he did not wish to have anything to do with the composition or subject of the picture, he did not even so much as glance at it.

Both Charles Arbuthnot and Priscilla Burghersh, who was also staying at Walmer, did look at the sketch, however, and both thought it a good likeness. Much gratified by this, Haydon wrote on the back of it, 'Never touched since it was left as it is, by desire of Lady Burghersh and Mr Arbuthnot. They thought I had hit the expression.'[34]

When the picture was almost complete, Count D'Orsay called on Haydon at his studio, wearing 'such a dress! white greatcoat, blue satin cravat, hair oiled and curling, hat of the primest curve, gloves scented with eau de Cologne, primrose in tint, skin in tightness'.

> He pointed out several things to correct in Copenhagen, [Haydon wrote.] I did them, and he took my brush in his dandy gloves, which made my heart ache, and . . . lowered the hindquarters by bringing over a bit of the sky . . . He took up a nasty, oily, dirty hog-tool and immortalised Copenhagen by touching the sky.
>
> I thought, after he had gone, this won't do – a Frenchman touch Copenhagen! So out I rubbed all he had touched, and modified his hints myself.[35]

42 Life at Walmer Castle

1830 – 50

'I'm considered a great favourite with children.'

THE DUKE clearly enjoyed his life at Walmer Castle. He rose early, as soon as he was awake, believing, as he said when asked how he managed to turn over in such a narrow bed, that 'when it's time to turn over, it's time to turn out'.*[1] He shaved himself carefully, using razors which he insisted on having sharpened either by a man in Jermyn Street, one of the few cutlers in London whom he considered capable of doing the job properly,[2] or by a man 'in a little cellar, subsequently a newspaper shop, in Piccadilly, close to the Burlington Arcade'.[3] After safety razors came into use he became one of the first men in England to experiment with them. He then dressed carefully, and, in his later years, extremely slowly, insisting on brushing his clothes himself and leaving only his boots – made for him by Mr Hoby of St James's Street – to the attention of his valet, Kendall, and the boot-boy; and he would have cleaned those too, so he told Lord Strangford, if he could have done so without the servants coming to bore him with their talk in the boot-room.†[4]

Soon after seven o'clock, and from time to time as early as half-past five, he could be seen, usually in blue coat with white trousers in summer, blue trousers in winter, walking briskly up and down the battlements, occasionally in company with Charles Arbuthnot – 'our two dear old gentlemen', as the housekeeper once fondly described them, 'so happy together'.[5]

---

* He slept on a travelling bed for preference but he did not insist upon it. His bed at Apsley House was 'an elaborate French mahogany one decorated with trophies of arms in gilt bronze' ('Wellington: Some Elucidations' in Gerald 7th Duke of Wellington, *Collected Works*, 92).

† He was as particular about his pictures. Colonel Gurwood told Benjamin Robert Haydon that he would not let anyone else have the key of the glass of his Correggio and when the glass was dirty he would dust it himself with his handkerchief. Gurwood once asked him if he would give him the key so that he could clean the glass for him. 'No,' the Duke said. 'I won't' (*Haydon Journals*, ed. Elwin, 30 November 1839).

From time to time the Duke would look out to sea, enjoying the prospect of it far more than sailing on it, which he did not like at all, being a very poor sailor. Although he needed spectacles for reading, he maintained that his eyesight was still so good that he could distinguish the nationality of the flags on the ships passing up and down the Channel at distances which made them quite unidentifiable to others, even making the improbable claim that on clear nights he could distinctly see the lights of Calais.[6]

After writing or reading for two or three hours in his room, he had breakfast at ten o'clock, 'making messes of rusks and bread in his tea, never [eating] meat or eggs';[7] then, having looked through the newspapers, he returned to his room a small, plain room with a bookshelf over the curtainless camp-bed and a 'stand up' writing desk in the recess by the window looking out to sea, a litter of papers everywhere as there was in his room at Apsley House where, entering by one of its five doors, a visitor once found not only the long table but also the sofa covered with them, leaving just enough room on the sofa for one person to sit down.[8]

In his room at Walmer he worked again until two, leaving his guests to have lunch on their own for he did not eat at that time himself, unless it were to have 'a jelly or a biscuit',[9] the kind of fare he thought quite sufficient for anyone in the middle of the day: Lady Salisbury was once asked what she would like for lunch when they went to Dover Races together. 'Oh, just a bit of bread,' she said; and she got precisely that.[10]

He would sometimes ride or drive along the coast into Dover or as far as Folkestone, where he was occasionally to be seen walking on the pier, or he would take a guest for a ride in his curricle, as he did in London, at high speed, seeming to take scant notice of other traffic on the road or of fog, talking unconcernedly with the reins loose in his hands, once frightening his son Charles by going to sleep in a phaeton on their way to a meet and almost toppling the carriage into a ditch, an accident averted by Lord Charles who gave a jerk on the rein, thus waking up his father who exclaimed 'in an angry voice', 'What are you about Charles? I wish you would mind your own business.'

One day at Walmer the Duke drove out with Lord Clanwilliam, who had been *chef de chancellerie* to the Duke's mission at the Congress of Verona, horrifying his passenger, a good twenty-five years younger than himself, by the speed at which they hurtled down the narrow country lanes followed by George Gleig who soon lost sight of them. On their return Gleig apologized for the fact that the Duke had left him so far behind. 'I thought more than once,' Clanwilliam said, 'that he would have left me behind too!'

At dinner after these excursions the Duke appeared in boots if men only were present; but if ladies were of the party, or even one young lady, the daughter of a guest perhaps, he 'always wore shoes, silk stockings with his star and the Garter'. He was 'exceedingly polite to all, and particularly attentive to women, *la vieille cour personifiée*'. He ate fast but never very much, 'mixing meat, rice and vegetables into a mess on his plate', taking even less interest in what his French cook had prepared for him than he had done in his meals in the past – although insisting that he should have nothing fried in oil – 'accepting everything that was carried round', Lord Ellesmere said, and, in the flow of conversation, 'without thinking or caring about it', filling his plate with 'the most incongruous articles which, however, he scarcely tasted, but sent away almost untouched'.

He had so little sense of taste, Ellesmere added, that he could scarcely tell rancid butter from fresh or one wine from another and once consumed an egg for breakfast before declaring that it was 'quite rotten'. By general consent the food at his table was not very good, the French chef having, no doubt, grown tired of having the proposed menu for the day being returned to him without comment, or with 'pudding and tart' scrawled across the bottom, and then receiving no word of either commendation or complaint about the dishes that were served. One guest complained of the 'very worst turtle soup' he had ever tasted and 'the Punch as bad'. The Duke's wines were, however, 'excellent', so George Gleig testified. 'They were all mellow and ripe because he paid large prices for them, yet the oldest could not have been more than a couple of months in his possession. Of his reasons for thus acting he made no secret and he acted in a similar manner with every consumable article required in housekeeping. "At one time," he said, "I used to do as others do – gave my orders to the house-steward, and handed him the money to pay the bills. This went on for a year or two when [I discovered] the fellow had been gambling with my money . . . and from that day to this I have made it a point to pay my own bills, and to keep my accounts with tradesmen as short as possible."'

The Duke himself drank very little wine, in later years giving it up almost entirely in favour of iced water, two decanters of which were placed beside him and were usually empty when he went to bed. About nine o'clock, the ladies having already gone to the drawing-room, he would say, 'Will anybody have any more wine?', then lead the way to the drawing-room himself, never remaining long at table for he never smoked, having only once in his life tried a pipe and once a cigar, neither of which he liked, and he never indulged in the kind of bawdy talk common at other tables on these occasions. Lord Ellesmere never heard from anyone 'in his society, still less from him anything which might not have been repeated before ladies'.

In the drawing-room he sat in his armchair by the fire where guests would come up to talk to him. Cards were not played at Walmer; but there were books and newspapers lying on the tables.* About eleven the ladies retired and, half an hour later, their host would light his candle and say, 'I am going to bed. Whoever leaves the room last will ring for the lights to be put out.' In his room he was soon asleep in his narrow bed, his head resting on 'an exceedingly hard pillow, stuffed with horsehair and lined with wash leather'.

Occasionally there were duties connected with his Wardenship of the Cinque Ports to perform: he had, for instance, to see that the countersign to the Dover garrison was given every day, and from time to time he had to march in procession through Walmer with the Cinque Port pilots when the court was in session. But none of his duties was arduous and, once his correspondence had been dealt with, he found time to walk along the beach, to take pot shots at woodcock in the castle grounds or throw crumbs of bread to the robins which hopped about in the hawthorn hedges, or to inspect his kitchen garden in the castle moat and discuss the progress of the vegetables with his head gardener, Townshend, a former sergeant, whom he had employed on the spur of the moment when the man had called at Stratfield Saye in the hope of finding work.

'Do you know anything about gardening?'

'No, your Grace.'

'Then *learn* – *learn* and return here this day fortnight at the same hour. Take the place of gardener at Walmer Castle.'

'But I know nothing of gardening.'

'Neither do I. Neither do I.'[11]

He still read, or at least looked into, a wide variety of books, declining to finish those of whose contents he disapproved or which he believed

---

* There was never a dearth of books in any of the Duke's houses, since it had become common practice for authors to send him copies of their works. So many arrived, indeed, that he felt constrained to give orders that no parcels of books should be taken in unless he was given the opportunity of declining those he did not want. Requests for him to subscribe to books in preparation met with the standard response: 'F.M. the Duke of Wellington begs to decline to give his name as a subscriber to the book in question. If he learns that it is a good book he may become a purchaser.'

to be false.* When he reached the pages dealing with Julius Caesar's cruelty to his prisoners in Niebuhr's *Roman History* he declined to continue, refusing to have one of his idols so thrown down; and in the middle of reading P.A. Fleury de Chaboulon's *Mémoires. . . de Napoléon* he exclaimed, 'There is not a word of truth in all this bombast' and angrily set the book aside.

While deprecating the discussion by laymen of sacred subjects, he was particularly interested in books of theology, warmly recommending Cardinal Wiseman's *Lectures on Science and Revealed Religion* to one friend, and telling another that Alexander Keith's *Evidence of the Truth of the Christian Religion from the Fulfilment of Prophecy* was 'the most interesting Work upon any Subject' that he had 'ever perused'. He was also much impressed by a work which advanced the thesis that the original inhabitants of America had reached that continent across the Atlantic Ocean from Phoenicia; and he was once found carefully studying a dissertation by the architect Matthew Habershon on prophecy. He was much intrigued by P.F. Curie's *Principles of Homeopathy*, confessed that the horrors described in the *Histoire des Girondins* made him feel 'quite miserable' and ashamed that 'Human Nature should be so bad', and, although he rarely read novels now, he did once read aloud to his guests the instalment of the *Pickwick Papers* in which is recounted the eponymous hero's defence of the breach of promise action brought against him by Mrs Bardell.[12]

The Duke still had many visitors both at Walmer and at Stratfield Saye, not all of them welcome. A notice was fixed to the front door at Stratfield Saye: 'Those desirous of seeing the Interior of the House are requested to ring at the door of entrance and to express their desire. It is wished that the practice of stopping on the paved walk to look in at the windows should be discontinued.' Uninvited visitors were not always turned away, however. A woman with two children, who had wandered into the shrubbery at Walmer and been warned off by a servant, was stopped by the Duke who happened to be riding by. She apologized nervously.

> 'Oh, never mind, never mind,' was his answer. 'You're quite welcome to go where you will. And, by the by, bring the children here tomorrow at one o'clock, and I'll show them all about the place myself.'

---

* He declined, however, to read accounts of his own times. 'I have not read Sir David Baird's *Life*,' he declared characteristically. 'I never read these modern productions called histories, in which my name must be made use of, because I do not wish to be tempted to write myself' (WP/H1, WP2/6/42, 22 Oct. 1833).

The lady came as desired, and was delighted to find that the Duke had prepared a dinner for her children, and lunch for herself, with fruit. The young people ate their fill, and the Duke, after showing them through the castle, and over the garden, hung a half-sovereign suspended from a blue ribbon round each of their necks before sending them away.[13]

Capable as he was of offering such hospitality to strangers, it was noted that 'though retaining to the last a warm regard for his old companions in arms, he entered very little with them into the amenities of social life. There is reason to believe that neither Lord Hill nor Sir George Murray ever visited the Duke at Stratfieldsaye; nor could they or others of similar standing, such as Lord Anglesey, Sir Edward Paget and Sir James Kempt, be reckoned among the habitués of Apsley House'.[14]

Charles Arbuthnot was, however, often a guest; so was Croker; so was Alava, amiable and amusing, hobbling about on crutches now, black toothed but still enjoying a reputation as an *héros de roman*, and, despite his long residence in England, still speaking English with an atrocious accent.*

The Duke's son, the Marquess of Douro, was also a frequent guest at Stratfield Saye, the more welcome there now because of his wife Elizabeth, the pretty, unaffected daughter of the eighth Marquess of Tweeddale, to whom the Duke was devoted.† Almost as often to be encountered there were Philip Stanhope, Lord Mahon, an assiduous recorder of the Duke's conversation, who had been Under-Secretary when the Duke was Peel's Minister for Foreign Affairs; and John Gurwood who came without his French wife, a Parisienne of dubious extraction, one of whose sisters was a dressmaker's assistant and another the mistress of the Director of the Comédie Française.

* Alava was not, however, as welcome as he had been in the past, which was 'easily to be accounted for, for many reasons,' Lady Salisbury said: 'but among others from his love of gossiping which, of all other propensities the Duke most detests' (Hatfield House Papers, June 1835). Exasperated by the Duke's reticence, Lady Georgiana Fane once burst out, 'Oh, do pray speak ill of somebody' (*Ibid.* 18 July 1836).
† When he was told of Douro's proposal of marriage to Lady Elizabeth Hay, the Duke wrote immediately to her father to tell him how pleased he was: 'No connection which Douro could form could be more agreeable to me: We have for many years been connected in Service; and by friendly Relations; and I entertain no doubt that the closer connection about to be formed between our families will tend to our mutual satisfaction. You will find me disposed to make every arrangement which may be desirable for the Comfort Happiness and Honor of Lady Elizabeth' (Yester Papers, MS. 14448, 57, 23 Nov. 1839).

Colonel Gurwood himself was becoming increasingly strange, over-worked amidst the Duke's voluminous papers, obsessed by animal magnetism and mesmerism, insomniac and depressed. The Duke, who had appointed him Deputy-Lieutenant of the Tower at a salary of almost £800 a year, advised him to go down to Brighton for a rest; but he was more miserable than ever there and one Christmas Day in his lodgings he cut his throat.

The Duke wrote to his widow to express his condolences, at the same time asking her to return to him the papers on which, so he had been told, her late husband had been in the habit of making notes of his conversation. Mrs Gurwood replied that 'from an overstrained sense of delicacy' towards his Grace, Colonel Gurwood had destroyed all his papers. The Duke took leave to doubt it: he had been informed by 'different persons, by some verbally by others in writing, that the Colonel had been in the habit . . . of retiring to his room early at night, or as soon as possible, in order to write down a memorandum' of what the Duke had said. The Duke – disregarding the activities of James Boswell and choosing to ignore those of Lord Mahon, if indeed he was aware of them – did not believe there was 'an instance in history of a similar act'. It was 'anti-social'; it put an end 'to all the charms of society, to all familiar and private communications of thought between man and man'.[15]

Mrs Gurwood was not a woman to bear submissively such a rebuke. She replied with spirit. Wellington responded with further reproofs, reminding her that, although her late husband had been a frequent guest in his house, the Duke had never had the honour of receiving Mrs Gurwood, excepting at balls, concerts or public breakfasts. So she could not be expected to be acquainted with her late husband's prac-tices. Whether or not there had been such practices, Mrs Gurwood replied, she had no papers to return to the Duke and there the matter must be allowed to rest. The Duke allowed it to rest after sending her a long letter of explanation and guarded apology.[16]

So the Duke never saw the Colonel's record of his talk; nor did he see Lord Mahon's *Notes of Conversations with the Duke of Wellington* which was published long after both of them were dead. Lord Mahon, the fifth Earl Stanhope as he became upon his father's death in 1855, had been indefatigable in his endeavours to record all that the Duke said which might be considered of the remotest interest, his stories about India and about the Peninsula, his encounters with Talleyrand, Blücher and Napoleon's marshals, his opinion of the Spanish armies, his views on Roman Catholics, the mob, conscription, estate management, indeed on anything upon which an opinion was expressed.

The Duke submitted patiently, some thought resignedly to Lord Mahon's promptings and interrogations; but there were occasions when it became clear to others that his patience was tried, when he would have preferred to have been left alone with a book. Taking pity on him one evening, a lady guest piled his reading table high with volume upon volume as a barrier between himself and the importunate Mahon whose habit it was to occupy a nearby seat. But, not in the least put off by this, Mahon removed all the books and settled himself down in his usual chair. The Duke murmured to the lady who had tried to help him, 'I don't think much of your fortifications.'[17]

He was much given to such remarks of sardonic humour; and, having once listened to the wiseacre J.W. Croker expatiate at length upon the science of fortification, he was obliged to receive a further lecture at dinner upon the respective merits of various percussion caps. 'My dear Croker,' he said with the utmost good nature, 'I can yield to your superior information on most points, and you may perhaps know a great deal more of what passed at Waterloo than myself; but, as a sportsman, I will maintain my point about the percussion caps.'[18]

With no one was his amiability more evident than it was in his encounters with children who were so often to be seen romping about his house. 'I'm considered a great favourite with children,' he was proud to say. He played hide-and-seek and football with them on the ramparts, indulged them with pillow fights, crawled about the floor with them under the dining-room table, allowed them to be 'eager attendants' when he opened his letters in the morning, made no protest when, as a signal for romps to begin, a cushion was hurled at the newspaper in his outstretched hands, or even, as Haydon had noticed, when, ignoring his injunction not to do so, they slopped tea over his coat at breakfast. Lady Salisbury thought it was 'quite *touchant*' the way in which the children surrounded his chair and rushed upon him in delight when he entered the room.[19] He was once seen playing draughts with the young son of his valet who, having been beaten twice at the game, was asked to have dinner with him; and once he agreed to look after a pet toad for a boy whom he came across in tears in his garden because he thought the creature would die of starvation when the holidays were over. The Duke was true to his word and sent a report of the toad's satisfactory progress when the boy had gone back to school.[20]

Strange children were treated as indulgently as the offspring of his guests and his own grandchildren. They might well be asked to a meal as were the children of the woman found wandering in the shrubbery. They were presented, as those children had been, with shillings or half sovereigns attached to red and blue ribbons kept in his pockets, blue ribbon for those who said they would like to join the Navy, red for those who declared a preference for the life of a soldier, and a red one once for a little girl to whom, mistaking her sex, he promised a commission in the Guards. They were allowed to pick fruit in his orchard; and, when staying in the house, were likely to receive letters from him by post. He wrote to them also when they returned home, being careful not to write by the same post as he wrote to their parents so that they were given the satisfaction of supposing that the postman had come especially to make deliveries to themselves.[21]

He delighted in making toys, and, indeed, in all manner of contraptions, some of them of his own invention, such as a sword-umbrella for dealing with footpads and would-be assassins in rainy weather, a mackintosh cape compact enough to be rolled up in his pocket, a teapot cum hot-water jug which his guests found impossible to manage, and a finger bandage which he invented at Woodford where, so Lord Ellesmere said, 'he did nothing but exhibit how he could tie and untie it for himself'. He also had a weakness for inventing or elaborating strange conveyances, like his exceptionally fast curricle, and for wearing the oddest of clothes designed to keep him dry and warm, including overalls, layered capes such as those worn by coach drivers, sleeveless cloaks like tents with immense pockets and fur collars. He also possessed a voluminous grey cloth coat lined with reindeer fur which he had presumably brought home from Russia. Charles Dickens once saw him in London wearing a 'bright white overcoat'.*

* The original Wellington boot was a high boot covering the knee in front and cut away behind so as to make it easier to bend the knee. The term was also used, from 1818, to denote a shorter boot worn under the trousers. It was later used to designate a waterproof rubber boot reaching to the knee. Wellington also gave his name to Wellingtonia, the popular name of a large coniferous tree, *sequoia gigantica*, to the Wellington chair and the Wellington chest, to coats, hats, trousers and apples. The adjective Wellingtonian entered the language in 1854. Wellington became a term in cards as, for instance, in nap when a call of *Wellington* doubles *Napoleon*. All over England – he never went to Scotland, entertaining a suspicion, so it was said, that some dreadful misfortune would overtake him if he did so – taverns, streets, avenues, squares, crescents, terraces, roads, gardens and bridges were named after him. In the Greater London area there are more of these bearing his name than there are commemorating any other person – sixty of them are named Wellington and twenty-two Wellesley. There are, in addition, nineteen avenues, courts, streets, roads and places commemorating Waterloo, and at least fourteen Wellington or Duke of Wellington public houses. There is, by comparison, only one Nelson's Arms and one Nelson's Head.

He had a touching tendency to suppose that these examples of unusual apparel and more or less useless contraptions were worthy of the most respectful regard, just as he was convinced that his geese were invariably swans. He once bought at a draper's shop in Ramsgate a white handkerchief with red spots which cost him a shilling and of which he seemed inordinately proud. Walmer Castle was the 'most charming marine residence' he had ever seen: there was nothing to be compared with it even in royal hands; the lime trees in its garden were 'the finest in the world'; Apsley House was without a defect; Stratfield Saye was 'perfect as a residence'. 'His pictures, his statuary, his furniture, his horses and his carriages, were all regarded in the same light'; while the rather clumsy and heavily ornate billiard table at Stratfield Saye was 'not only excellent as a Billiard-Table but the most beautiful piece of furniture' he had ever seen. His horses, likewise, were 'as good as any in London'. Indeed, like his guns, they were 'better than anybody's'.[22]

43   The Young Queen

1837 – 9

'Our Gracious is very much out of Temper.'

IN HIS PICTURE of her first Privy Council meeting, painted at the young Queen Victoria's instigation by Sir David Wilkie, the members of Lord Melbourne's Cabinet stare with fixed gaze upon her Majesty. At the other end of the table stands the Duke of Wellington, eyes cast down, a figure apart, *sui generis*.

He had already had much to do with the Queen who came to the throne on the death of her uncle, King William IV, in 1837. The Duke had been present at her birth and had subsequently watched her progress with interest; and, as was to be expected, had been much taken with her. At this first Council meeting she performed her part perfectly, he said: if she had been his own daughter he could not have been better pleased with her, concerned though he was that, even were she to be an angel from Heaven, she could not, at her age, be expected to have the knowledge to oppose the mischief the Whig Government was likely to propose to her. At her coronation he himself was warmly acclaimed with a burst of applause upon his appearance in Westminster Abbey – as was France's representative, Marshal Soult* – and there was 'a great shout and a clapping of hands' when he knelt to do homage to her.[1] He was applauded again when he left the Abbey and he looked back down the aisle 'with an air of vexation', Lady Salisbury thought, as if to say 'this should be for her'. He noted that she carried herself with charm, dignity and grace.[2]

He could not, however, forbear from voicing his later disapproval of her appearance on horseback at a review of her troops at Windsor. She would have been well advised to come in a carriage; it was a

---

* Out of deference to the feelings of Marshal Soult, the Duke asked for a delay in the publication of the volume of his *Dispatches* in which is described the Marshal's defeat at Toulouse. He also ordered the removal of the French trophies from his table when Soult attended a dinner at Apsley House, substituting for them some vases presented to him by Louis XVIII which bore no inscription (Sir Herbert Maxwell, *Life of Wellington*, ii, 321, quoting Lady Salisbury's journal).

'childish fancy' to come on a horse, attended by men only. She had evidently read about Queen Elizabeth at Tilbury Fort. 'But *then* there was threat of foreign invasion, which was an occasion calling for display.' 'What occasion,' he asked, 'is there now?'[3]

It was a rare criticism at that time, though her being surrounded by 'Whigs and Whiglings male and female' did not augur well for the future.[4] Nor did his being the only Tory guest at a Court banquet where his place-card, which he preserved as a 'real curiosity', read, 'Chancellor of Oxford'.[5] It was soon clear, however, that he was considered at Court to be far more influential and far more worldly than university chancellors were normally expected to be. So, when it was falsely rumoured that Lady Flora Hastings, the unmarried lady-in-waiting to the Queen's mother, the Duchess of Kent, was pregnant by the widely disliked and distrusted Comptroller of the Duchess's Household, Sir John Conroy, both the Duchess and Lady Flora's brother, the Marquess of Hastings, flew to the Duke for advice, as people so often did in circumstances such as these. The Duke, in Charles Greville's words, 'wrote a capital letter to the Duchess, advising conciliation and quiet'. He had already offered the same advice to Lord Hastings whom he told that, both for his sister's sake and the Queen's, the scandal was better hushed up.[6] For a time it seemed that this advice would be followed. The Queen, who had not been on speaking terms with her mother when the rumours were first spread abroad, who detested Sir John Conroy and who had been much inclined to believe that the pious, High Tory Lady Flora was, indeed, pregnant, agreed to receive her and to express the hope that all the unpleasantness of the past would soon be forgotten. But neither Lady Flora's mother nor her brother was prepared to allow the 'atrocious conspiracy' to be brushed aside in this way; and when Lady Flora died and a post-mortem revealed that the swelling of her stomach had been caused by a growth on her liver, newspapers expressed the outrage of the people.

For a long time now the Queen's early popularity had been fast slipping away. She was hissed at the theatre and at Ascot where two Tory ladies in the crowd cried out, 'Mrs Melbourne!' At Lady Flora's funeral her carriage was stoned. As Greville said, she had now become 'an object of indifference or of odium'.

She had already become embroiled in the first serious constitutional crisis of her reign. At the beginning of 1839 she had been horrified to hear from the Home Secretary that the Government of her dear Lord Melbourne, facing defeat on a colonial issue in the House of Commons, would have to resign. The Duke was shocked by her petulance, by her tearful distress at the prospect of having to deal with Tories which were one of the things, she said, like insects and turtle soup, that she hated most in all the world. And what if they demanded changes in her Household? She could not bear that. Lord Melbourne had assured her that they would not touch her Ladies; but she feared that they might want to do so, and she was determined to prevent them.

It would not have been so bad had she been able to have the Duke of Wellington as Melbourne's successor; but when she sent for him, as Melbourne advised her to do, the Duke maintained that he was now too old at seventy, as well as too deaf, to think of becoming Prime Minister again, that she must ask Sir Robert Peel to form a Government instead.[7] The prospect of Peel as Prime Minister depressed her still further: he was so difficult to talk to; his extreme shyness in her presence made her feel shy too, while his nervous mannerisms, his irritating habits of pointing his toes and thrusting out his hands to shake down his cuffs, reminded her of a dancing master.* She added that, even if Peel were to become Prime Minister, she would continue to see Melbourne whom she considered 'as a parent'. The Duke was perfectly agreeable to this, unusual as such an arrangement would be. When the Duke left her she burst into tears.

Her subsequent interview with Peel confirmed her worst fears. Melbourne had warned her that he would be 'close and stiff'; he was also, so she complained, embarrassed and 'disagreeable'. She reacted in the same way, taking childish pride in being austerely civil 'and high', and accepting with unconcealed distaste the names that Peel put forward as Ministers. When Peel tentatively suggested that there would have to be some changes in the Household to show that the new Government enjoyed her confidence, the Queen quickly rejoined that the only members she could be expected to part with were those gentlemen who were also in Parliament. For the moment Peel let the matter rest there, merely commenting that nothing would be done without her consent. He then awkwardly took his leave and, as the door closed behind him, she, yet again, gave vent to her feelings in further floods

---

* The accuracy of the second part of Wellington's celebrated comment about their respective unsuitability for the office of the Queen's first minister – 'I have no small talk and Peel has no manners' – was confirmed by Charles Greville: 'I never was so struck as yesterday [20 February 1835] by the vulgarity of Peel. In all his ways, his dress, his manner, he looks more like a dapper shopkeeper than a Prime Minister. He eats voraciously, and cuts cream and jellies with his knife ... Yet he has genius, and taste, and his thoughts are not vulgar though his manners are to such a degree' (The Greville Memoirs, iii, 162–3).

of tears. 'He is such a cold odd man,' she wrote to Melbourne. 'The Queen don't like his manner . . . How different, how dreadfully so, to that frank, open, natural and most kind warm manner of Lord Melbourne. The Duke I like by far better than Peel.'[8]

During his second audience, Peel came more firmly and directly to the question of the Household. 'Now, Ma'm,' he said, 'about the Ladies.' The Queen, bridling at the implied question, replied that she could never give up any of her Ladies, that she 'never had imagined such a thing'.

Did she intend to retain *all* of them? Peel asked.

'All.'

'The Mistress of the Robes and the Ladies of the Bedchamber?'

'All.'[9]

But some of these Ladies were married to his Whig opponents, protested Peel who, so the Queen afterwards wrote with satisfaction, began to look 'quite perturbed'. This did not matter, she riposted; she never talked politics with her Ladies, it did not matter to whom they were married. He would not ask her to change her younger Ladies, Peel persisted; it was only the more important, senior Ladies who would have to go. But these, she countered, were just the ones she could not spare; besides, queens had not been asked to make sacrifices in the past. Comparisons with past queens did not really apply, Peel pointed out; *they* had been queen consorts, *she* was a reigning queen: that made all the difference. 'Not here,' the Queen declared sharply, refusing to give way.

Forced to conclude that he himself could do nothing more to move her, Peel enlisted the support of the Duke who found that the Queen had now worked herself up into a state of 'high passion and excitement'.

'Well,' he began, 'I am very sorry to find there is a difficulty.'

'Oh, *he* began it and not me,' the Queen replied. 'It is offensive to me to suppose that I talk to any of my Ladies upon public affairs.'

'I know you do not . . . But the public does not know this.'[10]

The argument continued for some time; but the Duke was powerless in the face of the young girl's stubborn pertness. So was Peel when he made a further effort to persuade her to change her mind. Sir Robert must be very weak, she told the Duke tartly as she closed the discussion, if *even* the *Ladies* were required to share his political opinions.

'I was very calm but very decided and I think you would have been pleased to see my composure and great firmness,' the Queen reported to Melbourne who, in fact, had expressed the opinion that it would be very unwise to break off negotiation with Peel on such an issue. 'I never saw a man so frightened . . . but this is *infamous* . . . The Queen of England will not submit to such trickery. Keep yourself in readiness for you may soon be wanted.'[11]

Most of the senior members of his Cabinet were far readier than Melbourne himself to support the Queen in her stand against Peel's demands. Melbourne noted that Peel was asking for '*some* changes', not a complete replacement of the entire Household. But this did not much concern Lord John Russell, the Home Secretary, who considered it unthinkable to desert the Queen in her stand against unreasonable Tory demands, nor Lord Howick, later Earl Grey, Secretary at War, who believed her Majesty had 'the strongest claims' to the Government's support 'in the line which she [had] taken'. So Lord Melbourne, not unwillingly, allowed himself to be persuaded; and on 12 May, having approved a Cabinet Minute to the effect that his Ministers were prepared to remain in office to ensure that the Queen's wishes in the matter of her Ladies were respected, he appeared once more at dinner at Buckingham Palace, 'very much excited', in the Queen's words, 'talking to himself and pulling his hair about which always [made] him look so much handsomer'. At a ball given that week for the Tsarevich, who was on a state visit to England, she was seen to be much excited herself. She did not leave the ballroom until a quarter to three, 'much pleased' as her mind was 'happy'. The Duke and Peel, she noted in her journal, seemed 'very much put out'.[12]

So the Tories and the Duke remained in opposition. But, for the Duke, this as usual meant opposition on his own terms. Never having been a strictly party man, he certainly did not intend to become one now. He would continue to support the Government of the day when he considered that they needed his support and to oppose them when he felt called upon to do so.* He felt such a call when the Government proposed to accord the Queen's chosen husband, Prince Albert of Saxe-Coburg and Gotha, the same more than generous allowance of £50,000 a year that had been granted to Queen Anne's husband, Prince George of Denmark. The Duke insisted that £30,000 would be

---

* The Duke's view was that Lord Melbourne was 'the best Minister' the Queen could have. He told Lord Clarendon, 'I like Melbourne . . . and he has given her very good advice I've no doubt.' But, he added, 'I am afraid he jokes too much with her, and makes her treat things too lightly, which are very serious.' Melbourne heard of this remark and repeated it to the Queen who rejected its message. But Melbourne said there was unfortunately some truth in it.

quite enough, although, as Colonel Gurwood told the third Earl of Liverpool, he did not really care 'a fig about it'.*[13]

Supported by other Tories, he raised more determined objections when it was proposed to grant Prince Albert precedence over all other people in the country, including the royal dukes. On behalf of the Whigs, Lord Clarendon went to see the Duke in the hope that he might be persuaded to induce the Tories to be less intransigent. The Duke was not to be persuaded. The precedence of the Royal Family, he pointed out, was fixed by Act of Parliament. It was well known that he held no brief for the royal dukes; but it would be unfair to ask them to support a change of the law to interfere with their rights.[14] When Charles Greville asked the Duke what he thought should be done 'about the precedence', the Duke answered emphatically, 'Oh, give him the same which Prince George of Denmark had: place him next before the Archbishop of Canterbury.' 'That will by no means satisfy her,' Greville objected. At this the Duke 'tossed his head, and with an expression of extreme contempt said, "Satisfy her! What does that signify?"'[15]

Upon hearing of Tory objections to her granting Prince Albert the precedence she had in mind for him, the Queen was quite as cross as Melbourne had feared she would be. She 'raged away', 'perfectly frantic', in her own words, railing at her uncles and the 'vile, confounded, infernal' Tories as 'wretches', 'scoundrels' 'capable of every villainy [and] personal spite'.[16] Already they had deeply offended her by censuring her Whig Ministers for not having made it clear that Prince Albert was a Protestant and able to take Holy Communion in the form prescribed by the Church of England. In the House of Lords, Wellington, in leading the attack, had declared that the people ought to know something about Prince Albert other than his name, that they should be given the satisfaction of knowing that he 'was a Protestant – thus showing the public that this is still a Protestant state'.[17]

'Do what one will,' the Queen protested to her uncle Leopold, King of the Belgians, 'nothing will please these most religious, most hypocritical Tories whom I dislike (I use a very soft word), most heartily and warmly.' As for the 'wicked old foolish' Duke of Wellington, she would

---

* 'Everybody (except those who have an interest in defending it) thinks the allowance proposed for Prince Albert very exorbitant: £50,000 a year given for pocket money is quite monstrous, and it would have been prudent to propose a more moderate grant for the sake of his popularity' (*The Greville Memoirs*, iv, 231). Prince Albert was eventually granted £30,000 a year, over twenty times more, in present day terms, than the £65,000 which the Duke of Edinburgh received as a result of the Civil List Act of 1972.

never speak to him or look at him again, she would certainly not ask
him to her wedding. Nor would she send a message to Apsley House
when it was reported that the Duke was ill. Charles Greville called
there and found 'his people indignant that while all the Royal Family
have been sending continually to enquire after him, and all London
has been at his door, the Queen alone has never taken the slightest
notice of him'. Greville immediately sent Melbourne a note 'representing the injury it was to *herself* not to do so'. Melbourne asked
Greville to come to see him without delay and told him that the Queen
was 'very resentful, but that people pressed her too much, did not give
her time'. To this Greville replied that it 'really was lamentable' that
she did the things she did, that she would get into a great scrape. The
people of England would not endure that she should treat the Duke
of Wellington with disrespect. He had no scruple in saying so to
Melbourne since he knew that the Prime Minister was doing his utmost
to keep her straight. 'By God!' Melbourne said, 'I am moving noon and
night at it.'[18]

He wondered, though, if it were not now too late for the Queen to
send a message to Apsley House. 'Better late than not at all,' Greville
advised him; so Melbourne sat down and wrote to the Queen. 'I suppose
she will send now?' Greville asked. 'Oh, yes,' Melbourne replied. 'She
will send now.' Melbourne also persuaded the Queen to ask the Duke
to her wedding after warning her that the people of England would
never tolerate the absence of the Duke at such a national event. But
'that Old Rebel', the Duke, was the only Tory there, apart from the
two joint Great Chamberlains, Lord Liverpool, father of her friend
Lady Catherine Jenkinson, and Anthony Ashley Cooper, the husband
of Melbourne's niece, Lady Emily Cowper. But she did not intend to
ask the Duke to the wedding breakfast. 'Our Gracious,' Wellington
concluded, 'is very much out of Temper.'[19]

The Queen's angry displeasure with the Duke did not last long.
She looked upon him more favourably when, having read a pamphlet
prepared by Charles Greville, he changed his mind about Prince
Albert's precedence and infuriated the Queen's uncle, the Duke of
Cambridge, by declaring that she had, after all, 'a perfect right to give
her husband whatever precedence she pleased'.* He later supported

* He had evidently voiced a similar opinion as to the Queen's authority at the outset
of her reign when the Master of the Horse, Lord Albemarle, insisted that he had the
right to accompany her Majesty in her state coach on her way to St James's Palace to
be proclaimed, as he had done with William IV. The Queen wished to be accompanied
only by her mother and one of her Ladies. 'The point was submitted to the Duke of

the Queen against the old royal family by coming out in favour of Prince Albert's being appointed Sole Regent in the event of her Majesty's death. 'It could and ought,' he said, 'to be nobody but the Prince.' The Queen was also grateful to the Duke for the part she understood he had played in persuading the detested Sir John Conroy to leave the country.*

By the time her first child, Princess Victoria, was born, she was on such good terms with him that she asked him to represent the baby's godfather, the Duke of Saxe-Coburg, at the christening; and when her next child was born, the Duke expressed himself as being much flattered 'by her Majesty's most gracious desire that he should bear the Sword of State at the ceremony of the christening of His Royal Highness the Prince of Wales'.[20] 'The Duke,' the Queen wrote in her journal, encouraged in the belief by Prince Albert, 'is the best friend we have.'[21] 'I was never so well received,' the Duke wrote contentedly after a visit to Windsor in August 1840. 'I sat next to the Queen at Dinner. She drank wine repeatedly with me; in short if I was not a Milksop, I should become a Bottle Companion.'[22]

He went out of his way to please her. At a military review in Windsor Park he gave orders that the guns should remain silent until she had

---

Wellington, as a kind of universal referee in matters of precedence and usage. His judgement was delightfully unflattering to the outraged magnate – "The Queen can make you go inside the coach or outside the coach, or run behind like a tinker's dog"' (G.W.E. Russell, *Collections and Recollections*, 26).

* Although there were other reasons for Conroy's retirement, the Duke took full credit for it himself, telling Greville that he had persuaded the man to leave by means of cajoling and flattery, using 'plenty of butter' (*The Greville Memoirs*, iv, 198–9). He was certainly glad to see the last of him. He thought it probable that he was the Duchess of Kent's lover and believed that the Queen's hatred of him was the result of her having witnessed 'familiarities' between him and her mother (*The Greville Memoirs*, ii, 194–5). The Duke had already crossed swords with him and the Duchess when, as Prime Minister, he had declined to submit to the new King William IV her claim, formulated by Conroy, to be made Regent in the event of the King's death and, in the meantime, to be treated as Dowager Princess of Wales and be granted an income suitable to that rank. An Act of Parliament had, however, appointed the Duchess sole Regent for her daughter. This had much gratified Conroy and had prompted the Duchess to say that, when the news reached Buckingham Palace, it was the first happy day she had known for ten years. The King, on the contrary, had been much displeased; and at a dinner at Windsor Castle, at which the Duchess was sitting next to him and Princess Victoria opposite, he had rudely declared that he hoped his life would be spared for nine months longer until his niece came of age so that there could be no question of a Regency being placed in the hands of a woman sitting near him who was 'surrounded by evil advisers' and was 'incompetent to act with propriety in the station in which she would be placed'. The Princess had burst into tears; and the Duke of Wellington had commented, 'very awkward, by God!' (*The Greville Memoirs*, iii, 309–10).

left the ground, knowing that she hated the noise of artillery. There would be no firing, he assured her; but some mistake had been made and no sooner were the words out of his mouth than 'bang went the guns all down the line!' It was so irresistibly funny that the Queen 'burst into an uncontrollable fit of laughter'. But the Duke was furious; he positively 'blew up'; no one could appease him; and he gave orders for the gunners to leave the field immediately.[23]

He was more successful in his attentions to the Queen at a concert at Buckingham Palace. She had a bad cold and ran out of handkerchiefs before the performance was over. The Duke, who was sitting immediately behind her, noticed her plight; and, since he always carried a reserve supply in his pocket, he was able to help her. 'I immediately slipped one of mine into her hand,' he related contentedly, 'then a second, then a third; and whispered I had a fourth at her service should she require it.'[24]

44 Grand Old Man

1839 – 50

'There is not an affair of any kind in which I am
not required to be a party.'

AS WELL AS OPPOSING the Government when he felt that opposition
was called for, the Duke continued to write reports and memoranda
for their guidance upon matters on which he considered himself to be
peculiarly or uniquely qualified to speak. He had not been at all disposed to take a Cabinet post of any sort again, though when the Queen
asked him if he would consider becoming Foreign Secretary should
she ever be forced to accept Peel as Prime Minister, he had intimated
that his sense of duty might oblige him to undertake such a responsibility. Would not the work be too much for him? the Queen wondered.
'I'm able to do anything,' he said as he always did when his health and
strength were questioned.

He was thankful, though, that he had not been required to take up
office again. As it was, he was still constantly being bothered and
badgered by people who wanted his help or advice in one way or
another. 'I am the Duke of Wellington,' he was much given to complaining, 'and an officer of the army. But there is not an affair of any
kind in which I am not required to be a party ... There is not an
Individual who wants anything of any description; particularly money,
who does not apply to me for it. If a church or chapel, Glebe or School
House or even Pagoda is to be built, I must patronise and subscribe
for it: the same for Canals, Rail Roads, Harbours ... Rest! Every other
animal – even a donkey, a costermonger's donkey – is allowed some
rest, but the Duke of Wellington never! There is no help for it. As
long as I am able to go on, they will put the saddle upon my back and
make me go ... Every Animal in the creation is allowed some relaxation
from Exertion ... except for the Duke of Wellington ... It is like
everything else. Nobody else will do it. The Duke of Wellington
must... They forget that the Duke of Wellington has only one pair of
eyes, and only a certain number of hours in the day like other people

. . . On this very morning [30 November 1841] I have received not less than fifty letters . . . They will not understand that the whole labour and business and ceremony and everything else of the world cannot be thrown upon one man . . . I really think that people now and then should apply in the proper quarters and not come to me.'*[1]

Fears had already been expressed that the Duke had been overstraining his constitution when he had risen to make a speech in the House of Lords in the middle of May 1839, soon after his seventieth birthday. As he swayed on his feet, men leaned forward to catch his whispered sentences when, without warning and quite inappropriately stressed, a torrent of words issued from his lips in a voice of intimidating force. Six months later it was noticed by his servants at Walmer that he was losing his appetite, picking at his food with the fork in his left hand and keeping his right hand in his pocket. One day, after eating nothing but a morsel of dry bread for breakfast and, on returning from riding, a fragment of an Abernethy biscuit which he broke from a little parcel of them placed on his bureau, he found that he could not hold his newspaper properly. He had gone out for a brisk walk, hoping to shake the malady off. But, upon returning home, he had fallen to the floor of his room where his valet had discovered him unconscious. Lord Mahon had hurried down to find him on his camp bed 'apparently insensible; his face like monumental marble in colour and in fixedness, his eyes closed, his jaw dropped, and his breath loud and gasping'.[2] He had soon recovered from this stroke but his right arm and mouth were still stiff several days later.

The following year in February he had another stroke while riding over to see Lady Burghersh. When he got to Harley Street he could not make out the numbers on the doors; nor could he recognize his niece's house. His groom had to guide him home, holding the reins of

---

* Protest as he did, the Duke loved being consulted. 'The Duke,' Melbourne said one day to Queen Victoria, 'is amazingly sensible to attention; nothing pleases him so much as if one asks his opinion about anything' (Queen Victoria's Journal, Royal Archives, 6 February 1838).

Shortly before his marriage to Lady Elizabeth Hay, the Marquess of Tweeddale's daughter, Lord Douro urged his bride to consult his father as often as possible: 'Pray do not neglect to write to the Field Marshal on Sunday at farthest; He will like much to hear shortly from you often, for he likes to be in everyone's confidence and have his advice asked in things which are *not* his business. Consult him about your difficulties . . . He will answer you by return of post' (Wellington Private Papers, 15 March 1839; Gerald 7th Duke of Wellington (ed.), Roxburghe Club correspondence, 1952).

his horse which he could not grasp in his own chilled hands. On his arrival at Apsley House a servant was sent for Dr Hume who found him groaning in the drawing-room. He was immediately put to bed where he had a series of convulsions. The next day Lord Lyndhurst expressed the fear that he might now become 'a dotard like Marlborough, or a driveller like Swift'.[3] He recovered from that stroke, however, as quickly as he had recovered from the earlier one; but Lord Mahon now described him as being extremely thin, stooping 'a good deal on one side, his countenance careworn and pale, and the fire of his eagle eye much quenched'.[4]

Charles Greville had already made similar observations: 'It is a sad thing to see how the Duke is altered in appearance, and what a stride old age has made upon him. He is much deafer than he was, he is whiter, his head is bent, his shoulders are raised, and there are muscular twitches in his face, not altogether new, but of a more marked character.'[5]

In February 1841 he had another seizure in the House of Lords. Thomas Raikes heard that he had been 'conveyed in Lord Brougham's carriage to Apsley House where he remained for some hours in an alarming state'. 'It is really surprising', Raikes commented, 'that notwithstanding his previous warning the Duke will persist in taking so little care of [himself] . . . He had dined hastily at two o'clock, and went down to the House in an open carriage, with the weather at five or six degrees of frost.'[6]

It was remarked how deeply he had been affected by the death of Lady Salisbury just before the first of these strokes. Since then he had grown closer to Lady Wilton to whom he wrote numerous letters.[7] But she was neither as *simpatica* as Lady Salisbury, nor as tirelessly interested in his political life as Harriet Arbuthnot had been. He grew increasingly lonely; and considered it fortunate that he had so much to occupy his mind, that his opinion and influence were still considered well worth seeking, that, despite his recent strokes, he was able to go about his business, demonstrating what Mahon called 'a victory of mind over matter'.

He spoke in the House of Lords, if not as fluently as the Hansard reporters suggested at least upon as diverse a selection of topics as he had ever done, on Canada and the Middle East, on French insolence and Irish potatoes, on the 'lamentable state' of the magistracy and on penny postage, on the doubtful use of Indian missions and on Chartism which was 'neither more nor less than Combination to raise Wages: to force Industrious Men to discontinue Work by Violence and

Intimidation . . . the ultimate object being to obtain money, whether in the shape of Wages, pension or any other manner, without Work'.[8]

He even signified his willingness to take command of the armies of a German Confederation. At the same time he occupied himself far more conscientiously and tendentiously than had been expected with the affairs of Oxford University, supporting calls for the reform of college statutes; strongly urging the Hebdomadal Board to refrain from expressing an opinion upon a Bill to remove Jewish disabilities which was 'not required of them and was not their duty to give'; plunging into the dispute concerning the appointment of the Low Church Whig, Dr Renn Dickson Hampden, as Regius Professor of Divinity; endeavouring to calm the uproar occasioned by the proposal to erect a memorial to the three Protestant martyrs, Latimer, Cranmer and Ridley, and to soothe the passions roused by the tracts and sermons of J.H. Newman and Edward Pusey; and, when Convocation proposed to challenge the Duke's nomination of Dr Benjamin Symons as Vice-Chancellor, threatening to resign 'by return of the post'.[9]

Meanwhile, the Duke's correspondence showed no sign of flagging; and he continued to deal with it with as little help as possible, explaining to Lady Wilton that, since there was 'not a secret whether political or Private, in Europe or in the World at large' which did not come into his hands, anyone who saw his papers must be completely trustworthy.[10]

In any case, his correspondence remained a welcome if extremely demanding activity and an assurance that he was still a forceful presence in the state. He continued to answer an extraordinary number of letters in his own hand or to add pungent comments to the forms which were dispatched to those deemed unworthy of more detailed replies, often standing up at his desk, still preserved at Apsley House, for hours on end. To his secretary, Algernon Greville, he handed draft replies written on blank sheets of paper or scrawled across the writing on letters received or, as his handwriting shrank with age, squashed on to the corners of pages turned down for the purpose.[11]

His composition of lengthy memoranda also continued apace. Some of these were written for the guidance of Ministers or Government departments, others for the benefit of friends and acquaintances who sought his opinion on all manner of subjects and were given it in the most meticulous detail. Charles Greville was far from being alone in thinking that he often expressed himself at quite unnecessary length: when he was asked 'to be a party to the establishment of a college in Kent to teach agriculture', he declined to be associated with it on the grounds that it reminded him 'of a lady in Paris who had an opera dancer to teach her daughter how to walk in a garden', and that, in any case, he really knew very little about farming, the expression of this lack of confidence covering several large sheets of paper.[12]

When Lord Melbourne departed from office in 1841 and Sir Robert Peel became Prime Minister again, the Duke made it known that he was willing to 'do anything, go anywhere, and hold any office, or no office, as may be thought most desirable or expedient for the Queen's service'.[13] There were growing doubts, however, about his health: he often found it difficult to keep awake now, though he prided himself on needing little sleep. 'I am perfectly well,' he had told Lady Salisbury when she advised him that to get up at six o'clock was too early for a man who, in London, was rarely in bed before midnight. 'Whether a man has a little more sleep or a little less, what does it signify?'[14] He also suffered much from rheumatism and was more prone than ever to outbursts of alarming irritation as, for instance, when Lord Charles Manners, son of the Duke of Rutland, offered to act as his guide while they were riding together through the grounds of Belvoir Castle. 'I never wanted anyone to show me my way,' he snapped, 'and I don't now.'[15] A stranger who guided him through the traffic at Hyde Park Corner was given even shorter shrift. The man, having received the Duke's curt thanks, assured him that it was a privilege to be able to help him. 'My Lord,' he said, 'I have passed a long and not uneventful life; but never did I hope to reach the day when I might be of some assistance to the greatest man that ever lived.' The Duke cut such nonsense short: 'Don't be a damn fool!'[16] Later that evening, in Lady Lyttelton's drawing-room, having related this story of his crossing through the traffic at Hyde Park Corner, he added complacently, 'And I do believe, if it hadn't been for me, the fellow would have been run over.'[17]

The Duke, it seems, behaved quite as dismissively to a man who approached him after a service at Stratfield Saye parish church and asked to have the privilege of shaking hands with the victor of Waterloo. He, too, was told not to be a damned fool.[18]

A man who accosted him in the street with the greeting, 'Mr Jones,

I believe?' received the curt response, 'If you believe that, Sir, you will believe anything.'*

Written requests were quite as sharply put down, although his private secretary, Algernon Greville, did his best to soften their harshness when he could. One day a plea was received from a manufacturer in the north who asked the Duke to use his influence to persuade the nobility and gentlemen at Court to wear lighter coloured clothes, which did not last so long as dark coloured cloth, and thus help the cloth manufacturers of the north where unemployment was rife. This met with the blunt rejoinder that the Duke of Wellington was not a member of Prince Albert's household and it was no part of his duty to advise him what to wear. Similarly, a request for the Duke's intercession on behalf of another of his correspondents received this characteristic rebuff: 'Field Marshal the Duke of Wellington ... positively and distinctly declines to solicit favors for any Person whatever, but most particularly for a Gentleman of whom he knows nothing, not even whether or not he is trustworthy.'[19] A request from a philanthropist to present some petitions on behalf of chimney sweeps to the House of Lords was met with a similarly curt dismissal: 'Mr Stevens has *thought fit* to leave some petitions at Apsley House. They will be found with the porter.'[20] A correspondent who sought the Duke's opinion as to Bonaparte's behaviour in Egypt was brusquely informed that F.M. the Duke of Wellington was not the historian of the Wars of the French Republic.[21]

According to the second Duke's friend, Sir William Fraser, a similar reply was sent to a man who wrote on behalf of his mother, a washerwoman who, 'having washed for the Marquess of Douro for many years', had been unable to obtain payment for the last three:

> The Duke of Wellington regrets to find that his son has not paid his washerwoman's bill.
>
> The Duke of Wellington is not the Marquess of Douro.
>
> The Duke recommends that Mrs Tomkins places the matter in the hands of a respectable solicitor.[22]

Some weeks later, at a dinner party at Apsley House, the Duke was

---

* The Mr Jones for whom the Duke was mistaken was, no doubt, George Jones (1786–1869), the painter and Keeper of the Royal Academy from 1840 to 1850, who bore a remarkable resemblance to Wellington and was often pointed out as being the great Duke himself. He specialized in painting historical and military subjects in several of which Wellington is portrayed. The Royal Academy has a photograph of him which reveals his resemblance to the Duke.

asked if he was pestered for his autograph. 'Oh, yes, constantly,' replied the Duke who declined to accede to the requests. He must then, so Fraser thought, have been much put out to be told of a man who overcame the reluctance of eminent people in this respect by writing to them to accuse their sons of bilking their washerwomen.[23]

The impatience and anger of the Duke when responding to importunate or impertinent letters were reflected in the appearance as well as in the tone of his replies which became notably more emphatic, with words written in capitals and with exclamation marks liberally employed.[24] The handwriting itself became smaller and smaller as though to accord with the shrunken frame of the man so impatiently wielding the pen. It also became increasingly illegible, 'the despair of his friends,' Lord Ellesmere said, 'and also of himself when he had to recur to it'.[25] Even Algernon Greville could not read it on occasions; and when Croker sent one of the Duke's letters back to be deciphered, Greville had to confess he could not do so and wrote, 'The Duke always writes without spectacles; he fancies his eyes are much stronger and better than they were twenty years ago. He consequently often writes parts of words only and often omits them altogether. However, I have one consolation, and that is, that I am a much better hand at his own writing than he is himself.' Unfortunately, Algernon Greville's writing was much like the Duke's, and was sometimes quite as bad or even worse.[26] Once when asked to decipher one of his own illegible letters, the Duke protested, 'It was my business to write that letter. It is your duty to read it.'[27]

Members of the Duke's family were just as likely to be soundly admonished as were strangers. When, for example, he was invited to the wedding of one of his brother Richard's grandsons and the bridegroom's mother forgot to mention where the ceremony was to take place, he sent her a reply at once heavily sarcastic and angrily impatient: it was usual to indicate the venue as well as the time in such a communication; presumably it was not to be 'the open space in Piccadilly opposite the Gate of [his] House'. He could not really be expected to go about the streets 'seeking for the place at which W. Wellesley is to be married to Miss Drummond'. Besides if a man of his age was 'required to give his Attendance, care ought to be taken to fix a Season for his Attendance convenient to Himself'.[28]

To save time in answering letters and refusing applications, the Duke ordered lithographed forms to send out to decline all manner of requests from 'Applications for Employment and Places' and 'Applications for Patronage of Inventions' to 'Invitations to Dinner' and 'Duke's Autograph'. There were no forms, however, to refuse requests for money with which he was exceptionally generous, especially to soldiers' charities as well as orphanages. Indeed, as Charles Greville said, he was 'profuse but careless and undiscriminating in his charities, and was continually imposed upon, especially by people who pretended to have served under him, or to be the descendants or connexions of those who had; and it was very difficult to restrain his disposition to send money to every applicant who approached him under that pretence'. Occasionally, however, when in a grumpy mood, he would lose patience with a petitioner as he did with the importunate widow of an army officer who twice sent him a bundle of testimonials and was curtly informed on the second occasion that F.M. the Duke of Wellington was not a relieving-officer.[29] He also grew tetchily impatient with officers who approached him with requests for promotion or with pleas for him to stand as godfather to the children of parents he had never met.[30] Yet he made it a habit not to leave his house without a supply of sovereigns in his pocket so that he could distribute them to men or the wives of men who had, or claimed to have, served under him.

Charles Arbuthnot agreed with Greville that the Duke was as generous as he was indiscriminate in his charities, frequently sending money to applicants without enquiring as to the merits of their claims and giving wry accounts of the more preposterous of these applications. He once upbraided Lord Charles for his interference after he had informed his father that a letter the Duke had received, and to which he intended giving a favourable response, had been composed by a gang of swindlers, excusing his sending money to a barrack-master he had had to dismiss for dishonesty by declaring, 'What can one do? One can't leave a man to starve', and explaining his generous gifts to orphanages by saying that he had been involuntarily responsible for making so many orphans that he felt in duty bound to help them.*

---

* Wellington College, which was founded as a memorial to the Duke soon after his death, was originally intended, at the instigation of Prince Albert, as a charitable foundation for 'the education of orphan children of Indigent and Meritorious Officers of the Army'.

The Wellington family were much distressed when they heard of the Prince Consort's plan. They had themselves hoped that enough money would be raised by public subscription to erect a huge bronze statue of the great Duke in every large town in the country. So they were not altogether surprised or, indeed, disappointed when, despite the dispatch of 100,000 letters and a compulsory subscription of a day's pay by all the ranks in the Army, insufficient sums were raised for the proposed institution's endowment; and they were much relieved when it became clear that E.W. Benson, the future Archbishop of

One day Arbuthnot found him stuffing banknotes into several envel-
opes. 'What are you doing, Duke?' he asked him. 'Doing? Doing what
I am obliged to do every day. It would take the wealth of the Indies
to meet all the demands that are made upon me.'[31]

Often those who succeeded in obtaining an interview with the Duke
wished they had failed to do so. A baronet who had gained access to
Apsley House was abruptly asked, 'You stated you had something to
say to me.'

'Yes, my Lord. I have a question to put. I wish to ascertain whether,
if your Grace were to return to office, you would support principles of
moderate reform.'

'That is your question, is it?'

'Yes, my Lord.'

'Then allow me to put a question in return. What right have you to
ask me?'[32]

The Duke was often quite unaware of the distress or offence his
rebuffs occasioned. Whenever a wounded recipient of one of his blunt
letters wrote to protest, he would ask the victim to return the letter to
him with the objectionable passages marked. Even when conscious
that he had been rude or unreasonable he still never apologized though
his anger soon cooled and he would make it clear that there were no
feelings of lasting resentment towards the persons who had provoked
him. His servants were well aware of this. His valet recalled an occasion
when the Duke, having rung his bell with terrifying violence, upbraided
him furiously for moving a book he had left on a table. 'I laid it just
there,' he said, striking the table with his hand. 'You have taken it
away. What have you done with it?' When the servant had gone, he

---

Canterbury, who was appointed the first Master of the school, intended to create a great
public school like Rugby, where he had been an assistant master. To do so he was
prepared to ignore the wishes of the Court as expressed by Sir Charles Phipps, Prince
Albert's private secretary, who wrote to him to say that it was 'hardly worthwhile to
establish another public school in competition with those already existing'.

When Benson retired from Wellington College in 1872 the second Duke of Wellington
was called upon to make the farewell speech. It was a rather humdrum performance;
and the Duke afterwards took Benson aside to apologize for it and to tell him what he
'really meant to have said'.

'I and my family hoped that there would be a fine monument set up . . . And you can
fancy what our feelings were when we found that it was . . . a charity school . . . where
scrubby little orphans could be maintained and educated . . . But you have made the
college what it is – one of the finest public schools in England – and I and my family
are more than content at the result' (Jonathan Gathorne-Hardy, The Public School
Phenomenon, London, 1977, 138); David Newsome, A History of Wellington College,
1859–1959, London, 1959).

remembered that he had taken the book into another room. He rang the bell again; the servant returned to be asked some question nothing to do with the book. On receiving the man's reply, in 'a tone of marked kindness', the Duke said, 'Thank you, I am much obliged to you.'[33]

'It seemed to be a settled principle with him,' observed the Rev. G.R. Gleig when he himself had been unjustly upbraided, 'never to acknowledge that he had done wrong.'[34] George Napier made the same observation: 'He has always kept to that system never acknowledging he was wrong or mistaken.'[35]

'But sooner or later,' Gleig added, 'he made amends for whatever wrong was done by a process which, though indirect, was infinitely more agreeable to the sufferer than any apology could have been.'[36]

His great-niece, Lady Rose Weigall, did, however, recall one example of an apology. It was given, either at Walmer or at Stratfield Saye – she could not remember which – when she was a child. The Duke had several times rung the drawing-room bell and no servant had appeared. When a footman at last came, the Duke upbraided him angrily.

> So far from being frightened I thought it exceedingly funny to see the Duke angry and went into fits of laughter [Lady Rose remembered]. This checked him, and the footman then interposed saying, 'If your Grace will look you will see the bell is broken and never rang at all. I only came in for something else.'
>
> The Duke examined the bell and then turned to the footman and said, 'Yes, I was wrong, I am very sorry William, and I beg your pardon'; and then turning to me added in his gruff voice, 'Always own when you are in the wrong.'[37]

45 The Horse Guards and the House of Lords

1842 – 50

'It would be difficult to convey to the present
generation any idea of the veneration that was felt
for the Great Duke.'

IT WAS NOTICED, not unexpectedly, that the Duke was at his most
acerbic when his rheumatism was troubling him or he was suffering from
a cold, as he frequently was, a circumstance which his doctors considered
not in the least surprising since he thought nothing of driving up to
London, even in winter, in his open britska after a breakfast of dry bread
or an Abernethy biscuit. The very fact that the doctors advised him against
doing so made him determined not to give up the practice. In his opinion
'all doctors are more or less *Quacks*! . . . and what they talk is neither more
nor less than *nonsense & stuff*.[1] He preferred to stick to his own prophylac-
tics and cures, even though they were clearly not efficacious: he wore
Bengal muslin next to his skin to prevent colds, and, pulling on Indian
gloves, rubbed himself with vinegar and rose water every time he changed
his clothes, which he would do as often as seven times a day. To his
friends he recommended a whole range of cures or preventatives: Mrs
Arbuthnot had been enjoined to wear a paper cap he made for her when
she had a bad cold; Lady Salisbury was advised not to give her little son,
Sackville, 'a full Supper' before he went to bed at night and to warn her
brother to 'leave off Opiates';[2] Lady Burghersh was urged to wear 'eye
preservers' and sent large bottles of the acid he used himself to preserve
her from colds – they would not prevent her from catching colds entirely
but 'the attacks would be much less frequent and milder'. Also to be
recommended were 'Chili vinegar gargle', 'Lemon gruel & Stuff' and
keeping the head warm at night by putting 'Brown paper upon it'.*[3]

---

* His brother Richard was almost as full of medical advice as the Duke himself. Richard
told his brother more than once how to ensure he did not become deafer than he was
already. He must take care to see that the temperature of the ear was kept steady and must
'always wear cotton when outside' (Wellington Papers, Hartley Institute, WPI/750/19).

367

Since his strokes in 1839 and 1840 he had recovered his balance and his step was seen to be quite firm as he walked down Piccadilly or Constitution Hill; but he rolled alarmingly in his horse's saddle as he rode across the Park. Indeed, it was a 'wonder to all bystanders that he did not topple over', for he sometimes fell asleep as he rode along. His deafness was growing worse by the month and he was inclined to refuse invitations to shoot now, since the noise of the guns made it worse than ever. 'I am very sorry that you are so deaf,' he commiserated in a letter to Croker. 'I have been very bad lately . . . I suffer torments in the House of Lords, at meetings, etc., etc. when I am obliged to talk after listening, and endeavouring to hear and understand what others say. I should not mind it if I had only to understand the bawling of [my grandchildren].'[4] 'I am certain,' he told Lady Salisbury, 'I catch cold in my Ears at night! which causes Deafness as well as Rheumatism in my neck next day.'[5]

He was also now finding it increasingly difficult to read without spectacles, while the rheumatism in his neck made his stoop a deformity seized by caricaturists. Charles Greville went so far as to describe him as being 'only a ruin'.

The prospect of serving in Peel's Cabinet as a minister without office appeared to give him new strength, however; and when Lord Hill died in December 1842 he felt strong enough to return to the Horse Guards as Commander-in-Chief, his 'proper place', he said, the place to which he was 'destined by [his] trade'.[6] The next year he was described as surprising everybody by 'speaking with extraordinary vigour'. He was 'certainly a much better man in all respects this year than he was two years ago, mind and body more firm'. So that when Peel resigned in December 1845, and Lord John Russell was left with the difficult task of forming an alternative Government, the Duke had no hesitation in satisfying the Queen's 'STRONG desire' that he should remain 'at the head of her Army'.[7] It cannot be said, however, that he was as effective as a Commander-in-Chief as he was to be as the acknowledged leader of the House of Lords. Indeed, Prince Albert believed that there could be no reform in the Army so long as Wellington remained in command of it though when the Duke, anxious that it should not fall into the hands of the House of Commons, proposed that Prince Albert should succeed him, the Prince protested that he was quite unsuited to the task and was far from convinced by the Duke's assurance that he need not spend much time at the Horse Guards since subordinates would attend to all the details.[8]

Bringing a strongly conservative cast of mind to such matters as the

Oil sketch of the Duke aged fifty-nine by Sir Thomas Lawrence.

Left: 'Achilles in the Sulks after his Retreat or the Great Captain on the Stool of Repentance.' A caricature by Thomas Howell Jones, published on 7 May 1827, shows the Duke in a huff at Apsley House, having resigned his political office as well as that of Commander-in-Chief. His baton lies broken at his feet. On the table is a large letter: *'His M-j-sty accepts the resignation of his Grace the Duke of W-ll-ngt-n with the same regret that it is communicated.'* Outside the window is the Achilles statue, the first public nude statue in England, which was erected near Apsley House at the expense of 'the women of England to Arthur Duke of Wellington and his brave companions in arms'. The King was reported to have said that he would keep the command of the Army in his own hands until Arthur recovered his temper.

Right: *Repose*, a lithograph by H.B. (John Doyle) published on 10 July 1831 after Wellington's labours as Prime Minister had come to an end.

Left: 'Awful Apparition to a Gentleman whilst Shaving in the Edgeware Road.' A drawing in *Punch* of Matthew Cotes Wyatt's immense statue of the Duke, which weighed 40 tons and was 30 feet high, being dragged from Wyatt's workshop in 1846 to Hyde Park Corner where it was much ridiculed.

Walmer Castle, the Duke's residence on the Kentish coast when he became Lord Warden of the Cinque Ports. He died here in September 1852.

'The Field of Battersea', a caricature by William Heath published in March 1829 after Wellington had fought a duel with Lord Winchilsea. The Duke's face is a lobster's claw – soldiers being then known as lobsters because of their red coats. He wears a monk's robe and a rosary to indicate his support of Roman Catholic emancipation. Winchilsea fires in the air, while the Duke's doctor, J.R. Hume, sits on the grass to watch the contest.

A sketch by Haydon for his *Wellington Musing on the Field of Waterloo*, portraying the Duke in his seventy-first year. Haydon wrote on the back: 'Never touched since it was left as it is, by desire of Lady Burghersh and Mrs Arbuthnot. They thought I had hit the expression.'

Wellington Musing on the Field of Waterloo, painted by Benjamin Robert Haydon, who had stayed at Walmer Castle in 1839.

Queen Victoria's first Privy Council meeting in 1837 by Sir David Wilkie. The Queen is inaccurately portrayed in a white dress, as a symbol of innocence, instead of in the black dress she was actually wearing. Lord Melbourne, the Prime Minister, stands holding the pen; Peel is on his left; the Duke, in uniform as Commander-in-Chief, stands in front of the pillar with the Duke of Sussex seated to his left and the Duke of Cumberland to his right.

A miniature engraving of the Duke from a daguerreotype taken in 1844 when he was seventy-five.

Angela Georgina Burdett-Coutts, Baroness Burdett-Coutts, a portrait in watercolour upon ivory by Sir William Charles Ross done six years after the Duke's death in 1858 when she was forty-four. She had asked the Duke to marry her eleven years before when she was thirty-two and he seventy-seven.

Left: Franz Xaver Winterhalter's portrait of the Duke with Sir Robert Peel at Windsor Castle in 1844 when Peel was Prime Minister and Wellington a cabinet minister without portfolio.

Elizabeth Hay, daughter of the eighth Marquess
of Tweeddale, Marchioness Douro, afterwards
Duchess of Wellington, the first Duke's beloved
daughter-in-law. From a portrait by Sir George
Hayter.

Arthur Richard Wellesley, Marquess Douro,
Wellington's elder son, afterwards second
Duke of Wellington. A portrait by Spiridore
Gambardella.

The Duke opening his letters before breakfast in his library at Stratfield Saye and giving the covers to
his grandchildren. The picture was painted for Baroness Burdett-Coutts the year after the Duke's
death by Robert Thorburn. The four children are, from the left, Henry (later the third Duke, born in
1846 and died without issue in 1900), Mary Angela (married George Scott of Rotherfield Park,
Hampshire in 1875 and died in 1936), Arthur (later the fourth Duke, born in 1849 and died in 1934)
and Victoria Alexandrina (married the first Baron Holm Patrick in 1877 and died in 1933).

training of officers and the innovations in weapons and armaments, the Duke was as loath to deal effectively with such outrageously arrogant officers as the Earl of Cardigan – who had ordered the arrest of a junior officer for placing wine on the mess-table in a black bottle instead of a decanter – as he was to look favourably upon suggestions that flogging should be abolished in the Army.* He shared the view of many other senior officers that, despite public opinion which was running high against it, flogging was a necessary punishment as a deterrent in cases of gross ill discipline. The Duke was equally unwilling to consider abolishing the purchase of commissions – since the necessity to buy a commission 'brought into the service men of fortune and character' – and to countenance an increase in the soldiers' pay. This was not, however, because he thought the soldiers were unworthy of better treatment – the condition of their dreadful barracks was much improved while he was in office – but because he saw danger in 'overtaxing the liberality of Parliament' and arousing the anti-militarism of the British people. For this latter reason he strongly disapproved of officers parading about the streets in uniform when not on duty.[9]

He was also opposed to Prince Albert's proposal for the purchase of a large area of land as a military training ground and declined to consider the merits of such inventions as a new sight for muskets which was brought to his notice by the Rev. Patrick Brontë of Haworth Parsonage near Bradford. 'Field Marshal the Duke of Wellington presents his compliments to Mr Brontë,' the Commander-in-Chief wrote in a characteristic rebuff. 'He considers it his duty to refrain from interfering in the details of duties over which he has no control . . . Much time would be saved if others would follow the Duke's example.'[10]

In other words the old musket which had been so effective in the Peninsula was still perfectly serviceable and there was no need for its adjustment, still less for its replacement by the Minié rifle which had been invented by Captain Minié of the Chasseurs d'Orléans. Lord Fitzroy Somerset, the Duke's Military Secretary, had advised the Government to extend a factory at Enfield where rifles incorporating the best features of the Minié could be made; but it was not for some time that the Duke authorized the general use of Minié rifles in the Army and even then many of them were to be manufactured with smooth bores so that the old stocks of musket ammunition could be

---

* In a long memorandum on the subject of corporal punishment dated 4 March 1852 Wellington wrote, 'I cannot conceive that there is a man with information on the subject who will think otherwise than that if the state is to have an army, we must retain the use of corporal punishment' (Wellington Papers, Hartley Institute, WPI/1219/5).

used up. Nor must soldiers be allowed to fancy they were all likely to be turned into riflemen, otherwise they would become 'conceited and be wanting next to be dressed in green, or some other jack-a-dandy uniform'.[11] By the time the Crimean War broke out some two years after the Duke's death the whole Army had still not yet been issued with rifles or, indeed, with many other kinds of equipment which other armies considered essential. Watching a French regiment unloading its stores at Balaclava, its wagons and ambulances, planks for hutting, heaps of tents, crates of medical supplies and other material, a British officer demanded to know if their allies had come to colonize the country.[12]

While there were officers at the Horse Guards who expressed their concern at the Duke's old-fashioned prejudices, his colleagues in Parliament continued to treat him with the utmost respect and consideration, looking up to him as the self-styled, incorruptible 'Servant of the Sovereign of this Empire', standing up when they had anything of importance to say to him and going to sit in the empty chair beside him so that he might better hear the questions they wanted to ask him or the advice they sought.[13]

In the country at large he was as popular as he had ever been and more venerated than ever before. When he entered Exeter Hall one evening as the performance was almost at an end, 'the piece they were singing stopt at once; the whole audience rose, and a burst of acclamation and waving of handkerchiefs saluted the great old man, who is now the Idol of the people. It was grand and affecting, and seemed to move everybody but himself.'[14] In Hyde Park 'the air resounded with acclamations as the Old Warrior passed by' at a review attended by the Czar and the Queen;[15] and at Cambridge, when Prince Albert was installed as Chancellor, it seemed to Charles Greville that he was received with even more enthusiasm than the Queen. 'It is incredible what popularity environs him in his later days,' Greville commented. 'He is followed like a show wherever he goes.'[16] A young lady new to London was 'amazed to see "well-bred" ladies stretch out their hands to touch the hero as he passed down the stairs'.[17]

'It would be difficult to convey to the present generation any idea of the veneration that was felt for the great Duke,' wrote the painter William Frith in his autobiography.

> Everybody, down to the street boys, knew him, and vied with each other in offering marks of respect. I cannot refrain from describing an incident that came under my own observation. I was descending the

steps that lead from the Duke of York's column into St James's Park, when I saw the Duke on horseback, trotting slowly along, followed by his chocolate-coated groom, and attended by a dirty little boy who managed to keep pace with the Duke's horse, now and again looking up at the rider. The Duke's patience with his inquisitive follower failed as I descended the last step into the Park, for he stopped his horse and addressed the boy:

'What do you want?'

The boy put his hands into his pockets, was confused for a moment, and then looking up at the Duke said:

'I want to see where you are going.'

'I am going there,' said the Duke, pointing to the Horse Guards. 'Now go about your business!'[18]

One day Greville was walking with him down Piccadilly and observed that everyone looked at him, all the men took off their hats to him, and 'one woman came up and spoke to him. He did not seem to hear what she was saying, but assuming as a matter of course that she wanted something, he said, "Do me the favor, Madam, to write to me," and then moved on as quickly as he could.'[19]

Politicians and men in the public service who had occasion to consult him sometimes found him tiresomely difficult, for he was as abrupt as ever and on occasions extremely cantankerous, stating his views with a confidence that defied disagreement and brushing away objections with alarming vehemence. 'There is no knowing in what mood he may be found,' wrote Charles Greville who learned much of what went on at Apsley House from his brother, Algernon. 'Everybody is afraid of him, nobody dares to say anything to him. He is sometimes very amiable and good-humoured, sometimes very irritable and morose.' 'When anybody applies for an interview, he flies into a passion,' Greville added. 'He fancies he is so engaged that he cannot spare time to see anybody . . . This peculiarity is the more remarkable, because formerly his weakness was a love of being consulted by everybody and mixed up with everything . . . Innumerable were the quarrels, *tracasseries*, scandals, intrigues, and scrapes which he had to arrange and compose.'[20]

When the repeal of the Corn Laws became a burning issue, he entered into an acrimonious correspondence with Croker, insisting, as with Roman Catholic Emancipation and Parliamentary Reform, that, although he himself did not personally approve of repeal, the Government should make a tactical retreat on the issue rather than allow Cobden and his radical friends to force repeal on their own terms.

After surprising his fellow peers by making a highly effective speech in the Lords, the Duke helped to ensure that the Corn Bill was passed in June 1846; and, upon emerging from the House in the early hours of the morning, he was loudly cheered. 'God bless you Duke!' a workman shouted. 'For Heaven's sake, people,' the Duke responded, 'Let me get on my horse.'[21]

A few weeks later another Bill introduced by Peel's Government was defeated in the Commons. On 29 June the Prime Minister announced his resignation and was succeeded by Lord John Russell. But the Duke remained at the Horse Guards and, while disapproving of Palmerston's aggressive behaviour at the Foreign Office, seemed as much at ease with the new Cabinet as he had been with Peel's. In fact, Charles Greville thought that he 'was much more cordial and communicative' with the new Prime Minister than he had been with his former Tory colleagues. Certainly Lord John valued him as a reliable liaison officer between the Government and the Court, for the Queen never felt entirely at ease with her new Prime Minister: he was so very small for one thing, and she always felt more at home with taller men. Besides, Lord John was always consulting his colleagues instead of discussing matters in an intimate way with her as she thought a Prime Minister should and as Lord Melbourne had taught her to expect. So the Duke's regular attendance at Windsor was a comfort to Russell who hoped that the Queen and the Duke would continue to get on as well together while he was Prime Minister as they had done in Peel's time.

46 Hyde Park Corner

1845 – 6

'Lord Melbourne was very funny about the statue.'

AT THE BEGINNING of 1845 the Duke was busy preparing to receive the Queen and Prince Albert at Stratfield Saye. The Queen had already paid a brief visit to Walmer Castle to give her children a taste of the bracing sea air when an outbreak of scarlet fever had prevented them going to Brighton. On that occasion her carriage had got stuck in the Castle entrance; but otherwise the visit had been a success, even though the building had had to be 'pulled to Pieces' to suit her convenience and was a scene of the most utter confusion when she arrived, with trunks and baggage in every room and 'Abigails, Maids, Nurses of all ages and descriptions running about'.[1]

The Duke, however, had not been in attendance then, having merely lent the Castle to an attenuated Royal Household and moved out to the Ship Hotel in Dover. But he was now in 1845 to act as host at Stratfield Saye.

He would have liked to forgo the honour. It was not that he was concerned about the house's comforts: the central heating system he had installed was perfectly efficient. The windows were now doubly glazed. The principal rooms were lit by colza-oil lamps. The conservatory, where he was in the habit of dealing with his correspondence of a morning, was also kept warm by an Arnott stove; and every one of the guest bedrooms had its own water-closet of blue patterned china. But there were only nine of these bedrooms, and the reception rooms were by no means large: they would seem almost minute when compared with what the Queen was used to in her own castles and palaces. His protestations of inadequacy were brushed aside: her Majesty 'smiled and continued to be very gracious but did not give a Hint of postponing the Visit'.[2] So 'bells had to be hung from H.M. Apartments into those for Her Attendants, Walls broken through, etc.'[3] 'You recollect Poor Mrs Apostles the Housekeeper,' the Duke reported to Lady Wilton, 'I thought that she would have burst out crying while I was talking to Her of the Honour intended and the preparations to be made. She said to me, "My Lord, Your House is a very comfortable Residence for yourself, your Family and your Friends. But it is not fit for the Reception of the Sovereign and her Court." I answered, "Very true." '[4]

The Duke need not have worried. The visit went off very well. He was a most attentive host, showing the Queen to her room and returning to escort her down to dinner, where he amused her by helping her to the dishes himself, 'rather funnily giving such large portions & mixing up tarts and puddings, but being so kind and attentive about it'.[5] After dinner he sat near to the Queen on the sofa where the conversation was 'certainly rather to the benefit of the whole society'. But he was 'very well and in very good spirits', she told her mother; and he went upstairs before her 'in the eveᵍ: with two candles in his hand'.[6]

The house was 'low & not very large' to be sure; but 'warm and comfortable'. She had a 'nice little sitting-room', a 'snug bedroom', and she and Albert both had dressing rooms.* If she was to be critical she had to confess that the Duke's central heating system made the rooms rather too hot. She was not accustomed to this – the Duke confided in Lady Salisbury that he was 'never warm at Windsor, excepting in bed!'[7]

The Duke took Albert shooting and into the tennis court and the billiard room. Family prayers were said in the morning which had never been done before; and when, 'thank God!', the visitation was concluded, the Duke attended 'Her Majesty on Horseback to the Borders of the County'.[8]

He dutifully gave a report of the visit to the Prime Minister. Indeed, he wrote to Russell at length on all manner of subjects from the state of the Army to the Government of India; and grateful for the Duke's

---

* The walls, she noted, were covered with prints which, indeed, the Duke – who had told Mrs Arbuthnot she could have no idea of the number he had got – had had fixed to the walls of nine rooms in the house, the room which Mrs Arbuthnot had occupied being decorated instead with water-colour copies of the frescoes uncovered at Pompeii, part of the booty taken from Joseph Bonaparte's carriage at Vitoria. The prints in all the other rooms included one or two of the Duke himself, a choice on their host's part which his guests were inclined to ascribe to a sardonic humour rather than to vanity.

comments and advice on such matters, Russell was prepared to over-look those upon which the Duke's concern threatened to become obsessive.

Among these topics was the danger which the Duke believed to be posed by foreign invasion and the consequent need for national defence. He and Lord Anglesey, by now Master-General of the Ord-nance, made several excursions together – referred to by Anglesey as 'reconnoisances' – to inspect the coastal defences which, so the Duke feared, were now open to attack, 'at all times and in any state of weather [by] Steam Vessels'.[9] The Duke wrote to Sir John Burgoyne, Inspector-General of Fortifications, on the subject; and Burgoyne was so impressed by the force of the Duke's arguments that he got his wife and daughters to make copies of the letter. One of these copies found its way into the hands of Lady Shelley who passed it on to Lord Ellesmere, the rich poet who had been Secretary at War in a previous administration, with the suggestion that the Duke might like to see it published. Parts of it were published, which the Duke did not mind at first; but when he became the butt of jokes in the popular press, and found himself accused of endeavouring to create alarm in the public mind with the intention of bringing down Russell's Government, he was furious. He apologized at length to Russell and wrote a letter of the most angry reproach to Lady Shelley who remembered the pain of receiving it long after the Duke had put the matter out of mind.[10]

Worry about national defence constantly haunted him, Arbuthnot said. It 'deprived him of rest, and night and day he was occupied with the unhappy state of our foreign relations, the danger of war, and the defenceless state of our coasts'.

The Duke became equally concerned when it was proposed that the colossal bronze statue of him which had been erected at Hyde Park Corner on Decimus Burton's Constitution Arch, then known as Wellington Arch, should be removed. This statue of the Duke astride a horse supposed to represent Copenhagen had been modelled by Matthew Cotes Wyatt and his son, James. Weighing 40 tons and measuring 26 feet from nose to tail, it was 30 feet high and large enough to accommodate a party of twelve who dined in it the day before it was placed in position. Upon seeing it for the first time after its scaffolding had been removed, the Duke expressed his pleasure at its appearance: 'The colossal size of the Statue, so remarkable when near the Ground, has disappeared, and in fact it now appears small for the Height of the Arch on which it is placed.'[11] Few agreed with him. It was commonly agreed not only to be far too large but also to be hideous: *Punch* described it as a 'monstrosity in ironmongery', 'a gigantic triumph of bad taste'; a Frenchman, upon seeing it for the first time, was said to have exclaimed, 'We have been avenged!' But when the Duke learned of plans to remove it from Hyde Park Corner, he was distressed beyond measure, though he had previously expressed himself quite indifferent to its creation. 'The Duke of Marlborough, because he was an old man, was treated like an old woman,' he said to Colonel Gurwood. 'I won't be. And the reason I have a right never to have a liberty taken with me is because I never take a liberty with any man.'[12] 'Upon the whole,' commented Benjamin Robert Haydon, 'the Duke has been made too much of at the wrong period of his life and too little of at the fine time. Because he knows himself old, he fears people take liberties with him, poor dear old man.'[13] He was, indeed, as Charles Greville and Harriet Arbuthnot had both recognized, increasingly given to pique whenever he felt himself slighted. 'He is the best natured, most warm hearted man in the world,' Mrs Arbuthnot had commented, 'but when he thinks he has been ill used he certainly does not easily forgive it.'[14]

He became even more distressed about the statue when he was led to believe that the Queen herself approved of its removal, as, indeed, she did. 'The D. of W.'s statue is *a perfect disgrace*,' she wrote in a minute to her Private Secretary. 'Pray say it ought to be covered over & hidden from sight.'*[15] The Prime Minister, who also thought it should be removed, apprehensively asked Greville whether or not he ought to mention the delicate topic at Apsley House. Russell would have been well advised not to do so, for the Duke had by then become so agitated over what he took to be an unforgivable slight that it was feared he might resign as Commander-in-Chief. Rather than drive him

---

* 'Lord Melbourne was very funny about the Statue of the Duke of Wellington ... Which we think looks dreadful and much too large,' the Queen wrote. 'We then observed what a pity Wyatt should do the Statue, as we thought he did them so ill ... [Lord Melbourne] continued, "I never will have anything to do with Artists. I wished to keep out of it all; for they're a waspish set of people"' (Queen Victoria's Journal, Royal Archives, 12 August 1838).

Sir Robert Peel agreed that Wyatt was a very bad choice. 'How could you consent,' he protested to Croker, a member of the committee responsible for it, 'to such a job as selecting Mr Matthew Wyatt – a bad architect and worse sculptor – for the Duke of Wellington's trophy' (*The Croker Papers*, ii, 326).

to this, it was decided to allow the statue to stay where it was, the Duke's feelings on the matter, so Russell decided, being 'the best grounds for retaining the statue as an eye-sore in its present position'.*16

* The statue, the first equestrian statue of a person other than a monarch to be erected in London, remained at Hyde Park Corner until it was removed to Aldershot in 1883 and handed over to the Aldershot Division by the Prince of Wales. Constitution Arch was then moved to the top of Constitution Hill. The bronze group, the Quadriga, which now surmounts it is by Adrian Jones, a former officer in the 3rd Hussars. The bronze statue of Wellington on Copenhagen to be seen at Hyde Park Corner now is by J.E. Boehm (1888). At each corner of the granite plinth are bronze figures of soldiers, those to the north men of the 1st Foot Guards and 42nd Royal Highlanders, and to the south the 23rd Royal Welch Fusiliers and the 6th Inniskilling Dragoons.

The stone figure of the Duke at the Royal Arsenal, Woolwich is by Thomas Milnes (1848). This was originally erected at the Tower and was brought to Woolwich in 1863 to commemorate the Duke's Master-Generalship of the Ordnance. The equestrian bronze of Wellington at the Royal Exchange is by Sir Francis Chantrey who died soon after he had made the maquette. The work, the unveiling of which was attended by the Duke, was completed by Henry Weekes in 1844. The bronze is from captured French guns. This statue was erected by the Corporation of London in recognition of the Duke's support of the Bill for the rebuilding of London Bridge. Wellington is the only person not of royal blood to have two equestrian statues erected to his memory in London (Weinreb and Hibbert, The London Encyclopaedia, 822–3).

A letter to the Duke from the sculptor, John Charles Felix Rossi, refers to another 'Colossal Portrait' of Wellington in the form of a 'Medallion encircled by a wreath (done from the bust by the late Mr Nollekens) and held by a figure on each side representing Europe and Asia' (WP1 1/1020/1, 25 May 1829). This was to have been placed on the 'Triumphal arch now erecting for his Majesty's Grand Entrance to His New Palace in St James's Park'; and a representation of it can be seen on the model of Nash's Marble Arch in the Victoria and Albert Museum. But the huge relief was not used for the Arch and it was eventually placed – with the Duke's head expunged – within the portico of the National Gallery over the entrance door, where it can still be seen (History of the King's Works, vi, London, 1973, 296, note 14).

47 Disturbers of the Peace

1846 — 51

'I feel no want of confidence in my own powers
... to provide for the general safety without
requiring the assistance of French Officers.'

WHEN LORD JOHN RUSSELL had become Prime Minister in July
1846, the Duke was seventy-six years old. Most of his army contemporaries were dead or were soon to die; and, except Lord Goderich, by
now Earl of Ripon, few of his erstwhile leading political colleagues
were left. Lord Liverpool had never recovered from the stroke that had
incapacitated him. Peel was soon to die, having fallen from his horse
as he rode up Constitution Hill; and, although he had never been
intimate with him, the Duke, close to tears, his voice breaking, spoke
movingly in the House of Lords of Peel's great qualities. He had never
known a man in whose 'truth and justice' he had a 'more lively confidence' or in whom he saw 'a more invariable desire to promote the
public service'.[1] John Cam Hobhouse, who saw the Duke at a levee
the day after Peel's death, found him 'sitting alone in a window seat,
leaning on his hands and looking pensively into the garden'. 'He was
more than usually grave, and when I went up to speak to him, he held
my hand for some time in his and spoke with great kindness. He was
evidently much affected.'[2]

Like Liverpool, Melbourne also had suffered from a stroke and had
had to concede that he was not capable of accepting it anyway when
Russell declined to offer him a place in his ministry. All the Duke's
brothers, as well as his sister Anne, died in the 1840s, his eldest brother
Richard being the first to go in 1842. His quarrel with the Duke had
been made up some years before with the help of Lady Wellesley who,
having received a call from her brother-in-law, had told her husband
that he would like to go to see him. 'I write this to prepare you to do
as you may like,' Lady Wellesley had written. 'But I am sure peace
with him is the wisest thing. He is most anxious for it.'[3]

The meeting had been a success and, having seen the Duke after it, Lady Wellesley had reported to her husband, 'He says nothing could be more gratifying than your reception of him . . . He was much affected and evidently highly pleased . . . Thank God you are now on good terms, and that nothing will ever change it.'[4]

As the Duke stood, looking 'pale and thoughtful', beside the grave at the funeral – which was conducted with great pomp at Wellesley's request at Eton College – William Fraser, then a boy at the school, passed by the grave and saw the Duke standing beside it, looking down into it. 'His upper lip quivered,' Fraser wrote. 'This I observed distinctly.'[5] The Marquess's grandson was also a witness of the scene which moved several mourners to tears. 'The Iron Duke,' he commented, 'folded his arms and looked sternly on the whole scene; what he felt he was determined not to show'.[6] He had, however, been unable to conceal his distress during a long delay before the interment and had burst out furiously to the undertaker, 'Sir, I don't know how it is, but these things are never done with punctuality in England. Had you informed *me* that the funeral would not take place till eleven I could have been doing other THINGS!'[7] On his return to Apsley House – having left the college by way of the Upper School and Flogging Room, rather than the Long Walk, so as to avoid the acclamations of the boys – he blamed the Provost of Eton also for the tedious delay: the man would never get a bishopric if he had anything to do with it.[8]

Lord Wellesley's death was followed by that of his brother William, Lord Mornington, in 1845. The Duke often went to see William in his dying days and reported regularly to William's daughter, Lady Burghersh. A fortnight before his death the Duke wrote to her, 'He was mightily pleased at seeing me; and thanked me repeatedly for my constant attention to him . . . He kissed me when I came away from him!'[9]

The Duke was equally attentive to Lady Burghersh's invalid son, George, who died at the age of twenty-eight, going to see him regularly while his mother was with her husband who had been appointed British Ambassador in Berlin, and promising to continue to do so whenever he 'had a moment to spare'.[10] 'I shall never forget all they tell me of his kindness to poor George in his last days,' Lady Burghersh wrote, 'and how much feeling he showed, kissing him and calling him "his dear child" with tears running down his face.'[11]

In August 1850 the Duke's dear friend Charles Arbuthnot fell seriously ill. 'No, no,' the Duke said, grasping the doctor's hand and looking him closely in the eye with earnest hope. 'He's not very ill, not very bad. He'll get better . . . It's only his stomach which is out of order.

He'll not die.'[12] But, on 18 August, on returning from a Sunday service in the Chapel Royal and entering his friend's room, he 'felt the cold at the ends of his fingers'. The Duke's hand in his, Arbuthnot died 'without a struggle, convulsion or apparent pain, just as a flame or candle would expire from extinction'.[13] The Duke was seen to be in tears at his funeral. 'I really feel that he would have died sixteen years ago if I had not gone on to him from Hatfield when I was apprised of her Death!' he wrote to Lady Salisbury. 'I have kept him alive; and, in general, good health and tolerable comfort ever since.'[14]

'He is a great and irreparable loss to the Duke who is now left alone in the world,' Charles Greville commented. 'Arbuthnot was almost always with him and had his entire confidence . . . The Duke, who has for a long time been growing gradually more solitary and unsocial, more irritable and unapproachable, is now left without any friend and companion with whom he can talk over past events, and to whom he can confide present grievances and complaints.'[15]

The Duke sought refuge in his grief and loneliness in his correspondence and public duties. Fortunately he was still consulted; his opinions were still valued. At the time of the proposed Chartist demonstration in London in 1848, when it had been expected that immense crowds of menacing people would march through the streets, when a number of noblemen had summoned men from their country estates to defend their London homes, when the Queen – in tears, suffering from postnatal depression after the birth of Princess Louise, and shivering with fright after the lamps outside Buckingham Palace had been smashed to shouts of *'Vive la république!'* – had been advised by Wellington to leave for her house at Osborne on the Isle of Wight, and several regiments had been called up, the Duke had suggested that reliance should be placed upon 170,000 special constables rather than upon the military.[16]

He had long been deeply worried about the Chartists. In 1839 he had angrily complained about the lack of authority of the magistrates in Birmingham where a demonstration had degenerated into a riot, where 'property was taken out of many houses and burnt in the public streets, before the faces of the owners, notwithstanding the presence of the police and troops with ample means of putting an end to these disgraceful disorders'.[17] He had subsequently thought it as well to go to a Chartist meeting. 'I was alone there,' he reported to a friend, 'the only one of my Caste.' However, he was not molested. In fact, the Chartists turned out to be 'better people than their fellows in the U. States who threw a Stranger over the bannister of their Stairs and broke his Ribs'.[18] Yet he did not underestimate the threat the English Chartists posed to the kind of society he wished to see preserved in his own country. He had no doubt that strong measures must be taken against them; and when he heard that some seven thousand armed men, mostly miners and iron-workers, had marched through the streets of Newport demanding the release of a Chartist orator from the local gaol, that they were fired upon by soldiers, that at least twenty-two had been killed, and that one of the demonstrators' leaders was a magistrate, he threw up his hands and declared, 'Oh! If I were twenty years younger!'[19]

He was determined to do all he could to ensure that such scenes should not be repeated in London in 1848. On a visit to Apsley House, Charles Greville found him 'in a prodigious state of excitement' as he formulated his plans.[20] Anxious not to provoke riots, he proposed that the Army should be ready to take action if necessary – and detailed plans were drawn up for such an emergency – but the troops, nine thousand of them, should be kept out of sight: there was to be no excuse for violence. As it happened, all went off quietly, as the Duke had predicted it would provided he was 'allowed to proceed' with his precautionary measures. Feargus O'Connor, the Irish orator and journalist, a leading figure in the Chartist movement, urged the crowds to disperse. Another Chartist leader gloomily conceded that the Government had proved too strong for the workers.

Thereafter, Chartism gradually declined; and Queen Victoria expressed her profound relief that the trouble was over and that the workmen, misled by professional agitators and the 'criminals and refuse of London', remained loyal after all.

She was deeply grateful to the Duke for the calm he had displayed during the crisis and the advice he had given; and not long afterwards, when her third son was born on his own birthday, she and her husband decided to call him Arthur 'in compliment to the good old Duke'. The Duke had already stood proxy not only for the Queen's father-in-law at the birth of her first child, the Princess Royal, but also for Prince Charles of Leiningen at the baptism of Prince Alfred. Now he was to be godfather himself to Prince Arthur who was, appropriately enough, to become a field marshal in the next century.[21]

'The Exhibition,' the Prince Consort added to the letter conveying the news of Prince Arthur's name to Baron Stockmar, 'is making good progress.'

The Duke rather wished it had not; for he had recently added to his other appointments that of the Ranger of the Royal Parks and, as such, he was responsible for Hyde Park where the Great Exhibition was to be held. He had to confess that he could not clearly understand 'the Benefit an Exhibition of Works of Art and Manufacture' was intended to produce, though he could well envisage the trouble its organization would entail. There was, first of all, the niggling problem of an old woman who had for years been occupying a shack on the banks of the Serpentine where she sold oranges, drinks and cakes. An official of the Department of Woods and Forests informed the Deputy Ranger of the Royal Parks that the 'female Squatter' would have to be moved. Annoyed by having received orders from a department of Government by way of his own Deputy, the Duke protested against such gross discourtesy, before riding over to talk to the old woman whose removal, he had no doubt, would be 'a troublesome job'.[22] As it happened, however, she was quite content to leave provided she received due compensation. She did leave and her ramshackle premises were demolished, but, months later, she had received no compensation. Instead, the Duke received a letter from the North London Anti-Enclosure Social and Sanitary Improvement Society whose indignant official enquired how the Duke would like it if his own dwelling were to be demolished likewise. The Duke replied that he did not understand what connection was supposed to exist 'between His Mansion in Piccadilly and Mrs Hicks's Cottage. The Duke purchased from the Crown his property . . . Mrs Hicks was neither more nor less than a Squatter on the bank of the Serpentine.'[23]

While dealing with Mrs Hicks's removal, the Duke had also to consider the problems of controlling the enormous crowds – many of them foreigners or of 'the lowish order' – which the Exhibition was likely to attract. Already an Arab camp, occupied by exhibitors from Tunis, had sprung up in the Park and had had to be contained within stout palings. Who was to keep an eye on less controlled foreigners who would be coming over to London in their hundreds, if not thousands?[24] The Duke thought that soldiers, largely cavalry, should be employed for this task, but kept out of sight, as he had suggested at the time of the Chartist demonstration in 1848. If they were needed, it should be remembered that it was always 'bad policy to *hem in a Mob*. The force should be applied in *one direction and as many avenues for* escape left open as possible.'[25] Prince Albert did not like this talk of soldiers: he argued that the presence of the military would not be in keeping with the tone and purpose of the Exhibition. So the Prime

Minister, Lord John Russell, suggested enlisting policemen from Paris. The Duke might as well have been advised to send for bashi-bazouks. He replied to Russell's proposition in a letter which made the Prime Minister hastily and apologetically explain that he was only trying to be helpful: 'I feel,' the Duke protested, 'no want of confidence in my own powers to preserve the public peace and to provide for the general safety without requiring the assistance of French Officers.'[26]

He felt no such confidence in the specially constructed Crystal Palace, or Glass Palace as he called it, which had been designed by Joseph Paxton on the lines of a conservatory which had been created for the Duke of Devonshire at Chatsworth. For one thing the glass was 'very thin', and for another it had been decreed that no trees should be cut down in the Park, so the Crystal Palace enclosed a tree from whose branches large numbers of sparrows flew about casting their droppings upon the 100,000 objects from all over the world being prepared for display. What was to be done? the Queen asked the Prime Minister, according to a fictitious story printed in a provincial newspaper. Lord John Russell proposed that the Foot Guards should be called upon to shoot the birds. Prince Albert pointed out that this was out of the question: the shot would shatter the glass roof. A solution proposed by the Foreign Secretary, Lord Palmerston, that birdlime should be put on the branches of the trees was equally impracticable: the sparrows had left the trees for the iron girders. The Duke, the time-honoured problem solver, was then asked for his opinion, and replied with a characteristic rebuff: 'The Duke of Wellington has the honour to be Commander-in-Chief of her Majesty's forces, but the Duke of Wellington is not a bird-catcher.' Immediately regretting the snub, the Duke recalled the letter and went in person to the palace where, so this invented story related, he delivered himself of his celebrated solution with typical directness and brevity: 'Try sparrow hawks, Ma'am.'[27]

Sceptical as he had been when the Great Exhibition had first been proposed, the Duke had by then become an enthusiast, and was often to be seen on the site talking to the workmen. When doubts were expressed that the construction would be finished in time, he announced with brisk authority, 'I know it will be ready. Paxton has said it will.'[28]

The Exhibition was opened on 1 May 1851 with a visit by the Queen who was much touched by the sight of the two old warriors, the Duke of Wellington and the Marquess of Anglesey, long since reconciled, walking up and down a trifle unsteadily arm in arm between the exhibits, the Duke bent with arthritis, Anglesey limping on his artificial leg, both talking in the loud voices of the deaf as they did so often in the House of Lords.[29] Ticket-holders were touched, too, and cheered the two men heartily, some of them wishing the Duke a happy birthday. He did not forget it was Prince Arthur's birthday, too, and he went to the Palace to take him a present of a cup and a model of the throne. These objects were replaced by Franz Winterhalter with a casket in his painting of the presentation, a painting which, the Duke grumpily complained, cost him, in travelling time and sittings, three valuable hours a day.

48   Growing Old

1850 — 1

'I really believe that there is not a youth in
London who could enjoy the world more than
myself.'

HAVING EXPRESSED strong reservations about the whole concept of
the Exhibition, the Duke was pleased to be able to say that, while the
show's usefulness might still be questioned, it was certain that 'nothing
could be more successful'. He went to it frequently himself, on the
last occasion getting 'such a rubbing, scrubbing and mashing' from the
other visitors that he expected at 'every moment to be crushed' and
had to be saved by the police.[1] He was fascinated by the strange
exhibits, the ingenious inventions, the collapsible piano, the knife with
three hundred blades and the assorted timepieces.

He was particularly interested in clocks and watches, and always
had six or seven ticking away in his room. He was particularly fond of
three of his watches: one was an old English one which had belonged
to Tippu Sultan, another had been Marshal Junot's, the third, with a
map of Spain on the back, had been made by the Swiss watchmaker
Abraham Louis Bréguet for Napoleon who gave it to his brother Joseph.
Bréguet, who was always a welcome visitor at Apsley House, made
him a watch with small knobs on the dial by which he could tell the
time without giving offence by taking it out of his pocket.[2]

Intrigued as he always was by such contraptions as were displayed
in the Crystal Palace, he was extremely wary of newfangled inventions
which upset the traditional tenor of the country's life. He could not
bear railways, for example, and railed against them often in his letters
to his lady friends.

> In my opinion people never acted so foolishly as we did in allowing
> of the Destruction of our excellent and commodious [post roads] in
> order to expend Millions Sterling on these Rail Roads! [he wrote to
> Miss Angela Burdett-Coutts, who was investing heavily in them in
> September 1848]. It appears to me to be the Vulgarest, most indelicate,

most inconvenient, most injurious to Health of any mode of convey-
ance that I have seen in any part of the World! Mobs of well-dressed
Ladies and Gentlemen are collected at every Station, to examine and
pry into every Carriage and actions of every Traveller.[3]

I cannot bear seeing or hearing of ladies going alone by the Trains on
the Rail Roads [he added in a letter to Lady Salisbury] . . . If I could
attain the object, no lady should ever go by a Train, at all events
without protection. It is horrible altogether . . . England did not require
Rail Roads.[4]

Yet less intrusive inventions and gadgets always appealed to him.
He was intrigued by the submarine telegraph which he went to see at
Dover and which prompted the observation, 'I should not be surprised
if I lived to fly in the air!'[5] and he was fascinated by a 'delightful
instrument' known as a 'Baby Jumper', an example of which he sent
to the young Lady Salisbury with detailed instructions as to how to fix
it to the nursery ceiling and with warnings to have it well tested before
her babies were placed inside it.[6] He was also much taken with Charles
Babbage's 'Calculating Engine' and with the idea of a 'rational dress'
for women advocated by the American reformer Amelia Jenks Bloomer.
It was 'impossible', he thought, that such a costume of baggy Turkish
trousers gathered at the ankle beneath a knee-length skirt should be
adopted; but he was 'vastly amused' by the 'Bloomer discussions'. He
understood all about them, he said, 'being somewhat of a Taylor'.[7]

Indeed, he found much to amuse him in these last years of his life,
despite the constant bugbear of his deafness which made it so difficult
for him to talk to, for instance, Adolphe Thiers when the exiled statesman came to London in 1851, and so frustrating to gather so little of
what was said in the House of Lords where he still spoke occasionally
and, indeed, made a long speech on the Militia Bill in the summer of
1852. The deafness was a grievous impediment which he sometimes
endeavoured to disguise. Once asked what he thought of a play by
Lord Lytton which he had attended, he replied emphatically, 'Very
good indeed. Very good indeed. Capital, capital'; but asked a few
minutes later what the play was about he had to confess, 'Couldn't
hear a word, not a word.'[8] When Lord John Russell resigned in February
1852 and the Tories came in under the Earl of Derby, the Duke kept
asking Derby, 'Who? Who?' in penetrating tones as he vainly strove to
catch the names of the men appointed to the Cabinet of what subsequently became known as the 'Who? Who? Ministry'.[9] When he did
catch a name it was as likely as not to be unknown to him. Sir John

Pakington, he was told, was appointed Secretary for War. '"Who?" said the Duke in a loud voice. "Never heard of the gentleman."'[10]

Yet there were many pleasures left to the Duke. He still enjoyed shopping for presents, often buying the oddest things, a pair of galoshes for a lady friend, for example.* He was still partial to country house parties, provided the company was congenial, even though he could never 'conceive how people contrive to pass their time so totally without occupation';[11] and he still enjoyed balls and continued to do so even when well into his eighties. Thomas Carlyle, who saw him at one in London, was much taken with his appearance.

> Truly a beautiful old man. I had never seen till now how beautiful, and what an expression of graceful simplicity, veracity, and nobleness there is about the old hero when you see him close at hand. His very size had hitherto deceived me. He is a shortish, slightish figure, about five feet eight, of good breadth, however, and all muscle and bone. His legs, I think, must be the short part of him, for certainly on horseback I have always taken him to be tall. Eyes beautiful light blue ... the face wholly gentle, wise, valiant, and venerable. The voice clear ... almost musical, essentially tenor or almost treble ... He glided slowly along, slightly saluting this and that other ... till the silver buckle of his stock vanished into the door of the next room and I saw him no more.[12]

The Duke also enjoyed fancy dress balls, attending one in a powdered wig, a tricorne hat and such a coat as might have been worn by the first Duke of Marlborough. Before leaving for the ball he showed the children staying in his house how to perform a minuet. He delighted in the company of his grandchildren, at whose birth, so Lord Ellesmere said, he displayed as 'great an agitation as a young husband';†[13] and he continued to relish the company of his lady friends. He took exasperating pleasure in comparing what he liked to suppose was his own

---

* These had been a present for Mrs Arbuthnot. She was better pleased, no doubt, with an emerald and pearl bracelet which the Duke had had made for her, as he said, 'from Stones strung upon a sword given to me by a Mahratta Chief upon the occasion of the first Battle I ever won upon my own Bottom [the defeat of Dhoondiah Waugh in 1800]' (Gerald 7th Duke of Wellington, ed., *Wellington and his Friends*, 30).

† These were all Charles's children (Douro and his wife had none). There were two boys, Henry, born in 1846, who became the third Duke, and Arthur Charles, born in 1849, who became the fourth. A third son, born in 1845, died the following year. There were also three girls, Victoria Alexandrina, for whom Queen Victoria was sponsor, Mary Angela and Georgina. They married respectively the first Baron Holmpatrick, George Arthur Jervoise Scott and William Rolle Malcolm.

vigour with the decrepitude of his contemporaries. A few months before his death he was present when the Queen invested four generals of about his own age with the Order of the Bath. As the last of them stumbled backwards from her Majesty, so she recorded in her journal, the Duke observed in a voice loud enough to reach the far corners of the room, 'None of these generals seem able to walk.' He himself had been looking of late far better than he had been in the early 1840s. On his visits to Apsley House to see his brother Algernon, Charles Greville had found him 'remarkably well, strong, hearty and of a good colour . . . certainly a much better man in all respects . . . in wonderful vigour of body'.[14]

'I really believe that there is not a youth in London who could enjoy the world more than myself,' he said. 'But being deaf, the spirit, not the body tires . . . one gets bored in boring others, and one becomes too happy to get home.'[15]

There were certain ladies from whose company he always longed to escape by riding home. The most troublesome of these was Harriet Arbuthnot's cousin, Lady Georgiana Fane, daughter of the Earl of Westmorland, who had once declined an offer of marriage made to her by Lord Palmerston. This woman, 'a half-cracked, tiresome, trouble-some, crazy old maid', in Charles Greville's opinion, had in the past received from the Duke some extremely compromising letters which she showed to Lady Georgiana Bathurst, lady in waiting to the Duchess of Gloucester, in the hope that the Duchess might bring pressure to bear upon Wellington to fulfil the promises he had made to her. The Duchess of Gloucester refused to become involved; so Lady Georgiana consulted her solicitors who advised her that there were, indeed, grounds for a breach of promise action. No case was brought, however, much to the relief of the Duke and his friends: it would have been painful, as Charles Greville said, to see the Duke 'an object of ridicule and contempt in the last years of his illustrious life during the earlier stages of which he had been extremely addicted to gallantry and had great success with some women of fashion whose weaknesses have never been known, though perhaps suspected'.[16]

Lady Georgiana created enough scandal as it was, pursuing the Duke so persistently that he felt compelled to ask his daughter-in-law, Lady Charles Wellesley, who had an apartment at Apsley House, not to let the woman in. 'I have long been under the necessity of declining to allow this house to be made a show on the 18th of June! [Waterloo Day]. People however still persevere! and this morning I learned that Lady Georgiana Fane, knowing that I will not receive her visits, intends to apply to you to receive her! I shall be very much obliged if you will refuse to receive her.'[17] He could not, however, prevent her attending services at the Chapel Royal and once she succeeded in making an embarrassing scene when he himself was there.

The Duke complained of her behaviour to her mother, the Countess Dowager of Westmorland, asking her to do what she could to 'prevail upon her Ladyship to cease to molest [him] with daily vituperative letters' and to persuade her to destroy those letters which he had formerly addressed to her and which she had 'shown to others with a view to calumniate, to injure, to vex and torment' him.[18]

The Duke's protest, and his assurance to the Countess that there was nothing 'in the nature of a *mistake* or *misunderstanding*' between himself and Lady Georgiana, seem to have had little effect. But by this time the Duke had at least heard the last of another woman who had once plagued him remorselessly. This was Harriette Wilson who had decided to solve her financial problems by writing her memoirs and offering to leave the names of certain of her numerous lovers out of them if she were to be paid for doing so. Her unscrupulous publisher, J.J. Stockdale, the son of a man who had twice been a defendant in actions for libel, informed the Duke of his author's intentions:

> My Lord Duke,
>   In Harriette Wilson's Memoirs, which I am about to publish are various anecdotes of your Grace which it would be more desirable to withhold, at least such is my opinion. I have stopped the Press for the moment; but as the publication will take place next week, little delay can necessarily take place.
>   I have the honour to be,
>   My Lord Duke,
>   Your Grace's ever attached Servant,
>   John Joseph Stockdale.[19]

It is commonly supposed that the Duke returned this letter to the sender with the four words, 'Publish and be damned', scrawled across it; but the letter survives among the Wellington Papers with no such message upon it. Also among the Papers is another letter from Stockdale which indicates that Wellington may have threatened to take him to court. The threat was not carried out, though other persons defamed in his publication did take action against him and succeeded in ruining him after the *Memoirs* had appeared with their malicious portrait of the Duke as one of Harriette Wilson's more boring admirers. Yet the publication of the *Memoirs* did little damage to the Duke's reputation;

and, while huge crowds had assembled outside Stockdale's premises when their appearance was announced, and thirty editions were said to have been issued, they had by the 1850s come to be regarded as little more than a literary curiosity. Harriette Wilson married a M. Rochfort and went to live in France; and by the time of her death twenty years later she had been largely forgotten; and the Duke heard no more of her.[20]

He had other, younger women friends by then. There was, for instance, Lord Salisbury's second wife, Mary Catherine, daughter of the fifth Earl De la Warr, who, well over fifty years younger than the Duke, was often to be seen walking arm in arm with him in St James's Park. He took much pleasure also in the company of Charlotte Jones, the young wife of a Member of Parliament whose 'Love Affair' with the aged Duke, according to John Ruskin's wife, made him look ridiculous and was a 'great grief to his family'.[21] Then there were the rumbustious Hatton sisters whose close attendance upon the Duke gave rise to one of those riddles of which his contemporaries were so fond:

'Why is the Duke the rudest man in London?'

'Because he always comes into a room with his *Hat On*.'[22]

Above all, he relished the friendship, indeed the love, of Angela Burdett-Coutts, daughter of Sir Francis Burdett and granddaughter and heiress of the banker Thomas Coutts, who lived at 79 Piccadilly, on the corner of Stratton Street, a few hundred yards from Apsley House, where she conducted the numerous philanthropic projects in which she was so deeply interested. The Duke had known her for several years, had sent her presents and received presents in return. He had asked her to dinner and invited her and her companion, Mrs Brown, to stay at Walmer Castle.[23] But it was not until 1847 that, having fallen in love with him, this shy, lonely and reserved young woman of thirty-two had astonished the world by asking the seventy-seven-year-old Duke to marry her. By then the Duke had become her confidential adviser not only on her many charities, displacing a rather disgruntled Charles Dickens in this capacity, but also on her dealings with her family's bank. She rarely took his advice. He told her that 'the Parent of generosity is Oeconomy', and thought that little good would come of the scheme for a 'Home for Fallen Women' which she had been planning with Dickens. He was 'much afraid' that there was but 'little hope of saving in this World that particular Class of Unfortunates'.[24] Certainly his own experience had led him to this sceptical view: most of the unmarried mothers he had tried to help had not spent the money he had allowed them in the manner he had hoped they would. Nor did the Duke believe that Miss Coutts should spend her money on the Irish Relief Fund after the failure of the Irish potato crop: 'Not an Irishman would work anywhere! All would flock to the spot at which he would receive His share of the Eleemosynary Gift without working for it!'[25] Nor yet did he approve of the proposed reduction in the working hours of the clerks in Coutts's bank: 'There never was anything more absurd; not one Clerk will seek Instruction at that Hour of the afternoon. He will go to the Publick House, the Play House or other place of resort of vice or Idleness, and the Hour lost to himself, His Employers and the Publick Interests will be passed in Dissipation and only lead to renewed Idleness and Mischief. This concession is like many others advocated and applauded by the News-papers, such as Feasts and Shews for the people which occasion only idleness and vice, loss of time, increase of Want.'[26]

Yet, if she did not often take his advice, Miss Coutts was clearly entranced by the pleasure of his company when receiving it. Still an attractive man, he was an ideal father-figure: her own father was dead and she had never seen much of him when he was alive. Moreover, there could be no suspicion in his case that he was attracted by her money. He declined her offer of marriage in a letter of affectionate regret:

> My dearest Angela, I have passed every Moment of the Evening and Night since I quitted you in reflecting upon our conversation of yester-day, Every Word of which I have considered repeatedly. My first Duty towards you is that of Friend, Guardian, Protector. You are Young, My Dearest! You have before you the prospect of at least twenty years of enjoyment of Happiness in Life. I entreat you again in this way, not to throw yourself upon a Man old enough to be your Grandfather, who, however strong, Hearty and Healthy at present, must and will certainly in time feel the consequences and Infirmities of Age. You cannot know, but I do, the dismal consequences to you of this certainty . . . My last days would be embittered by the reflection that your Life was uncomfortable and hopeless. God Bless you my Dearest![27]

They remained the most affectionate of friends, amazing everyone by what Charles Greville called their 'strange intimacy'. This intimacy was much closer than most people expected. The Duke told Miss Coutts that, 'in recollections of what you said to me some time ago as to your wishes', he was 'looking out and measuring walls' at Stratfield Saye 'with a view to break out doors and make passages [and create] fresh communication with my Apartment'.[28] Accordingly, or so her biographer suggests, a little winding staircase was built so that she could come down to his ground-floor rooms from the apartments she occupied above.*

When they were apart they wrote to each other regularly, pressing flowers between the sheets of their writing paper; and, when Miss Coutts went abroad, he made no secret of his longing for her return. A swatch of his white hair was bound up in a bow with strands of her own brown locks.

There were occasions when he grew irritated by the demands she made upon him, when he complained that he 'would never be able to prevail' upon her to consider him 'as quite unfit for social purposes, being deaf, eighty years old and seeking for repose'. He wished it would occasionally occur to her how old he was. 'It would save you a good deal of disappointment and be less trouble for me.'[29]

When she called one morning unexpectedly at Apsley House he delivered himself of one of his explosions of epistolary rage:

I must tell you that I don't admire your little Gentillesse of this morning! If we don't respect ourselves, How can we expect that our Servants will respect us?

The Queen's Servants, the Adjutant and Quarter Master General, the Military Secretary, private Secretary, my aides de Camp, acquaintances and relatives are in the Habit of calling at all Hours. Lord John Russell is frequently here before I have done breakfast shortly after ten o'clock. Other Ministers come also at an early Hour. They would be greatly surprised to find me still dressing, and a young Lady in possession of my room! . . .

If you wish to see my Room and every Article it contains, I have no objection. Fix your Hour regularly. Bring your friends with you. I will attend you. But do not be found here alone, like an *Enfant de la Maison*, and this by Official Men, entire Strangers to you. In short I tell you very firmly I will not allow it. I will lock up the Room as I would and as I do a writing desk or Secretaire, and will not allow it to be entered excepting when I am present. I am very sorry if this note should not be agreeable to you, but I cannot help it. I did not think it possible that you would be guilty of such folly![30]

---

* There is another explanation for the construction of this staircase which still exists at Stratfield Saye: the seventh Duke of Wellington believed that it was created so that his ancestor's valet could descend from his own room more easily and quickly when his services were required.

He was equally angry when Miss Coutts proposed bringing Lord Brougham with her on a visit to Walmer Castle. 'I shall certainly beg leave to decline to receive any excepting those whom I may myself invite,' he replied.* 'When a man comes to Eighty Years of Age he may claim the privilege of not receiving to his house those who he has not invited to it. God help me! The only favour I crave from the world is to leave me to repose in peace.' Nor did he look kindly upon the proposition that she should take Lord Mahon's house on Walmer beach: 'You may rely upon it that [you] cannot do so with Impunity. Your name will immediately be again in the Newspapers . . . It is very desirable to me to avoid these publications . . . They lead to my reception of numerous abusive anonymous letters, which do not contribute to one's comfort, however indifferent about them one may feel.'[31]

He immediately repented of the harshness of such letters, however. The day after the dispatch of the letter about Lord Mahon's house, he sent another, kinder one; and he followed his furious letter about her morning call with another which begged her to excuse him: he had been naked at the time and had been ashamed to have been caught by his servant 'in that state'.[32]

To the cross letter about Lord Brougham he added, 'God Bless you Dearest with much affection. Wn.' She remained his 'Dearest' to the end. When he died, his family treated her almost as though she were his widow. Lord Douro sent her a copy of his death mask with the assurance that he was sending one to 'no other ladies'. That, Douro said, is 'votre affaire'. He saw to it that she attended the funeral with the ladies of his family.[33]

---

* Lord Brougham became, in fact, a frequent guest at Walmer, often self-invited (Hatfield House Papers).

49 Last Days

1851 – 2

'On every face there was an expression of mixed
reverence and alarm.'

THE OLDER AND DEAFER the Duke grew, the less he enjoyed parties
in crowded country houses – being 'quite unfit for a large society', as
he said when declining an invitation to Stowe – and the more pleasure
he took in quiet days at home in the company of old friends who spoke
clearly into his ear and of children whose chatter had no need of
comprehension or response. He was hardly ever grumpy with children
even now, however tiring he might find them on what he called his
off days. On these days adults took care not to disturb him when he
fell asleep, as he often did now, not only in the high-backed wing chair
in his room but also in the drawing-room and even at balls at Apsley
House. He still attended the Horse Guards, difficult as he found it to
let himself down from the saddle on his arrival. 'Wearily the right leg
scrambled, so to speak, over the croup of the saddle. Slowly and painfully it sank towards the ground, and then the whole body came down
with a stagger . . . A little crowd always gathered to watch this proceeding, and on every face there was an expression of mixed reverence and
alarm . . . Yet nobody presumed to touch or even to approach him.'[1]
For it was well known that he hated being helped. 'You could scarcely
offend him more than by offering to hold his overcoat or button his
cloak when he was getting ready to return from a ball or a rout. "Let
me alone," was the usual recognition of civility of some evident admirer,
who sprang forward to help him out of a difficulty.'[2]

Algernon Greville said, 'If he drops his hat I should never think of
stooping to pick it up.'[3]

Well aware of his 'hatred of all assistance', Lord Ellesmere was
unsure what to do when he saw the Duke, who was then over eighty,
struggling to clamber up the bank of a canal on a visit to Worsley Hall.
'I saw the moment he would slip into the canal,' Ellesmere wrote, 'so
I seized hold of his hand and hauled him up. He did not say a word,

but when we got to the top, he solemnly shook hands with me, which was funny.'⁴

Ellesmere fared better than an ancient butler who presumed to help the Duke mount his horse outside the house of the Chairman of the Court of Directors with whom the Duke had had an argument about the recall of Lord Ellenborough as Governor-General of India.

> The Duke came down very much irritated [recalled a young member of the Chairman's family] and unfortunately the old butler, who was very shaky on his legs, went out to help him onto his horse . . . The Duke pushed him away, and poor old Hodges tumbled into the gutter, the sight of which appeared to restore his Grace's equanimity.⁵

The painter William Weigall was likewise sharply and physically rebuffed when he tried to help the Duke remove his boots. 'After many efforts the Duke succeeded in kicking off a boot, and with it went the dress-shoe; but the artist thought, from the rebuff he had already received, he had better not interfere, and allowed the Duke to pick it up himself, which he did; and then, says the artist, we got on capitally together.'⁶

Once inside the Horse Guards the Duke frequently fell asleep, and woke up much disgruntled. Lord Fitzroy Somerset, still his Military Secretary, was obliged to do most of his work. Sometimes the Duke would fall asleep in the middle of a discussion; and men would have to tiptoe from the room and ask Somerset what should be done.⁷ He appeared now to be a frail old man. His stoop had grown worse of late, and he was inclined to totter in his walk. His white hair was thin now, contrasting strongly with his eyebrows; his whole slight frame seemed shrunken.

On his better days the Duke could still enjoy a dinner party. 'When left to himself or engaged in thought, his head seems to droop on his breast,' Thomas Raikes wrote in his journal after a visit to Walmer; 'but the instant any subject is started that interests him, his eyes brighten, his head is raised, he puts his hand to his right ear to catch the sound, and enters into the argument with all the spirit, and judgement and penetration which form so striking a part of his character.'⁸

The Duke could also still enjoy a drive into Dover and even at the age of eighty-three he would walk from Folkestone railway station to Croker's house, a good three miles distant at the top of a steep hill.

> He said he had found it a rough walk [Croker recalled], and the ground intercepted in a way he had not expected; so I said to him, 'It seems

you forgot *to guess what was at the other side of the hill.*' This was an
allusion to a circumstance which had occurred some thirty years before
. . . when . . . we amused ourselves by guessing what sort of a country
we should find at the other side of the hills we drove up; and when
I expressed surprise at some extraordinary good guesses he had made,
he said, 'Why, I have spent all my life trying *to guess what was at the
other side of the hill*' . . . He turned round to Mrs. Croker to explain
to her, adding, 'All the business of war, and indeed all the business
of life, is to endeavour to find out what you don't know by what you
do; that's what I call "guessing what is at the other side of the hill" . . .'

Lady Barrow's five little girls were with us and he won their hearts
by writing his name in their albums; in the signature of *one* he wrote
his name with a single 1. His good humour and kindness to the children, and indeed to everybody was very pleasing. To *me* (evidently on
account of my precarious health) he was peculiarly affectionate . . .

Going down out of the house, there were two sets of steps, which
he went down very leisurely with Mrs. Croker on his arm, and counting
1, 2, 3, and 1, 2, 3 and 4, and then looked back and repeated the
numbers, as if for my use, for he thought me feebler than I really am.

How characteristic this trifle is both of his precision and his kind
attention to others![9]

This proved to be one of the Duke's last excursions. Soon afterwards,
on the morning of 14 September 1852, when Kendall entered his
master's bedroom at six o'clock, the Duke did not stir though the coal
was rattled in the grate and the poker clashed against the bars. There
seemed no cause for alarm, however: the previous night he had been
in good spirits and had dined unusually well on 'mock-turtle soup,
turbot and venison';[10] but soon afterwards one of the housemaids
thought she heard a groan. The valet went up again and, making more
noise with the shutters, told the Duke that it was getting quite late.

'Is it? Do you know where the apothecary lives?'

'Yes, at Deal, your Grace.'

'Then send for him. I wish to speak to him.'

When the apothecary arrived and asked what the trouble was, the
Duke raised his hand to his chest and complained of 'some derangement'. The apothecary, having felt his patient's pulse and prescribed
an ammonia stimulant, returned to his breakfast in Deal, undertaking
to come back to Walmer later on that morning. When he had gone
Kendall asked the Duke if he would like a cup of tea. 'Yes, if you
please,' he said. They were the last words he spoke.

When the apothecary returned with his son, the Duke was unconscious. The local doctor was sent for; a mustard emetic was prescribed,
followed by three grains of calomel and extract of colocynth. A mustard
poultice was applied to the patient's legs; and a feather brushed against
his jaw. But there was no sign of returning consciousness. Early in the
afternoon, Kendall proposed that the Duke should be lifted from his
narrow camp-bed and placed in his favourite wing chair; and, sitting
there, quiet and motionless, just before half past three, watched anxiously by the medical men, by his servants, his son Lord Charles and
Charles's wife, Sophia, he died. The apothecary's son held a small
looking-glass to his mouth, and, removing it, showed its surface to the
others unmarked.

An hour later Lady Burghersh arrived to find the whole household 'in
consternation'. She went up to the Duke's room and found him 'looking
just as if he was asleep, calm and placid'. 'I brought away a bit of his
hair,' she told her husband, 'and kissed his dear face which was still
warm. All the servants begged to see me before I left. It was most
moving to see their grief . . . I cannot yet recover from the shock, or
think of anything but him who during my whole life has given me such
kindness, confidence and affection.'[11]

The Queen was in Scotland enjoying an expedition from Balmoral
when she heard that the Duke was dead. At first she refused to believe
the report. She had mislaid a watch which he had given her; and she
sent a ghillie back to find it for her. He returned with the watch and
a letter from Lord Derby.

> Alas! [the Queen wrote in her journal] it contained the confirmation
> of the fatal news, that Britain's pride, her glory, her hero, one of the
> greatest men she ever produced was *no more*! What a great and irrepar-
> able loss . . . one cannot think of this country *without 'the Duke'*, our
> immortal hero! In him centred almost every earthly honour a subject
> could possess, his position was the highest a subject ever had, above
> all Party – looked up to by all, – revered by the whole nation, the
> trusted friend of the Sovereign! And how simply he carried these
> honours! By what singleness of purpose, what straightforwardness,
> what courage, were all the motives of his actions guided. The Crown
> *never* possessed, & I fear never will again, such a loyal, faithful subject,

& such a *staunch* supporter. To us . . . his loss will be quite irreparable
. . . There will be few dry eyes in the country, – We hastened home
on foot . . . A gloom cast over everything! Albert dreadfully sad at the
news.[12]

She and the Prince, she later decided, would now stand sadly alone.
Lord Aberdeen, who was to succeed Derby as Prime Minister in
December that year, was 'almost the only personal friend of that kind'
they had left. 'Melbourne, Peel, Liverpool – and now the Duke – *all*
gone!' She gave orders for her household to go into mourning, a mark
of respect most rarely accorded to a subject by the Sovereign.[13]

50 The Way to St Paul's

1852

'One cannot realize at all the possibility of his
being no longer with us, or think of *England
without him*.'

THE DUKE'S BODY lay embalmed at Walmer Castle where the Lord
Warden's flag flew above the battlements at half-mast as muffled
church bells tolled. Death masks were taken and, since the Duke's
false teeth had been removed, the casts, made by the sculptor George
Gammon Adams – who came to the castle equipped with a camera
lucida[1] – give to the mouth a sadly sunken appearance. The dead man's
hands were modelled – it was said that Lord Clanwilliam had asked
for the right hand itself – the false teeth of walrus ivory were given to
his daughter-in-law, Lady Douro, now Duchess of Wellington, who
had been abroad at the time of her father-in-law's death; locks of hair
were cut off for numerous friends and relations, so much hair, indeed,
that a manservant had to apologize to one recipient for the small
amount he was able to send, the demands from the family and other
friends 'being so great'.*[2]

'Lord Douro, the present Duke, told me that Her Majesty was desirous for a piece of the poor Duke's hair,' Kendall wrote on sending a
few strands to Windsor where the Queen was to have them enclosed
in a gold bracelet. 'The last Hand laid on the Body was mine to cut
off a Lock of Hair from the Head . . . The coffin was instantly soldered
down, the poor Duke's remains never to be seen more.'[3]

For two days in the second week of November hundreds of local
people were admitted to Walmer Castle to file past the coffin before

---

* The Duke had submitted to having locks of his hair cut off during his lifetime: 'We
dined today at Lady Shelley's. She has got a medallion of the Duke framed with a Garter
he has worn for some years, and she wanted some of his hair. So she had him to dinner
the first of the month, as he said that was his day for having his hair cut, and I cut off
two pieces for her, one quite brown & the other as white as silver, with which she was
quite overjoyed & meant to put into the frame and keep as an heirloom in the family
for ever' (*The Journal of Mrs Arbuthnot*, ii, 180).

it was taken to the railway station on the evening of 10 November, almost two months after the Duke's death, as minute guns boomed across the beach. In London, where nearly £30,000 was to be spent on a state funeral perhaps unparalleled in its grandeur, the remains of the Duke – encased in a mahogany coffin, itself encased in three other coffins of pine, oak and lead – were escorted to Chelsea Hospital. Here in the Great Hall, the walls of which were draped in black cloth, the coffin was to lie in state on a black bier decorated with all manner of trophies and escutcheons, banners, wreaths and plumes. On the coffin, which was placed on a dais covered with cloth of gold, lay the Duke's cocked hat and sword. At its foot were his medals and orders. Beneath eighty-three immense candelabra, representing the Duke's years, soldiers stood in pairs, motionless and silent. The scene was sombrely magnificent, too much so for the Queen who came with some of her children. She never got beyond the middle of the Hall, where she broke down in tears and had to be led back to her carriage, while the Princess Royal 'wept out loud'.[4]

The crowds who afterwards pushed their way into the Hall turned the lying-in-state into what Lord Douro – as he still signed himself in letters to her – told Miss Coutts was 'a really disgusting affair', an 'exhibition devoid of taste and feeling'. 'Seven people they say were killed by the crowds today [newspapers recorded three people crushed to death] and I shall certainly consider whether or not it will do for us to countenance such a disgraceful way of doing honor . . . Pray burn this disloyal letter.'[5]

'The screams of females and the shrieks of young children were heard in all directions,' the *Observer* reported of the distressing scenes in the Great Hall. 'The police held aloft their batons, threatening the dense, moving swaying mass. A cry was heard amidst the crowd . . . the lifeless form of a female was borne out . . . Another and another body was carried away, and yet the eagerness of the multitude was not restrained . . . A melancholy scene – the dead being borne over the shoulders of the living.'[6]

It had been raining nearly all night as the last stands erected along the route of the funeral procession and covered in black cloth were completed by the light of flares; and the streets were still glistening with water when, on the morning of 18 November, the sun came out again. Well over a million people, many of them clothed in black, had been gathering since dawn, 300,000 of them occupying long rows of seats in the stands. Charles Dickens's son, Alfred, remembered being woken at three o'clock in the morning to be taken with his brothers

and sisters to the office of *Household Words* to watch the great event
which their father thought was marred by the behaviour of the numerous 'ghouls' who made money 'out of the old hero's death by renting
windows and balconies along the route of the procession and selling
mementoes, autograph letters and locks of hair'.[7]

The crowds were so dense around St Paul's that the lamplighters
could not reach the lamps to turn them out. There were no disturbances, though, and few casualties. A man was killed by a cart as he
was crossing the street to his seat; another man fell from the high roof
of a bank on the west side of Charing Cross; and a woman was almost
crushed to death at the Old Bailey. But that was all.

Throughout the night men had been at work in a tent on Horse
Guards Parade, putting the finishing touches to a huge black and gold
funeral car on which a hundred men had already been working in shifts
for eighteen days. Heavy with elaborate allegory, sprouting lions' heads
and dolphins, swords, halberds, muskets and wreaths, the lower part
was made from guns captured at Waterloo. On the upper part were
vases in which incense was intended to burn and sputter. Lord Hardinge, the Duke's successor as Commander-in-Chief, considered the
contraption 'a most beautiful specimen of art'; but he was almost alone
in thinking so.[8] Charles Dickens thought that 'for forms of ugliness,
horrible combinations of colour, hideous motion and general failure,
there never was such a work achieved as the Car'.[9] Lady de Ros agreed
with him: it was 'so frightful' she couldn't describe it; she would have
to leave that to the *Morning Post*.[10] It was the 'abominably ugliest'
object which Thomas Carlyle had ever seen, 'an incoherent huddle of
expensive palls, flags, sheets and gilt emblems and cross poles', no fit
carriage for 'the one true man of official men in England' or, so far as
Carlyle knew, in Europe.[11]

Drawn by twelve dray horses draped in black and 'so loaded with
plumes and trappings' that in Dean Stanley's eyes they 'might have
been elephants', the unwieldy bronze structure – eighteen tons in
weight and over twenty feet long – rumbled down the Mall, but had
progressed no further than the Duke of York's Column when its wheels
sank into a hole in the road and the strenuous efforts of sixty police
constables were required to drag it out.*

The long cortège moved on down the Strand to the sound of military
bands, muffled drums and minute guns in the Park. Three thousand

---

* For many years the funeral car lay in a dark corner of the crypt of St Paul's Cathedral.
It is now at Stratfield Saye.

infantry marched by with slow step, their arms reversed. Eight squadrons of cavalry and three batteries of guns were followed by pensioners
from the Royal Hospital in Chelsea and a private from every regiment
in the British Army. Among the mourners were the Poet Laureate,
Alfred Tennyson, whose 'Ode on the Death of the Duke of Wellington',
published that morning, had been met with 'all but Universal depre-
cation';[12] and Napoleon's bastard son, Count Alexandre Walewski, who
had been persuaded to come by his cousin Louis-Napoleon, President
and, a fortnight later, Emperor of the French. Directors of the East
India Company were there and so were representatives of Trinity House
and the Tower of London, the Cinque Ports, Oxford University, bishops
and judges, and members of the Cabinet, including Benjamin Disraeli,
Chancellor of the Exchequer and Leader of the House, to whose lot
it had fallen to deliver an encomium upon the Duke and whose memory
of a panegyric pronounced by Thiers upon Marshal St Cyr had led
him to make a speech of embarrassing similarity.[13] Field marshal's
batons of Prussia and Russia, the Netherlands, Spain, Portugal and
Hanover were borne by distinguished representatives of these
countries.

The mourning coaches rolled by one after the other, containing the
Duke's servants and pall-bearers, his friends and relations, colleagues
and fellow officers. Prince Albert drove by in a coach and six; the
Queen's carriage was empty as royal protocol dictated; the Duchesses
of Kent, Gloucester and Cambridge rode behind it; Lord Anglesey bore
the Duke's field marshal's baton, Clarenceux King of Arms his ducal
coronet. The second Duke of Wellington's mourning cloak trailed along
the ground. The late Duke's old groom led his horse, from whose sides
hung, reversed, a pair of Wellington boots, the 'touching sight' of which
moved the Queen to tears. 'It was,' she wrote, 'the first funeral of
anyone I had known and who was dear to me that I had ever seen! To
realise that this great Hero, the most loyal and devoted subject that
ever lived, is really gone, makes me really sad[14]. . . . I cannot say *what*
a deep . . . impression it made on me! It was a beautiful sight . . . The
dear old Duke!'[15]

She was watching the procession from the balcony of Buckingham
Palace and had already 'wept unrestrainedly' as the bands, each playing
different dirges chosen by the Prince, announced the approach of the
funeral car. The Dead March from *Saul*, with its roll of muffled drums,
she found 'the most harrowing of all'. She noticed that few eyes were
not as wet as her own.[16]

Inside the Cathedral thousands of people – 10,000 of them in specially constructed stands – waited for the appearance of the coffin which remained for over an hour outside the west door where the funeral car had creaked to a halt again and men struggled to transfer its heavy load – six feet nine inches long and fifteen feet from the ground – to the waiting bier.* By the time it was passed into the hands of the Bishop of London and the Dean of St Paul's many of the congregation were shivering with cold from the icy wind which had blown through the open doors, and numbers of men had put their hats on again. Lord Anglesey complained that he had never been so cold in his life. They had all been provided with a form of service and as the thousands of pages were turned simultaneously there was 'a faint dull roar such as a sudden Gust causes in a forest in autumn'.[17]

At the conclusion of the burial service the Duke's numerous titles and styles were read out by Garter King of Arms. The Duke's Comptroller broke his staff of office and Garter King of Arms dropped the pieces into the grave as the Tower guns fired their salute. The Marquess of Anglesey, 'moved by an irresistible impulse, stepped forward and, with tears streaming down his cheeks, placed his hand upon [the slowly descending coffin] in a moving gesture of farewell'.[18]

Charles Greville, who had known and understood the Duke so well, and who had not hesitated in the past to specify his faults and foibles, provided a just and well-considered epitaph:

> He was beyond all doubt, a very great man – the only great man of the present time – and comparable, in point of greatness, to the most eminent of those who have lived before him. His greatness, was the result of a few striking qualities – a perfect simplicity of character without a particle of vanity or conceit, but with a thorough and strenuous self-reliance, a severe truthfulness, never misled by fancy or exaggeration, and an ever-abiding sense of duty and obligation which made him the humblest of citizens and most obedient of subjects. The Crown never possessed a more faithful, devoted, and disinterested subject. Without personal attachment to any of the Monarchs whom

---

* Steps had been taken to make a possibly long delay and a certainly long service tolerable. 'Louisa has had an invitation [from the Dean's wife] to see and hear all at St Paul's,' Lady Stanley of Alderley wrote to her daughter-in-law. 'But she is in great doubt whether she could undertake the fatigue – but I do think she ought to make the effort and would be well rewarded – *especially* as 200 *conveniences* are provided – how the world improves!' (Nancy Mitford, *The Stanleys of Alderley*, London, 1939, 63). The cloakrooms were provided not only with looking glasses but also with tortoiseshell combs.

he served, and fully understanding and appreciating their individual merits and demerits, he alike reverenced their great office in the persons of each of them, and would at any time have sacrificed his ease, his fortune, or his life, to serve the Sovereign and the State. He was treated with greater respect than any individual not of Royal birth, and the whole Royal Family admitted him to a peculiar and exclusive familiarity and intimacy in their intercourse with him, which, while he took it in the easiest manner, and as if naturally due to him, he never abused or presumed upon. No man was more respectful or deferential towards the Sovereign and other Royal personages, but at the same time he always gave them his opinions and counsels with perfect frankness and sincerity, and never condescended to modify them to suit their prejudices or wishes. Upon every occasion of difficulty, public or private, he was always appealed to, and he was always ready to come forward and give his assistance and advice in his characteristic plain, and straightforward manner. He had all his life long been accustomed to be consulted, and he certainly liked it to the last, and was pleased with the marks of deference and attention which were continually paid to him.[19]

For his country and for her, so the Queen told the King of the Belgians, the loss of the 'dear and great old Duke of Wellington' was 'irreparable. He was the pride and the bon génie, as it were, of this country! He was the GREATEST man this country ever produced, and the most devoted and loyal subject, and the staunchest supporter the Crown ever had ... To think that all this is gone; and that this great and immortal man belongs now to History.'[20]

'May his example ever live in our hearts, Dear Great Duke,' the Queen added in a letter to her cousin, the Duke of Cambridge, the future Commander-in-Chief of the Army. 'One cannot realize at all the possibility of his being no longer amongst us, or think of England without him.'[21]

REFERENCES

For full bibliographical details see Sources, pp. 426–38.

Abbreviations

Asp/P	Aspinall, ed., *Correspondence of George, Prince of Wales*
Asp/K	Aspinall, ed., *Letters of King George IV*
BM *Cat.*	British Museum *Catalogue of Political and Personal Satires*
HHP	Hatfield House Papers
RA	Royal Archives
RP	Raglan Papers
WD	Dispatches of . . . the Duke of Wellington (ed. Colonel Gurwood)
WDNS	Wellington Dispatches . . . New Series
WP (HI)	Wellington Papers, Hartley Institute
WP (SS)	Wellington Papers, Stratfield Saye
WSD	Wellington Supplementary Dispatches

CHAPTER 1: ETON, DUBLIN AND ANGERS, 1769–87

1 Daines Barrington, 317.
2 Delany, iii, 535, 539, 546; Guedalla, 11–12.
3 Calvert, 25.
4 John Hamilton, *Sixty Years' Experience as an Irish Landlord*, London, 1894, 12, quoted in Elizabeth Longford, *Wellington: The Years of the Sword*, 37.
5 Timbs, 4; Gleig, *Life*, 4; Longford, op. cit., 38.
6 Ellesmere, 81.
7 Lyte, 339.
8 William Fraser, 161.
9 Gleig, *Life*, 6; Longford, op. cit., 43.
10 Brialmont, *Life*, i, 6.
11 G. de la Villebiot, *L'Académie d'Equitation et les Origines de l'enseignement équestre à Angers*, Angers, 1909; Guedalla, 25.
12 Quoted in Longford, op. cit., 46.

CHAPTER 2: AN OFFICER IN THE 33RD, 1787–93

1 Herbert Maxwell, i, 5–6.
2 Quoted in Guedalla, 28.
3 Mavor, 76; Guedalla, 29.
4 Gleig, *Life*, 8; W.H. Maxwell, i, 12; Elizabeth Longford, *Wellington: The Years of the Sword*, 54; Guedalla, 29.
5 Butler, *passim*.
6 Longford, op. cit., 54.
7 Lt-Gen. William Napier, i, 52.
8 Jonah Barrington, 176.
9 Joan Wilson, 14; Croker, i, 337.
10 Herbert Maxwell, i, 8.

11 Gleig, *Reminiscences*, 27.

CHAPTER 3: THE FIRST
CAMPAIGN, 1794−5
1 Stanhope, *Conversations*, 111.
2 WSD, xii, 2; Herbert Maxwell, i, 13.
3 Stanhope, *Conversations*, 182.
4 Ellesmere, 161.
5 Gleig, *Life*, 13.
6 Stanhope, *Conversations*, 182.
7 WP (SS), 15 Sept. 1793; Guedalla, 52.
8 WP (SS), 30 Sept. 1795; Elizabeth
   Longford, *Wellington: The Years of the
   Sword*, 70−1.
9 Ellesmere, 161.

CHAPTER 4: A VOYAGE TO INDIA,
1796−8
1 WP (SS) quoted in Guedalla, 55−64.
2 Elers, 46−7.
3 Ibid.
4 Guedalla, 75.
5 Hickey, i, 154.
6 Ibid., i, 155.
7 Ibid., i, 190−1.
8 WP (SS), 17 April 1797.
9 Hickey, i, 171−2.

CHAPTER 5: THE TIGER OF
MYSORE, 1799
1 Quoted in Guedalla, 75.
2 WSD, xiii, 3.
3 WSD, i, 18.
4 Quoted in Elizabeth Longford,
   Wellington. The Years of the Sword,
   80.
5 WSD, i, 4−8
6 WSD, i, 20−1; Longford, op. cit., 82.
7 Roberts, 48.
8 WSD, i, 4−6 87 109.
9 WSD, i, 111−12.
10 WSD, i, 160−5.
11 WSD, i, 160−70.
12 WSD, i, 203.
13 WSD, i, 195−6.
14 WSD, i, 187−8.
15 WSD, i, 209; Herbert Maxwell, i,
   32−3; Fortescue, *History*, iv, 736.

16 Elers, 102−3.
17 WD, i, 24.
18 Elers, 100.
19 Hook, i, 72.
20 Ibid., i, 174.
21 Ibid., i, 157; Herbert Maxwell, i,
   62−3.

CHAPTER 6: THE GOVERNOR OF
MYSORE, 1799
1 Croker, ii, 102−3.
2 Elers, 103.
3 Hook, i, 205, 216.
4 WSD, i, 16.
5 Ibid.
6 Ibid., ii, 567.
7 Ibid., iii, 151.
8 Ibid., i, 419.
9 Ibid., i, 215.
10 Ibid., i, 246
11 Guedalla, 91−2.
12 Elizabeth Longford, *Wellington: The
   Years of the Sword*, 106.
13 WSD, ii, 143.
14 WD, i, 37.
15 Roberts, 75.
16 WSD, ii, 314−33, 334−43.
17 Bulter, 245.
18 WSD, ii, 323−6; WP (HI), WPI/71,
   WP3/2/16; Halliwell.
19 WD, i, 307, 321; WSD, ii, 345−6, 347,
   352−61.
20 WSD, ii, 355; Stanhope,
   Conversations, 103.
21 WSD, ii, 364.

CHAPTER 7: THE SULTAN'S
PALACE, 1800−1
1 Walker, i, 525−33.
2 Elers, 124.
3 Ibid., 116−7.
4 Ibid., 118.
5 WSD, ii, 487−9.
6 WSD, ii, 592; Elizabeth Longford,
   Wellington: The Years of the Sword,
   118.
7 WSD, ii, 7, 36, 55, 83; iii, 301, 314−16;
   iv, 43.

8 WSD, iii, Letter to Major Elliot, 33rd, 15 May 1802.
9 Elers, 129.
10 Ibid., 126.
11 Rogers, 82; Griffiths, 39.
12 WP (SS) quoted in Guedalla, 104.
13 Elers, 123.
14 WSD, ii, 501.
15 Elers, 122.
16 WSD, i, 595–6.

CHAPTER 8: ASSAYE, 1802–5
1 WD, i, 520–1.
2 WD, ii, 257.
3 Croker, i, 354; Stanhope, Conversations, 182.
4 WD, ii, 356; Croker, i, 354.
5 WSD, iv, 186–7.
6 WSD, iv, 185–8, 210–14; Elizabeth Longford, Wellington: The Years of the Sword, 131
7 Stanhope, op. cit., 142.
8 WSD, iv, 295–300.
9 WD, ii, 647.
10 WP(SS); Longford, op. cit., 141–2; Guedalla, 112.
11 WP(SS); Guedalla, 113.
12 Ibid.
13 WD, iii, 444, 593–4.
14 WSD, iv, 487.
15 WP(SS); Guedalla, 117.
16 Stanhope, op. cit., 130.
17 WSD, iv, 507.
18 RP, 13 Sept. 1809.
19 WD, ii, 345.

CHAPTER 9: RETURN TO LONDON, 1805–6
1 WSD, iv, 508.
2 Elers, 57.
3 Elizabeth Longford, Wellington: The Years of the Sword, 213.
4 Lockhart, 585.
5 Blanch, 58–9.
6 Ibid.
7 Croker, ii, 233–4.
8 WSD, iv, 538.
9 WSD, iv, 539.

10 WSD, iv, 540.
11 WP(SS), 18 May 1801; Longford, op. cit., 147.
12 Elers, 103.
13 J.H. Rose, 556; Guedalla, 124.
14 Stanhope, Pitt, iv, 346–7; Ehrman, 806.
15 Stanhope, op. cit., iv, 346.
16 Ibid., iv, 369; Ehrman, 820.
17 WSD, xiii, 279.

CHAPTER 10: KITTY PAKENHAM, 1790–1806
1 Joan Wilson, 2.
2 Edgeworth, Life and Letters, i, 151.
3 Joan Wilson, 47.
4 Ibid., 49.
5 Cole and Gwynn, 27; Joan Wilson, 59.
6 Joan Wilson, 69.
7 Ibid., 69–70.
8 Calvert, 67.
9 Joan Wilson, 72.
10 Ibid., 65.
11 Edgeworth, op.cit., i, 149–50.
12 Calvert, 66–7.
13 Joan Wilson, xiv; Elizabeth Longford, Wellington: The Years of the Sword, 163.
14 London Encyclopaedia, 365.
15 Joan Wilson, 75.

CHAPTER 11: IRELAND AND DENMARK, 1806–7
1 WP(SS); Elizabeth Longford, Wellington: The Years of the Sword, 163, 167.
2 Hansard's Parliamentary Debates, 24 April 1806; Guedalla, 130.
3 WSD, iv, 546–86.
4 BM Add. MSS 37415, f. 17, letter to Marquess Wellesley, 26 October 1806, quoted in Guedalla, 132.
5 BM Add. MSS 37415, f. 23, 26 Oct. 1806, quoted in Guedalla, 133.
6 WSD, vi, 39–82.
7 WSD, xiii, 285–6; Longford, op. cit., 167; Guedalla, 135.

8 Brooke and Gandy; WSD, v, 33, 108, 124; vii, 124, 353; Larpent, 75.
9 WSD, v, 68, 28–36, 71, 202–10.
10 WP(SS), July 1807; Joan Wilson, 90; Longford, op.cit., 168.
11 WP(SS); Joan Wilson, 97–8; Longford, op. cit., 169–70; Wellington (Roxburghe Club selection), 11–14.
12 Arbuthnot, i, 168–9.
13 WSD, 66–7.
14 Croker, i, 342–3.
15 Ibid.
16 Ibid.
17 WSD, vi, 9, 12–13, 18–19, 25; Croker, ii, 120.
18 WSD, vi, 1–26.

CHAPTER 12: PORTUGAL, 1808
1 WSD, xiii, 288.
2 WSD, v, 139.
3 WSD, v, 151, 185.
4 WSD, v, 341; iv, 592–601; v, 330.
5 Stanhope, Conversations, 68–9; Creevey, 86.
6 Stanhope, op. cit., 69.
7 WD, iv, 16.
8 Croker, i, 12–13.
9 Mavor, 139; Wellington, Friends, 281.
10 WSD, vi, 89.
11 Griffiths, 16.
12 General Orders, 31 July 1808: WSD, vi, 91–2.
13 WD, v, 134–5.
14 Arbuthnot, i, 141.
15 WD, iv, 107.
16 Croker, ii, 122; Gleig, Reminiscences, 430.
17 Gates, 91.
18 Proceedings upon the Inquiry relative to the Armistice and Convention . . . between the British and French Armies, 1809, 87.
19 Fortescue, History, vi, 231; WSD, 162.
20 Hibbert, Corunna, 26.
21 Ibid.

22 Elizabeth Longford, Wellington: The Years of the Sword, 200.
23 WSD, vi, 122–4.
24 WD, iv, 158; Brett-James, Wellington at War, 144; RP, 19 Aug. 1808.
25 WD, iv, 156–7; Diary of Sir John Moore (ed. Sir J.F. Maurice, 1904), ii, 256–9.
26 WD, iv, 147; RP, 16 Sept. 1908.
27 BM Add. MSS 37415 f. 47, letter to Marquess Wellesley, 5 Oct. 1808; Guedalla, 172.
28 Quoted in Longford, op. cit., 205.
29 Creevey, 54.
30 Longford, op. cit., 207.
31 Blanch, 69–70.

CHAPTER 13: BOARD OF ENQUIRY, 1808
1 Croker, i, 344.
2 Arbuthnot, i, 234; Croker, i, 344; Stanhope, Conversations, 243.
3 BM Cat., 11215, 3 Feb. 1809.
4 BM Cat., 11035, 29 Sept. 1808.
5 BM Cat., 11042, Oct. 1808.
6 Castalia Granville, ii, 332.
7 WD, iv, 193.
8 Proceedings upon the Inquiry relative to the Armistice and Convention . . . between the British and French Armies, 1809, 120–1.
9 WSD, v, 515; vi, 122–4, 157.
10 WSD, v, 525.
11 WSD, v, 575, 601.
12 Vane, vii, 43–4.
13 Blanch, 71.
14 Arbuthnot, i, 378.
15 Rogers, 112.

CHAPTER 14: ACROSS THE DOURO, 1809
1 Wellington, Friends, 124.
2 Fortescue, History, vii, 146–9; Charles Oman, Wellington's Army, 82–7.
3 WD, iv, 371.
4 Mackesy, 28–9.
5 WD, iv, 276.

6 WD, iv, 412.
7 Guedalla, 183.
8 Croker, iii, 276.
9 Stanhope, *Conversations*, 9.
10 WD, iv, 430.
11 Stanhope, op. cit., 10.
12 WD, iv, 380.
13 WSD, vi, 349, 353, 505, 529; vii, 83, 345, 470.
14 Gleig, *Life*, 430–1.
15 Ibid.
16 Ellesmere, 221.
17 WD, iv, 385.
18 RP, 11 Jan. 1811.
19 WD, iii, 143; Muir and Esdaile, 15.
20 Canning Papers, Canning to Frere, quoted in Muir, 94.
21 RP, William Wellesley-Pole to Sir Arthur Wellesley, 1 Feb. 1811.
22 RP, Sir Arthur Wellesley to William Wellesley-Pole, 22 May 1809.
23 WD, iv, 526.
24 WD, iii, 367–8.
25 Chad, 17.
26 WD, iv, 543.
27 Brett-James, *Wellington at War*, 159.
28 Gates, 185.
29 Quoted in Elizabeth Longford, *Wellington: The Years of the Sword*, 243.
30 WD, v, 59.
31 WD, v, 15.
32 WD, v, 31, 73.
33 Fortescue, *Wellington*, 12.

CHAPTER 15: 'A WHOLE HOST OF MARSHALS', 1809–10.
1 WD, v, 8.
2 WSD, vi, 383.
3 *Independent Whig*, 20 Aug. 1809, quoted in M.D. George, BM *Cat.*, viii, 846.
4 BM *Cat.*, 11381, 'Preparation for the Jubilee or Theatricals Extraordinary', 24 Oct. 1809.
5 Muir, 113.
6 WD, v, 384, 196.

7 WSD, vi, 451–8, 459–62, 537–49, 649–72.
8 Letter to C. Flint, 7 Dec. 1809, quoted in Guedalla, 193.
9 WP (SS), 7 Nov. 1809.
10 Quoted in Elizabeth Longford, *Wellington: The Years of the Sword*, 267.
11 Shelley, i, 40.
12 Lord William Lennox, 216.
13 Longford, op. cit., 275.
14 Stanhope, *Conversations*, 17.
15 Quoted in Bryant, *The Age of Elegance*, 16.
16 RP, 6 Sept, 1808.
17 Cole and Gwynn, 60.
18 WD, vi, 33.
19 RP, 8 Aug. 1809.
20 WSD, vi, 588; WSD, vii, 470.
21 Schaumann, 395.
22 WSD, vi, 330, 353; Schaumann, 202.
23 Longford, op. cit., 252.
24 Hibbert, *A Soldier of the 71st*, 74–5.
25 WSD, vi, 582.
26 Ibid.
27 Schaumann, 365–6.
28 Croker, ii, 123.
29 WSD, vi, 61–2.
30 WSD, vii, 549.
31 Croker, i, 346.
32 RP, 6 April 1810.
33 WSD, vi, 493.
34 WSD, vi, 511, 592.
35 WD, vi, 6–9.
36 Gleig, *Life*, 147; Stanhope, op. cit., 19–20; Ellesmere, 97.
37 Marshall-Cornwall, 188.

CHAPTER 16: FROM BUSSACO TO EI BODON, 1810–11.
1 Gates, 235; Donald D. Horward, *The Battle of Bussaco*, 173, quoted in Muir, 133.
2 Stanhope, *Conversations*, 162.
3 Marshall-Cornwall, 219.
4 Fortescue, *History*, vii, 547.
5 WSD, vi, 612.

6 WSD, vi, 641.
7 Quoted in Muir, 135.
8 Ibid.
9 Castalia Granville, ii, 372–3.
10 Buckingham, *Memoirs of Court and Cabinets of George III*, iv, 458.
11 WSD, vii, 1–2.
12 Ibid.
13 Lowry Cole Papers, quoted in Guedalla, 200.
14 WD, vii, 59–60.
15 Marshall-Cornwall, 221.
16 WD, vii, 66.
17 WSD, xiii, 652–64; Gates, 263–9.
18 Charles Oman, *History*, vii, 178.
19 WSD, vii, 123.
20 WD, vii, 546.
21 WSD, vii, 123; WD, vii, 547.
22 WSD, vii, 176–7.
23 RP, 6 March 1811.
24 WSD, vii, 177.
25 WD, vii, 503.
26 Stanhope, op. cit., 90; Griffiths, 307–8.
27 RP, 2 July 1811; WSD, vii, 177.
28 WD, vii, 558.
29 Ellesmere, 107.
30 *Courier*, 20 April 1811, quoted in Haythornthwaite, *Armies of Wellington*, 245.
31 Griffiths, 131.
32 Larpent, i, 85; William Fraser, 164.
33 WD, viii, 232–3.

CHAPTER 17: LIFE AT
HEADQUARTERS, 1810–12
1 McGrigor, 304–5.
2 Letter to Major-General Stopford, quoted in Guedalla, 211.
3 WSD, vii, 172; Guedalla, 212.
4 WSD, xiv, 13.
5 Larpent, i, 86.
6 Ibid., i, 403.
7 Ponsonby, 9.
8 Larpent, i, 35.
9 Ibid., i, 403.
10 Charles Oman, *Wellington's Army*, 295.

11 WD, viii, 378–9.
12 Schaumann, 317.
13 Thornton, 107.
14 Ibid.
15 Cole and Gwynn, 59.
16 Fergusson, *Hounds are Home*, xvi, 6–7; Brett-James, *Wellington at War*, 199–201; Malmesbury, ii, 240; Larpent, *passim*.
17 Schaumann, 397–8.
18 Kincaid, 201.
19 Thornton, 74.
20 Stanhope, *Conversations*, 29.
21 McGrigor, 263.
22 Gleig, *Life*, 161–2.
23 Mills, 88.
24 Gleig, op. cit., 187–8.
25 Larpent, i, 197.
26 Gates, 35.
27 WD, v, 466.
28 McGrigor, 283; Gronow, i, 14–16; Elizabeth Longford, *Wellington: The Years of the Sword*, 265.
29 Gates, 326–31; Muir, 199–200.
30 Quoted in Longford, op. cit., 328.
31 WD, viii, 557.
32 Lionel G. Robinson, ii, 79.
33 William Fraser, 165; Gates, 326–31.

CHAPTER 18: BADAJOZ,
SALAMANCA AND MADRID, 1812
1 Wilkins, i, 131.
2 Muir, 216.
3 Gates, 336–7.
4 McGrigor, 121; Gleig, *Life*, 153–4.
5 Arbuthnot, i, 143.
6 WSD, vii, 311–13; Muir, 201.
7 Blakeney, 270–1, 273–5; McGrigor, 276–7.
8 Stanhope, *Conversations*, 9.
9 WD, ix, 173.
10 Fortescue, *History*, viii, 462.
11 Ibid., 471.
12 Bragge, 10.
13 WP (SS), 7 July 1801, Wellington to Henry Wellesley, quoted in Elizabeth Longford, *Wellington: The Years of the Sword*, 114.

14 Cole and Gwynn, 83.
15 Stanhope, op. cit., 51–2.
16 Croker, ii, 310.
17 Ibid,
18 Tomkinson, 165.
19 Greville, iv, 4; Croker, ii, 120.
20 Greville, iv, 98.
21 Ellesmere, 159; Longford, op. cit., 352.
22 Combermere and Knollys, i, 274.
23 Gates, 351–8.
24 RP, 25 July 1812, letter from
   Wellington to William
   Wellesley-Pole.
25 *Pakenham Letters*, 23 July 1812, quoted
   in Longford, op. cit., 356.
26 W.F.P. Napier, iv, Book xviii, chap. 4,
   299.
27 Wheeler, 90.
28 Bragge, 69.
29 Wheeler, 91.
30 Cole and Gwynn, 87.
31 Mills, 199, 207, 211.
32 Muir, 265.
33 Guedalla, 224.
34 WSD, vii, 406, 414, 432; WD, ix, 378,
   434; Muir, 265.

CHAPTER 19: RETREAT TO
PORTUGAL, 1812
1 WD, ix, 378.
2 WD, ix, 434.
3 WD, ix, 465.
4 Gates, 366, 371; Muir, 214–15.
5 Wheeler, 105–6.
6 Fortescue, *History*, viii, 608.
7 McGrigor, 302–3; Gleig, *Life*, 177.
8 Greville, iv, 99
9 WD, ix, 582–5; x, 574–7
10 Larpent, i, 226.
11 Bragge, 99–100.
12 WD, x, 73, 371.
13 WD, iv, 53–4, 63–5.
14 WSD, vii, 495.
15 S.G.P. Ward, 156–7.

CHAPTER 20: FROM VITORIA TO
THE FRONTIER, 1812–13
1 Herbert Maxwell, i, 310.
2 Gates, 386.
3 Elizabeth Longford, *Wellington: The
   Years of the Sword*, 385.
4 Kincaid, 162.
5 WSD, xiv, 236–40.
6 Stanhope, *Conversations*, 144.
7 Schaumann, 380.
8 Quoted in Guedalla, 237.
9 Gates, 390.
10 Wheeler, 119.
11 Schaumann, 379–81.
12 Wheeler, 119.
13 WSD, vii, 14 July 1813, 30 Aug. 1813;
   Asp/P. viii, 412.
14 Tomkinson, 252–3.
15 Longford, op. cit., 393–4, WD, x, 539;
   Frazer; Tomkinson; E.M. Lloyd,
   Dictionary of National Biography, xvi
   706–8; Bragge, 89.
16 Schaumann, 381.
17 WD, 29 June 1813.
18 Fortescue, *History*, ix, 255–6
19 Quoted in Longford, op. cit., 402,
20 WD, x, 596.
21 Quoted in Longford, op. cit., 404
22 Larpent, i, 304.
23 R P, 18 Aug. 1813.
24 Gates, 414–22; Stanhope, op. cit., 14,
   18.
25 Muir, 269.
26 WD, x, 496; Fortescue, *History*, ix,
   199; Stanhope, op. cit., 14, 18.
27 Gates, 429.
28 WSD, vii, 309–12
29 W.F.P. Napier, v, 278; WSD, vii,
   309–10.
30 Schaumann, 396.
31 Herbert Maxwell, i, 373.
32 Ibid., i, 327
33 William Fraser, 166.
34 Greville, iv, 5.
35 Stanhope, op. cit., 79
36 WD, vii, 406.
37 Ellesmere, 129; Tomkinson, 117.

38 Gash, *Anecdotes*, 28.
39 J.S. Cooper, *Rough Notes of Seven Campaigns* (Carlisle, 1869), 63.
40 Kincaid, 10, 53.
41 Quoted in Guedalla, 240.
42 William Fraser, 208.
43 Gronow, i, 3.

CHAPTER 21: ST JEAN DE LUZ, 1813
1 Larpent, ii, 187.
2 RP, 19 March 1814.
3 WSD, xiv, 314, 490.
4 Bragge, 125.
5 Stanhope, *Conversations*, 22.
6 Schaumann, 394−5, 402.
7 Sir Harry Smith, i, 136−7.
8 Wheatley, 30.
9 Schaumann, 382.
10 Ibid., 386, 388.
11 Croker, i, 433.
12 Brett-James, *Life in Wellington's Army*, 292−309.
13 Surtees, 257−8.
14 Wheatley, 34−5.
15 Rogers, 242.
16 RP, 3 August 1813; Shelley, i, 96; Stanhope, op. cit., 184.
17 Herbert Maxwell, i, 366; Gleig, *Life*, 494; Larpent, ii, 187, 422, 425; Stanhope, op. cit., 184.
18 WD, xi, 645.
19 WSD, vii, 743−6; Gates, 461−6.
20 Broughton, i, 190.
21 Larpent, ii, 267.

CHAPTER 22: IN LONDON AGAIN, 1814
1 WSD, ix, 100.
2 WD, xi, 668, 681; xii, 688; WSD, ix, 74.
3 *Letters of Sir Walter Scott* (ed. H.J.C. Grierson, 1932), 95.
4 Broughton, i, 111−14.
5 Stanhope, *Conversations*, 79; Croker, i, 333−4; Herbert Maxwell, i, 379.
6 Leach, 370.

7 WD, xii, 62.
8 Bruce, i, 165.
9 William Napier, *Life and Opinions of General Sir Charles Napier*, iv, 306.
10 Gleig, *Life*, 246; McGrigor, 278.
11 Gleig, op. cit., 272.
12 Chad, 7.
13 Duchess of Wellington's Journal, WP (SS), quoted in Elizabeth Longford, *Wellington: The Years of the Sword*, 304.
14 Harriet Granville, ii, 449.
15 Berry, ii, 506.
16 Duchess of Wellington's Journal, WP (SS).
17 Joan Wilson, 120.
18 Duchess of Wellington's Journal, WP (SS); Joan Wilson, 125−6, 143.
19 Duchess of Wellington's Journal, WP (SS).
20 Shelley, i, 71.
21 Marchand, i, 459−60.
22 Gronow, i, 32.
23 Warrenne Blake, 234.
24 Shelley, i, 70.
25 Ibid., 68−9.
26 Howard Colvin, 937.
27 Elizabeth Longford, 'The Duke of Wellington's Search'; Gerald Wellington (Roxburghe Club Correspondence), 142.
28 Stanhope, op. cit., 167.
29 Desmond Seward, *Napoleon's Family* (1986), 168; Lord William Lennox, 24−5.

CHAPTER 23: PARIS AND VIENNA, 1814−15
1 WSD, ix, 241.
2 WSD, ix, 173−6, 625−7, 228−33, 277, 293−5, 319−24.
3 Stanhope, *Conversations*, 36, 31
4 Ibid., 216.
5 Ibid., 126.
6 Gleig, *Life*, 250.
7 Byron to Lady Melbourne, 8 January 1814.

8 Stanhope, op. cit., 218.
9 Castalia Granville, ii, 507.
10 Quoted in Elizabeth Longford, *Wellington: The Years of the Sword*, 457.
11 Blanch, 334–5.
12 Cronin, 394.
13 Castalia Granville, ii, 516.
14 Joan Wilson, 158.
15 Castalia Granville, ii, 507.
16 Foy MSS, 26 Oct. 1814, quoted in Longford, op. cit., 461.
17 Letter to Earl Bathurst, 19 Nov. 1814, quoted in Guedalla, 258.
18 WSD, ix, 405, 407–8, 425, 430, 458; RP, 9 Nov. 1814.
19 Quoted in Longford, op. cit., 462.
20 WSD, ix, 422–3, 425–6; RP, 17 Nov. 1814.
21 Quoted in Longford, op. cit., 463.
22 Lord William Lennox, 90–1.
23 Gronow, ii, 322.

CHAPTER 24: BRUSSELS, 1815
1 Palmer, 144.
2 Byron's letters to Lady Melbourne, 1, 8, 10, 17 Oct. 1813.
3 Jackson, 11.
4 Creevey, 226–7.
5 Ibid., 227–8.
6 WD, xii, 291–2.
7 WSD, x, 49.
8 Anglesey, *One-Leg*, 119.
9 William Fraser, 170.
10 Quoted in Elizabeth Longford, *Wellington: The Years of the Sword*, 482.
11 Stanhope, *Conversations*, 68.
12 Quoted in Longford, op. cit., 483.
13 WSD, x, 219.
14 WD, xii, 358; WSD, x, 219.
15 WD, xii, 346.
16 Greville, v, 125.
17 Croker, i, 277.
18 Creevey, 228.
19 Captain William Verner, 7th Hussars, quoted in Brett-James, *The Hundred Days*, 39.

20 Herbert Maxwell, ii, 13.
21 Captain Verner, in Brett-James, op. cit., 40.
22 *Extracts from the Notebook of the Comtesse d'Assche, née d'Ives*, quoted in Longford, op. cit., 506.
23 Malmesbury, ii, 445–6.
24 Ibid.

CHAPTER 25: WATERLOO, 1815
1 Ellesmere, 170.
2 Stanhope, *Conversations*, 109.
3 Chad, 5.
4 Herbert Maxwell, ii, 37–8.
5 Mercer, i, 160.
6 Edward Cotton, *A Voice from Waterloo* (1849), quoted in Hibbert, *Napoleon's Last Campaign*, 132.
7 Herbert Maxwell, ii, 57.
8 Gronow, i, 70.
9 Mercer, i, 166.
10 William Fraser, 2–4.
11 Quoted in Elizabeth Longford, *Wellington: The Years of the Sword*, 541.
12 *Wieder Napoleon! Ein deutsches Reiterleben 1806–1815* (Stuttgart, 2 vols, 1911), 320–1, quoted in Brett-James, *The Hundred Days*, 86.
13 Houssaye, ii, 318–20; Brett-James, op. cit., 99–100; Chandler, 1066; Longford, op. cit., 546–7; Cronin, 400; Hamilton-Williams, 262–3.
14 WD, xii, 529.
15 Gronow, i, 190–1, 69–70.
16 Quoted in Hibbert, op. cit., 192.
17 Gronow, i, 76.
18 Colonel Auguste-Louis Pétiet, *Souvenirs militaires de l'Histoire Contemporaine* (Paris, 1844), quoted in Hibbert, op. cit., 273.
19 Ernest F. Henderson, *Blücher and the Uprising of Prussia against Napoleon, 1806–1815* (New York, 1911) quoted in Hibbert, op. cit., 235.
20 Stanhope, op. cit., 245.
21 Gleig, *Life*, 273.
22 Thornton, 87.

23 John Barrow, *The Life and Correspondence of Admiral Sir William Sidney Smith* (2 vols, 1848), ii, 57.
24 Lord William Lennox, 217–8; Brett-James, op. cit., 182; Ellesmere, 172; Longford, op. cit., 584.
25 WSD, x, 531.
26 Horatia Durant, *The Somerset Sequence* (1951), 171–2.
27 Anglesey, *One-Leg*, 149.
28 Anglesey, *Capel Letters*, 116; *One-Leg*, 150.
29 Quoted in Longford, op. cit., 582.
30 Anglesey, *Capel Letters*, 122.
31 Leeke, i, 62.
32 Ibid., 97.
33 WD, xii, 484.
34 *Samuel Rogers's Recollections*, 215.
35 Shelley, i, 102.
36 Carola Oman, 214.
37 Creevey, 236–7.
38 Quoted in Brett-James, op. cit., 183; RP, 19 June 1815.
39 Shelley, i, 102.

CHAPTER 26: THE AMBASSADOR, 1815
1 WSD, xi, 24–5.
2 WD, xii, 534.
3 Stanhope, *Conversations*, 119; Houssaye, 238–41; Shelley, i, 106; Elizabeth Longford, *Wellington: Pillar of State*, 16.
4 Nicolson, *The Congress of Vienna*, 81.
5 Gronow, i, 206–7.
6 Ibid., i, 81.
7 Mercer, 284.
8 Gronow, i, 97–8.
9 Ibid., i, 98.
10 D'Arblay, ii, 45.
11 Gronow, i, 85.
12 WD, xii, 516.
13 Holland, 220.
14 Nicolson, 232.
15 Wellington College Archives.
16 Shelley, i, 99–144.
17 Ibid., i, 110; Cole and Gwynn, 148.
18 Shelley, i, 106.

19 Ibid., i, 113.
20 Ibid., i, 125, 144 and *passim*.
21 Harriet Granville, i, 62.
22 Maria Edgeworth to Lady Romilly, 13 Aug. 1815, Irish National Library, quoted in Longford, op. cit., 21.
23 Quennell, 132.
24 Quoted in Longford, op. cit., 19.
25 Lord William Lennox, 181–3.
26 Aspinall, *Politics and the Press*, 342.
27 T.A.J. Burnett, *The Rise and Fall of a Regency Dandy: The Life and Times of Scrope Berdmore Davies* (London, 1981), 38, 230–1.
28 Harriet Granville, i, 74.
29 Stone, *Broken Lives*, 300; *Narrative of the Case of the Marchioness of Westmeath; Reply to the Narrative.*
30 Stone, op. cit., 301.
31 Hinde, *Castlereagh*; WSD, xi, 175–80.
32 WSD, xi, 33–4, Liverpool to Castlereagh, 15 July 1815.
33 Broughton, i, 325; WD, xii, 641–6.
34 Grattan, ii, 96–8; Broughton, i, 325; Longford, op. cit., 26.
35 Cole and Gwynn, 177.
36 Ibid.
37 WSD, ix, 231–6; Longford, op. cit., 28–9.

CHAPTER 27: CAMBRAI AND VITRY 1815–18
1 Berry, iii, 78–9.
2 Lord William Lennox, 191, 206.
3 Shelley, i, 202.
4 Carola Oman, 91.
5 Letter from the Duchess of Wellington to Lady Eleanor Butler and Miss Ponsonby, 18 July 1816, quoted in Guedalla, 299.
6 Haydon, ii, 288–90, Sir David Wilkie's letter to Haydon, 18 Aug. 1816.
7 Timbs, 70.
8 Frith, i, 322.
9 Arbuthnot, ii, 347.
10 Frith, i, 323.

11 WSD, xii, 77.
12 WSD, xii, 141–2, 153, 146.
13 Quoted in Guedalla, 303.
14 Cole and Gwynn, 187.
15 Gerald Wellington, *Wellington and His Friends*, 286.
16 Hibbert, *The Grand Tour* (1969), 217.
17 Carver Papers, quoted in Butler, 497.
18 Ibid.
19 Harriet Granville, i, 108.
20 Arbuthnot, i, 301; E.A. Smith, *Wellington and the Arbuthnots*, 63.
21 WP (SS) 6 March 1817; Elizabeth Longford, *Wellington: Pillar of State*, 45–6.
22 Creevey, 280–1.
23 WSD, x, 455–6, 502–4.
24 WSD, xii, 271.
25 WSD, xii, 406.
26 BM Add. MSS 37315, f. 256, the Duchess of Wellington to Lord Wellesley, quoted in Guedalla, 306.
27 WSD, xii, 325, 363.
28 Asp/P, viii, 428.
29 RP, 20 Feb. 1816.
30 WSD, xii, 273, 292–3, 33–5, 363.

CHAPTER 28: STRATFIELD SAYE, 1818–20
1 *London Encyclopaedia*, 932.
2 Scott, 2–4; Howard Colvin, 127, 639, 938; Peel, 87–8; Arbuthnot, i, 63; Wharncliffe, ii, 295; Elizabeth Longford, *Wellington: Pillar of State*, 89.
3 Howard Colvin, 808; *Country Life*, 26 Nov. 1948, 1107 and 25 May 1972, 1322.
4 Butler, 492.
5 Campbell, *Lives of the Lord Chancellors* (1846).
6 Jervis and Tomlin, 5–7, 19–20, 44–7; *London Encyclopaedia*, 936; Howard Colvin, 51, 938.
7 Lord Palmerston, *Selections from Private Journals of Tours in France* (1871), 54.

8 Vane, xi, 5; Cookson, 22.
9 WSD, xii, 813.
10 WP (SS), Wellington to Mrs Arbuthnot, 27 Aug. 1819; Longford, op. cit., 62.
11 Gash, *Life of the Earl of Liverpool*, 154; Thomas Lawrence, 271; Johnson, 95; HHP, 13 Sept. 1834.
12 Arbuthnot, i, 70; Johnson, 69.
13 Arbuthnot, i, 70; Johnson, 89.
14 Ellesmere, 132; Gleig, *Life*, 292.

CHAPTER 29: KING GEORGE AND QUEEN CAROLINE, 1820–1
1 Creevey, 279.
2 Ibid., 277.
3 Hibbert, *George IV: Regent and King*, 154.
4 Carola Oman, 207.
5 Bartlett, 176.
6 Flora Fraser, 399–400.
7 Hibbert, op. cit., 154; Arbuthnot, i, 26.
8 William Cobbett, *History of the Regency and the Reign of King George IV* (1830), 425.
9 Lever, 36.
10 Greville, i, 97, 100; E. Tangye Lean, *The Napoleonists* (Oxford, 1970), 118.
11 Quennell, 69.
12 Arbuthnot, i, 36; Lever, 41.
13 Palmerston Papers c 1V/4/3, 22 Aug. 1820, quoted in Hibbert, op. cit., 161.
14 Quennell, 62.
15 G.W.E. Russell; Hibbert, op. cit., 161–2; Longford, op. cit., 68.
16 Gerald Wellington, *Wellington and His Friends*, 100, 103, 7.
17 Creevey, 337.
18 Greville, i, 107.
19 Arbuthnot, i, 53.
20 Ibid., i, 78.
21 Ibid., i, 79.
22 WP (SS), 29 July 1821; Lever, 86.
23 Quoted in Hibbert, op. cit., 192.

24 Arbuthnot, i, 108.
25 Denbigh MSS, Pailton House, f. 40–1, 20 July 1821.
26 Quoted in Hibbert, op. cit., 208.

CHAPTER 30: HUSBAND AND WIFE, 1821

1 Gerald Wellington, *The Collected Works of the 7th Duke*.
2 Joan Wilson, 128, 143.
3 Arbuthnot, i, 168–9.
4 Ibid.
5 Ibid., 422–3.
6 WP (SS).
7 Elizabeth Longford, *Wellington: Pillar of State*, 79.
8 WP (SS), Agreement with J.J. Angerstein dated 1822.
9 WP (SS); Longford, op. cit., 76–7.
10 Gerald Wellington, Roxburghe Club correspondence, 2 May 1822, 14–15.
11 Arbuthnot, ii, 5–6.
12 Carola Oman, 223.
13 Gerald Wellington, Roxburghe Club correspondence, 20–1.
14 Augustus Hare, *The Story of My Life* (1900), quoted in Longford, op. cit., 85.
15 Hare, op. cit., 13 Nov. 1879, iv, 344.
16 Gerald Wellington, Roxburghe Club correspondence, 25, 52–3.
17 Hare, op. cit., v, 11–12.
18 Quennell, 101–2.
19 Quoted in E.A. Smith, *Wellington and the Arbuthnots*, 67.
20 Peel, 61.
21 Quennell, 103–4.
22 Ibid.
23 G.W.E. Russell.
24 Gronow, ii, 14.
25 Arbuthnot, i, 260.
26 Carola Oman, 183.
27 Calvert, 233.
28 Harriet Granville, i, 203.
29 Raikes, *Journal*, iii, 27.
30 Wharncliffe, ii, 167–8.
31 Arbuthnot, i, 137.
32 Ibid.
33 Shelley, ii, 95.
34 Croker, i, 282, letter to Lord Hertford, 22 Sept. 1825.
35 Shelley, ii, 81.
36 Lever, 118.
37 Shelley, ii, 73–4.
38 Ibid., ii, 310.
39 Pückler-Muskau quoted by E.A. Smith, op. cit., 161.
40 Lever, 118.
41 Ibid., 138.
42 Quoted in E.A. Smith, op. cit., 87, 108.
43 Ibid., 87.
44 Ibid., 65.
45 Shelley, ii, 95.
46 Quennell, 116.
47 Arbuthnot, i, 142.
48 Quennell, 120–1.
49 Gleig, *Life*, 297; Shelley, ii, 110; Hibbert, *George IV: Regent and King*, 229.
50 Londonderry MSS quoted in Asp/K ii, 472.
51 Quennell, 189.
52 Hyde, *Castlereagh*.
53 Gerald Wellington, *Wellington and His Friends*, 24; Stanhope, *Conversations*, 126, 272–3; HHP, 19 June 1835.
54 WDNS, i, 251–4, Bankhead to Wellington, 9 Aug. 1822; Hinde, *Castlereagh*, 279; Arbuthnot, i, 180.
55 BM Add. MSS 38190, f. 56 quoted in Cookson, 368–9.
56 Greville, i, 184.
57 Arbuthnot, i, 238.
58 Cookson, 372–3; WDNS, i, 272–6.
59 Quoted in Longford, op. cit., 99; Hibbert, op. cit., 254.
60 Parker, i, 336; Yonge, iii, 200.
61 Quennell, 168–9.
62 Quoted in Guedalla, 335.

CHAPTER 31: VIENNA AND
VERONA, 1822−4

1 Gleig, *Life*, 313.
2 Ibid., 314.
3 Gerald Wellington, *Wellington and His Friends*, 29.
4 BM Add. MSS 37415 f. 71
5 Haydon, ii, 347.
6 Arbuthnot, i, 209.
7 Ibid., ii, 75; Colchester, iii, 553.
8 Carola Oman, 205.
9 WP (SS), Wellington to Mrs Arbuthnot, 4 Oct. 1822.
10 *Courier*, 19 Oct. 1822, quoted in Elizabeth Longford, *Wellington: Pillar of State*, 102.
11 Creevey, 409.
12 Nicolson, 'Wellington: The Diplomatist', 43−5.
13 Palmer, 211−19; Longford, op. cit., 102−3; Hyde, *Princess Lieven*, 144−6; Quennell, 218−31, WP (HI), WPI/724/23, 724/24.
14 Aspinall, *Correspondence of Charles Arbuthnot*, 85.
15 Arbuthnot, i, 209.
16 Shelley, ii, 41.
17 Gerald Wellington, op. cit., 48.
18 Hibbert, *George IV: Regent and King*, 277.
19 Gerald Wellington, op. cit., 22, 46−8; Quennell, 271.
20 Wharncliffe, ii, 296.
21 Quennell, 103.
22 Ibid., 19, 26.
23 Peel, 87−8.
24 Gerald Wellington, op. cit., 263.
25 Rose Weigall, *Correspondence of Lady Burghersh*, 132.
26 Gerald Wellington, op. cit., 49−50.
27 Ibid., 110.
28 Greville, ii, 304.
29 WDNS, i, 385.
30 Rolo, 134; Temperley, 147; Guedalla, 341−2.
31 Harold Temperley, *The Foreign Policy of Canning, 1822−1827* (1925).
32 Lionel G. Robinson, ii, 71.

33 Arbuthnot, i, 258; Hibbert, op. cit., 257, 286, 294.
34 Quennell, 218−19.
35 Arbuthnot, i, 309.
36 Ibid., i, 319.
37 Ibid., i, 307.
38 Ibid., i, 262.
39 WP (HI), WPI/796/15, 23 July 1824.
40 Woodward, 211.
41 Thompson, 55; Yonge, ii, 383−93.

CHAPTER 32: ST PETERSBURG
AND THE NORTHERN COUNTIES,
1825−7

1 Arbuthnot, i, 335.
2 Elizabeth Longford, *Wellington: Pillar of State*, 124; Temperley, 352.
3 Greville, i, 155.
4 Arbuthnot, ii, 10
5 Ibid.
6 Gerald Wellington, *Wellington and His Friends*, ii, 143.
7 Shelley, ii, 143.
8 Gerald Wellington, op. cit., 56−64; Guedalla, 346−8.
9 Chamberlain, 202; Guedalla, 348.
10 Nicolson, 'Wellington: The Diplomatist', 53.
11 Lionel G. Robinson, ii, 33, 47, 82;
12 Ibid., 133, 137.
13 Ibid., 108, 133; Raikes, *Journal*, 23 Dec. 1840.
14 E.V. Ashley, *Life of Lord Palmerston*, quoted in Lionel G. Robinson, ii, 129.
15 Lionel G. Robinson, ii, 149, 157, 266.
16 Lever, 148; Longford, op. cit, 126; Arbuthnot, ii, 23.
17 Gerald Wellington, Roxburghe Club correspondence, 10 Oct. 1824, 26−7.
18 Gleig, *Life*, 435.
19 W.R. Ward, 85; Gerald Wellington, Roxburghe Club correspondence, Dean of Christ Church to Wellington, 22 March 1825; Arbuthnot, i, 387.
20 Gerald Wellington, Roxburghe Club correspondence, Wellington to Dean, 21 March 1825, 29.

21 Arbuthnot, ii, 36.
22 Gerald Wellington, *Wellington and His Friends*, 111.
23 Arbuthnot, i, 422.
24 Ibid., ii, 56.
25 Gerald Wellington, *Wellington and His Friends*, 66.
26 Ibid., 111.
27 Gerald Wellington, Roxburghe Club correspondence, 47–52.
28 Gash, *Mr Secretary Peel*, 425; Stapleton, ii, 578.
29 Peel, 95–6.
30 Ibid.
31 Ibid., 110.
32 *The Times*, 24 Jan. 1827; Creevey, 450–1.
33 Gerald Wellington, *Wellington and His Friends*, 70.
34 Ibid., 67.
35 Creevey, 450–1.
36 Aspinall, 'The Formation of Canning's Ministry, February to August 1827' (Camden Third Series, vol. lix, Royal Historical Society, 1937), xxxl-xxxll; Croker, i, 363.
37 Guedalla, 356.
38 Temperley, 206–7.
39 Lionel G. Robinson, ii, 286–7.
40 WDNS, iii, 629.
41 Shelley, ii, 155.
42 Creevey, 464.
43 Gash, *Life of Lord Liverpool*, 222.
44 Arbuthnot, ii, 109.
45 Aspinall, op. cit., 206; Rolo, 154.
46 Pückler-Muskau, 116.
47 Buckingham, *Memoirs of the Court and Cabinets of George IV*, ii, 237.
48 Hyde, *Princess Lieven*, 180.
49 M.A. Richardson, *The Local Historian's Table Book* (Newcastle, 1843), 358–63; files of the *Durham County Advertiser*, County Record Office, Durham.
50 Brock, *Great Reform Act*, 59.
51 Quoted in Longford, op. cit., 155.
52 Hibbert, *George IV: Regent and King*, 301.

CHAPTER 33: THE PRIME MINISTER, 1828–9

1 Raikes, *Journal*, iv, 292.
2 Croker, i, 431; Raikes, op. cit., iv, 292; RA 23101: Asp/K, iii, 57.
3 Woodward, 76.
4 Lionel G. Robinson, ii, 152.
5 Arbuthnot, ii, 160–1.
6 Quoted in Thompson, 72–3.
7 Elers, 273.
8 Ibid., 274.
9 Croker, i, 404.
10 Sir H. Lytton Bulmer, *Life of Lord Palmerston* (1870), i, 246, 250, quoted in Guedalla, 370.
11 Greville, i, 214.
12 Brock, *Great Reform Act*, 64.
13 Peel, 103.
14 Creevey, 498.
15 Brock, op. cit., 65.
16 Greville, i, 216.
17 WP (SS), Wellington to Mrs Arbuthnot, 5 April 1828.
18 Anglesey, *One-Leg*, Frederick Lamb to Anglesey, 24 March 1828.
19 *Wellington Anecdotes*, 63.
20 Peel, 62.
21 RA 24110–11: Asp/K, iii, 275–6.
22 Gash, *Sir Robert Peel*, 525.
23 Quoted in Elizabeth Longford, *Wellington: Pillar of State*, 166.
24 Anglesey, op. cit., 210.
25 Lionel G. Robinson, ii, 146.
26 Arbuthnot, ii, 161.
27 Lionel G. Robinson, ii, 152.
28 Colchester, iii, 594.
29 Greville, i, 301.
30 Ibid., 239.
31 Ellenborough, i, 139.
32 Greville, i, 302.
33 Ibid., i, 236.
34 Arbuthnot, ii, 254.
35 Ibid., ii, 246.
36 Ibid., i, 301.
37 Rogers, 221.
38 WSD, v, 467.
39 Arbuthnot, ii, 266.

40 WP (SS), 30 March 1829.
41 Broughton, iii, 315–16.
42 WP (SS), 1 April 1829.
43 Greville, i, 249–253.

CHAPTER 34: BATTERSEA FIELDS
AND SCOTLAND YARD, 1829
1 J.S. Harford, *Life of Bishop Burgess* (1941).
2 Greville, ii, 35.
3 Twiss, iii, 95.
4 Anglesey, *One-Leg, passim.*
5 WDNS, v, 527, 531, 533–8.
6 Ellenborough, i, 403; Herbert Maxwell, ii, 234; Greville, i, 276–7; Elizabeth Longford, *Wellington: Pillar of State*, 186–90; Guedalla, 382–3; WP (SS); WDNS, v, 538–45.
7 BM *Cat.* 15696, 15697, 15703.
8 Martineau, 25.
9 Creevey, 542.
10 Arbuthnot, ii, 257.
11 WP (SS), 26 March 1829.
12 Greville, i, 277–9.
13 Quoted in Charles Reith, *The Police Idea* (1938), 215.
14 Charles Reith, op. cit., 224.
15 *Hansard's Parliamentary Debates* (1828), XLVI.
16 Reith, op. cit., 131; W.L. Melville Lee, *A History of Police in England* (1901), 243.
17 William Fraser, 136.
18 Peel, 108, 114.
19 Anglesey, op. cit., 222.

CHAPTER 35: THE DEATH OF THE
KING, 1829–30
1 Shelley, iii, 313.
2 Arbuthnot, ii, 5–6.
3 Asp/Geo IV, iii, 1564, 20 June 1829.
4 Quoted in E.A. Smith, *Wellington and the Arbuthnots*, 126.
5 Ellenborough, ii, 15.
6 Carola Oman, 175–6; Ellenborough, ii, 225.
7 Croker, i, 430–1; Ellenborough, ii, 225.

8 RA 24703–4; Asp/K, iii, 461.
9 RA 24771; Asp/K, iii, 468; Ellenborough, ii, 35.
10 HHP, notes by the Marchioness of Salisbury; Eldon Papers, copy in RA under reference RA 21/179/327, 20 Jan. 1830; RA Add. 21/179, 20 Jan. 1830.
11 Ellenborough, ii, 174; RA 24771; Asp/K, iii, 468.
12 Croker, ii, 4.
13 Lionel G. Robinson, ii, 163.
14 Greville, i, 293–4.
15 Gerald Wellington, *Wellington and His Friends*, 270.
16 Greville, i, 351.
17 Guedalla, 389.
18 Greville, ii, 111.
19 Mavor, 272.
20 Sadleir, 279.
21 Hubert Cole, 155, 164; Greville, i, 341.
22 Stone, *Broken Lives*, 327.
23 HHP (Westmeath Papers); Stone, op. cit., 335; 'Reply to the Narrative of the Case of the Marchioness of Westmeath'; Anglesey, *One-Leg*, 206.
24 Elizabeth Longford, *Wellington: Pillar of State*, 204
25 Arbuthnot, ii, 357.
26 Ibid., ii, 340.
27 Ibid., ii, 343.
28 WDNS, vi, 294.
29 Greville, i, 362.
30 Ibid., i, 365.
31 Arbuthnot, ii, 352.
32 Carola Oman, 177.
33 WP (HI), 1186/27.
34 Waller of Woodcote MSS (Warwick) CR 341/206; Hibbert, *George IV: Regent and King*, 335.

CHAPTER 36: RIOTS AND
REPRESSION, 1830–2
1 Quennell, 309.
2 Greville, ii, 3.
3 Ibid., ii, 14–15.
4 Arbuthnot, ii, 386; Shelley, ii, 202; Ellenborough, ii, 370.
5 WP (SS), 9 Oct. 1830.

6 Elizabeth Longford, *Wellington: Pillar of State*, 224.

7 Arbuthnot, ii, 399.

8 *Hansard's Parliamentary Debates*, 2 Nov. 1830.

9 WDNS, vii, 352–3.

10 Greville, ii, 52.

11 Chamberlain, 252.

12 Greville, ii, 92.

13 Ibid., ii, 56.

14 WDNS, vi, 354–5; *Precautions ... to be taken to defend Apsley House in Case of Attack*, 7 Nov. 1830; Thompson, 107.

15 Ellenborough, ii, 417; Arbuthnot, ii, 400; Greville, ii, 53–4.

16 Greville, ii, 40, 42, 78.

17 Ibid., ii, 61.

18 Ibid., ii, 62.

19 Hyde, *Princess Lieven*, 199; Lionel G. Robinson, ii, 277.

20 Rogers, 220.

21 Greville, iv, 65–6.

22 Arbuthnot, ii, 407.

23 Duke of Wellington's Lieutenancy Papers, WP (HI).

24 Ibid.

25 Ibid.

26 Ibid.

27 Croker, ii, 80–1.

28 Aspinall, *Three Diaries* (Ellenborough), 27 Jan. 1831.

29 WP (SS), 12 Jan. 1831.

CHAPTER 37: A BOGY TO THE MOB, 1832

1 Le Strange, ii, 392.

2 Lionel G. Robinson, ii, 278.

3 Rose Weigall, *Correspondence of Lady Burghersh*, 51.

4 Herbert Maxwell, ii, 259.

5 WDNS, vii, 409–10.

6 *Hansard's Parliamentary Debates*, 24 March 1831.

7 WP (HI), 1186/27.

8 Elizabeth Longford, *Wellington: Pillar of State*, 250–2, 254; BM *Cat.* 15928, 15929.

9 Maria Edgeworth, *Life and Letters*, ii, 522.

10 Greville, vi, 361.

11 WP (SS), 8 April 1831; Longford, op. cit., 267.

12 Maria Edgeworth, op. cit., ii, 533–4.

13 Gerald Wellington, *Wellington and His Friends*, 94–5.

14 Ibid., 95–6.

15 WP (HI), 1186/11.

16 WP (HI), 1186/18.

17 WP (HI), 1186/9.

18 WP (SS), 17 Jan. 1832; Longford, op. cit., 409.

19 Stanhope, *Conversations*, 13.

20 Arbuthnot, ii, 298; Stanhope, op. cit., 86; Greville, i, 306; WDNS, vii, 557–8.

21 Gerald Wellington, op. cit., 99.

22 Ellesmere, 14.

23 Croker, ii, 124.

24 Gleig, *Life*, 362–3.

25 Gleig, *Reminiscences*, 101–2.

26 WDNS, viii, 98–9.

27 Ibid., viii, 304.

28 Ibid., viii, 280.

29 Croker, ii, 157.

30 Guedalla, 413.

31 Ibid., 414.

32 Quoted in Longford, op. cit., 275.

33 J.R.M. Butler, *The Passing of the Great Reform Bill* (1914), 396–7; HHP, 27 May 1831.

34 William Fraser, 206.

35 Stanhope, op. cit., 176; Gleig, *Life*, 376; William Fraser, 23–5; Rogers, 224–5; Herbert Maxwell, ii, 271; Raikes, *Journal*, i, 33.

36 Herbert Maxwell, ii, 270–1.

37 WDNS, viii, 492.

38 Brooke and Gandy, 345.

39 William Fraser, 11.

CHAPTER 38: OXFORD UNIVERSITY AND APSLEY HOUSE, 1832–4

1 Stanhope, *Conversations*, 36.

2 Croker, ii, 212.

3 Ibid., ii, 224.

4 Shelley, ii, 101.
5 W.R. Ward, 85.
6 Croker, ii, 225.
7 Bumpus, 6.
8 Mozley, 41
9 Shelley, ii, 253; Ellesmere, 46; William
   Fraser, 156–61; Raikes, *Journal*, ii, 373;
   W.R. Ward, 86.
10 Greville, iii, 47.
11 Croker, ii, 228.
12 Carola Oman, 119–20.
13 Ibid., 122.
14 Christopher Hibbert, *Tower of London*
   (New York, 1971), 133.
15 WP (SS).
16 Stanhope, *Conversations*, 241.
17 Elizabeth Longford, *Wellington: Pillar*
   of State, 280.
18 WP (SS).
19 Arbuthnot, ii, 335–6.
20 Jervis and Tomlin, 6; Gerald
   Wellington, *Collected Works of the 7th*
   Duke of Wellington, 96.
21 Gerald Wellington, Roxburghe Club
   correspondence, 154.
22 Ibid.
23 Creevey, 551.
24 WP (SS), 21 Aug. 1832
25 Raikes, *Journal*, i, 143.
26 William Fraser, 213.

CHAPTER 39: LADY FRIENDS, 1834
1 Carola Oman, 132.
2 HHP, 18 Aug. 1834.
3 WP (SS), 28 July 1834.
4 Gerald Wellington, *Wellington and His*
   Friends, 120.
5 Quennell, 335.
6 Carola Oman, 145.
7 Herrick; Elizabeth Longford,
   Wellington: Pillar of State, 300–2;
   Guedalla, 422–9.

CHAPTER 40: THE FOREIGN
SECRETARY, 1834–6
1 Rogers, 237.
2 Gleig, *Life*, 431.
3 Carola Oman, 109.

4 WDNS, viii, 147–9.
5 Bennett, 134.
6 Philip Magnus, *Gladstone: A*
   Biography (1958), 33.
7 Parker, i, 252.
8 Jane Ridley, 154.
9 Maria Edgeworth, *Letters from*
   England, quoted in Elizabeth
   Longford, *Wellington: Pillar of State*,
   307.
10 Brialmont, *Life of Wellington*, iv, 168.
11 Raikes, *Journal*, ii, 69–70.
12 HHP, 13 Sept. 1834.
13 Le Strange, ii, 47.
14 Quoted in Thompson, 148.
15 William Fraser, 206.
16 Lionel G. Robinson, ii, 172.
17 Quoted in Longford, op. cit., 303.
18 Greville, iii, 193.
19 Ibid., iii, 175.
20 HHP, 28 March 1835.
21 Herbert Maxwell, ii, 306.
22 Carola Oman, 165.
23 Ibid., 177.
24 HHP, 24 Jan. 1836.
25 Morley, i, 133.
26 Stanhope, *Conversations*, 272.
27 Greville, iii, 178–9.
28 Ibid., iii, 152.
29 Jane Ridley, 155; Robert Blake, 123;
   Norman Gash, *Politics in the Age of*
   Peel, 436.
30 W.E. Gladstone, *Gladstone Papers*
   (1930), 20 Jan. 1836.

CHAPTER 41: PORTRAITS AND
PAINTERS, 1830–50
1 Greville, v, 25.
2 Ibid., v, 460. '
3 Ellesmere, 177.
4 Wharncliffe, ii, 262.
5 Redesdale, i, 88.
6 Arbuthnot, i, 30, 39, 55; ii, 145.
7 Greville, iv, 10.
8 Carola Oman, 109.
9 Rose Weigall, *Correspondence of Lady*
   Burghersh, 84.
10 Helen Smailes, 'Thomas Campbell

and the "Camera Lucida": the Buccleuch statue of the first Duke of Wellington', *Burlington Magazine*, vol. CXXiX, No. 10016, Nov. 1987, 709–14.

11 WP (SS); Walker, i, 530.
12 Ibid.
13 Haydon, ii, 564.
14 Arbuthnot, ii, 50.
15 Gerald Wellington, *Wellington and His Friends*, 12.
16 Haydon, ii, 400.
17 Carola Oman, 166.
18 Gerald Wellington, op. cit., 166.
19 Carola Oman, 166.
20 Walker, i, 535–42.
21 Wellesley and Steegman, *Iconography of the Duke of Wellington*.
22 Gleig, *Life*, 242; *Wellington Anecdotes*, 93.
23 Sadleir, 257.
24 Willard Connelly, *The Dandy of Dandies* (1952), 409–11; Sadleir, 334.
25 Connelly, op. cit., 411; Walker, i, 532.
26 Griffiths, 255.
27 Wellesley and Steegman, op. cit., 60.
28 Rose Weigall, op. cit., 156–9.
29 William Fraser, 69.
30 Gerald Wellington, op. cit., 163.
31 Gerald Wellington, *Collected Works of the 7th Duke*.
32 Rose Weigall, op. cit., 112.
33 Stanhope, *Conversations*, 93.
34 Haydon, ii, 567–73.
35 Ibid., ii, 565.

CHAPTER 42: LIFE AT WALMER CASTLE, 1830–50

1 Gleig, *Life*, 427.
2 Gronow, i, 213.
3 William Fraser, 31.
4 *Wellington Anecdotes*, 99; Gronow, i, 213; Fraser, 26.
5 Rose Weigall, *Correspondence of Lady Burghersh*, 192.
6 Gleig, op. cit., 433; Gerald Wellington, *Wellington and His Friends*, 171.
7 Raikes, *Journal*, iv, 318.

8 *Wellington Anecdotes*; Muriel Wellesley, *Wellington in Civil Life*, 192–3; Burghclere, 105; Ellesmere, 88, 91; Curzon, *Walmer Castle and its Lord Wardens*, 255.
9 Carola Oman, 183.
10 Ibid., 137.
11 Gash, *Anecdotes*, 6; Ellesmere, 85–6; Brialmont, *Life of Wellington*, 238; Raikes, *Journal*, iv, 318–19; Gleig, *Reminiscences*, 141–2, 427–8; Ellesmere, 78, 94; *Wellington Anecdotes*, 10, 21, 36, 99; Muriel Wellesley, op. cit., 239; Raikes, *Journal*, iv, 318; Rose Weigall, op. cit., 200; Elvin, 24; Chad, 2.
12 Gerald Wellington, op. cit., 183, 249, 280; William Fraser, 203.
13 Gleig, *Reminiscences*, 438.
14 Ibid., 424.
15 Stanhope, *Conversations*, vii; WP (HI), WP2/136/86, WP2/136/87–9.
16 WP (SS), 27 Jan., 2 Feb. 1846; Woolgar, 'Wellington's *Dispatches*', 8
17 Stanhope, op. cit., viii.
18 Raikes, *Journal*, iii, 43.
19 Carola Oman, 280.
20 *Wellington Anecdotes*, 67, 83.
21 Stanhope, op. cit., 107; Rose Weigall, op. cit., 200.
22 Gleig, *Reminiscences*, 423; Gerald Wellington, op. cit., 185, 288; Ellesmere, 17.

CHAPTER 43: THE YOUNG QUEEN, 1837–9

1 Broughton, v, 145.
2 Arbuthnot, ii, 428–9; Carola Oman, 287; Rose Weigall, *Correspondence of Lady Burghersh*, 98–9; Charlot, 84.
3 HHP, 9 Sept. 1837.
4 Gerald Wellington, Roxburghe Club correspondence, 204.
5 WP (SS), Wellington to Arbuthnot, 20 July 1837.
6 Greville, iv, 134.
7 *Victoria Letters*, i, 155, 157–8.

8 Esher, ii, 166–7.
9 Elizabeth Longford, *Victoria RI*, 111.
10 Woodham-Smith, 174; Elizabeth Longford, op. cit., 112; Greville, iv, 200–1.
11 Woodham-Smith, 172; Greville, iv, 200–1.
12 RA, Queen Victoria's Journal, 16 April 1839.
13 BM Add. MSS 38303 (Liverpool Papers), Gurwood to Liverpool, 20 Jan. 1840; Thompson, 190.
14 Bennett, 49.
15 Greville, iv, 236.
16 Woodham-Smith, 198–9.
17 Charlot, 172–3.
18 Greville, iv, 244.
19 Gerald Wellington, *Wellington and His Friends*, 131.
20 *Victoria Letters*, i, 376.
21 Quoted in Woodham-Smith, 220.
22 Gerald Wellington, *Wellington and His Friends*, 139–40.
23 Ramsay, *Rough Recollections*, i, 66.
24 Burghclere, 197; Muriel Wellesley, *Wellington in Civil Life*, 306.

CHAPTER 44: GRAND OLD MAN, 1839–50
1 WP (SS), Wellington to Lady Burghersh, 30 Nov. 1841; Stanhope, *Conversations*, 194; Rose Weigall, *Correspondence of Lady Burghersh*, 139, 143; WP (SS), Wellington to Gleig, 28 Feb. 1841.
2 Stanhope, op. cit. 197, 204.
3 Greville, iv, 242.
4 Stanhope, op. cit. 27 Sept 1840.
5 Greville, iv, 66.
6 Raikes, *Journal*, iv, 123.
7 WP (SS), Lady Wilton Correspondence.
8 WP (SS), Wellington to Sir James Graham, 22 Aug. 1842.
9 WP (SS), 29 Sept. 1844.
10 Gerald Wellington, *Wellington and His Friends*, 172.
11 Thompson, 14.

12 Stanhope, op. cit., 133–4.
13 WP (SS), Wellington to Peel, 17 May 1841.
14 HHP, 26 Nov. 1834.
15 RA, Y. 55, 64 quoted in Elizabeth Longford, *Wellington: Pillar of State*, 372.
16 William Fraser, 108; Calvert, 234.
17 Griffiths, 262.
18 Gash, *Anecdotes*.
19 Quoted in Longford, op. cit., 352.
20 G.W.E. Russell, 321.
21 Gash, op. cit., 72.
22 William Fraser, 213.
23 Ibid., 194–5.
24 Thompson, 189.
25 Ellesmere, 90.
26 Croker, iii, 213.
27 Herbert Maxwell, ii, 288.
28 WP (SS), Wellington to Mrs Richard Wellesley, quoted in Thompson, 250.
29 Gash, op. cit., 74.
30 WP (HI), WPI/758/12, WPI/801/11, WPI/822/9.
31 Gleig, *Reminiscences*, 441, 294, 439–41.
32 Carola Oman, 245–6.
33 Gleig, op. cit., 319.
34 Ibid.
35 Griffiths, 233.
36 Gleig, op. cit., 319; Brialmont, *Life of Wellington*, iv, 270.
37 Weigall, op. cit., 214–15.

CHAPTER 45: THE HORSE GUARDS AND THE HOUSE OF LORDS, 1842–50
1 Gerald Wellington, *Wellington and His Friends*, 37, 38.
2 HHP, *passim*.
3 Gerald Wellington, op. cit., 41, 243; Arbuthnot, i, 425; Rose Weigall, *Correspondence of Lady Burghersh*, 39, 40–1, 85; Burghclere, 300.
4 Croker, ii, 329.
5 HHP, 5 Oct. 1849.
6 Howard, 85.

7 WP (SS), Queen Victoria to Wellington, 12 Dec. 1845.
8 Bennett, 224.
9 Howard, 86.
10 WP (SS), Wellington to the Rev. Patrick Brontë, 15 Nov. 1841.
11 Gleig, *Reminiscences*, 398.
12 Christopher Hibbert, *The Destruction of Lord Raglan* (1961), 18.
13 Greville, v, 157–8.
14 Ibid., v, 25.
15 Ibid., v, 176–7.
16 Ibid., v, 460.
17 Alexander, 92.
18 Frith, i, 235.
19 Greville, iv, 413–14.
20 Ibid., iv, 427.
21 Herbert Maxwell, ii, 352.

CHAPTER 46: HYDE PARK CORNER, 1845–6

1 Gerald Wellington, *Wellington and His Friends*, 185.
2 Ibid., 197.
3 Thompson, 209.
4 Gerald Wellington, op. cit., 197–8.
5 RA, Queen Victoria's Journal, 21 Jan. 1845.
6 Ibid.
7 HHP, 8 Oct. 1849.
8 Gerald Wellington, op. cit., 198.
9 Quoted in Anglesey, *One-Leg*, 222.
10 Shelley, ii, 281–9.
11 Gerald Wellington, op. cit., 238.
12 Haydon, ii, 582.
13 Ibid.
14 Greville, iii, 262; Arbuthnot, i, 282.
15 Ponsonby, 50.
16 John Blackwood, *London's Immortals* (1989), 243–9; *London Encyclopaedia*, 846

CHAPTER 47: DISTURBERS OF THE PEACE, 1846–51

1 *Hansard's Parliamentary Debates*, 14 July 1850; Thompson, 248.
2 Broughton, vi, 259–60.

3 BM Add. MSS 37316 f. 81.
4 BM Add. MSS, quoted in Muriel Wellesley, *Wellington in Civil Life*, 264.
5 William Fraser, 6.
6 Carver Papers, quoted in Butler, 578; Gleig, *Reminiscences*, 426.
7 Lord Hatherton's diary entry 8 Oct. 1843, quoted in Butler, 576.
8 BM Add. MSS 38308, 8 Oct. 1842, Colonel Gurwood to Lord Liverpool; Thompson, 210.
9 Rose Weigall, *Correspondence of Lady Burghersh*, 193.
10 Ibid., 190–1.
11 Ibid., 122.
12 Brialmont, *Life of Wellington*, iv, 251–2.
13 Burghclere, 193.
14 Ibid.
15 Greville, vi, 255.
16 Lever, 300.
17 *Hansard's Parliamentary Debates*, vol. xlix, cols 373–5; Thompson, 182.
18 WP (SS), 4 April 1840, 26 Aug. 1839; Ellesmere, 190.
19 J.V. Jones, *The Last Rising: The Newport Insurrection of 1839* (1985); Stanhope, *Conversations*, 195.
20 Greville, vi, 49.
21 Elizabeth Longford, *Victoria RI*, 196–8; Woodham-Smith, 288–90.
22 HHP, 23 Aug. 1851.
23 WD (SS), 25 Aug. 1851.
24 Bennett, 204.
25 Quoted in Thompson, 253.
26 WP (HI), 2 April 1851.
27 Gash, *Anecdotes*, 8–9.
28 Bennett, 204.
29 Anglesey, *One-Leg*, 332.

CHAPTER 48: GROWING OLD, 1850–1

1 Burghclere, 180; Elizabeth Longford, *Wellington: Pillar of State*, 391.
2 Griffiths, 257
3 Gerald Wellington, *Wellington and His Friends*, 266–7.

4 Burghclere, 93.
5 Ibid.
6 Ibid., 226.
7 Ibid., 208.
8 William Fraser, 153.
9 Robert Blake, *Disraeli*, 313.
10 William Fraser, 49.
11· Quoted in Thompson, 6.
12 J.A. Froude, ii, 48–9.
13 Ellesmere, 179.
14 Greville, v, 70, 77, 311, 460.
15 Burghclere, 312–5.
16 Greville, vi, 297–8, 361.
17 WP (SS), 18 June 1849.
18 Fane MSS 22 Oct. 1851.
19 WP (SS), 16 Dec. 1824.
20 Elizabeth Longford, *Wellington: The Years of the Sword*, 211–13.
21 Mary Lutyens, *Effie in Venice: Unpublished letters of Mrs John Ruskin* (1965), 164; Longford, op. cit., 385.
22 Lutyens, op. cit., 29 April 1851.
23 Healey, 84.
24 Ibid., 89, 95.
25 Ibid., 89.
26 Ibid., 86–7.
27 WP (SS), 8 Feb. 1847.
28 Healey, 91.
29 Healey, 111.
30 Gerald Wellington, op cit., 264–5.
31 Ibid., 276.
32 Healey, 104.
33 Ibid., 113.

CHAPTER 49: LAST DAYS, 1851–2
1 Gleig, *Reminiscences*, 237.
2 Ibid., 336.
3 Raikes, *Journal*, iv, 310.
4 Ellesmere, 201.

5 Ramsay, *Rough Recollections*.
6 Ibid.
7 Gleig, op. cit., 338.
8 Raikes, *Journal*, iv, 319.
9 Croker, iii, 280.
10 Stocqueler, ii, 260.
11 Rose Weigall, *Correspondence of Lady Burghersh*, 303–5.
12 RA, Queen Victoria's Journal; Woodham-Smith, 325.
13 Charlot, 341.

CHAPTER 50: THE WAY TO ST PAUL'S, 1852
1 Walker, i, 532.
2 Spicer MSS, 4 Oct. 1852 quoted in Elizabeth Longford, *Wellington: Pillar of State*, 400.
3 Quoted in Thompson, 277.
4 Stanley, 47.
5 Healey, 113.
6 Charlot, 342.
7 Edgar Johnson, *Charles Dickens: His Tragedy and Triumph* (1953), ii, 756.
8 Croker, iii, 283.
9 Johnson, op. cit., ii, 756.
10 Swinton, 272; Longford, op. cit., 403.
11 Quoted in Guedalla, 476.
12 Alfred Ainger, *DNB*, xix, 550.
13 Robert Blake, *Disraeli*, 335.
14 Charlot, 342.
15 *Victoria Letters*, ii, 402.
16 Elizabeth Longford, *Victoria RI*, 231.
17 Gerald Wellington, *Collected Works of the 7th Duke*, 85.
18 Anglesey, *One-Leg*, 333.
19 Greville, vi, 360–4.
20 *Victoria Letters*, ii, 394.
21 FitzGeorge Papers, quoted in St Aubyn, *The Royal George*, 49.

SOURCES

Manuscripts

Bathurst Papers, Beresford Papers, Croker Papers, Peel Papers, Marquess Wellesley
    Papers, British Library
George Canning Papers, West Yorkshire Archives, Leeds
Dalhousie Muniments, Scottish Record Office, Edinburgh
Fane Papers, Fulbeck Hall
Hatfield House Papers
Account of the Services of Corporal John Parker, 20th Foot
Raglan Papers, Gwent County Record Office, Cwmbrân
Royal Archives, Windsor Castle
Lord Fitzroy Somerset's Account of the Battle of Waterloo
Benjamin Symons Papers, Bodleian Library
Tweeddale of Yester Papers, National Library of Scotland
Wellington College Archives
Wellington Papers, Hartley Institute, Southampton University
Wellington Papers, Stratfield Saye, Hampshire
Wellington's Lieutenancy Papers (microfilm), Hampshire Record Office

Newspapers and Journals

Daily Advertiser, Examiner, General Advertiser, Gentleman's Magazine, London Evening
    Post, Morning Post, Public Advertiser, St James's Chronicle, The Times, The World;
    Durham County Advertiser, Edinburgh Evening Post, Hampshire Chronicle,
    Hertfordshire Guardian, Liverpool Mercury

Books and Articles

Unless otherwise stated, the place of publication is London.
Airlie, Mabell, Countess of, *Lady Palmerston and Her Times* (2 vols, 1922).
Albemarle, George Thomas, Earl of, *Fifty Years of My Life* (1877).
Alexander, Eleanor (ed.), *Primate Alexander, Archbishop of Armagh: A Memoir* (1914).
Anderson, Joseph, *Recollections of a Peninsular Veteran* (1913).
Anglesey, Marquess of (ed.), *The Capel Letters, 1814–17* (1955).
    One-Leg: The Life and Letters of Henry William Paget, First Marquess of Anglesey
    K.G. 1768–1854 (1961).

'Apsley House', *Quarterly Review*, March 1853.

Arbuthnot see Bamford.

Archives de Joseph Bonaparte roi de Naples, puis d'Espagne (Archives Nationales, Paris, 1982).

Aspinall, A (ed.), *The Correspondence of Charles Arbuthnot* (1941).

(ed.), *The Correspondence of George, Prince of Wales, 1770–1812* (8 vols, 1963–71).

(ed.), *The Diary of Henry Hobhouse 1820–1827* (1947).

(ed.), *The Later Correspondence of King George III* (5 vols, Cambridge, 1962–1970).

(ed.), *The Letters of King George IV* (3 vols, Cambridge, 1938).

Lord Brougham and the Whig Party (Manchester, 1927).

Politics and the Press c. 1780–1850 (1949).

(ed.), *Three Early Nineteenth-Century Diaries* (1952).

Bamford, Francis (ed.), *The Journal of Mrs Arbuthnot, 1820–1832* (2 vols, 1950).

Barnett, Correlli, *Britain and Her Army 1509–1970: A Military, Political and Social Survey* (1970).

Barrington, Daines, *Miscellanies* (1781).

Barrington, Sir Jonah, *Personal Sketches of His Own Times* (2 vols, 1827).

Bartlett, C.J., *Castlereagh* (1967).

Beatson, F.C., *With Wellington in the Pyrenees* (1914).

Bell, Herbert C.F., *Lord Palmerston* (2 vols, 1922).

Bennett, Daphne, *King without a Crown: Albert, Prince Consort of England, 1819–1861* (1977).

Benson, A.C. and Viscount Esher, *The Letters of Queen Victoria: A Selection from Her Majesty's Correspondence Between the Years 1837 and 1861* (3 vols, 1908).

Berry, Mary, *Journal and Correspondence of Miss Berry, 1783–1852* (ed. Lady Theresa Lewis, 1865).

Bessborough, Earl of (ed.), *Lady Bessborough and Her Family Circle* (1940).

(ed.), *Lady Charlotte Guest: Extracts from Her Journals 1833–1852* (1950).

Bishop, Morchard (ed.), *Recollections of the Table-Talk of Samuel Rogers* (first collected by the Revd. Alexander Dyce) (1859).

Blake, Robert, *The Conservative Party from Peel to Churchill* (1970).

Disraeli (1966).

Blake, Mrs Warrenne, *An Irish Beauty of the Regency: Compiled from the Unpublished Journals of the Hon. Mrs Calvert* (1911).

Blakeney see Sturgis.

Blanch, Lesley (ed.), *The Game of Hearts: Harriette Wilson and Her Memoirs* (1957).

Blanco, Richard L., *Wellington's Surgeon General: Sir James McGrigor* (1974).

Blessington, Countess of, *The Literary Life and Correspondence of the Countess of Blessington* (ed. R.R. Madden, 2 vols, 1855).

Bourne, Kenneth, *Palmerston: The Early Years 1784–1841* (1982).

Bragge see Cassels.

Brett-James, Antony (ed.), *Edward Costello: The Peninsular and Waterloo Campaigns* (1967).

(ed.), *General Wilson's Journal 1812–1814* (1964).

(ed.), *The Hundred Days: Napoleon's Last Campaign from Eye-Witness Accounts* (1964).

Life in Wellington's Army (1972).

(ed.), *Wellington at War, 1794–1815* (1961).

Brewer, John, *The Sinews of Power: War, Money and the English State, 1688–1783* (1989).

Brialmont, A.H., *Histoire du duc de Wellington* (3 vols, Paris, 1856–7).
History of the Life of Arthur, Duke of Wellington (from the French with emendations and additions by the Rev. G.R. Gleig, 4 vols, 1858–60).

Briggs, Asa, *The Age of Improvement* (1965).

British Museum *Catalogue of Political and Personal Satires* (ed. M. Dorothy George, vols vi-xi, 1938–54).

Brock, Michael, *The Great Reform Act*, (1973).
'Wellington: The Statesman' in *Wellingtonian Studies* (ed. Michael Howard, Wellington, 1959).

Brooke, John and Julia Gandy, *The Prime Minister's Papers: Wellington, Political Correspondence 1. 1833–November 1834*, Royal Commission on Historical Manuscripts (1974).

Broughton, Lord, *Recollections of a Long Life* (6 vols, 1911).

Bruce, H.A. (ed.), *Life and Letters of Sir William Napier* (2 vols, 1865).

Bryant, Arthur, *The Age of Elegance, 1812–1822* (1950).
The Great Duke (1971).
The Years of Endurance, 1793–1802 (1942).
Years of Victory, 1802–1812 (1944).

Buckingham and Chandos, Duke of, *Memoirs of the Court and Cabinets of George IV, 1820–1830* (2 vols, 1859).
Memoirs of the Court and Cabinets of George III, 1756–1810 (4 vols, 1855).
Memoirs of the Court and Cabinets of William IV and Victoria (2 vols, 1861).
Memoirs of the Court of England during the Regency, 1811–1820 (2 vols, 1856).

Bumpus, George C., *The Life of Frank Buckland* (1885).

Burghclere, Lady, *A Great Man's Friendship: Letters of the Duke of Wellington to Mary, Marchioness of Salisbury, 1850–1852* (ed. Lady Burghclere, 1927).

Burghersh, see Weigall.

Burnett, T.A.J., *The Rise and Fall of a Regency Dandy: The Life and Times of Scrope Berdmore Davies* (1981).

Butler, Iris, *The Eldest Brother: The Marquess Wellesley, The Duke of Wellington's Eldest Brother* (1973).

Calvert see Blake, Mrs Warrenne.

Cassels, S.A.C., *Peninsular Portrait: The Letters of Captain William Bragge, 3rd King's Own Dragoons* (1963).

Castlereagh see Vane.

Cecil, David, *The Young Melbourne* (1939).
Lord M (1954).

Chad see Wellington, Gerald 7th Duke of.

Chalfont, Lord (ed.), *Waterloo: Battle of Three Armies: Anglo-Dutch* by William Seymour; *French* by Jacques Champagne; *Prussian* by E. Kaulbach (1979).

Chamberlain, Muriel E., *Lord Aberdeen: A Political Biography* (1983).

Chandler, David, *The Campaigns of Napoleon* (1967).

Charlot, Monica, *Victoria: The Young Queen* (Oxford, 1991).

Cholmondeley, R.H., *The Hever Letters 1783–1832* (1950).

Clark, George Kitson, *Peel and the Conservative Party: A Study in Politics, 1832–1841* (1964).

Cockton, Peter, *The Wellington Pamphlet Collection: Introduction and Catalogue* (2 vols, Southampton, 1978).

Colby, Reginald (with Notes by Victor Percival), *The Waterloo Dispatch* (1965).

Colchester, Charles Abbot, Lord, *The Diary and Correspondence of Charles Abbot, Lord Colchester* (3 vols, 1861).

Cole, Hubert, *Beau Brummell* (1978).

Cole, Maud Lowry and Stephen Gwynn (eds), *Memoirs of Sir Galbraith Lowry Cole* (1934).

Colley, Linda, *Britons: The Forging of the Nation, 1707–1837* (1952).

Colvin, Christina see Edgeworth.

Colvin, Howard, *A Biographical Dictionary of British Architects 1600–1840* (1978).

Combermere, Lady and W. Knollys, *Memoirs and Correspondence of Field Marshal Viscount Combermere* (2 vols, 1866).

Cookson, J.E., *Lord Liverpool's Administration 1815–1822* (Edinburgh, 1975).

Costello, Edward, *Adventures of a Soldier* (1841).

Cowell, John Stepney, *Leaves from the Diary of an Officer of the Guards* (1854).

Creevey, Thomas, *The Creevey Papers: A Selection from the Correspondence and Diaries of the Late Thomas Creevey, M.P.* (ed. Sir Herbert Maxwell, 3rd edn, 1905).

Croker, John Wilson, *The Croker Papers: The Correspondence and Diaries of John Wilson Croker, Secretary to the Admiralty from 1809 to 1830* (ed. Louis J. Jennings, 3 vols, 1885).

Cronin, Vincent, *Napoleon* (1971).

Curzon of Kedleston, Marquess, *The Personal History of Walmer Castle and its Lords Warden* (ed. Stephen Gwynn, 1927).

D'Arblay, Madame, *The Diaries of Madame D'Arblay* (edited by her niece, 7 vols, 1854).

Davis, H.W.C., *The Age of Grey and Peel* (Oxford, 1929).

De Grey, Earl, *Characteristics of the Duke of Wellington apart from his Military Talents* (1853).

Delany, Mary, *The Autobiography and Correspondence of Mary Granville, Mrs Delany* (6 vols, ed. Lady Llanover, 1861–62).

Dickinson, Violet, *Miss Eden's Letters* (1919).

The Dispatches of Field Marshal the Duke of Wellington during His Various Campaigns in India, Denmark, Portugal, Spain, The Low Countries and France (compiled from official and other authentic documents by the late Colonel Gurwood (new and enlarged edn, 8 vols, 1852) (see also Wellington)

Dixon, Peter, *Canning: Politician and Statesman* (1976).

Eden see Dickinson.

Edgcumbe, Richard, (ed.), *The Diary of Frances, Lady Shelley 1787–1817* (2 vols, 1912).

Edgeworth, Maria, *Letters from England 1833–1844* (ed. Christina Colvin, Oxford, 1971).

The Life and Letters of Maria Edgeworth (ed. Augustus Hare, 2 vols, 1894).

Ehrman, John, *The Younger Pitt: The Consuming Struggle* (1996).

Eimer, Christopher, *Medallic Portraits of the Duke of Wellington* (1994).

Elers see Monson.

Ellenborough, Lord, *A Political Diary, 1828–1830* (ed. Lord Colchester, 2 vols, 1881).

Ellesmere, Lord, *Personal Reminiscences of the Duke of Wellington by Francis, First Earl of Ellesmere* (ed. Alice, Countess of Strafford, 1903).

Elvin, Charles, *Walmer and Walmer Castle* (privately printed, 1894).

Elwin, Malcolm (ed.), *The Autobiography and Journals of Benjamin Robert Haydon (1786–1846)* (1950).

Esher, Viscount (ed.), *The Girlhood of Queen Victoria: A Selection from Her Majesty's Diaries between the Years 1832–1840* (2 vols, 1912).
   See also Benson.

Farington, Joseph, *The Farington Diary by Joseph Farington RA* (8 vols, ed. James Grieg, 1922–8).

Fay, C.R., *Huskisson and His Age* (1951).

Fergusson, Gordon, *The Green Collars: The Tarporley Hunt Club and Cheshire Hunting History* (1993).
   Hounds are Home: The History of the Royal Calpe Hunt (1979).

Fletcher, Ian, *Craufurd's Light Division* (Tunbridge Wells, 1991).
   (ed.), *For King and Country: The Letters and Diaries of John Mills, Coldstream Guards, 1811–14* (Staplehurst, 1995).
   (ed.), *A Guards Officer in the Peninsula: The Peninsular War Letters of John Edward Cornwallis Rous, Coldstream Guards, 1812–1814* (Tunbridge Wells, 1992).
   In Hell Before Daylight: The Siege and Storming of the Fortress of Badajoz, 1812 (Tunbridge Wells, 1994).
   Wellington's Regiments: The Men and Their Battles from Roliça to Waterloo, 1808–15 (Staplehurst, 1996).
   with Andy Cook, *Fields of Fire: Battlefields of the Peninsular War* (Staplehurst, 1996).

Fortescue, Sir John, *History of the British Army* (vols iv–x, 1906–20).
   Wellington (1925).

Fox see Ilchester.

Fraser, Flora, *The Unruly Queen: The Life of Queen Caroline* (1996).

Fraser, Sir William, *Words on Wellington: The Duke – Waterloo – The Ball* (1889).

Frazer see Sabine.

Frith, W.P., *My Autobiography and Reminiscences* (2 vols, 1888).

Froude, J.A., *Carlyle's Life in London* (2 vols, 1884).

Fulford, Roger, *George IV* (1935).
   The Royal Dukes (1933).
   The Trial of Queen Caroline (1967).
   See also Greville

Gandy see Brooke.

Gash, Norman, *The Life and Political Career of Robert Banks Jenkinson, Second Earl of Liverpool 1770–1828* (1984).
   Politics in the Age of Peel (1953).
   Mr Secretary Peel (1961).
   Sir Robert Peel (1972).
   Wellington Anecdotes: A Critical Survey (Southampton, 1992).
   (ed.), *Wellington: Studies in the Political and Military Career of the First Duke of Wellington* (Manchester, 1990).

Gates, David, *The Spanish Ulcer: A History of the Peninsular War* (1986).

George see Abbreviations.

Gleig, G.R., *Life of Arthur, Duke of Wellington* (new edn, 1891).
   Personal Reminiscences of the Duke of Wellington (ed. Mary E. Gleig, new edn, 1914).

Glover, Michael, 'An Excellent Young Man: The Rev. Samuel Briscall, 1788–1848', *History Today* 18 (1968).

Peninsular Preparation (Cambridge, 1963).

Wellington as Military Commander (1973).

Wellington's Peninsular Victories (1968).

Gooch, G.D., (ed.), *The Later Correspondence of Lord John Russell 1840–1878* (2 vols, 1925).

Gordon, Pryse Lockhart, *Personal Memoirs or Reminiscences of Men and Manners at Home and Abroad during the last Half Century* (2 vols, 1830).

Gower, Lord Ronald, *My Reminiscences* (1883).

Grant, James, *Random Recollections of the House of Lords* (2nd edn, 1836).

Granville, Castalia, Countess (ed.), *Lord Granville Leveson Gower, First Earl of Granville, Private Correspondence 1781–1821* (2 vols, 1916).

Granville, Harriet, Countess, *Letters of Harriet, Countess Granville 1810–1845* (ed. the Hon. F. Leveson Gower (2 vols, 1894).

Grattan, William, *Adventures with the Connaught Rangers* (ed. Sir Charles Oman, 4 vols, 1902).

Gray, Denis, *Spencer Perceval* (1963).

Greville, Charles, *The Greville Memoirs 1814–1860* (ed. Lytton Strachey and Roger Fulford (8 vols, 1938).

Grieg see Farington.

Griffiths, Major Arthur, *The Wellington Memorial. His Comrades and Contemporaries* (1897).

Gronow, R.H., *The Reminiscences and Recollections of Captain Gronow* (2 vols, 1889).

Grosvenor, Caroline and Charles Beilby, Lord Stuart of Wortley, *The First Lady Wharncliffe and Her Family* (2 vols, 1927).

Guedalla, Philip, *The Duke* (1931).

Guest see Bessborough.

Gurwood see *Dispatches*.

Halliwell, W.A.C., 'The Passage to Bombay' (Southampton University, 1996).

Hamilton-Williams, David, *Waterloo: New Perspectives: The Great Battle Reappraised* (1993).

Hansard's Parliamentary Debates, 3rd series (1814–50).

Harcourt see George Rose.

Hare, Augustus, *The Story of My Life* (5 vols, 1900).

Harris, [Benjamin], *Recollections of Rifleman Harris as told to Henry Curling* (ed. Christopher Hibbert, 1970).

Hastings, Max (ed.), *The Oxford Book of Military Anecdotes* (Oxford, 1985).

Haswell, C.J.D., *The First Respectable Spy: The Life and Times of Colquhoun Grant, Wellington's Head of Intelligence* (1969).

Hathaway, Eileen (ed.), *A Dorset Soldier: The Autobiography of Sergeant William Lawrence, 1790–1869* (new edn, Staplehurst, 1995).

Hay, Captain William, *Reminiscences, 1808–1815* (1901).

Haydon, Benjamin Robert, *Correspondence and Table Talk* (2 vols, 1876). See also Elwin.

Haythornthwaite, Philip J., *The Armies of Wellington* (1994).

Wellington's Military Machine (Staplehurst, 1996).

Healey, Edna, *Lady Unknown: The Life of Angela Burdett-Coutts* (1978).

Herrick, C.T. (ed.), *The Letters of the Duke of Wellington to Miss Jenkins, 1834–1851* (1924).

Hibbert, Christopher, *Corunna* (1961).

George IV: Prince of Wales, 1762–1811 (1972).

George IV: Regent and King, 1811–1830 (1973).

(ed.), *The Recollections of Rifleman Harris* (1970).

(ed.), *A Soldier of the 71st: A Journal of a Soldier of the Highland Light Infantry 1806–1815* (1975).

(ed.), *Waterloo: Napoleon's Last Campaign* (New York, 1967).

(ed.), *The Whealey Diary: A Journal and Sketchbook kept during the Peninsular War and the Waterloo Campaign* (1964).

Hickey, William, *Memoirs of William Hickey* (ed. Alfred Spencer, 4 vols, 1925).

Hill, The Rev. Edwin Sidney, *The Life of Lord Hill* (1845).

Hinde, Wendy, *George Canning* (1973).

Castlereagh (1981).

Hobhouse, J.C., *Recollections of a Long Life* (4 vols, ed. Lady Dorchester, 1910–11).

Holland, Henry Richard, Lord, *Further Memoirs of the Whig Party 1807–1821* (ed. Lord Stavordale, 1905).

Hook, Theodore, *Life of Sir David Baird* (2 vols, 1833).

Houssaye, Henry, *1815 – Waterloo* (ed. A. Euan-Smith. trans. A.E. Mann, 1900).

Howard, Michael (ed.), *Wellingtonian Studies: Essays on the Duke of Wellington by Five Old Wellingtonians* (Wellington, 1959).

Howarth, David, *A Near Run Thing* (1968).

Hyde, H. Montgomery, *Princess Lieven* (1938).

The Strange Death of Lord Castlereagh (1959).

Ilchester, Lord (ed.), *Journal of the Hon. Henry Edward Fox, 4th and Last Lord Holland, 1818–1830* (1923).

Lady Holland's Journal (2 vols, 1908).

See also Lady Sarah Lennox.

Jackson, Basil, *Notes and Reminiscences of a Staff Officer* (ed. R.C. Seaton, 1903).

James, Lawrence, *The Iron Duke: Military Biography of Arthur Wellesley, Duke of Wellington* (1992).

Jennings see Croker.

Jerningham Letters (1780–1843) (ed. Egerton Castle, 2 vols, 1896).

Jervis, Simon and Maurice Tomlin (revised by Jonathan Voak), *Apsley House: Wellington Museum* (1995).

Johnson, David, *Regency Revolution: The Case of Arthur Thistlewood* (Compton Chamberlayne, 1974).

Jones, Sir John, *Journals of the Sieges in Spain 1811–1814* (1846).

Jones, W.D. *'Prosperity' Robinson: The Life of Viscount Goderich 1782–1859* (1967).

Journal of a Soldier of the 71st or Glasgow Regiment, Highland Light Infantry from 1806 to 1815 (Edinburgh, 1822, reprinted as *A Soldier of the 71st*, ed. Christopher Hibbert, 1975).

Kaye see Malcolm.

Keegan, John, *The Face of Battle* (1976).

The Mask of Command (1987).

Kincaid, Captain John, *Adventures in the Rifle Brigade* (1929).

Knighton, Lady, *Memoirs of Sir William Knighton* (1838).

Kurtz, Harold, 'Madame de Staël and the Duke of Wellington,' *History Today*, 13 (1963). *The Trial of Marshal Ney* (1957).

Larpent, Sir George, *The Private Journal of Judge-Advocate Larpent: Attached to the Head-Quarters of Lord Wellington during the Peninsular War* (3rd edn, 2 vols, 1854).

Lawrence, Sir Thomas, *Sir Thomas Lawrence's Letter Bag* (ed. George Somes Layard, 1906).

Lawrence, William, *The Autobiography of Sergeant William Lawrence* (ed. G.N. Bankes, London, 1886).

Layard see Sir Thomas Lawrence.

Leach, Lt. Col. J., *Rough Sketches of the Life of an Old Soldier* (1831).

Lecky, W.E.H., *History of Ireland in the Eighteenth Century* (1892)

Leeke, William, *The History of Lord Seaton's Regiment at the Battle of Waterloo* (2 vols, 1866, 1871).

Lennox, Lady Sarah, *The Life and Letters of Lady Sarah Lennox* (ed. the Countess of Ilchester and Lord Stavordale, 1902).

[Lennox, Lord William Pitt], *Three Years with the Duke, or Wellington in Private Life by an Ex-Aide-de-Camp* (1853).

Le Strange, Guy (ed.), *Correspondence of Princess Lieven and Earl Grey* (3 vols, 1890).

Lever, Sir Tresham (ed.), *The Letters of Lady Palmerston* (1957).

Leveson Gower see Granville.

Lewis, Lady Theresa see Berry.

Liddell Hart see Wheeler.

Lieven see Quennell and Lionel G. Robinson.

Lincoln, L.J. and R.L. McEwen, *Lord Eldon's Anecdote Book* (1960).

Llanover see Delany.

Lockhart, J.G., *Memoirs of the Life of Sir Walter Scott* (1893).

London Encyclopaedia see Weinreb.

Long, Robert Ballard, *A Peninsular Cavalry General: The Correspondence of Lt.-Gen. Robert Long* (ed. T.H. McGuffie, 1951).

Longford, Elizabeth, 'The Duke of Wellington's Books', *History Today* 17 (1967).
'The Duke of Wellington's Search for a Palace', *Horizon*, vol. xi, no. 2, Spring 1969.
Victoria RI (1964).
Wellington: Pillar of State (1972).
Wellington: The Years of the Sword (1969 and paperback 1971).

Longford, 5th Earl of, *Pakenham Letters* (privately printed, 1914).

Ludovici see Schaumann.

Lyte, H.C. Maxwell, *A History of Eton College 1440–1875* (1875).

McGrigor, James, *The Autobiography and Services of Sir James McGrigor* (1861).

McGuffie, T.H. (ed.), *Rank and File: The Common Soldier at Peace and War* (1964).
(ed.), *Peninsular Cavalry General: The Correspondence of Lt. Gen. R.B. Long* (1951).

Mackesy, Piers, 'Wellington The General' in *Wellingtonian Studies* (ed. Michael Howard, Wellington, 1959).

Malcolm, John, *The Life and Correspondence of Maj.-Gen. Sir John Malcolm* (ed. J.W. Kaye, 2 vols, 1856).

Malmesbury, 3rd Earl of (ed.), *The Diaries and Correspondence of James Harris, First Earl of Malmesbury* (4 vols, 1844).

Marchand, Leslie A., *Byron: A Critical Introduction with an Annotated Bibliography* (3 vols, 1957).

Marshall-Cornwall, Sir James, *Marshal Massena* (Oxford, 1965).

Martin, Sir Theodore, *A Life of Lord Lyndhurst* (1883).

Martineau, John, *The Life of Henry Pelham Clinton, 5th Duke of Newcastle 1811–1864* (1908).

Mavor, Elizabeth, *The Ladies of Llangollen: A Study in Romantic Friendship* (1971).

Maxwell, Sir Herbert, *The Life of Wellington* (2 vols, 1899).
See also Creevey.

Maxwell, W.H., *The Life of Field-Marshal His Grace the Duke of Wellington* (3 vols, 1839–41).
Peninsular Sketches by Actors on the Scene (2 vols, 1845).

Melville, Lewis (ed.), *The Huskisson Papers* (1931).
(ed.), *The Wellesley Papers: The Life and Correspondence of Richard Colley Wellesley 1760–1842* (2 vols, 1914).

Mercer, General Cavalié, *Journal of the Waterloo Campaign* (2 vols, 1870).

Mills see Fletcher.

Monson, Lord and George Leveson-Gower (eds), *Memoirs of George Elers, Captain in the 12th Regiment of Foot, 1774–1842* (1903).

Monypenny, W.F. and G.E. Buckle, *The Life of Benjamin Disraeli, Earl of Beaconsfield* (2 vols, 1929).

Moore Smith, G.C., *Life of Sir John Colbourne, Field Marshal Lord Seaton* (1903).
See also Smith, Sir Harry

Morley, John, *The Life of William Ewart Gladstone* (2 vols, 1905).

Mozley, Anne (ed.), *Letters of the Rev. J.B. Mozley D.D.* (1885).

Müffling, Baron Von, *Passages from My Life* (trans. and ed. Philip Yorke, 1853).

Muir, R.J.B. and C.J. Esdaile, 'Strategic Planning in a time of Small Government: the Wars against Revolutionary and Napoleonic France' (Southampton University, 1996).

Muir, Rory, *Britain and the Defeat of Napoleon, 1807–1815* (New Haven, 1996).

Myatt, Frederick, *British Sieges of the Peninsular War* (new edn Staplehurst, 1995).

My Dear Mrs Jones: The Letters of the Duke of Wellington to Mrs Jones of Pantglas (ed. Mrs Davies-Evans, 1889).

Napier, Lt. General William, *The Life and Opinions of General Sir Charles Napier* (4 vols, 1857).

Napier, Major General Sir W.F.P., *History of the War in the Peninsula and in the South of France from the Year 1807 to the Year 1814* (new edn, 6 vols, 1882).

Napier, General William, (ed.), *Passages in the Early Life of General Sir George Napier* (1884).

Napier see also Bruce.

Narrative of the Case of the Marchioness of Westmeath (1857).

Naylor, John, *Waterloo* (1968).

Neillands, Robin, *Wellington and Napoleon: Clash of Arms* (1994).

Nicolson, Harold, *The Congress of Vienna: A Study in Allied Unity 1812–1822* (1946).
'Wellington: The Diplomatist' in *Wellingtonian Studies* (ed. Michael Howard, Wellington, 1959).

Oman, Carola, *The Gascoyne Heiress: The Life and Diaries of Frances May Gascoyne-Cecil 1802–39* (1968).

Oman, Sir Charles, *A History of the Peninsular War* (7 vols, Oxford, 1902–30).
Wellington's Army, 1809–1814 (1913).

Page, Julia (ed.), *Intelligence Officer in the Peninsula: Letters and Diaries of Major the Hon. Edward Charles Cocks, 1786–1812* (Staplehurst, 1996).

Paget, Julian, *Wellington's Peninsular War* (1990).

Palmer, Alan, *Metternich: Councillor of Europe* (1972).

Pange, Victor De, *The Unpublished Correspondence of Mme. de Staël and the Duke of Wellington* (1965).

Parker, Charles Stuart, *Sir Robert Peel, from his Private Papers* (3 vols, 1891–99).

Parkinson, Roger, *The Peninsular War* (1973).

Partridge, Michael S., *The Duke of Wellington 1769–1852: A Bibliography* (Westport, CT, 1990).

Peel, George (ed.), *The Private Letters of Sir Robert Peel* (1920).

Petrie, Sir Charles, *Wellington: A Reassessment* (1956).

Petty, S., 'Wellington's General Orders, 1808–1814' (Southampton University, 1996).

Physick, John, *The Duke of Wellington in Caricature* (1965).
    The Wellington Monument (1970).

Ponsonby, Arthur, *Henry Ponsonby: Queen Victoria's Private Secretary: His Life from His Letters* (1942).

Prothero, Roland E. (ed.), *The Life and Correspondence of Arthur Penryn Stanley* (2 vols, 1893).

Pückler-Muskau, Prince, *Pückler's Progress: The Adventures of Prince Pückler-Muskau in England, Wales and Ireland as Told in Letters to his Former Wife* (trans. Flora Brennan, 1987).

Quennell, Peter (ed.), *The Private Letters of Princess Lieven to Prince Metternich 1820–1826* (1937).

Raikes, Thomas, *A Portion of the Journal kept by Thomas Raikes 1831 to 1847* (2nd edn. 4 vols, 1856–57).
    Private Correspondence of Thomas Raikes with the Duke of Wellington and Other Distinguished Contemporaries (1861).

Rathbone, Julian (ed.), *Wellington's War: His Peninsular Despatches* (1994).

Redding, Cyrus, *Personal Reminiscences of Eminent Men* (3 vols, 1867).

Redesdale, Lord, *Memoirs of Lord Redesdale* (2 vols, 1915).

Reid, T. Wemyss, *The Life, Letters and Friendships of Richard Monckton Milnes, First Lord Houghton* (1890).

Reply to the 'Narrative of the Case of the Marchioness of Westmeath' (1857).

Ridley, Jane, *The Young Disraeli 1804–1846* (1995).

Ridley, Jasper, *Lord Palmerston* (1970).

Roberts, P.E., *India under Wellesley* (1929).

Robinson, H.B., *Memoirs of Sir Thomas Picton* (2 vols, 1836).

Robinson, Lionel G., *Letters of Dorothea, Princess Lieven during Her Residence in London 1812–1834* (2 vols, 1902).

Rogers see Bishop.

Rolo, P.J.V., *George Canning: Three Biographical Studies* (1965).

Rose, George, *Diaries and Correspondence of the Rt Hon. George Rose* (ed. L.V. Harcourt, 2 vols, 1860).

Rose J.H., *William Pitt and the Great War* (1911).

Russell, G.W.B., *Collections and Recollections* (1898).

Russell, Rollo (ed.), *Early Correspondence of Lord John Russell 1805–1840* (2 vols, 1913).

Sabine, General Sir Edward (ed.), *Letters of Colonel Sir Augustus Frazer* (1859).

Sadleir, Michael, *Blessington-D'Orsay: A Masquerade* (1933).

St Aubyn, Giles, *Queen Victoria: A Portrait* (1991).

The Royal George: The Life of HRH Prince George, Duke of Cambridge (1963).
'Wellington: The Man' in *Wellingtonian Studies* (ed. Michael Howard, Wellington, 1959).

Sanger, Ernest, *Englishmen at War: A Social History in Letters* (Far Thrupp, Stroud, 1993).

Saunders, Edith, *The Hundred Days* (1964).

Schaumann, A.L.F., *On the Road with Wellington: The Diary of a War Commissary in the Peninsular Campaigns* (trans. by A. Ludovici, 1924).

Scott, Christopher, *Stratfield Saye* (n.d.).

Seaton see Jackson.

Sharpe, W., *Recollections by Samuel Rogers* (1859)

Shelley see Edgcumbe.

Sherer, Moyle, *Recollections of the Peninsula* (1825).

Siborne, William, *History of the War in France and Belgium in 1815* (2 vols, 1844).

Smith, E.A., *Lord Grey 1764–1845* (Oxford, 1990).
Reform or Revolution: A Diary of Reform in England 1830–32 (Far Thrupp, Stroud, 1972).
Wellington and the Arbuthnots: A Triangular Friendship (Far Thrupp, Stroud, 1994).

Smith, Sir Harry, *Autobiography of Lt.-Gen. Sir Harry Smith* (ed. G.C. Moore Smith, 2 vols, 1901).

Spencer see Hickey.

Spencer-Stanhope, Lady Elizabeth, *The Letter-Bag of Lady Elizabeth Spencer Stanhope* (2 vols, 1912).

Stanhope, Philip Henry, 5th Earl, *Life of Pitt* (4 vols, 1879).
Notes of Conversations with the Duke of Wellington (privately printed, 1886; new edn, 1938).

Stanley, Lady Augusta, *Letters of Lady Augusta Stanley: A Young Lady at Court, 1849–1863* (ed. The Dean of Windsor and Hector Bolitho, 1927).

Stapleton, A.G., *The Political Life of George Canning* (2 vols, 1831).

Stavordale see Holland and Lady Sarah Lennox.

Steegmann, John see Wellesley, Lord Gerald.

Stewart, Robert, *Henry Brougham: His Public Career, 1778–1868* (1985).

Stocqueler, J.H., *The Life of Field Marshal the Duke of Wellington* (2 vols, 1852).

Stone, Lawrence, *Broken Lives: Separation and Divorce in England 1660–1857* (Oxford, 1993).
(ed.), *An Imperial State at War: Britain from 1689 to 1815* (1994).

Strachey see Greville.

Strafford, Alice, Countess of see Ellesmeres.

Strawson, John, *Beggars in Red: The British Army, 1789–1889* (1991).
The Duke and the Emperor: Wellington and Napoleon (1994).

Sturgis, Julian (ed.), *A Boy in the Peninsular War: The Services, Adventures and Experiences of Robert Blakeney, Subaltern in the 28th Regiment* (1899).

Surtees, William, *Twenty-five Years in the Rifle Brigade* (1833).

Sutton, Denys, 'The Great Duke and the Arts', *Apollo*, Sept. 1973.

Swinton, The Hon Mrs J.R., *A Sketch of the Life of Georgiana, Lady de Ros* (1893).

Temperley, Harold, *The Unpublished Diary and Political Sketches of Princess Lieven Together with Some of Her Letters* (1925).

Thompson, Neville, *Wellington after Waterloo* (1986).

Thornton, James, *Your Most Obedient Servant: James Thornton, Cook to the Duke of Wellington* (Exeter, 1985).

Timbs, John, *Wellingtoniana* (1852).

Tomkinson, Lt.-Col. William, *The Diary of a Cavalry Officer in the Peninsular and Waterloo Campaigns, 1809–1815* (ed. James Tomkinson, 1894).

Tomlin see Jervis.

Trench, Richard, *The Remains of the late Mrs Richard Trench being Selections from Her Journals* (ed. Richard Chenevix Trench, 1862).

Turbeville, A.S., *The House of Lords in the Age of Reform 1784–1837* (1958).

Twiss, Horace, *The Public and Private Life of Lord Chancellor Eldon* (3 vols, 1844).

Vane, Charles (ed.), *Memoirs and Correspondence of Viscount Castlereagh, Second Marquess of Londonderry* (12 vols, 1850–53).

Vansittart, Jane (ed.), *The Journal of Surgeon James* (1964).

Van Thal, Herbert (ed.), *The Prime Ministers: Vol 1. From Sir Robert Walpole to Sir Robert Peel* (1974).

Verner, Willoughby, *A British Rifleman: The Journals and Correspondence of Major George Simmons* (1899).

Victoria see Benson.

Walker, Richard, *Regency Portraits* (2 vols, 1985).

Ward, B.R. (ed.), *A Week at Waterloo: Lady de Lancey's Narrative* (1906).

Ward, S.G.P., *Wellington's Headquarters: A Study of the Administrative Problems in the Peninsula 1809–1814* (Oxford, 1957).

Ward, W.R., *Victorian Oxford* (1965).

Webster, Sir C. (ed.), *Some Letters of the Duke of Wellington to His Brother, William Wellesley Pole*, Camden Miscellany, Royal Historical Society, vol. xviii, 1948.

Weigall, Rachel, *Lady Rose Weigall: A Memoir* (1923).

Weigall, Lady Rose (ed.), *The Correspondence of Lady Burghersh with the Duke of Wellington* (1903).

(ed.), *The Correspondence of Priscilla, Countess of Westmorland* (1909).

Weinreb, Ben and Christopher Hibbert, *The London Encyclopaedia* (1983).

Weller, Jac, *Wellington in India* (1993).

Wellington in the Peninsula 1805–1814 (1962).

Wellesley, F.A. (ed.), *The Diary and Correspondence of Henry Wellesley, 1st Lord Cowley, 1790–1846* (n.d.).

Wellesley, Lord Gerald and Steegmann, John, *The Iconography of the Duke of Wellington* (1935).

Wellesley, Muriel, *The Man Wellington Through the Eyes of Those Who Knew Him* (1937).

Wellington in Civil Life Through the Eyes of Those Who Knew Him (1939).

The Wellesley Papers: The Life and Correspondence of Richard Colley Wellesley, Marquess Wellesley 1760–1842 (by the editor of *The Wyndham Papers*, 2 vols, 1914).

Wellington Anecdotes: A Collection of Sayings and Doings of the Great Duke (2nd edn, 1852).

Wellington, Gerald 7th Duke of, *The Collected Works of Gerald 7th Duke of Wellington* (privately printed, Glasgow, 1970).

(ed.), *The Conversations of the First Duke of Wellington with George William Chad* (Cambridge, 1956).

(ed.), *A Selection from the Private Correspondence of the First Duke of Wellington* (privately printed for the Roxburghe Club, 1952).

(ed.), *Wellington and His Friends: Letters of the First Duke of Wellington to the Rt Hon. Charles and Mrs Arbuthnot, the Earl and Countess of Wilton, Princess Lieven and Miss Burdett-Coutts* (1965).

Wellington, 2nd Duke of (ed.), *Despatches, Correspondence and Memoranda of Field Marshal Arthur Duke of Wellington (New Series) 1819–1832* (8 vols, 1867–1880). *Supplementary Despatches and Memoranda of Field Marshal Arthur Duke of Wellington KG* (15 vols, 1858–1872).
See also Dispatches.

Wharncliffe see Grosvenor.

Wheatley, Edmund, *The Wheatley Diary: A Journal and Sketchbook kept during the Peninsular War and the Waterloo Campaign* (ed. Christopher Hibbert, 1964).

Wheeler, Private William, *The Letters of Private Wheeler, 1809–1828* (ed. B.H. Liddell Hart, 1951).

Wilkins, W.H., *Mrs Fitzherbert and George IV* (2 vols, 1905).

Williams, Noel St John, *Judy O'Grady and the Colonel's Lady: The Army Wife and Camp Follower Since 1660* (1988).

Wilson, Harriette, *Harriette Wilson's Memoirs Written by Herself* (4 vols, 1825).
See also Blanch.

Wilson, Joan, *A Soldier's Wife: Wellington's Marriage* (1987).

Witt, John George, *Three Villages* (1804).

Woodham-Smith, Cecil, *Queen Victoria: Her Life and Times, vol. 1, 1819–1861* (1972).

Woodward, Sir Llewllyn, *The Age of Reform 1815–1870* (2nd edn, Oxford, 1962).

Woolgar, C.M., *A Summary Catalogue of the Wellington Papers* (Southampton, 1984). 'Wellington's *Dispatches* and their Editor, Colonel Gurwood' (Southampton University 1996).

Wyndham, The Hon. Mrs Hugh, *The Correspondence of Sarah Lady Lyttelton, 1787–1870* (1912).

Yonge, C.D., *Life and Administration of Robert Banks Jenkinson, 2nd Earl of Liverpool* (3 vols, 1868).

Ziegler, Philip, *A Life of Henry Addington, First Viscount Sidmouth* (1965). *Melbourne: A Biography of William Lamb, 2nd Viscount Melbourne* (1976). *William IV* (1971).

INDEX

The Duke of Wellington's name is abbreviated to W, the Duchess's to the Duchess, and the Marquess Wellesley's to Marquess W.